Jesus as God

Other Books by Murray J. Harris

3 Crucial Questions about Jesus
Colossians and Philemon
Easter in Durham: Bishop Jenkins and the Resurrection of Jesus
From Grave to Glory: Resurrection in the New Testament
Pauline Studies: Essays Presented to Professor F. F. Bruce on His 70th Birthday (edited with Donald A. Hagner)
Raised Immortal: Resurrection and Immortality in the New Testament

Jesus as God

The New Testament Use of Theos in Reference to Jesus

Murray J. Harris

Published by Baker Books
a division of Baker Book House Company
P.O. Box 6287, Grand Rapids, MI 49516-6287

First hardcover edition published 1992

First paperback edition published 1998

Printed in the United States of America

Library of Congress Cataloging-in-Publication Data

Harris, Murray J.
Jesus as God : the New Testament use of theos in reference to Jesus / Murray J. Harris.
p. cm.
Includes bibliographical references and index.
ISBN 0-8010-2195-2
1. Jesus Christ—Divinity—History of doctrines—Early church, ca. 30–600. 2. Bible. N.T.—Criticism, interpretation, etc. 3. Theos (the Greek word) I. Title.
BT216.H37 1992
232′.8′09015–dc2092-30780

For information about academic books, resources for Christian leaders, and all new releases available from Baker Book House, visit our web site:
http://www.bakerbooks.com

To David Burt,
Christian brother,
Esteemed friend

Contents

Tables

Preface

No one who turns from reading a church father such as Ignatius back to the NT can help being impressed by the remarkable reserve of the NT writers in applying the term θεός to Jesus. Nowhere in the Gospels or Epistles or the Apocalypse does one find expressions such as those of Ignatius:[1] "for our God, Jesus the Christ (ὁ γὰρ θεὸς ἡμῶν Ἰησοῦς ὁ Χριστός), was conceived by Mary" (*Eph.* 18:2); "love for Jesus Christ, our God (ἀγάπην Ἰησοῦ Χριστοῦ τοῦ θεοῦ ἡμῶν)" (*Rom. prooem.*); "permit me to be an imitator of the passion of my God (τοῦ πάθους τοῦ θεοῦ μου)" (*Rom.* 6.3); "I give glory to Jesus Christ, the God who granted you such wisdom (Ἰησοῦν Χριστὸν τὸν θεὸν . . . σοφίσαντα)" (*Smyr.* 1:1).[2] And in the spurious fourth *Oration against the Arians*, Pseudo-Athanasius inveighs principally against the Marcellians in a treatise that begins "the Word is God from God (ἐκ θεοῦ θεός ἐστιν ὁ λόγος)"[3] and closes "so then he himself is God the Word. So Christ is the God-man, born of Mary (εἶτα οὖν καὶ αὐτὸς ὁ θεὸς λόγος. Χριστὸς οὖν ὁ ἐκ Μαρίας θεὸς ἄνθρωπος)."[4]

The questions that arise jostle for attention. Does the NT *ever* parallel the boldness of Ignatius in designating Jesus as ὁ θεός?[5] If the writers of the NT were persuaded of the deity of Christ, what accounts for their reticence to ascribe to him the title that, of all the divine names, would seem most

1. On the Christology of Ignatius, see Lebreton, "Théologie" esp. 115–22; W. Grundmann, *TDNT* 9:574–75; on his use of (ὁ) θεός in reference to Christ, see Richardson 40–45; Paulsen 23–24; Schoedel 39.

2. Other relevant passages in Ignatius include the following: "by the will of the Father and of Jesus Christ our God (Ἰησοῦ Χριστοῦ τοῦ θεοῦ ἡμῶν)" (*Eph.* 1:1); "being imitators of God and stimulated to activity by the blood of God (ἐν αἵματι θεοῦ)" (*Eph.* 1:1); "God in man (ἐν ἀνθρώπῳ θεός)" (*Eph.* 7:2); "when God appeared as a man (θεοῦ ἀνθρωπίνως φανερουμένου) to bring newness, namely eternal life" (*Eph.* 19:3); "warm greetings in Jesus Christ our God (ἐν Ἰησοῦ Χριστῷ τῷ θεῷ ἡμῶν) in blamelessness" (*Rom. prooem.*); "for our God, Jesus Christ (ὁ γὰρ θεὸς ἡμῶν Ἰησοῦς Χριστός), being in the Father, is the more plainly visible" (*Rom.* 3:3); "I bid you farewell always in our God, Jesus Christ (ἐν θεῷ ἡμῶν Ἰησοῦ Χριστῷ)" (*Poly.* 8:3).

3. *Orat. c. Ar.* 4:1 (*PG* 26:468).

4. *Orat. c. Ar.* 4:36 (*PG* 26:524).

5. J. B. Lightfoot observes (II 2:26) that, where θεός is used of Christ in the Ignatian epistles, generally a genitive limitation or some further definition follows.

explicitly to affirm that deity? Have the fathers and the creeds of the church outstripped the NT evidence in speaking so plainly and so often of Jesus Christ as "God"?

The aim of the present study is to examine all those NT verses in which it has been thought possible that θεός or ὁ θεός refers to Jesus. This rather arbitrary criterion for choosing the verses to be discussed has, of course, excluded from consideration many other verses, passages, and themes that would be directly relevant in any exhaustive treatment of the biblical testimony concerning the person of Christ. What is offered here is in no sense a NT Christology nor even a treatment of the deity of Christ in the NT, but merely a detailed analysis of one aspect of NT christological thought.

One of the characteristics of the study of NT Christology during the last two decades has been a movement away from the analysis of the titles of Jesus in the NT as a key to the understanding of his person. This movement is part of a general preference for a so-called implicit Christology over an explicit Christology. In a paper read at the 1985 meeting of the Society of New Testament Studies, L. E. Keck alleged that "probably no other factor has contributed more to the current aridity of the discipline" of NT Christology than "fascination with the palaeontology of Christological titles" ("Renewal" 368).[6] Few, indeed, would want to suggest that the history of the titles applied to Jesus by NT writers is the essence of Christology, or that words are concepts; nor would anyone wish to deny that there are many significant christological passages in which no title is used. Nonetheless it is my contention that the titles of Jesus again and again encapsulate the early Christian understanding of the role and status of Jesus. While no single title sums up the full revelation of God contained in Jesus, each title contributes distinctively to the multifaceted picture of the man from Nazareth drawn by NT authors.

What is surprising is that even in the writings of scholars who have approached NT Christology by way of a study of the titles of Jesus there has not always been a treatment of the title θεός. One thinks, for example, of the monographs by V. Taylor (*Names*), F. Hahn (*Titles*), and R. H. Fuller (*Foundations*). What is more, as far as I have been able to determine, there has never been a full-scale study of the NT use of θεός as a christological term. Brief treatments abound, particularly in the standard systematic theologies, and even the longer discussions—such as the articles by

6. Cf. Keck, "Jesus" 9–15, where he argues that christological titles should be interpreted as metaphors ("similes leave the inherited meanings intact in order to compare two known realities but metaphors live by the disparity of what is identified," 12) and observes that "the inherited, traditional meanings of the titles do not really fit Jesus. He was a very unmessianic Messiah, a very non-regal Son of David, a very humble Son of Man, a very human Son of God, a very lowly Lord" (12–13).

A. W. Wainwright ("Confession") and R. E. Brown ("Jesus")—seem hampered by considerations of space. Only when a single verse has been the focus of attention in an article or book has justice been done to a verse or passage—as in the analyses of Romans 9:5 by T. Dwight ("Romans"), E. Abbot ("Construction" and "Discussions"), A. Durand ("Divinité"), H. M. Faccio (*De Divinitate*), B. M. Metzger ("Punctuation"), and O. Kuss ("Römer").

In the final chapter of his 1982 volume on *Jesus and the Constraints of History*, A. E. Harvey claims "that the New Testament writers appear to have submitted to this constraint [of monotheism], and to have avoided using the word 'god' or 'divine' of Jesus" (157).[7] Even when scholars allow that NT writers sometimes apply the title θεός to Jesus, it is not infrequently asserted or assumed that, as G. H. Boobyer expresses the claim (260), "they were not assigning Jesus equality of status with God, and certainly did not intend to say that ontologically he *was* truly God. They meant that he was God functionally."

Here, then, is the *apologia* for my topic—my unease concerning three matters: the retreat from "title Christology," the relative neglect of the study of θεός as a christological title, and the claim that NT writers avoid using θεός of Jesus or that θεός has a purely functional meaning when applied to Jesus.

Two writers (both writing in 1975) have highlighted the need for a study of this type. In the course of a succinct analysis of "The Neglected Factor in New Testament Theology" (viz., the doctrine of God), N. A. Dahl writes: "Most treatments of New Testament Christology pay astonishingly little attention to the relationship between faith in Christ and faith in God, or to the *transfer of divine names*, attributes and predicates *to Jesus*, or to the emergence of 'trinitarian' formulations. The provocative thesis of A. C. McGiffert, that Jesus was 'The God of the Early Christians', seems to have been forgotten" (5; italics mine). Again, a commentator on John's Gospel, B. A. Mastin,[8] begins his article on "A Neglected Feature of the Christology of the Fourth Gospel" (viz., the christological use of θεός by the fourth evangelist) with the observation that "because the term θεός is used so infrequently of Jesus in the New Testament, it is not surprising to find that there are relatively few discussions of it as a Christological title" ("Christology" 32).

It is a curious fact that each of the texts to be examined contains an interpretative problem of some description; actually, most contain two or three.

7. Similarly 178. In his belief that the NT data about a christological use of θεός are ambiguous, Harvey is followed by Austin 272–73. Cf. Cupitt 108–9: "The full coequal deity of Jesus is nowhere taught in the New Testament."

8. Mastin edited and completed J. N. Sanders's *Commentary on the Gospel According to St. John.*

It may be helpful at this point to anticipate what is to come by classifying these various problems:

1. Textual: John 1:18; Acts 20:28; Gal. 2:20; Col. 2:2; 1 Tim. 3:16; Heb. 1:8; 2 Pet. 1:1; 1 John 5:20
2. Punctuation: John 1:1; Rom. 9:5
3. Grammatical:
   a. Problems relating to the presence or absence or the repetition of the article: John 1:1, 18; 20:28; Rom. 9:5; 2 Thess. 1:12; Titus 2:13; 2 Pet. 1:1
   b. General syntactical problems:
      (1) Whether καί is epexegetic or two nouns are in epexegetic apposition: John 17:3; Gal. 2:20; Eph. 5:5; Col. 2:2; 2 Thess. 1:12; Titus 2:13; 2 Pet. 1:1
      (2) Whether a case is nominative or vocative: John 20:28; Heb. 1:8–9
      (3) Whether a word is substantival or adjectival: John 1:1, 18; Acts 20:28
4. Contextual:
   a. Immediate: I John 5:20
   b. Old Testament: Matt. 1:23; Heb. 1:8–9

The sixteen passages that will be considered are treated in canonical order within two groups—nine major texts and seven "other texts."

Throughout this monograph I use the terms *Deity*, *God*, and *Godhead* synonymously, in reference to the one true God of the Judeo-Christian tradition; *godhood* (corresponding to *manhood*) refers to the divine essence/nature and qualities, or *god-ness*; *deity* and *divinity* are likewise used synonymously, in reference either to the godhood of the Deity or to a particular pagan god (see the discussions of these terms by B. B. Warfield in *ISBE* 2:1268–70 and by Broyles).

Attention should also be drawn to an important distinction in terminology. A (proper) *name* is taken to be an identifying appellation that belongs only to one individual or to a restricted number of individuals, whereas a *title* is a descriptive appellation that is based on nature, character, function, status, or attainment and is potentially applicable to any number of individuals. For instance, in the sentence "Yahweh is my shepherd" (Ps. 23:1 JB), "Yahweh" is a name and "shepherd" a title.

In the footnotes, references to scholars and English translations are generally listed in chronological order. References to BDR are given only when this 1976 edition differs from BDF (1961). References to BAGD are generally by page number and quadrant on the page, *a* indicating the upper half and *b* the lower half of the left-hand column, and *c* and *d* the upper and lower halves of the right-hand column. Classical references and references to church fathers are generally cited according to the abbreviation list in *TDNT*. To conserve space, works are cited by authors' surnames or, where there are several works by one author, by surname and an abbreviated title. If reference is made to a scholar's whole book or article, usually no page numbers are given; the bibliography contains the necessary information. Initials of scholars are omitted in footnotes and in parentheses in the text, except when ambiguity would result and when dictionary articles are cited (these are not listed in the bibliography). Unless otherwise indicated, the translations of ancient texts are my own.

It gives me great pleasure to dedicate this volume to David Burt, whose Christian friendship over many years has been greatly enriching and whose legal acumen helped to sharpen my critical faculties during university years.

December 1991

Acknowledgments

This book has been in the making for many years so that its completion has brought me not a little sense of relief. Warm gratitude is due to several friends who have helped with typing—Carol Pederson, Eric Svendsen, Michael Vanlaningham, Michael Combs, Sung-Min Park, and Paul Winters (who also helped to prepare the indexes). Jon Gutierrez gave valuable assistance in tracking down various bibliographic items and Eleanor Warner diligently secured books and articles through interlibrary loan. To all these people I give my sincere thanks. My family has shown great patience and given constant support during this prolonged venture—my wife Jennifer and our children Oliver and Jessie Jane.

I also wish to thank Allan Fisher of Baker Book House for his willingness to accept this technical manuscript for publication, Jim Weaver for overseeing the editorial process, and David Aiken for his meticulous editorial work.

In preparing this volume I have benefited greatly from interaction with students in the U.S.A., the U.K., and Germany where I have conducted seminars and given lectures on "Jesus as θεός in the New Testament" or "A Neglected Feature of New Testament Christology."

Permission was granted by Paternoster Press and William B. Eerdmans Publishing Company to reproduce an earlier form of chapter VII (Titus 2:13) from *Pauline Studies: Essays Presented to Professor F. F. Bruce*, edited by D. A. Hagner and M. J. Harris (1980), and by the editor of the *Tyndale Bulletin* to reprint, with the necessary updating, the articles on Psalm 45:7–8 and Hebrews 1:8–9 (chapters VIII–IX) that appeared in volume 35 (1984) and volume 36 (1985).

Abbreviations

ASV	*American Standard Version* (1901)
BAGD	W. Bauer, *A Greek-English Lexicon of the New Testament and Other Early Christian Literature* (ETr. adapted by W. F. Arndt and F. W. Gingrich; 2d edition revised and augmented by F. W. Gingrich and F. W. Danker; Chicago: University of Chicago Press, 1979)
Barclay	W. Barclay, *The New Testament: A New Translation* (2 vols.; New York: Collins, 1968)
BC	F. J. Foakes-Jackson and K. Lake (eds.), *The Beginnings of Christianity* (5 vols.; London: Macmillan, 1920–33)
BDB	F. Brown, S. R. Driver, and C. A. Briggs, *A Hebrew and English Lexicon of the Old Testament* (Oxford: Clarendon, 1953)
BDF	F. Blass and A. Debrunner, *A Greek Grammar of the New Testament and Other Early Christian Literature* (ETr. edited by R. W. Funk; Chicago: University of Chicago Press, 1961)
BDR	F. Blass and A. Debrunner, *Grammatik des neutestamentlichen Griechisch* (14th ed.; revised by F. Rehkopf; Göttingen: Vandenhoeck & Ruprecht, 1976)
Berkeley	*The Holy Bible: The Berkeley Version in Modern English* (1959)
Cassirer	H. W. Cassirer, *God's New Covenant: A New Testament Translation* (Grand Rapids: Eerdmans, 1989)
COED	*The Compact Edition of the Oxford English Dictionary* (2 vols.; New York: Oxford University Press, 1971)
DCG	J. Hastings (ed.), *A Dictionary of Christ and the Gospels* (2 vols.; Edinburgh: Clark, 1906–8)
EBC	F. E. Gaebelein (ed.), *The Expositor's Bible Commentary* (to be completed in 12 vols.; Grand Rapids: Zondervan, 1976–)

EGT	W. R. Nicoll (ed.), *The Expositor's Greek New Testament* (5 vols.; reprinted Grand Rapids: Eerdmans, 1970 [= 1907–10 original])
EJ	*Encyclopaedia Judaica* (1971)
ETr.	English translation
GKC	*Gesenius' Hebrew Grammar* (edited and enlarged by E. Kautzsch; ETr. revised by A. E. Cowley; Oxford: Clarendon, 1910)
GNB	*Good News Bible* (1976)
Goodspeed	E. J. Goodspeed, *The New Testament: An American Translation* (Chicago: University of Chicago Press, 1923)
HDB	J. Hastings (ed.), *A Dictionary of the Bible* (5 vols.; Edinburgh: Clark, 1898–1904)
HR	E. Hatch and H. A. Redpath, *A Concordance to the Septuagint* (2 vols.; reprinted Graz: Akademische Verlag, 1975 [= 1897 original])
IB	G. A. Buttrick et al. (eds.), *The Interpreter's Bible* (12 vols.; New York: Abingdon, 1952–57)
IDB	G. A. Buttrick et al. (eds.), *The Interpreter's Dictionary of the Bible* (5 vols.; New York: Abingdon, 1962–76)
ISBE	J. Orr et al. (eds.), *The International Standard Bible Encyclopedia* (5 vols.; reprinted Grand Rapids: Eerdmans, 1955 [= 1915 original])
JB	*Jerusalem Bible* (1966)
KB	L. Koehler and W. Baumgartner, *Lexicon in Veteris Testamenti Libros* (Leiden: Brill, 1958)
KJV	*King James Version* (= *Authorized Version*)
κτλ.	καὶ τὰ λοιπά (and the rest)
LSJ	H. G. Liddell and R. Scott, *A Greek-English Lexicon* (9th ed. by H. S. Jones et al.; 2 vols.; Oxford: Clarendon, 1940; supplement in 1968)
LXX	Septuagint
mg	margin
MH	J. H. Moulton, *A Grammar of New Testament Greek*, vol. 2: *Accidence and Word-Formation* (edited by W. F. Howard; Edinburgh: Clark, 1919–29)
MM	J. H. Moulton and G. Milligan, *The Vocabulary of the Greek Testament Illustrated from the Papyri and Other Non-Literary Sources* (reprinted Grand Rapids: Eerdmans, 1972 [= 1930 original])

Moffatt	J. Moffatt, *The Moffatt Translation of the Bible* (London: Hodder, 1935)
MT	Masoretic Text
NA^{26}	K. Aland et al. (eds.), *Novum Testamentum Graece* (26th ed.; Stuttgart: Deutsche Bibelstiftung, 1979)
NAB^{1}	*New American Bible* (1970)
NAB^{2}	*New American Bible: Revised New Testament* (1988)
NASB	*New American Standard Bible* (1977)
NEB	*New English Bible* (1970)
NIDNTT	C. Brown (ed.), *The New International Dictionary of New Testament Theology* (3 vols.; Grand Rapids: Zondervan/ Exeter: Paternoster, 1975–78)
NIV	*New International Version* (1983)
NJB	*New Jerusalem Bible* (1985)
NRSV	*New Revised Standard Version* (1990)
NT	New Testament
OCD	M. Cary et al. (eds.), *The Oxford Classical Dictionary* (Oxford: Clarendon, 1949)
OGIS	Orientis Graeci Inscriptiones Selectae
OT	Old Testament
PG	J.-P. Migne (ed.), *Patrologia graeca*
PGM	K. Preisendanz (ed.), *Papyri graecae magicae*
Phillips	J. B. Phillips, *The New Testament in Modern English* (London: Bles, 1958)
POxy	B. P. Grenfell, A. S. Hunt, and H. I. Bell (eds.), *The Oxyrhynchus Papyri* (17 vols.; London: Egypt Exploration Fund, 1898–1927)
Rahlfs	A. Rahlfs (ed.), *Septuaginta* (8th ed.; 2 vols.; Stuttgart: Württembergische Bibelanstalt, 1965)
REB	*Revised English Bible* (1990)
RSV	*Revised Standard Version* (1952)
RV	*Revised Version* (NT, 1881; OT, 1885; Apoc., 1895)
SB	H. L. Strack and P. Billerbeck, *Kommentar zum Neuen Testament aus Talmud und Midrash* (4 vols.; Munich: Beck, 1922–28)
Segond	L. Segond, *La Sainte Bible* (2d ed.; 1955)
TBNT	L. Coenen, E. Beyreuther, and H. Bietenhard (eds.), *Theologisches Begriffslexikon zum Neuen Testament* (3 vols.; Wuppertal: Brockhaus, 1967–71)
TCNT	*Twentieth Century New Testament* (1904)

TDNT	G. Kittel and G. Friedrich (eds.), *Theological Dictionary of the New Testament* (9 vols.; ETr.; Grand Rapids: Eerdmans, 1964–74)
TDOT	G. J. Botterweck and H. Ringgren (eds.), *Theological Dictionary of the Old Testament* (6 vols. to date; ETr.; Grand Rapids: Eerdmans, 1974–)
TEV	*Today's English Version of the New Testament* (1966)
Tricot	A. Tricot, *La Sainte Bible du Chanoine Crampon: Nouveau Testament* (Paris: Desclée, 1960)
UBS/UBS^3	K. Aland, M. Black, C. M. Martini, B. M. Metzger, and A. Wikgren (eds.), *The Greek New Testament* (3d ed.; New York: United Bible Societies, 1975; 1st ed. in 1966 [= UBS^1]; 2d ed. in 1968 [= UBS^2])
v.l.	variant reading
Weymouth	R. F. Weymouth, *The New Testament in Modern Speech* (3d ed.; London: Clarke, 1909)
WH	B. F. Westcott and F. J. A. Hort, *The New Testament in the Original Greek*, vol. 1: *Text*; vol. 2: *Introduction, Appendix* (London: Macmillan, 1881)
Williams	C. B. Williams, *The New Testament: A Translation in the Language of the People* (Chicago: Moody, 1950)

I

Introduction: *Theos* in the New Testament

A satisfactory analysis and classification of the NT use of θεός would be impossible without first sketching its earlier use in biblical and extrabiblical contexts.

A. Background to the New Testament Use of θεός

1. θεός in the Septuagint

In the LXX θεός renders some twelve different Hebrew words.[1] But of these only three are sufficiently often rendered by θεός to warrant consideration when examining the LXX background to the NT use of the term, viz., אל (rendered by θεός 163 times), אלהים (rendered by θεός more than 2,280 times),[2] and יהוה (rendered by θεός 353 times,[3] although by far the most common LXX rendering of יהוה is (ὁ) κύριος).[4]

1. HR lists another nine distinct Hebrew words or phrases which the LXX only once renders by θεός or a phrase involving θεός.

2. There are also 33 instances where אלהים is rendered by κύριος ὁ θεός, and 4 times it is rendered by κύριος θεός. The related singular form (אֱלוֹהַּ or אֱלֹהַּ) is translated by θεός 21 times; the Aramaic term אֱלָהּ, 65 times (see below, n. 12).

3. In addition there are 189 instances where יהוה is rendered by κύριος ὁ θεός; 4 times it is rendered by ὁ κύριος θεός, and 3 times by κύριος θεός.

4. The other nine Hebrew words rendered by θεός are צוּר (19 times), אֲדֹנָי (11), שַׁדַּי (10), אָבִיר (3), יָהּ (2), אֱלִיל (1), עִלַּי (1), עָצָב (1), and קֹדֶשׁ (1).

a. As Rendering אֵל

In comparison with the more than 2,600 uses of the word אלהים in the MT, the word אל occurs relatively rarely, except in poetry that exhibits an archaizing tendency.[5] Basically, אל was used[6] (1) as an appellative or generic title denoting deity, whether the true God (Ps. 18:33), an "alien god" (Exod. 34:14) that is "no god" (Deut. 32:21), or deity in general (Exod. 15:11; Hos. 11:9); and (2) as a proper name of the God of Israel, equivalent to יהוה (see especially Num. 23:8, where יהוה is parallel to אל; Job 5:8; 8:5; Isa. 40:18).

However, the term appears in several other interesting contexts: (1) in the formation of epithets descriptive of Yahweh (e.g., Exod. 34:6: "the God (אל) of compassion and mercy" = "a compassionate and merciful God"; Deut. 7:21; Ps. 84:3); (2) as the first element in certain divine names found in the patriarchal narratives of Genesis (e.g., אל עולם); (3) describing people of valor or rank (e.g., 2 Kings 24:15; Ezek. 31:11; 32:21) and in the expression בני אלים, "angels" (Ps. 29:1; 89:7); (4) as the equivalent of an adjective expressing magnitude or power (e.g., Ps. 80:11: "cedars of אל" = "mighty cedars"); (5) in divine-human contrasts (Isa. 31:3; Ezek. 28:9); and (6) as the first or last element in theophoric names (e.g., Elisha and Samuel).

b. As Rendering אֱלֹהִים

Old Testament usage of אלהים[7] may be summed up under three headings.[8]

5. Perhaps not strangely, the etymology of this oldest Semitic term for God remains obscure (see Murtonen 34–39; Pope 16–21). A common explanation derives the term from the root אל, which means "to be strong" or "to be preeminent." That the idea of power was basic to the Semitic understanding of deity seems to be indicated also by the comparable divine appellatives בעל and אדון, both of which imply the possession and exercise of authority (cf. G. Quell, *TDNT* 3:84).

6. See the discussion of F. M. Cross, *TDOT* 1:253–61. In the specific examples cited in the text with regard to the use of אל and אלהים, these words are always rendered by θεός in the LXX.

7. If אלהים is a plural form of אל expanded with ה (on this view אלה [or אלוה] is a singular form inferred from the plural אלהים), like אל it could derive from the root אל, which denotes strength or priority in status (see n. 5 above), or the root אלה, "to be strong." Some (e.g., Murtonen 41–42), however, regard אלהים as the plural of אֱלֹהַּ (originally meaning "revered one") from the root אלה (cf. BDB 41–42; H. Ringgren, *TDOT* 1:273). Various explanations have been given of the curious fact that the regular term for God in the monotheistic faith of Yahwism is plural in form. The most probable explanations are that אלהים is (1) an abstract plural ("the Deity") which sums up the qualities inherent in the idea of the stem (cf. the plurals זקנים, "old age"; בשרים, "fleshliness"; cf. GKC §124d); (2) a plural of amplification which intensifies the idea of the stem: "Then *ʾelohim* would mean the 'great,' 'highest,' and finally 'only' God, i.e., God in general" (H. Ringgren, *TDOT* 1:273; cf. GKC §124e); or (3) a plural of excellence or majesty which seems a combination of the two ideas above, since it sums up the characteristics of and also intensifies the original idea (GKC §124g): "That the language has entirely rejected the idea of numerical plurality in אֱלֹהִים (whenever it denotes *one* God), is proved especially by its being almost invariably joined with a singular attribute . . . , e.g. אֱלֹהִים צַדִּיק" (Ps. 7:10 [Engl. v. 9]; GKC §124g; cf. §132h).

8. This summary is a modification of the entry under אלהים in BDB 43–44.

1. As a numerical plural
   a. Human rulers or judges, regarded as divine representatives or as bearers of divine authority and majesty (Exod. 21:6; 22:8 [cf. 1 Sam. 2:25]; Judg. 5:8; Ps. 82:1, 6)
   b. Spiritual or heavenly beings, including God (Gen. 1:27) and angels (Ps. 8:6 [Engl. v. 5])
   c. Angels (Ps. 97:7; 138:1)
   d. Heathen gods (Exod. 22:19 [Engl. v. 22]; Jer. 5:7) or "foreign gods" (Josh. 24:20, 23), along with their images (Exod. 20:23; Jer. 16:20)
2. As an intensive plural
   a. A god or goddess (1 Kings 11:5 [Ashtoreth], 33 [Chemosh])
   b. The deity in general (Ps. 14:1; Mic. 3:7; Mal. 3:14–15, 18)
   c. A representative of God (Exod. 4:16; 7:1; Ps. 45:7 [Engl. v. 6])
   d. A spiritual being (1 Sam. 28:13)
   e. To express magnitude (1 Kings 3:28; Jon. 3:3)
3. As a plural of excellence or majesty[9]
   a. The (one true) God (Deut. 7:9; 1 Chron. 6:34)
   b. The God of Israel
      (1) In absolute state (Gen. 9:27; Isa. 35:4), often with adjectives (Deut. 4:31; 5:26)
      (2) In construct state
         (a) With proper names: Israel (Gen. 33:20), Abraham (Gen. 31:42), Elijah (2 Kings 2:14)
         (b) With abstract nouns, to express divine attributes (2 Chron. 15:3), functions (2 Sam. 22:3), or sphere of authority (Gen. 24:3)
      (3) With suffixes (especially in Deut. and in conjunction with יהוה) (Exod. 20:2; Ruth 1:16)

c. As Rendering יְהוָה

Although the tetragrammaton יהוה occurs some 6,823 times in the Hebrew Bible (BDB 217b), it is rendered by θεός in the LXX only 353 times.[10] These instances are scattered sparsely throughout all four sections

9. The examples listed under no. 3 represent the predominant use of אלהים (more than 2,000 instances).

10. The four consonants יהוה, which form the *nomen ineffabile* (known to Jews simply as השם, "the name," or as שם המיוחד, "the proper name" of God), are usually thought to have been originally pronounced יַהְוֶה (Yahweh), on the basis of (1) the contracted and poetic form יה (e.g., Isa. 38:11); (2) the suffixes יהו־ and (in shortened form) יה־ which appear in compound Hebrew proper names; (3) the Greek transliteration Ιαουαι found in Clement of Alexandria (*Strom.* 5:6:34) and Ιαβε found in Theodoret and Epiphanius (see G. R. Driver, "Yahweh"); and (4) the parallel אהיה in Exod. 3:14.

of the LXX, although the equation יהוה = θεός sometimes occurs frequently in particular sections (e.g., the 20 examples in Prov. 1–21). But, as noted above, by far the most common LXX rendering of יהוה is (ὁ) κύριος (6,156 instances).[11]

Being a proper noun and the covenant name of Israel's God, יהוה is invariably the name of a person who sustains relationships with other persons. This name is never used generically of deity but always personally and individually of "the God of Abraham, the God of Isaac, and the God of Jacob" (Exod. 3:15).[12]

d. The Interrelationship of אֵל, אֱלֹהִים, and יַהְוֶה

The primary distinction between אל and אלהים is not with regard to etymology (the terms are probably related and could derive from the root אול or the root אלה) or range of application (both may be used of either the Israelite Deity or a pagan god),[13] but in the matter of (1) form and (2) frequency and distribution of usage. The plural form אלהים occurs some 2,570 times (BDB 43a), occurring in all OT books, whereas אל is found only 217 times (in reference to the one true God; BDB 42b), rarely in the plural (only 4 instances), and particularly in early poetry and archaizing texts (witness the 55 occurrences in Job).

Whereas אל and אלהים, like יהוה, are used of the God of Israel, they can also, unlike יהוה, be appellatives designating deity as such or a particular pagan deity. יהוה, on the other hand, functions exclusively as a proper noun, denoting an individual divine Being (viz., Israel's covenant God), never as a common noun, denoting divinity in general or a nameless divinity (similarly Cassuto 18–19).

The derivation of יהוה has been variously explained (for further details and proposals, see Murtonen 61–67; Parke-Taylor 46-62, 98–100; Gianotti 41–51): (1) as a substantive from the root הוה (an old form of היה), formed with the preformative *yod* (KB 369b), meaning "the self-existent One," the *Ens a se*; (2) as an archaic imperfect qal form of הוה (equivalent to יִהְיֶה), meaning "he exists" and alluding to the divine self-existence and immutability; or "he (who) is (truly present)," alluding to his creative and redemptive action; (3) as the imperfect hiphil of this same root (הוה), meaning either "he (who) brings into existence" (a reference to the creative activity of God) or "he (who) causes to come to pass" (a reference to the divine providence or to God's performance of his promises); or (4) as an abbreviation of יַהְוֶה אֲשֶׁר יִהְוֶה (cf. Exod. 3:14), "he brings into existence whatever exists."

11. Vigorous debate continues over the question whether the LXX originally read κύριος as a surrogate for יהוה, with the tetragram in Greek manuscripts as evidence of a secondary archaizing stage (thus, e.g., Pietersma), or whether the divine name was originally written in Aramaic or in paleo-Hebrew letters or else was transliterated into Greek letters (thus, e.g., G. E. Howard, "Tetragram" 63–72).

12. But Obermann (301–23) argues that originally יהוה was an epithet, a *nomen agentis*, viz., "Sustainer, Maintainer, Establisher" (of strength or weakness, victory or defeat, life or death).

13. The same is true of אלוה and אלה (see above, n. 2). The former word may refer to Israel's God (Deut. 32:15) or to a heathen god (Dan. 11:37b). The Aramaic term אלה is used of heathen deities (Jer. 10:11), the God of Israel (Ezra 5:2), or deity in general (Dan. 6:8, 13 [Engl. vv. 7, 12]). The LXX has either θεός or θεοί in these passages (the plural is used in Jer. 10:11).

Even when אלהים stands as a virtual proper name equivalent to יהוה, it should not be regarded as identical in sense with יהוה.[14] יהוה is more appropriately used to emphasize the direct and personal character of God's merciful and loving relationship with his covenant people and his immediate lordship over nature and history, while אלהים highlights God's transcendence and power as the universal, majestic, eternal God who created the world and rules and judges it in righteousness.[15] If the former term points to God's reality as one who speaks and acts in self-disclosure and salvation, the latter term suggests his absolute deity as the Creator and one true God before whom all persons must tremble and as the only one who has the property of "godhood."[16]

While יהוה is never applied (in a secondary sense) to angels or human beings, both אל and אלהים have extended or "irregular" applications to angels or to persons who represent on earth divine power, judgment, or majesty.

2. θεός in Extrabiblical Literature

a. As Applied to Gods

Since originally θεός was a predicative term, its use encompassed the whole range of Greek religious thought.[17] Sometimes the term (with or without the article) refers to deity in general; that is, the divine power and qualities that are the common possession of all gods. W. H. S. Jones observes (253) that the articular ὁ θεός (like ὁ ἄνθρωπος, "mankind") is "very often generic" in sense ("god-kind," "a god," "any god *qua* god"), as in the well-known definition of Epicurus: "First of all reckoning a god (τὸν θεόν) to be living, immortal and blessed."[18]

14. Cf. Eichrodt 185–92; Cassuto 17–18, 27–41.

15. Cf. the rabbinic distinction (Exodus Rabbah 3 on 3:14): "When I judge men, I am called אלהים . . . when I have mercy on them I am called יהוה" (cited by E. Stauffer, *TDNT* 3:90 n. 113). See further G. F. Moore 1:387. Marmorstein (43) contrasts the rabbinic and the Philonic understanding of these two terms: "Rabbinic lore preserved the teaching that the Tetragrammaton implies or expresses the measure of love and mercy; the name Elohim, that of judgement. Philo taught just the reverse; the term θεός = אלהים means εὐεργέτης, the good, the God of love and benevolence; κύριος = אדני expresses God's Lordship, Rulership, Judgement." See further Dahl and Segal.

16. Concerning the explanatory term אלהים in the expression יהוה אלהים, G. Quell (*TDNT* 3:81) comments that it signifies "the God of all ages, . . . the unique bearer of divine essence who has made the world." Later he observes: "The אֱלֹהִים possesses the אֵל quality in full measure" (*TDNT* 3:87). See further M. H. Segal.

17. H. Kleinknecht, *TDNT* 3:67. On the etymology of the term θεός, see Chantraine 429–30. In a brief survey of the Greek concept of θεός, Harnack (*Dogma* 119 n. 2 = 119–21) speaks of its "variability and elasticity." G. Murray (12) vividly illustrates this diversity in the use of θεός when he observes that "τὸ εὐτυχεῖν, 'the fact of success', is 'a god and more than a god' (Aesch. *Choeph.* 60); τὸ γιγνώσκειν φίλους, 'the thrill of recognizing a friend' after long absence, is a 'god' (Eur. *Hel.* 560); wine is a 'god' whose body is poured out in libation to gods (Eur. *Bacch.* 284); and in the unwritten law of the human conscience 'a great god liveth and groweth not old' (Soph. *Oed. Tyr.* 871)."

18. Diogenes Laertius 10:123.

Again, (ὁ) θεός may signify a particular god (or, as ἡ θεός, goddess),[19] who may or may not be named in the context. When ὁ θεός stands unspecified, it will sometimes denote the supreme god, Zeus,[20] "father of both men and gods"[21] and "the best of men or gods."[22] Certainly, in extrabiblical Greek literature the presence of the article with θεός will not generally testify to an articulated philosophical monotheism but rather to a divine hierarchy among a plurality of gods who reflect the diversity and manifold character of reality. Given this hierarchy of deities, it is not surprising that a Greek could so readily oscillate from θεοί to ὁ θεός to (for example) Ζεύς in speaking of deity, without intending that subtle distinctions should be drawn between the three.[23]

In the progressive refining of the Greek idea of θεός, the movement was away from Homeric anthropomorphism toward a deification of metaphysical powers that finds its climax in the monism of Plotinus. The gods are less eternal beings with human form and passions who live in felicity far above worldly anguish than impersonal cosmic forces that guarantee permanence of being; οἱ θεοί ("the gods") have, to a large extent, become τὸ θεῖον ("the divine") or even τὸ ὄν ("that which exists") or τὸ ἕν ("the one") (cf. H. Kleinknecht, *TDNT* 3:69–79).

b. As Applied to Human Beings

But θεός (or *deus*) was not a term reserved exclusively for divinities that might inhabit heaven (θεοὶ οὐράνιοι)[24] or the lower realms (νέρτεροι θεοί).[25] In the pre-Christian era and in the first century A.D. this title was also applied to many human figures:

1. Renowned heroes, such as Chiron[26] and Colonos[27]
2. Skillful politicians, such as Demetrius Poliorketes and his father Antigonos[28]

19. Such as Athena (Plato, *Tim.* 21A) or Thetis (Plato, *Ap.* 28C). These two references and some of the following are cited in LSJ 791 s.v. θεός.

20. Herodotus 2:13: ὁ θεὸς ὕει; cf. the explicit identification θεὸς Ζεύς in Homer, *Odyssey* 4:236; 14:327.

21. Homer, *Iliad* 1:544; 15:47.

22. Ibid., 19:96.

23. Cf. Nilsson 1:216, 219, 364, 739–40; 2:197. To illustrate this oscillation, Jones cites (*inter alios*) Semonides 1:5; 7(8):1, 21, 72, 104 (Ζεύς = θεός = Ὀλύμπιοι); Aeschylus, *Pers.* 739 (Ζεύς = θεοί = ὁ θεός); Sophocles, *El.* 199, 1264–66 (θεοί = θεός); and the comment of Cicero (*Nat. Deor.* 1:12): "Xenophon has Socrates saying that there is only one god, but then that there are several."

24. Aeschylus, *Ag.* 90.

25. Sophocles, *Ant.* 602; cf. 1070: οἱ κάτωθεν θεοί.

26. Sophocles, *Trach.* 714.

27. Sophocles, *Oed. Col.* 65.

28. Athenaeus 6:63: "That the greatest of the gods and those most friendly to our city are here to help."

3. Founders or heads of philosophical schools, such as Diogenes and Heraclitus[29]
4. Rulers, such as Ptolemy V (Epiphanes),[30] Julius Caesar,[31] Augustus,[32] Herod Agrippa I,[33] Nero,[34] and Domitian[35]
5. Exalted patriarchs, such as Moses[36]
6. Self-styled servants of God, such as Mariccus[37]
7. Human beings as the possessors of νοῦς ("intelligence")[38]

While all this indicates the widespread use of the appellation θεός for certain persons, care should be taken not to read theological doctrine into statements that were often merely the product of obsequious flattery or profound respect. The emperor Vespasian's deathbed jest (A.D. 79) is relevant in this regard: "Woe is me. I think I am becoming a god."[39]

c. As Applied to the God of Israel

Philo, who prefers the abstract philosophical term τὸ θεῖον to denote Deity, distinguishes between ὁ θεός (God as the Creator who is good, loving, and benevolent),[40] θεός (the Logos,[41] or a man such as Moses),[42] and ὁ κύριος (God as the King who rules and judges).[43] Josephus, on the other

29. Epictetus, *Moral.* 15 (cited by Harnack, *Dogma* 120 n. 2, who also notes that even Christians in Syria are reproached by Lucian for venerating their teacher Peregrinus as a god [*Peregr. Mort.* 11]).

30. Πτολεμαῖος ὑπάρχων θεὸς ἐκ θεοῦ καὶ θεᾶς καθάπερ Ὧρος ὁ τῆς Ἴσιος καὶ Ὀσίριος υἱός, "Ptolemy who is god of god and of goddess, as Horus the son of Isis and Osiris" (Rosetta Stone, 196 B.C.; OGIS 90:10).

31. Τὸν ἀπὸ Ἄρεως καὶ Ἀφροδε[ί]της θεὸν ἐπιφανῆ καὶ κοινὸν τοῦ ἀνθρωπίνου βίου σωτῆρα, "God made manifest, offspring of Ares and Aphrodite, and common savior of human life" (Ephesus, 48 B.C.; Dittenberger 760:7). On the "divinity" of Julius Caesar, see L. R. Taylor 58–99, 267–69; Fowler 107–33.

32. Καίσαρ[α] θεὸν ἐκ θεοῦ, "by Caesar, god of god" (Egypt, 27 B.C.; P Oxy 1453:11); θεοῦ ἐκ θεοῦ, "god of god" (Egypt, 24 B.C.; OGIS 655:2); ὁ θεὸς Καῖσαρ, "the god Caesar" (Strabo 4:177, 193, 199). See further L. R. Taylor 142–246, 270–83.

33. Josephus, *Ant.* 19:345: "Immediately his flatterers raised their voices from different directions (though not for his good), addressing him as a god θεὸν προσαγορεύοντες)." Cf. Acts 12:22: "And the people shouted out, 'The voice of a god (θεοῦ φωνή), and not of a man.'"

34. Ἀγαθῷ θεῷ, "(to) the good god" (the address in a votive inscription of Gaius Stertinius Xenophon of Cos) (Deissmann 345 and n. 4).

35. (Δεσπότης ἡμῶν καὶ θεός =) dominus et deus noster, "our lord and god" (Suetonius, *Domit.* 13:2). Cf. Dio Cassius 67:4:7; Dio Chrysostomus 45:1.

36. Philo, *Sacr. AC.* 9. But see Holladay 136–41.

37. Tacitus, *Hist.* 2:51: "Mariccus . . . already a deliverer of the Gauls and a god (*deus*)—a name he had attached to himself."

38. Epictetus, *Diss.* 2:8:12; cf. Marcus Aurelius 3:5 (ὁ ἐν σοὶ θεός, "God in you"); Plotinus, *Enn.* 6:5:1 (τὸν ἐν ἑκάστῳ ἡμῶν θεόν, "the God in each of us").

39. Suetonius, *Vesp.* 23:4. See also H. F. Burton 80.

40. *Fug.* 97; *Sacr. AC.* 9.

41. *Som.* 1:229–30.

42. *Vit. Mos.* 1:158; *Det. Pot. Ins.* 161–62.

43. *Leg. All.* 3:73. Cf. Marmorstein 43.

hand, who prefers the articular over the anarthrous θεός, can employ θεός and ὁ θεός interchangeably, without apparent distinction.[44]

3. Conclusion

To those Jews or Gentile "God-fearers" of the first century A.D. who became the first converts to Christianity and who knew the Scriptures in their Greek dress, the term θεός would probably have seemed extremely rich in its connotations and yet at the same time very varied in its applicability. Rich in meaning, because it summed up everything that distinguished God from humans, signifying godhood as opposed to manhood and representing in Greek the two basic generic terms for God (אֵל and אֱלֹהִים) that were used in the Hebrew OT; it denoted the one supreme God whom Jews worshiped as Creator and Redeemer; it was not infrequently found in the LXX where the sacred name יהוה stood in the Hebrew text.[45] Varied in application, because it could be used to refer to deity in general, a particular heathen god or goddess, pagan deities at large (along with their images), angels, human rulers or judges, persons of valor or rank, godlike persons, as well as the one true God of Israel. What was more, on occasion it was simply equivalent (in the form τοῦ θεοῦ) to the adjective "mighty."

Neither in LXX Greek nor in secular Greek is a firm or a fine distinction drawn between the articular and the anarthrous θεός,[46] with ὁ θεός denoting, for example, a specific god or the supreme Deity (however conceived), and θεός designating deity in general or emphasizing the qualities of godhood. This is not to say that the use of the article is totally capricious or that the above distinctions are never drawn. But it does mean that in certain contexts it is as possible for ὁ θεός to refer generically to divinity as it is for θεός to denote God or a particular god.

B. Analysis of the New Testament Use of θεός

1. Statistical Summary

The statistics in table 1 reflect the uses of θεός in NA[26] (= UBS[3]). Words bracketed in these editions of the Greek text have been included in the statistics. These statistics prompt some general observations.

44. To illustrate this interchangeable use, E. Stauffer (*TDNT* 3:90) cites *Ap*. 2:168, and compares περὶ θεοῦ in *Ap*. 2:169, 179, 256 with περὶ τοῦ θεοῦ in 2:254 (*TDNT* 3:90 n. 116).

45. Paap (124) goes so far as to claim that for Grecized Jews of the Diaspora "the Greek word for 'God' had exactly the same value as the tetragram."

46. This judgment is confirmed, as far as Hellenistic Greek writings contemporaneous with the NT are concerned, by Meecham, who cites specific examples from the Epistle to Diognetus.

TABLE 1. *Statistical Summary of the New Testament Use of θεός*

	Singular												*Plural*				*Totals*		
	ὁ θεός as subject	ὁ θεός as predicate	θεός as subject	θεός as predicate	θεέ	ὁ θεός as vocative	τὸν θεόν	θεόν	τοῦ θεοῦ	θεοῦ	τῷ θεῷ	θεῷ	οἱ θεοί as subject	θεοί as predicate	θεούς	θεοῖς	articular θεός	anarthrous θεός	**Totals**
Matt.	5	4			2		7		24	6	1	2					41	10	51
Mark	6	3		1		2	3		27	3	2	1					43	5	48
Luke	12			1		2	22	3	66	6	7	3					109	13	122
John	14		1	2		1	9	4	36	10	3	1		1	1		63	20	83
Acts	62	1					27	3	54	4	12	1	1	1	1		157	10	167
Rom.	29		1	1			11	4	44	33	26	3					110	42	152
1 Cor.	29		2				3		29	27	11	3		2			72	34	106
2 Cor.	15	1	1	3			4	3	21	19	10	2					51	28	79
Gal.	7		1				2	2	8	7	2	1				1	19	12	31
Eph.	4	1		1				1	14	6	4						23	8	31
Phil.	7		1				1		2	8	3	1					13	10	23
Col.	2								13	2	4						19	2	21
1 Thess.	6		1				4		12	3	5	5					27	9	36
2 Thess.	4		1					2	6	1	2	2					12	6	18
1 Tim.	1		1					1	6	10		3					7	15	22
2 Tim.	2								6	3	2						10	3	13
Titus	1							1	6	4		1					7	6	13
Philem.										1	1						1	1	2
Heb.	20		1	1		2	3	2	22	7	8	2					55	13	68
James	3	1							3	5	4						11	5	16
1 Pet.	4	1					3	6	11	10	1	3					20	19	39
2 Pet.	1								4	2							5	2	7
1 John	12	1					9	1	34	2	3						59	3	62
2 John								1		1							0	2	2
3 John							1		2								3	0	3
Jude									1	1		2					1	3	4
Rev.	16			2		3	5		56	1	13						93	3	96
Totals	262	13	11	12	2	10	114	34	507	182	124	36	1	4	2	1	1,031	284	
	275		23																
	298				12		148		689		160		5		2	1	1,315		1,315

1. Of the 1,315 uses of θεός in the NT, 78.4% are articular and 21.6% anarthrous.
2. Only in 1 Timothy, 2 John, and Jude is the anarthrous θεός used more frequently than the articular. Whereas in 1 Peter, Titus, and Philemon (and, to a lesser extent, Philippians and Galatians) the usage is evenly balanced, in Revelation, 1 John, and Acts there is a marked predominance of the articular form.
3. By far the most common case is the genitive (689 uses), its most frequent use being in the (ὁ) ναὸς (τοῦ) θεοῦ construction.
4. In the nominative singular θεός rarely lacks the article when it is subject (11 times out of 273).
5. The plural occurs infrequently (8 times; singular, 1,307 times), a reflection of Judeo-Christian monotheism.

2. The Nominative Singular (ὁ) θεός

In the majority of cases (ὁ) θεός is followed by a verb denoting past, present, or future action (e.g., μονογενῆ ἀπέσταλκεν ὁ θεός, 1 John 4:9; ὁ θεὸς τρέφει αὐτούς, Luke 12:24; ὁ . . . θεὸς . . . ἡμᾶς ἐξεγερεῖ, 1 Cor. 6:14). However, in this study of the application to Christ of the term (ὁ) θεός, it is of more importance to examine the use of the term when it is accompanied by some form of εἶναι or when this verb is in ellipse.[47] The number that follows each verse (in parentheses) indicates the particular category to which the example belongs within the two broad classes discussed below under points *c* and *d*.

a. (ὁ) θεός with εἶναι Expressed

(1) ὁ θεός as Subject (24 Examples)[48]

John 3:2	οὐδεὶς γὰρ δύναται ταῦτα τὰ σημεῖα ποιεῖν ἃ σὺ ποιεῖς, ἐὰν μὴ ᾖ ὁ θεὸς μετ' αὐτοῦ (3).
John 3:33	ὁ θεὸς ἀληθής ἐστιν (cf. Rom. 3:4a) (2a).
John 8:42a	εἰ ὁ θεὸς πατὴρ ὑμῶν ἦν ἠγαπᾶτε ἂν ἐμέ (1a).
Acts 7:9	καὶ ἦν ὁ θεὸς μετ' αὐτοῦ (3).
Acts 10:34	οὐκ ἔστιν προσωπολήμπτης ὁ θεός (2a).
Acts 10:38b	ὁ θεὸς ἦν μετ' αὐτοῦ (3).
Rom. 1:9	μάρτυς γάρ μού ἐστιν ὁ θεός (cf. Phil. 1:8) (1a).
Rom. 11:23	δυνατὸς γάρ ἐστιν ὁ θεὸς πάλιν ἐγκεντρίσαι αὐτούς (2b).
1 Cor. 14:25b	ὄντως ὁ θεὸς ἐν ὑμῖν ἐστιν (4).

47. On the ellipsis of εἶναι, see BDF §§127–28.

48. This excludes Mark 12:29 (ἄκουε, Ἰσραήλ, κύριος ὁ θεὸς ἡμῶν κύριος εἷς ἐστιν), where ὁ θεὸς ἡμῶν is in apposition to the subject κύριος.

1 Cor. 14:33	οὐ γάρ ἐστιν ἀκαταστασίας ὁ θεὸς ἀλλὰ εἰρήνης (5).
1 Cor. 15:28	ἵνα ᾖ ὁ θεὸς τὰ πάντα ἐν πᾶσιν (1).[49]
2 Cor. 11:31	ὁ θεὸς καὶ πατὴρ τοῦ κυρίου Ἰησοῦ οἶδεν, ὁ ὢν[50] εὐλογητὸς εἰς τοὺς αἰῶνας (2b).
2 Cor. 13:11	ὁ θεὸς τῆς ἀγάπης καὶ εἰρήνης ἔσται μεθ' ὑμῶν (3).
Gal. 3:20	ὁ δὲ θεὸς εἷς ἐστιν (2a).
Eph. 2:4	ὁ δὲ θεὸς πλούσιος ὢν ἐν ἐλέει (2b).
Phil. 4:9	καὶ ὁ θεὸς τῆς εἰρήνης ἔσται μεθ' ὑμῶν (3).
James 1:13	ὁ γὰρ θεὸς ἀπείραστός ἐστιν κακῶν (2b).
James 2:19	εἷς ἐστιν ὁ θεός (v.l.) (2a).
1 John 1:5	ὁ θεὸς φῶς ἐστιν (1a).
1 John 3:20	μείζων ἐστὶν ὁ θεὸς τῆς καρδίας ἡμῶν (2b).
1 John 4:8b	ὁ θεὸς ἀγάπη ἐστίν (1a).
1 John 4:16b	ὁ θεὸς ἀγάπη ἐστίν (1a).
Rev. 21:3b	καὶ αὐτὸς ὁ θεὸς μετ' αὐτῶν ἔσται (3).
Rev. 21:22	ὁ γὰρ κύριος ὁ θεὸς ὁ παντοκράτωρ ναὸς αὐτῆς ἐστιν (1a).

(2) θεός as Subject (3 Examples)

John 1:18b	μονογενὴς θεὸς[51] ὁ ὢν[52] εἰς τὸν κόλπον τοῦ πατρός (v.l.) (4).
2 Cor. 5:19	θεὸς ἦν ἐν Χριστῷ κόσμον καταλλάσσων ἑαυτῷ (4).[53]
Phil. 2:13	θεὸς γάρ ἐστιν ὁ ἐνεργῶν ἐν ὑμῖν (1b).

(3) ὁ θεός as Predicate (3 Examples)

Matt. 22:32a	ἐγώ εἰμι ὁ θεὸς Ἀβραὰμ καὶ ὁ θεὸς Ἰσαὰκ καὶ ὁ θεὸς Ἰακώβ (= Exod. 3:6, 15–16 LXX; cf. Luke 20:37) (1b).[54]
Matt. 22:32b	οὐκ ἔστιν ὁ θεὸς νεκρῶν ἀλλὰ ζώντων (v.l.) (2a).[55]
1 John 5:20b	οὗτός ἐστιν ὁ ἀληθινὸς θεὸς καὶ ζωὴ αἰώνιος (2d).

(4) θεός as Predicate (8 Examples)

Mark 12:27	οὐκ ἔστιν θεὸς νεκρῶν ἀλλὰ ζώντων (2a).

49. All three editions of the UBS text bracket τά before πάντα.

50. Since ὁ ὤν is here equivalent to ὅς ἐστιν, this example may be conveniently included at this point.

51. In chapter III (on John 1:18) I argue that θεός is in epexegetic apposition to a substantival μονογενής which forms the subject; θεός may therefore be regarded here as a virtual subject.

52. See n. 50 above.

53. That ἦν . . . καταλλάσσων is probably not a periphrastic imperfect is shown by (1) the distance between the auxiliary and the participle; (2) the apparently fixed order of καταλλάσσειν–object–goal (with agency being expressed before or after these three elements) that appears elsewhere in Paul (e.g., 2 Cor. 5:18; Col. 1:20); and (3) with the verb καταλλάσσω agency is usually expressed by διά (as in the two verses cited above), not ἐν.

54. This is reckoned as a single example since (ἐγώ) εἰμι occurs only once.

55. All three editions of the UBS text bracket ὁ before θεός.

Luke 20:38	θεὸς[56] δὲ οὐκ ἔστιν νεκρῶν ἀλλὰ ζώντων (2a).
John 1:1b	θεὸς ἦν ὁ λόγος (3a).
John 8:54	ὃν ὑμεῖς λέγετε ὅτι θεὸς ἡμῶν ἐστιν (2a).
Rom. 9:5	ἐξ ὧν ὁ Χριστὸς τὸ κατὰ σάρκα, ὁ ὢν ἐπὶ πάντων θεὸς εὐλογητὸς εἰς τοὺς αἰῶνας, ἀμήν (2a).[57]
2 Cor. 6:16d	ἔσομαι αὐτῶν θεός (cf. Jer. 32:38; Ezek. 37:27) (1c).
2 Thess. 2:4c	ἀποδεικνύντα ἑαυτὸν ὅτι ἔστιν θεός (2a).
Rev. 21:7	ὁ νικῶν κληρονομήσει ταῦτα, καὶ ἔσομαι αὐτῷ θεὸς καὶ αὐτὸς ἔσται μοι υἱός (cf. 2 Sam. 7:14 and Heb. 8:10: ἔσομαι αὐτοῖς εἰς θεόν) (1c).

b. (ὁ) θεός with εἶναι Unexpressed

(1) ὁ θεός as Subject (21 Examples)[58]

Luke 1:68	εὐλογητὸς κύριος ὁ θεὸς τοῦ Ἰσραήλ (v.l.) (2a).
John 4:24	πνεῦμα ὁ θεός (1a).
Rom. 3:5b	μὴ ἄδικος ὁ θεὸς ὁ ἐπιφέρων τὴν ὀργήν; (2a).
Rom. 3:29	ἢ Ἰουδαίων ὁ θεὸς μόνον; (5).[59]
Rom. 3:30	εἷς ὁ θεὸς (2a).
Rom. 8:31	εἰ ὁ θεὸς ὑπὲρ ἡμῶν, τίς καθ' ἡμῶν; (4).
Rom. 15:33	ὁ δὲ θεὸς τῆς εἰρήνης μετὰ πάντων ὑμῶν (3).
1 Cor. 1:9	πιστὸς ὁ θεός (2a).
1 Cor. 10:13	πιστὸς δὲ ὁ θεός (2a).
1 Cor. 11:3	κεφαλὴ δὲ τοῦ Χριστοῦ ὁ θεός (1a).[60]
2 Cor. 1:3	εὐλογητὸς ὁ θεὸς καὶ πατὴρ τοῦ κυρίου ἡμῶν Ἰησοῦ Χριστοῦ (2a).
2 Cor. 1:18	πιστὸς δὲ ὁ θεός (2a).

56. Θεός is here predicative, since (1) in the Synoptic parallels (Matt. 22:32; Mark 12:27), (ὁ) θεός follows ἔστιν; and (2) θεός is anarthrous, not articular, and therefore is more likely to be the predicate than the subject since there are only two certain NT examples of an anarthrous θεός as subject with εἶναι following (viz., 2 Cor. 5:19; Phil. 2:13).

57. This takes ὁ ὤν as the equivalent of ὅς ἐστιν. Alternatively, if ὤν be regarded as otiose, one would have ὁ Χριστὸς . . . [ἐστιν] ὁ . . . ἐπὶ πάντων θεός. Again, the phrase θεὸς εὐλογητὸς εἰς τοὺς αἰῶνας, ἀμήν could be in apposition to ὁ Χριστός. See further chapter VI below.

58. Some render Heb. 1:8 as "God is your throne (ὁ θρόνος σου ὁ θεός)" (see below, chapter IX); and some translate Matt. 1:23 as "God is with us (μεθ' ἡμῶν ὁ θεός)" (see below, chapter XII §A). In 1 Thess. 2:10 (ὑμεῖς μάρτυρες καὶ ὁ θεός), both ἐστιν *and* μάρτυς are in ellipse. Similarly in Mark 10:18 = Luke 18:19 (cf. Mark 2:7), which reads οὐδεὶς ἀγαθὸς εἰ μὴ εἷς ὁ θεός, the phrase ὁ ὢν ἀγαθός or ὅς ἐστιν ἀγαθός is suppressed after ὁ θεός. See also 1 Cor. 3:7.

59. In full this would probably read ἢ θεὸς Ἰουδαίων ἐστιν ὁ θεὸς μόνον; (cf. Matt. 22:32 [according to K Π Θ f^{13} syr^{h} Or Chrys]: οὐκ ἔστιν (δὲ) ὁ θεὸς θεὸς νεκρῶν ἀλλὰ ζώντων).

60. Although the parallelism of ἡ κεφαλὴ . . . κεφαλὴ . . . κεφαλή might suggest that ὁ θεός is predicative in v. 3c, the anarthrous state of κεφαλή and the articular state of θεός make this improbable (cf. v. 3b).

Eph. 1:3	εὐλογητὸς ὁ θεὸς καὶ πατὴρ τοῦ κυρίου ἡμῶν Ἰησοῦ Χριστοῦ (2a).
Phil. 1:8	μάρτυς γάρ μου ὁ θεός (cf. Rom. 1:9) (1a).
Phil. 3:19	ὧν ὁ θεὸς ἡ κοιλία (1b).
Heb. 6:10	οὐ γὰρ ἄδικος ὁ θεὸς ἐπιλαθέσθαι (2b).
Heb. 11:19	λογισάμενος ὅτι καὶ ἐκ νεκρῶν ἐγείρειν δυνατὸς ὁ θεός (2b).
Heb. 12:29	καὶ γὰρ ὁ θεὸς ἡμῶν πῦρ καταναλίσκον (1a).
1 Pet. 1:3	εὐλογητὸς ὁ θεὸς καὶ πατὴρ τοῦ κυρίου ἡμῶν Ἰησοῦ Χριστοῦ (2a).
Rev. 4:8	ἅγιος ἅγιος ἅγιος κύριος ὁ θεὸς ὁ παντοκράτωρ (2a).
Rev. 18:8	ἰσχυρὸς κύριος ὁ θεὸς ὁ κρίνας αὐτήν (v.l.) (2a).

(2) θεός as Subject (2 Examples)[61]

Rom. 8:33b	θεὸς ὁ δικαιῶν (1c).[62]
1 Thess. 2:5	θεὸς μάρτυς (1a).

(3) ὁ θεός as Predicate (5 Examples)[63]

Mark 12:26b	ἐγὼ ὁ θεὸς Ἀβραὰμ καὶ ὁ θεὸς Ἰσαὰκ καὶ ὁ θεὸς Ἰακώβ (1a).[64]
Acts 7:32	ἐγὼ ὁ θεὸς τῶν πατέρων σου, ὁ θεὸς Ἀβραὰμ καὶ Ἰσαὰκ καὶ Ἰακώβ (v.l.) (1a).[65]
1 Cor. 12:6	καὶ διαιρέσεις ἐνεργημάτων· εἰσίν, ὁ δὲ αὐτὸς θεός, ὁ ἐνεργῶν τὰ πάντα ἐν πᾶσιν (2b).
2 Cor. 4:6	ὅτι ὁ θεὸς ὁ εἰπών . . . ὃς ἔλαμψεν (2b).
Heb. 11:10	τὴν . . . πόλιν ἧς τεχνίτης καὶ δημιουργὸς ὁ θεός (3a).

(4) θεός as Predicate (8 Examples)

1 Cor. 8:4	οὐδεὶς θεὸς εἰ μὴ εἷς (2c).
1 Cor. 8:6	ἀλλ' ἡμῖν εἷς θεὸς ὁ πατήρ (2c).
2 Cor. 1:21	ὁ δὲ βεβαιῶν ἡμᾶς σὺν ὑμῖν εἰς Χριστὸν καὶ χρίσας ἡμᾶς θεός (3b).
2 Cor. 5:5	ὁ δὲ κατεργασάμενος ἡμᾶς εἰς αὐτὸ τοῦτο θεός (3b).
Eph. 4:6	εἷς θεὸς καὶ πατὴρ πάντων (2c).

61. Some render Rom. 9:5 as "God(, who is over all,) be blessed for ever" (see below, chapter VI §D).

62. This may be punctuated as a question or exclamation rather than as a statement.

63. Some render Heb. 1:8 as "your throne is God" (see below, chapter IX §C.1).

64. This is reckoned as a single example since ἐγώ occurs only once. NA^{26}/UBS^{3} brackets the final two occurrences of ὁ before θεός.

65. Here the second ὁ θεός is appositional and introduces an explicative phrase, not a second separate predicate.

1 Tim. 2:5a	εἷς γὰρ θεός (2c).
Heb. 3:4	ὁ δὲ πάντα κατασκευάσας θεός (3b).
Rev. 21:3b	(καὶ αὐτὸς ὁ θεὸς μετ' αὐτῶν ἔσται) αὐτῶν θεός (v.l.) (2e).[66]

c. (ὁ) θεός as Subject (= nos. a.(1)–(2) and b.(1)–(2))

When ὁ θεός or θεός forms the *subject* of the sentence (50 times), the *predicate*[67] may be:

1. A substantive (e.g., φῶς), that is (a) anarthrous, *unless* (b) the proposition is reciprocating (as in Phil. 3:19) or (c) substantival participles are used (as in Rom. 8:33; 1 Cor. 12:6; Phil. 2:13)
2. An adjective (e.g., πιστός), either (a) standing alone or (b) introducing a clause or phrase
3. A μετά τινος construction (e.g., μεθ' ὑμῶν)
4. A prepositional phrase (e.g., ὑπὲρ ἡμῶν)
5. Introduced by an elliptical θεός (e.g., "or [is] God [the God] of Jews only?" Rom. 3:29)[68]

d. (ὁ) θεός as Predicate (= nos. a.(3)–(4) and b.(3)–(4))

When ὁ θεός or θεός is used predicatively (24 times), the subject of the sentence (whether expressed or unexpressed) may be:

1. First person singular: (a) ἐγώ, (b) ἐγώ εἰμι, or (c) ἔσομαι
2. Third person singular: ἐστίν (or ἔστιν) meaning (a) "he is," (b) "it is," (c) "there is"; or (d) οὗτός ἐστιν, "this is"; or (e) ἔσται, "he will be"
3. A substantive, either (a) a noun or (b) a substantival participle

On the basis of the data set out above, two observations may be made. First, it is apparent that, whether εἶναι be expressed or unexpressed, the NT writers prefer (1) the articular nominative ὁ θεός (45 times) to the anarthrous (5 uses) when "God" is the subject;[69] and (2) the anarthrous nominative θεός (16 uses) to the articular (8 uses)[70] when "God" is predicative.[71] Second, when the term θεός is used predicatively in the NT (24 times), it is usually qualified if articular (7 out of 8 examples), often qualified if anarthrous (11 out of 16 instances), this qualification being (1) a noun in the genitive (e.g., Acts 7:32: ὁ θεὸς τῶν πατέρων σου); (2) a personal pronoun in the

66. NA[26]/UBS[3] brackets αὐτῶν θεός.

67. Or further description of the subject (as in John 1:18; 2 Cor. 11:31; Eph. 2:4).

68. See n. 59 above.

69. This ratio (90% : 10%) is slightly higher than the general NT preponderance of articular over anarthrous uses of θεός (78.4% : 21.6%) (see above, §B.1).

70. Three of the eight uses relate to NT citations of Exod. 3:6, 15–16 (LXX).

71. This is not surprising, since predicative nouns are often anarthrous in the NT.

genitive (e.g., John 8:54: θεὸς ἡμῶν ἐστιν); (3) a substantival participle (as in 2 Cor. 4:6: ὁ θεὸς ὁ εἰπών); or (4) an adjective (e.g., 1 Cor. 8:6: εἷς θεός). Such qualification is lacking only in John 1:1; 2 Corinthians 1:21; 5:5; 2 Thessalonians 2:4; and Hebrews 3:4; 11:10. It appears, therefore, that NT writers generally avoid a statement such as "X is ὁ θεός" and prefer to qualify the affirmation that "X is θεός."

3. The Relation between ὁ θεός and θεός

Does NT usage make it antecedently probable that Jesus Christ could be called θεός but that the designation ὁ θεός would be denied him? Is there any evidence to suggest that the NT writers carefully distinguish between the articular and the anarthrous states of θεός?

a. Suggested Distinctions

It is well known that on several occasions Philo distinguished between the one true God (ὁ θεός) and the Logos (θεός).[72] Origen, too, drew a sharp distinction between θεός and ὁ θεός.[73] As θεός, the Son is not only distinct from ("numerically distinct")[74] but also inferior to the Father who is ὁ θεός and αὐτόθεος (i.e., God in an absolute sense). The Son is divine in a derivative sense, for he gains his deity by communication from the Father, "the only true God" (John 17:3) who is preeminent as the single source or fountain of deity.[75] As further evidence of a tendency, early in the Christian era, to distinguish between ὁ θεός and θεός, appeal could be made to the textual variants in the NT that evidently arose either from a scribal desire to create an incontestable "proof text" of the deity of Christ by adding the Greek article before θεός,[76] or from a belief that ὁ θεός was the more personal and θεός the more qualitative of the two terms.[77]

In the modern era, in his treatment of Sabellianism and the beginning of the trinitarian discussion, W. P. du Bose remarks (72; similarly Liddon, *Romans* 154) that "the Christian doctrine of the Trinity was perhaps before anything else an effort to express how Jesus was God (θεός) and yet in another sense was not God (ὁ θεός), that is to say, was not the whole Godhead." Again, R. Knight (42) finds a contrast in the first verse of the Prologue

72. For example, *Som.* 1:229–30. On Philonic use, see Goodenough 243–44.

73. *In Johannem* 2:2.

74. Ibid., 10:37.

75. See further Pollard, *Christology* 86–105.

76. For example, in John 1:18 all regard the articular ὁ μονογενὴς θεός read by $\mathfrak{P}^{75}$ $\aleph^{c}$ 33 cop^{bo} as secondary, whether the true reading be μονογενὴς θεός or ὁ μονογενὴς υἱός (see below, chapter III §A). Or again, in 1 Tim. 3:16 the twelfth-century minuscule 88 has refined the secondary variant θεὸς (ἐφανερώθη ἐν σαρκί) into ὁ θεὸς κτλ.

77. The spate of variants in James 2:19 may be divided into those in which ὁ θεός is found (UBS^3 gives a "C" preference to εἷς ἐστιν ὁ θεός) and those which have merely θεός (UBS^2 expressed a "C" preference for εἷς θεός ἐστιν, "there is one deity").

to the Fourth Gospel between God Unmanifest (ὁ θεός) and God Manifest (θεός). Finally, in particular reference to Johannine usage (which is found to be representative of the NT in general), B. F. Westcott claims that "the difference between ὁ θεός and θεός is such as might have been expected antecedently. The former brings before us the Personal God who has been revealed to us in a personal relation to ourselves: the latter fixes our thoughts on the general conception of the Divine Character and Being" (*Epistles* 172).

These representative statements of suggested distinctions may now be summarized. A difference has been thought to exist between (1) the Father (ὁ θεός) and the Son or Logos (θεός); (2) the Godhead (ὁ θεός) and any one member of the Godhead (θεός); (3) God unrevealed (ὁ θεός) and God in his self-revelation (θεός); and (4) God in personal relationship with human beings (ὁ θεός) and the general concept of deity (θεός).

b. Frequently Interchangeable

How valid are such distinctions? From three converging lines of evidence it becomes abundantly clear that in NT usage ὁ θεός and θεός are often interchangeable.

First, when it is a dependent genitive, θεός will be articular or anarthrous, generally depending on the state of the preceding noun; this is the canon of Apollonius.[78] Thus in 1 Corinthians 3:16a (οὐκ οἴδατε ὅτι ναὸς θεοῦ ἐστε;), θεοῦ is anarthrous because ναός is anarthrous, and ναός is anarthrous because it is predicative. In the following verse (1 Cor. 3:17), however, Paul twice uses ὁ ναὸς τοῦ θεοῦ. Examples are too numerous to be cited in full where either τοῦ θεοῦ or θεοῦ is attached to the same noun occurring twice or more within the same book.[79] While this oscillation may

78. See below, appendix I §B.1.

79. Examples are as follows:

		τοῦ θεοῦ	θεοῦ
Matt.	υἱός	16:16; 26:63	14:33; 27:43, 54
John	υἱός	1:34, 49; 3:18; 5:25; 11:4, 27; 20:31	19:7
	τέκνα	11:52	1:12
Rom.	υἱοί	8:19	8:14; 9:26
	τέκνα	8:21	8:16
	ἀλήθεια	1:25; 3:7	15:8
	νόμος	7:22; 8:7	7:25
	δικαιοσύνη	10:3 *bis*	1:17; 3:5, 21, 22
	θέλημα	1:10; 12:2	15:32
1 Cor.	πνεῦμα	2:11, 14; 3:16; 6:11	7:40; 12:3
	μυστήριον	2:1	4:1
	σοφία	1:21	1:24; 2:7
	βασιλεία	4:20	6:10; 15:50
Eph.	θέλημα	6:6	1:1
Heb.	χάρις	12:15	2:9 v.l.
1 Pet.	θέλημα	2:15; 3:17; 4:19	4:2
1 John	τέκνα	3:10; 5:2	3:1, 2
Rev.	σφραγίς	9:4	7:2

Table 2. *Prepositions with (ὁ) θεός*

Preposition	*Articular*	*Anarthrous*
1. ἀπό	Rom. 15:15[a]	Rom. 1:7
	1 Cor. 4:5	1 Cor. 1:3, 30; 6:19
	Heb. 6:7	Heb. 3:12
2. ἐκ	John 7:17, 8:42, 47 *bis*	John 1:13
	1 Cor. 2:12; 11:12	1 Cor. 7:7
	2 Cor. 3:5, 5:18	2 Cor. 2:17; 5:1
3. παρά (+ dat.)	Mark 10:27b	Mark 10:27a
	Luke 1:30; 18:27	Luke 2:52
	1 Cor. 3:19	1 Cor. 7:24
4. ἐν	Rom. 5:11	Rom. 2:17
	1 Thess. 2:2	1 Thess. 1:1
5. εἰς	Acts 6:11; 24:15	Acts 20:21
6. ἐπί (+ acc.)[b]	Acts 15:19; 26:18, 20	Acts 14:15
7. παρά (+ gen.)	John 5:44; 6:46; 8:40; 16:27[c]	John 1:6; 9:16, 33
8. πρός (+ acc.)	Rom. 5:1; 10:1; 15:17, 30	Rom. 4:2
9. ὑπό	Gal. 3:17	Gal. 4:9

a. ℵ* B F read ἀπό; other manuscripts read ὑπό, the reading preferred by NA[26].

b. In each of these four instances in Acts, the prepositional phrase follows ἐπιστρέφειν.

c. 𝔓[5] ℵ*,b A N Θ 33 *al* do not have the article in John 16:27, which is bracketed in UBS[3] and NA[26].

often be grammatically or theologically conditioned,[80] and not capricious, the fact of the possible interchangeability remains.[81]

Second, table 2 lists examples where the same preposition is used with both articular and anarthrous θεός within one NT book (or, in the case of Mark 10:27, within a single verse). Even though a definite grammatical or stylistic principle sometimes accounts for the presence or absence of the article, it remains true that the same basic fact (such as divine origin or agency) may be expressed by articular θεός or by anarthrous θεός.

In the third place, in the NT θεός (like κύριος) is virtually a proper name and consequently shares the imprecision with regard to the use of the article that seems to mark all proper names.[82]

It is therefore not possible to maintain that whenever θεός is anarthrous, it differs from ὁ θεός in meaning or emphasis.

c. Occasionally Distinguishable

That an important distinction is on occasion drawn between ὁ θεός and θεός is perhaps most evident from the NT use of the anarthrous accusative

80. See, e.g., the discussion of νόμος by E. D. Burton 443–60; and of δικαιοσύνη by Oepke.

81. That no *consistent* pattern of usage may be discerned is well illustrated by the use of ἐν with τῷ πνεύματι τοῦ θεοῦ in 1 Cor. 6:11 and with πνεύματι θεοῦ in 1 Cor. 12:3. Examination of all the instances shows that neither the case of the noun on which (τοῦ) θεοῦ is dependent nor the meaning of the preposition used with that noun is an adequate criterion for determining whether the noun will be articular or anarthrous.

82. See BDF §§254.(1), 260; Robertson, *Grammar* 761, 795; N. Turner, *Syntax* 165–66, 174.

θεόν.[83] Sometimes the change from τὸν θεόν to θεόν is clearly without importance, according with certain well-known grammatical principles (such as Granville Sharp's "rule"), as in Luke 20:37 (ὡς λέγει κύριον τὸν θεὸν Ἀβραὰμ καὶ θεὸν Ἰσαὰκ καὶ θεὸν Ἰακώβ) where the God of Abraham cannot be considered in any sense distinct from the God of Isaac and Jacob (see Acts 7:32). Yet in Romans 1:21 the same change cannot be deemed insignificant. Those who clearly perceived, through the visible creation, that God exists and that he possesses "eternal power and deity" (= "they knew God," γνόντες τὸν θεόν) are without excuse for they failed to give him the glory that is his due because of who he is (= "they did not honor him as God," οὐχ ὡς θεὸν ἐδόξασαν). In this context the anarthrous θεόν seems to denote "God as he is in himself," the one who possesses divine qualities, and τὸν θεόν "what may be known of God" (τὸ γνωστὸν τοῦ θεοῦ, v. 19),[84] the one who has manifested his invisible nature.[85]

Γνόντες τὸν θεόν of Romans 1:21 should be compared with (νῦν δὲ) γνόντες θεόν in Galatians 4:9. Although formerly the Galatians had been without any real knowledge of the God of whom alone deity may be predicated (τότε . . . οὐκ εἰδότες θεόν)[86]—in comparison with gods who lack true deity (τοῖς φύσει μὴ οὖσιν θεοῖς) (Gal. 4:8)—now they had come to know God as the sole possessor of deity. Similarly in John 1:18a (θεὸν οὐδεὶς ἑώρακεν πώποτε) and 1 John 4:12a (θεὸν οὐδεὶς πώποτε τεθέαται), θεός emphasizes God as he is in himself, God in his divine essence and attributes, God who cannot be directly known. That John expected his readers to find in θεός in these passages some such distinctive meaning seems confirmed by the fact that in the Fourth Gospel τὸν θεόν occurs nine times and θεόν only four times, while in his first epistle τὸν θεόν occurs nine times and θεόν this once. Again, in Titus 1:16 the corrupt and unbelieving are said to profess to know God as he really is in himself (θεὸν ὁμολογοῦσιν εἰδέναι) but their deeds belie any such knowledge. Finally, Paul avers that those who lack any knowledge of God in his reality (τοῖς μὴ εἰδόσιν θεόν), who refuse to obey the gospel of the Lord Jesus, will become the objects of the Lord's flaming vengeance when he is revealed from heaven (2 Thess. 1:8). The phrase οἱ μὴ εἰδότες θεόν differs from τὰ ἔθνη τὰ μὴ εἰδότα τὸν θεόν (1 Thess. 4:5) only in connotation, not denotation: in the former case the apostle is emphasizing their ignorance of the God who alone possesses deity, who alone is God, while in the latter case he is stressing their ignorance of God as he has made himself known.

From all this one may enunciate the general principle that when a writer wishes to highlight divine qualities (viz., godhood), θεός (not ὁ θεός) will

83. Generally (114 times out of 148) the articular form τὸν θεόν is found. Often τὸν θεόν or θεόν follows one of the following verbs: δοξάζω, ὁράω, εὐλογέω, αἰνέω, φοβέομαι, σέβομαι, οἶδα, γινώσκω, ἀγαπάω.

84. Cf. the τὸν θεόν that follows γινώσκειν in John 17:3; 1 Cor. 1:21; 1 John 4:6, 7, 8.

85. This oxymoron is clear from vv. 19–20a.

86. Cf. 2 John 9: πᾶς ὁ προάγων καὶ μὴ μένων ἐν τῇ διδαχῇ τοῦ Χριστοῦ θεὸν οὐκ ἔχει.

often be used.[87] This accords with the fact that the anarthrous state of a noun may draw attention to the characteristic quality of the person or thing specified.

A further indication that ὁ θεός and θεός are not always interchangeable may be seen in the uniform use of articular θεός with certain words[88] and its customary use with personal pronouns.[89]

Thus it is evident that the use or nonuse of the article with θεός does not usually, but on occasion may, give the term a special connotation.[90] If, within a single sentence (e.g., John 1:1), an author uses both θεός and ὁ θεός, it would seem *a priori* likely that he intends a distinction to be drawn that will be apparent from the context.

4. *The Principal Referent(s) of (ὁ) θεός*

Even if a consistent distinction is not drawn between θεός and ὁ θεός in NT usage, does the term, in either its articular or its anarthrous form, consistently have the same referent when it is applied to the Deity? What is the customary conceptual content of θεός in the NT?

87. So also in the papyri (Mayser §58).

88. Viz., ἐνώπιον (26 uses; but cf. ἐνώπιον κυρίου in Luke 1:15, 76; 2 Cor. 8:21; James 4:10), εὐχαριστέω, κύριος (in the phrase κύριος ὁ θεός = יהוה אלהים), ἔμπροσθεν (4 uses), ἐναντίον (2 uses), ἔναντι (2 uses); also ὁ λόγος (except for 1 Thess. 2:13b; 1 Tim. 4:5; 1 Pet. 1:23) and ἡ βασιλεία in the Gospels and Acts.

89. With regard to word order, the personal pronoun invariably follows θεός, which is generally (43 out of 50 cases) articular. The 7 cases where a personal pronoun follows an anarthrous θεός are only apparent exceptions. In Matt. 27:46 *bis*, μου follows the vocative θεέ (which cannot be articular). In John 20:17b (ἀναβαίνω πρὸς τὸν πατέρα μου καὶ πατέρα ὑμῶν καὶ θεόν μου καὶ θεὸν ὑμῶν), the 2 instances of θεόν are virtually articular, being linked to the preceding nouns (πατέρα, *bis*) by the common bond of πρὸς τόν. Since there is a single referent (ὁ πατήρ = ὁ θεός), the preposition and article would not normally be repeated. Then θεοῦ is anarthrous in Luke 1:78 (διὰ σπλάγχνα ἐλέους θεοῦ ἡμῶν) because the preceding noun on which it is dependent (ἐλέους) is without the article (Apollonius's canon). Finally, both John 8:54 (ὃν ὑμεῖς λέγετε ὅτι θεὸς ἡμῶν ἐστιν) and Heb. 11:16 (διὸ οὐκ ἐπαισχύνεται αὐτοὺς ὁ θεὸς ἐπικαλεῖσθαι αὐτῶν) afford examples of the predicative θεός (which accordingly is anarthrous).

90. With this conclusion compare the detailed distinction ("hints . . . worthy of attention") proposed by Webster (29), which, it would seem, is based primarily on *a priori* considerations rather than on an explanation of all the data.

> Θεός occurs without the article (1), where the Deity is contrasted with what is human, or with the universe as distinct from its Creator, or with the nature and acts of evil spirits; (2), when the essential attributes of Deity are spoken of; (3), when operations proceeding from God are appropriated to one of the three Divine Persons; (4), when the Deity is spoken of as heathens would speak, or a Jew who denied the existence of the Son and of the Holy Spirit. But the article seems to be used (1), when the Deity is spoken of in the Christian point of view, as the one true God, opposed to the gods of Heathenism; (2), when the First Person of the blessed Trinity is specially designated, unless its insertion is unnecessary by the addition of πατήρ, or some distinctive epithet.

For a critique of B. Weiss's analysis ("Gebrauch") of the NT use or nonuse of the article with θεός, see Funk 146–67. It was the opinion of Meecham with regard to Hellenistic Greek writings contemporary with the NT that no differentiation can be made between the articular θεός and the anarthrous θεός.

Those who read the NT in the light of trinitarian controversies or scholastic theology aver that ὁ θεός denotes the Triune God in general or any one person of the Trinity in particular. Since "God" *signifies* the person who inherently possesses the divine nature, this term also can *stand for* each of the three persons to whom this nature is proper and for all three persons considered together. Such logic is built on a distinction important in medieval scholasticism. There are two possible levels of "meaning" in words. *Signification* is the basic conception connected with a word; thus "scripture" *signifies* (*significat*) something that is written. *Supposition*, on the other hand, is the application of a word whose signification is known to a particular instance; thus "Scripture" *stands for* (*supponitur*), or actually refers to, the Bible.

Addressing the problem of whether this interpretation of the NT evidence that reads the data through the spectacles of trinitarian formulation fairly represents the NT usage, K. Rahner has proposed a radically different solution while still employing the terminology of scholastic logic (125–48). In the NT, Rahner argues, ὁ θεός *signifies* the Father and does not simply *stand for* him (126, 143–44). In the First Person of the Trinity one finds the "inner signification" of the word ὁ θεός, not merely a "suppositional application" (132, 144). Ὁ θεός does not stand for any one of the three persons of the Trinity or all three persons together but generally signifies and consequently stands for the Father alone (126, 146).

Significantly, Rahner prefaces the exposition of his thesis with an explanation of its importance for practical theology. In praying to "God," Christians are not addressing God in general or the God of natural theology or even the three persons of the Trinity indifferently. Prayer is to be directed specifically to the Father through the mediation of Christ by those who are "children of God" (not children of the Son or Spirit) (128–30).

To begin, Rahner states two *prima facie* objections to his thesis (130). Although in the phrases *Son of God* and *Spirit of God*, the term *God* obviously stands for the Father, when the NT refers to the God of the OT, the God of creation, or the God of natural theology, the Triune God is signified. This argument Rahner answers (132–35) by observing that the "absolutely Unoriginate" to whom natural theology ascends must be the Father (though he is not known as such) and also the Creator, who is, in NT usage, none other than the Ruler of the Old Covenant. The second objection, confesses Rahner, may seem more weighty. The texts in which (ὁ) θεός is used of the Son show that in the NT ὁ θεός only stands for the Father but does not signify him. Acknowledging that there are six such texts, Rahner finds in their relative fewness an indication (1) that the word θεός does not have that quasi-generic signification which would have allowed the term to be used much more frequently when the NT speaks of Christ's divinity, and (2) that originally ὁ θεός signified the Father alone (135–38).

Then there follows Rahner's positive demonstration of his thesis, which falls into two parts. First, he has little difficulty in demonstrating that ὁ θεός nearly always refers exclusively to the Father (138–44). For example, where the terms ὁ θεός and κύριος Ἰησοῦς Χριστός stand side by side, as in the so-called trinitarian formulas, ὁ θεός stands for the Father. Juxtaposition implies distinction. This constant and almost exclusive suppositional use of ὁ θεός for the Father amounts to proof that the word actually signifies that for which it so frequently stands suppositionally. Second, he claims (144–45) that ὁ θεός must have the significative meaning of Father because, in certain "critical instances" where precision and clarity demanded the use of a word that signified the thing meant, ὁ θεός is found, although ὁ πατήρ was available. Thus, in many decisive NT statements regarding the person of Christ, he is called ὁ υἱὸς τοῦ θεοῦ (not ὁ υἱὸς τοῦ πατρός).

Such a brief synopsis of Rahner's view scarcely does justice to his closely reasoned argument. But it will be obvious that he has squarely faced the basic issue: To whom are the NT writers referring when they speak of ὁ θεός? And, stripped of its philosophical—some would say, casuistical—casing, his answer may stand.[91] Customarily, (ὁ) θεός denotes the Father, but exceptionally it refers to the Son.[92] That (ὁ) θεός generally refers specifically to the trinitarian Father is clearly seen in each strand of the NT, but particularly in the testimony of John and Paul.

Before examining these strands separately, I should isolate the general bases for this conclusion. First, there is the use of the compound appellative θεὸς πατήρ in various combinations (see §4d below), each of which implies that θεός is identified with the Father. When this πατήρ lacks a defining genitive, it is invidious to choose between Jesus Christ and believers as the person or persons to whom that fatherhood is exhibited. Both are probably included, since on occasion each is joined to the word pair (ὁ) θεός (καὶ) πατήρ[93] and the sonship of believers is based on the sonship of Jesus.[94] Second, in embryonic trinitarian formulas of the NT where the Father, Jesus, and the Holy Spirit are mentioned in conjunction, the term θεός is reserved for the Father and is never applied to the Son or the Spirit.[95] Third, there are numerous passages in which ὁ θεός is distinguished from κύριος Ἰησοῦς Χριστός (or various combinations of these

91. Rahner's translator, C. Ernst, delineates a third level of "meaning" in words—significative, suppositional, *and* contextual (i.e., meaning in use; "what ordinarily comes to mind")—and avers that Rahner has shown that ὁ θεός "means" the Father only in this latter sense (which, he believes, is not properly *significatio*) (127–28 n. 1).

92. Concurrence with Rahner in this latter point (with regard to the Son) presupposes the discussion of subsequent chapters.

93. For example, Eph. 1:3: ὁ θεὸς καὶ πατὴρ τοῦ κυρίου ἡμῶν Ἰησοῦ Χριστοῦ; and Col. 1:2: χάρις ὑμῖν καὶ εἰρήνη ἀπὸ θεοῦ πατρὸς ἡμῶν.

94. Matt. 11:27; Gal. 4:4–6.

95. For example, Rom. 15:30; Eph. 4:4–6.

names). Often the names are simply juxtaposed, implying a distinction between them (e.g., Rom. 8:17: believers are "heirs of God and coheirs with Christ"). Sometimes God's action is related to Christ (e.g., Acts 2:36: "God has made this Jesus, whom you crucified, both Lord and Christ") or Christ's action is related to God (e.g., Luke 11:20: Jesus exorcised demons by the finger of God). Because the NT never uses ὁ θεός of the Holy Spirit, this θεός to whom Christ is in some way related must be the Father. Finally, in many texts θεός is defined as "Father" by a reference in the immediate context to ὁ πατήρ (e.g., John 6:32–33), sonship (e.g., John 3:17), regeneration (e.g., John 1:12–13), or brotherhood (e.g., 1 John 4:21).

a. Synoptic Gospels

Although the θεὸς πατήρ combination is never found in the Synoptic Gospels, the absolute ὁ πατήρ on occasion stands in contrast with ὁ υἱός and clearly denotes God the Father.[96] Then in 6:26 (= Luke 12:24) and 10:29 (= Luke 12:6), Matthew has ὁ πατὴρ ὑμῶν where Luke has ὁ θεός. "(Heavenly) Father" is apparently used as a synonym for God in Matthew 6:26, 32 (cf. the intervening 6:30) and 16:17 (cf. 16:15).

Baptism is to be administered in the name of the Father, the Son, and the Holy Spirit (Matt. 28:19). Just as the disciples of Jesus are designated "sons of God" (Matt. 5:9), so Jesus is called "the Son of God" (e.g., Mark 1:1; 5:7), and the Holy Spirit "the Spirit of God" (Matt. 3:16; 12:28). In these latter two cases ("Son of God" and "Spirit of God") (at least), θεός cannot mean "the Triune God."

With regard to the life and mission of Jesus, God was present in the virgin's Son (Matt. 1:23); Jesus was the Holy One of God (Mark 1:24) and "a prophet mighty in deed and word before God" (Luke 24:19); God's favor was on him (Luke 2:40) and he increased in favor with God (Luke 2:52); he offered prayer to God (Matt. 27:46; Luke 6:12); and he exorcised demons by the finger of God (Luke 11:20) or by the Spirit of God (Matt. 12:28).

b. Johannine Corpus

In four places in the Fourth Gospel the terms *God* and *Father* are actually conjoined. Jesus is accused of calling God his Father (5:18). God the Father is said to have set his seal on the Son of Man (6:27). To the Jews' assertion "we have one Father, even God" (8:41), Jesus replies, "If God were your Father, you would love me" (8:42). Often the equation "θεός = the Father" is clearly implicit because of a contextual connection with sonship (e.g., 3:16: "For God so loved the world that he gave his only Son"; cf. 1 John 4:9–10)[97] or an accompanying mention of the Father (e.g., "God is spirit,

96. Matt. 11:27 (= Luke 10:22); Matt. 24:36 (= Mark 13:32); Luke 9:26.
97. See also John 1:12–13, 34, 49; 3:17–18, 36; 5:25; 10:36; 11:4, 27, 52.

and those who worship him must worship in spirit and truth" [4:24] follows "true worshipers will worship the Father in spirit and truth" [4:23]).[98] In fact, of the 83 uses of (ὁ) θεός in the Fourth Gospel, the only places where the term could not or does not refer to the Father are 1:1b, 1:18b, 10:34–35,[99] and 20:28 (see chapters II–IV below).

A similar picture emerges from the Johannine Epistles and, to some extent, from the Apocalypse. One finds the actual conjunction of the terms θεός and πατήρ (2 John 3: "Grace, mercy, and peace will be with us, from God the Father and from Jesus Christ the Father's Son, in truth and love"; also Rev. 1:6), the contextual association of the terms (e.g., 2 John 9: "He who abides in the doctrine of Christ has both the Father and the Son"),[100] and the link between θεός and sonship (e.g., 1 John 3:1: "See what love the Father has lavished on us, that we should be called children of God"),[101] regeneration (e.g., 1 John 4:7b: "Everyone who loves has been born of God"),[102] and brotherhood (e.g., 1 John 4:21: "The person who loves God should love his brother also").[103] And in four texts in the Apocalypse, the terms ὁ θεός and Ἰησοῦς are closely linked yet not identified (Rev. 1:2; 14:12; 20:4, 6) and several times the risen Christ speaks of "my God" (Rev. 3:2, 12 [4×]; also John 20:17) and once of "my Father" (Rev. 3:21).

c. Acts

Repeatedly in the Book of Acts Jesus is the person involved in some action of θεός. He was anointed by God (10:38) and attested by God (2:22). God brought him to Israel as a Savior (13:23), raised him from the dead (e.g., 2:24, 32),[104] glorified him (3:13), exalted him by his right hand (2:33; 5:31; cf. 2:36), and ordained him to be judge of the living and the dead (10:42; cf. 17:31). Jesus was God's Christ (3:18), God's Son (9:20). The apostolic mission involved preaching the kingdom of God and teaching about the Lord Jesus Christ (28:31; cf. 8:12). But nowhere in Acts is this distinction between Jesus and God more pronounced than in 7:55–56 where at his martyrdom Stephen sees the glory of God and Jesus standing at God's right hand.[105]

98. See also John 5:42, 44; 6:28–29, 33, 45–46; 8:42, 54; 10:35; 11:40; 13:3 *bis*; 14:1; 16:2, 27; 17:3; 20:17.

99. On the use of Ps. 82:6 in John 10:34–36, see Neyrey, "Gods." Jesus' argument seems to be as follows: If there is scriptural precedent for the use of θεοί in reference to mere mortals who received God's word, how can the one whom the Father consecrated and sent into the world as the bearer of his Word be guilty of blasphemy when he claims to be υἱὸς θεοῦ?

100. See also 1 John 2:14–17; 3:1; 2 John 3.

101. See also 1 John 3:2, 8, 10a; 4:4, 9–10, 15; 5:1–2, 9–11, 13, 20; Rev. 2:18; 21:7.

102. See also 1 John 3:9 *bis*; 5:4, 18 *bis*.

103. See also 1 John 3:10b; 4:20.

104. See also Acts 3:15, 26; 4:10; 5:30; 10:40; 13:30, 33–34, 37; 17:31.

105. This passage remains relevant even if καί is epexegetic in Acts 7:55b (εἶδεν δόξαν θεοῦ καὶ Ἰησοῦν ἑστῶτα ἐκ δεξιῶν τοῦ θεοῦ).

d. Pauline Corpus

On no fewer than 33 occasions Paul directly links the terms θεός and πατήρ to form a single compound appellative.[106] His most common combination is θεὸς πατήρ (17 times, especially with prepositions) but ὁ θεός καὶ πατήρ is also frequently used (11 times). The other combinations are ὁ θεὸς πατήρ (Col. 1:3; 3:17), ὁ θεὸς ὁ πατήρ (2 Thess. 2:16), εἷς θεὸς ὁ πατήρ (1 Cor. 8:6), and εἷς θεὸς καὶ πατήρ (Eph. 4:6). Invariably πατήρ follows θεός:[107] whenever the combination occurs, the word *God* is being defined in terms of fatherhood, not fatherhood in terms of deity. When the apostle qualifies πατήρ, he uses ἡμῶν (18 times)[108] or τοῦ κυρίου Ἰησοῦ Χριστοῦ (5 times) or πάντων (Eph. 4:6). But 9 times πατήρ stands without any genitive limitation.[109] Moreover, as in John, so in Paul θεός and πατήρ are sometimes closely related in thought. For example, Christ has reconciled both Jews and Gentiles "to God in one body through the cross," so that through him "both have access in one Spirit to the Father" (Eph. 2:16, 18).

Another clear indication that for Paul ὁ θεός designated the Father is provided by the embryonic trinitarian formulations found in his letters. Second Corinthians 13:13 is the classic instance.[110] Paul invokes upon the Corinthians the grace that is given by the Lord Jesus Christ, the love that is shown by God, and the fellowship that is engendered by the Spirit. It is instructive, in this regard, to compare the trinitarian formulation in Matthew 28:19 with usage characteristic of Paul (e.g., Rom. 15:30; 1 Cor. 12:4–6; 2 Cor. 13:13). The Matthean ὁ πατήρ becomes the Pauline ὁ θεός, ὁ υἱός becomes ὁ κύριος (Ἰησοῦς Χριστός), and τὸ (ἅγιον) πνεῦμα remains unchanged.

Then there are many "binitarian" formulas that distinguish "God" from "the Lord," "his Son," or similar expressions.[111] "God sent forth his Son" (Gal. 4:4). Christ gave himself up for Christians, "a fragrant offering and sacrifice to God" (Eph. 5:2). "God raised the Lord" from the dead (1 Cor. 6:14). Believers have "peace with God through our Lord Jesus Christ" (Rom. 5:1) and are "heirs of God and coheirs with Christ" (Rom. 8:17). Most remarkable are the three passages in 1 Corinthians which not only distinguish Christ from God but also subordinate Christ to God the Father: 3:23 ("Christ is God's"), 11:3 ("God is the head of Christ"), and 15:28 (after delivering the

106. On θεὸς πατήρ as a compound name, see E. D. Burton 385–90; G. Schrenk, *TDNT* 5:1006–8.

107. See, however, the textual variant τῷ πατρὶ καὶ θεῷ in Eph. 5:20 read by 𝔓[46] D* G it syr[pal] goth arm Ambrosiaster.

108. Three of these eighteen are somewhat uncertain (viz., 1 Tim. 1:2; 2 Tim. 1:2; Titus 1:4) since ἡμῶν follows the reference to Christ Jesus and could be restricted in reference.

109. In these cases the fatherhood is probably related to both believers and Christ (thus E. D. Burton 388).

110. See also Rom. 8:11; 15:30; 1 Cor. 12:4–6; 2 Cor. 1:21–22; Eph. 4:4–6.

111. On the linguistic association of "God" and "Christ" in Paul, see R. R. Williams, "Binitarianisms."

kingdom "to God the Father" [v. 24], "the Son himself will also be subjected to him who put everything under him").

So closely are the concepts of deity and fatherhood related in Paul's thought that θεός has gained some of the distinctive connotations of πατήρ, and πατήρ of θεός. Thus in 2 Corinthians 1:3 Paul refers to the Father who shows mercy and also to the God *who gives comfort*. On the other hand, in Ephesians 1:17 "the God of our Lord Jesus Christ" is described as "the Father *of glory*." Deity involves paternal care and friendship as well as power and glory, while fatherhood involves majesty and sovereignty as well as benevolent love.

e. Hebrews, James, and Jude

In three General Epistles, too, there is ample evidence to support the thesis that θεός generally points to the Father of Jesus and of believers.

For the author of Hebrews, "God has spoken . . . by a Son" (1:1–2), Christ, who "was faithful over God's house as a Son" (3:6). Jesus came to do God's will (10:7), was "designated by God to be high priest in the order of Melchizedek" (5:10), and now serves as "a great priest over the house of God" (10:21). In making expiation for sin he was "a merciful and faithful high priest in the service of God" (2:17). "Through the eternal Spirit (Christ) offered himself without blemish to God" (9:14), "by God's grace" tasting death for everyone (2:9). After being raised by "the God of peace" (13:20), he sat down "at God's right hand" (10:12; cf. 12:2) and now appears "in the presence of God" on behalf of Christians (9:24) who "draw near to God through him" (7:25; cf. 13:15) and have come to "a judge who is God of all, . . . and to Jesus, the mediator of a new covenant" (12:23–24). Believers are God's sons (12:7), as Jesus is God's Son (4:14; 6:6; 7:3; 10:29). God's exercise of divine fatherhood is the theme of 12:3–11: "My son, do not make light of the discipline of the Lord. . . . God is treating you as sons. . . . Shall we not much more be subject to the Father of spirits and live?"

James 1:1 distinguishes God from the Lord Jesus Christ. A definition is given in 1:27 of pure and faultless religion "before God who is our Father (παρὰ τῷ θεῷ καὶ πατρί)," while in 3:9a ὁ κύριος καὶ πατήρ is a synonym for θεός (3:9b).

The addressees in Jude are "those who are called, who are loved by God the Father (ἐν θεῷ πατρί) and kept by Jesus Christ" (v. 1). "Our only Master and Lord, Jesus Christ" is distinguished from "our God" in verse 4 and later (v. 25) "the only God" is called "our Savior through Jesus Christ our Lord."

f. Petrine Epistles

First Peter begins with one of the clearest trinitarian formulations in the NT, and, like Ephesians 4:4–6, it is distinctive in that θεός is defined by πατήρ: "To the exiles . . . chosen on the basis of the foreknowledge of God the Father (θεοῦ πατρός), sanctified by the Spirit for obedience and the sprinkling of Jesus Christ's blood" (1 Pet. 1:1–2). Then follows an introductory benediction (identical with 2 Cor. 1:3 and Eph. 1:3) that again juxtaposes θεός and πατήρ ("blessed be the God and Father (ὁ θεὸς καὶ πατήρ) of our Lord Jesus Christ," 1 Pet. 1:3). And 2 Peter 1:17 states that Jesus "received honor and glory from God the Father (παρὰ θεοῦ πατρός)."

God and Christ are associated yet distinguished in references to the resurrection (1 Pet. 1:21), the offering of acceptable spiritual sacrifices (1 Pet. 2:5), the bringing of the unrighteous to God (1 Pet. 3:18), the session of Christ (1 Pet. 3:22), the glorification of God (1 Pet. 4:11c), the call to eternal glory (1 Pet. 5:10), and the object of the Christian's knowledge (2 Pet. 1:2).

g. Conclusion

No attempt has been made in the preceding survey to be exhaustive. But we have seen that throughout the NT (ὁ) θεός is so often associated with and yet differentiated from κύριος Ἰησοῦς Χριστός that the reader is forced to assume that there must be both a hypostatic distinction and an interpersonal relationship between the two. The writers of the NT themselves supply the key by speaking not only of ὁ θεός and Ἰησοῦς but also of ὁ πατήρ and ὁ υἱός, of ὁ υἱὸς τοῦ θεοῦ and of ὁ θεὸς καὶ πατὴρ κυρίου ἡμῶν Ἰησοῦ Χριστοῦ. God is the Father (in the trinitarian sense), Jesus is the Lord (1 Cor. 8:6). When (ὁ) θεός is used, we are to assume that the NT writers have ὁ πατήρ in mind unless the context makes this sense of (ὁ) θεός impossible.[112]

112. A related question demands brief treatment. To whom did the NT writers attribute the divine action described in the OT? To answer "the Lord God" (יהוה אלהים = LXX κύριος ὁ θεός) is to beg the question, for the authors of the NT wrote of OT events in the light of their trinitarian understanding of God. A clear distinction must be drawn between what the OT text meant to its authors and readers and how it was understood by the early Christians who lived after the advent of the Messiah and the coming of the Spirit. Certainly the person who projects the trinitarian teaching of the NT back into the OT and reads the OT through the spectacles of the dynamic or trinitarian monotheism of the NT is thinking anachronistically. On the other hand, it does not seem illegitimate to pose a question such as this: To whom was the author of Hebrews referring when he said (1:1), "At many times and in various ways *God* spoke in the past to our forefathers through the prophets"? That it was not the Holy Spirit in any ultimate sense is evident from the fact that in neither the OT nor the NT is the Spirit called "God" *expressis verbis*. And, in spite of the fact that the LXX equivalent of יהוה, viz., κύριος, is regularly applied to Jesus in the NT so that it becomes less a title than a proper name, it is not possible that ὁ θεός in Heb. 1:1 denotes Jesus Christ, for the same sentence (in Greek) contains "(the God who spoke . . .) in these last days has spoken to us in a Son (ἐν υἱῷ)." Since the author is emphasizing the continuity of the two phases of divine speech (ὁ θεὸς λαλήσας . . . ἐλάλησεν), this reference to a Son shows that ὁ θεός was understood to be "God the Father." Similarly, the differentiation made between ὁ θεός as the one who speaks in both eras and υἱός as his final means of speaking shows that in the author's mind it was not the Triune God of Christian theology who spoke to the forefathers by the prophets. That is to say, for the author of Hebrews (as for all NT writers, one may suggest) "the God of our fathers," Yahweh, was no other than "the God and Father of our Lord Jesus Christ" (compare Acts 2:30 and 2:33; 3:13 and 3:18; 3:25 and 3:26; note also 5:30). Such a conclusion is entirely consistent with the regular NT usage of ὁ θεός. It would be inappropriate for אלהים or יהוה ever to refer to the Trinity in the OT when in the NT θεός regularly refers to the Father alone and apparently never to the Trinity.

C. Classification of the New Testament Use of θεός

The following classification of the NT uses of θεός is representative but of course not exhaustive. Yet any particular NT example may be set under one (or on occasion, two) of the categories listed. In §3 this classification assumes the results of subsequent discussion regarding the particular texts in which (ὁ) θεός may refer to Christ.

1. A god or deity
   a. Singular, either of a particular god(dess) (Acts 7:43 [= Amos 5:26 LXX], Rephan; 19:37 v.l., Ephesian Artemis; cf. ἡ θεά in 19:27 and אלהים of the goddess Ashtoreth in 1 Kings 11:5) or of a divine being worthy of worship[113] (Acts 12:22; 17:23; 28:6; 1 Cor. 8:4; 2 Thess. 2:4a, c; and possibly John 10:33)
   b. Plural, of the gods of Gentile polytheistic religion (Acts 7:40 [= Exod. 32:1]; 14:11; 19:26; 1 Cor. 8:5 *bis*; Gal. 4:8)
2. The one true God of Jewish and Christian monotheism
   a. Used absolutely,[114] in any of the cases, with or without the article
      (1) Nominative
         (a) As subject, usually articular: Luke 16:15; Gal. 6:7
         (b) As predicate: Mark 12:26; 2 Cor. 1:21
         (c) Of address (equivalent to θεέ), always articular: Luke 18:11, 13
      (2) Vocative: Matt. 27:46 *bis*
      (3) Accusative
         (a) Direct object: Mark 2:12; John 1:18a
         (b) Subject of infinitive: Heb. 6:18
         (c) In oaths: Mark 5:7b
      (4) Genitive
         (a) Possessive: Luke 11:20; 2 Cor. 4:7
         (b) Objective: 1 Cor. 15:34; 1 Pet. 2:19
         (c) Subjective: John 3:36; Rom. 1:17
         (d) Descriptive: 2 Cor. 11:2
         (e) Familial: Luke 3:38

113. In Classical Greek τὸ θεῖον often signifies divine power or activity or the divine nature considered generically, without reference to one particular god. There appears to be no NT instance where θεός signifies merely τὸ θεῖον (= *numen divinum*, as in Xenophon, *Mem.* 1:4:18), deity in general, although both Philo (e.g., *Agric.* 17) and Josephus (e.g., *Ant.* 14:183; *Bell.* 3:352) use τὸ θεῖον of the one true God of Israel's monotheism. In Acts 17:29 (see also the reading of D in Acts 17:27 and the addition to Titus 1:9 found in minuscule 460) τὸ θεῖον is used of "the Deity" that is often represented "by the art and imagination of man." See further below, chapter XIII §I.

114. That is, without a modifier such as a preposition, or without a qualifier such as an adjective, substantive, or dependent genitive.

(f) With certain verbs: Acts 4:19b; 10:2b
(g) With ἀξίως: 1 Thess. 2:12; 3 John 6
(h) Τὰ τοῦ θεοῦ: Matt. 16:23; 22:21; 1 Cor. 2:11

(5) Dative
(a) Indirect object: Mark 12:17; 1 Cor. 15:24
(b) Of advantage:[115] Rom. 6:10–11; Rev. 1:6
(c) Ethic:[116] Acts 7:20; 2 Cor. 10:4 (?)
(d) With certain verbs: Acts 26:29; Rom. 1:8
(e) With ἴσος: John 5:18; Phil. 2:6

b. Followed by a dependent genitive, which may be a:
(1) Personal pronoun, almost always articular: e.g., μου, 2 Cor. 12:21; αὐτῶν, Heb. 11:16
(2) Substantive
(a) Proper noun:[117] Luke 1:68; Eph. 1:17
(b) Abstract noun:[118] Rom. 15:5, 13, 33
(c) Collective noun: Luke 20:38; Acts 13:17

c. With an accompanying:
(1) Substantive (in the same case)
(a) Κύριος: Matt. 4:7
(b) Πατήρ: Gal. 1:4; Col. 1:2; 1 Pet. 1:3
(c) Σωτήρ: 1 Tim. 1:1; 2:3
(2) Adjective
(a) Attributive: Matt. 16:16; Rom. 16:26
(b) Predicative: Rom. 3:30; 2 Cor. 1:18
(3) Participle (= genitive absolute): Acts 18:21; Heb. 2:4

d. After prepositions, with or without the article: e.g., ἐκ τοῦ θεοῦ, 2 Cor. 5:18; ἐκ θεοῦ, 2 Cor. 5:1

3. Jesus Christ
a. Certainly in John 1:1; 20:28
b. Very probably in Rom. 9:5; Titus 2:13; Heb. 1:8; 2 Pet. 1:1
c. Probably in John 1:18
d. Possibly in Acts 20:28; Heb. 1:9; 1 John 5:20

4. Figuratively
a. Of someone who acts as the representative of God: human magistrates and judges, John 10:34–35 (= Ps. 81:6 LXX [MT and Engl. 82:6])

115. With the sense, "to God's honor and praise."

116. Meaning "in God's estimation" or "God being judge" (= "exceedingly, very"; superlative in sense).

117. Ὁ θεός τινος, the God of anyone, i.e., his guardian, benefactor, and object of worship.

118. This expresses an action, benefit, or blessing of which God is the author or source.

b. Of something/someone that assumes the place of God or to which/whom one is completely devoted:
   (1) The stomach (= natural instincts): Phil. 3:19
   (2) The devil: 2 Cor. 4:4

II

The Word Was God (John 1:1)

Ἐν ἀρχῇ ἦν ὁ λόγος, καὶ ὁ λόγος ἦν πρὸς τὸν θεόν, καὶ θεὸς ἦν ὁ λόγος.

It is difficult to imagine the first sentence of a book that would be at one and the same time so simple and yet so profound, so brief and yet so stately as this exordium to the Johannine Prologue (1:1–18) and the Fourth Gospel as a whole. As a result, immense scholarly effort has been expended in seeking to analyze the structure, themes, sequence of thought, original language, and background of the Prologue which begins with this verse. But in spite of all this effort no consensus has emerged on these issues and in particular with regard to the extent of any "hymn" or hymnic material thought to be incorporated with the Prologue. Only verses 1, 3–4, and 10–11 appear in almost every reconstruction of the *Urprolog*, although verses 1–5, 9–11, 14, and 16 are commonly regarded as original.[1] For our present purposes it suffices to note that whether or not the Prologue had a literary "prehistory,"[2] all of verse 1 is almost unanimously regarded as an original part of the Prologue, not an interpolation or gloss added by a final redactor.[3] As it stands, the Prologue falls into four sections:[4]

vv. 1–5	the relation of the preexistent Logos to God and to creation
vv. 6–8	the relation of John the Baptist to the Logos
vv. 9–13	the Logos in the world of humankind
vv. 14–18	the incarnate Logos-Son as revealer of the Father

Before I proceed to the exegesis of each clause in John 1:1, it will be helpful to summarize the use of θεός in the whole Gospel.

1. For summaries of scholarly opinion, see Brown, *Gospel* 1:21–23; Feuillet, *Prologue* 180–90; Miller, *Prologue* 6, and the literature cited by him (2–3 n. 3). In addition to there being a lack of unanimity about the extent of the *Urprolog*, there is wide diversity of view regarding the position of the climax of the Prologue as it now stands, with vv. 13, 14, 16, 17, 18, or 14–18 being among the proposals (see J. S. King 373).

2. It is not impossible that the evangelist has incorporated within the Prologue material that he himself had composed at an earlier time (cf. Feuillet, *Prologue* 196–203).

3. But Miller, who regards the Prologue as "a mosaic or anthology consisting of hymnic material, narrative material, miscellaneous lines, and later interpolations" (*Prologue* 4), argues that 1:1a–b, 3–5 is a self-contained christological hymn of four strophes (with ὃ γέγονεν—rendered "what has appeared"—introducing the third) "in which the early Johannine community celebrated the salvation-history enacted through the Logos" (*Prologue* 96), with vv. 1c (καὶ θεὸς ἦν ὁ λόγος) and 2 as interpolations (*Prologue* 7–15, 90–109).

4. For a discussion of chiasmus in the Prologue, see Culpepper 2–17.

A. The Use of θεός in the Fourth Gospel

1. The term θεός appears in some form 83 times; of these, 63 are articular and 20 anarthrous.[5]
2. When the nominative singular ὁ θεός occurs, it is invariably the subject, never predicative. The plural forms θεοί and θεούς, however, are predicative in 10:34–35.
3. Apart from the textually and exegetically ambiguous θεός in 1:18, there is no instance of anarthrous θεός forming the subject of a sentence. In 8:54 θεός is predicative after εἶναι.
4. Several facts make it highly improbable that John intends any consistent distinction to be drawn between ὁ θεός and θεός (as if between the Father and the Son):
   a. In prepositional phrases θεός occurs 22 times, 12 times with the article and 10 times without.
   b. When it is used with the prepositions παρά (+ the genitive) and ἐκ, θεός sometimes has the article (παρά: 5:44; 6:46; 8:40; 16:27 v.l.; ἐκ: 7:17; 8:42, 47 *bis*) and sometimes lacks it (παρά: 1:6; 9:16, 33; ἐκ: 1:13).
   c. In 19:7 John has υἱὸς θεοῦ, but he writes ὁ υἱὸς τοῦ θεοῦ in 1:34, 49; 3:18; 5:25; 10:36 (υἱὸς τοῦ θεοῦ); 11:4, 27; 20:31. Similarly, compare τέκνα θεοῦ in 1:12 with τὰ τέκνα τοῦ θεοῦ in 11:52. See the discussion of the canon of Apollonius in appendix I §B.1.
5. Of these 83 uses of θεός, the only places where the word could not refer to the Father are 1:1 (second occurrence, referring to the Logos); 1:18 (second occurrence, referring to μονογενής—see chapter III §§B–C); 10:34–35 (both plurals); and 20:28 (addressed to Jesus).
6. Reference to the Father is explicit in 5:18, 6:27, and 8:41–42a, and it is clearly implicit in other passages because of (a) a contextual connection with sonship (1:12–13, 34, 49; 3:16–18, 36; 5:25; 10:36; 11:4, 27, 52); (b) an accompanying mention of the Father (4:24; 5:42, 44; 6:28–29, 33, 45–46; 8:42b, 54; 10:35b; 11:40; 13:3 *bis*; 14:1; 16:2, 27; 17:3; 20:17); and (c) the qualifying adjective μόνος (5:44 and 17:3). Elsewhere in John's Gospel, except for the exceptions listed above (#5), it is fair to assume that (ὁ) θεός means the Father.[6]

5. These figures are based on NA[26]/UBS[3] (see chapter I §B.1).

6. There are no references to (ὁ) θεός in chapters 2, 15, and 18 and only one in chapters 7, 12, 14, 17, 19, and 21. In the Farewell Discourse (13:31–16:33), there are 7 references to (ὁ) θεός and 43 to ὁ πατήρ. Such statistics tend to confirm the conclusion that for John (ὁ) θεός customarily meant the Father.

B. Verse 1a: ἐν ἀρχῇ ἦν ὁ λόγος

Since the Greek Bible begins with the expression ἐν ἀρχῇ ("in the beginning"), rendering בראשית, it seems likely that John is alluding to Genesis 1:1.[7] But whereas the first verse of the Torah continues "God created,"[8] John follows with "the Word [already] existed." In Genesis the creation of the world is contemporaneous with or marks "the beginning"; in John the existence of the Word is anterior to "the beginning."[9] In itself John 1:1a speaks only of the pretemporality or supratemporality of the Logos, but in his conjunction of ἐν ἀρχῇ and ἦν (not ἐγένετο) John implies the eternal preexistence of the Word.[10] He who existed "in the beginning" before creation was himself without a beginning and therefore uncreated. There was no time when he did not exist. John is hinting that all speculation about the origin of the Logos is pointless. The imperfect tense ἦν (= Latin *erat*), which here denotes continuous existence, is to be carefully distinguished from ἔστι ("he is"), which would have stressed his timelessness at the expense of any emphasis on his manifestation historically (cf. 1:14), and from ἐγένετο, which would have implied either that he was a created being ("he came into existence") or that by the time of writing he had ceased to exist (= Latin *fuit*).

Although the Johannine Logos concept has only superficial resemblances to the Heraclitean notion of the Logos as immanent divine Reason or the Stoic view of the Logos as the rational Principle of the universe (see H. Kleinknecht, *TDNT* 4:81, 84–85),[11] there is no need to deny that John's λόγος embraces the dual idea of reason (*ratio*) and speech (*oratio*).[12] Accordingly, H. R. Minn has proposed (17) that λόγος signifies "the Intelligent (reason) plus the Intelligible (word or speech). It is the intellect in action. . . . Christ is declared by the Apostle to be the Inward and Expressed Thought of the Eternal Mind." But, given John's demonstrable dependence

7. For a defense of the view that John the son of Zebedee was the author of the Fourth Gospel, see Morris, *Studies* 215–80; J. A. T. Robinson, *Redating* 254–311, esp. 298–311.

8. For a defense of the customary English translation of Gen. 1:1, see Hasel.

9. "In the beginning" means in effect "before the world was created" (cf. John 17:5, 24; Eph. 1:4). Brown (*Gospel* 4) comments: "The 'beginning' refers to the period before creation and is a designation, more qualitative than temporal, of the sphere of God." In Prov. 8:23 (LXX) ἐν ἀρχῇ clearly means "before time was" and "before he (the Lord) made the earth."

10. "'Ἐν ἀρχῇ ἦν is not said of an *act done* ἐν ἀρχῇ (as in Gen. i.1), but of a *state existing* ἐν ἀρχῇ, and therefore without beginning itself" (Alford 1:680). "His *eternity* is implied since he is unaffected by that process of coming-to-be which is creation, abiding, by contrast, in a changeless mode of being" (Boismard, *Prologue* 7).

11. For the etymology of λόγος, see Jendorff 43–52, and on the evolution of the idea of λόγος in Greek thought, see Šurjanský 134–59.

12. Boyle has shown that from the time of Tertullian until Théodore de Bèze there was a tradition of translating λόγος in John 1:1 as *sermo*, God's copious and eloquent discourse, rather than by *verbum*, God's single undivided utterance.

on the OT for his formative ideas (see Reim, *Studien*), one should assume that his Logos concept is informed principally by OT teaching concerning "the word of the Lord"[13] as God's agent in creation (Ps. 33:6), revelation (Jer. 1:4–5, 9), and salvation (Ezek. 37:4–6),[14] especially since the Prologue proceeds to emphasize precisely these three spheres as the areas in which the Logos is mediator.[15] He created the universe (1:3, 10), he personally and perfectly revealed the Father (1:4–5, 9, 14, 18), and he redeemed humankind (1:12, 16).[16]

C. Verse 1b: καὶ ὁ λόγος ἦν πρὸς τὸν θεόν

For several reasons there can be little doubt that ὁ θεός in 1:1b designates the Father: (1) John 1:18 expresses a thought similar to 1:1b, using the term πατήρ: the Logos, depicted as μονογενὴς θεός, is said to reside εἰς τὸν κόλπον τοῦ πατρός; (2) 1 John 1:2 also affords a close parallel: ἡ ζωὴ . . . ἦν πρὸς τὸν πατέρα; (3) in Johannine usage ὁ θεός customarily denotes the Father (see §A above); and (4) the articular θεός could not refer to the divine essence ("the Word was with the divine nature" is nonsensical) or to the trinitarian God (since ἦν πρὸς τὸν θεόν is predicated of the Logos-Son and the Spirit is not mentioned or alluded to elsewhere in the Prologue).

Considerable dispute has arisen over the meaning of πρός. There are four major possibilities.[17] First, following the term λόγος, the expression ἦν πρός could conceivably mean "spoke to." In questioning the customary translations "auprès de" or "avec" for πρός, C. Masson argues that since a "word" is spoken to a person, one might expect after verse 1a an answer to the question "*To whom* was the Word spoken?" (πρός + the accusative: ἦν πρὸς τὸν θεόν) rather than "*Where* was the Word?" (παρά + the dative: ἦν παρὰ τῷ θεῷ). Masson believes that his rendering of 1:1b, "et la Parole parlait (s'adressait) à Dieu," appropriately reflects the dynamic nature of the

13. See Feuillet, *Prologue* 225–36. Closely associated is the Hebraic wisdom concept (see Feuillet, *Prologue* 236–44). In a helpful chart (202) Šurjanský compares OT teaching about wisdom with Pauline affirmations about the Son of God and the Johannine concept of the Logos–*Deus unigenitus*.

14. See further O. Procksch, *TDNT* 4:91–100.

15. Indicating his intention to document his thesis in a future publication, Miller rejects all the theories which root the Johannine Logos in some pre-Johannine tradition ("without denying utterly some possible connections with these traditions") and proposes rather that "*Logos* here is a peculiarly Johannine idea, and that its Christological development may be traced from the many Christologically 'transparent' uses of *logos* and *rhema* in the Fourth Gospel 'proper,' to a more self-conscious Christological significance in the First Epistle, to the full-blown Christological title in the Prologue. It means 'Word,' the saving truth which is revealed in and is Jesus Christ" ("God" 67).

16. Pollard (*Christology* 14–15; "Cosmology" 147–53) interprets John 1:3a, which he translates "all things happened through him," as a summary of what the Prologue later declares in detail, the mediatorship of the Logos in all of God's external actions (viz., creation, revelation, and salvation).

17. In the discussion that follows I am drawing on and expanding my earlier treatment of πρός in John 1:1b found in *NIDNTT* 3:1204–5.

Word. "Thus, for faith, 'in the beginning' there is not an unknown and unknowable God, some indeterminate and nameless Being, enveloped by night and by silence: there is the God who speaks and whose Word in time, in creation, and in redemption is the eternal Word" (381).[18] However, it is just as reasonable to think that 1:1b answers the question "What was the relationship of the Logos to the Father at and before the beginning?" (cf. 1 John 1:2). Moreover, Masson is scarcely justified in filling out the meaning of ἦν πρός on the basis of an accompanying substantive (ὁ λόγος) that here functions as a proper noun.

Second, appealing to the common Classical Greek phrases πρὸς ταῦτα ("having regard to these things") and ζῆν πρός τινα ("to live in absolute devotion to anyone"), E. A. Abbott finds in the phrase πρὸς τὸν θεόν the meaning "having regard to God," "[looking] toward God,"[19] or "devoted to God," in addition to a secondary, local sense, "in converse with God" (*Grammar* §2366; cf. §§2308, 2365). These various meanings of πρός are all feasible, but it is the combination of εἶναι (not ζῆν or στρέφειν or any comparable verb) and πρός in 1:1b that renders Abbott's first three proposals inappropriate.

A third view takes πρός as equivalent to παρά, denoting position ("with").[20] The preposition does not imply any movement or action on the part of the Logos in his relation to the Father. Support for this view may be found in the NT parallels where πρός + the accusative, often following the verb εἶναι, denotes not linear motion but punctiliar rest.[21] But, as I. de la Potterie has pointed out ("L'emploi" 379), elsewhere John uses παρά τινι to

18. A comparable rendering was suggested earlier by Jannaris ("Logos" 24: "Now the utterance was *made* unto God") and Burkitt (*Church* 95: "The Word spoke to God").

19. With this compare the translation proposed by Braun (3.2:278 n. 5) and Feuillet (*Prologue* 20, 264–69; cf. 33; Feuillet, *Mystère* 65, 182): "tourné vers." "Il [le Fils de Dieu] est sans cesse en mouvement vers lui [le Père], si l'on peut ainsi parler; nous avons recours à ce langage déficient pour exprimer tout ce qu'a de dynamique la relation filiale intratrinitaire" (Feuillet, *Mystère* 107).

20. Thus BDF §239.(1); C. F. D. Moule, *Idiom Book* 52–53; N. Turner, *Syntax* 274; N. Turner, *Style* 71 (but cf. his earlier "Eternal Word" 246: "The strong preposition 'with' suggests that He [the Logos] existed in a living fellowship with the Father, His life going out to meet the Father's"); Bultmann, *John* 32 n. 3, 82 n. 2; Haenchen, *John* 109. Most English versions simply have "with God," but some emphasize the local sense: "in God's presence" (NAB[1], REB), "by the side of God" (Cassirer).

21. Mark 6:3 (= Matt. 13:56); Mark 9:19 (= Luke 9:41; but Matt. 17:17 has μεθ' ὑμῶν); Mark 14:49 (= Luke 22:53, which has μεθ' ὑμῶν); 1 Cor. 16:6–7; 2 Cor. 5:8; 11:9; Gal. 1:18; 4:18, 20; Phil. 1:26; 1 Thess. 3:4; 2 Thess. 2:5, 3:10; Philem. 13: Heb. 4:13; 1 John 1:2. This usage reflects (1) the blurring of the notions of movement and rest found in Hellenistic Greek; (2) the reduction of the dative case and the extension of the accusative case in Hellenistic Greek; and (3) "an extension of many classical usages, particularly in such phrases as ἐνθυμεῖσθαι πρὸς αὐτόν" (G. R. Driver, cited [without reference] in MH 467) rather than Aramaic influence (e.g., Burney [29] suggests that the translator of an Aramaic original, finding לות, rendered it by πρός rather than παρά under the influence of the more common use of this Aramaic preposition, viz., to express motion toward). Winer (405; cf. Abel §50m) notes that this usage in which πρός τινα = παρά τινι occurs particularly with personal names.

express the proximity of one person to another[22] or the nearness of the Son to the Father,[23] never πρός τινα.

According to the fourth alternative, the sense is "the Word was in active communion with God."[24] This seems to be the import of John's statement, whether or not πρός bears a dynamic sense, for when πρός describes a relationship[25] between persons it must connote personal intercourse rather than simply spatial juxtaposition or personal accompaniment.[26] Used of divine persons, this preposition points to eternal intercommunion.[27]

D. Verse 1c: καὶ θεὸς ἦν ὁ λόγος

1. Punctuation

A. N. Jannaris ("Logos" 20, 24) and J. N. Sanders (69–70) have proposed that a stop should be placed after καὶ θεὸς ἦν ("and was *theos*."), with verse 2 beginning ὁ λόγος οὗτος ("This Word . . ."). No grammatical objection may be raised against this proposal, especially since the phrase ὁ λόγος οὗτος (albeit in a different sense) is found in John 6:60 and 7:36 (cf. οὗτος ὁ λόγος in 21:23), while the resulting meaning does not differ materially from the sense of the words when the traditional punctuation is followed. However, this variant punctuation disrupts the balance of the verse (removing the

22. John 1:39; 4:40; 8:38a; 14:17, 23, 25; 19:25. Note also μετά τινος (e.g., John 3:22, 25–26).

23. John 8:35; 17:5.

24. Similarly Westcott, *Epistles* 219; Milligan and Moulton 4 (πρός "denotes not merely being beside, but maintaining communion and intercourse with (comp. Mark vi.3; 1 John i.2, ii.1)"); Robertson, *Grammar* 623; Robertson, *Divinity* 39 (πρὸς τὸν θεόν = "face to face with God"); cf. Zerwick, *Greek* §§102–3. Langbrandtner (42) distinguishes παρὰ τῷ θεῷ ("bei Gott") from πρὸς τὸν θεόν ("in Beziehung zu Gott"). But K. Barth argues that πρὸς τὸν θεόν must mean more than "for God" or "in communion with God" since these sentiments are applicable to others who were not "in the beginning" as the Logos was (*Dogmatics* 95–96).

25. The basic sense of πρός + the accusative is not "movement" but "relation" or "direction"; see Dewailly 123–25, who compares Aristotle's use of τὸ πρός τι to define one of his ten categories of existence.

26. Abbott usefully compares μετὰ τοῦ θεοῦ ("in companionship with God"), παρὰ τῷ θεῷ ("by the side of God"), σὺν τῷ θεῷ ("together with God"), and πρὸς τὸν θεόν ("in converse with God") (*Grammar* §§2363, 2365–66).

27. Dewailly (128) rightly warns against discovering in John 1:1b "all the patristic and conciliar christology which was much later attached to it, still less the speculation of Eastern or Western traditions concerning existential relations." Some commentators seem to have erred here. Bengel, for example, claims that "πρός . . . denotes a perpetual, as it were, tendency of the Son to the Father in the unity of essence" (2:234). Alford alleges that "both the inner substantial union, and the distinct personality of the λόγος are here [in 1:1b] asserted" (1:681). And while de la Potterie ("L'emploi" 381 n. 3) believes that the Son's "filiation" is expressed by the Johannine formula πρὸς τὸν θεόν, he rejects the view of Isaac (80) that the mutual belonging (*appartenance*) or immanence of the Father and Son is indicated, since this would presuppose that πρός had both a static and a dynamic sense at the same time.

thrice-repeated ὁ λόγος and the medial position of ἦν in each case) as well as the chiasmus within the verse (ABBA: ὁ λόγος [second occurrence] . . . θεόν, . . . θεὸς . . . ὁ λόγος). And, to emphasize θεός, John might have been expected, on this view, to write ὁ λόγος ἦν πρὸς τὸν θεόν καὶ ἦν θεός or ὁ λόγος πρὸς τὸν θεὸν καὶ θεὸς ἦν. Moreover, in the other three uses of ὁ λόγος in the Prologue (vv. 1a, 1b, 14), the word is unqualified. There is therefore no adequate reason to reject the customary punctuation: καὶ θεὸς ἦν ὁ λόγος.

Three further matters demand attention with regard to this clause. Can the Logos be identified with Jesus Christ? Why is θεός anarthrous? How should θεός be translated?

2. Identity of the Logos

One of the crucial ingredients in the Christology of J. A. T. Robinson is his thesis that the divine Logos or the Christ was defined in, but not confined to, Jesus of Nazareth: "The early Christian message was that Jesus is the Christ—not that the Christ, or the Logos, the meaning of the mystery of life, is exclusively or exhaustively to be found in Jesus, so that the two are simply interchangeable."[28] Only in John 1:14 does the preexistent, impersonal Logos become personalized in Jesus (*Face* 218): "The Logos was anhypostatic *until* the Word of God finally came to its full expression . . . in an individual historical person, and thus *became* hypostatic."[29] More recently, J. D. G. Dunn has expressed similar views: Until verse 14 "we are still dealing with the Wisdom and Logos figure of pre-Christian Judaism, that is, not as a personal being, but as the wise utterance of God personified" (*Christology* 242). But verse 14 may well mark "the transition from impersonal personification to actual person" (*Christology* 243; cf. "Christianity" 334). Accordingly "Christ is not the Logos *per se*; he is the Logos *become flesh.* We may quite properly say that the personified Logos, the impersonal Logos first became personal in the incarnation" ("Christianity" 331).[30]

By way of response, several observations are in order. Nowhere in the Prologue—not even in verse 14—is the Logos explicitly identified as Jesus Christ, who is first mentioned in 1:17, yet this identification is a necessary inference, for 1:18 makes the same three affirmations of Jesus Christ as 1:1

28. *Face* 10; cf. 113–14, 180–85, 209–10, 213–14; *Truth* 97–129.

29. "John" 334, citing Schoonenberg 54–66, 80–91.

30. Dunn presses his point further. Because the Logos Christology of the Prologue prefaces the whole Gospel, one may infer that the Son of God Christology of the discourses should be interpreted in the light of the Logos Christology. "In this case by pre-existent Son John means pre-existent Logos; that is to say, the Son is not another divine power but is the immanent presence of him who alone is God from all eternity" ("Christianity" 332; similarly *Partings* 244–46). But earlier Dunn had affirmed that "for John the pre-existent Logos was indeed a divine personal being" (*Christology* 244) and that "the Fourth Evangelist was the first Christian writer to conceive clearly of the personal pre-existence of the Logos-Son and to present it as a fundamental part of his message" (*Christology* 249).

does of the Logos (viz., timeless existence, intimate relationship with God, and participation in deity) and the themes of the Prologue are developed in the body of the Gospel in reference to Jesus of Nazareth.[31] But with this said, one should affirm that the one whom John envisaged as preexisting with God (1:1a–b; cf. 8:58; 17:4) was not Jesus of Nazareth but the preincarnate Son of God.[32] Another relevant point is that everywhere in the Prologue the Logos is portrayed as personal. The αὐτόν of 1:10–12[33] must refer to the Jesus of human history and in the Fourth Gospel the expression πιστεύειν εἰς τὸ ὄνομα αὐτοῦ (1:12) is always applied to belief in the historical or exalted Jesus. And although Word and Wisdom were hypostatized in pre-Christian Judaism and in the ancient Near East in general (see J. T. Sanders 29–57), there is no reason why John 1:1–2 should not represent an advance from any previous mere hypostatization of Logos. The ideas of existence (1:1a), relationship (1:1b), and identification (1:1c) accord perfectly with a concept of a personal Logos.

In 1:14 John is not affirming that an impersonal universal Logos became incarnate in the person of Jesus Christ, but rather that the personal individualized Logos assumed a complete and genuine human existence. If, for John, the Logos was the preincarnate Son, then Jesus Christ, the Son of God, is the incarnate Logos. There was personal continuity between the preexistent Logos and the historical Jesus: the λόγος ἔνσαρκος was personally none other than the λόγος ἄσαρκος. If this is so, what John says in 1:1 regarding the person of the Logos, he says, by implication, regarding the person of Jesus Christ.

3. Reasons for the Anarthrous State of θεός

In light of the fact that in the preceding clause John has written πρὸς <u>τὸν</u> θεόν, it would seem fair to assume that the anarthrous state of θεός in 1:1c is not without significance.[34] It would be improper to question this assumption by arguing that since no distinction can be drawn between θεός and ὁ

31. For example, life (1:4 and 5:26), light (1:5, 9 and 3:19; 8:12; 12:35, 46), glory (1:14 and 12:41), truth (1:14, 17 and 14:6).

32. But for Lampe the individual, personal identity of the historical Jesus of Nazareth has been "retrojected" on to the Logos who thus becomes for John a preexistent person: "Jesus writ large, a divine Jesus in heaven before he came down to earth" (39; cf. 128, 137). There is a "two-way projection of the Jesus of the Gospels on to the pre-existent Logos-Son, and of the pre-existent Jesus-Logos-Son on to the historical figure of the New Testament records" (141).

33. John 1:10: ὁ κόσμος αὐτὸν οὐκ ἔγνω; 1:11: οἱ ἴδιοι αὐτὸν οὐ παρέλαβον; 1:12: ὅσοι δὲ ἔλαβον αὐτόν.

34. It is unwise to speak, as some do, of the "omission" of the article with θεός, for this assumes without good reason that John either intended to write, or ought to have written, ὁ θεός, but for some reason failed to do so. Even the expression "absence of the article" tends to be pejorative, suggesting as it does that the presence of the article is normative with proper or common nouns (which, in fact, is not the case—see N. Turner, *Syntax* 165–74).

θεός in the usage of the Fourth Gospel (see §A above), John might equally well have written ὁ λόγος ἦν πρὸς τὸν θεόν, καὶ ὁ θεὸς ἦν ὁ λόγος. All that Johannine usage shows is that there is no *necessary* distinction between θεός and ὁ θεός, both terms generally referring to the Father. But an *actual* differentiation between the terms cannot be excluded at any point, especially here where an articular use and an anarthrous use of θεός occur in succession, the first θεός clearly referring to the Father (see §C above) and the second being predicated of the Logos.[35]

a. Grammatical Reasons

(1) To Indicate That θεός Is Indefinite

In appendix I §A.5 some of the reasons why a given noun may be anarthrous are listed. Since the basic function of the article is *deictic*, to add precision to thought by emphasizing individuality or identity, the nonoccurrence of the article with a noun may point to the nonparticularity, the indefiniteness, of the concept. Accordingly, from the point of view of grammar alone, θεὸς ἦν ὁ λόγος could be rendered "the Word was a god,"[36] just as, for example, if only grammatical considerations were taken into account, ὑμεῖς ἐκ τοῦ πατρὸς τοῦ διαβόλου ἐστέ (John 8:44) could mean "you belong to the father of the devil." But the theological context, viz., John's monotheism, makes this rendering of 1:1c impossible, for if a monotheist were speaking of the Deity he himself reverenced, the singular θεός could be applied only to the Supreme Being, not to an inferior divine being or emanation as if θεός were simply generic. That is, in reference to his *own* beliefs, a monotheist could not speak of θεοί nor could he use θεός in the singular (when giving any type of personal description) of any being other than the one true God whom he worshiped. On the other hand, when the polytheistic inhabitants of Malta affirmed that Paul was θεός, they were suggesting that he had or deserved a place among their *own* pantheon of gods. "They said that he was a god" is therefore a proper translation of ἔλεγον αὐτὸν εἶναι θεόν (Acts 28:6).

(2) To Indicate That θεός Is Predicative

Had John written καὶ ὁ θεὸς ἦν ὁ λόγος, there would have been room, it is argued, for some degree of uncertainty as to the subject, but as the text

35. Among NT verses which contain the term θεός, John 1:1 is unique with regard to its construction. The closest parallels are found in five (of the fifteen) verses which have an anarthrous predicative θεός. But, for example, John 1:1 differs from John 8:54 in that θεός is unqualified. It differs from 2 Cor. 1:21; 5:5; and Heb. 3:4 in that θεός precedes the subject. It differs from 2 Thess. 2:4 in that θεός precedes the copula. It differs from all five in that the subject is an articular noun.

36. Since the autograph of John's Gospel will have been written in uncials, no distinction would have been possible between θεός and Θεός.

stands, all real ambiguity is removed. That θεός, and not ὁ λόγος, is predicative is shown by the anarthrous state of the noun.[37]

This argument has *prima facie* plausibility. Θεός is anarthrous and apparently predicative. However, the relation between these two facts is not necessarily causal. It is certainly possible that in 1:18 the anarthrous θεός stands as subject (see chapter III §C.1), although in the closest parallel to 1:1c (viz., John 8:54), the anarthrous θεός is predicative (ὑμεῖς λέγετε ὅτι θεὸς ἡμῶν ἐστιν). Given the general interchangeability of ὁ θεός and θεός in the Fourth Gospel (see §A above), it would not be impossible, from the point of view of grammar alone, to translate 1:1c as "God was the Word,"[38] especially since the word order (with θεός preplaced) could indicate the subject. But what is grammatically admissible is contextually inadmissible. If θεός were taken as subject and as equivalent to ὁ θεός ("God was the Word"), the clause would contradict what precedes ("the Word was with God," distinguishing two persons) and would reduce the λόγος to merely a divine attribute (cf. 1 John 4:8: ὁ θεὸς ἀγάπη ἐστίν).[39] And what is more, ὁ λόγος is the subject and τὸν θεόν part of the predicate in the preceding clause (v. 1b) and in the sentence that follows (v. 2), while the principal subject of the whole Prologue is the Logos.

It is unlikely, therefore, that the sole or even the main reason for the anarthrous state of θεός was the need to distinguish predicate from subject. The articular λόγος and the context clearly point to the subject and thus the predicate is isolated.[40] If John had thought there would be any uncertainty as to subject and predicate, καὶ ὁ λόγος ἦν θεός would have settled the matter.

(3) To Accord with Principles of Word Order

In appendix I §B.3 I discuss and evaluate E. C. Colwell's "rules" concerning definite predicate nouns in the NT. One of his canons was that "definite predicate nouns which precede the verb usually lack the article" ("Rule" 20). Does this rule apply to John 1:1c? Colwell himself believed so, although

37. Similarly, e.g., Bultmann, *John* 33 n. 2; Wainwright, *Trinity* 60–61 (= "Confession" 288–89); J. N. Sanders 70.

38. Thus the translations of Wycliffe and Cranmer; also Burney (41), translating his postulated Aramaic original (viz., ואלהא הוא מימרא); Abbott (*Grammar* §2594: "And Divine Being was the Word," although in a footnote [443 n. 3] he observes that the more natural English would be "the Word was Divine Being"!).

39. Cf. Alford 1:681.

40. It is a moot point whether the article with λόγος indicates the subject (thus Bengel 2:239) and therefore the predicate, or whether the anarthrous state of θεός identifies the predicate and consequently the subject. In his detailed examination of the NT use of εἶναι as a copulative, McGaughy demonstrates that within a sentence containing an equative verb and a complement, when one unit is articular and the other anarthrous, "the word or word cluster determined by an article is the subject" (49; his rule 3c).

not as confidently as some who have appealed to the rule he enunciated, in order to defend the rendering "the Word was God":[41]

> The opening verse of John's Gospel contains one of the many passages where this rule suggests the translation of a predicate as a definite noun. Καὶ θεὸς ἦν ὁ λόγος looks much more like "And the Word was God" than "and the Word was divine" when viewed with reference to this rule. The absence of the article does *not* make the predicate indefinite or qualitative when it precedes the verb; it is indefinite in this position only when the context demands it. The context makes no such demand in the Gospel of John, for this statement cannot be regarded as strange in the prologue of the gospel which reaches its climax in the confession of Thomas ("Rule" 21).

It is clearly the context of the verse in the Fourth Gospel that encourages Colwell to see an application of the grammatical rule here.

Two considerations make one hesitate, however, to find in John 1:1c an instance of Colwell's rule. First, as I observe in appendix I (§B.3.b), it seems *a priori* unlikely that the largely mechanical and external factor of word order should itself account for the presence or absence of the article with definite predicate nouns. If word order alone determined the anarthrous state of what was a definite noun (ὁ θεός), the implication is that John could have written ὁ λόγος ἦν ὁ θεός (or even ὁ θεὸς ἦν ὁ λόγος) as a stylistic variant of θεὸς ἦν ὁ λόγος. But, in the context of John 1:1, this would have involved an intolerable equation of persons, with the Logos being personally identified, in a convertible proposition, with the Father (ὁ θεός in v. 1b). Such an affirmation—fitly described as embryonic Sabellianism—would contradict the unambiguous clause that immediately precedes: "The Word was *with* ὁ θεός." Whatever John's word order, ὁ θεός would have been inappropriate in verse 1c, given the immediate context.

Second, as he applies his rule to John 1:1c, Colwell wrongly assumes that definiteness and qualitativeness are mutually exclusive categories, that if θεός can be shown to be definite because of principles of word order, it cannot be qualitative in sense. In the expression πνεῦμα ὁ θεός (John 4:24), for example, πνεῦμα is both definite (referring to a specific *genus*) and qualitative (denoting a distinctive quality or inherent characteristic). In a similar way in John 1:1c, θεός could refer to the "god-ness" of the one true God.[42] If John, believing in the deity of Jesus as the Logos and yet also in his personal distinction from the Father (ὁ θεός in 1:1b), had wished here to *stress* that the Logos fully shared the divine nature, he could have expressed this

41. See, e.g., Metzger, "Translation"; Metzger, "Jehovah's Witnesses" 75–76; V. Perry, "Jehovah's Witnesses" 18; Countess; McGaughy 77 n. 1; Miller, "God" 69–70.

42. *Pace* Harner (87): "In John 1:1 I think that the qualitative force of the predicate is so prominent that the noun cannot be regarded as definite."

truth only by saying ὁ λόγος ἦν θεός or θεὸς ὁ λόγος ἦν or θεὸς ἦν ὁ λόγος (= 1:1c).[43] It must be allowed that John may not be identifying the person of the Logos in 1:1c but describing his nature.[44]

(4) To Indicate a Nonreciprocating Proposition

An eighth-century uncial, Codex Regius (L), reads in John 1:1c ὁ θεὸς ἦν ὁ λόγος. Whether this is rendered as "God was the Word" or "the Word was God," the presence of the article with both nouns identifies the proposition as convertible, true in both directions. If John had written this or ὁ λόγος ἦν ὁ θεός, he would be either identifying the Logos with the θεός of verse 1b ("the Word was this θεός," anaphoric ὁ), or affirming that no θεός existed apart from the Logos.[45]

As it stands, θεός is anarthrous to show that the statement "the Word was God" is not a convertible proposition. John thereby denies that "God was the Word." As C. K. Barrett expresses it: "The absence of the article indicates that the Word is God, but is not the only being of whom this is true."[46] Since John regularly uses ὁ θεός or θεός of the Father (see §A above), there is adequate reason for his avoidance of a construction that would, while affirming the deity of the Logos, exclude the Father from the Godhead. While the Logos can be included within the category of Deity, he is not coextensive with that whole category.

(5) To Give θεός an Adjectival Significance

On John 1:1c R. H. Strachan comments: "Here the word *theos* has no article, thus giving it the significance of an adjective."[47] Strachan is not, of course, suggesting that an author's choice not to use the article with a noun virtually converts that noun into an adjective. But it remains doubtful whether even an adjectival *significance* may attach to an anarthrous substantive (cf. Griffiths 315). Ἐγώ εἰμι ἄνθρωπος does not exactly mean "I am human" (ἀνθρώπινος). Similarly, θεὸς ἦν ὁ λόγος does not exactly mean

43. This assumes, on the basis of John 1:18a (θεὸν οὐδεὶς ἑώρακεν πώποτε), that John could allude to the divine nature or "essence" by the use of an anarthrous θεός (see chapter III §D.2).

44. This is the view of Westcott, *Gospel* 3. C. F. D. Moule cites it approvingly with the comment: "Westcott's note . . . , although it may require the addition of some reference to idiom, does still, perhaps, represent the writer's theological intention" (*Idiom Book* 116).

45. Cf. Hofius 16 n. 89. See appendix I §A.5.e.

46. *John* 156; similarly his *Essays on John* 23; Crawford, "Pittenger" 122 ("if ὁ θεός had been used it would identify the Logos with the totality of the divine existence . . . the Word does not by Himself make up the entire Godhead"); Miller, "God" 71–73, 77; Macquarrie 109–10 ("even if we are correct in speaking of the 'identification' of Jesus with the Word, we could not go on to infer an identification of Jesus with God").

47. *Fourth Gospel* 99. In a similar vein, Temple observes that "the term 'God' is fully substantival in the first clause—πρὸς τὸν Θεόν: it is predicative and not far from adjectival in the second—Θεὸς ἦν ὁ λόγος. Thus from the outset we are to understand that the Word has its whole being within Deity, but that it does not exhaust the being of Deity" (*John* 5). It is unclear whether Temple derived the quasi-adjectival sense of θεός from its being predicative or from its being anarthrous.

"the Word was divine" (θεῖος). Especially when there exists an adjective corresponding to the substantive, the anarthrous noun should not be deemed adjectival. A careful distinction should be drawn between the potentially *qualitative* sense of an anarthrous noun (see appendix I §A.5.c) and issues of translation that may be resolved by the use of an adjective.

b. Theological Reasons

(1) To Distinguish the Logos from the Father

Since it was John's custom to reserve the title ὁ θεός for the Father, it would have been impossible for him to have written ὁ λόγος ἦν ὁ θεός (or ὁ θεὸς ἦν ὁ λόγος) without suggesting a precise identification of the person of the Logos (the Son) with the person of the Father.[48] Having just distinguished the Logos from ὁ θεός in verse 1b, would he be likely immediately afterward to dissolve that personal distinction?[49] For him to have used ὁ θεός in the predicate of verse 1c would have implied either that subject and predicate were identical or coextensive or that this predicate referred to none other than the ὁ θεός of the preceding clause (the article being anaphoric; see §D.3.a.(4) above). As it is, in verse 1c John maintains the distinction between the Logos and the Father that he has drawn in verse 1b, while at the same time affirming the participation of the Logos in the divine essence (θεός).

This explanation of the anarthrous state of θεός has the advantage of arising from the immediate context. Nevertheless a potential difficulty should be met. Since John not infrequently uses the anarthrous θεός of the Father,[50] the anarthrous state of θεός in itself in no way reduces the possibility of a reference to the Father or guarantees that John is referring to someone other than the Father. However, the uniform distinction between Son and Father that John makes throughout the Gospel, as well as in 1:1b, effectively excludes any possible reference to the Father in the term θεός here. And, as well as repeating the salient points of verse 1, verse 2 may be aimed at averting a possible misinterpretation of verse 1c, viz., that there was no distinction between ὁ λόγος and ὁ θεός.[51]

(2) To Indicate the Subordination of the Logos

Appealing to the view of S. de Ausejo (385–403, 426 n. 136) that throughout the Prologue ὁ λόγος refers to the incarnate Jesus Christ, the Word-

48. Stevens, *Johannine Theology* 91; Brown, *Reflections* 26 (= "Jesus" 564); Brown, *Gospel* 1:24; and Theobald 44–45 share the view that one reason for the anarthrous state of θεός was to distinguish the Logos from the Father.

49. Noting the author's careful placement of θεὸς ἦν ὁ λόγος between two clauses that assert ἦν πρὸς τὸν θεόν, Bultmann (*John* 34) observes: "A *paradoxical* state of affairs is to be expressed which is inherent in the *concept of revelation* . . . : the paradox that in the Revealer God is really encountered, and yet that God is not directly encountered, but only in the Revealer."

50. John 1:6, 12, 13; 3:2, 21; 6:45; 8:54; 9:16, 33; 13:3a; 16:30; 19:7.

51. Cf. Bultmann, *John* 34; Cullmann, *Christology* 266.

become-flesh, R. E. Brown tentatively proposes that the anarthrous θεός may point to the humble status of the Word as one who had adopted "the form of a servant" (Phil. 2:5–7).[52]

No one will question that the subordinationist element is pronounced in the body of the Fourth Gospel, with its repeated references to the Father's sending of the Son and its blunt *verbum Christi*, "the Father is greater than I" (John 14:28; cf. 5:22, 26–27, 30; 10:18, 36; 17:22). But so far from prefacing his Gospel with a hint or reminder of the functional subordination of the incarnate Word to the Father, John seems intent to begin his work as he will end it (20:28), with an unqualified assertion of the supreme status of Jesus Christ, in both his preincarnate (1:1) and resurrection (20:28) states. He, equally with the Father, shares in the divine essence (1:1c). He, equally with the Father, is the legitimate object of human worship (20:28). In addition, it is not impossible that 1:1c was included by John in part to correct an erroneous inference that might be drawn from 1:1b, viz., that since the Word was said to be "with" the Father—not the Father "with" the Word—he was in some way inferior or subordinate to God. A further point is that in 1:1c John is not describing the relation of the Logos to the Father (as in 1:1b) but the relation of the Logos to the divine essence.

(3) To Indicate That θεός Is Qualitative in Meaning

One of the most frequently quoted *dicta* from J. H. Moulton's classic *Prolegomena* is his assertion that "for exegesis, there are few of the finer points of Greek which need more constant attention than this omission of the article when the writer would lay stress on the quality or character of the object" (83). Applied to John 1:1c, this principle would suggest that, being anarthrous, θεός describes the nature of the Logos rather than identifying his person.[53] Personally distinct from the Father (1:1b), he is yet essentially

52. *Reflections* 26 n. 43 (= "Jesus" 563 n. 43: "If de Ausejo's suggestion is true, there could be some justification in seeing in the anarthrous *theos* something more humble than the *ho theos* used of the Father, along the lines of Jn 14:28"); *Gospel* 1:23, 25. E. F. Scott (*Fourth Gospel* 201) finds in John 1:1b a hint of the Son's subordination: "The Logos was 'towards God,' derived from Him and dependent on Him."

53. This is by far the most common explanation of the anarthrous θεός in John 1:1c. In addition to §D.4.c below, see Alford 1:681 ("God, *in substance and essence*,—not ὁ θεός, 'the Father,' *in Person*"); A. B. D. Alexander, *ISBE* 3:1915 ("actually identical in essence with God"); Stevens, *Johannine Theology* 91 ("John here [in 1:1] uses ὁ θεός to denote specifically the Father—the central seat and fountain of divinity—and θεός to denote the category of divine nature or essence in which the Son, equally with the Father, partakes"); B. Weiss, "Gebrauch" 323; Lagrange, *Jean* 2 ("participation à la nature divine"); Barclay, "Themes" 114 ("the Word belongs to the same sphere of being as God"); Zerwick, *Greek* §172; Rahner 136 (the anarthrous θεός in John 1:1, 18 and Rom. 9:5 "suggests a kind of conceptual generality"); Zerwick and Grosvenor 285; Bruce, *John* 31; Fuller and Perkins 133 n. 2 (the anarthrous θεός indicates that the Logos "'shared the God-ness of God' but without being inexhaustibly what God was"); Harner 87; Ellis 29 n. 71 (the anarthrous θεός "stresses a qualitative identity while maintaining a numerical distinction from God the Father").

one with the Father (1:1c).[54] Not an identity of person but an identity of nature is affirmed. Verse 1c "attributes godhead to the Logos," so that "the Logos is God as truly as he with whom he exists in the closest union of being and life."[55] Between the Logos and God the Father, there is not simply a similarity of nature but an identity of essence. Nor does the text leave room for any notion of the Son's inferiority of essence such as was propounded by Eusebius of Caesarea who distinguished between the Son as αὐτὸς θεός and the Father as ἀληθινὸς θεός (cf. John 17:3) and ὁ ἐπὶ πάντων.[56] The unqualified θεός must mean no less than ἀληθῶς θεός. (How best to translate a qualitative θεός will be discussed below in §D.4.).

Two objections to taking θεός in a qualitative sense must be considered. It is sometimes claimed[57] that, if this had been John's meaning, he would have used either θεῖος or (τοῦ) θεοῦ in the place of θεός. In reply one may observe that (1) the use of θεῖος would have left the statement open to what from John's point of view was a grave misinterpretation, viz., that the Logos was nothing more than a δεύτερος θεός or θεῖος ἀνήρ or that the Son was essentially inferior to the Father; and (2) θεῖος may have sounded too philosophical or literary to John, particularly in the predicative position, and in any case says less than he believed (given John 20:28).[58] On the other hand, if John had written καὶ (τοῦ) θεοῦ ἦν ὁ λόγος, the sense would have been that the Word "belonged to God" or "was from God" rather than "was like God" (= "divine").

The second objection is this.[59] If a contrast were intended between 1:1b and 1:1c (viz., the Logos and the Father were personally distinct, *yet* the Logos, equally with the Father, shared the divine nature), John would have connected the two clauses not by the vague copulative καί but by an adversative such as ἀλλά or δέ. But this is to overlook the Johannine propensity for parataxis, his preference for καί,[60] and the fact that parataxis itself may have an adversative effect. What is more, 1:1b and 1:1c are perhaps complementary rather than antithetical: there is a unity between the Son and the Father (1:1c; cf. 10:30) as well as a difference (1:1b).

54. Macquarrie makes use of an analogy suggested by some remarks of B. Clarke regarding "mass terms" such as *gold*, *water*, or *matter*: "If I say . . . 'This bracelet is gold,' I am not identifying it with all the gold in the world, but I am saying that it is of 'the same substance' or that it is 'one in being' with gold" (110).

55. Schnackenburg, *John* 1:234; similarly Wikenhauser 41; Lagrange, *Jean* clvi.

56. For the reference to Eusebius, see Pollard, *Christology* 122–30, 172–76, 266–98 (esp. 172, 282).

57. Cullmann, *Christology* 266; Crawford, "Pittenger."

58. On θεῖος, see further below, chapter XIII §I.

59. According to Stevens (*Johannine Theology* 92), this objection was raised by G. C. F. Lücke.

60. It is also noteworthy that καί joins the successive elements in the "staircase" structure of vv. 1, 4, 5 in which the last element of a clause becomes the first of the next clause (ὁ λόγος, καὶ ὁ λόγος . . . τὸν θεόν, καὶ θεὸς . . . ζωὴ . . . , καὶ ἡ ζωὴ . . . τὸ φῶς . . . καὶ τὸ φῶς . . . τῇ σκοτίᾳ . . . , καὶ ἡ σκοτία). Cf. H. C. Green, who distinguishes between two types of antithetical parallelism found in the hymn embodied within the Prologue: "inverted synonymous parallelism and inverted step-parallelism" (294).

Why, then, is θεός anarthrous in John 1:1c? Although it is inappropriate to speak of John's "omission" of the article, one may justifiably speak of his purpose in writing θεός[61] rather than, say, ὁ θεός or θεῖος or θεοῦ.[62] Having distinguished the Logos from the Father (τὸν θεόν, 1:1b), John wished to point to their commonality, not merely in purpose but in being (θεός). Like the Father, and equally with him, the Logos may be included within the category of Deity as a partaker in the divine essence. If, then, a single reason is to be given for the anarthrous state of θεός, it is that this noun is qualitative, emphasizing nature rather than personal identity. In an incidental manner, this anarthrous θεός also confirms that the articular λόγος is the subject of the clause and excludes the inference that the Word exhausts the category of Deity or that the Son was the Father.

4. Translation

The complexity of the issues involved in the interpretation of John 1:1c is reflected in the varying translations of the verse that have been proposed. These may now be briefly evaluated in the light of the foregoing discussion.

a. "The Word was a god"

The translation "a god" is found in the New World Translation,[63] Jannaris ("Logos" 24, but "a God" on p. 20),[64] and Becker (65, 68, 70: "ein Gott").[65]

61. "That John designedly wrote θεός is apparent, partly from the distinct antithesis πρὸς τὸν θεόν verses 1, 2, and partly from the whole description of the λόγος" (Winer 122). Similarly Fennema notes that "the only two occurrences of the articular θεός [in the Prologue] are strategically placed, so as to bracket John's initial ascription of deity to the Logos" (130).

62. At different points in the foregoing discussion, three main alternative forms of expression that John may have used have been discussed (apart from the various possible positions of ἦν and of an anarthrous θεός, with the resulting changes of emphasis):

1a. ὁ θεὸς ἦν ὁ λόγος
1b. ὁ λόγος ἦν ὁ θεός
2. θεῖος ἦν ὁ λόγος (or, ὁ λόγος ἦν θεῖος)
3. (τοῦ) θεοῦ ἦν ὁ λόγος (or, ὁ λόγος ἦν (τοῦ) θεοῦ)

In 1a and 1b a precise equation of ὁ λόγος and ὁ θεός would be suggested, and in 1a there would be some ambiguity as to subject and predicate. The second could give rise to misunderstanding, viz., that the Logos was a "second god" or merely a "divine man" or was essentially inferior to the Father. The third would mean "the Logos was God's," denoting possession; or possibly "the Logos was from God," denoting origin.

63. *New World Translation of the Christian Greek Scriptures* (New York: Watchtower Bible & Tract Society, 1950) 282, with a justification of the rendering in the appendix (773–77). See Metzger, "Jehovah's Witnesses" 74–76; V. Perry, "Jehovah's Witnesses"; Countess.

64. According to Jannaris, the articular λόγος refers to the well-known cosmogonic *fiat* (εἶπεν ὁ θεός occurs nine times in Gen. 1) by which God created the world: "That well known oracular utterance which God made unto (πρὸς) Himself and which having been instrumental (δι' αὐτοῦ) in the creation, is naturally represented as a creative power, a creator, that is *a god*,—god and creator being two synonymous terms" ("Logos" 20–21).

65. Becker alludes to "eine philonische Differenzierung zwischen 'dem Gott' und dem Logos als 'Gott' (ohne Artikel)" (72).

The reasons for rejecting this rendering[66]—represented in none of the major English translations of the twentieth century—have been set out in §D.3.a.(1) above.

b. "The Word was divine"

Moffatt ("the Logos was divine"), Goodspeed, Schonfield,[67] Temple (3), Strachan (99), and Zerwick and Grosvenor (285) render θεός as "divine." I have already expressed doubts as to whether θεός may be treated as equivalent to θεῖος (§D.3.a.(5) above).[68] But if θεός bears a qualitative sense, the rendering "divine" should not be dismissed as altogether inappropriate.[69] The inadequacy of this translation arises from two considerations—contextual and linguistic. Bounded as it is on either side by a use of θεός (1:1b, 2) that clearly refers to "God" the Father, θεός in 1:1c is most naturally taken as substantival. Furthermore, if 1:1 and 20:28 form the two christological "bookends" of the Fourth Gospel, θεός in 1:1c, as in 20:28, is likely to be titular. On the matter of word usage, there can be no doubt that in English the word *divine* has a much wider range of applications and a more attenuated meaning than does the term *God.* In modern parlance, for instance, "divine" may describe a meal that is "supremely good" or "fit for a god" or may be used of human patience that is "God-like" or "of a sublime character." Only if "divine" is taken to mean "having the very nature of God" does the word accurately convey John's meaning.[70] In a religious context like the Fourth Gospel, such an interpretation of the English term certainly cannot be said to be forced, but it lacks the potency of a substantival rendering of θεός.

c. "The Word was God"

The rendering found in the vast majority of English translations, "the Word was God," also occurs in a comparable form in most other transla-

66. Perhaps reflecting his view that in John 1:1–13 the Logos is an "impersonal personification" (*Christology* 242), Dunn proposes the translation "god" for John 1:1 (*Christology* 58; but in his earlier *Unity* [226] he gives the rendering "God").

67. *Authentic NT* 389; *Original NT* 479.

68. De Kruijf proposes that in John 1:1, 18 θεός = θεῖος (121).

69. The negative reaction to this rendering has sometimes been prompted by assumptions about the motives of the translators or commentators. What Moffatt is supposed to have believed about the deity of Christ has on occasion become a more important factor in evaluating this translation than what the apostle John wished to say about the Logos. For instance, Simpson discusses Moffatt's rendering as an instance "in which theological prepossessions tend to warp the mind of the exegete" (*Words* 10) and as "a flagrant specimen of biassed translation" (*Words* 12–13).

70. In his commentary based on Moffatt's translation, Macgregor remarks: The "distinction of persons, so strongly emphasized by the second proposition of verse 1, though still implied, is resolved into a community of essence in the third proposition, *the Logos was divine.* John does not say 'the Logos was *God*'; still less does he imply merely that the Logos possessed certain divine *qualities.* He means that the Logos was partaker of the divine *essence*" (4). Note also Haenchen, *John* 110: "divine (in essence)."

tions. It has the advantage of being as simple as the original and of representing a definite Greek substantive by a definite English substantive, each being without an article.

It is remarkable how little the defenders of this translation differ when they come to paraphrase John's meaning. The Logos/Word was or is "divine in nature" (Lebreton, *History* 373–74; cf. 449); "God by nature" (K. Barth, *Dogmatics* 98; E. Stauffer, *TDNT* 3:106; Beasley-Murray 2 n. e); "ein Gottwesen das an der Gottheit Gottes teilhatte" (J. Schneider, *TBNT* 2:607; similarly Strathmann, *Johannes* 31); "Gott von Art" (Bauer 10; Schulz 19; Delling 61); "von göttlicher Art" (Richter 269; Blank 1:83; similarly J. Schneider, *Johannes* 50); "göttlichen Wesens" (B. Weiss, "Gebrauch" 323); "what God was" (Pollard);[71] "possessed of divine essence" (Milligan and Moulton 4); "One who in His essence is and continues to be God" (Zahn, *Introduction* 3:326 n. 3); "in His essential nature . . . Deity" (G. T. Purves, *HDB* 3:133); "partaker of the Godhead" (Ebrard 347).

From this sample of paraphrases it is clear that in the translation "the Word was God" the term *God* is being used to denote his nature or essence and not his person. But in normal English usage "God" is a proper noun, referring to the person of the Father or corporately to the three persons of the Godhead. Moreover, "the Word was God" suggests that "the Word" and "God" are convertible terms, that the proposition is reciprocating. But the Word is neither the Father nor the Trinity. Therefore few will doubt that this time-honored translation needs careful exegesis, since it places a distinctive sense upon a common English word. The rendering cannot stand without explanation. I shall return to this important point in chapter XIII §J.

d. "The Word was deity"

Dana and Mantey (148), A. M. Perry (331), Tenney (65), and Fennema (135 n. 58: "the Word was [himself] Deity") have proposed the translation "the Word was deity." There is much to commend it for it largely avoids the ambiguities of the previous two versions. The word *deity*, as opposed to "the Deity" or "a deity," does not refer to a person (cf. "God") nor is it in common use with a diluted meaning (cf. "divine"). As a translation it seems to strike middle ground between "the Word was God" and "the Word was divine." Nevertheless, the suggestion is not entirely successful, since (1) "deity," without either a definite or an indefinite article, is not nearly as common a word in English as the anarthrous θεός is in Greek; (2) it has an abstract flavor ("divine status, quality, or nature") that is absent from θεός; and (3) it accords better with the verb *possessed* than with the verb *was*.

71. Pollard renders θεός by "God" (*Christology* 14, 16) but later (19) supports his statement that the "Logos-Son clearly belongs to the sphere of the divine" by citing the NEB ("what God was, the Word was").

e. "What God was, the Word was"

The translation found in the NEB and the REB[72] is "what God was, the Word was." Similar renderings include the following:

TEV	What God was, the Word also was[73]
Barclay	the nature of the Word was the same as the nature of God
GNB	he was the same as God
Cassirer	the Word was the very same as God
P. B. Harner	the Word had the same nature as God

None of these translations suggests any identity between two proper nouns ("Word" and "God"), for the reference to nature or essence is explicit in Barclay and Harner and implicit in the translations of the NEB/REB, GNB, and Cassirer ("what God was," not "who God was"). All aim at a thought-for-thought rather than a word-for-word translation, and, if John's theological intention is to describe the nature of the Logos rather than to identify his person, they are all defensible. If they are paraphrastic, it is because no word-for-word rendering could possibly capture John's meaning as precisely as a careful paraphrase does. On the other hand, no one will doubt that all these renderings lack Johannine succinctness and force. One should also observe that those versions which begin with "What God was," while reproducing the Greek word order, have converted the predicate into the subject.

From this brief survey of proposed renderings of John 1:1c, I conclude that the most common translation ("the Word was God") remains the most adequate, although it requires that "God" be carefully defined or qualified. Harner's paraphrastic translation "the Word had the same nature as God" (87), or the paraphrase "the Word was identical with God the Father in nature," most accurately represents the evangelist's intended meaning.

E. Conclusion

John 1:1 is clearly triadic: each of the three clauses has the same subject (ὁ λόγος) and an identical verb (ἦν).[74] So far from being tautological, verse 2 gathers together these three separate affirmations and declares them all to be true ἐν ἀρχῇ: "This Logos who was θεός was in the beginning with God." Even though Jesus Christ is not explicitly mentioned until verse 17,

72. This rendering is endorsed by Dodd ("Problems" 103–4) and J. A. T. Robinson (*Face* 182; *Honest* 71; *Truth* 110), both of whom were NEB translators; and by Fuller, "Christology" 33, who paraphrases θεός in John 1:1c as "a personal reality sharing the being of God" (similarly his "Jesus" 114 and Fuller and Perkins 122). Cf. Loader, *Christology* 161.

73. Another TEV edition of the same year (1966) has "he was the same as God" (= GNB).

74. The first two instances of ἦν relate to existence; the third to predication. In John 1:1b it is the conjunction of ἦν and πρός, not πρός itself, that connotes relationship.

the evangelist clearly assumes throughout the Prologue that the Logos is none other than the "only Son" (μονογενής, 1:14, 18) of the Father. In the first proposition of verse 1 John affirms that the Logos existed before time and creation and therefore implicitly denies that the Logos was a created being.[75] In the second, he declares that the Logos always was in active communion with the Father and thereby implies that the Logos cannot be personally identified with the Father. In the third, he states that the Logos always was a partaker of deity and so implicitly denies that the Logos was ever elevated to divine status. The thought of the verse moves from eternal preexistence to personal intercommunion to intrinsic deity. Verse 1c states the basis on which verses 1a and 1b can be said to be true:[76] only because the Logos participated inherently in the divine nature could he be said to be already in existence when time began or creation occurred and to be in unbroken and eternal fellowship with the Father. This would justify regarding θεός as emphatic, standing as it does at the head of its clause.[77]

Wherever one places the pivotal point in the Prologue, verses 14 and 18 are of paramount importance. Verse 1 stands in antithetical parallelism to verse 14 and in synthetic and climactic parallelism to verse 18. The Logos who "existed in the beginning" (v. 1a), "came on the human scene (ἐγένετο)" in time (v. 14a). The one who was eternally "in communion with God" (v. 1b), temporarily "sojourned among us" (v. 14b). "The Word had the same nature as God" (v. 1c) is paralleled by the contrasting thought that "the Word assumed the same nature as humans (σὰρξ ἐγένετο)" (v. 14a). Verses 1 and 18 share references to timeless existence (ἦν *ter*, v. 1; ὁ ὤν, v. 18c), intimate fellowship (πρὸς τὸν θεόν, v. 1b; εἰς τὸν κόλπον τοῦ πατρός, v. 18c), and predicated deity (θεός, vv. 1c, 18b). Where verse 18 advances beyond verse 1 is in its grounding of the validity and accuracy of the Son's revelation (ἐξηγήσατο) of the Father in his oneness with the Father in nature (θεός) and fellowship (εἰς τὸν κόλπον).[78] And, as we shall see, within the Fourth Gospel as a whole, John 1:1c is the first of three strategically positioned statements (viz., 1:1, 18; 20:28) that unequivocally affirm the essential divinity of Jesus Christ.[79]

75. It is perfectly plausible, as Kysar has argued (358–62), that the Christology of the Prologue was occasioned by Jewish-Christian controversy about Christ.

76. Cf. Hofius 16: "Der Stichos v. 1c erklärt zunächst, dass das ἐν ἀρχῇ—Sein und das präexistente Bei-Gott-Sein des Logos in seinem Gott-Sein gründen." Cf. Schnackenburg's comment (*John* 1:235) that the deity of the Logos forms the basis for his functions as depicted in the Prologue.

77. Yet it remains true that the subject often follows the verb in John, as in the papyri (see MH 417–18; Colwell, *Greek* 13–15).

78. But cf. Loader ("Structure" 202; cf. *Christology* 159, 161, 166), who argues that the Fourth Gospel defines the relationship of Jesus to God "not in substantial but in highly functional terms. Jesus is qualified as the revealer not on grounds of his being, but on grounds of where he has been and the relationship which he has" to God as one sent by him.

79. See below, chapter III §D.5.c, chapter IV §D, and chapter XIII §H.

III

The Only Son, Who Is God (John 1:18)

Θεὸν οὐδεὶς ἑώρακεν πώποτε· μονογενὴς θεὸς ὁ ὢν εἰς τὸν κόλπον τοῦ πατρὸς ἐκεῖνος ἐξηγήσατο.

Probably no verse has a more strategic position in the Fourth Gospel than 1:18, looking back as it does over the Prologue from its peak and also forward to the expansive plain of the Gospel narrative. Of crucial import, therefore, is the interpretation of this verse and, in particular, the determination of its original text.[1]

A. The Original Text

Four variant readings call for consideration.[2]

1. ὁ μονογενής

vg^{ms} Diatessaron Aphrahat Ephraem Ps-Athanasius[3]

a. Pro

(1) On the principle *lectio brevior potior*, the reading ὁ μονογενής is to be preferred over the other three.

1. The majority of those who seek to isolate an original hymn within the Prologue regard v. 18 as a secondary addition. But several (e.g., Bernard, *John* 1:cxlv; H. C. Green; de Ausejo 403) see v. 18 as part of the original poem. See the introductory paragraph in chapter II.

2. The reading ὁ μονογενὴς υἱὸς θεοῦ, read by it^{q} (cop$^{sa?}$ θεός), is obviously secondary, as a scribal expansion of ὁ μονογενὴς υἱός or (less probably) ὁ μονογενής. See also McReynolds 110 and n. 47.

3. The collation of evidence is reproduced from UBS^{3}, with the corrections noted by McReynolds 108 nn. 10, 12, 15; 110–11.

(2) It may also account for the other variants.[4] J. N. Sanders (85 n. 1) maintains that "at a very early stage in the tradition" the ΣΟ in ΜΟΝΟΓΕΝΗΣΟΩΝ was accidentally repeated, and the resulting additional ΟΣ was "corrected" to ΘΣ (as in 1 Tim. 3:16), the regular abbreviation for θεός. This reading (ὁ μονογενὴς θεός), in turn, was emended to the simpler ὁ μονογενὴς υἱός.[5] An alternative explanation of the rise of the variants (*ex hypothesi*) is simply that an explanatory υἱός (in the West) or θεός (in Egypt) was consciously added,[6] presumably by a scribe who was aware of the Johannine expression ὁ μονογενὴς υἱός or by a scribe who was intent on introducing into the text an incontestable affirmation of Christ's deity (θεός).

(3) M. E. Boismard goes further.[7] He follows ℵ* it$^{a,\delta}$ and (he claims, "Sein" 23–26) syr^{c} arm Tatian Novatian Tertullian Irenaeus(?) Aphraates Ephraem in omitting ὁ ὢν before εἰς τὸν κόλπον, and W it^{pl} arm eth Tatian in their insertion of εἰ μή before ὁ μονογενής. The preferred text that emerges (viz., the Greek text presupposed by Codex Vercellensis [it^{a}]) is θεὸν οὐδεὶς ἑώρακεν πώποτε, εἰ μὴ ὁ μονογενής· εἰς τὸν κόλπον τοῦ πατρός, ἐνεῖνος ἐξηγήσατο,[8] which Boismard renders, "No one has ever seen God, except the Only Son; he it is who has led the way into the Father's bosom"[9] (= into the kingdom of God).[10] "*Jo.*, 1,18 forme une excellente transition entre les vv. 14–17 du Prologue et le reste de l'évangile: après avoir été constitué médiateur de la Nouvelle Alliance, le Messie prend la tête du nouvel Exode vers le Royaume de l'Esprit" ("Sein" 37).

b. Contra

(1) In comparison with the support for the readings ὁ μονογενὴς υἱός and μονογενὴς θεός, the external evidence favoring ὁ μονογενής is decidedly weak:[11] at most, two manuscripts of the Vulgate, Tatian's Diatessaron, and Aphrahat and Ephraem as witnesses to the Diatessaron (McReynolds 110–11), but no Greek manuscript. F. J. A. Hort (*Dissertations* 11) accounted for the "stray instances" of ὁ μονογενής and *unigenitus* by noting the great frequency of these expressions in patristic writings of the

4. This view was thought "possible" by the NEB translators (Tasker 425).

5. Sanders fails to distinguish between μονογενὴς θεός and ὁ μονογενὴς θεός, listing 𝔓[66] ℵ B C* L W* Θ (*sic*) as manuscripts that support the latter reading.

6. Such is the tentative suggestion of Bousset 318 n. 292.

7. "Sein"; cf. his *Prologue* 91–92.

8. For an appraisal of Boismard's preference for a short text as the primitive text of the Fourth Gospel, see Fee, "Critique," esp. 165, 170–72.

9. "Dieu, personne ne l'a jamais vu, sinon le Fils Unique; dans le sein du Père, c'est lui qui a conduit" ("Sein" 31). But Boismard acknowledges (39) that a crucial difficulty in his interpretation is that no church father ever understood the verse in this sense. One may note that even Novatian and Tertullian make sinum patris the object of a verb such as *enarravit*, *exposuit*, or *disseruit*.

10. On Boismard's interpretation of ἐξηγήσατο see below, §D.4.

11. Hort (*Dissertations* 11) speaks of "unsubstantial shreds of authority."

fourth and fifth centuries. More recently, G. D. Fee has drawn attention to the danger of using patristic citations as *primary* evidence in establishing the primitive text ("Contribution").

(2) While ὁ μονογενής is the shortest reading, it is not the most difficult, being a natural development from the anarthrous (ὡς) μονογενοῦς of verse 14.

(3) Although ὁ μονογενὴς υἱός may easily derive from an original ὁ μονογενής (see John 3:16, 18; 1 John 4:9), the same cannot be said concerning μονογενὴς θεός. It seems improbable that a *second*-century scribe would have created a linguistic and theological *hapax legomenon* by adding θεός to ὁ μονογενής.[12] Only a transcriptional error is likely to account for the variant ὁ μονογενὴς θεός, although the loss of the article would still need explanation.[13]

2. ὁ μονογενὴς υἱός

A C[3] K W[supp] X Δ Θ Π Ψ 063 *f*[1] *f*[13] 28 565 700 892 1009 1010 1071 1079 1195 1216 1230 1241 1242 1253 1344 1365 1546 1646 2148 *Byz Lect* it[a,aur,b,c,e,f,ff2,l] vg syr[c,h,pal] arm eth[pp] geo [Irenaeus[lat]] [Clement[2/4]] [Origen[lat]] Tertullian Alexander Eusebius Ambrosiaster Victorinus-Rome Hilary Athanasius Basil Gregory-Nazianzus [Gregory-Nyssa] Chrysostom Synesius Theodore Nonnus [Cyril-Alexandria] Proclus Theodoret Fulgentius Caesarius[14]

a. Pro

(1) The witnesses supporting ὁ μονογενὴς υἱός are geographically widespread:[15] (later) Alexandrian (892 1241), Western (W[supp] it vg syr[c] Irenaeus[lat] Tertullian),[16] pre-Caesarean (*f*[1] *f*[13] 28), Caesarean proper (Θ 565 700 arm geo Eusebius), and Byzantine (A K Π most minuscules).

(2) The reading accords with Johannine usage (John 3:16, 18; 1 John 4:9), whereas μονογενὴς θεός is unparalleled.

(3) The clause that follows (ὁ ὢν εἰς τὸν κόλπον τοῦ πατρός) seems to demand an antecedent reference to υἱός.[17]

(4) At least three explanations of the origin of the other principal variant (μονογενὴς θεός) have been given. It arose (a) as an accidental misreading

12. On the significance of this point, see below §A.4.a.(4).

13. It is conceivable that a scribe may have wished to ease what he regarded as a theological irregularity (cf. the anarthrous θεός in John 1:1).

14. The bracketed witnesses "are Fathers whose text of John 1:18 almost certainly read θεός, but whose text has suffered corruption in the transmission process" (McReynolds 108 n. 9).

15. This point weighs heavily in the judgment of Abbot, *Authorship* 269, 281.

16. Finegan (§§86, 167) regards W[supp] as Western in John 1:1–5:11.

17. Thus Hoskyns 152; cf. Tasker 425 (the NEB translators regarded ὁ μονογενὴς Υἱός as "intrinsically more probable").

of abbreviations (Θ̄C for Ῡ C),[18] (b) as an error in dictation,[19] or (c) as an assimilation to John 1:1c (θεὸς ἦν ὁ λόγος).[20] The other two variants would thereafter (presumably) result from deliberate omission (ὁ μονογενής, the article being added to avoid having an articular participial phrase [ὁ ὢν κτλ.] dependent on an anarthrous noun) or deliberate addition for doctrinal reasons (ὁ μονογενὴς θεός).

b. Contra

(1) However, ὁ μονογενὴς υἱός lacks proto-Alexandrian manuscript support and B. F. Westcott contends that "the most ancient authorities for the reading, . . . the *Old Latin* and *Old Syriac* versions, are those which are inclined to introduce interpretative glosses" (*Gospel* 32).

(2) The three Johannine uses of μονογενής in conjunction with υἱός (John 3:16, 18; 1 John 4:9) relate these words to ὁ θεός, not ὁ πατήρ; that is, τοῦ πατρός in John 1:18 does not "require" the reading υἱός (Fennema 125–26).

(3) If Θ̄C was accidentally substituted for Ῡ C, how is one to account for the omission of the article in the reading μονογενὴς θεός? John 1:1c is not exactly parallel, for there θεός is predicative, not the subject or in apposition to the subject (as in John 1:18).[21] On the other hand, however, if υἱός replaced an anarthrous θεός, the article would have been naturally added to accord with Johannine use of the expression μονογενὴς υἱός (John 3:16, 18; 1 John 4:9).[22]

(4) A copyist who intentionally altered υἱός to θεός in order to grant Jesus the divine name would probably have eliminated the clause ὁ ὢν εἰς τὸν κόλπον τοῦ πατρός (Cullmann, *Christology* 309). With regard to the whole possibility that ὁ μονογενὴς υἱός was ever consciously changed to μονογενὴς θεός, Hort reminds us that "the single fact that μονογενὴς θεός was put to polemical use by hardly any of those writers of the fourth century who possessed it, either as a reading or as a phrase, shews how unlikely it is that the writers of our earliest extant MSS. were mastered by any such dogmatic impulse in its favour as would overpower the standing habits of their craft" (*Dissertations* 10).

3. ὁ μονογενὴς θεός

𝔓[75] ℵ[c] 33 cop[bo]

18. So Scrivener 358; Abbot, *Authorship* 270, 283; A. Wikgren in Metzger, *Commentary* 198.
19. Bultmann, *John* 81 n. 2.
20. Stevens, *Johannine Theology* 109.
21. This point is discussed below in §C.
22. Similarly Hort, *Dissertations* 10; WH 2: appendix 74; Westcott, *Gospel* 33.

a. Pro

(1) A third variant, ὁ μονογενὴς θεός, has both proto-Alexandrian (𝔓[75]) and later Alexandrian (33 cop[bo]) support and is the most difficult of the verse's five variant readings.[23]

(2) The other variants may all be derived from this reading: ὁ μονογενὴς υἱός could have arisen through a primitive transcriptional error (Υ̅C for Θ̅C) or through assimilation to Johannine usage; μονογενὴς θεός, through harmonization with John 1:1c or to accord with Johannine avoidance of ὁ θεός as a title of the Son; ὁ μονογενής, through an omission due to homoeoteleuton (ΜΟΝΟΓΕΝΗC for ΜΟΝΟΓΕΝΗCΘ̅C) or (more probably) an amelioration of what seemed theologically harsh.

b. Contra

(1) Relatively weakly attested, ὁ μονογενὴς θεός probably represents a combination of μονογενὴς θεός and ὁ μονογενὴς υἱός (Westcott, *Gospel* 32).

(2) It destroys the precise distinction the evangelist has already drawn at the outset of the Prologue between the Father as ὁ θεός (1:1b) and the Logos as θεός (1:1c); it also nullifies his uniform reservation for the Father of an articular θεός as subject.[24] And whereas the anarthrous θεόν in 1:18a may have a qualitative force, ὁ μονογενὴς θεός in 1:18b could only be personal.

4. *μονογενὴς θεός*

𝔓[66] ℵ* B C* L syr[p,hmg] eth[ro] Valentinians[acc. to Irenaeus and Clement] Diatessaron[a] Irenaeus[lat] Clement[2/4] Origen[gr,lat] Arius[acc. to Epiphanius] Hilary Basil Apostolic Constitutions Didymus Gregory-Nyssa Epiphanius Synesius[acc. to Epiphanius] Jerome Cyril Ps-Ignatius

a. Pro

(1) The witnesses that have μονογενὴς θεός belong mainly to the Alexandrian family (proto-Alexandrian: 𝔓[66] B; later Alexandrian: C* L), with ℵ* being the only manuscript representing the Western text type.[25] If the textual support for ὁ μονογενὴς θεός (𝔓[75] ℵ[c] 33 cop[bo]) is added, the superiority of the reading θεός over υἱός with regard to external evidence is confirmed.[26]

23. On the reading ὁ μονογενὴς υἱὸς θεοῦ, see above n. 2.

24. See above, chapter II.

25. Fee ("Sinaiticus") has shown that from John 1:1 to about 8:38 ℵ represents a Western text closely akin to D.

26. While ὁ μονογενὴς θεός obviously supports the presence of θεός in the text and therefore the reading μονογενὴς θεός, it does not follow, conversely, that external attestation for μονογενὴς θεός is evidence for ὁ μονογενὴς θεός, for this wrongly assumes that the article is insignificant.

(2) There can be little doubt that μονογενὴς θεός is a more difficult reading than either ὁ μονογενής or ὁ μονογενὴς υἱός, given its immediate context in the Prologue and the wider background of Johannine thought and style. Ὁ μονογενὴς υἱός is certainly the least difficult variant, for a person who is related to a πατήρ (cf. εἰς τὸν κόλπον τοῦ πατρός, 1:18) as μονογενής must be a son (or daughter).

(3) Μονογενὴς θεός forms a suitable climax to the Prologue, catching up (by *inclusio*)[27] the two crucial designations of the Logos[28] in the two principal preceding verses (viz., vv. 1 and 14)[29] and attributing deity (θεός) to the Son (cf. μονογενής), as earlier it had been predicated of the Logos (v. 1). On the other hand, although making explicit what was merely implicit in verse 14, the reading ὁ μονογενὴς υἱός is pedestrian by comparison, for, used personally, the term μονογενής itself suggests sonship and the addition of υἱός actually weakens the emphasis on the uniqueness (cf. μονογενής) of the Son in comparison with τέκνα θεοῦ (v. 12).[30]

(4) The supposition that μονογενὴς θεός was the original reading seems best to account for the other variants. An *unintentional* "error of eye" in misreading a contraction of a *nomen sacrum* (viz., Θ̄C or Ῡ̄C)[31] might as easily explain a change from θεός to υἱός as from υἱός to θεός.[32] And, although "the phrase ὁ μονογενὴς θεός being familiar to copyists of the third and following centuries, θεός would easily be unconsciously substituted for υἱός, especially as the θεόν which precedes would *suggest* the word" (Abbot, *Authorship* 283; cf. 270), the fact that both $\mathfrak{P}^{66}$ and $\mathfrak{P}^{75}$

27. On *inclusio* in the Fourth Gospel, see Lagrange, *Jean* xcix.

28. In v. 1 θεός is a direct designation of the Logos, but in v. 14 only inferentially is the Logos designated μονογενής (that is, if C. H. Dodd is right in rendering μονογενοῦς παρὰ πατρός parabolically as "a father's only son"—cited, from a letter, by J. A. T. Robinson, "Use" 78 n. 99). If, however, ὡς defines an actual and characteristic quality or states an actual fact (cf. ὡς θεόν, Rom. 1:21; see BAGD 898a) and does not introduce a comparison, μονογενής is a direct designation.

29. Similarly Zahn, *Johannes* 94; Hort, *Dissertations* 14–15 (who speaks of "the pregnant and uniting force" of μονογενὴς θεός, 11); WH 2: appendix 74. See, *per contra*, Abbot, *Authorship* 283, who avers that "forming the grand conclusion of the Prologue which began with predicating θεός of ὁ λόγος, θεός would be a natural marginal gloss, which would easily find its way into the text."

30. Cf. Hort, *Dissertations* 14. In his preface (v), Hort confesses that it was only "a more careful study" of the whole context of 1:18—that is, study of what he termed "intrinsic probabilities"—that caused him to abandon an earlier tentative acceptance of ὁ μονογενής as the original reading (cf. 11) and to decide in favor of μονογενὴς θεός.

31. As to the origin of the contraction of *nomina sacra*, Paap (2, 124–26) theorizes that Grecized Christian Jews of the Diaspora (possibly at Alexandria), wanting a distinctive written form for their tetragram, borrowed (in the first half of the second century) the Hebrew principle of consonantal writing (θεός becoming θς) so that later similar sacral words were also written with first and last letters only.

32. This observation meets Abbot's objection (*Authorship* 270, 284) that, had μονογενὴς θεός been the original text, scribal reverence for this unique and dogmatically significant reading would have preserved it from change, making its widespread corruption to ὁ μονογενὴς υἱός incredible.

read θεός shows that it was *before* 200[33] that any such change from an original ὁ μονογενὴς υἱός to (ὁ) μονογενὴς θεός must have been made.[34] But the phrase (ὁ) μονογενὴς θεός was certainly not a theological commonplace in the second century.

Alternatively, a *conscious* scribal change from (ὁ) μονογενὴς θεός to ὁ μονογενὴς υἱός is more probable and therefore less remarkable than a change in the opposite direction, since (a) in the Johannine corpus there is *one* other instance of ὁ μονογενὴς υἱός (John 3:18) and two of ὁ υἱός ὁ μονογενής (John 3:16; 1 John 4:9);[35] (b) (ὁ) μονογενὴς θεός is a *hapax legomenon* both in the Fourth Gospel and in the NT as a whole; (c) in his understanding of John 1:14 a scribe might well have supplied υἱοῦ with μονογενοῦς, making an explicit reference to υἱός natural in 1:18; (d) the reference to "the Father's heart" that follows immediately after the disputed phrase accords better with υἱός than with θεός, which is therefore less likely to be secondary; and (e) "the universal agreement of the later copies in the reading, *the only-begotten Son*, shews that there was no tendency in scribes to change it, while the correction of ℵ (*the only-begotten God*) shews us the reading, *God*, *only-begotten*, modified under the influence of the common reading."[36]

As for the other variants, their introduction into the textual tradition may be attributable to (a) a copyist's desire to combine the readings μονογενὴς θεός and ὁ μονογενὴς υἱός and thus produce ὁ μονογενὴς

33. 𝔓[66] is generally dated ca. 200 (see Metzger, *Studies* 145–46, 146 n. 1; *Text* 254), but by one distinguished papyrologist, H. Hunger, it has been dated to the middle or even the first half of the second century, while 𝔓[75] belongs within the period 175–225 (Metzger, *Studies* 147, 157–58; cf. his *Text* 255 [beginning of third century]; as also Aland 308).

34. It is therefore now inappropriate to object to μονογενὴς θεός on the ground that "it savours too much of later dogmatics" (Godet, *John* 1:378, writing before the papyri era). In any case, later theological discussion might well have been influenced by this Johannine text (*si vera lectio*), rather than the reverse. But certainly the popularity of (ὁ) μονογενὴς θεός in the third to the fifth centuries no more demonstrates that John 1:18 originally read θεός than the common patristic appellation ὁ θεὸς λόγος proves that this was the way John 1:1 was understood (a similar point is made by Abbot, *Authorship* 267, 282).

35. That ὁ μονογενὴς υἱός was the result of scribal assimilation to these passages is the view of (*inter alios*) a majority of the UBS Committee (Metzger, *Commentary* 198) and Feuillet (*Prologue* 129).

36. Westcott, *Gospel* 32–33. "The publication of critical editions has shown that a Father's text often suffered corruption toward ὁ μονογενὴς υἱός, but *never* in the other direction [viz., toward (ὁ) μονογενὴς θεός]" (McReynolds 113). It is significant that μονογενὴς θεός never became a controversial expression, but was used, for example, by Arius and Eunomius (albeit sparingly) as by Athanasius (apparently only twice) and Gregory of Nyssa (repeatedly) (see Hort, *Dissertations* 18–28). Accordingly, the reading would not have arisen in anti-Arian polemic (even if the date of its origin allowed this). Nor is it likely that the reading originated among the Valentinian Gnostics (see the suggestion of F. Büchsel, *TDNT* 4:740 n. 14; and for the relevant data, Hort, *Dissertations* 9, 30–33) as an attempt to support their ascription of deity to the Logos by an appeal to the deity of the *Monogenes* (= *Arche* = *Nous*) (see Hort, *Dissertations* 32 n. 2), for no church father accuses them of altering the text (similarly Lagrange, *Jean* 26).

υἱὸς θεοῦ (Westcott, *Gospel* 32) or to make incontestable (by the addition of the article) the reference to the deity of Christ (in the case of the reading ὁ μονογενὴς θεός);[37] or (b) harmonization of the reading ὁ μονογενὴς υἱός with the substantival μονογενής in verse 14 (in the case of ὁ μονογενής).[38]

b. Contra

(1) Support for the reading μονογενὴς θεός is largely Alexandrian. But as other examples of Alexandrian readings which are "terse or somewhat rough" or "superficially more difficult" but which commend themselves as original on closer examination, J. H. Greenlee cites λέγω ὑμῖν ἀπέχουσιν in Matthew 6:16, προσέχετε (without δέ) in Matthew 7:15, and ἐν αὐτῷ in John 3:15.[39]

(2) When intrinsic probabilities make the more (or most) difficult reading seem well-nigh impossible, the canon *praestat procliviori ardua* is inapplicable.[40] To some, θεός appears not to accord with the preceding anarthrous θεόν (which cannot refer exclusively, if at all, to the person of the Son), or with the following ὁ ὢν εἰς τὸν κόλπον τοῦ πατρός. Granted, υἱός better suits what follows, but it should not be overlooked that John did not write εἰς τὸν κόλπον τοῦ θεοῦ (which might have made a preceding μονογενὴς θεός virtually impossible). With regard to what precedes, θεός seems as appropriate as υἱός. Had John written θεὸν οὐδεὶς ἑώρακεν πώποτε· θεὸς κτλ., there would have been a difficulty comparable to the hypothetical μονογενὴς θεὸς ὁ ὢν εἰς τὸν κόλπον τοῦ θεοῦ mentioned above. But θεός is qualified in sense, whether μονογενής be adjectival or substantival.[41] In addition, if verse 17 as well as verse 18a be considered, μονογενὴς θεός highlights the difference between Christ and Moses. It was not simply another human mediator—such as Moses—who revealed God, but a being whose nature was divine. Christ had not merely seen God (a privilege denied even Moses); as himself θεός, he had always resided near the Father.

(3) Ὁ μονογενὴς υἱός corresponds to Johannine diction (John 3:16, 18; 1 John 4:9) (Abbot, *Authorship* 284). This argument is two-edged, however, since it may also account for a change from the unparalleled μονογενὴς θεός to ὁ μονογενὴς υἱός.

37. Cf. the "improvement" of the secondary variant θεός by the addition of the article in minuscule 88 in 1 Tim. 3:16.

38. On scribal propensity for "harmonization to the immediate context," see Colwell, "Papyri" 377–78.

39. Greenlee, *Introduction* 87; cf. Metzger, *Text* 218.

40. F. Büchsel (*TDNT* 4:740 n. 14), for example, says of μονογενὴς θεός, "It can hardly be credited of Jn., who is distinguished by monumental simplicity of expression."

41. On this latter point, see below, §C.

5. Final Evaluation of the Evidence

Whether one considers external evidence or transcriptional probabilities, μονογενὴς θεός has a considerably stronger claim to originality than ὁ μονογενὴς υἱός, the other principal variant. External attestation for μονογενὴς θεός is admittedly restricted in extent, representing, as it does, mainly the Alexandrian textual tradition, but it is not uncommon for this text type alone to have preserved the original reading. In regard to the single matter of derivation of other variants, no one of the four readings discussed is *distinctly* better than the others, although μονογενὴς θεός has the edge on its rivals. Nevertheless, the greater the weight given to considerations of intrinsic probability, the more evenly matched do the two main readings become. In summary, the superior manuscript support for μονογενὴς θεός and matters related to scribal habits more than counterbalance any arguments based on Johannine vocabulary or the immediate context that seem to favor ὁ μονογενὴς υἱός. A strong preference may therefore be expressed for μονογενής θεός as the primitive text, an Alexandrian reading that resisted the general tendency toward amelioration. This is not, however, to endorse the verdict that Hort established the originality of μονογενὴς θεός beyond contradiction.

But is the emphasis or meaning of the passage materially altered if θεός be preferred? Defenders of the originality of υἱός seem more ready to answer in the negative[42] than are defenders of θεός.[43] In fact, no part of Hort's carefully worded essay, "On Μονογενὴς Θεός in Scripture and Tradition," is more eloquent than his vigorous argument that only this reading suitably climaxes the Prologue (*Dissertations* 12–16). It has been argued above[44] that ὁ μονογενὴς υἱός is less climactic than μονογενὴς θεός. And in sense, too, there seems to be a not insignificant difference between the two readings. It was not simply the only Son (ὁ μονογενὴς υἱός) who knew and revealed the Father. It was an only Son (μονογενής) who himself possessed deity (θεός) and therefore both knew the Father and was qualified to make him known.

6. Support for the Principal Variants

The list in table 3 is representative, not exhaustive. Only a sampling of scholarly opinion is offered and many of the older textual critics are not listed.

42. Schnackenburg, *John* 1:279.
43. But note Westcott, *Gospel* 15.
44. See above, §A.4.a.(3).

Table 3. *Support for the Principal Variants in John 1:18*

Variant	*Textual Critics*	*Commentators*	*General Studies*	*Translations*[a]
ὁ μονογενής	M. E. Boismard (*Prologue* 91–92; "Sein" 23–31)	J. N. Sanders (85 n. 1)	W. Bousset (318 n. 292) E. Hirsch (3)	
ὁ μονογενὴς υἱός	F. H. A. Scrivener (358–60) A. Wikgren (in Metzger, *Commentary* 198)[b]	E. C. Hoskyns (151–52) R. Bultmann (*John* 81 n. 2) R. H. Lightfoot (90) R. Schnackenburg (*John* 1:279–80) S. Schulz (34)	E. Abbot (*Authorship* 241–85) F. Büchsel (*TDNT* 4:740 n. 14) I. de la Potterie (*Vérité* 189)	RV ASV Weymouth Berkeley RSV NEB (cf. Tasker 424–25) JB NJB Cassirer REB
ὁ μονογενὴς θεός	H. J. Vogels (288)			
μονογενὴς θεός	B. F. Westcott—F. J. A. Hort (WH 2: appendix 74; Westcott, *Gospel* 15, 32–33; Hort, *Dissertations* 1–29) NA[26] J. H. Greenlee (*Introduction* 123–26) UBS[1,2,3] J. Finegan (§§211–17) P. R. McReynolds (105–16)	T. Zahn (*Johannes* 94–95, 703–8) M. J. Lagrange (*Jean* 26–28) J. H. Bernard (*John* 1:31) W. F. Howard ("Gospel" 479) C. K. Barrett (*John* 169)[c] R. E. Brown (*Reflections* 12–13 = "Jesus" 553–54; *Gospel* 1:17, 36) L. Morris (*John* 113) B. Lindars (*John* 98–99) J. Schneider (*Johannes* 63) F. F. Bruce (*John* 44–45) G. R. Beasley-Murray (2 n. e)	B. Weiss (*Johannes* 59–60; "Gebrauch" 323) E. Stauffer (114, 283 n. 352; *TDNT* 3:105) A. J. Surjansky (118– 23) O. Cullmann (*Christology* 309) A. W. Wainwright (*Trinity* 61–62 = "Confession" 292–93) K. Rahner (136, 137 n. 1) G. Richter (41) A. Feuillet (*Prologue* 129–30) T. E. Pollard (*Christology* 14 and n. 2; 15) G. Reim (*Studien* 259) B. A. Mastin ("Christology" 37–41) S. Pancaro (279) M. Theobald (16) D. A. Fennema (125–28) L. Morris (*Jesus* 64, 72, 95) J. Ashton (149)	TCNT Moffatt Goodspeed NASB GNB Barclay NAB[1] NIV NAB[2] NRSV

a. When a version reads "the only (begotten) Son," it is always possible that the Greek being rendered is simply ὁ μονογενής.
b. McReynolds (117) lists Souter (1910), von Soden (1913), Bover (1943), and the first three editions of Nestle as reading ὁ μονογενὴς υἱός.
c. But in the first edition of his commentary (141), Barrett favored ὁ μονογενὴς υἱός.

B. The Meaning of μονογενής

Whatever one's final decision concerning the textual problem in John 1:18, the question of the meaning of μονογενής remains, for all of the textual variants in the verse include this enigmatic term.

In compound adjectives, -γενής refers to derivation[45] or descent in general, rather than to birth in particular or to species. Etymologically it is related to γί(γ)νεσθαι, not γεννᾶσθαι.[46] The idea of birth, although congruous with μονογενής, is in no way an essential part of its meaning (see further below).

If the first element in compounds involving -γενής is a noun, the *source* of the derivation is thereby indicated (thus γηγενής, "sprung from the earth") (F. Büchsel, *TDNT* 4:738). Accordingly, μονογενής could mean "he who proceeded from the Unique One (= μόνος)" or "deriving from a single begetter" (where μονογενής = ἐκ μόνου γενόμενος). But there is no evidence that μόνος was a first-century title of God[47] that might have been used by Christians or borrowed by John, or that by employing the term μονογενής John was combating attacks of some description on the virgin birth of Jesus or else asserting the descent of Jesus from the one true God of Israel.

If, on the other hand, the first component in a -γενής compound is an adverb, the *nature* of the derivation is thus shown (so εὐγενής, "of noble descent") (F. Büchsel, *TDNT* 4:738). To this category the adjective μονογενής rightly belongs. It means "of sole descent,"[48] referring to the only child in a family, a meaning attested in secular Greek literature,[49] the LXX[50] and other Jewish literature,[51] and the NT.[52] So, for example, Tobit 3:15: "I am my father's only daughter (μονογενής) and he has no other child (ἕτερον τέκνον, ℵ) to be his heir."

45. Thus F. Büchsel, *TDNT* 4:737–38.

46. On the confusion between terms derived from γίνεσθαι and those from γεννᾶσθαι in the early Christian era, see Prestige, *God* 37–52, 135–40, 151–56, and his earlier detailed articles "Eusebius" and "Athanasius."

47. However, the phrase (ὁ) μόνος θεός occurs four times in the NT (John 5:44 v.l.; 17:3; Rom. 16:27; 1 Tim. 1:17; and cf. μόνος ὁ θεός in Luke 5:21).

48. F. Büchsel, *TDNT* 4:738. Most of the following examples (in nn. 49–51) are drawn from his article.

49. Hesiodius, *Op.* 376; Plato, *Critias* 113D; Aeschylus, *Ag.* 898.

50. Judg. 11:34; Tob. 3:15; 6:11 (A), 15 (ℵ); 8:17; Ps. 21:21; 24:16; 34:17; Wisd. Sol. 7:22.

51. Josephus, *Ant.* 1:222, 5:264. Israel is called μονογενής in Pss. Sol. 18:4; cf. 4 Ezra 6:58.

52. Luke 7:12; 8:42; 9:38. In Heb. 11:17 Isaac is designated the μονογενής of Abraham, not as the only son he fathered (cf. Ishmael, Gen. 16:15) but as the only "son of promise" or his "beloved son." Behind the use of μονογενής in later Hellenistic Jewish writings and in the NT outside John, de Kruijf finds the theme of paradoxical divine intervention to save an only child who is in a critical situation, intervention that calls for the utmost trust and fidelity (113–17).

Some, however, find the -γενής element insignificant and treat μονογενής merely as an emphatic or fuller form of μόνος,[53] meaning "unique, unparalleled, incomparable." Others argue for this sense on the ground that the components of the term μονογενής are μόνος ("alone, single") and γένος ("kind, species"). Whatever is μονογενής is unique with regard to γένος, the "only one of its kind."[54] Thus the phoenix, whose longevity was legendary, is described in 1 Clement 25:2 as μονογενές, "alone of its kind," while in a passage in the Wisdom of Solomon (7:22) that enumerates the various qualities of Wisdom, she is depicted as having in her "a spirit that is quick of understanding, holy, alone in kind (μονογενής)."

That μονογενής may bear the meaning "unique" when applied to nonpersonal objects is beyond dispute. But it is less clear that this is the predominant or primary sense of the word.[55] The meaning "without siblings" does not result from the application to the sphere of the family of the category of "singularity of kind." Rather, from the personal application of μονογενής to "the only member of a kin" there developed a nonfamilial and nonpersonal use in reference to "the only member of a kind."[56] Certainly in Johannine usage the conjunction of μονογενής and υἱός[57] shows that it is not the personal uniqueness of Jesus in itself that John is emphasizing but his being "of sole descent" as the Son of God.

There is, undoubtedly, a certain overlapping between the NT terms μονογενής, πρωτότοκος, and ἀγαπητός when applied to Christ, for each word *implies* his unique filial relation to God. But whereas μονογενής depicts the relation of the Son to the Father, πρωτότοκος is used to describe his relation to creation (Col. 1:15), including angels (Heb. 1:6), or to his spiritual kin (Rom. 8:29) by virtue of his resurrection (Col. 1:18; Rev. 1:5).[58] How the meaning of μονογενής could shade off into ἀγαπητός is clear. The child who is "without brothers or sisters" will naturally be the special object

53. Thus F. Kattenbusch, *DCG* 2:281b, citing the parallels of πρωτογενής = πρῶτος, ὁμογενής = ὅμοιος, and ἀειγενής = αἰώνιος. Further support for this view comes from (1) A and B read μόνος where ℵ reads μονογενής in Tob. 6:15 (μ. εἰμι τῷ πατρί); B and ℵ read μόνην where A reads μονογενῆν and R μονογενῆ in Bar. 4:16 (ἀπὸ τῶν θυγατέρων τὴν μ. ἠρήμωσαν); and (2) the adverb μονογενῶς means "only" or "in a unique manner" (LSJ 1144 s.v.).

54. Moody 213; D. Moody, *IDB* 3:604a; Dodd, *Interpretation* 305 n. 1. Similarly MM 416–17 s.v.; W. F. Howard, *John* 69–70; Roberts; de la Potterie, *Vérité* 181–91.

55. Hort traces instances where μονογενής = "unique" to a "rare laxity of popular speech" (*Dissertations* 17). This is a "rare secondary sense" of μονογενής, its "true usual sense" implying actual parentage (63 and n. 2).

56. LSJ 1144 gives as the basic meaning of μονογενής, "the only member of a kin *or* kind."

57. Υἱός accompanies μονογενής in John 3:16, 18; 1 John 4:9 but not in John 1:14, 18.

58. Interpreting μονογενής in the light of their view of πρωτότοκος, the Arians took the μονο- to indicate that only the Son was created directly by God, all other creatures being created through the Son (Pollard, *Christology* 158, 169, 212–13).

of parental affection.[59] An "only son" is a "beloved son."[60] For C. H. Turner the link is still closer. Adducing evidence for an old classical sense for ἀγαπητός of "only" and a new Judeo-Christian sense of "beloved," he defends the view that ἀγαπητὸς υἱός should be rendered "Only Son." Whatever verdict one passes on Turner's view,[61] it is of interest that the LXX renders יחיד ("alone, solitary") four times by μονογενής[62] and six times by ἀγαπητός.[63] Nevertheless, it may be that the Pauline ἴδιος υἱός (Rom. 8:32) is more nearly analogous to the Johannine μονογενὴς υἱός than is the Synoptic ἀγαπητὸς υἱός (thus Cremer 150).

Granted, then, that μονογενής is generally equivalent to *unicus* ("sole" or "unique"), can it ever mean *unigenitus* ("only begotten")? Etymologically μονογενής is not associated with begetting (γεννᾶσθαι)[64] but with existence (γίγνεσθαι). Yet it is not surprising that μονογενής soon came to acquire overtones of "begetting" or "generation,"[65] for in 1 John 5:18 Christ is described as ὁ γεννηθεὶς ἐκ τοῦ θεοῦ.[66] Indeed, Alexander of Alexandria and the Antiochenes understood (ὁ) μονογενὴς θεός as a reference to the uniqueness of the Son's generation by the Father (Pollard, *Christology* 149, 169). It seems that the impulse to render μονογενής by *unigenitus* rather than by *unicus* (as in the earlier Latin renderings) arose from christological dispute and in particular the desire to establish from Scripture the doctrine of the generation of the Son by and from the Father.[67] F. J. A. Hort speaks of "the almost uniform rule that *unicus* belongs to native Latin Creeds, *unigenitus* to comparatively late Greek Creeds translated into Latin" (*Dissertations* 51). As far as the evidence of

59. Concerning King Monobazus of Adiabene, Josephus (*Ant.* 20:20) writes: "By Helena he had an older son than Izates named Monobazus, and other children by his other wives, but it was obvious that all his favor was focused on Izates, *as if he were* an only son (ὡς εἰς μονογενῆ)."

60. Cf. Josephus, *Ant.* 1:222: "Now Isaac was very dearly loved by his father Abraham, since he was his only son (μονογενῆ ὄντα) and born to him on the threshold of old age through God's bounty." For evidence that in the Orphic hymns μονογενής is "a hyperbolic expression of affection" meaning "'darling' or as we say, Dear One," see J. R. Harris, "Athena" 65–69.

61. It is difficult, for example, to agree that the habitual combination of the words ἀγαπητός and μονογενής in Greek Christian writings of the first four centuries establishes their synonymity (cf. C. H. Turner 125–29). Μονογενής is concerned primarily with essential rather than ethical relations (cf. Lenski, *John* 80).

62. Judg. 11:34; Ps. 21:21 [MT 22:21]; 24:16 [MT 25:16]; 34:17 [MT 35:17]; cf. μονότροπος in Ps. 67:7.

63. Gen. 22:2, 12, 16; Judg. 11:34 (A); Jer. 6:26; Amos 8:10; Zech. 12:10; cf. ἀγαπώμενος in Prov. 4:3.

64. Yet it is inappropriate to dismiss, as some do, the possibility that μονογενής means "only begotten" on the ground that μονογέννητος would then have been used, for this word is never found in extant Greek literature.

65. See Westcott, *Epistles* 171 (in an additional note on the use of μονογενής); and also the comments of Grant .

66. Thus Brooke 148–49; but see *per contra* Beyer (216) who translates 1 John 5:18b as "Wer aus Gott gezeugt wurde, den bewahrt er (Gott)."

67. See further Hort, *Dissertations* 48–53; Moody 214–16. On the use of μονογενής in Orphic and Gnostic literature, see the extended footnote in Bultmann, *John* 72–73; for its use in christological controversy, see Pollard, *Christology* 149, 158, 167–69, 188, 212–13, 259–60.

the NT is concerned, it may be safely said that μονογενής is concerned with familial relations, not manner of birth. Neither the virgin birth of Jesus nor the "eternal generation" of the Son is in John's mind when he uses the adjective μονογενής.[68]

This leads us to conclude that μονογενής denotes "the only member of a kin or kind."[69] Applied to Jesus as the Son of God, it will mean that he is without spiritual siblings and without equals. He is "sole-born" and "peerless." No one else can lay claim to the title Son of God in the sense in which it applies to Christ.

But the connotations that μονογενής derives from Johannine usage greatly enrich the epithet or title. In the Johannine corpus,[70] Jesus is μονογενής because (1) he alone is υἱὸς θεοῦ, being "of sole 'descent.'" No one can call him brother. As in the First Epistle of John, so in the Fourth Gospel Jesus alone is υἱὸς θεοῦ[71] while believers are τέκνα θεοῦ[72] (υἱοὶ θεοῦ does not occur). This distinction might be expressed in a non-Johannine idiom by saying that Christ's sonship is essential, that of believers is adoptive. (2) He is "unique" (a) in relation to the Father, because (i) both before and after his incarnation he was in the most intimate fellowship with his Father (1:18), (ii) he was the sole and matchless Revealer of the Father's love (John 3:16; 1 John 4:9), and (iii) his origin is traceable to God the Father (John 1:14;[73] cf. 1 John 5:18); and (b) in relation to human beings, because he is the object of human faith, the means of eternal salvation, and the touchstone of divine judgment (John 3:16, 18).

68. That μονογενής does not relate to the virgin birth of Jesus is clear from the fact that Jesus' sonship was not inaugurated by the incarnation. First John 4:14 shows that the Son assumed the additional role of Savior of the world at the incarnation; the preexistent Son became the historical Savior. On the patristic concept of eternal generation and in particular on the role of Origen in the formulation of the concept, see Wiles, "Generation."

69. LSJ 1144 s.v. Although appeal is often made to this lexicon in support of the equation μονογενής = "unique," in fact it does not list John 1:14 (the only NT occurrence cited) under that meaning, but (with a "cf.") under "only, single."

70. The linking of the evidence of the Fourth Gospel and the First Epistle is justifiable on the ground of identity of authorship or identity of origin (viz., the Johannine circle). A distinction has not been drawn between John 1:14 and the remaining references in the Fourth Gospel (*pace* Bultmann, *John* 72n.).

71. John 1:34, 49; 3:18; 5:25; 9:35 v.l.; 10:36; 11:4, 27; 17:1 v.l.; 19:7; 20:31; 1 John 1:3, 7; 3:8, 23; 4:9, 10, 15; 5:5, 10 *bis*, 11, 12, 13, 20 *bis*.

72. John 1:12; 11:52; 1 John 3:1, 2, 10; 5:2. Note also the distinction drawn in 1 John 5:18 between the child of God as ὁ γεγεννημένος ἐκ τοῦ θεοῦ and the Son of God as ὁ γεννηθεὶς ἐκ τοῦ θεοῦ, and in John 20:17 between ὁ πατήρ μου and ὁ πατὴρ ὑμῶν (cf. John 5:18).

73. This assumes that παρὰ πατρός is to be construed with μονογενοῦς (not δόξαν) and is equivalent to τοῦ ἐξερχομένου παρὰ πατρός (cf. John 16:27; 17:8) (not simply πατρός). Brown (*Gospel* 1:14) translates the phrase as "coming from the Father" and observes that "the reference is to the mission of the Son, not his procession within the Trinity."

C. Translation of μονογενὴς θεός

There is a fairly general agreement that the most suitable English translation of ὁ μονογενὴς υἱός is "the only Son,"[74] but with the phrase μονογενὴς θεός it almost becomes a case of *tot homines, tot sententiae*, for both μονογενής and θεός may be understood adjectivally or substantivally. The plethora of proposed renderings—testimony to the difficulty of this *hapax legomenon*—will best be classified according to grammatical construction. All scholars cited prefer the reading μονογενὴς θεός, unless a name is followed by an asterisk. Those listed twice give variant translations.

1. μονογενής Construed as an Adjective Qualifying θεός

the only begotten God	NASB, T. Zahn[75]
an only-begotten God	F. Büchsel* (*TDNT* 4:740 n. 14)
ein einzigerzeugtes Gottwesen	H. J. Holtzmann–W. Bauer (49)
Only-Born God	J. R. Harris[76]
God Only-begotten	A. T. Robertson[77]
God, only-begotten	B. F. Westcott[78]
Deus unigenitus	A. J. Šurjanský (87, 118, 126, 202)[79]
un Dieu Monogène	A. Feuillet (*Prologue* 129)
a God begotten of the Only One	BAGD (527b s.v. μονογενής)
the unique God	R. N. Longenecker (*Christology* 137), R. Kysar (355)
One who is only-begotten God	F. J. A. Hort (*Dissertations* 17–18, apparently)
One who is God only begotten	E. C. Hoskyns* (152)
one who is God, only begotten	B. F. Westcott[80]
He who is in the bosom of the Father, only-begotten, divine	W. F. Howard ("Gospel" 479)

74. The rendering "the only begotten Son" is found in the KJV, RV, ASV, and Berkeley ("the only-begotten Son").

75. *Introduction* 3:312 ("the 'only-begotten God'"); cf. 3:326 n. 3; also *Johannes* 94.

76. J. R. Harris, "Athena" 69–70 ("it meant originally and as used by St. John, 'the dear God in the bosom of the Father,'" 70), citing the parallel expression μουνογενεῖα θεά in the Hymn to Persephone (*Orphic Hymns* 29:2).

77. *Divinity* 45; *Pictures* 5:17 ("God only begotten"); cf. his *Grammar* 656 (μονογενής is attributive).

78. *Gospel* 32–33. This is the rendering most frequently found in Westcott.

79. Šurjanský paraphrases the expression thus: "Persona divina, quae Filius est unigenitus Dei Patris" (127).

80. *Gospel* 32; cf. 15 ("one who is God only-begotten," *bis*). See also WH 2: appendix 74: "One who was both θεός and μονογενής," where θεός and μονογενής are termed "the two attributes of the Logos marked before (θεός v. 1, μονογενής v. 14)."

der Eingeborene Gott	J. Blank (72, 99)

2. μονογενής Construed as a Substantive

a. Equivalent to μονογενὴς υἱός

(1) With θεός Rendered Substantivally

God the only Son	TCNT,[81] NAB[1], NIV (1973, 1978), NRSV, B. F. Westcott,[82] R. E. Brown,[83] D. A. Fennema (124, 131), W. R. G. Loader (*Christology* 112, 161; cf. 35, 150)
un Dieu Fils unique	A. Feuillet (*Prologue* 129)
le fils unique, Dieu[84]	M. J. Lagrange[85]
the only Son, (himself) God	D. A. Fennema (131; cf. 135 n. 58)
the divine One, the only Son	Moffatt
the only Son, Deity Himself	Williams
the only Son, God	NAB[2]

(2) With θεός Rendered Adjectivally

the divine Only Son	Goodspeed[86]
the divine and only Son	Phillips

b. With θεός Rendered Substantivally

the only begotten, God	O. Cullmann (*Christology* 309)
the only-begotten one, God	B. Lindars (*John* 98)
an only-begotten one, God	BAGD (527b s.v. μονογενής)
Only begotten, God	E. A. Abbott[87]
the Only-Begotten, who is God	J. H. Bernard (*John* 1:32)
an only begotten, who is God	K. Rahner (1:137 n. 1)
the only one, who is himself God	J. A. T. Robinson[88]

81. TCNT has "God the Only Son."

82. *Gospel* 15 (apparently not Westcott's preferred rendering).

83. Brown, *Reflections* 12 (= "Jesus" 553); *Gospel* 1:4, 17, 36.

84. Similarly E. D. Burton 414 ("in 1[18] we should probably read μονογενὴς θεός, and interpret μονογενής as standing for μονογενὴς υἱός, with θεός in definitive apposition"). See further n. 99 below.

85. Lagrange, *Jean* 27: "Cette incapacité [to see God apart from representations] qui frappe tous les hommes n'atteint pas celui qui est le fils unique, Dieu comme son Père"; cf. 28: "né unique et Dieu."

86. So also de Kruijf 121: "The (divine) only Son," in a paraphrase of John 1:18.

87. Abbott, *Grammar* §§1938, 1964 ("Only begotten, *God*, HE THAT IS in the bosom of the Father—he hath declared him").

88. J. A. T. Robinson, *Face* 174 ("accepting the harder but best-attested reading," 174 n. 153; but cf. his *Truth* 110; *Priority* 372–73); "Use" 71 ("what is introduced as a simile in verse 14 is already fully allegorized by verse 18, especially if the astonishing μονογενὴς θεός, 'the only one who is himself God,' is indeed the right reading"). The NEB mg has "the only one, himself God."

God, the only-begotten	W. F. Howard (*John* 52)
God the One and Only	NIV (1984)
the unique one, [himself] God	D. A. Carson (*John* 135)

c. With θεός Rendered Adjectivally or Paraphrastically

the Only Begotten . . . who Himself is of divine nature	B. Weiss (*Commentary* 218)
un monogène divin	A. Loisy* (111)
ein Eingeborener göttlichen Wesens	B. Weiss (*Johannes* 60; "Gebrauch" 323 and n. 1)
the only-begotten, whose being is divine	R. Schnackenburg* (*John* 1:280)
the only-begotten one, who is divine in origin	B. Lindars (*John* 99)
the only One, who is the same as God	GNB (1966 and 1971 eds.)[89]
the unique one, He who is God	Barclay

Reference may be made at this point to the suggestion of C. F. Burney (39–40, 42), prompted by the difficulty of having μονογενὴς θεός after θεὸν κτλ., that, although μονογενὴς θεός ("the only begotten God") is the preferable reading, in fact an original Aramaic יְחִיד אֱלָהָא ("the only begotten of God") was misunderstood as יָחִיד אֱלָהָא and therefore rendered μονογενὴς θεός (instead of μονογενὴς θεοῦ).[90] This proposal, that effectively removes the "difficulty" of the Greek, gains or loses credibility depending on one's assessment of the difficulty of the unparalleled phrase μονογενὴς θεός. The more difficult this expression is felt to be, the more attractive Burney's conjecture. However, the first prerequisite to be met before one must consider the possibility of a mistranslation from a putative Aramaic original is that the Greek as it stands is not simply difficult or without precise parallel, but impossible. Yet such cannot be said about this phrase, particularly if μονογενής is substantival. Moreover, since there is no evidence of other similarly crass mistranslations in the Prologue,[91] it seems unlikely that the postulated translator would here be capable of so elementary a blunder as failing to distinguish between absolute and construct states.[92] In any case, it is by no means impossible that

89. Cf. Greenlee, *Introduction* 124, who renders the anarthrous θεός as "He who himself is deity."

90. On the reading ὁ μονογενὴς υἱὸς θεοῦ, see above n. 2.

91. *Pace* Burney 28–43.

92. Discussing the criteria for evaluating conjectural misrenderings of original Aramaic in the Greek text of the Gospels and Acts, Black (8–9) delineates two demands that must be met: the mistranslation must be credible and the conjectured Aramaic must be possible. Concerning Burney's

the Prologue or any hymn it incorporates was originally written in Greek.[93] There is therefore no need to regard μονογενὴς θεός as a translational error and to translate or exegete John 1:18 as though the text read μονογενὴς θεοῦ.

All of the above translations are possible renderings of the Greek. How then is one to decide between so many proposals? Several guidelines will help to restrict the choice.

1. As seen above (§B), μονογενής here bears its primary sense of "only" (with respect to filial status), not the meaning "unique" or its later sense of "only begotten" (where that means not simply "sole-born" or "the only child in a family" but "uniquely generated" or "eternally begotten").
2. There is no reason to suppose that μονογενὴς θεός is equivalent to ὁ μόνος θεός (John 5:44;[94] 17:3; cf. Rom. 16:27; 1 Tim. 1:17; Jude 25), especially since in John 17:3 Ἰησοῦς Χριστός is distinguished from ὁ μόνος ἀληθινὸς θεός.[95] By using this phrase the evangelist is not merely reaffirming Jewish monotheism in the context of his Logos theology.
3. John did not write θεὸς μονογενής,[96] which makes it doubtful that the popular translation "God the only Son" is the most accurate. Nor did he write ὁ μονογενὴς θεός,[97] which renders difficult (although not, of course, impossible) the translation "the only begotten God" or "the unique God," for elsewhere in the Johannine corpus when μονογενής is an attributive adjective (viz., John 3:16, 18; 1 John 4:9), the noun it qualifies is articular.[98]
4. Μονογενής should be treated as equivalent to (ὁ) μονογενὴς υἱός, since (a) in four of the other eight uses of μονογενής in the NT (viz., Luke 7:12; John 3:16, 18; 1 John 4:9), it functions as an attributive adjective before υἱός. On three further occasions μονογενής stands alone but in each case the context makes it clear that it means "only son" (John 1:14; Heb. 11:17 RSV) or "only child" (Luke 9:38 RSV, doubtless to distinguish μονογενής μοι from the preced-

suggestion regarding 1:18 Black writes (11): "It has an attractive simplicity, is free from philological difficulties, and the Greek reading is unusual. Equally remarkable, however, would be the ignorance of the translator who made the blunder, unless we look on his 'version' as a deliberate theological interpretation of the Aramaic."

93. So Barrett, *NT Essays* 35–36; see also Käsemann, *Questions* 140–41.

94. 𝔓[66] 𝔓[75] B W it[a] cop[sa] Origen *et al* omit θεοῦ after παρὰ τοῦ μόνου.

95. On John 17:3 see below, chapter XII §B.

96. An expression used, for example, by Bishop Alexander of Alexandria (*apud* Theodoret, *EH* 1:4).

97. On this reading in John 1:18, see §A.3 above.

98. In Luke 7:12 one finds μονογενὴς υἱός, but the reference is nonetheless definite, although not to Jesus Christ (as in each of the Johannine examples).

ing ὁ υἱός μου). The only occasion in the NT where μονογενής is not used of an "only son" is Luke 8:42, where it qualifies θυγάτηρ. (b) The phrase that qualifies μονογενής or (μονογενὴς θεός), viz., ὁ ὢν εἰς τὸν κόλπον τοῦ πατρός, indicates that μονογενής denotes not simply "the only one" but "an/the only Son." (c) In its primary sense μονογενής designates a familial relation ("sole-born, without siblings") whether or not υἱός or θυγάτηρ is expressed (see §B above).

5. If μονογενής is equivalent to (ὁ) μονογενὴς υἱός in John 1:18, the corollary is that θεός stands in epexegetic apposition to μονογενής:[99] "The only Son, who is θεός."
6. The anarthrous θεός is not indefinite. Since ἐκεῖνος in John 1:18 is specific, its antecedent μονογενής, further defined as θεὸς ὁ ὢν κτλ., must be definite. The absence of the article before μονογενής and before θεός is not without significance,[100] for it draws attention (in the case of μονογενής) to the uniqueness of the familial status of Jesus Christ as the one and only Son of God and (in the case of θεός) to his possession of the attributes of Deity,[101] all that makes God God (as in John 1:1c).[102] In any case it is John's custom to reserve ὁ θεός for the Father.[103]

These considerations point to the aptness of translating μονογενὴς θεός as "the only Son, who is[104] God" (cf. NAB², M. J. Lagrange, and D. A. Fennema under §C.2.a.(1) above).[105]

99. That θεός is in apposition to a substantival μονογενής is recognized, *inter alios*, by E. D. Burton 414; du Plessis 27; de Kruijf 120–21 ("if θεός is the original reading"); Finegan §§199, 217; Theobald 17, 49; Fennema 128, 131; Beasley-Murray (2 n. e); Carson, *John* 139; Carson, *Responsibility* 147. McReynolds notes (108 n. 13) that one of Origen's four citations of the reading μονογενὴς θεός (viz., *Cels.* 2:71: καὶ μονογενής γε ὢν θεὸς κτλ.) is "a clear early witness as to how one should understand the reading μονογενὴς θεός" (cf. 115).

100. Hort (*Dissertations* 14, 18) believed that the anarthrous state of μονογενὴς θεός gives the expression "predicative force" (viz., "one who is μονογενὴς θεός"; cf. WH 2: appendix 74). In rejecting the reading ὁ μονογενὴς υἱός, he avers that "the article would mar the integrity of the Prologue by giving its crowning sentence a new subject in place of ὁ λόγος; and in any case a designative name would serve the argument less than a recital of attributes" (18).

101. Milligan and Moulton (10) expound θεός thus: the Son is "Himself divine, not in a metaphorical sense, but possessing all the attributes of true and real divinity."

102. This answers Loisy's objection (111) that the reading μονογενὴς θεός ("un monogène divin") is too indefinite to describe the Revealer already known from the context.

103. See above, chapter II §A.

104. Although John 1:1c reads θεὸς ἦν ὁ λόγος, it seems more appropriate to supply "who is" than "who was" (to bring out the appositive force of θεός), in view of the following ὁ ὢν κτλ. that affords a second definition of μονογενής.

105. Loisy's second objection (111) to the reading μονογενὴς θεός (for the first, see above, n. 102) is that in the course of the same sentence an anarthrous θεός must then be construed in two different ways—once as a substantive ("la divinité"), once as an attributive adjective ("divin"). My reply is that θεός is in both cases substantival ("God"). However, it would not be illegitimate to render the second use adjectivally or paraphrastically. B. Weiss renders θεός in 1:1c and 1:18b by "göttlichen Wesens" and θεόν in 1:18a by "das göttliche Wesen" ("Gebrauch" 323, 349).

D. The Meaning and Significance of John 1:18

1. Its Old Testament Background

Several writers have found the background of John 1:14–18 in certain themes expressed in Exodus 29 and 33–34, such as the revelation of divine glory in a dramatic self-proclamation.[106] Whether John develops these themes in terms of similarities between the two economies or in terms of contrasts is hotly debated. The bold antithesis between ἐδόθη ("was given" [by God]) and ἐγένετο ("came on the scene") in verse 17 implies that, while the giving of the law stands apart from the person of Moses, grace and truth are realized only through the person of Jesus Christ (cf. John 14:6). He is not only the mediator but also the source of grace and truth. Yet the overall relation between verse 17a and verse 17b may be synthetic not antithetical parallelism, since both Moses and Christ were mediators of divine revelation.[107] Then again, following verse 17, verse 18 suggests that John has in mind a contrast between Moses, who was given a vision of God's back (Exod. 33:18–23) or form (תמנה, Num. 12:6–8) but denied a vision of God's face (Exod. 33:20; but cf. 24:9–10), and Jesus Christ, who, sharing the divine nature (θεός) as the only Son (μονογενής), had not simply seen God on one isolated occasion but had always known him intimately as Father (ὁ ὢν εἰς τὸν κόλπον τοῦ πατρός).

2. θεὸν οὐδεὶς ἑώρακεν πώποτε

That God as he is in himself cannot be seen by the physical or even the spiritual eye[108] was axiomatic in Judaism.[109] At the same time, no Jew would have denied that on occasion, through self-disclosure, God permitted himself to be seen in some "form," that is, indirectly or partially.[110] Consequently John's thought may be either that it has always been and will always be impossible for humans to see God in his essence or that God is not immediately accessible to human knowledge apart from his self-disclosure in Christ the Revealer. The former view stresses God's invisibility and incomprehensibility. No human being has ever seen

106. See, e.g., Sahlin 74; Boismard, *Prologue* 136–40; Boismard, "Sein" 36–37. Note also the wider treatment in Enz.

107. So J. Jeremias, *TDNT* 4:873. See also Glasson, *Moses* 24–26, esp. 24 n. 2; and the extensive discussion in Pancaro 534–46, esp. 537.

108. Bultmann rightly observes (*John* 79; cf. 69 n. 2) that, given Johannine usage (see the discussions of Tarelli 176–77; Abbott, *Vocabulary* §§1597–1611), ὁρᾶν should not be restricted to visual perception.

109. See, e.g., Exod. 33:20, 23; Deut. 4:12; Ps. 97:2; Sir. 43:31; Philo, *Poster. C.* 5; Josephus, *Bell.* 7:346). See further Bultmann, "Untersuchungen"; Amiot; and SB 4:939–40.

110. See, e.g., Gen. 32:30; Exod. 24:9–10; Num. 12:6, 8; Deut. 34:10; Isa. 6:1, 5. On the prophetic, theophanic, or *post mortem* vision of God, see W. Michaelis, *TDNT* 5:329–34; Pancaro 219–26.

God—or ever will[111]—since only a divine being can sustain such a *visio* (cf. v. 18; 6:46). The latter view emphasizes God's inaccessibility and hiddenness (cf. John 5:37). God cannot be directly known by humans unless God himself take the initiative in a self-revelation. While both views suit the context, perhaps the former is to be preferred, since it better accounts for the emphatic anarthrous θεόν,[112] which has been variously rendered "God in his being,"[113] "God as God,"[114] "the divine nature,"[115] "the Godhead."[116]

3. (μονογενὴς θεὸς) ὁ ὢν εἰς τὸν κόλπον τοῦ πατρός

a. The Meaning of ὁ ὢν

At least five different views have been held regarding the meaning of the articular participle ὁ ὤν.[117]

1. E. A. Abbott (*Grammar* §§1938, 1964) believes that in John 1:18b the evangelist enumerates three distinct titles of the Logos:[118] μονογενής ("the only begotten" or, as a proper name, Monogenes), θεός ("God"), and ὁ ὤν ("He That Is").[119] This latter title, presumably regarded by Abbott as the third-person equivalent of the ἐγώ εἰμι of the Fourth Gospel, is qualified by εἰς τὸν κόλπον τοῦ πατρός "to indicate a Person, in whom the defining characteristic is not strength or wisdom but filial union with a Father"

111. This may be the implication of ἑώρακεν, which, used with πώποτε, is a "present perfect of broken continuity" (Robertson, *Grammar* 896, 905–6 [cf. 893], developing the suggestion of Moulton, *Prolegomena* 144), since a (constative) aorist εἶδεν might have been expected with πώποτε (as in *PGM* 5:102: Osiris ὃν οὐδεὶς εἶδε πώποτε, and cf. τούτων οὐδεὶς πώποτε . . . εἶπεν in Josephus, *Ap.* 2:124—cited in BAGD 592a s.v. οὐδείς). The implication is even clearer if ἑώρακεν is a gnomic perfect ("can see"; for this category, see BDF §344). Against this may be set the suggestion of J. N. Sanders (86, possibly depending on Origen [see Wiles, *Gospel* 92–93] or Westcott, *Gospel* 15) that John added πώποτε after οὐδείς ("no one . . . ever yet") to leave open the possibility of some future direct vision of God when the faithful have been united with God in Christ (citing John 17:21ff. and 1 Cor. 13:12). But it is doubtful whether πώποτε ("at any time" [in the past or future], see BAGD 732a s.v.) may bear the sense of οὔπω or οὐδέπω ("not yet"; cf. οὐδεὶς οὔπω in Luke 23:53 and οὐδέπω οὐδείς in John 19:41, both of which mean "no one . . . [ever] yet"; see BAGD 592a s.v. οὐδείς).

112. As in John 1:1c, so in 1:18 the position of the term θεός at the head of its clause makes it emphatic, especially since John customarily places οὐδείς in this position.

113. B. Weiss, *Johannes* 59; Holtzmann 49; Bauer 18.

114. Westcott, *Gospel* 15; Hort, *Dissertations* 14 ("God as being God"); Beasley-Murray 2 n. e ("God by nature"; cf. 15).

115. Lagrange, *Jean* 28; Westcott, *Gospel* 15.

116. Loisy 110.

117. This phrase is omitted by ℵ it$^{a,\delta}$ and possibly some other witnesses; see above, §A.1.a.(3).

118. On this point, Abbott is followed by Bernard, *John* 1:31.

119. The relation between θεός and ὁ ὤν illustrates Abbott's general observation (*Grammar* §1937) that "apposition between a noun and a participle with the article may be ambiguous" (citing the expression ὁ χριστὸς ὁ ἐρχόμενος).

(§1964).[120] There are two difficulties with this proposal: (a) While this interpretation may enhance the symmetry of the Prologue,[121] it is certainly awkward to have an absolute title of Deity (ὁ ὤν) qualified by a prepositional phrase;[122] and (2) ὁ ὤν as a designation of God, expressive of not merely his supratemporality but also his eternality (F. Büchsel, *TDNT* 2:398–400), occurs in the NT only in the Book of Revelation (five times)[123] and there it is always accompanied by ὁ ἦν and three times[124] also by ὁ ἐρχόμενος.

2. The phrase expresses the simultaneous presence of Jesus in heaven and on earth during his earthly ministry[125] or, on the other hand, his uninterrupted fellowship with the Father while on earth.[126] The former view seems likely only if ὁ ὢν ἐν τῷ οὐρανῷ be the preferred reading in John 3:13—which is improbable.[127] And elsewhere John distinguishes the descent from the ascent of the Son of Man as successive acts (3:13, 31; 6:62; 8:14; 13:1, 3; 16:28; Schnackenburg, *John* 1:281, 394). However, numerous verses in the Fourth Gospel show that the latter view conforms with Johannine thought.[128]
3. Ὁ ὤν alludes to the session of Christ after his ascension, John expressing himself from his own standpoint in time.[129] Thus the Prologue gains a certain roundness of form, with verse 18 completing the cycle of preexistence (v. 1), incarnation (v. 14), and ascension. Attractive though this view is, it blurs the logical con-

120. With this one may compare Barclay's rendering: "It is the unique one, He who is God, He who is in the bosom of the Father, who has told us all about God."

121. For Abbott, the three names of 1:18 correspond to the three clauses in 1:1: "This is far more symmetrical than the view that the Prologue begins with three clauses describing the Word, and ends with two" (*Grammar* §2615).

122. Cf. ὁ ὢν ἐν τῷ οὐρανῷ (v.l.) in John 3:13 and ὁ ὢν ἐπὶ πάντων in Rom. 9:5.

123. Rev. 1:4, 8; 4:8; 11:17; 16:5.

124. Rev. 1:4, 8; 4:8.

125. Thus (apparently) Winer 429 and Morris, *John* 114 ("the only begotten is continually in the bosom of the Father. When the Word became flesh His cosmic activities did not remain in abeyance until the time of the earthly life was ended"). Although believing that ὁ ὢν ἐν τῷ οὐρανῷ in John 3:13 "should probably be omitted," Morris contends that "only a crassly literal localization of heaven would require us to think that Jesus had to leave heaven to come to earth" (*John* 224).

126. So Godet, *John* 1:379; Dodd, *Interpretation* 258–59; Brown, *Gospel* 1:133 (but cf. 1:17); de la Potterie, *Vérité* 236–37; Moloney, "John" 66–68.

127. See the discussion in Metzger, *Commentary* 203–4. It is interesting that in UBS[1] and UBS[2] the addition is rejected with an "A" rating, in UBS[3] with a "C" rating. On John 1:51, see Brown, *Gospel* 1:88–91.

128. See, e.g., 5:17–18; 6:46, 57; 7:29; 8:28–29, 38; 10:15, 30, 38; 14:10–11, 20; 15:15; 16:32; 17:21–23, 25.

129. H. A. W. Meyer, *John* 69–70, 72; Zahn, *Johannes* 96; Bultmann, *John* 82 n. 6; de Kruijf 121; Culpepper 10; Loader, *Christology* 152 (who also sees a reference to the Son's preincarnate relationship; see *per contra* Schillebeeckx, *Christ* 361, 366–67). Referring to this as a possible view, Cadman (9–19) maintains that an effective disclosure of the Father was impossible before Christ's passion and the Spirit's coming.

nection between ὁ ὤν and ἐξηγήσατο. True, Christ's exaltation by God may *confirm* the truth of his declaration of the Father (H. A. W. Meyer, *John* 70 n. 5) but John's point is rather that Christ's preincarnate fellowship with the Father *guarantees* the accuracy of that declaration.

4. Standing for the nonexistent past participle of εἶναι, ὁ ὤν has an imperfect sense (= ὃς ἦν),[130] "the one who was."[131] Before his incarnation, the Son dwelt with the Father (cf. 1:1b); after becoming flesh (1:14), he lived on earth.
5. A related interpretation takes ὁ ὤν as "the atemporal present of 'characterization' (generality),"[132] "indicating the eternal presence proper to the Son."[133] This quasi-metaphysical sense well accords with the two preceding ontological terms (μονογενής and θεός). In itself ὁ ὤν need say nothing about the relationship of the Son to the Father during Christ's earthly ministry.[134] Attention is focused on his premundane communion with God (as in ὁ λόγος ἦν πρὸς τὸν θεόν, 1:1) as the ground of the subsequent ἐξήγησις, but an allusion to his return to the Father's presence (cf. John 13:1, 3: 16:28; 17:5) need not be excluded.[135]

b. The Significance of εἰς τὸν κόλπον τοῦ πατρός

The imagery behind εἶναι εἰς τὸν κόλπον could be festal (of reclining at a meal, cf. John 13:23), familial (of the child on a parent's lap[136] or in a parent's or nurse's embrace),[137] or conjugal[138] (of the embrace of husband and wife).[139] Whatever the source of the image, its significance is clear. It denotes the exclusive and privileged intimacy of a deeply affectionate interpersonal relationship.

But what is the import of the preposition εἰς in this phrase? Does it denote direction and movement? or location? or a combination of motion and rest? Each of these three possibilities needs careful analysis. There is

130. Cf. John 12:17: ἐμαρτύρει οὖν ὁ ὄχλος ὁ ὢν μετ' αὐτοῦ. . . .

131. Thus Haenchen, "Probleme" 324 n. 75; *John* 121.

132. Zerwick, *Greek* §372. So also Alford 1:691; Westcott, *Gospel* 15.

133. Zerwick and Grosvenor 287. So also Lagrange, *Jean* 28 ("une présence éternelle"); G. Schrenk, *TDNT* 5:998 (ὁ ὤν refers "to what has always been and always is").

134. See *per contra* Stevens, *Johannine Theology* 107–8.

135. But Beasley-Murray places the focus elsewhere: "The prime reference is to the relationship to God of the Son in his life of flesh and blood, but it naturally extends to his pre-existent and post-Resurrection relationship to the Father" (16).

136. Ruth 4:16.

137. Num. 11:12; 1 Kings 3:20.

138. Mic. 7:5.

139. For classical references, see Wettstein 1:841; and for a general discussion, de la Potterie, *Vérité* 228–30.

also a variant punctuation, which permits εἰς to carry the common meaning of "into."[140]

(1) εἰς as Dynamic in Meaning

There can be little doubt that in both Classical and Hellenistic Greek εἰς frequently (some would say, normally or basically) denotes not simply orientation or direction but "movement toward or into," be it literal or metaphorical. Accordingly, although εἰς does not follow a verb of motion in 1:18, some maintain, with B. Lindars, that the preposition here "implies that Jesus has access to the innermost being of God" (*John* 99).

Others develop this notion considerably further. I. de la Potterie, for example, renders the whole phrase "turned toward the Father's bosom" and finds two theological truths expressed: (1) a personal distinction between Father and Son and (2) "the constant orientation of the Son toward the bosom of the Father as toward his origin (εἰς, not πρός), as toward the source of his own life (εἰς τὸν κόλπον)" ("L'emploi" 386; cf. *Vérité* 230–35). For de la Potterie, John 1:18 represents a climax in Johannine thought ("L'emploi" 385). In John 1:1b, which speaks in a general way of the orientation of the Logos toward God, and in 1 John 1:1, which depicts more precisely an orientation of the *life* of the Logos toward the *Father*, it is a matter of "filiation." But in John 1:18 where the *only Son* (ὁ μονογενὴς υἱός) is said to be turned toward the *bosom* of the *Father*, "vers ce sein dont il est engendré," it is a matter of "eternal generation" (cf. ὤν and John 6:57; "L'emploi" 385), "the eternal act of receiving divine life from the Father" ("L'emploi" 386; cf. *Vérité* 189–91).[141]

While de la Potterie rightly stresses that John seems to maintain a careful distinction between εἰς and ἐν,[142] his view is not without difficulties, two of which may be mentioned at this point. First, the idea of eternal generation would comport better with the prepositions παρά (cf. John 6:46: ὁ ὢν παρὰ τοῦ θεοῦ) or ἐκ (cf. the reading ἐκ τοῦ κόλπου reflected in syr[c]). If any element of movement is implied in εἰς, its direction is in effect reversed

140. In the discussion that follows, I am drawing on and expanding my comments in *NIDNTT* 3:1185–86.

141. Similarly Bonsirven, *Témoin* 43. Expressing his tentative approval of this view ("elle n'est pas au-dessus de toute discussion"), Feuillet comments thus: "Si la critique, par les méthodes qui lui sont propres, arrive à des conclusions qui peuvent servir de fondement à une doctrine théologique devenue traditionnelle, c'est là une rencontre des plus bienfaisantes, qui peut contribuer à refaire l'unité entre l'exégèse et la théologie, unité de continuité dynamique plutôt que d'égalité statique" (*Prologue* 268). Moloney renders John 1:18b as "the only Son, who is turned towards the Father," adding "in love and obedience throughout the whole of his *historical* presence among men and women" ("John," 68).

142. See §D.3.b.(2) below. However, de la Potterie's appeal ("L'emploi" 383 n. 3) to the Lucan distinction between εἰς τὸν κόλπον Ἀβραάμ (Luke 16:22) and ἐν τοῖς κόλποις αὐτοῦ (Luke 16:23) is scarcely relevant, since the former phrase follows a verb denoting movement (viz., ἀπενεχθῆναι), while in John one finds ἦν πρός (John 1:1) and ὁ ὢν εἰς (John 1:18).

according to this view. Second, the connotation "source of life" for κόλπος appears to be unparalleled.

(2) εἰς as Static in Meaning

If εἰς is static in meaning, then εἰς τὸν κόλπον is here equivalent to ἐν τῷ κόλπῳ (John 13:23),[143] in conformity with the general tendency of Hellenistic Greek to confuse the categories of movement and rest. This is the prevailing view among grammarians,[144] lexicographers,[145] and modern commentators.[146]

Etymologically, εἰς was a later variation of ἐν, being originally ἐνς, sigma having been added to ἐν on the analogy of ἐξ (= ἐκ-ς). With the disappearance of nu in ἐνς, a compensatory iota was added, giving εἰς (Robertson, *Grammar* 584–86, 591). The obsolescence of the dative case in Greek (see Humbert) meant the disappearance of ἐν so that in Modern Greek only εἰς (in the form 'ς or σέ) is found.[147]

In light, therefore, of the origin of εἰς as a variant of ἐν and its ultimate eclipse of ἐν, it is not surprising that there are instances in the NT (especially in Mark and Luke–Acts) where εἰς stands for ἐν and ἐν for εἰς (see N. Turner, *Syntax* 254–57). J. J. O'Rourke has examined all the apparent exceptions in the Fourth Gospel to the classical use of εἰς and ἐν[148] and concludes that only in John 1:18 and 19:13 does εἰς possibly stand for ἐν (1.09% of John's 183 uses of εἰς) and only in John 3:35 is ἐν (218 uses) possibly used for εἰς.

But few scholars are content to affirm that εἰς τὸν κόλπον denotes simply the personal juxtaposition of Son and Father. For G. B. Winer (415 and n. 1), the phrase indicates that the Son "is laid upon" or "rests against" the bosom of the Father, which would imply personal intercommunion. Some

143. But the evidence of this parallel is indecisive, for some use ἐν τῷ κόλπῳ to show that John distinguished εἰς from ἐν when these prepositions are found with κόλπος, while others find in this phrase in John 13:23 evidence of John's oscillation from εἰς to ἐν in conformity with his predilection for stylistic variation.

144. Thus Moulton, *Prolegomena* 234–35; cf. 62–63 (apparently); Jannaris, *Grammar* §1548; BDF §§205, 218; Robertson, *Grammar* 535–36 ("it is often impossible to insist on the idea of motion or extension in εἰς," citing John 1:18), 559, 586, 592–93; Abel §47(a); Zerwick, *Analysis* 212 (as one possibility; but cf. his *Greek* §§102–4 and Zerwick and Grosvenor 287); N. Turner, *Syntax* 254 (noting, however, that John [including Revelation] does not generally blur εἰς and ἐν).

145. Thus BAGD 230c s.v. εἰς 9a; Regard 157, 548; A. Oepke, *TDNT* 2:433 (here "εἰς and ἐν are fully interchangeable"); MM xiv, who cite the classic instance from P Oxy 2:294, lines 3 and 6: A certain Sarapion writes (A.D. 22) to his brother Dorion, "On coming to Alexandria (ἐπὶ τῷ γεγονέναι ἐν Ἀλεξανδρίᾳ) . . . I learned from some fishermen at Alexandria (εἰς Ἀλεξάνδρι [αν]) that. . . ."

146. So Bauer 18; Lagrange, *Jean* 28 (but noting that εἰς could mark "une pénétration plus complète comme il [Jean] a dit πρός et non παρά au v. 2"); Bultmann, *John* 82 n. 2; Hoskyns 151; Schnackenburg, *John* 1:281; Barrett, *John* 169–70; Morris, *John* 114 and n. 118 (with some hesitation); and apparently Brown, *Gospel* 1:4–5, 17 ("ever at the Father's side").

147. Cf. Hatzidakis 210–11; Thumb §160.

148. Ἐν in John 3:35; 5:7; εἰς in John 1:18; 8:26; 9:7; 19:13; 20:7, 19, 26; 21:4.

of the Greek fathers,[149] giving εἰς a static sense, believed that the verse described the consubstantiality of the Father and Son. Chrysostom, for example, speaks of the Son's dwelling (ἐνδιαιτᾶσθαι) in the Father's bosom as involving "affinity of essence": "The Father would not have in his bosom one of another essence."[150] Again, some scholars find in εἰς a hint of a preceding idea of movement.[151] But the difficulty with the suggestion that εἰς implies an earlier entrance *into* the Father's bosom[152] or points to the Son's *return* to his preincarnate state through the ascension (H. A. W. Meyer, *John* 70) is that the preceding ὁ ὢν probably depicts a supratemporal condition that had no beginning (see §D.3.a.(5) above).

(3) εἰς as Both Static and Dynamic in Sense

Commenting on the phrase εἰς τὸν κόλπον, B. F. Westcott wrote (in 1880): "There is the combination (as it were) of rest and motion, of a continuous relation, with a realisation of it (comp. i.1, ἦν πρός). The 'bosom of the Father' (like heaven) is a state and not a place" (*Gospel* 15). In making this observation Westcott betrays a tendency, characteristic of his times, to analyze NT Greek syntax in light of Classical Greek usage. Had he written twenty years later, after the serious and widespread study of the papyri had begun, he would doubtless have modified his remark about the significance of εἰς,[153] however correct the theology he had expressed.[154]

Yet Westcott's view persisted, for in 1906 E. A. Abbott argued for a "mystical" or "spiritual" understanding of εἰς,[155] claiming that the evangelist wished "to combine the notions of motion and rest as belonging to God and to the manifestations of God. From God, the Logos is ever coming *to* men and is also abiding *in* them. From Man the Logos is ever going up *to* God and is also abiding *in* Him" (*Grammar* §2309). According to Abbott, John is reacting to various "unprofitable and conflicting" ancient traditions

149. De la Potterie cites Chrysostom, Theophylact, Theodore of Mopsuestia, and Euthymius ("L'emploi" 384 and n. 2; 385).

150. *Homilies on the Gospel of St. John* 15:2.

151. See Abel §48(c) remark II, who cites a Classical Greek parallel, παρεῖναι εἰς Ἑλλήσποντον ("to be present in the Hellespont"); Zahn, *Johannes* 96; Loisy 111. Cf. LSJ 491 s.v. εἰς I.2: "With Verbs expressing *rest in* a place, when a previous motion *into* or *to* it is implied." The only biblical instance cited there (after the note "later used like ἐν") is Num. 35:33: τὴν γῆν εἰς ἣν ὑμεῖς κατοικεῖτε.

152. So Greenlee, "Preposition" 13; *Grammar* 32 (citing John 1:18: "who has gone into (and is now in) the Father's bosom").

153. Moulton declares this interpretation of εἰς in John 1:18 "impossible" (*Prolegomena* 234–35; cf. MM xiv), noting that "there are many NT passages where a real distinction between εἰς and ἐν is impossible to draw without excessive subtlety" (63).

154. Cf. the comments of A. Fox in his introduction to the 1958 reprint of Westcott's commentary (*Gospel* ii §§f–g).

155. Abbott, *Grammar* §2712. Abbott found a distinctive sense of εἰς in John 1:18 for three reasons: (1) "John generally avoids εἰς for ἐν"; (2) John 13:23 has ἐν τῷ κόλπῳ; and (3) εἰς κόλπον without a verb of motion cannot be paralleled in the Greek Bible or in Greek literature in general, while ἐν κόλπῳ is common (§§2706, 2712).

about Christ's "home" by asserting that his true residence—even while on earth—was in heaven, enabling him to lead people "to the bosom of God" (*Grammar* §2713).

(4) A Variant Punctuation

If εἰς τὸν κόλπον τοῦ πατρός is construed with ἐκεῖνος ἐξηγήσατο that follows rather than with ὁ ὢν that precedes, εἰς may bear its regular sense of "into." Thus J. R. Taylor translates verse 18: "No man hath seen God at any time; an only-begotten, God, he who is, he hath led the way into the bosom of the Father." Similar is M. E. Boismard's rendering: "No one has ever seen God, except the only Son; he it is who has led the way into the Father's bosom" ("Sein" 31).

These solutions have some merit but are not altogether satisfactory, for they solve one problem (viz., the apparently irregular meaning of εἰς) by introducing another, viz., the absolute use of ὁ ὢν in reference to Jesus (in the case of Taylor) and the implied preference for an inferior text (viz., θεὸν οὐδεὶς ἑώρακεν πώποτε, εἰ μὴ ὁ μονογενής· εἰς τὸν κόλπον κτλ.—in the case of Boismard).[156] Also, both proposals labor under the difficulty that John did not write ἐκεῖνος εἰς τὸν κόλπον τοῦ πατρὸς ἐξηγήσατο.

(5) Conclusion

In any discussion of the interrelation of εἰς and ἐν in NT Greek, two dangers are to be avoided: (1) to treat them as everywhere synonymous and (2) always to insist on a distinction between them (cf. Robertson, *Grammar* 559). Of the NT writers, only Matthew seems never to confuse εἰς and local ἐν (notwithstanding Matt. 28:19; see N. Turner, *Syntax* 254). Elsewhere, the exegete's presumption ought to be that, except for Luke (in the Third Gospel and Acts) and perhaps Mark, NT authors do not ordinarily use εἰς for ἐν (cf. Zerwick, *Greek* §106).

In the case of John 1:18 the real choice is not between εἰς = eternal generation and εἰς = ἐν = consubstantiality, but more generally between the static and dynamic senses of εἰς. While in John 1:1 πρὸς τὸν θεόν may point to an active relation of the Logos with God,[157] in 1:18 εἰς τὸν κόλπον τοῦ πατρός seems to stand for the passive notion ἐν τῷ κόλπῳ τοῦ πατρός (cf. John 13:23). The difference between the two verses is that between πρός + the accusative of the person (θεός) and εἰς + the accusative of the thing (κόλπος),[158] a distinction generally observed in NT Greek. Any notion of

156. See the discussion of this view above, §A.1. In his highly individualistic Greek text of the Fourth Gospel, based on the *lectio brevior potior* principle, Blass has the reading—not found in any extant Greek manuscript—μονογενὴς ὁ ὢν ἐκ τῶν κόλπων τοῦ πατρός, ἐκεῖνος ἐξηγήσατο. In his textual apparatus he explains that ἐκ became εἰς by a transcriptional error: "EIC fere = EK" (2). Blass also notes that syr[c] has ἐκ τοῦ κόλπου and that ἐκ κόλπων is found in *Acta Archelai* c.5.

157. See above, chapter II §D.1.

158. Cf. Godet, *John* 1:379: "The substitution of εἰς for πρός . . . arises from the difference between a strictly local regimen (κόλπος) and a personal regimen (θεός)."

dynamic interpersonal relationship found in verse 18 stems from the nouns κόλπος and πατήρ, not from the preposition εἰς.

The import of the whole clause ὁ ὢν εἰς τὸν κόλπον τοῦ πατρός is that, because of the unparalleled intimacy that existed (and still exists) between the Son and Father, the Son was qualified to reveal the Father.[159] Ὁ ὢν κτλ. introduces, not the confirmation of the ἐξήγησις,[160] but its ground. Jesus proclaimed what he had heard in the Father's presence.[161]

4. ἐκεῖνος ἐξηγήσατο

The antecedent of ἐκεῖνος cannot be restricted to μονογενής or θεός or ὁ ὢν κτλ. Although it is resumptive after an articular participial clause,[162] ἐκεῖνος catches up all three designations of the Logos; it is "he and no other" who has exegeted the Father.

If ἐξηγεῖσθαι is given its predominant classical meaning of "lead or show the way," it is natural to construe εἰς τὸν κόλπον τοῦ παρτός with ἐκεῖνος ἐξηγήσατο, as in the renderings "he hath led the way into the bosom of the Father" (J. R. Taylor) and "dans le sein du Père, c'est lui qui a conduit" (Boismard).[163] But in Jewish and Christian literature, the term gained the sense *praeire verbis*, "expound" or "recount,"[164] which suggests the translation "he has made [him] known" (as in most English versions)[165] or "der hat (von ihm) Kunde gebracht" (Wikenhauser 38; similarly many German commentators) or "he has narrated [the Father]" (Louw 32–38). A third meaning, however, is also possible. In secular Greek ἐξηγεῖσθαι was a common term for the communication of divine knowledge or the revelation of divine secrets by priests or soothsayers as *interpretes religionum*.[166] Ἐξηγήσατο in John 1:18 probably bears this sense: "He has revealed [him]."[167]

The unexpressed object[168] of ἐξηγήσατο may be (τὸν) θεόν from verse 18a[169] or τὸν πατέρα from verse 18b. Little hangs on the choice, for the referent is identical (God the Father) and the meaning would be similar in

159. Cf. Milligan and Moulton 10: The phrase describes "the conditions which make it possible for Jesus to be the complete Interpreter of the Father." But see *per contra* Cadman 9–10, 26–42.

160. *Pace* H. A. W. Meyer, *John* 70 n. 5.

161. Cf. John 3:11, 32; 7:16; 8:26, 28, 38, 47; 12:49; 14:10.

162. So also Robertson, *Grammar* 708; cf. 707 (ἐκεῖνος "refers to θεός followed by ὁ ὤν").

163. "Sein" 31; cf. *Prologue* 67–68.

164. As in Luke 24:35; Acts 10:8; 15:12, 14; 21:19.

165. Weymouth, Goodspeed, Phillips, Berkeley, RSV, NEB, GNB, JB, NIV, NJB, Cassirer, NRSV, REB. Cf. "declared" in KJV, RV, ASV; and "explained" in NASB.

166. For examples, see Wettstein 1:841–42.

167. So TCNT, NAB[1], NAB[2]; F. Büchsel, *TDNT* 2:908; J. N. Sanders 85.

168. W it[c] syr[c,pal] Tatian add the indirect object ἡμῖν.

169. But F. Büchsel (*TDNT* 2:908 n. 4) objects that "God is not an obj[ect] of explanation," and Bultmann (*John* 83 n. 3) alleges that no object is needed, since ἐξηγεῖσθαι can mean "give divine knowledge."

either case. Jesus Christ made visible the invisible nature of God (θεόν)[170] and laid bare the heart of the Father (τὸν πατέρα). It was the essential fatherhood of God that the Son disclosed.[171] Ἐξηγήσατο is a constative aorist,[172] encompassing in a single glance the whole span of Christ's earthly life together with his death[173] and resurrection.

5. The Significance of John 1:18

a. In the Section 1:14–18

The fullness which all believers have received in part (v. 16a) is grace and truth (vv. 16b, 17b) that came through and dwelt in Jesus Christ the Word (vv. 14, 17b). That is, the reference to grace and truth in verse 14 is taken up in verses 16 (grace) and 18 (truth), with the intervening transitional verse 17 again associating the two ideas (so Godet, *John* 1:374) by specifying the two occasions on which God preeminently displayed his grace.[174] Being asyndetic, verse 18 must be closely connected with verse 17. Truth became manifest on the human scene through Jesus Christ (v. 17b) because, although no earthly mortal can claim to have gained a perfect knowledge of God in his true being (v. 18a), Jesus Christ personally disclosed in time his own intimate, eternal knowledge of the Father (ὁ ὢν κτλ., v. 18b). Moreover, the divine nature is not foreign to the Son, for as μονογενὴς θεός he possesses it and is therefore qualified to reveal it.[175] Inasmuch as the only Son is God by nature and intimately acquainted with the Father by experience, he is uniquely qualified to reveal the nature and character of God.

170. H. A. W. Meyer (*John* 70) supplies with ἐξηγήσατο "the substance of His intuition of God."

171. "In Him God is revealed as Father; without Him He can be revealed only as God" (Milligan and Moulton 10). Barrett observes that in John 1:18 an anarthrous θεός "may point either to the invisible Father [θεόν] who is revealed, or to the visible Son [θεός] who reveals him" (*Essays on John* 8). Loader has rightly identified this theme, "the Son makes the Father known," as central to Johannine Christology (*Christology* 92). But not all agree that for the evangelist the Father is the content of the revelation that the Son brings. Bultmann, for example, alleges "that Jesus as the Revealer of God *reveals nothing but that he is the Revealer*." In his Gospel John "presents only the fact (*das Dass*) of the Revelation without describing its content (*ihr Was*)" (*Theology* 2:66). On the other hand, de la Potterie sees the Son as both the revealer and the revealed: "Connaître la révélation apportée par Jésus, c'est découvrir le mystère de Jésus lui-même" (*Vérité* 239; cf. 241).

172. Robertson calls this aorist constative (*Grammar* 829), effective (*Pictures* 5:18), and timeless (*Divinity* 45)!

173. De Kruijf (121–23) proposes that for the evangelist it is in the sacrificial death of Christ that the glory of the Word is seen (ἐθεασάμεθα, 1:14; cf. 19:35) and that God is manifested (ἐξηγήσατο, 1:18) "as a faithful and loving Saviour."

174. The ὅτι of v. 17a shows that the verse is giving proof of the constancy of God's grace (v. 16).

175. So also Lagrange, *Jean* 28. This theme, "only God can reveal God," is stressed by several commentators (e.g., Šurjanský 124; Feuillet, *Prologue* 130; Brown, *Gospel* 1:17; du Plessis 27; Mastin, "Christology" 41).

b. In the Prologue (1:1–18)

Verse 18 clearly forms the climax of the Prologue. First, it conjoins the two crucial terms θεός and μονογενής already used separately of the Logos or Son (viz., in vv. 1, 14). Second, whereas verse 1 asserts the deity of the Logos and affirms his pretemporal relation to God, verse 18 posits the deity of the Son and his intimate acquaintance with the Father as the basis of God's self-disclosure, a basis that ensures the reliability, indeed the perfection, of the divine revelation.[176]

c. In the Fourth Gospel as a Whole

In the whole of John's Gospel, verse 18 has a twofold function.[177] It links the Prologue and the remainder of the Gospel by highlighting the dual themes of the Father as directly and fully known to the Son and the Son as the unique Exegete of the Father—themes that are prominent throughout the Gospel. In the second place, together with the opening verse of the Prologue, verse 18 forms one of the two "bookends" that support and give shape to the whole Gospel, for 1:1 and 1:18 (at the beginning and the end of the Prologue) and 20:28 (at the end of the Gospel) all use θεός of Jesus, whether he be thought of as the eternally preexistent Logos (1:1), the incarnate Son (1:18), or the risen Christ (20:28). The evangelist thereby indicates that the acknowledgment of the messiahship of Jesus (20:31) necessarily involves belief in his deity.

176. Cf. Kysar 356: "As the prologue stands, it begins with the declaration of the intimacy of the *logos* and the Father and concludes with the functional results of that intimacy"; "Christ is the 'exegesis' of the very being of God."

177. It is not impossible that 1:18a may be polemic against any pious wish to see the glory or form of the Father (cf. John 5:37; 6:46; 14:8–9) or against any mystical attempt to arrive at a perfect knowledge of God apart from his self-disclosure in Christ (cf. 1 John 4:12, 20). Cf. Schnackenburg, *John* 1:278; and the thorough discussion of Bultmann, *John* 79–81.

IV

My Lord and My God! (John 20:28)

Ἀπεκρίθη Θωμᾶς καὶ εἶπεν αὐτῷ, Ὁ κύριός μου καὶ ὁ θεός μου.

John 20 contains four resurrection pericopes: the discovery of the empty tomb (vv. 1–10), the appearance of Jesus to Mary Magdalene (vv. 11–18), the impartation of the Spirit to the disciples (vv. 19–23), and the confession of Thomas (vv. 24–29). In this latter pericope the climax is reached when, in response to the invitation of Jesus to touch his wounds and the directive to display faith (v. 27), Thomas utters the words ὁ κύριός μου καὶ ὁ θεός μου (v. 28) and Jesus declares those who believe without seeing to be "blessed" (v. 29).

Four aspects of verse 28 call for attention. There is the grammatical problem (how is ὁ θεός μου to be construed?), the historical problem (did Thomas actually make this confession?), the theological issue (what are the sources, meaning, and theological significance of Thomas's confession?), and the literary issue (what is the significance of the Thomas episode in the Fourth Gospel?).

A. The Grammatical Problem

The crucial phrase ὁ θεός μου has been understood in several ways.

1. Predicative

a. Referring to God the Father: "Thomas answered him: '(Jesus, you are) my Lord; (Father, you are) my God.'"

On the first view each half of Thomas's affirmation is directed to a different addressee: ὁ κύριός μου to Jesus; ὁ θεός μου to the Father, either as indwelling Jesus[1] or as dwelling in heaven. This decidedly aberrant interpretation is rendered implausible by the presence of καί, by the absence of a distinguishing vocative (Ἰησοῦ or πάτερ), and by the frequent conjunction of κύριος and θεός in various combinations in the LXX in reference to one person (see below, §C.1.e). In addition, the immediate context (vv. 24–27, 29) contains numerous references to Jesus, but none to the Father, so that a sudden apostrophe is highly improbable, especially since the whole statement is introduced by εἶπεν αὐτῷ. Finally, the repeated μου, so far from necessarily indicating two distinct addressees, simply reflects the repetition of the pronominal suffix with copulated

1. Thus Artemonius, as cited by Bengel 2:494.

nouns in Hebrew and Aramaic[2] and has the effect of personalizing Thomas's response.[3]

b. Referring to Jesus: "Thomas answered him, 'My Lord is also my God.'"

E. A. Abbott (*Grammar* §2050), who at first defended the translation[4] "My Lord is also my God," adduced several lines of evidence in favor of his contention that κύριε would have been used if the vocative had been intended (*Grammar* §2049). (1) The one LXX instance of a vocatival ὁ κύριος (viz., Ps. 34:23: ἐξεγέρθητι, κύριε, καὶ πρόσχες τῇ κρίσει μου, ὁ θεός μου καὶ ὁ κύριός μου, εἰς τὴν δίκην μου) is explicable by its special context. That is, ὁ κύριός μου conforms to the preceding vocatival nominative (ὁ θεός μου). Apart from this one exceptional use, ὁ κύριος is never vocatival in the LXX, although the vocatival expressions ὁ θεός and κύριε ὁ θεὸς ἡμῶν (e.g., 2 Kings 19:19) are common. (2) In Classical Greek the vocatival nominative is (a) accompanied by οὗτος or σύ, (b) idiomatic, like the English "You, *Mr.* cricketer, *Mr.* Yorkshireman," or (c) found only in poetry (e.g., ὦ φίλος). (3) While using κύριε freely, the papyri never have a vocatival ὁ κύριος. (4) The Latin versions have *dominus* (not *domine*).

Abbott paraphrases the verse thus: "My dear Lord—is actually none other than my God." Thomas here "speaks *about* his Master in the act of replying *to* his Master."[5] Instead of continuing after "my dear Lord" with "has indeed risen from the dead" or "has been indeed restored to me," Thomas expresses his inspired conviction, in a moment when he was overcome by joy and amazement, that his Lord had become to him one with his God. According to Abbott, the omission of ἐστι might have been prompted by the evangelist's desire to force his readers to think out the full import of the confession, while the emphatic καί ("also") is frequent in John (§§2050–51).

First, one must admit that, judged by the usage of Classical Greek, the LXX, the NT, or the papyri, the use of ὁ κύριος as a vocative is uncommon. But that ὁ κύριος may be a nominative of address in Johannine usage is evident from John 13:13 (ὑμεῖς φωνεῖτέ με Ὁ διδάσκαλος καὶ Ὁ κύριος) and Revelation 4:11 (ἄξιος εἶ, ὁ κύριος καὶ ὁ θεὸς ἡμῶν); that it may be applied to Jesus is clear from the former verse. Second, it is extraordinary to treat καί as adjunctive when (a) it stands between two articular nouns in the

2. For example, the LXX renders the vocatival מלכי ואלהי (Ps. 5:3 [Engl. v. 2]) by ὁ βασιλεύς μου καὶ ὁ θεός μου and אלהי ואדני (Ps. 35:23) by ὁ θεός μου καὶ ὁ κύριός μου (LXX 34:23).

3. On μου, see further below, §C.2.a.

4. It is not generally recognized that Abbott later expressed a preference for the traditional view; see below.

5. *Grammar* §2050 and n. 2. In a later work Abbott remarks on John 20:28 thus: "The Jewish Shema declared that Jehovah was God and One; this Johannine Shema seems intended to suggest that the Lord Jesus and God are also One" (*Contributions* §3578c).

same case, each modified by μου, and (b) ἐστι is lacking. Third, there are at least two reasons why the evangelist may have written ὁ κύριος rather than κύριε. (a) In comparison with κύριε, which is not infrequently used in the Gospels in the sense "sir!,"[6] the vocatival ὁ κύριος is more formal and respectful, more sonorous and emphatic in tone (cf. John 13:13), and therefore would be appropriate when a disciple was addressing his Lord.[7] For John κύριε perhaps represented too mundane a usage, being often followed by a request for help[8] or a question.[9] (b) Although the nominative used in a vocatival sense was established Greek idiom,[10] John's two uses of ὁ κύριος in this sense (viz., John 13:13; 20:28) may owe something to the Semitic vocative,[11] expressed by the articular nominative in Hebrew (GKC §126e) and the emphatic state in Aramaic (Rosenthal §43). Fourth, it has not always been observed that Abbott later reversed his preference and took καί to mean "and" (not "also"): "Thomas said to him [the words], 'My lord—and my God,'" the vocatival ὁ κύριος being "exceptional Johannine usage."[12]

2. Exclamatory: "And Thomas exclaimed: 'My Lord and my God!'"

a. Referring to God the Father

Another interpretation, associated with the names of Theodore of Mopsuestia and Faustus Socinus, proposes that Thomas's cry was an exclamatory statement, expressing his astonishment and his praise to God for the miracle of the resurrection of Jesus:[13] "Praise (or, glory) be to my Lord and my God!" Accordingly, ὁ θεός μου sheds no light on the view of Jesus held by either Thomas or the evangelist.

6. For example, of persons other than Jesus, Matt. 21:30; Luke 13:8; John 12:21.

7. Cf. Gildersleeve and Miller 1.§12; N. Turner, *Syntax* 34. One may compare the Marcan preference for ῥαββί (9:5; 11:21; 14:45) over κύριε (only at 7:28) when disciples are addressing Jesus.

8. Matt. 8:25; 14:30; 15:25; Luke 11:1.

9. Luke 9:54; 10:40; 12:41.

10. See Gildersleeve and Miller 1:4–5, who, however, appear to distinguish between an anarthrous nominative (often preceded by ὦ) used as a vocative (§12) and an articular nominative in apposition to an expressed or unexpressed vocative that is identical with the subject of the verb (§13). Abel (§42.(g)) depicts the anarthrous vocatival nominative as typical of Classical Greek, the articular vocatival nominative as more common in Hellenistic Greek, although both are found in the NT.

11. Cf. BDF §147.(3); W. Foerster, *TDNT* 3:1086.

12. *Grammar* §§2679–82 (this change of viewpoint was anticipated in one of his earlier footnotes, 95 n. 3). Citing Origen's reference (in commenting on John 13:13) to τὸ καλῶς εἰπεῖν τῷ Σωτῆρι <u>τὸ</u> Ὁ διδάσκαλος, Abbott (*Grammar* 521 n. 3) suggests that "it is quite possible that in xx.28 the original was ΕΙΠΕΝΑΥΤΟΤΟΟΚΥΡΙΟΣ and that the second TO has been omitted." He seeks to justify his proposal by noting the frequent interchange of ο and ω in the first century and the liability of τό to scribal corruption when it was used in this or a similar way or when it was prefixed to interrogatives (e.g., Matt. 19:18; Gal. 4:25).

13. Cf. TCNT: "And Thomas exclaimed: 'My Master, and my God!'"

Insuperable objections attend this Socinian interpretation. (1) It renders the preceding (ἀπεκρίθη . . . καὶ εἶπεν) αὐτῷ (= Jesus) inexplicable (cf. Bauer 227). Why would John (or Thomas) introduce an indirect expression of praise to the Father by a phrase that directs the *ex hypothesi* praise to Jesus? The least he might have expressed in this case would be something like εἶπεν αὐτῷ, Εὐλογητὸς ὁ κύριός μου καὶ ὁ θεός μου (cf. Ps. 17:47 LXX [Engl. 18:47]; 143:1 LXX [Engl. 144:1]); εἶπεν αὐτῷ, Ὁ κύριός μου καὶ ὁ θεός μου τοῦτο ἐποίησεν (cf. Matt. 13:28); or εἶπεν αὐτῷ, Ὁ κύριός μου καὶ ὁ θεός μου, ὡς μεγάλη ἡ δύναμίς σου (cf. Rom. 11:33). (2) It is clear from the με after ἑώρακας in verse 29a and the parallelism between πιστεύσαντες in verse 29b (where εἰς ἐμέ must be inferred) and πεπίστευκας in verse 29a, that εἰς ἐμέ (or a phrase of similar import)[14] is to be supplied with πεπίστευκας. Verse 28 is therefore most naturally understood as an expression of Thomas's belief in the risen Jesus as his Lord and God. (3) All the previous uses of ὁ κύριος in John 20 (viz., vv. 2, 13, 18, 20, 25; cf. v. 15) refer to Jesus. In the literary artistry of the chapter, there seems to be a marked progress in meaning (but not in referent) from Mary Magdalene's ὁ κύριός μου (v. 13) to Thomas's ὁ κύριός μου καὶ ὁ θεός μου (cf. v. 17). (4) The preceding and following verses emphasize the relationship of Thomas to Jesus: λέγει τῷ Θωμᾷ (v. 27), λέγει αὐτῷ ὁ Ἰησοῦς (v. 29). It would be unlikely that the *oratio recta* that follows the intervening ἀπεκρίθη Θωμᾶς καὶ εἶπεν αὐτῷ (v. 28) would not be directed to Jesus.

b. Referring to Jesus

If Thomas's ejaculation is a statement about Jesus (and not a cry addressed to him), one must supply some such expression as (οὗτός) ἐστιν or ἐγήγερται ἐκ νεκρῶν. F. C. Burkitt paraphrased the confession thus: "It *is* Jesus Himself, and now I recognize Him as Divine" (48). But once again the presence of αὐτῷ is fatal to this interpretation.[15] Also, to understand Thomas's cry as a simple exclamation of surprise is to rob the cry of the ingredient of direct, personal encounter that is demanded by the context.

14. One might supply ὅτι ἐγήγερμαι ἐκ νεκρῶν (cf. Rom. 10:9) or εἰς τὸ ὄνομά μου (cf. John 3:18).

15. Winer has the curious comment: "Jno. xx:28, though directed to Jesus (εἶπεν αὐτῷ), is rather exclamation than address" (183).

3. Vocatival, Addressed to Jesus: "In response Thomas said to him, 'My Lord and my God!'"

Several observations support the interpretation that Thomas's words are vocatival and addressed to Jesus. This view prevails among grammarians,[16] lexicographers,[17] commentators[18] and English versions.[19]

a. Ἀπεκρίθη . . . καὶ εἶπεν implies a response *to Jesus* on the part of Thomas. While this phrase, representing the Biblical Aramaic ענה ואמר[20] or the Hebrew ויען ויאמר,[21] need not mean more than "he spoke up" (BAGD 93c), given the context and the presence of αὐτῷ, ἀπεκρίθη indicates that the *oratio recta* ὁ κύριός μου καὶ ὁ θεός μου is the response of Thomas to Jesus' invitation (v. 27). Thomas is not here replying to a formal question[22] ("Thomas replied," JB) but is reacting to a challenge to his faith ("Thomas said in response," NAB¹) in the form of a gentle command of Jesus (v. 27).

b. Εἶπεν αὐτῷ (v. 28) is clearly parallel to λέγει τῷ Θωμᾷ (v. 27) and λέγει αὐτῷ (v. 29) on the one hand and ἔλεγον . . . αὐτῷ (v. 25) on the other. In each case there is a speaker (or speakers), a statement that immediately follows, and a person addressed.[23] The whole phrase ἀπεκρίθη Θωμᾶς καὶ εἶπεν αὐτῷ may be rendered, "In response Thomas said to him."[24] What follows will be not simply an assertion or ejaculation made in the hearing of Jesus but an exclamation actually addressed to him.[25]

c. The articular nominative of address is an established NT usage (BDF §147), although the pre-Christian papyri seem to lack instances of this *enallage* of case (N. Turner, *Syntax* 34). It should be observed that the elements

16. Middleton 265–66; Abel §42.(g); Robertson, *Grammar* 461–62, 466; BDF §147.(3); Zerwick, *Analysis* 251 (but cf. Zerwick and Grosvenor 346: "if not rather an exclamation"); C. F. D. Moule, *Idiom Book* 116; N. Turner, *Insights* 16 (apparently).

17. Thayer 366 s.v. κύριος; BAGD 357b; W. Foerster, *TDNT* 3:1086.

18. Bengel 2:44; Godet, *John* 2:424; Loisy 511; Alford 1:912; H. A. W. Meyer, *John* 535; Milligan and Moulton 229; Bauer 227; Westcott, *Gospel* 297; Hoskyns 548; Brown, *Gospel* 2:1026, 1047; Brown, *Reflections* 28 (= "Jesus" 565); Morris, *John* 853 n. 76. Among general writers may be mentioned B. Weiss, "Gebrauch" 331, 508; Rahner 1:135; Sabourin, *Names* 302; Wainwright, *Trinity* 62 (= "Confession" 289); Boobyer 253; Fuller, *Foundations* 88.

19. RV, ASV, Moffatt, Goodspeed, RSV, NASB, GNB, Barclay, NIV, NAB², Cassirer, NRSV.

20. As in Dan. (Θ) 2:5, 8, 26; 3:14; 5:17.

21. BAGD 93c; F. Büchsel, *TDNT* 3:945.

22. As in John 1:48, where the same phrase (ἀπεκρίθη . . . καὶ εἶπεν αὐτῷ) occurs.

23. In only 3 cases (viz., John 9:20, 36; 12:30) out of the 29 instances of ἀπεκρίθη καὶ εἶπεν (or ἀπεκρίθησαν καὶ εἶπαν) in the Fourth Gospel (excluding 20:28) is this phrase not followed by a dative of the person(s) addressed. But even in these cases a dative is clearly implied (in John 9:20, 36 a question precedes the reply).

24. It is not impossible that εἶπεν αὐτῷ κτλ. is equivalent to ἐκάλεσεν αὐτὸν τὸν κύριον αὐτοῦ καὶ τὸν θεὸν αὐτοῦ (note especially Gen. 21:33: Ἀβραὰμ . . . ἐπεκαλέσατο ἐκεῖ τὸ ὄνομα κυρίου θεὸς αἰώνιος). But in no way could αὐτῷ be construed with what follows; in any case αὐτῷ (or εἰς αὐτόν) is regular Johannine diction for "to him" after λέγω.

25. It is possible, although unlikely, that following the address there is a suppressed statement ("I believe") or even a suppressed request ("forgive [or help] my unbelief").

of harshness, superiority, and impersonality that sometimes attach to the use of the idiom in Classical Greek are lacking in the almost sixty NT examples.[26] One finds ὁ θεός μου rather than θεέ μου (cf. Matt. 27:46)[27] because the expression is parallel to and therefore influenced by ὁ κύριός μου.[28] The article is used with θεός not merely because a vocatival nominative is commonly articular in Hellenistic Greek but in particular because when a possessive pronoun follows a vocatival nominative, the noun is always articular (cf. Abel §42g; C. F. D. Moule, *Idiom Book* 116).

I conclude that ὁ θεός μου is neither predicative nor simply exclamatory. It is neither an assertion made about the Father or Jesus, nor is it an ejaculation referring to the Father that was made in the presence of Jesus or referring to Jesus but not addressed to him. Rather it is an exclamatory address, an exclamation specifically directed to Jesus as its subject and recipient.

B. The Historical Problem

The historical issue may be stated thus: Does the christological confession of Thomas simply reflect the church's liturgy or the theology of the Johannine circle in the 90s without having a historical *Sitz im Leben Jesu*, or was the confession actually made by Thomas in the 30s and then incorporated into the emerging liturgical traditions of the church?

In the resurrection narratives of the Gospels, as in the records of the preresurrection ministry of Jesus, C. H. Dodd distinguishes two types of pericopes that originally stood as independent units of oral tradition: the "concise," which report the bare essentials of what occurred or what was said, and the "circumstantial," which report arresting details and traits of character in order to heighten interest.[29] While the story of Doubting Thomas (John 20:26–29) formally belongs to the class of concise narratives, it represents (according to Dodd) an intermediate type. Since it depends for its intelligibility on the connecting passage, 20:24–25, which itself presupposes 20:19–23, it could never have been an independent pericope. Thomas is not individualized in the way Mary Magdalene is. He typifies and acts as

26. Moulton, *Prolegomena* 70; N. Turner, *Syntax* 34.

27. But the parallel passage in Mark 15:34, following Ps. 21:2 (LXX [Engl. 22:1]), has ὁ θεός μου.

28. It has been observed above (§A.1.b) that ὁ κύριός μου was preferred over κύριέ μου probably because it was more emphatic in tone and elevated in style, κύριε often meaning merely "sir!" in the Synoptic Gospels (reflecting contemporary usage; cf. Matt. 21:30). Behind the words of Thomas could be the Hebrew אֲדֹנָי וֵאלֹהָי which might be rendered in Greek in at least four ways: (1) κύριέ μου καὶ ὁ θεός μου (cf. Rev. 18:20: οὐρανὲ καὶ οἱ ἅγιοι . . . , and the comment of Gildersleeve and Miller 1:4 n. 1), (2) κύριέ μου, θεός μου (cf. Matt. 15:22: κύριε υἱὸς Δαυίδ), (3) ὁ κύριος καὶ θεός μου, or (4) ὁ κύριός μου καὶ ὁ θεός μου, but *not* (5) κύριός μου καὶ θεός μου.

29. Dodd, *Studies* 102–3 (= "Appearances" 143).

spokesman for disciples who doubt (cf. Matt. 28:17; Luke 24:37–41).[30] Viewed thus as a dramatization of incredulity, this pericope, including the confession of verse 28, is a Johannine creation. The evangelist has expunged the reference to the disciples' doubt that was found in his source before verse 20 so that in a separate episode (vv. 24–29) he might personify apostolic doubt (Brown, *Gospel* 2:1031–32).

Such a theory would seem difficult to sustain on stylistic grounds. Of the 51 characteristics of Johannine style isolated by F. M. Braun (1:401–3) only two are in evidence in the Thomas pericope (John 20:24–29), viz., the expression ἀπεκρίθη καὶ εἶπεν (v. 28) (or equivalent), which is found some 33 times in the Fourth Gospel but only twice in the Synoptics,[31] and partitive ἐκ (v. 24), found 31 times in the Fourth Gospel and 26 times in the Synoptics.[32] This would suggest that the evangelist is here dependent on traditional material. Yet indications of John's editorial work are not lacking. The pericope builds on the previous episode (vv. 19–23) in the notes of time ("eight days later") and place ("once more in the house," "although the doors were locked," v. 26; cf. v. 19).

Since the Thomas episode displays this distinctive lack of Johannine stylistic characteristics, it is therefore unlikely to be purely a Johannine creation that was prompted by theological motives. Rather it embodies a pre-Johannine tradition unused by (or perhaps unknown to) the Synoptists in which Thomas was given a place of prominence. And since Thomas's confession is integral to the episode, forming its climax (along with v. 29), it too must be considered tradition and not a Johannine creation. It is scarcely conceivable that the evangelist would have inherited this Thomas tradition in a form similar to 20:24–27 (ending with the dominical rebuke: "Stop disbelieving; have faith!") and then added as his own contribution the climactic response of Thomas (v. 28) for which that dominical rebuke merely serves as a foil.[33] Verse 28 stands or falls with verses 24–27,[34] the whole pericope (vv. 24–29) being either a Johannine creation or (as I have argued) a pre-Johannine tradition.

If, then, neither the episode as a whole nor the christological confession in particular may be traced to the theological creativity of John, they must derive from an earlier written source or an earlier oral tradition. This does

30. Dodd, *Tradition* 145–46, 148; *Studies* 115–16.

31. For this expression as "an element of genuine biblical G[ree]k," see F. Büchsel, *TDNT* 3:945.

32. These statistics are from Braun 3.1:401–2. If, then, there are only two characteristics of Johannine style in these six verses (John 20:24–29), this represents an average of 0.33 characteristics per verse, a statistic which may be compared with Nicol's proposed range (25–26) for traditional material found within his "sēmeia source," viz., 0.30–0.75, with an average of 0.58 characteristics per verse.

33. Contra Reim, *Studien* 259–60, who sees John 20:28 with its reference to θεός as an editorial addition by the evangelist, although the Thomas episode as a whole is traditional material.

34. See below, §B.1.f.

not, of course, prove the historicity of the confession (v. 28) but it does establish that one should not look to the fertile and creative theological imagination of John for the original impulse behind the confession and it leaves open the possibility that the ultimate source of this pre-Johannine tradition was an actual encounter between Thomas and Jesus after the resurrection. I must now discuss the grounds for believing that the Thomas episode is rooted in history (without addressing the wider issue of the historical reliability of the Fourth Gospel in general)[35] and deal with the objections to the episode's historicity.

1. Grounds for the Historicity of the Thomas Episode

a. It is difficult to believe that the early church would have invented an incident in which Jesus publicly reproves "one of the Twelve" (John 20:24) for his disbelief (v. 27b) and even *after* his confession of faith (v. 28) gently chides him for demanding visual evidence for the reality of the resurrection (v. 29a) in addition to the verbal testimony he had already received (vv. 18, 25).[36] Moreover, there is a close verbal correspondence between John 4:48 (where Jesus condemns sign-seeking; cf. John 2:23–25) and John 20:25 (where Thomas demands signs).[37]

To render μὴ γίνου ἄπιστος ἀλλὰ πιστός (v. 27b) by "do not become unbelieving"[38] is to overlook Thomas's own admission of unbelief in verse 25: "Unless I see . . . I will not believe" implies that he did not then believe because he had not yet seen.[39] The phrase should be translated as "stop being an unbeliever,"[40] "do not persist in your disbelief,"[41] or "doubt no longer,"[42] implying Thomas's state of unbelief. And in verse 29a, whether

35. For a discussion of the problem of historicity in John, see Brown, "Historicity"; Morris, *Studies* 65–138.

36. One of the purposes of the Thomas episode is to show that for subsequent generations of Christians apostolic testimony is sufficient ground for faith in Christ. There is no need to repeat Thomas's demand for sensory confirmation or incontrovertible physical evidence. Two passages in Paul would seem to form his commentary on the Thomas incident and on the dominical logion found in John 20:29: ἡ πίστις ἐξ ἀκοῆς, ἡ δὲ ἀκοὴ διὰ ῥήματος Χριστοῦ (Rom. 10:17) and διὰ πίστεως . . . περιπατοῦμεν, οὐ διὰ εἴδους (2 Cor. 5:7).

37. Ἐὰν μὴ σημεῖα καὶ τέρατα ἴδητε, οὐ μὴ πιστεύσητε (John 4:48); ἐὰν μὴ ἴδω . . . οὐ μὴ πιστεύσω (John 20:25).

38. Temple, *John* 391; similarly H. A. W. Meyer, *John* 535; Loisy 511; Bernard, *John* 2:683.

39. To render γίνου by "become" is certainly not linguistically impossible; in fact, of the 51 uses of γίνομαι in the Fourth Gospel, 34 may be translated "become" (or an equivalent meaning such as "come into being, be made, take place"). The other 17 (including 20:27) are best rendered by "be" (1:6, 15, 30; 2:1; 3:9; 5:6, 14a; 6:21; 7:43; 8:58; 9:22; 10:16, 19, 22; 12:42; 13:2; 20:27).

40. Cf. J. N. Sanders 437; Bultmann, *John* 694 n. 1; Moulton, *Prolegomena* 124–25.

41. Brown, *Gospel* 2:1026.

42. Benoit 269. Significantly D has μὴ ἴσθι. If μὴ γίνου is rendered, "Do not show yourself [to be unbelieving]" (cf. Zerwick and Grosvenor 346), there is ambiguity as to Thomas's state of belief.

ὅτι ἑώρακάς με πεπίστευκας be construed as a question (as in RSV)[43] or a statement (as in NEB), there is not only an implied commendation for belief (which becomes explicit in v. 29b) but also an implied reproof for believing only after seeing, for rejecting the oral testimony of the witnesses to the resurrection.

b. Similarly, is it credible that one of the Twelve would be pictured as obstinately incredulous by the creative pen of some early Christian? The fact that Thomas finally confesses does not lessen the improbability that anyone would create and put into Thomas's mouth a demand (v. 25) that reflects obstinacy and self-assertiveness.

The evangelist records Thomas's unwillingness to believe as a vigorous denial (οὐ μὴ πιστεύσω, "I will certainly not believe"),[44] not simply as a polite refusal (οὐ πιστεύσω, "I shall not believe"). And what Thomas refused to believe for a week were the oft-repeated and detailed reports[45] of Mary Magdalene (vv. 17–18) and his trusted fellow disciples (v. 25a) concerning the resurrection appearances of Jesus. But he was not merely demanding that Jesus should appear to him personally to confirm the truth of others' testimony. In his insistence that he should touch as well as see the wounds of Jesus, he was seeking a privilege denied to Mary Magdalene (v. 17)[46] and not afforded to the other disciples (v. 20: "He showed them . . . they saw the Lord") or at least not sought by them (Luke 24:39).[47]

c. The incident as recorded contains several other indications of verisimilitude that are unlikely to be fabrications: the note regarding Thomas's absence from the previous meeting of the disciples (v. 24; this is an essential ingredient of the whole episode); the fact that Thomas had neither left nor been excluded from the company of the Ten (v. 26a) in spite of his rejection of their uniform and repeated testimony; the recognition that locked doors made an appearance of Jesus antecedently improbable ("in spite of the fact that the doors were locked,[48] Jesus came and stood among them," v. 26b); and the specific indications (v. 26a) of time ("eight days later") and place ("once more in the house"), which cannot naturally be interpreted symbolically.

43. So, e.g., Lagrange, *Jean* 518; N. Turner, *Syntax* 345. Parallelism with John 1:50a, where causal ὅτι introduces a direct question, supports this interpretation. See *per contra* Beasley-Murray 386.

44. It is significant that nearly 90% of the NT uses of οὐ μή to express an emphatic denial, a relatively rare construction in Hellenistic Greek (N. Turner, *Syntax* 96 n. 2), are found in Septuagintal quotations and sayings of Jesus (Moulton, *Prolegomena* 188–92).

45. Ἔλεγον (John 20:25) is probably iterative ("they kept telling").

46. On the meaning of μή μου ἅπτου (John 20:17), see Brown, *Gospel* 2:1011–12.

47. That Thomas did *not* in fact touch Jesus seems implied by the simple ἑώρακας in John 20:29 (not ἑώρακας καὶ ἐψηλάφωκας; cf. 1 John 1:1), although the invitation of Jesus was genuine, not ironical.

48. Τῶν θυρῶν κεκλεισμένων is a concessive use of the genitive absolute (cf. 2 Cor. 2:12).

d. Thomas's response to the testimony of the other disciples (John 20:25) is formulated in light of the invitation of Jesus reported in Luke 24:39. That is, "I refuse to believe it unless I see the mark of the nails on his hands and put my finger right into the mark of the nails and put my hand right into his side" presupposes the invitation, "See my hands and my feet—it is I myself; handle me and see." This complementarity that falls short of a precise verbal correspondence (witness John's "hands and side" and Luke's "hands and feet") argues for the historicity of Thomas's word in verse 25. Clearly Thomas had listened carefully to the full report of the disciples concerning the appearance of Jesus (Luke 24:36–43 = John 20:19–23).

e. There is a remarkable consonance between the character of Thomas expressed in the earlier episodes of the Fourth Gospel involving him (viz., 11:16; 14:5) and the personal traits exhibited in his encounter with Jesus recorded in John 20. In John 11:16 Thomas acts as spokesman for the disciples in saying, "Let us go [with Jesus into Judea to Lazarus], that we may die with him [Jesus]." Here Thomas expresses that intense desire for the uninterrupted companionship of Jesus and that willingness to die with him rather than abandon his cause, which at least partially account for his presence with the Ten one week after the resurrection in spite of his persistent unbelief (John 20:24–26). In John 14:5 Thomas responds to the simple assertion of Jesus, "You know the way to where I am going," by posing the question, "Lord, we don't know where you are going, so how can we know the way?" His faith could not advance beyond what he "saw" (cf. John 20:25). "How can we be expected to recognize the route if your destination remains unclear to us?" In addition, one finds in these earlier stories a streak of pessimism (John 11:16b) and a combination of forthright honesty and intellectual obtuseness (John 14:5) that are clearly reflected in John 20:25. Admittedly, this consistent picture of Thomas in the Fourth Gospel could have originated in a skillful evangelist's creative literary artistry, but the presence of certain negative elements in each portrayal of Thomas suggests rather that the Johannine depiction of Thomas corresponds to reality.

f. Finally, it may be noted that if the apostle John is the author of the Fourth Gospel[49] this Thomas episode will reflect eyewitness testimony.

The cumulative effect of these observations is to heighten the probability that John 20:24–29 embodies accurate historical reminiscence.

As for the historicity of the christological confession itself (v. 28), first, it seems arbitrary to acknowledge the historicity of the pericope in general but to deny the confession to Thomas, for within the pericope verse 28 is pivotal. Verses 24–27 look forward to verse 28 as their climax

49. For a defense of this position, see Morris, *Studies* 139–292.

and without it (in the pre-Johannine period of the tradition) they would simply have stood as an ugly torso, an indictment against one of the Twelve ("Do not persist in unbelief! Become a believer!," v. 27)—hardly a pericope worth enshrining in oral tradition! Similarly, verse 29 looks back to and presupposes verse 28, which then has the effect of defining "belief" as the recognition and confession of the lordship and deity of Jesus Christ (cf. v. 31). Second, if addressing Jesus as מרנא (= ὁ κύριος ἡμῶν) was characteristic of the primitive Palestinian church (1 Cor. 16:22),[50] why should a personal version of this address (ὁ κύριός μου) be denied to a member of the Jerusalem church? It is not a necessary corollary of this view that Thomas's understanding of the lordship of Jesus in A.D. 30 was identical with the Johannine view at the time of writing.[51] Third, if κύριος came to be an appropriate title to apply to Christ after the resurrection (Phil. 2:9–11),[52] there is no reason to deny either its suitability on the lips of one of the Twelve immediately after the resurrection with a christological sense or therefore the possibility that θεός too was an apposite term of address at that time (assuming that κύριος and θεός cannot be distinguished with regard to the status designated; see below, §C.2.c).

2. *Objections to the Historicity of the Thomas Episode*

a. It is claimed that in this pericope Thomas simply is the personification of the attitude of doubt shared to some extent by all the early disciples. The details of the narrative are literary rather than historical.[53]

In reply, it cannot be said that, simply because a person epitomizes an attitude or embodies an ideal, that figure must be fictitious. In any case Thomas does more than perform the negative role of dramatizing incredulity. He also represents those whose secure faith is hammered out on the anvil of vigorous skepticism. And his doubt was not complete, for he gathered with the disciples on the Sunday after he had publicly expressed his unwillingness to believe without tangible proof of Jesus' resurrection (John 20:19, 24–26) and his demand to see and touch before believing implied that he would believe after seeing and touching. The term Δίδυμος (v. 24) does not mean "doubter," symbolizing his character, but is the natural Greek equivalent (just as Θωμᾶς is a Greek transliteration) of the Ara-

50. See W. Foerster, *TDNT* 3:1094.

51. On this point, see further below, §C.2.b.

52. In Phil. 2:10 (ἐν τῷ ὀνόματι) Ἰησοῦ is a possessive rather than an epexegetic genitive: κύριος is the ὄνομα given Jesus at his resurrection.

53. Thus Suriano 309–10, 312; similarly Dodd, *Tradition* 145–46; *Studies* 115–16.

maic תאומא, "twin," and may have been the name of Thomas that had currency among Greek-speaking Christians in Asia Minor.[54]

b. The final verse of the pericope underscores the apologetic origin of the whole story. At a time when few eyewitnesses remained alive, it became inevitable that people came to faith apart from a personal encounter with the Jesus of history or his contemporaries. The survival of Christianity depended on "believing without seeing" (Suriano 314–15).

But apologetic value and historical reminiscence are not mutually exclusive categories. The apologetic significance and interest of a narrative do not in themselves demonstrate a writer's creativity but rather his judicious selection of an apologetically valuable story that may or may not be rooted in history.[55]

c. Perhaps the most serious objection is the assertion that Thomas's confession is too developed christologically to be possible in A.D. 30 and is anachronistic if the pericope is historical. Time must pass before any Jew could accommodate a divine Christ within the theological framework of monotheism.[56]

Now it is true that John 20:28 is more elevated and comprehensive than other christological confessions addressed to Jesus during his ministry. But one must not arbitrarily restrict the influence of the resurrection on the development of Christology.[57] Just as the title κύριος came to be used of Jesus in a titular sense after and because of the resurrection (Phil. 2:9–11),[58] so the title θεός, the Septuagintal equivalent of the generic appellative

54. Three times in the Fourth Gospel (11:16; 20:24; 21:2) Thomas is described by the phrase ὁ λεγόμενος Δίδυμος, "who is (commonly) called the Twin." In John 4:25 there is a similar movement from the Greek translation of a Semitic word (Μεσσίας) to the nearest Greek equivalent (Χριστός) after ὁ λεγόμενος. The Greek for "Doubter" would be Δίψυχος (cf. James 1:8). In papyri, the word δίδυμος (generally an adjective meaning "double" or "twofold") is used both as a proper name ("Twin") and as a common noun ("twin") (MM 159).

55. Similarly Benoit 285.

56. "Only little by little did they [the disciples] come to a clear formulation of what they had obscurely felt. It needed time to transpose this great mystery into human language. We must therefore distinguish that deep faith, which is very old, preceding even the resurrection and springing into new life very soon after it, from its intellectual formulation, which took longer to come to fruition" (Benoit 286).

57. See further, chapter XIII §E. While it is true that the confession "Jesus is Lord" (cf. John 20:28) postdates the giving of the Spirit (1 Cor. 12:3), it seems arbitrary in the context of John 20 to equate this pouring out of the Spirit with the Lucan Pentecost of Acts 2 when John 20:22 alludes to (at least) an anticipation of that effusion or to the regeneration (note ἐνεφύσησεν; cf. Gen. 2:7; Ezek. 37:9) of the disciples after the resurrection yet before Pentecost. (On the interpretation of John 20:22, see Dunn, *Baptism* 173–82.) While he holds that "it was the resurrection of Jesus which gave the decisive stimulus to Christological thinking," especially in regard to the terms "Lord" and "Messiah" (*Luke* 128), Marshall believes that "it took time" for the church to work out the full implications of the title "Son of God" until in the end it was recognized that Jesus might not inappropriately be called "God" (*Origins* 123).

58. On the resurrection as the primary influence leading to the application of the title ὁ κύριος to Jesus, see V. Taylor, *Person* 49–50.

אלהים, might well have been recognized as a suitable title by which to address Jesus once his divinity had been confirmed in the eyes of his followers by his resurrection.[59] Certainly no Jew would have regarded θεός as a less appropriate term of address to the Deity than κύριος. That is, if one admits κύριος as a postresurrection title of Jesus, on what grounds can one deny the possibility that θεός too was employed in addressing Jesus immediately after the resurrection?

d. How is it that Thomas's gloomy unbelief could be so quickly transformed into ecstatic faith?[60]

Several reasons may be given for this dramatic change in Thomas's attitude. (1) Thomas had been psychologically and spiritually prepared for a sudden emergence from the shadows of doubt into the light of faith by his week-long reflection on the reports of Mary Magdalene (v. 18) and the other disciples (v. 25). One reason he had rejected their testimony about the resurrection may have been his recognition (as he recalled Jesus' prophecies of the event) of the far-reaching implications of belief that Jesus had risen from the dead.[61] (2) The appearance of the risen and transformed Jesus would have seemed to Thomas a personal and gracious reply to his earlier semidefiant assertion, "Unless I see . . . I will never believe." (3) The personal invitation of Jesus to Thomas ("put your finger here and examine my hands; put out your hand and place it in my side," v. 27) was couched in terms that implied Jesus' preternatural knowledge of the language Thomas had used in rejecting the testimony of the other disciples that they had seen the Lord (v. 25).[62] It was this combination of more-than-human graciousness and knowledge, along with the sheer joy that comes from the relief of tension and uncertainty, that elicited Thomas's sublime confession. (4) Thomas became reassured of his Lord's continuing love through the accommodating manner of Jesus and his gentle yet firm rebuke (v. 27). (5) However, the ultimate stimulus behind Thomas's confession was the work of the Spirit (cf. Matt. 16:15–17; 1 Cor. 12:3). Although not present with the other ten disciples on the evening of the resurrection day, Thomas would hardly have been thereby deprived of the benefit of the "insufflation" (v. 22).

How may we summarize this issue of historicity? I have given reasons for believing that the Thomas episode (vv. 24–29) embodies a pre-Johannine tradition that the evangelist has blended into the previous

59. Pseudo-Athanasius perceptively argued that one may deduce from the resurrection of Christ and his victory over death that he is "very Lord and God" (*De Incarnatione* 45:4).

60. An objection of Theodore of Mopsuestia (*Commentary on St. John's Gospel* 256:29–35), cited by Wiles, *Gospel* 30–31.

61. For a fine discussion of what led up to Thomas's confession, see Milligan and Moulton 229.

62. It is just possible, of course, that the disciples had had an opportunity to inform Jesus of the content of Thomas's indirect challenge to him.

pericope (vv. 19–23) by adding the references to time and place necessary for the flow of the narrative. As it stands, the pericope has so many signs of verisimilitude that its historicity may be confidently assumed, and since the confession in verse 28 is pivotal and climactic in the story it may be reckoned *ipsissima verba Thomae*. Certainly the theological sentiments expressed in the confession are in keeping with the postresurrection setting of the narrative.

C. The Theological Issue

1. The Sources of Thomas's Cry

The meaning given to Thomas's devotional cry will be largely determined by one's appraisal of the originating impulse behind the confession or the source behind its particular formulation. At least five different (but not necessarily mutually exclusive) impulses or sources have been proposed.

a. Apologetic or Polemical

The confession arose as a defensive counterblast to the grandiose claims made by the imperial cult on behalf of Domitian (A.D. 81–96) who was called *dominus et deus noster* (Suetonius, *Domit.* 13:2; Mastin, "Cult").[63] This view presupposes that the Fourth Gospel was composed and published in the 90s of the first century A.D. and that the Thomas episode is not historical. Both assumptions are at least open to question.[64]

b. Liturgical

This expression of belief in the deity of Christ arose from the veneration of the κύριος in worship (Bousset 317, 322 n. 309, 330–31) or, more generally, this confession of faith may have had a liturgical origin or at least setting.[65] R. E. Brown (*Gospel* 2:1048) discerns in Thomas's words a combination of a covenantal confession ("you are my God," Hos. 2:25 [LXX]; cf. John 20:17) and a baptismal profession ("Jesus is Lord"). While the liturgi-

63. For a more tentative statement of this view, in light of his further proposal that the evangelist's threefold use of θεός in reference to Jesus (John 1:1, 18; 20:28) may have arisen as a result of controversy between church and synagogue over Christian claims about the person of Jesus, see Mastin, "Christology" 46.

64. On the Gospel's date, see J. A. T. Robinson, *Redating* 254–311, who dates the formation of the Johannine tradition and the proto-Gospel in Jerusalem between 30 and 50, the first edition 50–55 in Asia Minor, while the final form of the Gospel (with the Prologue and Epilogue added) may be dated around 65; on the historicity of the Thomas pericope, see above, §B.

65. Barrett, *John* 573, followed by Wainwright, *Trinity* 63 (= "Confession" 290).

cal setting of John 20:19–29 is unmistakable,[66] this does not necessarily imply the liturgical origin or shaping of the confession.

c. Theological

The christological affirmation, like the Thomas scene in general, is the product of Johannine theology and expresses the identity of the Jesus of history (ὁ κύριός μου) with the incarnate Logos (ὁ θεός μου; cf. John 1:1; Dodd, *Interpretation* 430–31). Questions have already been raised about this radical discounting of the historicity of the Thomas episode. It is true that the theological import of the affirmation remains intact whether or not the incident is historical, but it is of crucial significance whether the theology is that of Thomas or solely that of the evangelist and his circle.

d. Septuagintal

The combination κύριος καὶ θεός used in Christian worship probably arose directly from the common Septuagintal conjunction κύριε ὁ θεός (Deissmann 361, citing Ps. 85:15 LXX [Engl. 86:15]; 87:2 LXX [Engl. 88:1]). Given the frequency of this OT formula and comparable phrases involving ἡμῶν and μου (see next section), it is likely that OT usage influenced, either consciously or unconsciously, the particular choice of terms found in John 20:28, whether or not Thomas actually uttered these or similar words.

e. Experiential

Personally confronted by the risen Lord after a traumatic week of uncertainty as he wrestled with the implications of the report that Mary Magdalene and his fellow apostles had delivered to him, Thomas suddenly finds his doubt put to flight and sums up his new, liberating conviction, born of experience, in the worshipful cry, "My Lord and my God!"

As noted above, these suggested origins of Thomas's affirmation are not mutually exclusive.[67] The one indisputable influence is the Septuagint. Not only is there the κύριε ὁ θεός (3 examples)[68] that Deissmann cited, but also (more pertinently) κύριε ὁ θεός μου (20 examples),[69] κύριε ὁ θεὸς ἡμῶν

66. Liturgical features include the gathering of believers on the first day of the week, the Lord's day (vv. 19, 26; cf. Acts 20:7; Rev. 1:10), the presence of Christ (vv. 19, 26), the blessing (vv. 19, 21, 26), the coming of the Spirit (v. 22), the absolution (v. 23), the confession of faith (v. 28), and the benediction (v. 29).

67. See, for example, the discussions of Barrett, *John* 572–73, and Brown, *Gospel* 2:1047–48.

68. Ps. 9:33 [10:12]; 85:15 [86:15]; 87:2 [88:1]. In this and the following notes, references are to LXX verse numbers; English verse numbers, where different, are bracketed.

69. 2 Kgdms. [2 Sam.] 15:31; 3 Kgdms. [1 Kings] 17:21; Esther 4:17*l* (A); Tob. 3:11; Ps. 7:2, 4, 7 [vv. 1, 3, 6]; 9:33 (A ℵ[2]) [10:12]; 12:4 [13:3]; 29:3, 13 [30:2, 12]; 34:24 [35:24]; 37:16 [38:15]; 39:6 [40:5]; 85:12 [86:12]; 103:1 [104:1]; 108:26 [109:26]; Jonah 2:7 [v. 6]; Hab. 1:12 [A]; Isa. 25:1.

(14),[70] and κύριος ὁ θεός σου (1),[71] and also the frequent expressions κύριος ὁ θεός μου[72] and κύριος ὁ θεὸς ἡμῶν[73] and those instances where σύ (3)[74] or σὺ εἶ (or εἶ σύ) (10)[75] accompanies a phrase such as θεός μου or κύριος ὁ θεὸς ἡμῶν. The closest LXX parallel to John 20:28 is Psalm 34:23 [Engl. 35:23]: ὁ θεός μου καὶ ὁ κύριός μου. The inverted order in John 20:28 may be due to the frequency of κύριε ὁ θεός μου in the LXX. Another close parallel is Psalm 5:3 (LXX [Engl. 5:2]; cf. 83:3 LXX [Engl. 84:2]), which has the vocatival ὁ βασιλεύς μου καὶ ὁ θεός μου.

My suggestion regarding the genesis of Thomas's confession is this. In his attempt to depict the significance of the risen Jesus for himself personally, Thomas used a liturgical form ultimately drawn from the LXX, which later came to serve admirably as the crowning christological affirmation of the Fourth Gospel, as a confessional formula in the church, and as a rebuttal of the imperial cult.

2. *The Meaning and Theological Significance of Thomas's Cry*

a. The Implications of an Exclamatory Address and of μου

No one will contest that an exclamatory address differs in form from a doctrinal statement, yet it seems arbitrary to say that Thomas *addressed* Jesus as his Lord and God but did not believe that Jesus *was* his Lord and God. That is, there is a formal but not a material difference between saying "my Lord and my God!" and "Jesus is (or, you are) my Lord and my God."[76] In addition, one may legitimately extrapolate from Thomas's words the fact that he believed Jesus to be his Lord and his God because in verse 29a Jesus commends him for "believing," for having confessed his faith in his exclamation addressed to Jesus. From this

70. 4 Kgdms. [2 Kings] 19:19; 1 Chron. 29:16; 2 Chron. 14:10 *bis* [v. 11]; 20:12; Ps. 98:8 [99:8]; 105:47 [106:47]; Isa. 26:12, 13; Bar. 2:12, 19, 27; Dan. 9:15, 17 [A].

71. Ps. 80:11 [81:10].

72. For example, Ps. 143:1 [144:1]; Jer. 38:18 [31:18].

73. For example, 2 Esdras [Ezra] 9:9; Ps. 98:9 [99:9].

74. Jer. 38:18 [31:18]; Bar. 2:15; 3:6.

75. 2 Macc. 1:27; Ps. 15:2 [16:2]; 96:9 [97:9]; 117:28 *bis* [118:28]; 139:7 [140:6]; 142:10 (B א) [143:10]; Hos. 2:25 [Engl. v. 23]; Isa. 44:17; Jer. 3:22.

76. Note the comments of Bengel (2:494: "The absolute appellation has the force of an enunciation"), Hoskyns (548: "The words are addressed to Jesus, and are therefore a statement of faith in Him"), and Brown (*Gospel* 2:1026: "The expression, as used in John, is a cross between a vocative and a proclamation of faith ['You are my Lord and my God']"). Similarly Middleton 265–66; Westcott, *Gospel* 297. One wonders, therefore, whether John 20:28 is being ignored or overlooked when it is claimed that the *homologia* κύριος Ἰησοῦς is absent from the Fourth Gospel (see Neufeld 81–82, who cites the reasons that have been advanced to explain the alleged absence).

viewpoint verse 28 is the last of a series of confessions scattered throughout the Gospel.[77]

But does the presence of μου prevent one's affirming that, for Thomas and John, Jesus was Lord and God in an absolute sense? Probably not. The effect of μου is to convert perception into faith (cf. Schlatter, *Johannes* 362) and to personalize Thomas's response, just as Jesus had approached him personally in the presence of the other disciples (v. 27).[78] One could not affirm that Jesus was "Lord and God" only for Thomas or John without calling into question the evangelist's choice and use of this saying as the summation of his Christology and his whole purpose in writing. It was precisely because Jesus was believed to be *universally* Lord and God that John was motivated to write and carefully placed this significant devotional cry at the end of his Gospel[79] as the point of confession to which he wished to lead his readers. The theological significance of Thomas's response would differ little or not at all had the vocative been ὁ θεός or θεέ instead of ὁ θεός μου. The repeated μου does not convert into a functional assertion what otherwise would be an affirmation of deity. That is, ὁ κύριός μου καὶ ὁ θεός μου should not be read as ἐμοὶ σὺ εἶ κύριος καὶ θεός ("for me [or, in my experience] you are Lord and God"). As it is, one might paraphrase the sense, "O Lord and God, I worship you."

b. The Meaning of κύριος

As already noted, it is unnecessary to insist that if the Thomas episode is historical the understanding of Thomas as he uttered the words ὁ κύριός μου καὶ ὁ θεός μου must correspond to the Johannine perception of the theological import of the confession. On the other hand, it seems invidious to place *a priori* limitations on the theological insight of one like Thomas who was illumined by the Spirit. What must remain improbable is that John would use Thomas simply as a mouthpiece for a christological affirmation that in fact had not been used in the church before (or much before) the time of writing.

Certainly κύριος here means more than "sir" or "master," as the conjunction with θεός conclusively indicates.[80] And if the phrase were merely a synonym for the Jesus of history[81] (as in John 20:13; cf. 20:2), the μου and

77. "Lamb of God" (1:29, 36), "Messiah" (1:41), "Son of God, King of Israel" (1:49), "teacher" (3:2), "prophet" (4:19; 7:40), "Holy One of God" (6:69), "Son of Man" (9:35), "the Messiah, the Son of God" (11:27), "King of the Jews" (19:19).

78. It is remarkable that μου, not ἡμῶν, is found, for other disciples were present. Such a pronoun belongs to the confessional style, not to any polemical interest (cf. Kramer 222, speaking of the significance of ἡμῶν with ὁ κύριος Ἰησοῦς Χριστός). On "My God" in the OT, see Eissfeldt.

79. On this point, see §D below.

80. Cf. Bultmann, *John* 695 n. 1; Strathmann, *Johannes* 259–60.

81. So Dodd, *Interpretation* 430.

the following καί would become inexplicable. Because it is followed by ὁ θεός μου and because it cannot be construed as a nominative ("my Lord [Jesus] is also my God"),[82] the phrase must be accorded a religious significance.[83]

Given the pre-Christian Jewish custom of reading אדני (= κύριος) for יהוה in synagogue worship,[84] ὁ κύριός μου could conceivably mean, "You represent for me the presence of Yahweh," but scarcely, "To me, you (personally) are Yahweh."[85] But more is implied than mere representation. Thomas was addressing Jesus as one who shared Yahweh's authority and functions and exercised Yahweh's rights.[86] It was a case of καθὼς . . . ὁ πατήρ, κἀγώ (cf. John 20:21). Jesus deserved human worship as the one in whom was vested the ultimate authority to forgive sins (John 20:23; cf. Mark 2:5–10), the one who dispensed the Holy Spirit to his followers (John 20:22) and commissioned them to divine service (John 20:21), the one who by virtue of his resurrection possessed "the keys that unlock death and Hades" (Rev. 1:18 Moffatt), and the one who was to climax his resurrection by ascension to the Father (John 20:17).[87] Now it is true that Thomas was not present at the appearance of Jesus to Mary Magdalene and the disciples, but it is inconceivable that the report of Mary to all the disciples and of the disciples to Thomas should not have included, along with the central

82. See above, §A.1.b.

83. W. Foerster has observed (*TDNT* 3:1091 and n. 266) that in the world contemporary with primitive Christianity there are no instances of a distinction in rank between θεός and κύριος in which κύριος is an intermediary god.

84. In postexilic Judaism the practice arose of avoiding the pronunciation of the "proper name" of God. Thus the tetragrammaton יהוה was replaced (probably early in the third century B.C.) by אדני ("Lord") whenever Scripture was read, recited, or quoted or by השמים ("heaven") in free speech (apart from references to Scripture). Subsequently (probably after the early second century A.D.) the use of אדני as a substitute for יהוה was restricted to liturgical reading in synagogue worship, with השם ("the name") being used in other situations involving Scripture, such as private reading or quotation. Even the use of השמים in general speech outside Scripture quotations became taboo and was replaced by המקום ("the place" = heaven = God), except in certain stereotyped expressions such as לשם שמים, "for God's sake." This reverential avoidance of the "ineffable name" may have arisen from a particular understanding of the third commandment (Exod. 20:7; Deut. 5:11), from the belief that the simple utterance of the sacred tetragrammaton was a capital offense (Lev. 24:16), or from a fear that to pronounce the divine name would be to reduce God to the status of a pagan deity who was addressed by a personal name. Or perhaps later Judaism was simply fulfilling the rabbinic injunction: "Make a hedge about the law" (*Pirke Aboth* 1:1). On the other hand, אל, אלוה, and אלהים were freely used in the reading or quoting of Scripture, in religious texts, and in prayers, although probably not in free speech. This information is drawn largely from K. G. Kuhn, *TDNT* 3:92–94. Cf. also SB 2:308–19; Parke-Taylor 79–96.

85. Behind ὁ κύριός μου may lie אדני (see above, n. 28), but not יהוה (which never takes pronominal suffixes).

86. A careful distinction should be drawn between the Father as κύριος ὁ θεός (= יהוה אלהים)—a designation never used of Christ in the NT—and Christ as ὁ κύριός μου καὶ ὁ θεός μου. While distinct from Yahweh, Christ shares his status and his nature.

87. It is unnecessary to assume that the ascension occurs between John 20:17 and 20:19, so that 20:22 is the Johannine Pentecost (see Dunn, *Baptism* 174–77).

announcement "I (we) have seen the Lord" (John 20:18, 25; cf. v. 20), a recitation of *all* Jesus said and did on each occasion. I am not suggesting that Thomas necessarily realized at the time that the resurrection and ascension of Jesus involved his elevation to cosmic dominion that would be recalled in Christian worship (Eph. 1:20–22a; Phil. 2:9–11; 1 Pet. 3:22). But a perceptive understanding of the theological import of the words and deeds of Jesus after his resurrection, not to speak of those during his ministry, would have led Thomas to recognize (during his week of intense thought) that if Jesus had in fact risen from the dead he was indeed κύριος *par excellence*, Lord of both physical and spiritual life.[88] The meaning of ὁ κύριός μου on the lips of Mary Magdalene (John 20:13) differs altogether from its significance for Thomas. For Mary κύριος was a courteous and tender appellative, referring to the deceased Jesus. For Thomas it was an exalted and confessional title of address, referring to the risen Jesus. The radical, new ingredient that explains the difference between the two uses of the same phrase was the resurrection.

c. The Meaning of θεός

Although in customary Johannine and NT usage (ὁ) θεός refers to the Father,[89] it is impossible that Thomas and John would be personally equating Jesus with the Father, for in the immediate historical and literary context Jesus himself has explicitly distinguished himself from God his Father (John 20:17). Clearly, then, θεός is a title, not a proper name.[90] Nor is it fitting to argue that, since John aimed in his Gospel to prove merely the messiahship of Jesus (John 20:31), ὁ θεός μου of verse 28 cannot mean "my God" but must bear a diluted, descriptive sense such as "my divine one,"[91] as in F. C. Burkitt's paraphrase, "It *is* Jesus Himself, and now I recognize Him as divine" (48). As elsewhere in John, the title ὁ υἱὸς τοῦ θεοῦ,

88. Although κύριος is the distinctive title and name that the NT uses of the resurrected and ascended Jesus (e.g., 2 Cor. 5:6, 8; 1 Thess. 4:15–17) as universal sovereign and as head of the church, the concept of his being "Lord" doubtless arose during his earthly life as a consequence of his authoritative teaching and divine power (see Mark 11:3; 12:35–37, citing Ps. 110:1; cf. John 13:13–14). That is, the preresurrection historical experience of the lordship of Jesus foreshadowed the postresurrection theological confession of Jesus as Lord. But some believe that the disciples advanced beyond unitarian monotheism even before the resurrection. For instance, Dreyfus affirms that no Jew on his own initiative could conceive of anything as apparently contrary to monotheism as the adoration of a divine being distinct from God the Father, but he finds the stimulus that surrounded this monotheistic obstacle for the early Christians not in the resurrection of Jesus—"it postulated neither divinization nor preexistence" (59)—but in the teaching of Jesus himself regarding his preexistence and divinity, teaching that God confirmed by the resurrection (53–71). For a convincing defense of the thesis that NT Christology is best regarded as the development and articulation of "what was already there from the beginning" (3), rather than as an evolutionary process involving the emergence of new species or the accretion of elements alien to the historical Jesus, see C. F. D. Moule, *Origin*.

89. See above, chapter I §B.4.

90. So also B. Weiss, "Gebrauch" 331.

91. This point is made by Brown, *Gospel* 2:1060.

which is in apposition to ὁ Χριστός in John 20:31, denotes more than simply the Davidic Messiah. The Gospel was written to produce belief that Jesus was the promised Jewish Messiah and that this Messiah was none other than the "one and only"[92] Son of God who had come from the Father (John 11:42; 17:8), who shared his nature (John 1:1, 18; 10:30) and fellowship (John 1:18; 14:11), and who therefore might appropriately be addressed and worshiped as ὁ θεός μου.[93] Unique sonship implies deity (John 5:18; cf. 19:7).

Following the term κύριος used as a religious title with rich christological overtones, the title θεός could scarcely bear a less exalted sense. It is inadequate, therefore, to say simply that Thomas (or John) recognized that God was active in and through Jesus, or that in Jesus the eschatological presence of God was at work. Jesus was more than God's man appointed to become a redeemer, more than some suprahuman being who was a legitimate object of worship, more than the "inhistorized" divine *Agapē*. As used by a monotheistic Jew in reference to a person who was demonstrably human, θεός will denote oneness with the Father in being (cf. John 10:30),[94] not merely in purpose and action.[95] In other words, Thomas's cry expresses the substantial divinity of Jesus.[96] Thomas has penetrated beyond the σημεῖον—the appearance of the risen Jesus—to its implication, viz., the deity of Christ.[97] While not couched as an ontological affirmation (σὺ εἶ ὁ θεός μου), the apostle's exclamatory address has inescapable ontological implications. Even as it is expressed, the confession embodies less functional than ontological truth: Jesus was wor-

92. See the discussion of μονογενής above, chapter III §B.

93. Fortna, however, finds a tension between the "high christology" of v. 28 and the "more primitive messianism" of v. 31 (197–98).

94. Given John 1:1 and 1:18, it is quite admissible to discern in ἐγὼ καὶ ὁ πατὴρ ἕν ἐσμεν (John 10:30; cf. 17:11, 22–23; 1 Cor. 3:8) more than unity of will or purpose but less than identity of person. Equality of divine power (10:28–29) points to unity of divine essence (10:30: ἕν ἐσμεν). Šurjanský finds in ἕν ἐσμεν a unity of nature and existence (84–87). On the exegesis of John 10:30 in early trinitarian controversies, see Pollard, "Exegesis."

95. The inadequacy of Harvey's "agent Christology" may be seen in his comment on the implications of θεός in John 20:28: Thomas is there portrayed as addressing Jesus as the fully accredited divine agent "to speak to whom was *as if* to speak to God himself" (*Jesus* 172; cf. 166; italics mine).

96. That Thomas here acknowledges the deity of Jesus is recognized, *inter alios*, by Wikenhauser 344–45; Lagrange, *Jean* 518; Godet, *John* 2:424–25; Westcott, *Gospel* 297; Milligan and Moulton 229; Schultz 246; Wainwright, *Trinity* 6 (= "Confession" 289); Schnackenburg, *John* 3:333; J. Schneider, *Johannes* 324 ("ein Wesen göttlicher Art"); Pollard, *Christology* 16. It is interesting that in the Acts of Thomas (26) Jesus Christ is described as κύριος καὶ θεὸς πάντων (cf. θεὸς καὶ κύριος ἡμῶν Ἰησοῦς Χριστός in Eusebius, *HE* 5:28:11; cited by Neufeld 80 n. 9).

97. For John σημεῖα are miraculous evidences that point to spiritual truths and may prompt faith (compare John 20:25 and 4:48), doubt, or simply amazement. Once he had been convinced of the reality of the resurrected one, Thomas recognized in the resurrection appearances a token of the godhood of Jesus. The word ἄλλα (σημεῖα) in John 20:30, occurring immediately after the Thomas episode, seems to imply that the postresurrection appearances are among the σημεῖα (so also Brown, *Gospel* 2:1058–59; Mahoney 268–70; see *per contra* K. H. Rengstorf, *TDNT* 7:254–55.

shiped by Thomas as a sharer in the divine nature, not simply as a mediator of divine blessing.

From this viewpoint, John 20:28 represents an advance on John 1:1. Jesus not only already *was* θεός at the beginning of creation (John 1:1). At the time when Thomas spoke and John wrote, it could be said (by implication),[98] "Jesus *is* Lord and God." According to John, the essential deity of Christ was a present fact as well as a past reality.[99] On the other hand, θεὸς ἦν ὁ λόγος in John 1:1 shows that whereas one may rightly affirm that Jesus became κύριος (in the full sense of the term) through and after the resurrection (Acts 2:36; Phil. 2:9–11),[100] the same cannot be said concerning Jesus as θεός. That is, before his resurrection Jesus was κύριος *de iure* but θεός *de facto*; after his resurrection, he was both θεός and κύριος *de facto*.

That Thomas's cry was not an extravagant acclamation, spoken in a moment of spiritual exaltation when his exuberance exceeded his theological sense, is apparent from two facts. First, the evangelist records no rebuke of Jesus to Thomas for his worship. Jesus' silence is tantamount to consent,[101] for as monotheists Jews considered the human acceptance of worship as blasphemous.[102] Thomas was not guilty of worshiping the creature over the Creator (cf. Rom. 1:25).[103] Indeed, Jesus' word to Thomas—πεπίστευκας (John 20:29a; cf. γίνου . . . πιστός in v. 27)[104]—implies the acceptance of his confession,[105] which is then indirectly commended to others (v. 29b).[106] Second, John has endorsed Thomas's confession as his own by making it his final and climactic christological affirmation before his statement of purpose, verse 31. The author found in Thomas's

98. See above, §C.2.a.

99. On this point, see further below, chapter XIII §H.

100. The name κύριος that Jesus received from the Father at his resurrection-exaltation was not only an appellation but also signified an office or rank (ὄνομα = שׁם) which had not been his previously, except *de iure*, viz., the exercise of the function of κυριότης (lordship) in the spiritual sphere, cosmic dominion over all sentient beings. See further, Martin 249–83.

101. Cf. Godet, *John* 2:425, who rightly observes that Thomas believes not merely in the fact of the resurrection but in the divinity of Jesus.

102. Note the comment of Josephus on the failure of Herod Agrippa I to repudiate the adulation of sycophants when they reverenced him "as superior to mortal nature": "The king did not rebuke them nor did he reject their flattery as impious" (*Ant.* 19:345). With this compare the reproof that Paul and Barnabas gave to the people of Lystra when they attempted to offer sacrifice to them (Acts 14:8–18) and the angelic remonstrance ("worship God!") delivered to John when he "fell down at his feet to worship him" (Rev. 19:9–10). See further Bauckham, "Worship" 322–31, 335.

103. Cf. Athanasius, *Orat. c. Ar.* 2:23–24 (= *PG* 26:196–97).

104. Verse 28 marks the cessation of Thomas's disbelief in the testimony of others and in Jesus himself as risen, plus the fulfillment of γίνου . . . πιστός (v. 27).

105. Warfield therefore finds in John 20:28 "an item of self-testimony on our Lord's part to His Godhead" (*Lord* 182).

106. In John 1:50 there is a similar implicit commendation by Jesus of a confession of faith (John 1:49; and note πιστεύεις in 1:50).

cry a convenient means by which he might bring into sharp focus at the end of his Gospel, as at the beginning (John 1:1, 18), the ultimate implications of his portrait of Jesus.[107]

D. The Literary Issue

It has been argued that John 20:28 forms the climax and pivot in the Thomas episode. But what role does this episode play in the whole Gospel? What value did the evangelist place on Thomas's confession as a vehicle for his own christological thought?

Not only the position of the Thomas story as the last of the four resurrection pericopes in John 20 but also its content suggests that it is climactic within the chapter. The reader is expectant. It was the second time that the disciples had met behind locked doors "in the house," the second time that Jesus "came and stood among them" and pronounced the blessing, "Peace be with you." The disciples were meeting a week after the resurrection had occurred, presumably to review together their individual appraisal of the Easter events and because their experience a week earlier had led them to expect a special blessing from the Lord on the first day of the week. But if a dominical commissioning (v. 21b) and an insufflation of the Spirit (vv. 22–23) had marked the first appearance of Jesus, what would mark the second appearance? The author answers: the recognition by Thomas of the deity of Christ (v. 28) and the delivery of the last and greatest beatitude (v. 29).

A second indication of the climactic function of verses 24–29 in John 20 is found in a special use of κύριος. The designation of Jesus as ὁ κύριος is rare in John 1–19 (only four uses),[108] although κύριε (of Jesus) is common,[109] whereas in John 20 some six examples of ὁ κύριος occur.[110] Mary Magdalene uses ὁ κύριός μου in 20:13 to describe her deceased Master but in 20:28 Thomas uses the same phrase in addressing his risen Lord. This delicate but crucial distinction in the import of the phrase ὁ κύριός μου (which occurs nowhere else in the Gospel) illustrates the movement of the chapter toward its climax, the personal acknowledgment of a personal, resurrected Lord.

107. The word of the centurion, "Truly this man was the Son of God" (Mark 15:39), represents a similar climax within Mark's Gospel, having the evangelist's endorsement as a fitting confession. See appendix I n. 56.

108. John 6:23 (but some Western witnesses omit); 11:2; 13:13–14 (4:1 probably should read Ἰησοῦς not κύριος).

109. Either in the sense "sir" (John 4:11, 15, 19, 49; 5:7; 9:36; 12:21) or "Lord" (John 6:34, 68; 9:38; 11:3, 12, 21, 27, 32, 34, 39; 13:6, 9, 25, 36, 37; 14:5, 8, 22).

110. John 20:2, 13, 18, 20, 25, 28; cf. 21:7, 12. Κύριε means "sir" in John 20:15, but "Lord" in John 21:15, 16, 17, 20, 21.

Standing at the end of John 20 immediately before the author's statement of the purpose of his Gospel (vv. 30–31), the narrative about Thomas might naturally be thought to represent the climax of the whole Gospel as well, were it not for the following chapter that also deals with certain resurrection appearances of Jesus.

Many scholars are convinced, however, that regardless of whoever authored and added chapter 21, chapter 20 originally stood as the conclusion of the Gospel,[111] the evangelist envisaging no sequel at the time chapters 1–20 were written.[112] There are several compelling reasons for this view.[113] (1) Verse 28 forms a christological climax to the whole Gospel, reflecting 1:1. (2) Verse 29 creates a link between the text of the Gospel and the readership that would naturally be found at the close of the Gospel. Would a further recitation of appearances (chap. 21) be expected to follow the recorded blessing on those who believe without seeing (20:29)? (3) Verses 30–31 review the purpose of the recorded signs of "this book," a statement suitable for the conclusion of the Gospel. (4) Chapter 20 as a whole is a self-contained literary unit that needs no supplement.

But whether one adopts this prevailing view or argues that the evangelist himself added chapter 21 as an integral part of the Gospel or as an Epilogue that balances the Prologue (1:1–18),[114] one may justifiably conclude that he regarded the words of Thomas addressed to Jesus as the final pinnacle of his Gospel and the zenith of his Christology.

Such a conclusion is confirmed by the author's strategic placement in his Gospel of those verses in which Christ is designated as θεός. Not only the Prologue, but the Gospel as a whole, is enclosed by these literary "bookends." The Prologue ends (1:18) as it begins (1:1), and the Gospel ends (20:28) as it begins (1:1), with an assertion of the deity of Jesus.[115] We move from θεός (1:1) to μονογενὴς θεός (1:18) to ὁ θεός μου (20:28); from Jesus Christ as a participant in the divine essence to his being "the only Son, who fully shares the Divine nature" to his being the God who is worshiped by believers; from the preexistent Logos who eternally enjoyed active communion with the Father (1:1a–b) to the incarnate Son who always resides in the Father's heart and on earth revealed him (1:18) to the resurrected Lord who may be rightfully hailed by his devotee as "my God." That is, for

111. But the Gospel probably never circulated without chapter 21, for no extant manuscript omits chapter 21 and 𝔓[66] (which may be dated ca. 200) contains 20:25–21:9.

112. For a contrary view, see Lagrange, *Jean* 520 (John 20:30–31, originally the concluding verses of the Gospel, at first followed 21:23 but was displaced to its present position through the addition of 21:24–25 by John's disciples), and, at greater length, Vaganay (who develops Lagrange's theory but regards John 21:24 as authentic); also Fortna 7 n. 1, 87–88.

113. These are adapted from Mahoney 15–16.

114. See the judicious discussion of Carson, *John* 665–68.

115. It is these two examples of *inclusio* that prevent the dismissal of John 1:1 and 20:28 as merely "isolated instances" within Johannine Christology (the view of Granbery 105).

John, Jesus is appropriately designated θεός in his preexistent, incarnate, and postresurrection states.[116] Of all the titles used of Jesus in the Fourth Gospel, θεός would therefore seem to represent the culmination.[117]

E. Conclusion

One week after his resurrection, and because of a resurrection appearance, Jesus was adoringly addressed by Thomas with the exclamation, "My Lord and my God!," a confessional invocation that not only marks the climax (along with the accompanying beatitude) of the Thomas pericope and John 20, but also forms the culmination of the entire Gospel. Just as Israel had honored Yahweh as κύριος ὁ θεὸς ἡμῶν (e.g., Ps. 98:8 LXX [Engl. 99:8]) and Christians honored the Father as ὁ κύριος καὶ ὁ θεὸς ἡμῶν (Rev. 4:11), so now people were to "honor the Son, even as they honor the Father" (John 5:23), by addressing him with the words ὁ κύριός μου καὶ ὁ θεός μου. In uttering this confessional cry Thomas recognized the lordship of Jesus in the physical and spiritual realms as well as over his own life (ὁ κύριός μου) and the essential oneness of Jesus with the Father which made his worship of Jesus legitimate (ὁ θεός μου). As used in this verse, κύριος and θεός are titles, not proper names, the first implying and the second explicitly affirming the substantial deity of the risen Jesus.

116. Cf. Mastin, "Christology" 42–43; Carson, *Responsibility* 147.

117. So also Cullmann, *Christology* 308. But H. E. W. Turner (28) goes further: "Even the words of Thomas draw out the implications of the language of Phil. 2:6; Tit. 2:13 and possibly Rom. 9:5."

V

The Church of God (Acts 20:28)

Προσέχετε ἑαυτοῖς καὶ παντὶ τῷ ποιμνίῳ, ἐν ᾧ ὑμᾶς τὸ πνεῦμα τὸ ἅγιον ἔθετο ἐπισκόπους ποιμαίνειν τὴν ἐκκλησίαν τοῦ θεοῦ, ἣν περιεποιήσατο διὰ τοῦ αἵματος τοῦ ἰδίου.

A. Paul's Milesian Speech (Acts 20:18–35)

Acts 20:3–21:6 narrates Paul's journey to Judea in the company of the delegates of the Gentile churches (Acts 20:4; cf. 1 Cor. 16:3) for the purpose of delivering the collection for "the poor among the saints at Jerusalem" (Rom. 15:26). Because he was eager to be in Jerusalem with these Gentile believers on the day of Pentecost, the day on which the firstfruits of the wheat harvest were offered to God (Exod. 34:22; Num. 28:26; cf. Rom. 15:16), Paul chose to sail to Jerusalem without a further visit to Ephesus (Acts 20:16). But while his ship was harbored at Miletus for several days, some thirty miles from Ephesus, he summoned the Ephesian elders (Acts 20:17) and delivered to them the "farewell speech"[1] that Luke records in abbreviated form in Acts 20:18–35,[2] the only Pauline speech in Acts that is directed to a Christian audience.

Because the speech contains both distinctively Lucan and distinctively Pauline vocabulary,[3] there has always been scholarly disagreement as to whether the speech witnesses primarily to Pauline theology (e.g., Franklin 66, 199 n. 33) or to Lucan theology (e.g., Lambrecht 319–28). The former view is often associated with the assumption that the Lucan précis of the speech is historically reliable; the latter, with the assumption that to a considerable extent the speech is a free Lucan composition. It would seem that the theory that does greatest justice to both the Pauline characteristics[4] and the Lucan language, motifs, and style[5] is that Luke is summarizing in his own words an actual Pauline speech.[6] Specific indications that Luke is reporting this Milesian address accurately include the following. (1) Acts

1. On the literary genre of the "farewell discourse" in the OT, late Judaism, and the NT, see Munck, "Discours"; and H. J. Michel 35–72.

2. For a survey of scholarly views on this Pauline speech, see Lambrecht 308–14; Watson 184–91; and esp. H. J. Michel 23–34.

3. See the comprehensive lists and general NT statistics for the words involved found in Aejmelaeus 90–91.

4. See Cadbury in *BC* 5:412–13; Aejmelaeus 91 (who identifies 14 Pauline words). But for the view that 20:28 is "Lucan deuteropaulinism," see Barrett, "Elders" 113–15.

5. See H. J. Michel 28–33; Aejmelaeus 90–91 (who lists 39 Lucan words). Dupont cites (*Discours* 29) the earlier statistics of Bethge (119–20): 34 Lucan features, 43 traits that are both Lucan and Pauline, and 12 Pauline characteristics. Commenting on these data, Dupont remarks that "d'une façon générale, le style et le vocabulaire sont ceux de Luc, mais on ne peut nier que la rédaction ait subi l'influence de Paul" (*Discours* 29).

6. For a general defense of this position, see Hemer, *Acts* 418–27, esp. 425–26.

21:1 (cf. 20:15) implies that the author of the "we-passages" (Luke) was present with Paul and the Ephesian elders at Miletus. If so, Luke was doubtless fully aware of the solemnity and strategic importance of the occasion (cf. Acts 20:25, 29–30, 38), so that it would be no surprise if he had taken notes of Paul's address, possibly in shorthand.[7] (2) The parallels between this speech and the Pauline Epistles, especially the later ones, are more remarkable and striking than is the case with any other Pauline speech in Acts.[8] This fact gains in significance when we remember that the Book of Acts betrays no knowledge of the Pauline Epistles as such, even where such firsthand information would have supplemented Luke's other sources.

Many diverse proposals have been made concerning the structure of the speech.[9] One of the simplest and most attractive outlines is prompted by the thrice-repeated νῦν:[10]

vv. 18b–21	ὑμεῖς ἐπίστασθε	the past—Paul's ministry in Ephesus
vv. 22–24	καὶ νῦν ἰδού	the present—plans regarding Jerusalem
vv. 25–31	καὶ νῦν ἰδού	the future—Paul's expected death and dangers confronting the church
vv. 32–35	καὶ τὰ νῦν	blessing (32), apology (33–34), exhortation (35)

B. Textual Issues

In verses 25–31 Paul issues his challenge to the Ephesian elders to be alert (γρηγορεῖτε, v. 31) to their responsibilities as guardians of the flock. He reinforces his challenge by informing them that this would be the last time they saw him (v. 25; cf. v. 38), by recalling his own devoted attention to pastoral tasks at Ephesus (vv. 25–27, 31), by warning them of dangers that would confront the church from outside and from within (vv. 29–30), and preeminently by reminding them of their divine appointment to shepherd a church that had been acquired by divine blood (v. 28). But did Paul (or Luke) describe the church as τὴν ἐκκλησίαν τοῦ θεοῦ or as τὴν ἐκκλησίαν τοῦ κυρίου, and was the acquisition διὰ τοῦ αἵματος τοῦ ἰδίου or διὰ τοῦ ἰδίου αἵματος? These are the two textual issues in Acts 20:28.

7. Similarly Bruce, "Speeches" 63. On the use of shorthand in the first century A.D., see Bahr 471–75.

8. Cf. Cadbury in *BC* 5:412; Hemer, "Speeches" 84–85; and esp. Chase 234–88. This argument is not invalidated, as Cadbury suggests (*BC* 5:413), by the similarities he notes (*BC* 5:415) between the Milesian speech and 1 Peter 2:25 and 5:2, for these similarities relate to the common shepherding motif.

9. See the survey in Dupont, *Discours* 21–26 and Lambrecht 314–18. For the view that the speech is structured in accordance with Greco-Roman conventions of epideictic rhetoric, see Watson 191–208.

10. Similarly Haenchen, *Acts* 595; Bauernfeind 238.

1. θεοῦ or κυρίου?

There are, in fact, not two but more than nine variant readings following τὴν ἐκκλησίαν. All but two of these lack weighty manuscript support and arose *either* as a conflation of the two earliest readings (viz., θεοῦ and κυρίου) with the copula καί (thus κυρίου καὶ θεοῦ and θεοῦ καὶ κυρίου and similar variations) or without καί (thus κυρίου θεοῦ and κυρίου τοῦ θεοῦ and similar variations), *or* as an expansion or explanation of κυρίου (thus κυρίου Ἰησοῦ and Ἰησοῦ Χριστοῦ and Χριστοῦ).

It is impossible to decide between the two main variants on the basis of external evidence, for θεοῦ has proto-Alexandrian (ℵ B), later Alexandrian (104), and Western (614 vg) support, just as κυρίου has proto-Alexandrian (𝔓^{74} A), later Alexandrian (C* Ψ 33), and Western (D E 1739 syr^{hmg} Irenaeus) witnesses in its favor. With regard to paleography, the two readings differ only by a single letter: Θ̄Υ and K̄Υ. A final choice between the two readings will therefore rest largely on internal evidence, to which we now turn.

First, transcriptional probabilities. Κυρίου can lay claim to being the original reading on the principle *difficilior lectio potior*, for nowhere else does the NT speak of ἡ ἐκκλησία τοῦ κυρίου, the nearest parallel being αἱ ἐκκλησίαι πᾶσαι τοῦ Χριστοῦ (Rom. 16:16; cf. Ropes, *BC* 3:98). On the other hand, θεοῦ is also a difficult reading, for if διὰ τοῦ αἵματος τοῦ ἰδίου (or the variant) is taken to mean "through his own blood," the concept of "the blood of God" arises from the text, a concept that is unparalleled in the NT and would have been potentially offensive to the sensibilities of a scribe whose theological understanding was shaped more by the NT than by Ignatius and others.[11] Nor can a clear decision in favor of one reading or the other be reached by considering the derivation of variants. Scribes could easily have substituted θεοῦ for κυρίου, for the expression ἡ ἐκκλησία τοῦ θεοῦ is a common Pauline phrase (eleven uses)[12] and copyists sometimes unconsciously replaced an unfamiliar expression (such as ἡ ἐκκλησία τοῦ κυρίου) by a familiar.[13] A scribe may have been unaware

11. One cannot say that this concept was *certain* to be offensive, for language such as αἷμα θεοῦ or παθήματα θεοῦ was not uncommon in the second and third centuries, although it was repudiated even by the orthodox in subsequent centuries (see the detailed discussion in Abbot, "Reading" 320–26; Lightfoot i 2:14–15). For the explicit phrase "the blood of God" (= Jesus), see Ignatius, *Eph.* 1:1 (ἀναζωπυρήσαντες ἐν αἵματι θεοῦ); Tertullian, *ad Uxor.* 2:3 (*sumus pretio empti: et quali pretio? sanguine Dei*); Clement of Alexandria, *Quis dives salvetur* 34 (αἵματι θεοῦ παιδός).

12. 1 Cor. 1:2; 10:32; 11:16, 22; 15:9; 2 Cor. 1:1; Gal. 1:13; 1 Thess. 2:14; 2 Thess. 1:4; 1 Tim. 3:5, 15.

13. Cf. Abbot, "Reading" 315–17, who suggests, following Tregelles, that the similarity between 1 Pet. 5:2 (ποιμάνατε τὸ ἐν ὑμῖν ποίμνιον τοῦ θεοῦ, ἐπισκοποῦντες [omitted by ℵ B, "and perhaps derived from ἐπισκόπους in Acts xx.28"]) and the present passage might have facilitated the change to θεοῦ. Alford (2:231) argues that a *deliberate* alteration from κυρίου to θεοῦ is improbable, since Codex Vaticanus (B), as representative of the great manuscripts, shows no bias for θεός where other manuscripts read κύριος, and sometimes has κύριος or Χριστός (as do other major uncials) where other manuscripts have θεός.

that the idea of "the blood of God" could be inferred from the text as a result of the substitution or he may have found the idea perfectly orthodox and inoffensive. Alternatively, if θεοῦ was original, the change to κυρίου might have been occasioned by LXX usage of the phrase (ἡ) ἐκκλησία (τοῦ) κυρίου (seven uses)[14] in the light of Jesus' own teaching about his church (e.g., Matt. 16:18) and his function as the Good Shepherd (e.g., John 10:11, 14–16; 21:15–17), by a desire to introduce into verses 27–28 a trinitarian reference (viz., God, v. 27; the Holy Spirit, the Lord, v. 28), or possibly by the desire of an orthodox scribe to avoid having to clear Paul or Luke of a charge of being patripassian.[15] With regard to a possible accidental error in transcription, the choice between these two variants must once again remain inconclusive, for writing ΘΥ instead of ΚΥ and ΚΥ instead of ΘΥ were both common scribal errors.

We may now turn to intrinsic probabilities. If one considers Paul's frequent use of the expression ἡ ἐκκλησία τοῦ θεοῦ (eleven times), a use which H. Alford claims "is in a manner *precisely similar to this*,—as the *consummation of a climax*, or in a position of peculiar solemnity" (2:231),[16] and the absence of the expression ἡ ἐκκλησία τοῦ κυρίου from the NT, one finds support for the originality of θεοῦ. This is further strengthened by tracing the combination of ποιμαίνειν τὴν ἐκκλησίαν τοῦ θεοῦ and ἣν περιεποιήσατο in 20:28 to Psalm 73:1–2a (LXX [Engl. 74:1–2a]), which reads, Ἵνα τί ἀπώσω, ὁ θεός, εἰς τέλος, ὠργίσθη ὁ θυμός σου ἐπὶ πρόβατα νομῆς σου; μνήσθητι τῆς συναγωγῆς[17] σου, ἧς ἐκτήσω ἀπ' ἀρχῆς. If Paul (or Luke) is alluding to this psalm, it is ὁ θεός who is likely to be the "purchaser" of the church.[18]

So then, although the external evidence is evenly balanced and a consideration of transcriptional probabilities is indecisive, intrinsic probabilities

14. Deut. 23:2, 3, 4 *bis*, 9 [Engl. vv. 1, 2, 3 *bis*, 8]; 1 Chron. 28:8; Mic. 2:5.

15. Arguing that the reading θεοῦ was a stumbling block to Arianism but not to orthodoxy, Alford concludes that an alteration from θεοῦ to κυρίου was certain whereas a change from κυρίου to θεοῦ was uncertain and indeed unlikely (2:230–31). But this argument is almost certainly invalid, for the Arians readily applied the term θεός to Christ—albeit in an attenuated sense—so that they could speak of "the blood of God" or affirm that "God suffered through the flesh." Hence the comment of Pseudo-Athanasius (*De Incarnatione* 2:14) that "such audacious expressions (τολμήματα) are the preserve of the Arians." See further Abbot, "Reading" 313–14.

16. Alford cites 1 Cor. 10:32; 15:9; Gal. 1:13; 1 Tim. 3:5, 15 in support.

17. "The strong aversion to συναγωγή for the Chr. community may be seen from the emendation of LXX in Ac. 20:28. Ps. 74:2 has עֵדָה, LXX συναγωγή. Yet though עֵדָה is always transl. συναγωγή and never ἐκκλησία in LXX, Ac. 20:28 uses ἐκκλησία because the ref. is to the Chr. community" (W. Schrage, *TDNT* 7:829 n. 199).

18. Similarly WH 2: appendix 99.

tip the scales in favor of the originality of θεοῦ, a judgment supported by the majority of textual critics,[19] commentators,[20] and English versions,[21] although the reading κυρίου has not been without its defenders.[22]

2. *τοῦ αἵματος τοῦ ἰδίου or τοῦ ἰδίου αἵματος?*

With regard to this second textual issue in Acts 20:28, there is far less uncertainty. Whereas τοῦ αἵματος τοῦ ἰδίου has proto-Alexandrian (𝔓^{74} ℵ B), later Alexandrian (A C Ψ 33 326 945), and Western (D E 1739) support, τοῦ ἰδίου αἵματος is a largely Byzantine variant (P 049 056 0142 and most minuscules). It is also significant, as Metzger (*Commentary* 482) notes, that many of the Byzantine witnesses (e.g., P 049 2127 2492) that have the clearly secondary conflation κυρίου καὶ θεοῦ in the preceding variant, support τοῦ ἰδίου αἵματος here.

If, on the basis of this compelling external evidence, we prefer τοῦ αἵματος τοῦ ἰδίου as original, we may account for the rise of the variant in one of two ways. Construing ἰδίου as an adjective ("his own blood"), a scribe may have been influenced to write τοῦ ἰδίου αἵματος by the much more common position for this adjective when it is used attributively.[23] Alternatively, but less probably, once the title ὁ ἴδιος ("his [= God's] own [Son]")[24] ceased to be commonly used of Jesus,[25] τοῦ ἰδίου would naturally be construed as adjectival rather than substantival[26] and would assume the normal position of ἴδιος as an attributive adjective (cf. διὰ τοῦ ἰδίου αἵματος in Heb. 9:12; 13:12).

19. WH 1:564, 575; 2: appendix 98; Metzger, *Text* 234–36; UBS[1,2,3] (see Metzger, *Commentary* 480–81); NA[26] (and at an earlier time Vogels, Merk, and Bover—see DeVine 395).

20. Alford 2:230–31 (reversing a preference for κυρίου in his first and second editions); Jacquier 614; K. Lake and H. J. Cadbury, *BC* 4:261; DeVine 395–97; Bruce, *Acts* 434; Dupont, *Discours* 150–51; R. P. C. Hanson 205; Schmeichel 504; E. Stauffer, *TDNT* 3:101 and n. 230; 106 and n. 273; K. L. Schmidt, *TDNT* 3:504–5, 507.

21. RV, TCNT, Weymouth, Goodspeed, Berkeley, NASB, GNB, JB, Barclay, NAB[1], NIV, NJB, NAB[2], Cassirer, NRSV (reversing the RSV [1946, 1952] preference for κυρίου).

22. Among the textual critics one finds Ropes, *BC* 3:198; Clark 134 (and Lachmann, Tischendorf, Tregelles, and von Soden at an earlier time—for details, see DeVine 392–93). The most detailed defense is that of Abbot, "Reading" 310–20; Abbot, "Construction" 115–16; see also Farrar, "Readings" 377–82. English versions preferring κυρίου include ASV, Moffatt, RSV (until 1972), NEB ("by a majority vote," Tasker 433), and REB.

23. As an attributive adjective ἴδιος is found (apart from Acts 20:28) in the word order (article–) ἴδιος–substantive 68 times in the NT, 7 times in the order (article–)substantive–ἴδιος, and only 4 times (3 in the Fourth Gospel, once at Acts 1:25) in the order article–substantive–article–ἴδιος.

24. See the discussion of ὁ ἴδιος below, §C.4.

25. Harnack claims that "this antique ὁ ἴδιος, which practically coincides with ὁ ἀγαπητός, and like ὁ παῖς is of Messianic significance, soon fell out of use" (*Date* 107).

26. Cf. Lake and Cadbury in *BC* 4:261.

To express a preference for the readings θεοῦ and τοῦ αἵματος τοῦ ἰδίου[27] is not to decide without further discussion that θεός is here a christological appellation, for τοῦ θεοῦ may not refer to Jesus and τοῦ ἰδίου may not be adjectival ("his own blood").

C. Translational Problems

There are four ways of translating or understanding the text as established:[28] ποιμαίνειν τὴν ἐκκλησίαν τοῦ θεοῦ, ἣν περιεποιήσατο διὰ τοῦ αἵματος τοῦ ἰδίου.[29]

1. "To shepherd the church of God (= Jesus) which he acquired with his own blood"

There can be no objection (on broad *a priori* grounds) to understanding the verse to refer to Jesus,[30] for elsewhere the NT refers to Jesus as θεός and depicts him as acquiring the church through his death.[31] But it is the startling collocation of θεός and αἷμα that prompts a legitimate objection to this view. Although the concepts of αἷμα θεοῦ and παθήματα θεοῦ are common fare in the second and third centuries,[32] nothing resembling these expressions is found in the first century.[33] New Testament descriptions of Christ's redemptive death as well as of his life always avoid blending unqualified affirmations of his deity (such as θεός) with terms that can be related only to his humanness (such as αἷμα). Nowhere, for instance, do we read of "the cross of God" (cf. John 19:25; Gal. 6:14) or that at Golgotha "they crucified God" (cf. John 19:18) or that "God died and rose

27. Very few scholars, whether textual critics or commentators, support the reading τοῦ ἰδίου αἵματος (preferred by the NEB translators "by a majority vote," Tasker 433). Clark, who prefers Κυρίου, nevertheless reads τοῦ αἵματος τοῦ ἰδίου (134). Even Scrivener, who expresses the opinion that the Textus Receptus (θεοῦ, . . . τοῦ ἰδίου αἵματος) "is pretty sure to be correct" (374), later notes that "it is right to mention that, in the place of τοῦ ἰδίου αἵματος, the more emphatic form τοῦ αἵματος τοῦ ἰδίου ought to be adopted" (377, where also he objects to the rendering "the blood of his own").

28. For a brief history of the interpretation of Acts 20:28, see DeVine 398–404.

29. If κυρίου be preferred, the sense will be "the Lord (Jesus) . . . through his own blood" (similarly ASV, Moffatt, RSV [until 1972], NEB, REB); "the Lord (= Yahweh) . . . through his Own (Son)"; or "the church of the Lord (= Yahweh) which he (Jesus) obtained through his own blood."

30. This understanding of the verse is found in Calvin, *Acts* 184; Alexander 250; Lumby 279–80; Liddon, *Divinity* 437 and n. k; Rackham 392–93; Warfield, *Lord* 70, 218; Jacquier 614–15; Robertson, *Pictures* 3:353; Robertson, "Article" 187–88; Lebreton, *History* 371; Stauffer 283 n. 349; E. Stauffer, *TDNT* 3:106 and n. 273; Faccio 118–19; DeVine 404; Renié 282–83; Bonsirven, *Theology* 229; N. Turner, *Insights* 14–15; Stählin 270; R. N. Longenecker, "Acts" 513.

31. Titus 2:14; 1 Pet. 1:18–19; 2:9; Heb. 13:12; Rev. 1:5–6.

32. See above, n. 11 and esp. Abbot, "Reading" 320–26.

33. In 1 Clement (ca. 96) θεός denotes only the Father and αἷμα is only that of Christ (7:4; 21:6; 49:6) although it is "precious to God his Father" (7:4) (Lightfoot I 2:15).

again" (cf. 1 Thess. 4:14). On the other hand, early in the second century Ignatius can write with unembarrassed directness of "the blood of God (αἵματι θεοῦ)" (*Eph.* 1:1) and "the passion of my God (τοῦ πάθους τοῦ θεοῦ μου)" (*Rom.* 6:3).[34]

2. *"To shepherd the church of God (the Father) which he acquired with his own blood"*

On another view the blood shed was not actually that of the Father, but since it was the blood of his dearly loved Son (Rom. 8:32), it was in effect his own or as if it were his own. W. de Boor expresses it this way: "Father and Son are so united in intimacy and nature that the blood of the Son is also the heart blood (*Herzblut*) of the Father. And conversely God can shed his 'blood' only in the incarnate Son" (*Apostelgeschichte* 376). J. V. Bartlet paraphrases his rendering "the blood that was His own" with the words "as being that of His Messiah . . . or Son" (330–31).[35] He cites as a parallel Romans 5:8: "God commends his own love (τὴν ἑαυτοῦ ἀγάπην) to us, in that . . . Christ died for us" (331). The Achilles' heel of this interpretation is the presence of (τοῦ) ἰδίου, which implies that the αἷμα is the actual possession, the personal property, of the subject of περιεποιήσατο. In Romans 5:8 the love mentioned is actually that of God, not Christ, just as the death is actually that of Christ, not God. In Acts 20:28 αἷμα signifies real blood (not "heart blood"), which by metonymy stands for death, while ἴδιος denotes real and not merely pregnant possession.

3. *"To shepherd the church of God (the Father) which he (Christ) obtained through his own blood"*

J. Dupont argues that in the latter clause of verse 28 "one may recognize a sliding (*glissement*) in thought: the action of the Father (= 'God')

34. When I argue that the concept of αἷμα θεοῦ is anachronistic in the first century so far as extant records indicate, this is not because such a concept grazes the edge of patripassianism; only if θεοῦ in this phrase were misinterpreted to refer to the Father rather than Christ would there be danger of that doctrinal deviation. Rather, it is because the NT stops short of predicating human attributes or characteristics of Christ *as God* (such as "the blood of God") and divine attributes or characteristics of Christ *as man* (such as "the omnipotence of Jesus of Nazareth"). But it was inevitable that, as the church later grappled with the implications of the "hypostatic union" of the human and divine natures in Christ, there should arise some such doctrine as *communicatio idiomatum* (κοινωνία ἰδιωμάτων, "sharing of attributes") as a means of safeguarding both the reality of Christ's humanity and deity and the unity of his person. All this makes one uneasy with the reasoning of Renié (282) regarding Acts 20:28: "The duality of nature in Jesus is clearly indicated"—since Jesus is both God and man, one may speak of the "blood of God." Like Calvin (*Acts* 184), Renié refers to the doctrine of *communicatio idiomatum* (282–83).

35. The same view was expressed earlier by Hort ("on the supposition that the text is incorrupt"): "'Through the blood that was His own,' *i.e.* as being His Son's" (in WH 2: appendix 99).

and the action of the Son are so intimately associated and unified . . . that you pass over from one to the other without any mark of transition."[36] Dupont appeals to a parallel *glissement* in Romans 8:31–39 where Paul moves imperceptibly from the love of Christ (8:35) to the love of God displayed in Christ (8:39). An alternative explanation of the change of subject at περιεποιήσατο finds in the relative clause ἣν κτλ. a traditional formula in which Christ actually was the subject of the verb and which was coalesced with the common expression ἡ ἐκκλησία τοῦ θεοῦ without any indication of the change of subject.[37] Neither of these proposals can be pronounced impossible, although the latter explanation presupposes that the speech is a mosaic of traditional elements redacted by Luke. It is conceivable that the mention of "shepherding" (ποιμαίνειν) would have prompted the image of Jesus as the Good Shepherd surrendering his life for his sheep (cf. John 10:11, 14) and thereby procuring "the church of God." But the fact remains that there is no explicit change of subject and God the Father may be said to have "acquired" the church (e.g., Eph. 1:4–6; 1 Pet. 2:9–10).

4. *"To shepherd the church of God (the Father) which he obtained with the blood of his own Son/one"*

It was F. J. A. Hort who proposed that "it is by no means impossible that ΥΙΟΥ dropped out after ΤΟΥΙΔΙΟΥ [by haplography] at some very early transcription affecting all existing documents. Its insertion leaves the whole passage free from difficulty of any kind" (WH 2: appendix 99–100).[38] But one does not need to have recourse to this conjectural emendation to arrive at the meaning "his own Son";[39] ὁ ἴδιος may be regarded simply as an abbreviation of ὁ ἴδιος υἱός (cf. Rom. 8:32).[40] Among scholars who read θεοῦ and τοῦ αἵματος τοῦ ἰδίου it has become common to regard ὁ ἴδιος as substantival, and not simply as standing for ὁ ἴδιος υἱός but as a christological title, either "his Own",[41] "one who was his

36. In Cerfaux and Dupont 178 n. b; cf. NJB, p. 1835 n. r. But subsequently (in 1962) Dupont rendered διὰ τοῦ αἵματος τοῦ ἰδίου by "par le sang de son propre Fils" (*Discours* 159; similarly 182, 197).

37. Roloff 306; similarly Conzelmann 175 (who is followed by R. P. C. Hanson 205); Aejmelaeus 133.

38. Hort is followed, *inter alios*, by Chase 284; H J. Michel 24–25.

39. This is the rendering found in GNB, NJB, NRSV, and Bruce, *Acts (NIC)* 391 and n. 56; Haenchen, *Acts* 589; Munck, *Acts* 202, 204; Lohfink 89, 91; Prast 127–28; G. Schneider 292, 297.

40. Harnack, *Date* 107. In John 1:18 μονογενής may stand for (ὁ) μονογενὴς υἱός; see chapter III §C.2.

41. RSV mg; Bengel 2:689; Lake and Cadbury, *BC* 4:262 (as a possibility; ὁ ἴδιος = "his Chosen one," *BC* 4:261), but Cadbury believed that the titular ὁ ἴδιος is not lexicographically justified ("Titles" 372); R. R. Williams, *Acts* 142; C. S. C. Williams 234; Marshall, *Acts* 334; Zehnle 440; Watson 202 n. 2.

Own,"[42] or "his own One."[43] Such a substantive usage has been dismissed as "pure fantasy" (Jacquier 615) or "mere supposition" (Bauernfeind 239), but support for this sense of ὁ ἴδιος may be found in three directions.

First, there are fifteen substantival uses of ἴδιος in the NT: τὸ ἴδιον (once), τὰ ἴδια (nine times), and οἱ ἴδιοι (five times), the latter expression describing compatriots (John 1:11b), disciples (John 13:1), fellow believers (Acts 4:23; 24:23), and relatives (1 Tim. 5:8). Second, although the singular ὁ ἴδιος is not found elsewhere in the NT, it is used in the papyri as a term of endearment and close relationship; a letter may be addressed to so-and-so τῷ ἰδίῳ.[44] Third, the NT witnesses to several parallel coinages in which a substantival adjective or participle has become a christological title: ὁ δίκαιος, "the Righteous One" (RSV: Acts 3:14; 7:52; 22:14; cf. 1 Pet. 3:18; 1 John 2:1, 29; 3:7); ὁ ἀγαπητός (μου), "my Beloved" (NEB: Matt. 3:17; 12:18; 17:5; 2 Pet. 1:17);[45] ὁ ἠγαπημένος, "the Beloved" (Eph. 1:6 RSV); ὁ ἐκλελεγμένος, "my Chosen" (Luke 9:35 NEB); ὁ ἐκλεκτός, "his Chosen One" (Luke 23:35 RSV).

If, then, ὁ ἴδιος is here a christological title, it carries the connotation of uniqueness ("only") and endearment ("dearly loved") associated with the Greek term μονογενής and the Hebrew term יחיד.[46]

Not without reason does J. Dupont identify verse 28 as "the center of the speech and its culminating point" (*Discours* 156). Paul here emphasizes the high privilege and onerous responsibility of the pastoral office. The congregation which the Ephesian elders were to shepherd[47] as the Spirit's appointees[48] was nothing other than the church of God[49] which he

42. Moulton, *Prolegomena* 90; Moulton, "Notes" 277. In what he terms "a possible variant understanding" (513), Schmeichel (510) takes ὁ ἴδιος to be a veiled reference to Paul himself (507–14): "The blood of one who was His [= God's] own" is "a summary reference to the review of Paul's ministry just completed (vss. 18–27)." According to Schmeichel (511) the emphasis in 20:28c is theocentric, apologetic, and biographical (Luke knew Paul had been martyred): God obtained the churches of Asia for himself by the toil and martyrdom of someone who was his own chosen instrument (Acts 9:15).

43. Barclay ("His own One"); Lake in *BC* 5:220; Bruce, *Acts* 434 ("his own one"); Bruce, *Acts (NIC)* 391 n. 56 ("His own one"); Neil 215 ("his Own One"); Marshall, *Luke* 173 ("His own One"); Marshall, "Redemption" 161.

44. Moulton, *Prolegomena* 90; Moulton, "Notes" 277; cf. MM 298.

45. On ὁ ἀγαπητός as a pre-Christian messianic title, see J. A. Robinson, *HDB* 2:501.

46. Cf. Bruce, *Acts* 434; Bruce, "Speeches" 63 ("by the blood of his Beloved"). It is also significant that τοῦ ἰδίου υἱοῦ in Rom. 8:32 alludes to Gen. 22:16 where the LXX reads τοῦ ἀγαπητοῦ . . . υἱοῦ (Metzger, *Text* 236).

47. "Shepherding" (ποιμαίνειν) involves protection (v. 29) and superintendence (ἐπισκόπους) as well as feeding (cf. John 21:15–17; 1 Pet. 2:25; 5:2).

48. One may equate the Spirit's appointment of these elders to guardianship with the bestowal of qualifications for ministry, especially spiritual gifts (cf. 1 Cor. 12:7–11), or with prophetic utterances that designated them as guardians (cf. Acts 13:2, 4; 1 Tim. 4:14; cf. Bruce, *Acts* 433). D. J. Williams goes a step further: "On the basis of 6:3ff. and 14:23 we may suppose that they had been formally appointed by the laying on of hands with prayer" (355).

49. Ἡ ἐκκλησία τοῦ θεοῦ here need not be restricted to the church of Ephesus, as Cerfaux (*Church* 114 n. 39), O'Toole (110), and Giles (141 n. 11) argue, or to the churches of Asia, as Schmeichel (511) proposes. The referent may be first the church of Ephesus, then the universal church (cf. Jacquier 614): God's "acquisition" was wider than the Ephesian congregation.

acquired[50] by means of the shed blood[51] of his own dearly loved Son.[52] Eldership involves participation in a trinitarian enterprise.[53]

D. Conclusion

I have argued that the original text of Acts 20:28 read τὴν ἐκκλησίαν τοῦ θεοῦ, ἣν περιεποιήσατο διὰ τοῦ αἵματος τοῦ ἰδίου and that the most appropriate translation of these words is "the church of God which he acquired through the blood of his own one" or "the Church of God which he bought with the blood of his own Son" (NJB), with ὁ ἴδιος construed as a christological title. According to this view, ὁ θεός refers to God the Father, not Jesus Christ.[54] If, however, one follows many English versions in construing ἴδιος adjectivally ("through his own blood"), ὁ θεός could refer to Jesus and the verse could therefore allude to "the blood of God," although on this construction of ἴδιος it is more probable that θεός is God the Father and the unexpressed subject of περιεποιήσατο is Jesus. So it remains unlikely, although not impossible, that in Acts 20:28 ὁ θεός denotes Jesus.

50. Although περιποιέομαι may mean "preserve for oneself" (something already possessed), here it means "acquire/purchase for oneself" (something not yet possessed) (Lyonnet in Lyonnet and Sabourin 113–14, who translates περιεποιήσατο by "he purchased for himself," 113). Since the acquisition does not have to be regarded as a "purchase," one need not follow Renié (283) in seeing a possible allusion to a bride price (*môhar*) paid by Christ in order to espouse the church.

51. Since περιεποιήσατο is followed by διὰ τοῦ αἵματος and not ἐν τῷ αἵματι (indicating price, as in Rev. 5:9; see Robertson, *Grammar* 589) or simply τοῦ αἵματος (genitive of price, after a verb denoting purchase; see BDF §179), αἷμα (= *Kreuzestod*, H. J. Michel 88) should probably be regarded, not as "the price of acquisition" (Bruce, "Speeches" 63; cf. Morris, *Preaching* 57, 120: "price paid"; Kränke 123: *Kaufpreis*), but as the means by which the acquisition was made (so also BAGD 180a; Harnack, *Date* 109; Lyonnet in Lyonnet and Sabourin 114; Louw and Nida §57:61). Just as God had originally acquired a people to be his treasured possession through a covenant ratified by blood (Exod. 19:5–6; 24:3–8), so now he had secured for himself the church to be his distinctive people by means of the shed blood of his own Son.

52. On the question of whether Acts 20:28c is evidence of a Lucan *theologia crucis*, see H. J. Michel 88–89; Zehnle; and, for a summary of positions, Schmeichel 501–3.

53. Cf. the trinitarian reference in Acts 20:21–23.

54. If τοῦ κυρίου be read, the verse is not relevant to present considerations.

VI

God Blessed Forever (Romans 9:5)

(. . . τῶν συγγενῶν μου κατὰ σάρκα, . . .) ὧν οἱ πατέρες καὶ ἐξ ὧν ὁ Χριστὸς τὸ κατὰ σάρκα, ὁ ὢν ἐπὶ πάντων θεὸς εὐλογητὸς εἰς τοὺς αἰῶνας, ἀμήν.

A. Introduction

In the study of θεός as a christological title, Romans 9:5 holds a distinctive place. It is the one verse in the indisputably Pauline Epistles (F. C. Baur's *Hauptbriefe*: Romans, 1 and 2 Corinthians, Galatians) in which θεός may be applied to Christ, and among all the NT passages where Christ may be called θεός this verse has generated more studies devoted exclusively to its exegetical problems than has any other. During the last century or so, in addition to a detailed monograph by H. M. Faccio, there have been substantial articles on this verse alone written by T. Dwight ("Romans"), E. Abbot ("Construction" and "Discussions"), A. Durand, B. M. Metzger ("Punctuation"), and O. Kuss ("Römer"). What is more, the punctuation of this verse has come under more intense scrutiny than has any other NT verse and perhaps any other sentence in literature.[1]

Recent study of the relation between Romans 1–8 and 9–11 has moved away from the once prevailing view that chapters 9–11 form a misplaced postscript or awkward interlude, interrupting the natural flow of thought from 8:39 to 12:1. It has become increasingly apparent to scholars that these three chapters form an integral part of the epistle.[2] As Paul grapples with the problem of how God's faithfulness and justice are related to Jewish unbelief and Gentile belief he is expanding his abbreviated treatment of these themes in 3:1–9, 22, 29–30, as well as facing the wide-ranging implications of his thematic statement in 1:16b–17. If God's sovereign purpose for Israel and election of Israel did not guarantee the nation's salvation, how can the Christian be confident that the divine purpose for the church will not be frustrated and that the divine election of the church will not be nullified? These problems of theodicy that arose from the general Jewish rejection of the messianic salvation that had been depicted in the Jewish Scriptures and fulfilled in Jesus Christ prompted several agonizing ques-

1. The most comprehensive treatments of the history of the exegesis of Rom. 9:5 are found in Abbot, "Construction" 133–49; Abbot, "Discussions" 103–11; Durand 552–62; Faccio 64–108; Kuss, *Römerbrief* 683–88; and Kuss, "Römer" 292–301. Briefer accounts are given in Liddon, *Romans* 151–52; Sanday and Headlam 234; and Cranfield, *Romans* 469–70. In his survey of the data down to the end of the ninth century, Faccio aims to demonstrate that the application of all of v. 5b to Christ was accepted without dispute in the writings of the fathers and other ecclesiastical authors (64–101, 135). Then he shows that J. J. Wettstein and other modern critics are mistaken in their claim that many fathers refer v. 5b to God the Father (102–8).

2. See, e.g., Cranfield, *Romans* 445–47, 820; and esp. E. E. Johnson 110–47, for a review of the various proposals regarding the relation of Rom. 9–11 to 1–8.

tions. Have God's promises concerning Israel in fact proved empty (cf. 9:6)? How is it that the Gentiles who did not pursue righteousness nevertheless gained it whereas the Jews who pursued a law of righteousness failed to reach the goal of righteousness (cf. 9:30–31)? Has God repudiated his people (11:1)? Have the Jews stumbled so as to fall (11:11)?

As he begins his "Christian philosophy of history" (as Rom. 9–11 has been called), Paul solemnly affirms his truthfulness (v. 1) when he declares that he has intense sorrow and perpetual anguish at the failure of the majority of his fellow Jews to embrace the salvation found in Christ (v. 2). If it were possible and permissible to do so, he would pray (ηὐχόμην) that he himself were cursed and therefore cut off from Christ if that would bring about the salvation of his fellow countrymen (v. 3). To explain why his grief at general Jewish unbelief was so intense, Paul lists the incomparable privileges and distinctive advantages that belonged to the Jewish race, his kinsfolk by blood and nationality (vv. 4–5). After he has enumerated six impersonal blessings that belong (ὧν) to the Israelites (v. 4), he cites two personal blessings, the second representing their consummate privilege: "To them belong (ὧν) the patriarchs, and from their ranks (καὶ ἐξ ὧν) came the Messiah as far as human descent is concerned" (v. 5a).

However one punctuates and translates verse 5b, it forms a doxology, relating either to God or to Christ. Because some scholars doubt the presence of a "doxology" here, it becomes necessary to define this term and justify this position.

A doxology (δοξολογία) is a formal ascription of praise, honor, glory, or blessing to God or Christ. It is usually expressed in the third person; it often incorporates a reference to the divine attributes or actions that give rise to the utterance of praise (e.g., 1 Pet. 4:11; Jude 24–25); and it sometimes concludes with εἰς τοὺς αἰῶνας or the equivalent and a final ἀμήν. New Testament doxologies are of two types. There is the *volitive or exclamatory doxology*, usually introduced by εὐλογητός, in which a wish is expressed, with an optative such as εἴη or γένοιτο ("may he/it be") or an imperative such as ἔστω/ἤτω ("let him/it be") implied.[3] Then there is the *descriptive or declar-*

3. Luke 1:68; 2 Cor. 1:3; Eph. 1:3; 1 Pet. 1:3. Cf. Robertson, *Grammar* 396. But if one followed Abbot (*Authorship* 355–61, 409–10 = "Construction" 107–11, 152–54) and insisted on the distinction εὐλογητός = *laudandus* or *laude dignus* and εὐλογημένος = *laudatus*, only the indicative would be possible with εὐλογητός (as Abbot indeed argues; so also H. W. Beyer, *TDNT* 2:764; see *per contra* Winer 586). But whatever be said about the meaning of other verbal adjectives ending in -τέος or -τός (see the discussion in Caragounis 79 n. 3), it seems *a priori* unlikely that εὐλογητὸς ὁ θεός merely states that God is worthy of praise (εὐλογίας ἄξιος); the phrase expresses the wish that God be praised and, by doing so, actually praises him. This point seems to be tacitly acknowledged by Abbot when he comments that a doxology with εὐλογητός is, "grammatically considered, declarative, not optative, though the whole *effect* of the original is perhaps better given by rendering 'be blessed' than 'is to be praised'" (*Authorship* 410 = "Construction" 153). O'Brien, on the other hand, prefers to call 2 Cor. 1:3–4, Eph. 1:3ff., and 1 Pet. 1:3ff. "introductory eulogies" (233 n. 4), distinguishing

ative doxology, usually involving the term εὐλογητός or εὐλογημένος, in which an affirmation is made, with an indicative form such as ἐστίν ("he is") or a participial form such as ὁ ὤν ("[he] who is") expressed or implied. The word ἀμήν regularly appears at the end of both types of doxology,[4] whether the doxology be directed to God[5] or to Christ.[6] If θεός in Romans 9:5b refers to God the Father, there may be either a volitive doxology ("may God . . . be blessed . . . !") or a descriptive doxology ("God . . . is blessed . . ."). But if θεός applies to Christ, there is a descriptive doxology ("who is blessed . . ." or "he is blessed . . .").[7]

B. The Text of Romans 9:5

Textual critics have never entertained doubts about the text of Romans 9:5. Their disagreements have focused on the question of how to punctuate the established Greek text, witness the unusual disagreement between B. F. Westcott and F. J. A. Hort on this point in their "Notes on Select Readings" (WH 2: appendix 110). However, the grammatical ambiguities of the text have prompted at least three conjectural emendations, although only the first has a history attached to it and needs to be seriously considered.

1. J. Schlichting (1592–1661), a Socinian scholar, was apparently the first to mention the possibility that Paul originally wrote (or dictated) ὧν ὁ rather than ὁ ὤν, although he himself did not accept this conjectural emendation.[8] The proposal was adopted by L. M. Artemonius (= Samuel Crell) in 1726, whose defense of it elicited a detailed rejoinder from J. A. Bengel

"doxologies, in which δόξα or synonyms such as τιμή, κράτος, etc. appear, and eulogies (= *berakoth*) in which εὐλογητός occurs" (236 n. 19); similarly Mullins, who isolates three types of "ascription" in the LXX and NT—woes, beatitudes, and eulogies, the four formal eulogies or "didactic ascriptions" in the NT being Luke 1:68; 2 Cor. 1:3; Eph. 1:3; 1 Pet. 1:3 (195, 201–3).

4. *Contra* Burkitt (*Beginnings* 452), who, apparently recognizing only exclamatory doxologies, claims that the presence of ἀμήν in Rom. 9:5 shows that Paul's words "are not a description but an ascription."

5. Rom. 1:25; 11:36; 16:27; Gal. 1:5; Eph. 3:20–21; Phil. 4:20; 1 Tim. 1:17; 6:15–16; Heb. 13:21; 1 Pet. 4:11; 5:11; Jude 24–25; Rev. 7:11–12.

6. 2 Tim. 4:18; 2 Pet. 3:18; Rev. 1:5b–6.

7. It is a matter of interest that Abbot, denying the application of θεός to Christ in Rom. 9:5, expressly allows for both the volitive and declarative types of doxologies (*Authorship* 355 and n. = "Construction" 107 and n.), whereas Gifford, applying θεός to Christ in Rom. 9:5, insists that the verse contains no doxology at all but rather "a solemn declaration of Deity, exactly similar in form to 2 Cor. xi.31" (179). The only English version which refers θεός to Christ and has a volitive doxology is that of Cassirer: "To them the patriarchs belong, and theirs is the human stock from which Christ came, he who rules as God over all things. May he be blessed for ever. Amen." B. Weiss is an example of a scholar who views Rom. 9:5b as a doxology to Christ (*Theology* 1:393).

8. See Cranfield, *Romans* 465 n. 2 for details.

(3:122–24). More recently the conjecture has been accepted by K. Barth (*Romans* 330–31, 339; but later rejected in his *Dogmatics* 205), G. Harder, J. Schniewind,[9] H.-W. Bartsch, W. L. Lorimer (with a modification), and J. Ziesler (with reservations).

This suggestion has a *prima facie* attractiveness, for it produces a precise threefold parallelism (ὧν ἡ . . . ὧν οἱ . . . ὧν ὁ . . .) and an original ΩΝΟ could easily have become ΟΩΝ through a scribal transposition of the one letter omicron. Nevertheless the conjecture labors under some serious difficulties that have justifiably prevented its adoption by commentators on Romans.

a. The phrase καὶ ἐξ ὧν in verse 5a breaks the proposed sequence of parallel expressions, with its καί which suggests the end of a series (thus Bengel 3:123) and its ἐξ ὧν which denotes origin, not possession (ὧν).
b. E. Stauffer contends that "this formally brilliant conjecture is shattered materially by R[om]. 3:29, where Paul expressly declares that God is not just the God of the Jews" (*TDNT* 3:105). This appeal to Romans 3:29 loses its potency if the phrase "the Supreme God belongs to them" refers to his unique covenantal relationship with Israel (cf. "I will be their God," e.g., Jer. 32:38) or to his unique self-revelation to Moses (Exod. 3:6–15) (cf. Kirk 104; Barrett, *Romans* 179). But one may agree with H. M. Faccio (15) that "God cannot be called the property (*proprietas*) of the chosen people in the same sense as the privileges enumerated by the apostle," and one may well ask, with W. de Boor (*Römer* 224), whether Paul is likely to have reckoned the living God, along with the other benefits, among the "possessions" of Israel, when the Messiah himself is said not to "belong" to Israel but only to have "arisen from" Israel. Moreover, J. C. O'Neill (*Romans* 153) notes that "the whole list otherwise assumes that God is the author of the gifts entrusted to the Israelites."
c. If the article ὁ is attached to θεός, as this conjecture (viz., ὧν ὁ ἐπὶ πάντων θεός) demands, a further article would be required before εὐλογητός (Middleton 248).[10]
d. Because the almost unanimous reading of the Greek manuscripts (viz., ὁ ὤν) yields a perfectly intelligible sense from a grammatical point of view, either as "who is" or as "he who is," there is no reason to entertain a conjectural emendation of the text.

9. See Bartsch 406 nn. 9–11 for bibliographical details on Harder and Schniewind.

10. It was perhaps awareness of this, along with the parallel ὁ θεὸς . . . ὁ ὢν εὐλογητὸς εἰς τοὺς αἰῶνας in 2 Cor. 11:31, that prompted Lorimer (385) to amend the conjecture of Schlichting to read ὧν ὁ ἐπὶ πάντων θεός, <ὁ ὢν> εὐλογητὸς εἰς τοὺς αἰῶνας, ἀμήν.

e. H.-W. Bartsch (408–9) attempts to support this conjecture by arguing that 1 Clement 32:4 is a paraphrase of Romans 9:5. Certainly 1 Clement 32:2 contains clear allusions to Romans 9:4–5: Clement lists the various blessings that may be traced back to Jacob, one of which was that ἐξ αὐτοῦ ['Ιακώβ] ὁ κύριος Ἰησοῦς τὸ κατὰ σάρκα. Although the conceptual and verbal reminiscences in 32:2 are patent, it is far less evident (in spite of Bartsch 408) that in 32:4 Clement has "replaced" the putative ὁ ἐπὶ πάντων θεός of Romans 9:5 with the expression ὁ παντοκράτωρ θεός. As D. A. Hagner observes (*Use* 216 n. 2), the title παντοκράτωρ is common in Clement's epistle[11] so that no allusion to Romans 9:5 is necessary.

2. K. E. Kirk raises the possibility that θεός was a scribal insertion: "Its omission would bring the passage into line with S. Paul's usual custom of speaking of Christ in language appropriate to the mention of God, without explicitly assigning deity to Him" (104). But significant textual support for such an omission is lacking,[12] and one suspects that Kirk's mention of this "possibility" and of Schlichting's conjecture was triggered by his rather cavalier dismissal of the traditional reference of ὁ ὢν κτλ. to Christ: "It is a curiously crude statement of a great truth, and singularly unlike S. Paul's general manner of dealing with such profound questions" (104).

3. Ἐξ ὧν ὁ Χριστός, ὁ ὢν ἐπὶ πάντων εὐλογητὸς εἰς τοὺς αἰῶνας is the original text according to the conjecture of J. C. O'Neill, who notes that τὸ κατὰ σάρκα is omitted by D and θεός by G, while Irenaeus's text presupposes θεὸς ἐπὶ πάντων. To this putative original a glossator naturally added the restriction τὸ κατὰ σάρκα and an explicit reference to Christ's divine nature (θεός). But what O'Neill calls grammatical "objections" to the traditional text amounts merely to ambiguities or, at the most, difficulties. Since the text as it stands cannot be deemed impossible, the principle *lectio difficilior potior* is applicable even here; the traditional text, however translated, is certainly more difficult than O'Neill's conjecture.

C. Punctuation and Translation Variants

1. The Punctuation of Romans 9:5 in Greek Manuscripts

Regarding the papyri and uncials that contain Romans 9:5, K. Aland and K. Junack of the Münster Institute for New Testament Textual Research

11. See 1 Clem. introduction; 32:4; 56:6; 60:4; 62:2.

12. On the integrity of Rom. 9:5, and especially the alleged omission of θεός in the Syriac versions, see Faccio 12–15.

report[13] that there is no punctuation mark in this verse in 𝔓46 (ca. 200), ℵ (fourth century), or Dp (sixth century). A mid-point colon after σάρκα is found in A (fifth century), B (in the second hand), Fp (ninth century), Gp (ninth century), Ψ (eighth or ninth century), 049 (ninth century), and 056 (tenth century). A high-point colon occurs after σάρκα in L (ninth century), 0142 (tenth century), and 0151 (ninth century). A space was left following the point in 0151 and following σάρκα in C (fifth century).[14]

As far as minuscules are concerned, E. Abbot summarizes the findings of C. R. Gregory by reporting that at least twenty-six "have a stop after σάρκα, the same in general which they have after αἰῶνας or Ἀμήν (*Authorship* 432 = "Discussions" 107). Abbot estimates that a complete examination of the minuscule Greek manuscripts that contain Romans 9:5 would very probably show that three-quarters or four-fifths of them have a stop after σάρκα.

What is the significance of these data? It is incontestable that in the early centuries the scribes responsible for the transmission of the NT used marks of punctuation in an inconsistent and erratic fashion. For instance, according to C. Lattey ("Codex Vaticanus"), in Romans 9 Codex Vaticanus (B) has a colon after σάρκα in verse 3, after both occurrences of Ἰσραήλ in verse 6, after Ἀβραάμ in verse 7, after Ῥεβέκκα in verse 10, and after αὐτοῦ in verse 22. And B. M. Metzger notes that in this same chapter Codex Alexandrinus (A) has a colon after μεγάλη in verse 2, one after Χριστοῦ and another after σάρκα in verse 3, and one after Ἰσραηλῖται in verse 4 ("Punctuation" 99). Even if consistency were apparent, one could not move with any degree of confidence from the presence of a punctuation mark in a manuscript to the exegetical view of the scribe. Nor is there manuscript evidence of a colon after σάρκα before the fifth century. At most one may say that many ancient scribes regarded a pause after σάρκα as natural or necessary.

2. Modern Punctuation and Translation of Romans 9:5b

The analysis in table 4 shows the principal ways in which Romans 9:5b has been punctuated by modern editors and translators of the Greek text[15] or by representative commentators.[16]

13. In a communication to Metzger ("Punctuation" 97–98).

14. According to information supplied to Lattey by Père Boudon, in the palimpsest C a small cross (+), equivalent to a colon, is found between σάρκα and ὁ ὤν (Lattey, "Codex Ephraemi").

15. Skilton (104–15) has classified about one hundred English versions published between 1881 and 1973 into two groups—those favoring the KJV rendering in which ὁ ὤν κτλ. is referred to Christ and those preferring the construction adopted by the RSV and therefore place a colon or a period after σάρκα.

16. On the translation of Rom. 9:5 in the early versions (viz., Latin, Syriac, Coptic, Gothic, Armenian, Ethiopic), see Metzger, "Punctuation" 100–101, who discovered "a certain amount of variation in the manner in which the several translators have handled ἐπὶ πάντων, some putting it before 'God' and some after, and the Ethiopic omitting the phrase entirely. But almost all of the versions (the Latin is ambiguous) agree in taking ὁ ὤν κ.τ.λ. as describing Christ" (101).

Table 4. *Modern Punctuation and Translation of Romans 9:5b*

Punctuation after σάρκα, πάντων, and θεός[a]	*Editions*[b]	*Translations and Commentaries*
1. major—none—none	J. Scaliger WH mg Nestle-Kilpatrick BF[2] NA[25] UBS[1,2]	God who is over all be blessed for ever (RSV; similarly Goodspeed, NIV mg, NAB[2]; Käsemann, *Romans* 256; von der Osten-Sacken 20) He who is God over all be (is) blessed for ever (RV mg; Abbot, *Authorship* 334, 353n. = "Construction" 89, 104n.) Blessed forever be God who is over all! (NAB[1]; similarly Moffatt, Barclay)[c] May he who is God over all be blessed forever (NRSV mg) Der über allen waltende Gott sei gelobt in Ewigkeit (Schmithals 327)
2. major—minor—minor		He who is over all, God *be* blessed for ever (ASV mg; similarly Abbot, *Authorship* 334, 353n. = "Construction" 89, 104n.) May God, supreme over all, be blessed for ever! (NEB; similarly REB) May God, who rules over all, be for ever praised! (GNB) Der über allem ist, nämlich Gott, (sei) gepriesen in die Aionen (Kuss, *Römerbrief* 678) (. . . Christus . . . ;) der über allem waltet, Gott, (er sei) gepriesen in Ewigkeit (Zeller 172) Gott, der über das All herrscht, sei gepriesen in alle Ewigkeit (Stuhlmacher 131)
3. major—none—minor		He who is over all is God, blessed for ever (RV mg; similarly B. H. Kennedy [as cited by Abbot, "Discussions" 91]) The one who is God above all, is blessed for all time (Cerfaux, *Christ* 518)
4. minor—none—none	Textus Receptus B. Weiss H. von Soden H. J. Vogels A. Merk J. M. Bover G. Nolli NA[26] UBS[3]	English versions that are based on this punctuation usually place a comma after "all" (see under next variant).
5. minor—minor—none	WH	(. . . Christ . . . ,) who is over all, God blessed for ever (KJV, RV, AV; similarly NASB, NRSV, Sanday and Headlam 238) (. . . the Messiah,) supreme above all, God blessed for ever (NEB mg) (. . . Christ) who is above all, God for ever blessed! (JB, with no punctuation after σάρκα, unlike the French original) (. . . le Christ,) qui est au-dessus de toutes choses, Dieu béni éternellement (Segond) (. . . the Christ—) he who is supreme over all things, God for ever blessed (TCNT) (. . . the Christ,) who is exalted above all, God blessed throughout the Ages (Weymouth; similarly Williams) (. . . le Christ,—) lui qui est au-dessus de tout, Dieu à jamais béni (Tricot)

Punctuation	*Editions*	*Translations and Commentaries*
6. minor—none—minor		(. . . Christ,) who is God over all, blessed for ever (RSV mg; similarly NRSV mg) (. . . Christus . . . ,) der da ist Gott über alles, gelobt in Ewigkeit (Luther; similarly Althaus 98, 100; Schlier 284) (. . . Christ,) who is God over all, forever praised! (NIV) (. . . the Christ,) He who is God over all, blessed forever (Berkeley) (. . . Christus . . . ,) qui est super omnia Deus, benedictus in saecula (Faccio 16, 135) (. . . the Messiah,) who is God, supreme above all and blessed for ever (REB mg)[d]
7. minor—major—none		(. . . Christ . . . ,) who is over all. God be (is) blessed for ever (RV mg; similarly NIV mg) (. . . the Messiah,) who is supreme over all. Blessed be God for ever! (NEB mg, REB mg)
8. none—minor—minor		(. . . Christ) who is above all, God, blessed for ever (NJB; similarly Fahy 262)
9. minor—none—major		(. . . Christ . . . ,) he who rules as God over all things. May he be blessed for ever (Cassirer)

a. In the use of the terms major, minor, and none, I am following the tradition established in the punctuation apparatus of the UBS text (all editions), where major denotes a break that is "often equivalent to a period or full stop, a colon, or a semicolon," whereas a minor break is usually indicated by a comma, and none indicates there is no punctuation (UBS^{3} xliii).

b. Some of the information about the punctuation of various editions of the Greek NT is drawn from Metzger, "Punctuation" 95–96, and UBS^{3} 553.

c. Barrett's distinctive translation perhaps best fits here: "To them belong the fathers of the race and from them (on the human side) springs the Christ himself—Blessed for ever be God, who stands over the whole process!" (*Romans* 175). Similarly B. W. Longenecker 252 and n. 2.

d. This rendering (somewhat awkwardly) construes θεός directly with ὁ ὤν, and ἐπὶ πάντων with εὐλογητὸς κτλ., as though καί preceded εὐλογητός.

A comparison of the various editions of the Greek text and of the major translations of Romans 9:5 reveals two major reversals. First, whereas NA^{25} and UBS^{1,2} punctuate the text with a colon (raised period) after σάρκα, UBS^{3} (1975) and NA^{26} (1979) print a comma after σάρκα, which has the effect of referring ὁ ὢν κτλ. to the preceding ὁ Χριστός. Second, both the 1946 and 1971 editions of the RSV presuppose a period or full stop after σάρκα, "God who is over all be blessed for ever," with the footnote reading "*Or* Christ, who is God over all, blessed for ever." The NRSV of 1989, however, presupposes a comma after σάρκα (and perhaps also after πάντων): "The Messiah, who is over all, God blessed forever."[17] The NRSV mg (second alternative) now has essentially the 1946 and 1971 RSV text.

17. It cannot be deemed coincidental that the scholar who authored an influential article on Rom. 9:5 (Metzger, "Punctuation") which argued in favor of the Greek text found in UBS^{3} and reflected in the NRSV was himself a member of that UBS committee and the chairperson of that NRSV committee.

D. God the Father as the Referent of θεός

I now briefly state the main reasons that have convinced many commentators on Romans[18] and authors of general works[19] that Paul concluded his recital of the privileges accorded to his "kinsfolk by race" in Romans 9:4–5 with a doxology addressed to God the Father. (These arguments will be examined under §E.)

1. The biblical use of εὐλογητός supports a reference to God the Father.
   a. In LXX usage εὐλογητός is almost always used of God and εὐλογημένος of humans.
   b. Everywhere else in the NT (seven uses) εὐλογητός is applied to God (Kuss, "Römer" 297–98, 303).[20]
   c. The apparently irregular word order (ὁ . . .) θεὸς εὐλογητός, as opposed to the customary εὐλογητὸς ὁ θεός, may be explained (1) by Paul's wish to make prominent the concept of God as ruler over all (Abbot, *Authorship* 356–60 = "Construction" 108–11); and (2) by appeal to Psalm 67:19–20 (LXX [Engl. 68:18–19]), κύριος ὁ θεὸς εὐλογητός, εὐλογητὸς κύριος ἡμέραν καθ' ἡμέραν (Champion 125), where a similar emphasis on the subject is apparent (H. A. W. Meyer, *Romans* 363 n. 1).
   d. In the indisputable Pauline Epistles there are no doxologies to Christ; in the Pastorals, only one (2 Tim. 4:18) which is itself contested (Abbot, *Authorship* 342, 361–63 = "Construction" 95, 112–13).
2. The closest Pauline or NT parallel to ὁ ὢν ἐπὶ πάντων is Ephesians 4:6, εἷς θεὸς καὶ πατὴρ πάντων, ὁ ἐπὶ πάντων, where the "one God"

18. H. A. W. Meyer, *Romans* 360–64; Denney 658–59; Lietzmann 90; K. Barth, *Romans* 339; Dodd, *Romans* 152–53, 165; Kirk 103–4; V. Taylor, *Romans* 61–62; Kuss, *Römerbrief* 678–96; Käsemann, *Romans* 259–60; Wilckens 189; Zeller 173–74; Dunn, *Romans* 521, 529, 535–36; Schmithals 327, 333; Stuhlmacher 131–32.

19. Abbot, *Authorship* 332–438 = "Construction"; Abbot, "Discussions"; Burkitt, "Romans" 452–54; Burkitt, "Punctuation" 398; Bousset 210; Champion 124–26; Andrews 126–27; Bultmann, *Essays* 275; Bultmann, *Theology* 1:129n.; Funk 157–58; K. Barth, *Dogmatics* 205; V. Taylor, *Essays* 84–85 (= "Jesus" 55–57); Cerfaux, *Christ* 517–20; Barclay, *Jesus* 28–29; E. Schweizer, *TDNT* 7:128 n. 238; Kümmel 164; J. Schneider, *NIDNTT* 2:80; Kuss, *Römer* 302–3; Goppelt 2:79; von der Osten-Sacken 20, 221 n. 55; Dunn, *Partings* 203–4.

20. The 1978 excursus of Kuss in volume 3 of his commentary on Romans (679–96) is largely identical with his 1976 essay "Zur Römer 9,5" in the Käsemann *Festschrift*, although it gives more detailed attention to recent interpreters of Rom. 9:5 (683–87), usefully summarizing the views of some of the major exponents of the two basic exegetical positions; however, the most detailed treatment in any language—Faccio's treatise in Latin—is not mentioned.

is explicitly distinguished from Christ (εἷς κύριος, Eph. 4:5) (Abbot, *Authorship* 363 = "Construction" 113).

3. Given Paul's uniform reservation of the term θεός to designate the Father, it is highly improbable that, almost incidentally, he would on a single occasion speak of Christ not only as θεός, but also as being ἐπὶ πάντων and εὐλογητὸς εἰς τοὺς αἰῶνας (cf. Abbot, *Authorship* 363–74 = "Construction" 113–22). H. A. W. Meyer expresses the point potently: "Here Christ would be called not merely and simply θεός, but even *God over all*, and consequently would be designated as θεὸς παντοκράτωρ, which is absolutely incompatible with the entire view of the N.T. as to the dependence of the Son on the Father . . . , and especially with passages like viii.34 (ἐντυγχάνει), 1 Cor. iii.23, viii.6, xi.3, Eph. iv.5, 6, and notably 1 Cor. xv.28" (*Romans* 362; similarly Schmithals 333).

4. The context accords perfectly with an independent doxology addressed to God: "(i) A Jew thinking of God's blessings to Israel would naturally end with such a benediction to the God of Israel; (ii) 'God *over all*' is precisely what we would expect Paul to say, since he enumerates Israel's blessings not as theirs alone but as God's blessings for all (cf. 3:29–30; 4:13–17; and the converse argument of 3:1–6); (iii) the titular reference to Christ, 'the Messiah,' ranks him as one of Israel's privileges, indeed, in Paul's perspective, the greatest (the climactic point in the list), whereas a jump to describe the Messiah as 'God over all' would be unexpected, to say the least; (iv) and if some kind of contrast is intended between Christ's earthly and heavenly state (Cranfield, Schlier) we would have expected that to be more clearly marked, either by some kind of antithetic parallelism (1:3–4) or by some adversative" (Dunn, *Romans* 529).[21]

5. The absence of a christological focus in the doxology of Romans 11:36 at the end of Romans 9–11 suggests that Paul wished to confine his christological statements to "uncontroversial Jewish categories" (Dunn, *Romans* 702; cf. 529, 535–36).

21. In his 1988 commentary on Romans (528–29, 535–36), Dunn argues strongly against referring θεός to Christ, but earlier he entertained—although finally rejecting— "the very real possibility" that Paul here refers to Christ as God or "god" (*Christology* 45; cf. *Unity* 53, 405 n. 37).

E. Christ as the Referent of θεός

Rather than simply summarizing the arguments that have led many to conclude that θεός in verse 5b does in fact refer to Christ,[22] I shall engage in a detailed phrase-by-phrase exegesis of the verse to show that this conclusion is more convincing than the view that verse 5b is a doxology directed to God the Father.

1. ὧν οἱ πατέρες καὶ ἐξ ὧν ὁ Χριστός

All three instances of ὧν in verses 4–5 have the same antecedent, viz., τῶν συγγενῶν μου κατὰ σάρκα,[23] "my human kinsfolk," whom Paul has already called "my brothers" and proceeds to identify as "Israelites." The καί before ἐξ ὧν marks not merely the last member of the threefold listing (ὧν . . . ὧν . . . καὶ ἐξ ὧν) but also the transition from the idea of possession (ὧν) to that of derivation (ἐκ). The Messiah does not belong in any exclusive or ultimate sense to the Israelites either as individuals or as a nation, but he did arise[24] from their stock or race. F. Godet observes that if "the fathers" belong to the Jewish people as "national property," the same cannot be said of the Messiah: "He proceeds from them as to origin, but He does not belong to them exclusively as to His destination" (*Romans* 136).

22. Among these "many" are the following:

a. *Grammarians*: Middleton 314–19; Moulton, *Prolegomena* 228; B. Weiss, "Gebrauch" 323; Robertson, *Grammar* 1108; Robertson, *Pictures* 4:381; Zerwick, *Analysis* 350; N. Turner, *Insights* 15.

b. *Commentators*: Bengel 3:124–25; Olshausen 324–26; Hodge, *Romans* 300–302; Vaughan 175; H. C. G. Moule, *Epistle* 248, 261–62; H. C. G. Moule, *Romans* 164–65; Godet, *Romans* 136–43; Philippi 68–78; Shedd 278–79; B. Weiss, *Römer* 436–39; Gifford 168–69, 178–79; Alford 2:404–6; Liddon, *Romans* 151–54; Sanday and Headlam 232–38; Zahn, *Römer* 432–35; Lagrange, *Romains* 227; Haering 89; Sickenberger 249; Schlatter, *Gerechtigkeit* 295–96; Lenski, *Romans* 590–93; Nygren 358–59; Althaus 98, 100; O. Michel, *Römer* 229; Leenhardt 245–47; J. Murray 6–7, 245–48; Bruce, *Romans* 186–87; Bruce, *Paraphrase* 211; Best 107; de Boor, *Römer* 224; Cranfield, *Romans* 465–70, 840; Cranfield, *Shorter Commentary* 222–24; Schlier 288; H. N. Ridderbos, *Romeinen* 208–9; Harrison 103; Hendriksen, *Romans* 315–16; Morris, *Romans* 350. Harvey (*Jesus* 176) was unjustified in claiming (in 1982) that "the great majority of recent commentators and translators take Rom. 9:5 as an independent doxology to God" (citing, as an example, Lietzmann's *An die Römer* [1928]). See also n. 98.

c. *Authors of general works*: Dwight, "Romans" 24–50; Dwight, "Notes" 396–99; Westcott in WH 2: appendix 110; Liddon, *Divinity* 316–19 and nn. s, t, u, x; 437 and n. k; Durand 563–70; Warfield, *Lord* 70, 250, 254–55, 259; Stevens, *Theology* 397–98; Stevens, *Pauline Theology* 201–2; Rostron 180–84; McGiffert 27; Prat 1:251, 2:125–27; Warfield, *Christology* 267–70; Lebreton, *History* 371; Cotter 262–64; Faccio, esp. 17, 25–61, 134; Warner; Stauffer 283 n. 348, 324 n. 803; E. Stauffer, *TDNT* 3:105; Munck, *Christ* 32–33; Wainwright, *Trinity* 54–58 (= "Confession" 278–82); Cullmann, *Christology* 312–13; Prümm 140; Rahner 135; Lyonnet 26–30; Bonsirven, *Theology* 229 n. 10, 381; Whiteley 119; Fahy 262; Brown, *Reflections* 20–22 (= "Jesus" 559–60); Sabourin, *Names* 301, 304 n. 6; Sabourin, *Christology* 126–27; R. N. Longenecker, *Christology* 138–39; Metzger, *Commentary* 520–22; Metzger, "Punctuation" 103–12; Fortman 20, 27; Feuillet, *Christologie* 26; H. N. Ridderbos, *Theology* 68; H. N. Ridderbos, *Jesus* 73; Elwell 306; Thüsing 147–50; Siegert 119, 122–23; Morris, *Theology* 48; Piper 28; Cranfield, "Comments" 273; Reymond 272–75.

23. Καί before ἐξ ὧν (v. 5) indicates that this third ὧν does not refer to οἱ πατέρες (B. Weiss, *Römer* 435; but cf. *per contra* Zahn, *Römer* 435).

24. A verb such as ἦλθεν (cf. 1 Tim. 1:15), ἐγένετο (cf. Gal. 4:4), or even simply ἦν may be supplied.

J. Piper perceives in καὶ ἐξ ὧν "a climactic ring": "The fathers, at the beginning, give rise to the people of Israel; the Christ, at the end, comes *from* the people." With Christ's coming, the privileges of Israel have reached their climax both temporally and qualitatively (27).

Given the contrast between οἱ πατέρες ("the patriarchs") and ὁ Χριστός and the fact that Paul is enumerating distinctively Israelite privileges, it is not surprising that the majority of English versions render ὁ Χριστός by "the Messiah" (NEB, NAB[1,2], REB, NRSV) or "the Christ" (TCNT, Weymouth, Moffatt, Berkeley, RSV, NASB, NRSV mg; also Kramer 210 §62e). On the other hand, since Paul recognized the crucified and exalted Jesus of Nazareth as none other than God's Messiah (Gal. 3:1; Col 2:6; cf. Acts 9:22; 17:3), it is not inappropriate to translate ὁ Χριστός simply by the proper noun "Christ" (KJV, RV, ASV, Goodspeed, NIV).[25]

2. τὸ κατὰ σάρκα

Although the prepositional phrase κατὰ σάρκα is common in the Pauline Epistles (19 uses), there is no parallel in the whole Greek Bible for this phrase in a substantivized form. Τὸ "strongly emphasizes the limitation ('insofar as the physical is concerned')" (BDF §266.(2)), "as far as physical descent is concerned" (C. F. D. Moule, *Idiom Book* 58; similarly BAGD 744a).[26] But there is no reason to restrict σάρξ here to mere corporeality, as M. Rese (217) does in his rendering, "soweit seine Leiblichkeit in Betracht kommt," for Christ derived more than his physical body from Israelite stock (ἐξ ὧν). Σάρξ signifies "la nature humaine dans son intégrité" and is here synonymous with ἄνθρωπος (Durand 564; similarly Godet, *Romans* 136, adducing Rom. 15:8 and John 1:14 as parallels). That this limitation needs no correction, one may concede with Kuss (*Römerbrief* 690, 696; "Römer" 297, 303), but does it suggest that a complementary statement or even an antithesis will follow? Certainly the absence in verse 5b of an adversative particle such as δέ or of a formal antithesis such as τὸ δὲ κατὰ πνεῦμα (cf. Rom. 1:3–4)[27] shows that τὸ κατὰ σάρκα does not necessitate an expressed antithesis, but three considerations compel one to allow that ὁ ὢν κτλ. may express an informal contrast to τὸ κατὰ σάρκα.[28]

25. Although the NT epistles usually omit the article with Χριστός when it is a proper noun (cf. BDF §260.(1); Robertson, *Grammar* 760), an articular Χριστός may be a personal name rather than a title (e.g., Col. 3:1–4 [4×]). "Use of the article does not help us to decide when Χριστός is a title and when it is a name" (W. Grundmann, *TDNT* 9:540, citing [541] Rom. 14:15 and 14:18; 15:7 and 15:8; 1 Cor. 1:12 and 1:13; 1:17 *bis*).

26. Faccio usefully compares τὸ ἐξ ὑμῶν (= ἐξ ὑμῶν γε) in Rom. 12:18, "so far as it depends on you" (30).

27. Cf. Xenophon, *Cyrop.* 5:4:11: νῦν τὸ μὲν ἐπ' ἐμοὶ οἴχομαι, τὸ δ' ἐπὶ σοὶ σέσωσμαι (cited by H. A. W. Meyer, *Romans* 361 n. 2).

28. Cf. the slightly different argumentation toward the same conclusion found in Dwight, "Romans" 25–31.

a. If there was no sense in which ὁ Χριστός was not purely of Jewish stock, Paul would have concluded his statement with Χριστός. As it is, τὸ κατὰ σάρκα suggests that there is another aspect of Christ's person to which the category of human descent is inapplicable. Such a limiting phrase could not be applied to οἱ πατέρες.

b. If Paul *had* ended the sentence with ὁ Χριστός, this would have formed an eminently suitable climax to his recitation of Israelite privileges. But with the addition of τὸ κατὰ σάρκα, there would be a diminution of these stated privileges unless a complementary contrast followed which testified to the elevated status of the Messiah. As F. A. Philippi (69–70) argues the point: "That the Messiah springs from the Jews is a higher privilege than that He springs from them after the flesh merely. But that *He* springs from them after the flesh who is God over all [or, over all as God], this is the highest conceivable prerogative."

c. Paul is "speaking of Christ in the current schema of the διπλοῦν κήρυγμα. In R[om]. 1:3f. he calls Christ the Son of David κατὰ σάρκα and the Son of God κατὰ πνεῦμα. In R[om]. 9:5 he has spoken of Christ as the Son of Israel κατὰ σάρκα, and he now logically pursues his thinking in that schema to the final conclusion of calling Him the θεός who is over all things" (E. Stauffer, *TDNT* 3:105).[29] The substantivizing τό, then, relates κατὰ σάρκα back to ἐξ ὧν [ἦλθεν]; Paul was not here writing concerning "the human Christ," ὁ Χριστὸς (ὁ) κατὰ σάρκα. But it also looks forward, not to a suppressed τὸ κατὰ πνεῦμα, but to ὁ ὢν ἐπὶ πάντων θεός. What is being contrasted is not exactly two disparate origins of the Messiah, human and divine (as Godet, *Romans* 137, believes), but, on the one hand, his Jewish descent (ἐξ ὧν) and his universal supremacy (ὁ ὢν ἐπὶ πάντων)[30] and, on the other, his humanity (κατὰ σάρκα) and his deity (θεός), the human side of his being and the divine.[31] A comparable σάρξ–θεός antithesis is found in Romans 3:20, Romans 9:8, Matthew 16:17, Luke 3:6, and 1 Corinthians 1:29.

29. Stauffer observes that "the same twofold schema as the framework of *Theos* predication" is found in Ignatius, *Eph.* 7:2; 18:2 (*TDNT* 3:105 n. 264).

30. Cf. the paraphrase of Sanday and Headlam (225): "From them [the patriarchs] in these last days has come the Messiah as regards his natural descent—that Messiah who although sprung from a human parent is supreme over all things, none other than God, the eternal object of human praise!"

31. This contrast is recognized by many commentators, who express it as an antithesis between the two sides of Christ's being (B. Weiss, *Römer* 435; Sickenberger 249; Best 107) or between his human and his divine (or "higher") nature (Bengel 3:124; Olshausen 325; Hodge, *Romans* 300–301; H. C. G. Moule, *Epistle* 262; B. Weiss, *Theology* 1:343; Alford 2:404; Liddon, *Romans* 152–53, who sees the contrast as also between Christ's assumed humanity and his eternal person [ὁ ὢν], 150; Faccio 29 n. 1, 61, 134). But one need not endorse O. Bardenhewer's verdict (cited without reference by Cotter 262) that Rom. 9:5 is "a classical testimony to the duality of nature in the unity of Person."

3. ὁ ὤν

At this point one reaches the watershed in the verse. Is this articular participle prospective, beginning a sentence, or is it retrospective, continuing a sentence? In other NT uses these are the two principal functions of ὁ ὤν (or οἱ ὄντες): to introduce a new subject ("the person who is," "he who is")[32] or to further a description of an existing subject ("who is").[33] Grammatically, either case may obtain in Romans 9:5, so that one's decision must rest on other grounds. There are, in fact, not two but three ways in which ὁ ὤν has been understood here.

a. ὤν as Otiose and θεός Articular

If the participle ὤν is regarded as "unnecessary,"[34] the way is open to construe ὁ with θεός (Champion 125) and render the whole phrase "God who is over all" (RSV).[35] But such a rendering accords better with ὁ θεὸς ὁ ἐπὶ πάντων. It is insufficient to observe, as L. G. Champion does (124–25), that in postexilic Jewish writings there was a tendency to insert words between the article and the substantive and that participles are frequently used in doxologies (e.g., 2 Cor. 11:31), for in none of the alleged parallels are the inserted words or the participles otiose.[36] F. Prat is right when he affirms that "one can say ὁ ἐπὶ πάντων, or ὁ ἐπὶ πάντων Θεός, or again ὁ ὢν επὶ πάντων but not ὁ ὢν ἐπὶ πάντων Θεός, taking ὁ for the article of Θεός" (2:127 n. 1).

b. ὁ ὤν as Substantival ("He who is," "The Eternal," or "I AM")

As already seen, in NT usage ὁ ὤν may introduce a new subject. Other considerations apart, there can therefore be no objection to the renderings that begin a new sentence with ὁ ὤν: "He who is over all, God, *be* blessed for ever" (ASV mg), "Der über allem ist, nämlich Gott, (sei) gepriesen in die Aionen" (Kuss, *Römerbrief* 678), or "He who is over all is God, blessed for ever" (RV mg). But the overriding difficulty with this understanding is that it awkwardly separates ὁ ὤν from its natural antecedent ὁ Χριστός. True, τὸ κατὰ σάρκα intervenes, and elsewhere in the NT when ὁ ὤν is relatival it usually follows immediately after its anteced-

32. Matt. 12:30; Luke 6:3; 11:23; John 3:31; 6:46; 8:47; 9:40; 18:37; Acts 22:9; Rom. 8:5, 8; 13:1.

33. John 1:18; 3:13 v.l.; 11:31; 12:17; Acts 11:1; 2 Cor. (5:4); 11:31; Eph. 2:13; Col. 4:11.

34. "The use of ὤν, which is itself unnecessary, emphasises ἐπὶ πάντων" (Denney 659).

35. Similarly Goodspeed, NAB[2]; Käsemann, *Romans* 256.

36. The participle ὤν can be redundant or relatively colorless ("existing, current, present") when the word order is article–ὤν–substantive; e.g., Acts 5:17: ἡ οὖσα αἵρεσις τῶν Σαδδουκαίων, "the Sadducean party as it then was" (NEB). Cf. N. Turner, *Syntax* 151–52. BAGD cites P Mich. 155:3 (2d cent. A.D.): ὁ ὢν θεὸς ὁ Ἰάω κύριος παντοκράτωρ, "the god who exists . . ." (223a).

ent,[37] but one may account for the position of τὸ κατὰ σάρκα by noting the parallelism of ὧν ἡ υἱοθεσία . . . ὧν οἱ πατέρες . . . ἐξ ὧν ὁ Χριστός in verses 4–5 and by the fact that in Paul κατὰ σάρκα never precedes a substantive that it in any sense qualifies.[38] So my point stands—that to promote a divorce of ὁ ὤν from the grammatically consonant ὁ Χριστός is unconscionable.

There is also the consideration that in all NT doxologies an explicit link is found between the doxology itself and some preceding word or words; one never finds asyndetic doxologies.[39] For instance, in Romans 1:25 ὅς ἐστιν εὐλογητὸς εἰς τοὺς αἰῶνας looks back to τὸν κτίσαντα, while in Romans 11:36 αὐτῷ ἡ δόξα εἰς τοὺς αἰῶνας finds an antecedent in κυρίου (Rom. 11:34). But Romans 9:5b lacks any syntactical link with what precedes if it is construed as a doxology to God the Father.

F. C. Burkitt regarded verse 5b as a parenthesis in Paul's argument in which he solemnly invokes the God of Israel as a witness to the truth of his dramatic assertions in 9:2–5a, 6ff. The expression ὁ ὤν derives from Exodus 3:14–15[40] and is the Greek equivalent of the sacred tetragrammaton, which, when implicitly pronounced, naturally prompts the standing benedictory formula, εὐλογητὸς εἰς τοὺς αἰῶνας, ἀμήν ("Romans" 452–53; "Punctuation" 398). He paraphrased 9:1, 5b, "I lie not . . . , The Eternal (Blessed is His Name!), I call Him to witness" ("Romans" 454).[41] Apparently independently of Burkitt, H. J. Warner proposed that ὁ ὤν should be understood absolutely as a proper name, "I AM," "the familiar and official rendering of אֶהְיֶה" in Exodus 3:14, and that verse 5b should be punctuated as κατὰ σάρκα, ὁ ὤν, ἐπὶ πάντων Θεός, εὐλογητὸς εἰς τοὺς αἰῶνας.

Against this proposed titular sense of ὁ ὤν, I would urge two points. (1) The only unambiguous titular uses of ὁ ὤν in the NT are found in Revelation (five occurrences): twice in conjunction with ὁ ἦν alone (Rev. 11:17; 16:5) and three times in conjunction with ὁ ἦν and ὁ ἐρχόμενος (Rev. 1:4, 8; 4:8), but *never alone.* (2) Even if ὁ ὤν was the traditional Greek equivalent of אהיה, the title is not common in the LXX (only five occurrences),[42] so that Greek speakers would be much more likely to pause for sense after ἐπὶ πάντων, "(he) who is over all," than after ὤν.[43]

37. This point is pressed by Abbot (*Authorship* 345 = "Construction" 98) who regards the "parenthetic insertion" of ὁ ὢν κτλ. after ὁ θεὸς . . . οἶδεν in 2 Cor. 11:31 as the single NT exception to this rule concerning word order.

38. This prepositional phrase follows the substantive (e.g., Rom. 4:1) but may intervene between article and substantive (e.g., Rom. 8:4–5). In 2 Cor. 5:16 it qualifies ἐγνώκαμεν, not Χριστόν.

39. See Zahn, *Römer* 433 and n. 78; Metzger, "Punctuation" 106.

40. Καὶ εἶπεν ὁ θεὸς πρὸς Μωυσῆν Ἐγώ εἰμι ὁ ὤν (אהיה אשר אהיה). καὶ εἶπεν Οὕτως ἐρεῖς τοῖς υἱοῖς Ἰσραὴλ Ὁ ὢν (אהיה) ἀπέσταλκέν με πρὸς ὑμᾶς . . . τοῦτό μού ἐστιν ὄνομα αἰώνιον.

41. Consistently, Burkitt regards ὁ ὢν in 2 Cor. 11:31 as titular: "The God and Father of our Lord Jesus knows, even the Eternal Himself (Blessed is His Name!), that I lie not" ("Romans" 454).

42. Exod. 3:14 *bis*; Jer. 1:6; 14:13; 39:17 [Engl. 32:17].

43. See further the critique of Burkitt's view in Faccio 57–61.

c. ὁ ὢν as Relatival ("who is" = ὅς ἐστι)

The relatival use of an articular participle is common in NT Greek (see BDF §412) and I have cited above (n. 37) the eight NT uses of ὁ ὢν in this sense. But why is this the preferable way to construe this phrase in verse 5b[44] and why does the burden of proof rest with those who would construe it otherwise? First, a proper name (ὁ Χριστός) precedes and agrees with ὁ ὢν, so that a change of subject is antecedently improbable.[45] Second, whatever might be said regarding θεὸς εὐλογητὸς κτλ., the description "who is over all" is not inappropriate when applied to Christ (cf. Col. 1:17; Eph. 4:10), so that a reader would be likely to assume an identity of subject at least as far as ἐπὶ πάντων.[46] Third, 2 Corinthians 11:31 is a close parallel: ὁ θεὸς καὶ πατὴρ τοῦ κυρίου Ἰησοῦ οἶδεν, ὁ ὢν εὐλογητὸς εἰς τοὺς αἰῶνας, ὅτι οὐ ψεύδομαι. As T. Dwight astutely remarks, if the construction of this verse were altered to read ὁ πατὴρ τοῦ κυρίου Ἰησοῦ οἶδεν ὅτι οὐ ψεύδομαι, ὁ ὢν ἐπὶ πάντων θεὸς εὐλογητὸς εἰς τοὺς αἰῶνας, no one would hesitate to refer the participial clause back to ὁ πατήρ ("Romans" 24). Fourth, adequate reasons may be proposed to explain the unusual placement of τὸ κατὰ σάρκα between the *ex hypothesi* antecedent (ὁ Χριστός) and the articular participle that functions as a relative (see §E.3.b above).[47]

4. *ἐπὶ πάντων*

The next phrase, ἐπὶ πάντων, which should be taken with ὁ ὤν,[48] signifies universal supremacy: "[Is] over all" points to a status that involves authority,[49] "is supreme over all things" (TCNT), "is . . . Lord over all things" (Cranfield, "Comments" 273).[50] Implied, but only implied, in this status of authority

44. The relatival sense of ὁ ὢν is advocated by the great majority of those who refer θεός to Christ. But some within this category take ὁ ὢν as an appositional substantive ("he who is") (e.g., H. C. G. Moule, *Epistle* 248; Lenski, *Romans* 591; Fahy 262). See also table 4, no. 7.

45. N. Turner's comment (*Insights* 15) that "there is no grammatical reason why a participle agreeing with 'Messiah' should first be divorced from it and then be given the force of a wish, receiving a different person as its subject" is puzzling, for no commentator suggests that the *participle* has become volitive.

46. The translations found in RV mg, NEB mg, NIV mg, and REB mg (see table 4, no. 7) refer ὁ ὢν ἐπὶ πάντων to Christ and conclude with a doxology to God the Father.

47. If one asks why Paul here prefers ὁ ὢν over ὅς ἐστιν, one may surmise that the timelessness or perpetuity of Christ's universal reign was more unambiguously expressed by a nonfinite and atemporal participle than by a finite present tense (cf. John 1:18; 3:13 v.l.).

48. There are three other NT instances of a prepositional phrase being directly attached to a relatival ὁ ὢν/οἱ ὄντες (viz., John 1:18; 11:31; Col. 4:11).

49. Εἶναι ἐπί (+ the genitive) means "to be on" (of literal position; e.g., Luke 17:31; John 20:7) or "to be over" (of metaphorical position; e.g., Judith 14:13: ὁ ὢν ἐπὶ πάντων τῶν αὐτοῦ) (BAGD 225c); cf. BDF §234.(5). In Rom. 9:5 εἶναι ἐπί (cf. Acts 8:27) has the same sense as ἐξουσίαν ἔχειν ἐπί (cf. Rev. 20:6).

50. The rendering "exalted above all" (Weymouth; Prat 2:125) may stand, provided it is not taken to imply that only after the resurrection did Jesus become universally supreme.

is the exercise of rule.[51] If πάντων is masculine, the reference in the context will be to all persons without exception—patriarchs, both believing and unbelieving Jews, and all Gentiles (cf. Rom. 1:16; 3:29–30; 10:12; 11:32). So far from "belonging to" (cf. ὢν) the Jewish nation alone, or even to Jews and Gentiles, God or the Messiah is supreme over all. More probably πάντων is neuter, specifying not *simply* the inanimate universe (Hodge, *Romans* 300) or all creatures (B. Reicke, *TDNT* 5:889, 894) or people and events (Abbot, *Authorship* 353 = "Construction" 105) or human history (Käsemann, *Romans* 260; Zeller 173), but both persons and things (Cranfield, *Romans* 469 n.2), the entire universe, animate and inanimate, including their distinctive histories.[52]

In itself this phrase affords no help in determining the referent, for both the Father and the Son may be said to be ἐπὶ πάντων. It is true that this is expressly said only of the Father (Eph. 4:6: εἷς θεὸς καὶ πατὴρ πάντων, ὁ ἐπὶ πάντων), but one should not therefore conclude that Paul would never predicate ἐπὶ πάντων of Jesus, for the apostle depicts Jesus as κύριος πάντων (Rom. 10:12; cf. Acts 10:36), the supreme Lord of the universe and the church (Eph. 1:20–23; Phil. 2:9–11), "Lord both of the dead and of the living" (Rom. 14:9), and πρὸ πάντων (Col. 1:17a) as the one who created and now sustains the universe (τὰ πάντα, Col. 1:16, 17b).[53] If Paul is asserting the eternal and cosmic sovereignty of Christ, he need not be compromising his belief in the subordination of the Son to the Father that is so clearly stated in 1 Corinthians 3:23, 11:3, and 15:28, for he would obviously be excluding the Father from the πάντες or πάντα over which Christ is sovereign, as he explicitly does in 1 Corinthians 15:27. Nor need he be compromising his reservation of titles such as κύριος παντοκράτωρ (2 Cor. 6:18) or ὁ . . . μόνος δυνάστης (1 Tim. 6:15) for God the Father. For even if one construes θεός with ἐπὶ πάντων, the actual expression θεὸς παντοκράτωρ is not being applied to Christ, just as no NT writer uses the titles κύριος ὁ θεός or ὁ μόνος ἀληθινὸς θεός in reference to Jesus.

5. εὐλογητὸς εἰς τοὺς αἰῶνας, ἀμήν

One major difficulty faces the interpreter who refers the εὐλογητός phrase to God the Father in a volitive ("blessed be . . .") or descriptive (". . .

51. Cf. βασιλεύειν ἐπί + accusative (Luke 1:33; 19:14, 27). BAGD 632d and GNB have "who rules over all" (similarly Cassirer; Stuhlmacher 132, although his translation, using *herrschen*, retains the ambiguity: "Gott, der über das All herrscht," 131).

52. Barrett translates v. 5b, "Blessed for ever be God, who stands over the whole process" (*Romans* 175, 177), "leaving open the question whether the doxology refers to Christ or to God the Father" (179).

53. Some of these passages appear to "date" Christ's universal lordship from the resurrection (Rom. 14:9; Eph. 1:20–23; Phil. 2:9–11), but a distinction may be drawn between Christ's intrinsic lordship and its recognition after the resurrection. One may compare the role of the resurrection in openly declaring "with power," rather than inaugurating, the sonship of Jesus (Rom. 1:4).

is blessed") doxology.[54] Throughout the Greek Bible, whenever εὐλογητός occurs in an independent or asyndetic doxology, it always precedes the name of God.[55] Thus, for instance, εὐλογητὸς ὁ θεὸς ὁ ὕψιστος (Gen. 14:20) and εὐλογητὸς ὁ θεὸς καὶ πατὴρ τοῦ κυρίου ἡμῶν Ἰησοῦ Χριστοῦ (2 Cor. 1:3; Eph. 1:3; 1 Pet. 1:3).[56] But in Romans 9:5 εὐλογητός follows θεός. If normal biblical word order for independent doxologies were followed in Romans 9:5, one would expect either εὐλογητὸς ὁ θεὸς εἰς τοὺς αἰῶνας, ἀμήν (if ὁ ὢν ἐπὶ πάντων is construed with ὁ Χριστός) or εὐλογητὸς ὁ θεὸς ὁ ὢν ἐπὶ πάντων εἰς τοὺς αἰῶνας, ἀμήν.

Relief from the pressure of this potent argument, which C. E. B. Cranfield rightly calls "in itself almost conclusive" (*Romans* 468), is usually sought in two directions. Appeal is made to the apparent exception to the normal word order found in Psalm 67:19d–20a (LXX):[57] κύριος ὁ θεὸς εὐλογητός, εὐλογητὸς κυριος ἡμέραν καθ' ἡμέραν, which renders the Hebrew ברוך אדני יום יום (68:20). The second εὐλογητός occupies the regular position; the first, which represents no Hebrew, is exceptional. Various explanations have been offered: the first phrase may be an interpolation (Alford 2:405); ברוך must have occurred twice in the original text (H. A. W. Meyer, *Romans* 363 n. 1); there has been an erroneous duplicate translation (Metzger, "Punctuation" 107 n. 24; Cranfield, *Romans* 467); "the LXX is a free paraphrase with a designed rhetorical emphasis (with the inverted order of words, the doubled εὐλογητός, the stronger form of blessing following the weaker one)" (Liddon, *Romans* 152, who also suggests that the first phrase may be interpolated; similarly Hodge, *Theology* 512). But the most detailed and perceptive treatment of the LXX rendering is that of T. Dwight ("Romans" 32–33), who discounts this passage as a genuine parallel to Romans 9:5[58] on two grounds: (1) a double doxology is unparalleled in the Greek Bible and (2) once the failure of the LXX

54. Because εὐλογητός is not preceded by the article, the meaning cannot be "the blessed God" or "the Blessed One," which would require (ὁ) θεὸς ὁ εὐλογητός.

55. The situation is otherwise with εὐλογημένος (מבורך) in the LXX, where a verbal form such as εἴη or ἔστω or γένοιτο and the subject may precede εὐλογημένος (e.g., 2 Chron. 9:8: ἔστω κύριος ὁ θεός σου ηὐλογημένος). In the NT εὐλογημένος always precedes the subject (often in a quotation of Ps. 118:26 [LXX = 117:26]).

56. The same word order is found with ברוך or בריך in the Hebrew Bible and Jewish literature. For example, each of the Eighteen Benedictions begins "Blessed art thou, O Lord. . . ."

57. See, e.g., Schlier 288.

58. Significantly, this point is also recognized by Abbot, *Authorship* 356 (= "Construction" 107), author of the most comprehensive defense of Rom. 9:5b as a doxology to God the Father. The only other exception involving εὐλογητός (as opposed to εὐλογημένος) is Gen. 26:29, καὶ νῦν σὺ εὐλογητὸς ὑπὸ κυρίου (cited by Abbot, *Authorship* 357 = "Construction" 108), the reading preferred by Rahlfs and by Wevers (in the Göttingen LXX). It is a testimony to scribal awareness of normal word order that instead of σὺ εὐλογητός some witnesses read εὐλογητὸς σύ or εὐλογημένος σύ or simply εὐλογητός or εὐλογημένος (see Wevers 255). But what distinguishes Gen. 26:29 from Rom. 9:5 is that in the former verse εὐλογητός is applied to a mere mortal (Isaac), not to θεός, so that it is in no sense a doxology.

translators to understand the Hebrew text had given rise to the repeated εὐλογητός (see his reasoning, 32n.), the chiastic order κύριος . . . εὐλογητός, εὐλογητὸς κύριος served to give that same prominence to the doxological words which in a single exclamatory clause is achieved by placing εὐλογητός at the beginning. Dwight concludes: "So far, then, from being an exception which proves that the doxological word may stand after the subject of the sentence, . . . this verse from the Septuagint, in our judgment, strengthens the opposite view, inasmuch as it shows that, even in this peculiar case, this word is made to have the greatest possible prominence" (33). Certainly the word order in Psalm 67:19d shows that there is no inviolable law of Greek usage that prevents the subject from preceding εὐλογητός in a doxology, but it is surely arbitrary to make the single LXX exception to a pattern of biblical usage—which in fact is only an apparent exception—the regulative key for the interpretation of a contested NT passage.

The alternative way of explaining the extraordinary inversion (on the assumption that v. 5b is a doxology to God the Father) is to suggest that when the subject contains the dominant thought or is prominent in the writer's mind, it may precede the predicate. So it is proposed that Paul wishes to stress "the universality of God's embrace" (Dunn, *Romans* 536) or the overruling providence of God as "the Ruler over All" (Abbot, *Authorship* 360 = "Construction" 111): "He who is God *over all*, may *he* be blessed for ever. Amen." In a similar vein, G. B. Winer (551) declares that "only an empirical expositor could regard this position [the predicate placed first] as an unalterable rule; for, when the subject constitutes the principle [*sic*] notion, especially when it is antithetical to another subject, the predicate may and must be placed after it, cf. Ps. lxvii.20 [*sic*] Sept." F. A. Philippi's response is apt: "In the interpretation of a formula that has become fixed, empiricism is altogether in its right place, and still more where, for the established usage, a sufficient *ratio* can be alleged. Directly that a doxology, omitting the verb substant., appears in a purely exclamatory form, the idea of praise becomes so predominant that the word expressing the praise necessarily stands at the head" (2:76). If Paul had wished to address a doxology to God the Father, he must have realized that the unique position of εὐλογητός was a potential stumbling block to the right understanding of the verse. If he desired to stress the idea of universality or of the divine providence, and at the same time remove all possible ambiguity of interpretation, he might be expected to have written τῷ δὲ (ὄντι) ἐπὶ πάντων θεῷ δόξα εἰς τοὺς αἰῶνας, ἀμήν or τῷ δὲ θεῷ τῷ ἐπὶ πάντων (ὄντι) δόξα εἰς τοὺς αἰῶνας, ἀμήν,[59] which would accord with

59. Similarly Dwight, "Romans" 38; Dwight, "Notes" 398; Faccio 53.

doxologies employing the dative that are not uncommon in the Pauline corpus at the end of a paragraph.[60] Moreover, it is hard to imagine that nowhere else in the Greek Bible does the subject in a doxology bear an emphasis comparable to that in Romans 9:5 so that the customary word order is reversed.[61]

We may conclude that the position of εὐλογητός after ὁ ὢν and θεός makes it extremely unlikely that ὁ ὢν κτλ. is an independent doxology, whether volitive ("God who is over all be blessed for ever!") or descriptive ("he who is God over all is blessed for ever"). This leaves two options—that εὐλογητός introduces an exclamatory doxology to Christ ("May he be blessed for ever," Cassirer) or that it forms part of a descriptive doxology concerning Christ (". . . who is . . . blessed for ever"). The former view is improbable, since it is unparalleled for the subject of a volitive doxology to remain unexpressed and it is unnatural to separate εὐλογητός from a juxtaposed θεός. Some have objected to the latter view, which I espouse, on the ground that εὐλογητός is never elsewhere used of Christ, only of the Father,[62] and that ἀμήν implies that an exclamatory doxology precedes.[63] To these objections we now turn.

It is incontestable that each of the other seven NT uses of εὐλογητός is applied to God the Father,[64] whereas εὐλογημένος is used of Christ six times.[65] But no objection can be raised in principle against the use of εὐλογητός in reference to Christ, for while in LXX usage εὐλογητός is generally used of God and εὐλογημένος of humans, there are examples where εὐλογημένος is used of God[66] and εὐλογητός of humans.[67]

An examination of Paul's use of ἀμήν reveals that apart from its use with benedictions,[68] it usually stands at the end of volitive doxologies.[69] But in two cases it follows a declaration (Rom. 1:25; 1 Thess. 3:13 v.l.). The former passage affords a parallel relevant to Romans 9:5, for there ἀμήν concludes a declarative doxology which occurs earlier in the same letter, which is a relative clause, and which employs the word εὐλογητός[70] and

60. Rom. 11:36; Gal. 1:5; Eph. 3:21; Phil. 4:20; 1 Tim. 1:17; 2 Tim. 4:18; cf. Heb. 13:21; 1 Pet. 4:11; 5:11; 2 Pet. 3:18.

61. Dwight ("Romans" 36–37) cites several LXX passages where an inversion might be expected on this principle, but is not found (e.g., εὐλογητός in 1 Sam. 25:33 and 2 Macc. 15:34).

62. Abbot, *Authorship* 361 = "Construction" 112.

63. Cf. Burkitt, "Romans" 452; Barclay, *Jesus* 29.

64. Mark 14:61; Luke 1:68; Rom. 1:25; 2 Cor. 1:3; 11:31; Eph. 1:3; 1 Pet. 1:3.

65. Matt. 21:9 (// Mark 11:9; Luke 19:38; John 12:13); Matt. 23:39 (// Luke 13:35).

66. 1 Kings 10:9; 1 Chron. 16:36; 2 Chron. 9:8; Judith 13:18; Dan. 3:53.

67. Gen. 12:2; 26:29; 43:28; Deut. 7:14; 28:6 *bis* (A); 33:24; Judg. 17:2; Ruth 2:20; 1 Sam. 15:13; Judith 13:18; 2 Macc. 15:34.

68. Rom. 15:33; 16:24 v.l.; 1 Cor. 16:24 v.l.; Gal. 6:18; Philem. 25 v.l.

69. Rom. 11:36; 16:27; Gal. 1:5; Eph. 3:21; Phil. 4:20; 1 Tim. 1:17; 6:16; 2 Tim. 4:18. For the distinction between "volitive/exclamatory" and "descriptive/declarative" doxologies, see §A in this chapter.

70. As opposed to δόξα, which is found in seven of the eight volitive doxologies.

the phrase εἰς τοὺς αἰῶνας:[71] (. . . τὸν κτίσαντα,) ὅς ἐστιν εὐλογητὸς εἰς τοὺς αἰῶνας, ἀμήν. From these data one may see that while the presence of ἀμήν in Romans 9:5 may *prima facie* suggest that a volitive doxology has preceded, this is by no means a necessary conclusion, for ἀμήν may also express solemn assent to a prior affirmation such as is found in a descriptive doxology.

What light is thrown on this matter of the referent of θεός by a consideration of the immediate context in Romans 9?

Opinions differ dramatically concerning the appropriateness of a doxology to God the Father at the end of Romans 9:1–5. H. A. W. Meyer believes that Paul was impelled "by the recital of the distinctions of his nation to devote a doxology to God, the Author of these privileges, who therefore was not responsible for the deeply-lamented unbelief of the Jews" (*Romans* 361). But this tends to overlook the fact that Paul's recital of Israelite privilege was prompted by his desire "to emphasize the grievousness of the Jews' disobedience" (Cranfield, *Romans* 468); in verses 1–5 he is basically expressing sorrow over Jewish disobedience rather than joy over Jewish privilege, so that an ascription of praise to God the Father would seem out of place.[72] How could an ever-deepening sorrow, as Israel's privileges are detailed, give rise to praise?[73] The climactic privilege—hosting the Messiah—also prompted the deepest anguish, for those dignified with this incomparable honor had in general failed to embrace their Messiah. E. H. Gifford poignantly asks (169), "How could the Apostle bless God that Christ was born a Jew, in his anguish that the Jews had rejected Him?"[74]

If Romans 9:5b were an independent doxology, one would have expected δέ to be used, if not to mark a contrast, at least as a sign of transition ("now"; cf. Rom. 16:25; Jude 24) from one subject (ὁ Χριστός) to

71. This phrase, an abbreviation of εἰς τοὺς αἰῶνας τῶν αἰώνων (Gal. 1:5; Phil. 4:20; 1 Tim. 1:17; 2 Tim. 4:18), may be rendered "to all eternity" (BAGD 27c, citing Rom. 1:25; 9:5; 2 Cor. 11:31; cf. BDF §141.(1)), for "the plur. presupposes knowledge of a plurality of αἰῶνες, of ages and periods of time whose infinite series constitutes eternity" (H. Sasse, *TDNT* 1:199).

72. It is true that in Rom. 1:25 one finds a doxology to God set in a context of sorrow, but there, as in 2 Cor. 11:31, the doxology is added in rabbinic fashion when the name of God has *actually* occurred (Sanday and Headlam 236–37).

73. Hendriksen drives home this point with a modern analogy: "Today it is unlikely that a missionary, reporting back to his board, would say, 'Even though the people among whom I carry on my evangelistic activity have been blessed with many advantages—such as prosperity, good health, intelligence, etc.—there have been very few conversions. *Praise the Lord!*'" (*Romans* 316).

74. To argue as Kuss does (*Römerbrief* 690, 696; "Römer" 297, 302), that in Rom. 9–11 Paul is addressing first and foremost non-Christian Jews and is arguing purely on Jewish grounds so that Rom. 9:5b is probably a doxology to God the Father, assumes without warrant that there is a change of addressees at Rom. 9:1 from Christians to Jews, that to cite the OT means to adopt Jewish argumentation, and that Paul's aim in Rom. 9–11 is to win Jews over to faith in Christ rather than to explain to both Jewish and Gentile Christians in Rome why most Jews have rejected their Messiah. Cf. Cranfield, *Romans* 466 n. 7.

another (θεός).[75] Again, an asyndetic doxology to God following a reference to Christ would tend to reflect adversely on the person of Christ: "But he who is over all is not Christ, but God the Father who alone is blessed for ever!" (Lyonnet 28). On the other hand, if verse 5b is a doxology describing Christ, there is a natural climax that elevates the person of the Messiah as well as an antithesis that complements the limitation signified by τὸ κατὰ σάρκα (see above, §E.2). Not only did the Messiah come from Jewish stock; he is a universal monarch who will be eternally worshiped as God. To refer θεός to Christ accords perfectly with the immediate context. What is more, one should entertain seriously the possibility that the wording of Psalm 45 is echoed in Romans 9:5b: the king to whom it is said εὐλόγησέν σε ὁ θεὸς εἰς τὸν αἰῶνα (Ps. 44:3c LXX) is himself later addressed as "God": ὁ θρόνος σου, ὁ θεός, εἰς τὸν αἰῶνα τοῦ αἰῶνος (Ps. 44:7a LXX).[76]

F. The Meaning of θεός

This review of each phrase in Romans 9:5b has shown that it is exegetically more satisfactory to apply the second part of the verse to Christ than to God the Father. And it has shown that the immediate context supports such a conclusion. If this is so, it follows that at least two distinct affirmations are made regarding Christ: he is "over all" and "blessed for ever." Each is dependent on an atemporal articular participle ὁ ὤν. Christ is a universal sovereign and the object of eternal adoration.

But poised between these two affirmations is the term θεός. Should it be construed with what precedes, ὁ ὢν ἐπὶ πάντων, or with what follows, εὐλογητὸς εἰς τοὺς αἰῶνας, or does it stand independently as a third affirmation?

Grammatically it is not impossible that there are three separate predicates of ὁ ὤν.[77] In this case Paul would be asserting that Christ is universally supreme, divine by nature, and eternally the object of human praise; the first and second affirmations would be genuinely timeless,[78] while the third would have become true after the resurrection. However, the conjunction of θεός and εὐλογητός is so frequent in the Greek Bible that to construe

75. Abbot's objection (*Authorship* 342 = "Construction" 95) that a transitional δέ "would make the doxology too formal" seems purely arbitrary.

76. See Kidner 171; Bruce, *Romans* 187.

77. This is the view of Liddon, *Romans* 150; H. C. G. Moule, *Epistle* 248, 261–62; Haering 88. See also table 4, no. 8.

78. Against the view that restricts Christ's deity to his glorified state, Godet notes (*Romans* 143) that "Paul requires to complete the idea of the Israelitish *origin* of Jesus by that of a higher *origin*. The matter in question, therefore, is not His *exaltation*, but His divine *pre-existence*. . . . From the standpoint of biblical monotheism *to become* God, without *being* so by nature, is a monstrosity."

these two words separately would be highly irregular, especially when no καί precedes εὐλογητός.

Not a few scholars who find a reference to Christ in Romans 9:5b, construe θεός with ὁ ὢν ἐπὶ πάντων,[79] "(Christ,) who is God over all." Alternatively, θεός could be taken as being in apposition to ὁ ὢν ἐπὶ πάντων (Prümm 140): "(Christ,) who, as God, is/rules over all."[80] Both of these constructions sever the natural association of θεός with εὐλογητός and cohere better with the word order ὁ ὢν θεὸς ἐπὶ πάντων. Also, as Cranfield notes (*Romans* 469), if Paul had said that Christ is "God over all," he could have been misunderstood to suggest "that Christ is God to the exclusion of, or in superiority over, the Father."

I therefore prefer to construe θεός with the following phrase, εὐλογητὸς εἰς τοὺς αἰῶνας.[81] Two possible translations result: "(Christ,) who is over all, God blessed forever."[82] This makes θεὸς κτλ. a second predicate dependent on ὁ ὤν;[83] or the sense may be, "(Christ,) who is supreme above all as God blessed for ever." On this latter view, which I adopt, θεός is in apposition to ὁ ὢν ἐπὶ πάντων[84] and εὐλογητὸς κτλ. is descriptive of θεός.

But what does θεός here signify as applied to Christ? Θεός is anarthrous not only because it is appositional (or predicative) but also because it functions as a qualitative noun, highlighting Christ's inherent divinity, not as a proper noun, identifying Christ with God the Father. It is not simply that Christ "has the rank of God" (Harrison 103), true though that is; he intrinsically shares the divine nature.[85] Since Paul has already described Christ as

79. Olshausen 326; Philippi 68; B. Weiss, *Theology* 1:393 and n. 5; Alford 2:405; Schlatter, *Gerechtigkeit* 295; Nygren 358; Faccio 110, 135; O. Michel, *Römer* 229. See also table 4, no. 6.

80. Cf. Cassirer: "(Christ . . . ,) he who rules as God over all things."

81. So also Godet, *Romans* 142; Sanday and Headlam 232, 238; Lagrange, *Romains* 227; Leenhardt 247; J. Murray 2:248; Feuillet, *Christologie* 26; H. N. Ridderbos, *Romeinen* 208; Cranfield, *Romans* 451, 469. See also table 4, no. 5. If Paul intended θεός to be construed with εὐλογητὸς κτλ. and not with ἐπὶ πάντων, he avoided any suggestion that Christ was to be identified with θεὸς παντοκράτωρ.

82. For representative translations in the category, see table 4, no. 5.

83. Lenski (*Romans* 591) prefers to regard θεός alone as the second predicate of ὁ ὤν, with εὐλογητὸς κτλ. attached attributively to θεός.

84. So also Zahn, *Römer* 434; Prat 2:127 n. 1. Cf. Bengel's paraphrase (3:124): "Christ is of the fathers, according to the flesh; and at the same time was, is, and shall be over all, inasmuch as He is God blessed for ever"; similarly Godet, *Romans* 142.

85. This interpretation is held, *inter alios*, by B. Weiss, "Gebrauch" 323; Lagrange, *Romains* 227; Prat 2:127; O. Michel, *Römer* 224; Leenhardt 247; Lyonnet 28; de Boor, *Römer* 224; Cranfield, *Romans* 469 and n. 3, 840; Cranfield, "Comments" 273. H. A. W. Meyer concedes that if θεός here refers to Christ (a position he rejects), "Christ is not *nuncupative*, but *naturaliter* God" (*Romans* 363), that is, God by nature, not merely by name.

being “over all,” that is, as having preeminent status and dignity, θεός cannot be taken in a diluted or polytheistic sense.[86]

As Paul concludes his enumeration of the privileges that belong to Israel (Rom. 5:4–5), he focuses on two crowning benefits that are persons—the patriarchs and the Messiah (v. 5). Verse 5 contains two sets of contrasts:

1. ὧν—possession (the patriarchs belong to the Israelites)	ἐξ ὧν—origin (the Messiah arose from Israelite stock)
2. ἐξ ὧν—national descent	ἐπὶ πάντων—universal supremacy
[ἦλθεν]—origin	ὁ ὤν—status
τὸ κατὰ σάρκα—humanity (the Messiah came from the ranks of the Israelites as far as his human nature was concerned)	θεός—deity (the Messiah is supreme over all things and people as possessor of the divine nature)

In Romans 9:5b one may isolate three distinct affirmations about Christ: he is Lord of all, he is God by nature, and he will be eternally praised. But as they are stated by Paul, these three affirmations are interrelated.[87] Christ exercises dominion over the whole universe, animate and inanimate, inasmuch as he is God by nature (θεός) and the worthy recipient of the everlasting worship generally reserved for the Father (Rom. 1:25; 2 Cor. 11:31). It is in his capacity and because of his status as a divine being who will be worshiped forever that Christ enjoys universal supremacy. In this incidental reference to Christ as θεός, Paul shows that his Christian experience and reflection have forced him to redefine his hereditary monotheism so as to include Christ within the category of Deity.[88]

But before this exegetical conclusion finally stands, one must consider objections that arise from the wider context of Pauline Christology. They are three in number.

First, would a Jewish monotheist such as Paul ever contemplate using θεός of a figure other than Yahweh, the God of Israel?[89] In chapter I, we dis-

86. Similarly Cotter 262. Prat astutely comments: “Jesus Christ is not God in an unwarranted, participated, or analogous way; he is exalted above everything that is not God. As this quality of sovereign God can belong to one being only, the Son must necessarily be consubstantial with the Father and identical with him in nature” (2:127).

87. It is possible that “who is over all” and “God blessed forever” may simply stand side by side as separate declarations, but the anarthrous state of θεός and the absence of καί before or after θεός lead me to believe that Paul intended to express or imply some relation between the two or the three affirmations.

88. But cf. C. A. A. Scott: “What we do seem to see [in the Pauline Epistles] is the Apostle being pressed by his experience and urged by his convictions up to the verge of acknowledging that Christ is God, but finally precluded from making such acknowledgement by his hereditary monotheism” (*Christianity* 274; similarly in his *Dominus* 182, 216–20).

89. Cf. the view of C. A. A. Scott mentioned above, n. 88.

covered that in Pauline usage θεός was a sufficiently broad term to allow for its application to figures other than Yahweh. If he could apply the term to any being thought worthy of worship (1 Cor. 8:4; 2 Thess. 2:4c; cf. Acts 17:23) or to the so-called gods of polytheistic religion (1 Cor. 8:5 *bis*; Gal. 4:8b; 2 Thess. 2:4a), if he could depict the inordinate quest to satisfy all natural instincts (ἡ κοιλία, by metonymy) as ὁ θεός (Phil. 3:19), and if he could describe Satan as ὁ θεὸς τοῦ αἰῶνος τούτου (2 Cor. 4:4), there is no *a priori* reason why he should not use the term of a being whom he considered to have identity of nature and parity of status with the one true God, particularly because θεός could be used qualitatively and as a generic title as well as the personal name of God the Father.[90] To express the point another way, it cannot be deemed incongruous for Paul, who taught that one of the signs of the *Antichrist* would be his laying claim to the title θεός (2 Thess. 2:4), on one or two occasions himself to speak of the true Christ as θεός.

Moreover, Pauline Christology was sufficiently "high" to permit the application of θεός to Jesus as a title. Indications of Paul's exalted conception of Christ include the following (see also appendix I; Elwell):

1. Christ shares the divine nature (Phil. 2:6) and attributes (Eph. 4:10; Col. 1:19; 2:9).
2. Old Testament passages and titles (such as κύριος) that refer to Yahweh are applied to Christ (e.g., Joel 2:32 [MT 3:5] in Rom. 10:13; cf. 1 Cor. 1:2; Isa. 45:23 in Phil. 2:10–11).[91]
3. God and Christ jointly form a single source of divine grace and peace (e.g., Rom. 1:7; Philem. 3), direction (1 Thess. 3:11), and comfort (2 Thess. 2:16–17).[92]
4. Christ is the object of saving faith (Rom. 10:8–13; cf. Acts 16:31) and of human and angelic worship (Phil. 2:9–11).
5. Christ is the addressee in petitionary prayer (1 Cor. 1:2; 16:22; 2 Cor. 12:8).
6. Christ exercises exclusively divine functions, such as creational agency (Col. 1:16), the forgiveness of sins (Col. 3:13), and final judgment (1 Cor. 4:4–5; 2 Cor. 5:10; 2 Thess. 1:7–9).

The second objection is this. Since Paul nowhere else applies the term θεός to Christ, should not his *uniform* usage, according to which θεός

90. Cotter makes the interesting observation that "Paul uses none of the three titles θεός, κύριος, πνεῦμα as exclusively proper to one of the three divine Persons" (285).

91. One might also note here the similarity between Rom. 9:5b and Ps. 40:14 (LXX [Engl. 41:13]), which reads Εὐλογητὸς κύριος ὁ θεὸς Ἰσραὴλ ἀπὸ τοῦ αἰῶνος καὶ εἰς τὸν αἰῶνα.

92. These two Thessalonian passages contain remarkable instances of "*enallage* of number" and reversal of word order, both features that emphasize the intimate conjunction of God and Christ.

denotes God the Father, be decisive in the case of an ambiguous construction such as in Romans 9:5b (Abbot, *Authorship* 363–74 = "Construction" 113–22)?[93] In the next chapter I shall rehearse the reasons for believing that in Titus 2:13 Jesus Christ is in fact called ὁ μέγας θεὸς καὶ σωτὴρ ἡμῶν. Of course not all scholars regard that letter as genuinely Pauline, but even for such Titus 2:13 may represent an inevitable or legitimate development of Pauline tradition. Romans 9:5 and Titus 2:13 are the only two places in the Pauline corpus where it is at all probable that θεός is a christological title.[94]

No one can doubt that Paul generally—in fact, almost always—reserves the term θεός for God the Father (see chapter I). But dominant usage is not exclusive usage. Since there are several passages where θεός clearly does not refer to the Father,[95] we cannot speak of uniformity of usage. In the realm of lexicography one readily allows Paul *hapax legomena* (such as χειρόγραφον, Col. 2:14) or *dis legomena* (such as θριαμβεύειν, 2 Cor. 2:14; Col. 2:15). Why deny to him in the realm of theological diction the luxury of occasional *hapax* or *dis legomena* that might reflect a view (viz., regarding the deity of Christ) that he expressed linguistically throughout his letters in a variety of complementary ways?[96] To call Christ θεός was not the only way Paul could express his belief in the divinity of Christ. Other titles such as κύριος and υἱὸς θεοῦ also admirably served that purpose and in the early church were much more commonly used this way than was θεός, since they were less prone to misunderstanding. But this is to anticipate the third objection.

"It is difficult to imagine that if he [Paul] were content to speak so frankly here [of Christ as θεός] he should not have done so elsewhere in his epistles, where countless opportunities for such a course presented themselves" (Kirk 104). I address this general matter in chapter XIII so it must

93. Abbot concludes his detailed discussion of this objection with a powerful rhetorical question: "Can we believe that he who has throughout his writings placed Christ in such a relation of *subordination* to the Father, and has habitually used the name of GOD as the peculiar designation of the Father in distinction from Christ, who also calls the Father the one God, the only wise God (Rom. xvi.27), the only God (1 Tim. i.17), and the God of Christ, has here, in opposition to the usage elsewhere uniform of a word occurring 500 times, suddenly designated *Christ* as 'over all, God blessed for ever'?" (*Authorship* 374 = "Construction" 122). Abbot calls these considerations "absolutely decisive" (*Authorship* 363 = "Construction" 113). An allied objection alleges that there are no christological doxologies in the NT, "for which the acclamations of the Kyrios in 1 Cor. 8:6; 12:3; Phil. 2:11 in Paul, and the δόξα acclamations in Rev. 1:6; 2 Pet. 3:18, only prepare the way" (Käsemann, *Romans* 260). But it is difficult to identify what elements of genuine doxologies are absent from those addressed to Christ in 2 Tim. 4:18 (here the "kingdom" mentioned in v. 18a is that of Christ Jesus [v. 1], so that the "Lord" is Jesus); 2 Pet. 3:18; Rev. 1:5b–6; 5:12–13.

94. Regarding Gal. 2:20; Eph. 5:5; Col. 2:2; 2 Thess. 1:12; 1 Tim. 3:16, see chapter XII §§C–G; on 1 Tim. 1:17; 5:21; 2 Tim. 4:1, see chapter XII n. 1.

95. 1 Cor. 8:5 *bis*; 2 Cor. 4:4; Gal. 4:8b; Phil. 3:19; 2 Thess. 2:4a.

96. Cf. the similar observations of Metzger, "Punctuation" 110–12.

suffice at this point to state summarily some possible reasons why Paul so rarely speaks of Jesus as θεός:

1. As applied to the Father, θεός is a proper name. If Jesus were regularly called θεός, so that, like Χριστός, this term ceased to be a title and became a proper noun, linguistic confusion would prevail.
2. With the general reservation of the term θεός for the Father, the distinction between the Son and the Father remains intact—the Father is εἷς θεός, the Son εἷς κύριος (1 Cor. 8:6)—and there is no possible compromise of the doctrine of the Son's subordination to the Father.
3. If θεός had become the personal name of the Son as well as of the Father, it would have proved difficult for the early Christians to defend themselves against the accusation that they were ditheistic and that Jesus was in fact a δεύτερος θεός.[97]
4. Belief in the real humanity of Jesus would have been jeopardized if Jesus had perpetually been called θεός, not to speak of the theological conundrums that would have been created by expressions such as "God died for us" (cf. Rom. 5:8) or "God's physical body" (cf. Col. 1:22).

But quite apart from these proposed explanations, one may ask why, in principle, if the author of the Fourth Gospel, in which θεός is used 83 times, can apply the term θεός to Jesus on three occasions (John 1:1, 18; 20:28), should Paul not do so once (Rom. 9:5) or twice (Rom. 9:5; Titus 2:13) when he has used the word θεός over 500 times.

These then, are the three broad objections that have been brought against the conclusion that in Romans 9:5 θεός is a christological title: that Paul *would* not have called Jesus θεός; that Paul *did* not ever use θεός of Jesus; and that if Paul *had* applied this title to Jesus, he would have done so frequently. None of these objections is sufficiently compelling to force one to surrender or modify the conclusion reached on narrowly exegetical grounds.

G. Conclusion

The main arguments that favor the conclusion that θεός refers back to ὁ Χριστός in Romans 9:5 may therefore be summarized as follows.

97. Wainwright (*Trinity* 57 = "Confession" 276–77) suggests that "it is quite possible . . . that he [Paul] believed that Christ was God, and communicated this belief privately to his followers, but was reluctant to include it in his letters because he had not yet reconciled it in thought with his Jewish monotheism."

1. It is easier and more natural to maintain an identity of subject from ὁ Χριστός to ὁ ὤν, since there is grammatical concord between the noun and the participle, than it is to assume a change of subject.
2. Although the phrase τὸ κατὰ σάρκα in itself does not necessitate a complementary antithesis, it naturally suggests a matching contrast, and when ὁ ὢν κτλ. actually fulfills that expectation by supplying an appropriate antithesis, the possibility that the phrases are antithetical and complementary is raised to the level of high probability. This implies that ὁ Χριστός is the referent in ὁ ὢν κτλ.
3. If verse 5b is a doxology to God the Father, it is difficult to account for:
   a. The asyndeton, since Paul's doxologies are always explicitly linked to a preceding subject.
   b. The presence of ὤν, which is superfluous if ὁ ὢν ἐπὶ πάντων θεός means "God over all," while word order militates against the rendering, "He who is God over all."
   c. The word order, since in the Greek Bible εὐλογητός invariably (Ps. 67:19 LXX notwithstanding) precedes the name of God in independent doxologies.

   On the contrary, if verse 5b is a doxology descriptive of Christ:
   d. The relatival ὁ ὤν forms the connection with what precedes, so the doxology is not asyndetic.
   e. Ὁ ὤν is equivalent to ὅς ἐστιν, so ὤν is not superfluous.
   f. Εὐλογητός is descriptive of θεός and, with εἰς τοὺς αἰῶνας added, naturally follows θεός, so εὐλογητός is not in an irregular position.
4. Since the notion of Christ's universal sovereignty is not foreign to Pauline thought, there is no difficulty with relating the phrase ὁ ὢν ἐπὶ πάντων to Christ, while reserving the actual title θεὸς παντοκράτωρ for the Father.
5. If the controlling tone of 9:1–4 is Paul's λύπη and ὀδύνη at the predominant unbelief of his compatriots, it would be wholly appropriate for the apostle to end the paragraph with a reference to the exalted status and nature of the rejected Messiah, but singularly inapposite to conclude with a joyful ascription of praise to God that is introduced without an adversative.
6. Given the high Christology of the Pauline letters, according to which Jesus shares the divine name and nature, exercises divine functions, and is the object of human faith and adoration, it should generate no surprise if on occasion Paul should refer to Jesus by the generic title θεός.

It is therefore highly probable that the term θεός is applied to ὁ Χριστός in Romans 9:5.[98] Even on this understanding, some uncertainty remains concerning the most appropriate punctuation and translation of the verse. I follow the NA^{26} = UBS^{3} punctuation (table 4, no. 4 above), placing a comma after σάρκα, and render the verse, "To them belong the patriarchs, and from their ranks, as far as human descent is concerned, came Christ, who is supreme over all as God blessed forever." What the apostle is affirming at the end of 9:1–5 is this. As opposed to the indignity of rejection accorded him by most of his fellow Israelites, the Messiah, Jesus Christ, is in fact exalted over the whole universe, animate and inanimate, including the Jews who reject him, in that he is God by nature, eternally the object of worship.

98. Of the fifty-six principal commentators consulted, thirteen favored a reference to God the Father and thirty-six a reference to Christ, while seven were reluctant to express a clear preference for either interpretation. The dominant view, found in commentators of widely divergent theological persuasions, may now claim the support of the textual editors of NA^{26} and UBS^{3} and the translators of the NRSV in their significant reversals of previous positions.

VII

Our Great God and Savior (Titus 2:13)

> . . . προσδεχόμενοι τὴν μακαρίαν ἐλπίδα καὶ ἐπιφάνειαν τῆς δόξης τοῦ μεγάλου θεοῦ καὶ σωτῆρος ἡμῶν Ἰησοῦ Χριστοῦ.

How Christianity reached Crete remains shrouded in mystery. Paul's brief stopover at Fair Havens on the south side of Crete (Acts 27:7–8) would have afforded no opportunity for evangelism; he was a prisoner traveling to Rome. Perhaps Cretan Jews, converted at Pentecost (cf. Acts 2:11), had returned home and established the faith there. By the time Paul addresses his "pastoral letter" to Titus (ca. 63),[1] there were Christian communities in several towns in Crete (Titus 1:5), churches that needed official leadership (Titus 1:5–9), protection from divisive heresy (Titus 1:10–16; 3:9–11), and ethical instruction (Titus 2:1–3:8). In Titus 2:13 Paul specifies the ground (γάρ, v. 11) for his injunctions to holy living that Titus was to communicate to the old and the young in the church, including slaves (vv. 1–10). God's grace had appeared with a view to achieving the salvation of all people (v. 11), viz., their ransom from evil and their purification as the new people of God (v. 14), their repudiation of irreligion and worldly passions (v. 12), and their devotion to the doing of good (v. 14).

From an analysis of the syntax of the crucial phrase, ἐπιφάνειαν τῆς δόξης τοῦ μεγάλου θεοῦ καὶ σωτῆρος ἡμῶν Ἰησοῦ Χριστοῦ, several different translations may be proposed that will be assessed in turn.

A. The Grammatical Construction

1. δόξης and σωτῆρος as Dependent on ἐπιφάνειαν

The first alternative (in which θεοῦ is dependent on δόξης) may be translated as "the appearing of the glory of the great God (= the Father) and (the appearing) of our Savior, Jesus Christ." While there are NT parallels for the idea of a future ἐπιφάνεια of Christ (2 Thess. 2:8; 1 Tim. 6:14; 2 Tim. 4:1, 8) and a concomitant display of the Father's glory (Matt. 16:27; Mark 8:38; Luke 9:26), it would be strange for any NT writer to conjoin an impersonal or quasi-personal subject (δόξα) and a distinctly personal subject (σωτήρ) in a double epiphany. The only exit from this dilemma is to take ἡ δόξα τοῦ μεγάλου θεοῦ as a christological title and treat καί as epexegetic ("the appearing of the glory of the great God, namely [or, which glory is] our Savior, Jesus Christ")[2] or, with J. N. D. Kelly (*Pastoral Epistles* 246–47), to

1. The Pauline authorship of the Pastoral Epistles is here assumed. See the defense of this position by Guthrie, *Mind*; Metzger, "Reconsideration"; Jeremias 4–9; Spicq, *Épîtres Pastorales* 1:157–214.

2. This is a variation of the view associated with the name of Hort, on which see §A.4.a.

regard "the glory of the great God" as a description of "the divine radiance with which Christ is invested at his coming." Two distinct manifestations are therefore not contemplated.

Another difficulty with this view is the anarthrous state of σωτῆρος, which tends to associate this noun closely with either δόξης or θεοῦ.[3] One might have expected, *ex hypothesi*, that καὶ τοῦ σωτῆρος ἡμῶν Ἰησοῦ Χριστοῦ would balance τῆς δόξης τοῦ μεγάλου θεοῦ as a second subject, especially since the phrase σωτὴρ ἡμῶν is articular in the NT unless it follows an anarthrous θεός,[4] a point which also counts against the first proposed "exit."[5] Moreover, given the widespread use of the phrase θεὸς καὶ σωτήρ in first-century cultic terminology[6]—"no living person could escape contact with some *theos soter*" (Moehlmann 32)—it seems unnatural to separate σωτῆρος from θεοῦ. And Kelly's proposal would better accord with some such expression as ἐπιφάνειαν τοῦ σωτῆρος ἡμῶν Ἰησοῦ Χριστοῦ ἐν τῇ δόξῃ τοῦ μεγάλου θεοῦ.

2. *θεοῦ and σωτῆρος as Dependent on ἐπιφάνειαν*

Under a second view τῆς δόξης is treated as a "Hebrew" genitive[7] and θεοῦ and σωτῆρος may refer to either *one* or *two persons*: "the glorious appearing of our great God and Savior, Jesus Christ" (NIV; similarly Goodspeed and Berkeley) or "the glorious appearing of the great God and [of] our Savior Jesus Christ" (KJV). Within the thirteen letters of the Pauline corpus the genitive form δόξης occurs twenty times as *nomen rectum*. In seven of these cases (excluding the present verse), the genitive is possibly or probably "Hebrew" or adjectival ("glorious, resplendent").[8] But although it is grammatically admissible to understand τῆς δόξης in this sense,[9] there remain two objections to this rendering.

First, the verbal parallelism between verse 11 and verse 13 is compromised. As things stand, (ἡ) ἐπιφάνεια τῆς δόξης τοῦ μεγάλου θεοῦ (v. 13) clearly corresponds to ἐπεφάνη . . . ἡ χάρις τοῦ θεοῦ (v. 11). The first advent of Christ was an appearance of God's grace; the second advent of

3. On the reasons for the anarthrous σωτῆρος, see below, §B.2.

4. 1 Tim. 2:3; 2 Tim. 1:10; Titus 1:3, 4; 2:10; 3:4, 6. In each case where σωτὴρ ἡμῶν is anarthrous (1 Tim. 1:1; Jude 25), it follows an anarthrous θεός.

5. That is, one might have expected ἐπιφάνειαν τῆς δόξης τοῦ μεγάλου θεοῦ, τοῦ σωτῆρος ἡμῶν Ἰησοῦ Χριστοῦ.

6. See below, nn. 23–24.

7. On this "Hebrew" genitive (also called "adjectival," "qualitative," or "attributive"), see Zerwick, *Greek* §§40–41.

8. Rom. 8:21 (RSV, NAB[1], NIV, NAB[2], REB); 2 Cor. 4:4 (KJV); Eph. 1:17 (TCNT, NIV, [REB]); 3:16 (Phillips, NIV); Phil. 3:21 (KJV, RSV, JB, NEB, NIV, REB); Col. 1:11 (KJV, Weymouth, Moffatt, RSV, JB, NIV, NAB[2], NRSV, REB); 1 Tim. 1:11 (KJV, TCNT, Goodspeed, RSV, NAB[1], NIV, NAB[2], NRSV).

9. Since ἐλπίδα and ἐπιφάνειαν are joined by a single article, it would be possible to argue that τῆς δόξης is parallel to μακαρίαν and therefore adjectival in sense.

Christ will be an appearance of God's glory. Second, to render τῆς δόξης by the adjective "glorious" not only obscures the relation between verses 11 and 13 but also weakens the import of the term δόξα. Embedded in the church's tradition regarding the parousia of Christ was the belief that it would involve an open display of his Father's δόξα (Matt. 16:27; Mark 8:38; Luke 9:26). It is one thing to say that a person's appearance will be "resplendent" or "attended by glory." It is another thing to assert that his *own* "glory" will be revealed. A further problem with the KJV rendering is that nowhere in the NT is ἐπιφάνεια used of the Father (but five times of Christ)—or are two persons said to appear at the Last Day?[10]

The question of whether θεὸς καὶ σωτήρ refers to one or two persons will be discussed below (under §B.1–2).

3. θεοῦ and σωτῆρος as Dependent on δόξης and as Referring to Two Persons

The third view yields "the appearing of the glory of the great God and [the glory of] our Savior Jesus Christ" (RSV mg; similarly RV mg, ASV, Moffatt, NEB mg, NAB[1], and NAB[2]). There are two principal arguments generally cited in support of this translation.

First, "in *no single* passage is θεός connected directly with Ἰησοῦς Χριστός as an attribute" (Huther, *Timothy–Titus* 360).[11] Now it is true that no NT writer refers to Jesus Christ as Ἰησοῦς Χριστὸς ὁ θεὸς ἡμῶν, not to speak of the undefined ὁ θεὸς ἡμῶν. But it must be allowed that the first step toward the bold christological expressions of Ignatius would be the use of θεός in a titular sense in reference to Christ, particularly if the term θεός were incorporated within a traditional formula. The phrases ὁ θεὸς ἡμῶν καὶ σωτὴρ Ἰησοῦς Χριστός in 2 Peter 1:1 and ὁ μέγας θεὸς καὶ σωτὴρ ἡμῶν Ἰησοῦς Χριστός in Titus 2:13 may be just such an intermediate step. Here θεός is a descriptive title, not a proper name; it is part of the stereotyped formula θεὸς καὶ σωτήρ; it is not used absolutely but is followed by an identification of the person so titled. No one will doubt that if these two verses afford instances of a christological use of θεός, such usage is exceptional in the NT. But there is an ever-present danger in literary research of making a writer's "habitual usage" so normative that he is disallowed the

10. These two points are further developed in §B.5.b.

11. A similar but less precise statement of this argument is found in Abbot: "While the word θεός occurs more than five hundred times in the Epistles of Paul . . . , there is not a single instance in which it is *clearly* applied to Christ" ("Titus" 447); "the habitual, and I believe *uniform*, usage of Paul corresponds with his language [in] 1 Cor. viii.6" (447n.). Note also Winer's candid comment (130 n. 2): "Doctrinal conviction, deduced from Paul's teaching, that this apostle could not have called Christ *the great God*, induced me to show that there is . . . no grammatical obstacle to taking καὶ σωτ. . . Χριστοῦ by itself as a second subject."

privilege of creating the exception that proves the rule. Every NT author must be permitted the luxury of some stylistic, verbal, or theological *hapax* (or *dis* or *tris*) *legomena*. In the case of Paul in Titus 2:13, there is a comparable (very probable) application of the title θεός to Jesus in Romans 9:5 (see chapter VI above).[12]

Second, "is it probable that within one (Greek) sentence the same word once denotes the Father (v. 11) and once the Son (v. 13)?" (a summary of E. Abbot's point, "Titus" 448). Abbot reinforces his argument by pointing to the parallelism between verse 11 and verse 13, which, it is implied, would be destroyed if θεός referred to two persons: Christ's first advent was a visible manifestation of God the Father's grace; his second advent would be an appearing of God the Father's (and his own) glory. There are, however, several elements in the parallelism besides the reference to θεός, viz., the χάρις–δόξα antithesis and the ἐπεφάνη–ἐπιφάνεια and σωτήριος–σωτήρ correspondences. It is no more necessary to make θεός in verse 13 refer to the Father on the basis of the undoubted reference to him in verse 11 than it is to argue, from the identification of the σωτήρ as Jesus Christ in verse 13, that ἡ χάρις τοῦ θεοῦ σωτήριος is to be equated with the salvific grace of Christ (= τοῦ θεοῦ) in verse 11.

Any NT use of θεός as a christological title will produce certain linguistic anomalies and ambiguities, for in all strands of the NT θεός generally signifies the Father. Short of coining a new theological term to denote deity, writers who believed in the divinity of Jesus were forced to employ current terminology and run the risk of being branded worshipers of two gods. One reason for the relative infrequency of the NT use of θεός in reference to Jesus may in fact have been the recognition among early Christians that, if θεός were applied to Jesus as regularly as to the Father, Jews would naturally tend to view Christianity as ditheistic and Gentiles would probably regard it as polytheistic. Also significant is the fact that in those cases in which (ὁ) θεός certainly or probably refers to Jesus, the usage is usually accompanied by a statement in the immediate context that makes an explicit personal distinction between the Son and God the Father.[13] Thus, for example, one finds ὁ λόγος ἦν πρὸς τὸν θεόν immediately before θεὸς ἦν ὁ λόγος (John 1:1).

12. If θεοῦ be read in Acts 20:28 (which is part of Luke's account of Paul's speech to the Ephesian elders), it is possible that the referent is Jesus, but it seems more likely that God the Father is referred to and that either Ἰησοῦς Χριστός is the unexpressed subject of περιεποιήσατο or ὁ ἴδιος is a christological title (see chapter V above).

13. The one exception is Rom. 9:5. But even though this verse lacks any explicit distinction between Son and Father, ὁ Χριστός is qualified by τὸ κατὰ σάρκα, a phrase that could not be predicated of the Father.

4. θεοῦ and σωτῆρος as Dependent on δόξης and as Referring to One Person

a. With Ἰησοῦ Χριστοῦ in Apposition to τῆς δόξης

The fourth view opens up two possibilities. If Ἰησοῦ Χριστοῦ stands in apposition to τῆς δόξης, the translation would read "the appearing of [him who is] the Glory of our great God and Saviour [= the Father], [which Glory is/that is] Jesus Christ" (Hort, *James* 47, 103–4).[14] This novel interpretation has a *prima facie* attractiveness, since (1) it preserves intact the θεὸς καὶ σωτήρ formula; (2) in identifying "our great God and Savior" as the Father, it reflects the usage of the Pastorals (1 Tim. 1:1; 2:3; Titus 1:3; 2:10; 3:4) where the phrases ὁ σωτὴρ ἡμῶν θεός and θεὸς σωτὴρ ἡμῶν denote the Father; and (3) δόξα θεοῦ may have been a primitive christological title.[15]

Although this view is attractive, it is not without difficulties. (1) While nouns in epexegetic apposition need not be juxtaposed, ἥτις ἐστιν might have removed the ambiguity that arises, *ex hypothesi*, from the genitives that occur between δόξης and Ἰησοῦ Χριστοῦ.[16] (2) Since the relative clause following Ἰησοῦ Χριστοῦ (viz., "who gave himself for us . . .") defines the work of Jesus Christ as Savior, it is unnatural to dissociate σωτῆρος from Ἰησοῦ Χριστοῦ. (3) The title σωτήρ is elsewhere applied to Jesus in the Pastorals (2 Tim. 1:10; Titus 1:4; 3:6), but nowhere in the NT is the title δόξα θεοῦ explicitly used of Jesus.

b. With Ἰησοῦ Χριστοῦ in Apposition to θεοῦ καὶ σωτῆρος

The second alternative under the fourth view yields the sense "the appearing of the glory of our great God and Savior Jesus Christ" (RSV; similarly RV, TCNT, ASV mg, Weymouth, Williams, NEB, NASB, GNB, JB, Barclay, NJB, NRSV, REB). Several considerations support this rendering and will be discussed in the next section.

B. Support for the Rendering "our great God and Savior, Jesus Christ" (= §A.4.b)

1. The θεὸς καὶ σωτήρ Formula

The expression θεὸς καὶ σωτήρ was a stereotyped formula common in first-century religious terminology (see Wendland), was (apparently) used

14. Similarly Parry 81; Hasler, "Epiphanie" 201; cf. Hasler, *Briefe* 93; Fee, *Timothy–Titus* 196, 199; Dunn, *Romans* 529; and (apparently) Rawlinson 172 n. 3. Hort adduces Titus 2:13 in support of his interpretation of τῆς δόξης in James 2:1 in a titular sense (". . . who is the Glory").

15. See John 1:14; 12:41; Acts 7:55; 2 Cor. 4:6; Eph. 1:3 compared with 1:17; Heb. 1:3.

16. In Col. 2:2, for instance, τοῦ θεοῦ intervenes between τοῦ μυστηρίου and Χριστοῦ, yet the sense is "God's mystery, which is Christ." See chapter XII §E.

by both Diaspora and Palestinian Jews in reference to Yahweh,[17] and invariably denoted one deity, not two.[18] If the name Ἰησοῦς Χριστός did not follow the expression, undoubtedly it would be taken to refer to one person; yet Ἰησοῦς Χριστός is simply added in epexegesis.

That Paul is here borrowing and applying to Christ a formula derived from the current terminology of pagan apotheosis cannot of course be finally demonstrated but seems probable for two reasons. (1) In the immediate context Paul uses several semitechnical terms associated with the royal epiphany, viz., ἐπιφαίνομαι ("appear," v. 11), ἐπιφάνεια ("appearance," v. 13), χάρις ("favor," v. 11), σωτήριος ("bringing aid," v. 11), and ἐλπίς ("high expectation," v. 13).[19] (2) Some seven or eight years earlier, Paul had been personally confronted with the Demetrius riot at Ephesus when the people had chanted their *credo*, Μεγάλη ἡ Ἄρτεμις Ἐφεσίων (Acts 19:28, 34). Provoked by this pagan profession of faith which may have awakened memories of the cult of Artemis in Tarsus,[20] Paul had wished to mingle with the crowd, gain a hearing (Acts 19:30), and, one may suggest, speak of ὁ μέγας θεὸς καὶ σωτὴρ ἡμῶν, Ἰησοῦς Χριστός. Even if, as B. S. Easton (94) suggests, verse 13 is a citation of a Christian liturgical formula or credal hymn,[21] it is difficult to avoid the conclusion that, whatever the date of Titus, one impulse behind this particular verse was the desire to combat the extravagant titular endowment that had been accorded to human rulers such as Antiochus Epiphanes (θεὸς ἐπιφανής), Ptolemy I (σωτὴρ καὶ θεός), or Julius Caesar (θεὸς καὶ σωτήρ), or to claim exclusively for the Christians' Lord the divine honors freely granted to goddesses such as Aphrodite and Artemis or to gods such as Asclepius and Zeus.[22]

Consequently, if one reason for the use of the phrase θεὸς καὶ σωτήρ was polemical, it is unlikely that the two elements in the phrase should be divorced, with θεός denoting God the Father and σωτήρ Jesus Christ.

2. The Anarthrous σωτῆρος

The most satisfactory explanation of the anarthrous σωτῆρος is that two coordinate nouns referring to the same person are customarily linked by a

17. Dibelius and Conzelmann 100–102 (in an excursus on "Savior" in the Pastoral Epistles).

18. Θεός and σωτήρ are two separate titles of one and the same deity. This is why the καί in the formula is not epexegetic (which would produce the sense "the appearing of the glory of the great God, our Savior Jesus Christ").

19. Cf. Spicq, *Épîtres Pastorales* 2:251–52, 396–403, 640. It would seem illegitimate to argue, as Karris (117) does, that since the author of the Pastorals espouses a "low-Christology" and Jesus is not called "God" in the two parallel passages that speak of "manifestation" and "appearance" (viz., 1 Tim. 6:14–16; 2 Tim. 1:8–10), θεός is not applied to him in Titus 2:13.

20. See references in Spicq, *Épîtres Pastorales* 2:251–52, 640.

21. Cf. the observation of Spicq (*Épîtres Pastorales* 2:245) that the Christology of the Pastorals is expressed in traditional terminology.

22. On this theme, see Cerfaux and Tondriau; A. T. Hanson, *Pastoral Letters* 186–88.

single article (see appendix I §B.2). When two (or more) nouns in the same case are linked by καί, the repetition of the article with the second noun shows unambiguously that the nouns are separate items, while its nonrepetition indicates that the nouns are being considered corporately, not separately, or that they have a single referent.[23] For example, the repeated article in the phrase ὁ ἀπόστολοι καὶ οἱ πρεσβύτεροι (Acts 15:4, 6, 22, 23) shows that the apostles of the Jerusalem church were a group distinct from the elders. On the other hand the single article in the expression οἱ ἀπόστολοι καὶ πρεσβύτεροι (Acts 15:2; 16:4) indicates that the Jerusalem apostles and elders could also be regarded (by the Antiochian church?) as a single administrative unit, not as two distinct groups. But in the case of the combination ὁ θεὸς καὶ πατὴρ (τοῦ κυρίου ἡμῶν Ἰησοῦ Χριστοῦ) (2 Cor. 1:3) it is clearly a matter of personal identity—God *is* the Father, as the preceding phrase ἀπὸ θεοῦ πατρὸς ἡμῶν (2 Cor. 1:2) shows—not simply a matter of conceptual unity. In Titus 2:13 the difficulty lies in deciding whether the nonrepetition of the article before σωτῆρος points to a conceptual association of two separate items or to their actual equation, with the second element affording an additional description of the first. That is, are θεός and σωτήρ here distinct entities being conceived of unitarily as joint possessors of δόξα, or is σωτήρ a further description of one and the same θεός? The reason for preferring the second of these alternatives is that in contemporary usage the θεὸς καὶ σωτήρ formula never referred to two persons or deities.

Alternative ways of accounting for the anarthrous σωτῆρος are not lacking but they fail to carry comparable conviction:

a. Σωτήρ was already a semitechnical term (so Bernard, *Pastoral Epistles* 172) or "a quasi proper name" (Alford 3:420) and as such tended to be anarthrous. The absence of the article is therefore insignificant.

   But, to judge from the NT use of σωτήρ, evidence is wanting that in the first century σωτήρ was a proper name as well as a title of Jesus. Apart from Titus 2:13, the word is used only fifteen times in reference to Jesus.[24] In nine of these cases it is a title accompanying

23. For a discussion of these issues, see Zerwick, *Greek* §§183–85; and esp. Robertson, *Grammar* 785–88.

24. V. Taylor (*Names* 109) explains the sparing use of σωτήρ as a title of Jesus for more than half a century by suggesting that the use of the name in Greek religion and especially in the emperor cult "restricted and delayed its currency in the primitive tradition." But Moehlmann (40–41) rejects such an explanation, proposing rather that not until Jesus had been called θεός (subsequent to the death of Paul, according to Moehlmann) did the early church give him the title σωτήρ (42–65; cf. the similar sentiment expressed earlier by Bousset 317): "During the first decades of its life, Christianity promulgated a soterless soteriology" (2). The association of the terms θεός and σωτήρ in the θεὸς σωτήρ formula of Greco-Roman civilization forms the key for Moehlmann's hypothesis (see esp. 25–39). But in substantiating his thesis, Moehlmann rejects the apostolic authorship of Titus and 2 Peter.

proper names (such as Ἰησοῦς Χριστός);[25] in the remaining six cases it is used simply as a descriptive title.[26] Nor is there proof that as a quasi-technical word σωτήρ "speedily became anarthrous."[27] In fact, in the Pastorals σωτήρ is articular seven times[28] but anarthrous only twice (excluding Titus 2:13).[29] Only if it could be established that σωτὴρ (ἡμῶν) Ἰησοῦς Χριστός was an early credal formula comparable to κύριος Ἰησοῦς Χριστός could one argue that σωτήρ was anarthrous in Titus 2:13 because of its widespread technical use (similarly Wainwright, "Confession" 283–84).

b. Σωτήρ is anarthrous because there was no need to distinguish different subjects, the writer assuming a distinction between ὁ μέγας θεός and σωτὴρ ἡμῶν Ἰησοῦς Χριστός.[30]

No one will deny that the repetition of the article is not essential to ensure that two items be considered separately,[31] but it is difficult to prove what an author was or was not assuming. What is indisputable is that the combination σωτὴρ ἡμῶν is generally articular in the Pastorals (seven examples), being anarthrous only in 1 Timothy 1:1 (where there is no possibility that two persons are referred to) and in Titus 2:13. Consequently the exceptional nature of the usage in this verse calls for a positive explanation. But the affirmation that the article is absent because it was not needed does not account for this departure from the idiom of the Pastorals, which suggests that the article would normally be found with σωτὴρ ἡμῶν.[32]

Perhaps the relevant data are better accommodated by saying that Christ was given σωτήρ as a *proper name* and as a *frequent* appellation only when he was regularly called θεός, i.e., not until the second century.

25. Phil. 3:20; 2 Tim. 1:10; Titus 1:4; 3:6; 2 Pet. 1:1, 11; 2:20; 3:2, 18. Moehlmann, however, believes (20) that in 2 Pet. 3:2 σωτήρ is a proper name but that even there it occurs with another title (κύριος). From the data of the Pastoral Epistles and 2 Peter, Moehlmann traces the evolution of the early Christian use of σωτήρ: God our *soter*; Jesus Christ our *soter*; our Lord and *soter*, Jesus Christ; our God and *soter*, Jesus Christ (17). Significantly, in each case σωτήρ is found with a proper name.

26. Luke 2:11; John 4:42; Acts 5:31; 13:23; Eph. 5:23; 1 John 4:14.

27. As Bernard (*Pastoral Epistles* 172) claims.

28. Ὁ σωτὴρ ἡμῶν occurs in 1 Tim. 2:3; 2 Tim. 1:10; Titus 1:3, 4; 2:10; 3:4, 6 (the fact that ἡμῶν is generally attached to an articular noun does not diminish the force of this statistic).

29. 1 Tim. 1:1, where σωτήρ is anarthrous as being in apposition to θεός which lacks the article in accordance with the canon of Apollonius; 4:10, where σωτήρ is anarthrous because it is predicative and adjectival.

30. Abbot ("Titus" 451) formulates the general principle thus: "The definite article is inserted before the second attributive when it is *felt to be needed to distinguish different subjects*; but when the two terms connected by a copulative are *shown by any circumstance* to denote distinct subjects, then the article may be omitted, for the excellent reason that it is not needed."

31. N. Turner, *Syntax* 181. Cremer (280) cites (among other passages) Matt. 16:21; 20:18; 27:3; and Acts 15:22 in support of this principle.

32. The same objection may be leveled against Winer's proposal (130) that since ἡμῶν makes σωτῆρος definite the article is superfluous with σωτῆρος.

c. A single article is found with θεός and σωτήρ because Father and Son are regarded as equal sharers in or joint possessors of the divine glory to be manifested at Christ's parousia (Abbot, "Titus" 452).

   Luke 9:26 shows this to be a permissible view, although it fails to take sufficiently seriously the *ex hypothesi* ambiguity of diction that arises from the nonuse of the second article. The inference that a first-century reader or hearer would first draw from the phrase ἡ δόξα τοῦ μεγάλου θεοῦ καὶ σωτῆρος ἡμῶν would probably not be that two divine figures jointly possessed δόξα but that the θεός who was also their σωτήρ possessed δόξα.

d. By using the anarthrous σωτήρ the writer is stressing the saviorhood of Jesus Christ, his distinctive character as σωτήρ (Abbot, "Titus" 441, 452–53). This explanation would be more convincing if θεοῦ also were anarthrous: τὴν μακαρίαν ἐλπίδα καὶ ἐπιφάνειαν τῆς δόξης μεγάλου θεοῦ καὶ σωτῆρος ἡμῶν Ἰησοῦ Χριστοῦ.

e. The prefixing of the appositional substantive σωτῆρος to the proper name Ἰησοῦ Χριστοῦ has led to the anarthrous state of σωτῆρος.[33] It is not clear, however, that an appositional noun that precedes a proper name is necessarily anarthrous. Second Timothy 1:10 has διὰ τῆς ἐπιφανείας τοῦ σωτῆρος ἡμῶν Χριστοῦ Ἰησοῦ,[34] while in four other passages in the Pastorals σωτὴρ ἡμῶν is articular preceding the anarthrous quasi–proper name θεός.[35]

Two observations may fitly conclude this discussion of a complex grammatical point. First, if Paul had wished to speak unambiguously of two persons, he could have written either τοῦ μεγάλου θεοῦ καὶ Ἰησοῦ Χριστοῦ τοῦ σωτῆρος ἡμῶν or τοῦ μεγάλου θεοῦ ἡμῶν καὶ τοῦ σωτῆρος Ἰησοῦ Χριστου.[36] Second, it must remain improbable that Paul would have acquiesced in a form of words that would naturally be construed as depicting Jesus as ὁ μέγας θεὸς καὶ σωτὴρ ἡμῶν if in fact he believed that Jesus was in no sense θεός.

3. The Presence of μέγας

The exceptional use of μέγας with θεός may be more easily explained if θεός refers to Christ than if it signifies the Father (cf. Ellicott 207).

33. An argument of Winer (130) that is followed by Alford (3:420). An anarthrous σωτήρ precedes Ἰησοῦς Χριστός or Χριστὸς Ἰησοῦς in 2 Pet. 1:1, 11; 3:18 (as in Titus 2:13), while in Titus 1:4; 3:6 this name precedes the articular ὁ σωτὴρ ἡμῶν.

34. Here the presence of the article with σωτῆρος illustrates the canon of Apollonius that nouns in *regimen* generally either both have the article or both lack it.

35. 1 Tim. 2:3; Titus 1:3; 2:10; 3:4 (each rendered in the RSV by "God our Savior," which construes τοῦ σωτῆρος as an appositional substantive).

36. In the latter case, the article inserted before σωτῆρος, in addition to the altered position of ἡμῶν, would indicate two distinct subjects.

As a description of the Father, μέγας is not elsewhere used in the NT,[37] although it occurs relatively often in the LXX (especially in the Psalms) as a divine epithet.[38] Given the Jews' widespread use of this epithet in reference to Yahweh, one cannot say that μέγας would be redundant if applied to the Father, especially since it aptly summarizes the description of God given in 1 Timothy 6:15–16 in connection with the ἐπιφάνεια of Jesus Christ (cf. Abbot, "Titus" 443–44). Yet against this must be set two points. (1) If there is a use of the θεὸς καὶ σωτήρ formula and therefore exclusive reference to Christ,[39] it would occasion no surprise if μέγας (and ἡμῶν) was added in opposition to the pagan applications of the formula: "*Our great* God and Savior, Jesus Christ."[40] (2) In describing the atoning work of Christ, verse 14 explicates that in which the greatness of Jesus Christ as "our God and Savior" is displayed. Not only will Jesus Christ as Savior fulfill Christians' "hope of glory" (cf. Rom. 5:2) at his appearance (v. 13) by transforming their lowly bodies into glorious bodies like his own body (Phil. 3:20–21), but he has already proved himself a μέγας σωτήρ, a unique bearer of God's saving grace (v. 11), by his sacrificial self-surrender to achieve their redemption and sanctification (v. 14).

4. The Parallelism in Verse 13

There is significant parallelism between the two parts of verse 13, viz., τὴν . . . δόξης and τοῦ . . . ἡμῶν. In each case there is article–adjective–noun–καί–anarthrous noun–genitive. Whether τὴν . . . ἐλπίδα καὶ ἐπιφάνειαν is a hendiadys[41] or καί is epexegetic,[42] the sense of verse 13a seems to be "we wait for the hope[43] that brings and will bring blessing[44]—the appearing of the glory. . . ." If the parallelism is intentional, ὁ μέγας θεός is the σωτήρ, just as ἡ μακαρία ἐλπίς is the ἐπιφάνεια.

37. The substantival form μεγαλειότης is used of Christ in 2 Pet. 1:16, of God in Luke 9:43; and μεγαλωσύνη of God in Heb. 1:3; 8:1; Jude 25.

38. Deut. 10:17; 2 Esdras 14:8 [Neh. 4:14]; 18:6 [Neh. 8:6]; 19:32 [Neh. 9:32]; Ps. 47:2 [Engl. 48:1]; 76:14 [Engl. 77:13]; 85:10 [Engl. 86:10]; Isa. 26:4; Jer. 39:19 [Engl. 32:19]; Dan. 2:45; 9:4; Mal. 1:14.

39. Only on Hort's view (discussed above, §A.4.a) could θεοῦ and σωτῆρος both refer to the Father.

40. E. F. Scott (*Pastoral Epistles* 170) maintains that the idea of "greatness" really belongs to δόξα but has been transferred to θεός from whom the δόξα emanates.

41. According to Ellicott (207), Theodoret construed the whole phrase as a hendiadys: "The hope of his glorious coming"; similarly BDF §442.(16).

42. This understanding of the verse is reflected in several English versions: TCNT, Weymouth, Moffatt, Berkeley, RSV, NAB[1], NAB[2], Cassirer.

43. Ἐλπίς here is no subjective sentiment but the objective fulfillment of divine promise, *res sperata* not *spes* (cf. Col. 1:5). Goodspeed has the rendering "the fulfilment of our blessed hope" (similarly Cassirer); and NEB and REB, "the happy fulfilment of our hope."

44. The present expectation of realized hope brings blessing, as does the actual future realization of hope.

5. Dubious Support

Sometimes adduced in favor of understanding θεός of Jesus Christ in this verse are four further arguments, each of which is of dubious validity.

a. W. Lock (145) alleges that the relative clause ὃς ἔδωκεν κτλ. (v. 14) implies a single referent, θεὸς καὶ σωτήρ, or a second article would seem to be required before σωτῆρος if θεός designated the Father but σωτὴρ ἡμῶν . . . ὃς ἔδωκεν denoted Jesus.[45]

   However, a similar conjunction of two persons (this time under the bond of a single preposition, not a single article) followed by a predicate referring to only one of the two is found in Galatians 1:3–4: χάρις ὑμῖν καὶ εἰρήνη ἀπὸ θεοῦ πατρὸς ἡμῶν καὶ κυρίου Ἰησοῦ Χριστοῦ τοῦ δόντος ἑαυτὸν κτλ.

b. In the NT the word ἐπιφάνεια is never applied to the Father, but on several occasions to the Son, in reference to his first advent (2 Tim. 1:10) or his second advent (2 Thess. 2:8; 1 Tim. 6:14; 2 Tim. 4:1, 8).

   What this argument overlooks is that it is not the Father himself who will be visibly manifested but the *glory* that belongs to the great God. It is unlikely that τῆς δόξης is a "Hebrew" genitive ("the glorious appearing of the great God")[46] or that "the appearance of the glory of the great God" is simply a circumlocution for "the great God will appear."[47] In any case, nowhere does a NT writer speak of a dual epiphany of Father and Son. And in Jewish apocalyptic, where appearances of Yahweh and of the Messiah are mentioned, never are both said to appear together (Spicq, *Épîtres Pastorales* 2:640).

c. In the OT the work of redemption and purification is attributed to Yahweh (e.g., Exod. 19:5; Deut.7:6; 14:2), but in Titus 2:14 Christ is said to have redeemed and purified his people: Christ and his church replace Yahweh and Israel. Consequently it would be natural for Paul to apply to Jesus two of the OT appellations of Yahweh, viz., θεός and σωτήρ.[48]

   In reply, one may observe that what is "natural" for a writer to say is not always what he does say. Moreover, similarity of function does not prove interchangeability of titles any more than identity of person.

45. Similarly Spicq, *Épîtres Pastorales* 2:640. But Parry (81) refers ὃς ἔδωκεν to Ἰησοῦς Χριστός alone, because he finds in v. 14 an indication of the sense in which Christ is the glory of God, viz., in his manifestation of the grace of God.

46. For the reasons why it is improbable that τῆς δόξης is a "Hebrew" or attributive genitive ("glorious"), see above, §A.2.

47. *Pace* Easton 94, who compares Acts 7:55; 2 Pet. 1:17.

48. This argument is adduced by Cremer 281, Lock 145, and G. Kittel, *TDNT* 2:248.

d. The majority of post-Nicene writers support the identification of ὁ μέγας θεὸς καὶ σωτὴρ ἡμῶν as Christ.[49]

Against this, however, must be set the fact that the principal ancient versions (except the Ethiopic) distinguish θεός from σωτήρ, as does Justin Martyr (*Apol.* 1:61). If anything, the testimony of the versions is more important than that of the fathers on this point, given the widespread use of θεός as an appellation of Christ in the fourth century and the post-Nicene concern for the scriptural buttressing of orthodox teaching on the deity of Christ.

In the light of the foregoing evidence, it seems highly probable that in Titus 2:13 Jesus Christ is called "our great God and Savior," a verdict shared, with varying degrees of assurance, by almost all grammarians[50] and lexicographers,[51] many commentators,[52] and many writers on NT theology or Christology,[53] although there are some dissenting voices.[54]

49. Thus Ellicott (207), who also cites Clement of Alexandria and Hippolytus as supporting this identification, but Abbot ("Titus" 444) has shown their testimony to be suspect.

50. Middleton 393–96; H. J. Rose in Middleton 393; B. Weiss, "Gebrauch" 365; Moulton, *Prolegomena* 84; Robertson, *Grammar* 786; Robertson, "Article" 186–87; BDF §276.(3); Zerwick, *Greek* §185 (the single article "seem(s) to suggest the divinity of Christ"; cf. his *Analysis* 488); C. F. D. Moule, *Idiom Book* 109–10; C. F. D. Moule, *Origin* 137 ("probably"); N. Turner, *Insights* 15–16; cf. his *Syntax* 181.

51. Cremer 279–81; BAGD 357b, 552d, 801b; Stauffer 324 n. 803; E. Stauffer, *TDNT* 3:106; W. Grundmann, *TDNT* 4:538–40, 9:565 n. 464.

52. Ellicott 207–8 ("a direct, definite, and even *studied* declaration of the divinity of the Eternal Son"); Wiesinger 307–10; Bernard, *Pastoral Epistles* 171–73 ("with great hesitation"); Dibelius 90, 92; Easton 94–95; Lock 144–46; Spicq, *Épîtres Pastorales* 2:249, 251, 254, 640–41; Hendriksen, *Timothy–Titus* 373–75; Simpson, *Pastoral Epistles* 108–9 ("a studied assertion"); Gealy 539–40; Guthrie, *Pastoral Epistles* 212; Leaney 123; Barrett, *Pastoral Epistles* 138; A. T. Hanson, *Pastoral Letters* 116; Houlden, *Pastoral Epistles* 150–51. Note also the translation of Cassirer, which divorces σωτήρ from θεός but applies both terms to Christ, taking καί as epexegetic: "The appearing in glory of him who is the great God, our Saviour Jesus Christ."

53. Bousset 314, 316; Warfield, *Studies* 245, 254–55; E. Meyer 3:396; Lebreton, *History* 371; Moehlmann 17, 39, 57; Prat 2:127–28; Bonsirven, *Theology* 251 and n. 10; Bultmann, *Theology* 1:129; Cerfaux, *Christ* 35 n. 10 (cf. 83); Rahner 135, 136 n. 2; Cullmann, *Christology* 313–14; Wainwright, *Trinity* 63–65 (= "Confession" 283–84); Barclay, *Jesus* 31–33; Brown, *Reflections* 16–18, 23 (= "Jesus" 556–57, 561); Bruce, *Paraphrase* 293; Bruce, "God" 51; Sabourin, *Names* 302; Deichgräber 180–81; R. N. Longenecker, *Christology* 138–39; Romaniuk 66–67.

54. The only grammarian seems to be Winer 130. Among the commentators one finds Alford 3:419–21; Huther, *Timothy–Titus* 359–62; Abbot, "Titus"; Hort, *James* 47, 103–4; White 195–96; Parry 81; E. F. Scott, *Pastoral Epistles* 169–70; Jeremias 64–65; Kelly, *Pastoral Epistles* 246–47; Conzelmann in Dibelius and Conzelmann 143. So also V. Taylor, *Person* 131–33; but cf. his *Essays* 86 (= "Jesus" 117); W. Foerster, *TDNT* 7:1018 n. 70.

VIII

The Throne of God (Psalm 45:7–8)

7 כסאך אלהים עולם ועד
שבט מישר שבט מלכותך
8 אהבת צדק ותשנא רשע
על־כן משחך אלהים אלהיך
שמן ששון מחבריך

Of the sixteen separate NT passages considered in detail in this volume, in only one case does the term θεός occur within an OT citation. In Hebrews 1:8–9 we find two uses of ὁ θεός that could refer to Jesus Christ, embedded within a citation of Psalm 45:7–8 (= LXX 44:7–8 = Engl. 45:6–7) that closely follows the LXX (verse numbers in this chapter refer to the Hebrew text). This being so, it is imperative that we examine the meaning of these two verses in their original setting in Hebrew and then in their LXX dress before seeking to discover how the author of Hebrews employs the quotation. This NT writer is citing the LXX, but does the LXX accurately reflect the probable meaning of the Hebrew text at this point or does it distort that meaning? These issues are the concern of the present chapter.

A. Setting and Structure

Psalm 45 is one of the forty-two psalms in the "Elohist Psalter" (Pss. 42–83), so-called because the term אלהים predominates as the divine name.[1] The psalm belongs to a group of some ten "royal psalms" in which the king is the central figure.[2] It is a wedding song (*epithalamium*) that was composed for some unspecified royal marriage[3] and that was included within

1. For the relevant statistics see M. H. Segal 104–05. See also Patterson 32–33.

2. Pss. 2, 18, 20, 21, 45, 72, 89, 101, 110, 132 (some would add 118 and 144).

3. The identity of the king and queen remains obscure, but some of the more common proposals are Jehoram of Judah and Athaliah of Israel (who was Tyrian [cf. v. 13] on her mother's side; cf. 2 Kings 8:16; see further Patterson 33–34, 45–46), Solomon and the daughter of Pharaoh (cf. 1 Kings 3:1–3; 11:1–2), or Ahab and Jezebel (see the summary of research in Jacquet 42). Because allusions to Nathan's oracles (2 Sam. 7:8–16) are scattered throughout the poem (e.g., vv. 3, 5, 7, 17; cf. Pss. 72, 89, 132), the king in question was probably king of Judah. After a thorough examination of the literary background of the psalm, Mulder concludes that "Ps. 45 was all but certainly written before the exile under the influence of the court style of the later Neo-Assyrian empire. It originated probably in the seventh century B.C. in the Southern kingdom, with a good chance that Josiah is the king who is celebrated in the psalm" (158). However, in the light of the common Near Eastern practice of treating a bridal couple as royalty T. H. Gaster has proposed that the psalm describes a conventional wedding ceremony, with a comparison between the characteristics of a bridegroom and the qualities of a king.

the Psalter probably because it epitomized an ideal king of the Davidic dynasty, the royal Messiah.[4]

As for the psalm's setting, M. E. Podechard (28) believes that the poet's thought follows the successive stages of the wedding ceremony, from the bridegroom's procession to the bride's home, to the meeting of the two groups, to the joyful return to the royal palace. Some suggest that this nuptial ode may have been sung as the new queen and her attendants entered the royal palace in splendid procession (Ewald, *Psalms* 165) or after the marriage ceremony had taken place and the king and queen were seated on thrones in their palace attended by the royal retinue and celebrating their wedding feast (with vv. 14–16 referring to an earlier event) (Kissane 196, 200–201).[5]

With regard to the structure of the psalm, verse 2 is a dedicatory preface in which the psalmist describes his pleasant task, while verse 18 forms a valedictory epilogue that indicates the desired outcome of the wedding song, viz., perpetual praise of the king among the nations. Within this structure verse 3 is an introduction that praises the beauty and graciousness of the king, and verse 17 a conclusion that foresees that illustrious descendants will come from the marriage union. The heart of the poem consists of two sections, verses 4–10 and verses 11–16.[6]

There are depicted in verses 4–10 the two preeminent characteristics of the king: martial prowess in the defense of truth and right (vv. 4–6) and a just administration in a dynasty that is destined to endure for ever, an administration that merits the divine pleasure and prompts the joyful homage of his court (vv. 7–10). Or as L. C. Allen expresses it (226), "Verses 4–6 focus upon the king engaged in a just war, wielding sword and bow in his right hand; verses 7–10 envisage him on his throne wielding his royal sceptre, symbol of justice, and in his palace precincts in festive garb with his new consort at his right hand."[7]

4. A messianic interpretation of Ps. 45 does not preclude an original particular historical setting (see vv. 9–10, 13–15) involving a royal marriage. On this question see Sabourin, *Psalms* 161–62. Tournay ("Ps. xlv" 173) sketches the three principal interpretations of the psalm: (1) a purely secular marriage song, incorporated into the Psalter owing to a messianic adaptation; (2) a marriage song for a king of Israel or Judah, regarded as a type of the Messiah; or (3) a directly messianic marriage song composed in the third or fourth century B.C. On the history of the interpretation of this psalm, see P. J. King 1–31, 15, 103–27, who concludes "that in ps. 45 the Messiah is typified by an earthly monarch who is the subject of this psalm in the literal proper sense. . . . In short, the king is the type, the Messiah is the antitype" (129; cf. 119–28).

5. Building on a suggestion of Eaton (*Psalms* 123; cf. 23, 31–32), Goulder sees in Psalm 45 a reflection of the day-long annual ritual surrounding the new marriage of the king on the fifteenth of Bul, the first day of an autumnal festival at Dan. The first half of the psalm is an enthronement hymn (vv. 3–9), the second half a prothalamium (vv. 10–17), the whole poem being sung in the evening (121–37).

6. Cf. the treatment of the psalm's structure in N. H. Ridderbos 69–74; Schedl; Mulder 22–29; Allen 221–27; and most recently Patterson 31, 35–45.

7. Podechard aptly observes (33) that this king excels in performing two essential functions of royalty—defense of the nation from without, the maintenance of justice within.

Verse 10 represents a climax and a transition, for the poet's thought has moved from the king himself (v. 3) as a mighty warrior (vv. 4–6) and just administrator (vv. 7–8) to the king's robes (v. 9a), to the royal musicians (v. 9b) and harem (v. 10a), to the king's consort (v. 10b), who is then immediately addressed in verses 11–13. In the second principal segment of the psalm (vv. 11–16), which is "an unfolding of the statement in v. 10b, 'the consort stands at your right hand'" (N. H. Ridderbos 74), the poet exhorts the new bride to give exclusive allegiance to her lordly husband (vv. 11–13) and describes the splendid pomp of the bridal train and the consummate joy of the bridal party as they enter the royal palace (vv. 14–16).

Verses 7 and 8 of Psalm 45 are bound together by עַל־כֵּן in verse 8b. God could be said to have anointed the king with the oil of incomparable exultation (v. 8b–c) precisely because the king's dynasty was permanent or eternal (v. 7a), his royal administration was marked by equity (v. 7b), and he himself loved righteousness and eschewed wickedness (v. 8a). If "the oil of gladness" (v. 8c) refers to a literal anointing, it could allude to an earlier consecration with oil at the king's coronation (cf. 1 Sam. 15:17; 2 Sam. 12:7; Ps. 89:20 [MT v. 21]) or possibly to the preparations for the wedding celebration or for the marriage bed. On the other hand, if the expression is metaphorical (as seems more probable, cf. Isa. 61:3), ששון will be epexegetic of שמן oil = gladness),[8] indicating that God had anointed the king on his marriage day with a joy such as no other king or friend of the bridegroom had ever experienced.[9]

B. אלהים in Psalm 45:7–8

One of the most celebrated *cruces interpretum* in the OT is found in verse 7a. How are the words כסאך אלהים to be understood? It should be noted immediately that not a few scholars, daunted by what they consider to be insuperable grammatical or conceptual difficulties in the text as it stands (such as the anarthrous state of אלהים or its application to a human being, if it is a vocative), have resorted to various conjectural emendations.

8. Thus also König 474 n. 3, comparing Ps. 95:1b. Alternatively שמן could symbolize consecration so that the phrase would mean "(God . . . has anointed you) in a consecration that brought you gladness." But Briggs construes שמן ששון as a vocative that begins the third strophe of the poem (vv. 8c–18), a strophe whose characteristic theme is the joy of the bridegroom: "O, oil of joy above thy fellows" (cf. Song of Sol. 1:3; 4:10–16). The king himself is thus seen (in vv. 8c–9a) as embodying "all precious ointments" and "delightful odours and plants" (*Psalms* 383, 387; *Prophecy* 142 and n. 1).

9. מחבריך here may mean (1) "above your fellow kings" (P. J. King xix, 86) (or, "wedding guests," cf. Matt. 9:15); (2) "in greater measure than other men" (cf. v. 3a); or less probably (3) "(God, your God, has anointed you,) rather than your companions." Craigie (336; cf. BDB 582 §6a, s.v. מן) supports this latter view.

For the sake of completeness these may be briefly listed, before considering in detail the main ways of understanding the MT.

1. Conjectural Emendations

a. C. Bruston suggests (91–92) that an original יִהְיֶה was read as יהוה which was then subject to an Elohistic alteration to אלהים. The text should therefore be rendered "your throne will be eternal" (cf. 2 Sam. 7:13, 16; Ps. 21:4 [MT v. 5]; 72:5; 89:4, 29, 36–37 [MT vv. 5, 30, 37–38]).[10] Cf. Moffatt's translation: "Your throne shall stand for evermore."

b. S. R. Driver expressed (at least in 1892) a hesitant preference for P. de Lagarde's conjecture of סָעַד for ועד (cf. Prov. 20:28): "Your throne Elohim has established for ever."[11]

c. T. K. Cheyne proposes נשאך יהוה: "Yahwè lifts thee up for ever and ever."[12]

d. אלהים could be omitted as a gloss or later addition to the text (GKC §128d, "most probably").

e. Following earlier suggestions, T. H. Gaster (244, 250) supplies the verb הכין: "Thy throne hath some god [set firm] to endure for all time."

f. Reading אלהי־ם עולם ועד (i.e., with enclitic *mēm*) and vocalizing כסאך as a denominative piel (כִּסֵּאֲךָ) from כסא, M. Dahood translates the phrase as "the eternal and everlasting God has enthroned you," a proposal which creates a parallelism between verses 3, 7, and 8 ("God has blessed you. . . . God has enthroned you. . . . God has anointed you").[13]

Confronted by all these conjectures and knowing that the text as it stands may be understood satisfactorily in several different ways and that the ancient versions uniformly construed אלהים as a vocative (see below), the exegete may be excused for viewing any resort to emendation as an ill-advised counsel of despair. There are, in fact, at least five ways of translating the phrase כסאך אלהים.

10. Bruston was followed, *inter alios*, by Wellhausen 45, 183; Duhm 129; and Podechard 28–29, 33. This view was subjected to a lengthy critique by Allis. On the whole matter of the "Elohist redaction" of the Psalter, see R. D. Wilson, "Psalms" (esp. 7–10) and "Old Testament" 472–75.

11. 260 §194 ii (referring to de Lagarde xlvii, who cites Prov. 20:28 and Isa. 9:6 in support).

12. *Psalms* 199, 203; but cf. his earlier edition (1888) 124 and his *Psalter* 182.

13. 273, followed by Craigie 336–37 and REB. On this proposal, see Mulder 70–72, 80; Harman 340–42.

2. *Translations of* כסאך אלהים

a. "Your divine throne"

On the first view אלהים is genitival—"your throne of God" means "your throne established and protected by God,"[14] "the throne that God has given you" (GNB), "your throne is from God" (NJB), or "your God-like (or, godly) throne."[15] Proponents of this view[16] frequently cite such parallels as the phrases בריתי יעקוב, literally "my covenant, Jacob," in Leviticus 26:42 and מחסי־עז, literally "my refuge, strength," in Psalm 71:7.

This translation, popularized by the RSV,[17] is not without serious difficulties. If כסא is in fact qualified by two different types of genitive (viz., a pronominal suffix *kap* denoting possession and an adjectival genitive, אלהים, meaning "divine"), this is a construction that is probably unparalleled in the OT (see GKC §128d).[18] With regard to Leviticus 26:42, if י is not simply an archaic marker of the construct state or a case of dittography, either ברית has the suffix because the following proper name (unlike אלהים) could not be so qualified or the expression is an ellipsis for בריתי ברית יעקוב.[19] What is more, "my covenant [made with] Jacob" is not parallel to "your throne [established by] God"; God may be said to establish a throne, but not Jacob the covenant. As for Psalm 71:7 and comparable parallels often adduced,[20] the two nouns involved are usually related by apposition, so that מחסי־עז means "my refuge, which is strength (or strong)." Sometimes the second noun may be classed as an accusative of definition: מדו בד (Lev. 6:3 [Engl. v. 10]) means "his garment, in (= made of) linen."[21] If, in these two instances, the second noun can be appropriately translated by an adjective ("my strong refuge," "his linen garment") this is not because the substantive thus rendered is genitival. Furthermore, if it be argued that כסאך אלהים stands for the more regular כסא אלהיך, this latter means "the throne of your God" (cf. 1 Kings 1:20, 27, 37; 2:12, 24), not "your throne is from God" or "your divine throne."

14. Thus Hupfeld and Nowack 627.

15. A variation of this is, "Your throne is like God (in that it is) for ever and ever," where אלהים is predicative and stands for כאלהים, the כ having been omitted by haplography or for the sake of euphony after the final כ of כסאך.

16. For example, Vriezen 220 n. 1.

17. The NRSV reverts to the RV and ASV rendering, "Your throne, O God," and in the margin gives only one alternative translation, "Your throne is a throne of God."

18. Cf. the view of H. L. Fleischer cited by S. R. Driver §§193–94.

19. See the discussion in GKC §§128d, 131r; Hengstenberg 133–34.

20. Viz., Lev. 6:3 [Engl. v. 10]; Num 25:12; 2 Sam. 22:18, 33; 2 Kings 23:17; Ps. 79:5; Ezek. 16:27; Hab. 3:8.

21. Cf. S. R. Driver §193.

b. "God is your throne" or "Your throne is God (or, divine)"

Under a second view אלהים is subject or predicate and the sense is either that God himself is the creator and sustainer of the king's rule or that regal power is securely founded on and supported by the immovable rock of divine authority.[22]

Grammatically, no valid objection may be raised against these renderings, but conceptually they are harsh. An Eliakim, son of Hilkiah, may "become a throne of honor to his father's house" (Isa. 22:23) but God could scarcely "be a throne" to a king, for the concept of "God" and the idea of "throne" (= dynasty) are too dissimilar to permit even a bold metaphor such as is found elsewhere in the Psalter: "You are my rock and my fortress" (Ps. 71:3; cf. 91:2, 9; Isa. 26:4), "Lord, you have been our dwelling place in all generations" (Ps. 90:1; cf. Deut. 33:27). And, given the Hebrew word order, "God is your throne" could not be taken as brachylogy for "God will establish (יכין) your throne." With regard to the translation "your throne is God," where אלהים is predicative, it seems unfitting to assert that any human throne, however כסא be interpreted, belongs to the category of divine beings ("is God"). And it is unlikely that the notion of "founded on God" or "protected by God" or "having divine qualities" may be abbreviated to the single word אלהים.

c. "Your throne is God's throne" or "Your throne will be a divine throne"

In the third case כסא has been supplied from כסאך before אלהים, yielding "your throne is God's throne"[23] or "your throne will be a divine throne."[24] The construction may be explained as follows.[25] In the expression קיר עץ, "a wall of wood," עץ is used absolutely as part of the subject. But the absolute עץ could also be used predicatively, without any copula, as in the phrase קירתיו עץ (Ezek. 41:22), literally "its walls, wood," that is, "its walls [were] wood(en)." This represents, in expanded form, "its walls [were walls of] wood," with קירות supplied from קירתיו before עץ. Similarly

22. Cf. Knox's rendering, "God is the support of your throne."

23. Kirkpatrick 248 (tentatively; "thy throne [is the throne of] God"); Tournay, "Psaume cx" 7–8; Tournay, "Ps. xlv" 185–88; cf. Robert and Tournay 434; Mulder 54–65, 73–80 (with the qualification that this is "an unusual construction, without any really reliable parallel in the Old Testament" [65]); Mettinger 264–65, 273; Eaton, *Kingship* 142–43 ("your throne, the throne of God"; cf. his *Psalms* 125). The RSV mg and the NRSV mg make the supplied כסא indefinite in meaning: "Your throne is a throne of God."

24. Similarly Gesenius 50 (who paraphrases "divine" as "guarded and made prosperous by God"); Ewald, *Syntax* 133; König 474. But Buttenwieser prefers to supply an optative (as also in vv. 6a–b, 7b; cf. GKC §§141–42): "May thy throne be a throne divine forever" (82, 91).

25. Cf. Ewald, *Syntax* 132–33.

כסאך אלהים, literally "your throne, God," means "your throne [is the throne of] God." This concept of a royal throne being God's throne is paralleled by 1 Chronicles 29:23 (cf. 28:5; 1 Kings 3:28) where Solomon is said to sit "on the throne of Yahweh." Psalm 45:7–8a would thus affirm that since the king rules in equity and righteousness his kingdom will always remain secure; it will be a kingdom of God.

The problem with this translation is less grammatical than conceptual. In the following texts that are sometimes adduced as parallels to Psalm 45:7 there are (in Hebrew) two or more nouns in juxtaposition without a copula, the first noun being the subject and the other(s) predicate(s). A literal translation is given to illustrate this point.

The whole earth [was] one language	Gen. 11:1
The barley [was] ear and the flax [was] flower	Exod. 9:31
Your bars [shall be] iron and bronze	Deut. 33:25
The season [is] heavy showers	Ezra 10:13
All your robes [are] myrrh and aloes and cassia	Ps. 45:9 [Engl. v. 8]
Our vineyards [are] blossom	Song of Sol. 2:15
One basket [was] very good figs	Jer. 24:2
Hamath and Arpad [are] confusion	Jer. 49:23
Its walls [were] wood	Ezek. 41:22

Although these instances may be considered formally parallel to Psalm 45:7, there is one significant difference. In each case there is implied a certain identity between subject and predicate, so that the second (and any subsequent) noun denotes the material of which an object is made or a characteristic which an object possesses. Thus the copula ("be") supplied in the literal translations may be paraphrased or better expressed by phrases such as "consists of," "is made of," "contains," "is filled with," or "is characterized by."[26] But God is neither the material of which the throne is composed nor a characteristic it possesses. Between this subject and predicate there may be certain likenesses (such as eternality) but any form of identity is lacking. What this rendering in fact presupposes is the ellipsis not simply of כסא but of ככסא "[is] *like* the throne of" (see §B.2.d below).[27]

Grammatically there is no objection to finding an ellipsis in verse 7a but it is remarkable that in verse 7b, where there would have been no ambiguity of meaning without the repetition of the nominative, the subject is actually repeated in the predicate (שבט . . . שבט), whereas in verse 7a, where the repetition would have removed any ambiguity, the subject is not repeated.[28]

26. Cf. the similar comments in S. R. Driver §§187–88, 194.
27. Herkenne renders v. 7a this way: "Dein Thron gleicht dem Jahves immer und ewig" (172).
28. This point is made by Pusey 476n.

That is, if in fact verse 7a meant "your throne is the throne of God," one might have expected (considerations of meter apart) the poet to have written either כסאך כסא אלהים in verse 7a[29] (to parallel v. 7b) or שבט מישר מלכותך in verse 7b[30] (to parallel v. 7a, *ex hypothesi*). In any case, as T. K. Cheyne remarks (*Psalms* 182), given the simple style of the poet, the idea of the king's sharing the rule of God might have been more directly expressed by "you sit beside Yahweh on his throne."

d. "Your throne is like God's throne"

The rendering of G. R. Driver[31] and the NEB, which reflects the conceptual tendency of §B.2.c above, represents a fusion of two distinct Hebrew idioms. After the preposition כ ("like") there may occur an ellipsis of a word or words necessary to the sense. Thus חציו כגבור (Jer. 50:9) means "his arrows will be like [those of] a warrior." Second, in comparisons Hebrew sometimes omits the preposition כ. For example, ראשו כתם פז (Song of Sol. 5:11), "his head is [like] the finest gold." Accordingly, Driver's translation of Psalm 45:7a simply "presupposes a natural development of idioms that are well attested in Hebrew."[32]

To support this translation appeal has been made to three main texts. C. R. North refers to the expression עיניך יונים, "your eyes are doves," in Song of Solomon 1:15 and 4:1, which, in light of 5:12a (עיניו כיונים, "his eyes are like doves"), he takes to mean "'thy eyes are like doves' eyes' for softness and innocence" (30). The comparison, however, may equally well be between the whiteness of the eyes and the whiteness of doves (cf. 5:12b: "bathed in milk"; 4:2: "your teeth are like a flock of shorn ewes")[33] or between the eyes and the gentleness and purity of doves themselves. In either case, "your eyes are doves" means simply "your eyes are like doves."

In appealing to Psalm 80:11 [Engl. v. 10], J. A. Emerton expands the RV (text) rendering of the verse to illustrate the parallel: "The mountains were covered with the shadow of it [viz., Israel as a vine planted in Canaan], And the boughs thereof were like *the boughs of* cedars of God" (similarly NEB). "Just as the boughs of the vine are said to be like cedar trees because they offer shade, so the king's throne may be compared to God either because he is eternal or because his throne is eternal (cf. Lam. v.19)."[34] But the

29. Perhaps Exod. 32:16 affords the closest parallel to this: המכתב מכתב אלהים הוא.

30. Or if שבט מלכותך were the subject of v. 7b, שבט מלכותך מישר might have been expected.

31. G. R. Driver, "Study" 115–16; "Psalms" 124. Driver was followed by North 30 (tentatively, since "it is still possible that *Elohim* is a vocative addressed to the king"); Noth 186–87; A. R. Johnson, *Kingship* 27 n. 1; D. W. Thomas 16; Emerton (whose aim is to defend Driver's rendering as a "possibility").

32. Emerton 60. My summary of this view is drawn from Emerton.

33. Porter 52–53.

34. Emerton 61–63 (citation from p. 63).

immediate context in verse 10b (the vine "filled the land") suggests that verses 11–12 together illustrate the remarkable expansiveness of the vine (rather than its compass [vv. 11a, 12]) *and* its protectiveness (v. 11b; "offering shade," as Emerton puts it). כסה (v. 11a) may indicate height and שלח (v. 12a) breadth, and just as the latter verb is to be supplied in verse 12b, so the former is to be supplied in verse 11b.[35] One may therefore safely follow the RSV (similarly RV mg) in its rendering of the verse: "The mountains were covered with its shade, the mighty cedars [were covered] with its branches."[36] But even if וענפיה ("and its boughs") is nominative, as Emerton alleges, there is more than one possible interpretation of the text: as JB notes (p. 865 n. f), "'The branches were cedars of God' (i.e. the highest of cedars, cf. 36:6; 68:15)."

I conclude that although both the Hebrew idioms referred to (viz., an ellipsis after כ; the omission of כ in comparisons) may be separately attested, the purported conflation of the two idioms in Psalm 45:7 lacks any unambiguous parallel in the OT[37] and therefore remains an unconvincing explanation.[38]

e. "Your throne, O God"

The traditional rendering, "your throne, O God," where אלהים is a vocative,[39] is found in all the ancient versions,[40] many English translations (KJV, RV, ASV, Berkeley, NASB, JB, NAB[1], NIV, NRSV), and many modern commentators. But to whom does אלהים refer? To regard this vocative as an address to God himself, as does the Targum,[41] is to ignore the presence of a series of second-person singular pronominal suffixes in the preceding and following verses that can refer only to the king. What is more, a sudden apostrophe to

35. I owe this observation to Craig C. Broyles.

36. The Hebrew word order on this view (nominative–accusative–accusative–nominative) is a case of ABBA.

37. G. R. Driver himself called the construction in Ps. 45:7 "an archaic form of *comparatio compendiaria* which has survived unaltered in an early poem . . . a rare relic of a primitive syntax" ("Study" 115–16). On Driver's appeal to an "identical construction" in the Babylonian Creation Epic (4:4, 6), see Porter 52.

38. It would be somewhat strange to have a simile in verse 7a ("your throne is like . . .") but an identification in v. 7b ("your royal scepter is . . .") (cf. Macintosh 182).

39. אלהים occurs as a vocative in some 47 other places in the Psalms, אדני 4 or 5 times, and יהוה 3 times (Allis 250 n. 30).

40. On Ps. 44:7–8 in the LXX, see §D below. It is not impossible that the uniform testimony of the ancient versions in support of the vocative may reflect "a messianic re-reading which stresses the transcendence of the King-Messiah" (Robert and Tournay 434), but it is at least equally possible that all these versions testify to the most natural way of construing אלהים, whether they understood the word in reference to the Messiah or, as Mulder believes (48), to God.

41. "Thy throne of glory, O Lord, endures for ever and ever." The targumist understands מלך in vv. 2, 6, 12, 15–16 as referring to God, "the King of the world" (v. 15), "the Eternal King" (v. 16). Verse 3 contains the one explicit reference to the Messiah: "Your beauty, O King Messiah, surpasses that of ordinary men." See Levey 109–13.

God in verse 7a would be singularly out of place when the next verse speaks of God in the third person (v. 8b). Only slightly less difficult is the suggestion that אלהים is an apostrophe to the messianic King, for it involves the unlikely supposition that embedded within a poem addressed to the royal couple is a brief messianic prophecy found in verse 7[42] or verses 7–8.[43]

But not all those who regard אלהים as an address to some contemporary king agree that this vocative should be rendered "O God."[44] Alternative translations include "o Ruler,"[45] "o majesty,"[46] "o divine one,"[47] "o Divine One,"[48] "O god,"[49] and "O Elohim."[50] Behind this variety of renderings are differing views about the meaning of אלהים when the term is applied to beings other than the sovereign God. (We shall return to this point below.)

C. Objections to the Traditional Interpretation

Perhaps the attempt to defend this traditional interpretation is best made by considering the various objections raised against it. Such objections fall naturally into four categories: grammatical, structural, contextual, and theological.

1. Grammatical

On the grammatical side it is alleged that אלהים as a vocative would "without doubt" have the article (Podechard 33).

Now it is true that since a person addressed is always definite the vocative is generally articular, but, as P. Joüon rightly points out, especially in poetry and elevated prose it is quite often omitted (§137g). In reference to the one true God, אלהים is a proper name and therefore is determinate in

42. Thus J. B. Payne 262.

43. Thus Harman 343–47 ("the eyes of the inspired psalmist were suddenly lifted beyond the contemporary occupant of the Davidic throne to the kingly glory of the messianic ruler," 344).

44. Scholars who render אלהים by "O God" include Hengstenberg 133–35; Pusey 473–78; Perowne 363; Gunkel 189–90; Allis; Oesterley 251–53; de Fraine 25 n. 4, 203; P. J. King xix, 77–78; Schedl 314, 316; Kidner 172; Patterson 40 and n. 48; Van Groningen 366–67.

45. S. R. Hirsch 326.

46. Macintosh, who, citing G. R. Driver's view that the Aramaic אלהיא could be used as an ideogram for the Persian *bagan* ("majesty") (*Documents* 85; but see the 1954 edition, p. 35), suggests that in the Hebrew term אלהים, as in the Aramaic equivalent, there might have been a confusion of the concepts of divinity and majesty.

47. Briggs, *Prophecy* 141 and n. 4 (but cf. his later *Psalms* 387: "Yahweh"); Goulder 129–30; Allen 225 (but cf. 226: "God").

48. Kittel 170, 175 ("du Göttlicher"); Jacquet 38 ("ô Divin"); Bentzen 40 (apparently; cf. 17, 38, 85–86, 96 n. 10); Mowinckel, *Psalmenstudien* 3:98 (cf. 2:302 and his *Psalms* 73, 75); Weiser 360, 363 ("divine king," translating *Göttlicher*); Ringgren 230 (the original has "o Göttlicher," 211; cf. *TDOT* 1:282); Kraus, *Psalmen* 486–87, 490 ("o Göttlicher"; similarly in his *Theologie* 138, 231).

49. Kissane 198, 200 ("'god' in the sense of 'magnate,' 'noble'").

50. Delitzsch, *Psalms* 84, 95–98; Calès 466–67, 470; Jacob 236, 237 n. 1.

itself and does not take the article (GKC §125a, f).[51] In reference to supernatural or nonearthly beings or to persons standing *in loco dei*, אלהים becomes titular and is always anarthrous.[52] So, as a vocative referring to the king, אלהים in verse 7 cannot be said to require the article. One might also note that the other two titular vocatives in the psalm (viz., גביר, v. 4; בת, v. 11) are anarthrous.

Another grammatical objection is this: if עולם ועד were a "direct predicate" ("[is] for ever and ever"), לעולם as in verse 3 (cf. v. 18) rather than the simple עולם would have been expected.[53]

It is a fact that the phrase עולם ועד is never used elsewhere in the Hebrew Bible as an adverbial accusative of time ("for ever and ever") in the predicate of a verbless sentence. In defense of this rendering, however, one may point out[54] that (1) this phrase is used adverbially in verbal sentences (Ps. 21:5 [Engl. v. 4]; 52:10 [Engl. v. 8]; 104:5) and as an adverbial modifier of the predicate in verbless sentences (Ps. 10:16; 48:15 [Engl. v. 14]); (2) a substantive used as an adverbial predicate may replace a prepositional phrase (e.g., 2 Sam. 2:32; Ps. 52:3 [Engl. v. 1]; Jer. 15:18); (3) elsewhere in the Psalter עולם is equivalent to לעולם (Ps. 61:8 [Engl. v. 7]; 66:7; 89:2–3, 38 [Engl. vv. 1–2, 37]); and (4) other temporal adverbs may stand as sole predicates in verbless sentences (Job 8:9; 2 Chron. 12:15).[55] While admitting that a prepositional phrase would have been a more regular construction in a direct predicate (cf. Lam. 5:19), one may fairly claim that the translation of עולם ועד by "(is) for ever and ever" is quite admissible from a grammatical point of view.[56] It is of interest that the LXX renders עולם in verse 7, as it does לע(ו)לם in verses 3 and 18, by εἰς τὸν αἰῶνα. But it is also possible that the phrase עולם ועד forms an emphatic predicate nominative,[57] "Your throne, O God, is perpetuity and eternity (i.e., permanent and eternal)."

51. The only case where אלהים as a vocative referring to God is articular is Judg. 16:28.

52. See the passages cited below.

53. Cf. Hupfeld and Nowack 627. In Ps. 106:1 לעולם is a "direct predicate" ("Yahweh's steadfast love endures forever"); in Ps. 10:16 עולם ועד is an "indirect predicate" ("Yahweh is king for ever and ever").

54. The four points listed are drawn largely from observations made by Allis 254–58 and Mulder 40–43.

55. The research of Andersen on Hebrew verbless clauses in the Pentateuch (42–45, "Rule 3") suggests that if עולם ועד were predicative, the word order would probably have been עולם ועד אלהים כסאך. It is uncertain, however, whether Andersen's rules apply outside the Pentateuch and to poetic material. See the extensive review of Andersen's book by Hoftijzer who points out that poetry often has a syntax pattern that is quite different from that of nonpoetic material.

56. Held cites examples of the poetic usage in Biblical Hebrew of נצח (as well as its synonym עולם) without a preposition where the meaning is "forever," showing that the same phenomenon is observable in Ugaritic and Moabite (50–51; I owe this reference to Philip P. Jenson).

57. Thus Allis 254–55, 258 (citing GKC §141b).

2. Structural

From the standpoint of structure, J. S. M. Mulder (13, 23, 25, 43–44, 46) has argued that a vocative in verse 7a would destroy the symmetry of the two halves (vv. 4–10, 11–16), each beginning with an address (v. 4, גבור; v. 11, בת).

L. C. Allen has issued the rejoinder (225) that while there is no second vocative in verses 11–16 to match a vocatival אלהים in verses 4–10, a double reference to the king in verses 4a and 7a would match the twofold reference to the princess in verses 11a and 14a, and that the personal nouns אלהים (v. 7a) and בת־מלך (v. 14a) may mark the beginning of the second half of their units. One might also observe that verse 7a is not only related to verses 3b and 8b by the use of אלהים, but is also connected with verses 3b and 18b by the occurrence of (ל)ע(ו)לם (ועד), just as verse 8b has על־כן in common with verses 3b and 18b. If, then, verses 7a and 18b are linked structurally, it should occasion no surprise that verse 7a applies the language of divinity to the king since the poet does precisely the same thing in verse 18 by his use of the two liturgical expressions "I will cause your name to be celebrated (אזכירה שמך)" and "(the peoples) will praise you (יהודך)."

3. Contextual

A third type of objection is drawn from contextual considerations. The studied parallelism of verses 3b, 7a, and 8b shows, it is said, that the word אלהים must have the same referent in verse 7a as it does in verses 3b and 8b, viz., God; by using אלהים of the king, the poet would have created an intolerable ambiguity (Mulder 43–47).[58]

That there is verbal parallelism between these three lines is incontestable.[59] But it does not necessarily follow that there must be an identity of reference in parallel terms. Indeed, one explanation of the somewhat awkward repetition in verse 8b (אלהים אלהיך), which actually destroys any precise parallelism, is that the poet recognizes that he has given the term אלהים a distinctive meaning in verse 7a and therefore seeks to clarify the relation between the king as אלהים and Yahweh as אלהים: the king himself, however elevated his person or office, must never forget that Yahweh is his אלהים.

58. In the 1888 edition of his *Psalms* Cheyne had argued that because אלהים in v. 8 refers distinctly and solely to Yahweh it would be unnatural to interpret the word differently in v. 7 (126).

59. This may be shown as follows:

v. 3b	לעולם		אלהים	ברכך	על־כן
v. 7a	עולם ועד		אלהים	כסאך	
v. 8b		אלהיך	אלהים	משחך	על־כן

4. Theological

The fourth and perhaps the major objection to the traditional view is theological: given the vigorous monotheism of Israelite religion, would any court poet ever have addressed an earthly monarch as אלהים?[60]

It should be observed, to begin with, that to address the king as אלהים was not to deify him. As surely as Israelites believed that the king was distinct from other men, they believed he was distinct from אלהים.[61] In whatever sense the king was "divine," it was not an actual or intrinsic divinity that he possessed.[62] Nor was the king regarded as an incarnation of Deity. Rather, he was "Yahweh's anointed," in the sense that he served as Yahweh's deputy on earth, exercising a delegated yet sovereign authority.[63] And as anointed leader of God's chosen people, the king was, by the gracious divine will, God's adopted son (2 Sam. 7:14; Ps. 2:7; 89:27–28 [Engl. vv. 26–27]). Yet, in accounting for this unique application of the title אלהים to a king, one must reckon with more than simply the king's divine election and his unique role in standing *in loco dei*. The king may exceptionally be addressed as "God" also because, endowed with the Spirit of Yahweh, he exhibits certain divine characteristics. In Psalm 45 "glory and majesty" are ascribed to him (vv. 4–5a), as they are to God (e.g., Ps. 96:6); he is a defender and lover of truth and right (vv. 5b, 8a), just as God is (Ps. 33:5; 99:4; Isa. 61:8); he judges with equity (v. 7b),[64] as God does (Ps. 67:5 [Engl. v. 4]; 99:4); just as God's rule is eternal (Ps. 10:16; 93:2; 145:13), so is the dynasty to which the Davidic king belongs (v. 7a).[65] Some weight must also

60. If the psalm is taken to be directly messianic (thus Allis 260–61), no difficulty is occasioned by the address "O God," but as long as the exegete sees the psalm as a nuptial ode for a particular king and אלהים is taken as vocative, a problem remains in the use of אלהים, whether or not the psalm be deemed messianic. Certainly it is preferable to find a second, messianic meaning in the whole psalm (cf. Craigie 340–41) than to restrict the messianic allusion to one or two verses within the psalm (see above, nn. 42–43).

61. Cf. Mowinckel, "Elements"; P. J. King 112–14; de Vaux 112, citing 2 Kings 5:7; Ezek. 28:2, 9; Bernhardt 304 (cf. 263); Kraus, *Psalmen* 491. Concerning Ps. 45:7 Jacob writes: "Royal ideology reaches its highest point in this passage, but doubtless it is entirely right to remember in connection with this text that 'one swallow does not make a summer,' and that Old Testament teaching viewed as a whole always clearly asserts the king's subordination to Yahweh" (237).

62. Similarly Schildenberger 37; Schedl 317 (אלהים here alludes to divine election). On conceptions of kingship in the ancient Near East, see de Fraine 217–63; de Vaux 111–12; Bernhardt 67–90.

63. See Mettinger 104, 259–65, who, commenting on the relation between vv. 20–28 [Engl. vv. 19–27] and vv. 6–19 [Engl. vv. 5–18] in Ps. 89, observes that since the king does on earth what God does in heaven "one is almost tempted to speak of the king as 'the image and likeness of God' on earth" (263). According to A. R. Johnson ("Divine Kingship" 42), "in Israelite thought the king was a *potential* 'extension' of the personality of Yahweh."

64. שבט ("scepter," v. 7) denotes the king's functions as judge (de Vaux 103).

65. Hengstenberg (133) proposes that v. 7b is the cause and v. 7a the effect: righteous judgment leads to eternal rule (cf. Isa. 9:7 [MT v. 6]; Prov. 29:14). On the permanence and stability of the Davidic (messianic) dynasty, see 2 Sam. 7:13, 16; Ps. 18:51 [Engl. v. 50]; 45:18 [Engl. v. 17]; 89:4–5, 21–22, 30, 37–38 [Engl. vv. 3–4, 20–21, 36–37]; 132:12; 1 Chron. 28:7; Isa. 16:5. Sometimes "the permanency attributed to the dynasty in the language of court etiquette was freely wished to the king himself"

be given to the influence of the exuberant style of an oriental court (cf. v. 2: "my heart is bubbling over"). Psalm 45 is noteworthy for its superlatives in its description of the qualities and achievements of the king (vv. 3–8); אלהים is not the only instance of hyperbolic language in the poem (see especially vv. 3, 6, 8). But verse 7 remains distinctive in that here "the royal compliments suddenly blossom into divine honors."[66] With this said, it should also be emphasized that an occupant of the Davidic throne represented a dynasty with which God had made an eternal covenant (2 Sam. 7:13, 16) and from which God's ideal vicegerent would come, so that these "divine honors" should not be explained simply as verbal extravagance. A king of David's line could be addressed as אלהים because he foreshadowed the coming one who would perfectly realize the dynastic ideal, a godlike ruler who would embody all the ideals described in the psalm.

The poet's exuberance is tempered, however, by his theological propriety. It has been suggested above that the insertion of אלהיך after אלהים in verse 8 may reflect the poet's awareness of an extraordinary use of אלהים in verse 7. He forestalls misunderstanding by indicating that the king is not אלהים without qualification.[67] Yahweh is the king's "God."[68] Such an explanation of the expression "your God" does not rule out the possibility that the poet is also stressing the intimate and unique relationship that exists between the king and Yahweh, although אלהיך is also used in reference to individual prophets (e.g., 1 Kings 17:12; see de Fraine 268–76). What is improbable, however, is that אלהים in verse 8 is a vocative and that אלהיך is the subject: "Therefore, O God, your God has anointed you."[69] Rarely, if ever, is the vocative אלהים found between the verb and the subject;[70] such a view would comport with a different word order, viz., על־כן אלהים משחך אלהיך (metrical considerations apart).

(Sabourin, *Psalms* 337). De Fraine goes further and finds in Ps. 45:7, along with Ps. 21:5 [Engl. v. 4]; 61:7 [Engl. v. 6]; 72:5, 17; 110:4 among the royal psalms, "exuberant promises of immortality" (25).

66. Kidner 170. For a judicious analysis of the Psalms and the king, see Clines.

67. Similarly Kittel 175; Bernhardt 255 n. 6; Kraus, *Psalmen* 491. On this phenomenon of "permutation" see GKC §131a, k.

68. This is not to endorse the commonly held view (e.g., Gunkel 189, 191; North 29; Mowinckel, *Psalmenstudien* 3:98; Anderson 350; cf. 336) that originally יהוה אלהיך stood in v. 8b, the present text being the Elohistic editor's equivalent.

69. This interpretation is espoused by N. H. Ridderbos 74; Jacquet 38 ("ô Divin"), 47 ("ô divin"); and tentatively by Couroyer, "Psaume xlv" 236 and "Review" 284–85. As Dahood rightly remarks (273), metrical considerations rule out the possibility that אלהים אלהיך is a case of dittography. In the opinion of P. J. King (84), in v. 8 "אלהים most probably stands for a primitive יהוה," so that he renders v. 8a as "therefore, the Lord, your God . . ." (84; cf. xix).

70. For example, although 49 of the 164 uses of אלהים in Book 2 of the Psalter (Pss. 42–72) are in the vocative case (Ps. 45:7–8 apart), there is no instance where אלהים stands after the verb and before the subject. (The nearest parallel is Ps. 69:30 [Engl. v. 29]: subject–אלהים–verb.) On the contrary, there are five cases where אלהים stands outside the subject–verb combination: once where the word order is אלהים–subject–verb (72:1) and four times where the order is verb–subject–אלהים (65:2 [Engl. v. 1]; 67:4, 6 [Engl. vv. 3, 5]; 68:25 [Engl. v. 24]).

Another consideration that may partially explain this unique form of address is the relative fluidity of the term אלהים in the Hebrew Bible,[71] where on occasion it is used of the heavenly beings around Yahweh's throne (Ps. 8:6 [Engl. v. 5] [LXX, ἀγγέλους]; 97:7; 138:1), judges (Ps. 82:1, 6; cf. Ps. 58:2 [Engl. v. 1], אלם, and also John 10:34–36),[72] Moses (Exod. 7:1; cf. 4:16), and the apparition of Samuel (1 Sam. 28:13; cf. Isa. 8:19). It is also relevant to note that Isaiah 9:5 [Engl. v. 6] combines the two terms used in Psalm 45 to address the king (viz., גבור v. 4; אלהים, v. 7) and applies the title to the ideal king of the future (אל גבור, "Mighty God," used of Yahweh himself in Isa. 10:21).

Because, then, Israelites regarded the king as God's viceroy on earth, his legitimated son who exhibited divine qualities, it is not altogether surprising that, in a burst of lyrical enthusiasm but with the appropriate qualification, a Davidic king should exceptionally be given a title that was in fact not reserved exclusively for Deity.[73]

5. Conclusion

The objections to taking אלהים as a vocative in Psalm 45:7, whether they are drawn from grammar, the structure of the poem, the context of verse 7, or from general theological considerations, are by no means insuperable. The traditional rendering, "Your throne, O God, is for ever and ever," is not simply readily defensible but remains the most satisfactory solution to the exegetical problems posed by the verse. In addition, I have proposed that in this verse it is a king of the Davidic dynasty who is addressed as אלהים.[74] In Psalm 45:8, on the other hand, אלהים should almost certainly be construed as a nominative: "Therefore God (אלהים), your God, has anointed you."

71. See the discussion of McKenzie, who rightly insists that poetic language shows a certain indifference to "the severe canons of logic and metaphysics" (177).

72. Against this category (in which Exod. 21:6 and 22:7–8 [Engl. vv. 8–9] are sometimes included) see Gordon, "אלהים" and "Psalm 82." On the other hand, Schedl believes that it is perhaps in Ps. 82:6 ("you are gods (אלהים), sons of the Most High") that one finds the spiritual milieu that most closely corresponds to the use of אלהים in Ps. 45:7a (316).

73. It is proper to speak of an "identity" between the king and God (as Engnell does, 175) only in the sense that ideally the king is godlike in his character and conduct. He is not "one" with God by nature but may become partially "one" with him in practice and may therefore not inappropriately, if only exceptionally, be called "God."

74. If this is so, Ps. 45 is unique not only as the one genuine hymn to the king found in the Psalter but also as an instance where the title אלהים is used in direct address to the king. Cf. Mowinckel, *Psalms* 74–75, who notes that elsewhere in Israelite psalm poetry the hymn is reserved for Yahweh himself.

D. Psalm 44:7–8 in the Septuagint

In general one may characterize the LXX rendering of this psalm as consistently literal. For instance, the thrice-repeated עַל־כֵּן, standing at the beginning of clauses in verses 3, 8, and 18, is rendered each time by διὰ τοῦτο in the same position, and the slight differences between לעולם (v. 3), עולם ועד (v. 7), and לעלם ועד (v. 18) are reflected by εἰς τὸν αἰῶνα (v. 3), εἰς τὸν αἰῶνα τοῦ αἰῶνος (v. 7), and εἰς τὸν αἰῶνα καὶ εἰς τὸν αἰῶνα τοῦ αἰῶνος (v. 18).[75] Or again, the translator reproduces the distinctively Hebrew word order (e.g., vv. 3c, 8b, 9b) and personal pronouns even when Greek would not normally require them (e.g., vv. 3–5, 10–11). The double accusative (σε . . . ἔλαιον) with ἔχρισεν in verse 8 reflects a Hebrew idiom with משח (see GKC §117dd–ee; BDF §155.(6)), although the normal LXX construction after χρίω would have led one to expect σε . . . (ἐν) ἐλαίῳ (cf. Ps. 88:21 [MT 89:21]; 151:4). Such examples could be multiplied.

Several features of the LXX translation are noteworthy, especially in light of the citation of verses 7–8 in Hebrews 1:8–9:

1. Verse 6a reads τὰ βέλη σου ἠκονημένα, δυνατέ ("your weapons are sharpened, O mighty warrior"), where δυνατέ has no corresponding גבור in the MT,[76] as it does in verse 4a.[77] This dual address to the king as a "mighty warrior" or "hero" in verses 4 and 6 of the LXX heightens the probability that in the next verse ὁ θεός is also a vocative.[78]
2. As in the MT, so in the LXX, it is extremely unlikely that God (not the king) is addressed in verse 7, for a sudden apostrophe of this sort would involve an awkward transition from an address to God in verse 7 to a statement about God in verse 8, and from σου as referring to God in verse 7 to σου as referring to the king in verse 8 (as in v. 6).
3. To render ὁ θρόνος σου ὁ θεός by "your throne is God" is implausible in light of the articular θεός: an anarthrous θεός would have been expected in the predicate (cf. ῥάβδος in v. 7b). No more probable is the translation "God is your throne," given the word order

75. On these uses of αἰών, see H. Sasse, *TDNT* 1:200.

76. But Briggs (*Psalms* 383, 386, 391) reads גבור in v. 6, following the LXX "as required by measure" (386) and assuming that a copyist has omitted the word from the Hebrew text.

77. La[R] and Augustine read *sagittae tuae acutae potentissimae* but La[G] has (correctly) *potentissime*. See Rahlfs 38; Caloz 141–43.

78. In the LXX the vocative of θεός is generally ὁ θεός (not θεός, as is usual in Attic Greek), although θεέ is sometimes found, even in the literary books (see Helbing 34). In Ps. 45:7 Symmachus and Theodotion have ὁ θεός, and Aquila θεέ (Field, *Origenis* 2:162).

and the ambiguity of subject if the two articular nouns θρόνος and θεός were both nominative.

4. In verse 7b the anarthrous state of ῥάβδος εὐθύτητος shows ἡ ῥάβδος τῆς βασιλείας σου to be the subject.
5. The exact parallelism of verses 8b and 3c (viz., διὰ τοῦτο–verb–σε–ὁ θεός) suggests that in verse 8b ὁ θεός is nominative, not vocatival: "Therefore God (ὁ θεός), your God, has anointed you."[79]

From all this one may confidently conclude that the LXX translation of Psalm 45:7–8 (MT) accurately represents the probable meaning of the Hebrew text. That is, ὁ θεός is a vocative in Psalm 44:7 and a nominative in Psalm 44:8b.

79. In Rahlfs's *Psalmi cum Odis* Ps. 44:7a is printed as ὁ θρόνος σου, ὁ θεός, εἰς τὸν αἰῶνα τοῦ αἰῶνος (152) and 44:8b as διὰ τοῦτο ἔχρισέν σε ὁ θεὸς ὁ θεός σου (153). That is, ὁ θεός is taken to be vocatival in v. 7 but not in v. 8 (so also in Rahlfs's edition of the whole LXX).

IX

The Throne of God (Hebrews 1:8–9)

[8]Πρὸς δὲ τὸν υἱόν,
Ὁ θρόνος σου ὁ θεὸς εἰς τὸν αἰῶνα τοῦ αἰῶνος,
καὶ ἡ ῥάβδος τῆς εὐθύτητος ῥάβδος τῆς βασιλείας σου.
[9]ἠγάπησας δικαιοσύνην καὶ ἐμίσησας ἀνομίαν·
διὰ τοῦτο ἔχρισέν σε ὁ θεὸς ὁ θεός σου
ἔλαιον ἀγαλλιάσεως παρὰ τοὺς μετόχους σου.

The Epistle to the Hebrews is a "word of exhortation" (Heb. 13:22) addressed to a group of Hellenistic Jewish Christians, probably in Rome, who were facing a crisis of loyalty during the rising tide of Jewish nationalism before the revolt of A.D. 66. The readers were in danger of losing their confidence and hope (Heb. 3:6, 14; 6:11–12, 19; 10:35), of suffering from spiritual malnutrition (6:1–2; 13:9) and sclerosis (3:7–8, 13; 5:11), and of relapsing into Judaism, if not drifting into virtual paganism (2:1–3; 3:12; 4:1; 6:4–6; 10:39). The author responds to this pastoral need first by a doctrinal exposition (1:1–10:39) that establishes the superiority and finality of Christ and Christianity[1] and then by sustained practical exhortation (11:1–13:25) that issues a clarion call to the pilgrim's life of faith and endurance.

In the author's presentation of his argument the OT plays a crucial role.[2] Drawing on the proposal of G. B. Caird ("Hebrews" 47), R. N. Longenecker points out that the argument of the letter revolves around five OT portions: (1) a chain of verses drawn from five psalms, 2 Samuel 7, and Deuteronomy 32 (LXX) that forms the basis of Hebrews 1:5–2:4; (2) Psalm 8:4–6 [MT vv. 5–7] (Heb. 2:5–18); (3) Psalm 95:7–11 (Heb. 3:1–4:13); (4) Psalm 110:4 (Heb. 4:14–7:28); and (5) Jeremiah 31:31–34 (Heb. 8:1–10:39). The exhortations found in Hebrews 11–13 depend on the exposition of these five portions (other OT verses cited are ancillary to these).[3]

1. Correspondingly the author demonstrates the inferiority and impermanence of the pre-Christian order. In a brief but influential article Caird shows that each of the four OT pillars on which the argument of the epistle is built (viz., Pss. 8, 95, 110, and Jer. 31) "declares the ineffectiveness and symbolic or provisional nature of the Old Testament religious institutions" ("Hebrews" 47).

2. A convenient summary and analysis of statistics regarding the author's use of the OT may be found in G. E. Howard, "Hebrews." For bibliographical data on the subject, see Combrink 33 n.1, to which may now be added R. N. Longenecker, *Exegesis* 158–85; and McCullough. M. Barth (54) distinguishes four types of reference to the OT in Hebrews: direct quotations (e.g., 1:5), indirect quotations or allusions (e.g., 11:5), summaries of or reflections on the OT (e.g., 1:1; 10:1–4), and names (such as "Jesus" or "Christ") and topics (such as "priest" or "blood").

3. *Exegesis* 175. Alternatively, Kistemaker (101, 130–31) finds in four Psalms citations (viz., 8:4–6 [MT vv. 5–7]; 95:7–11; 110:4; 40:6–8 [MT vv. 7–9]) the central core of the four successive stages of the letter's argument down to 10:18, the subject of each phase being mentioned consecutively in summary form in 2:17 (Jesus' humanity, faithfulness, priesthood, propitiation). These four subjects are then elaborated consecutively in the didactic part of the letter.

A. Background and Structure of Hebrews 1

Although Hebrews ends as a letter with the customary personal notes, greetings, and benediction (13:23–25), it begins as a sermon. Instead of giving the usual epistolary salutation and thanksgiving, the author begins with a stately exordium (1:1–4), comparable to the Prologue of the Fourth Gospel (1:1–18) or to the christological "hymns" in Philippians 2:6–11 and Colossians 1:15–20, in which he summarizes many of the themes that are developed in the course of the "sermon." In particular, verse 4 introduces the theme of the superiority of Christ to angels, an idea immediately developed in 1:5–2:4 (as Son of God Christ is superior to the angels in his deity) and then in 2:5–18 (as Son of Man Christ is superior to the angels even in his humanity).

Behind this emphasis on Christ's superiority to the angels may lie a heterodox view of Christ held by the letter's recipients.[4] If the letter was written to warn Christian Jews who were in danger of lapsing back into Judaism, they may have held a quasi-Ebonite view of Jesus, according to which he was an angel, more than human yet less than divine.[5] "If Philo the Jew could frequently write of the *Logos* as an angel, it would have been comparatively easy for a Christian of the Diaspora to think of the Incarnate Word as an angel."[6] Such a view would be attractive to Christian Jews for it would not compromise their belief in either the unity of God (since an angel was less than divine) (Montefiore, *Hebrews* 42) or the distinctiveness of Jesus (since an angel was more than human). Against any such misconception the author insists that Jesus was both fully divine (1:5–13) and truly human (2:5–18). Although this insistence on the real humanity of the Son might at first sight seem to invalidate the author's argument about Christ's superiority over angels, he affirms that it was precisely the Son's being made for a little while lower than the angels (2:9) that enabled him, as God's obedient servant, to become the pioneer of human salvation (2:10) and a merciful and faithful high priest (2:17), roles that were never granted to angels.

Others find the reason for the repeated references to angels in chapters 1–2 in the prevalence of a gnostic cult of angels (cf. Col. 2:18), in the exalted status and exceptional glory accorded angels as mediators of divine revelation (cf. 2:2; Acts 7:38; Gal. 3:19),[7] in the suitability of angels (who were

4. See Spicq, *Hébreux* 2:50–61.

5. For the views of the Ebionites and the Elkesaites, see Daniélou, *Theology* 55–67; and especially Klijn and Reinink, 19–43, 54–67.

6. Montefiore, *Hebrews* 40–43 (quotation from p. 41), followed by Hagner, *Hebrews* 10, 16. On the possible influence of Jewish angelology on the NT and the early Christian formulation of Christology, see Barbel; Michaelis; and Daniélou, *Anges*.

7. Spicq, *Hébreux* 2:14. Cf. Davidson (51) who believes that the author is interested in the angels "not in themselves but only as symbols of the pre-Christian age, to which they are mediators of revelation and over which they are heads."

commonly regarded by Jews and Christians of the early Christian era as quasi–divine beings) to serve as a foil for the truly divine Son of God,[8] or in a tradition in which Melchizedek was regarded as an angel (cf. 11 Q Mel).[9]

Within the section (1:5–2:4) that follows the exordium (1:1–4), 2:1–4 is the first of several exhortations that are interspersed throughout the doctrinal section of the letter.[10] Hebrews 1:5–14 elaborates verse 4[11] in demonstrating that Christ's exaltation gives him a dignity and status far superior to the angels (cf. Eph. 1:20; 1 Pet. 3:22), with verse 13 actually citing, in a form of *inclusio*, the passage (viz., Ps. 110:1) which lay behind verses 3b–4. An examination of repetitions, conjunctions, and particles in 1:5–14 shows that the passage falls into three segments. Each part begins with a form of λέγειν and a reference to οἱ ἄγγελοι.

1. Verses 5–6. In verse 5 γάρ shows that the name which Jesus has inherited (v. 4) is "Son"[12] (υἱός occurs at the beginning and end of the citations in v. 5), while καὶ πάλιν joins the two OT quotations that illustrate his sonship. In verse 6 δέ may be conjunctive ("moreover"), indicating the further point that the Son is also the firstborn whom angels worship, or adversative ("but"), highlighting the difference between the angels who are never called "sons" and the Son who is called firstborn.
2. Verses 7–12. In verse 7 καί introduces another contrast (vv. 7–8a) between the angels and the Son, which is marked by πρὸς μὲν (v. 7a) . . . πρὸς δέ (v. 8a). Two further affirmations about the Son (vv. 8b–9 and vv. 10–12) are each introduced by καί.

8. Swetnam, *Jesus* 149–50; "Form" 370–71.

9. Hamerton-Kelly 244–45, who believes that in Heb. 1:5–14 the author forestalls any possibility that his readers might confuse Christ with the angel Melchizedek because of his subsequent use of Ps. 110:4 and the Melchizedekian tradition to interpret the person of Christ. On the other hand, Rowland tentatively suggests that in arguing for the superiority of Jesus, especially as the possessor of the divine name (Heb. 1:4), the writer of Hebrews may have borrowed from Jewish angelology a tradition that tended to elevate into prominence one particular member of the heavenly hierarchy (111–13). But this assumes that in depicting the exaltation of Jesus the writer is propounding the apotheosis of an angelic figure rather than the elevation to full divine honors of an already divine figure, who, as a man, had secured the redemption of humanity.

10. 3:6b–4:13; 5:11–6:12; 10:19–39.

11. There is much to commend the suggestion of Manson (91–92) that the catena of OT quotations in vv. 5–14 forms a commentary on the christological confession of vv. 1–4, provided too precise a correlation between text (vv. 1–4) and commentary (vv. 5–14) is not sought.

12. Thus, e.g., Käsemann, *People* 58; O. Michel, *Hebräer* 104–6. For a defense of the view that the ὄνομα of v. 4 is κύριος (cf. v. 10), see Ulrichsen. Dey regards the "name" as in fact a series of names, viz., Son (v. 5), firstborn (v. 6), God (v. 8), Lord (v. 10), and, by implication, king (v. 9) (147, 149, 153–54)—and this against the background of the ascription to Moses of the titles "king" and "God" and of certain divine prerogatives (134–38).

3. Verses 13–14. Here δέ (v. 13) has the sense of καὶ πάλιν ("and again," v. 5), leading to fresh antitheses, many of them implicit, between the Son and the angels.[13]

B. The Text of Hebrews 1:8–9

Studies of the use of the LXX in Hebrews suggest that one may safely assume that the author was using a text of the Psalter that was almost identical with the primitive LXX text[14] (as represented, for the Psalms, by A. Rahlfs's text).[15] On this assumption, Hebrews 1:9 reproduces exactly the LXX text of Psalm 44:8 [MT 45:8]. In both places some authorities read ἀδικίαν instead of ἀνομίαν,[16] but the meaning is unaffected. In 1:8, on the other hand, there are two textual issues, which are interrelated and are sometimes thought to determine how ὁ θεός is to be construed in verses 8 and 9.

1. Relation of 1:8 to Psalm 44:7 (LXX)

Psalm 44:7a	ὁ θρόνος σου, ὁ θεός, εἰς τὸν αἰῶνα τοῦ αἰῶνος,
Hebrews 1:8a	ὁ θρόνος σου ὁ θεὸς εἰς τὸν αἰῶνα τοῦ αἰῶνος,[17]
Psalm 44:7b	ῥαβδος εὐθύτητος ἡ ῥάβδος τῆς βασιλείας σου.
Hebrews 1:8b	καὶ ἡ ῥάβδος τῆς εὐθύτητος ῥάβδος τῆς βασιλείας σου.[18]

Although the author reproduces the first line of the LXX exactly, there are two significant changes in the second line. First, there is the addition of καί at the beginning of the line.[19] In verse 10a καί joins separate quotations (Ps. 45:6–7 [MT vv. 7–8] in vv. 8–9, and Ps. 102:25–27 [MT vv. 26–28] in vv. 10–12) while in 2:13, 10:30, and 10:37–38 the insertion of καὶ (πάλιν) marks a division of a single quotation into two distinct parts. In a similar way the

13. See below, n. 68. Dussaut (19–24), however, finds four sections in vv. 5–14, dividing vv. 7–12 into vv. 7–9 and vv. 10–12. On the literary artistry of vv. 5–14, see Vanhoye 69–74.

14. Thus McCullough (367), who cites two unpublished theses: E. Ahlborn, *Die Septuaginta-Vorlage des Hebräerbriefes* (Göttingen, 1966) 135, and J. C. McCullough, *Hebrews and the Old Testament* (Queen's University, Belfast, 1971) 476. On the form of the LXX text used in Hebrews in general and the relation between LXX^{A} and LXX^{B} in the Prophets and the Writings (from which 19 of the 29 direct citations of the OT in Hebrews come), see K. J. Thomas 321–25 (who believes that the author used a more primitive form of the LXX than is represented by codices A and B); and Schröger 247–51.

15. *Psalmi cum Odis*, vol. 10 in the Göttingen LXX.

16. In the LXX, 2013′ A; in Hebrews, ℵ A pc Or.

17. B 33 t have only εἰς τὸν αἰῶνα. In Ps. 44:7 (LXX) B has εἰς αἰῶνα αἰῶνος. See Zuntz 111.

18. Thus $\mathfrak{P}^{46}$ ℵ A B 33 1739, but most manuscripts reproduce the LXX text (see Zuntz 64).

19. Καί is omitted, following the LXX text (although minuscules 39 and 142 have καί), by some manuscripts (see NA^{26} 564).

insertion of καί in verse 8 has the effect of separating two lines of a single quotation so that two distinct but complementary points are made: the unendingness of the rule of Jesus the Messiah (v. 8a) and the scrupulous rectitude of his administration (v. 8b).[20] Second, there is the transposition of the article from the second ῥάβδος to the first, with the dependent genitive εὐθύτητος then becoming articular (on the canon of Apollonius). This change has the effect of inverting subject and predicate: instead of the LXX's "the scepter of your kingdom is a scepter of equity," Hebrews 1:8 now reads "the scepter of equity is the scepter of your kingdom." Thus, parallelism is created between ὁ θρόνος σου and ἡ ῥάβδος τῆς εὐθύτητος, indicating that verse 8b is to be construed with verse 8a rather than with verse 9: in administering his kingdom that is eternal, "God" (whether ὁ θεός here refers to the Father or the Son) shows perfect equity.

2. αὐτοῦ/σου in 1:8

Does the verse end with the third-person or the second-person singular pronoun?[21] The arguments in favor of each variant may now be discussed.

a. Arguments in Favor of αὐτοῦ

1. This variant has proto-Alexandrian support in 𝔓[46] ℵ B, a combination of witnesses which, according to K. J. Thomas (305 n. 3),[22] has the original reading in eleven other cases of minority readings in Hebrews.
2. Αὐτοῦ is the more difficult reading, since it differs both from the MT (מלכותך) and from the LXX text being quoted (σου) and creates an awkward transition from ὁ θρόνος <u>σου</u> (v. 8a) to ῥάβδος τῆς βασιλείας <u>αὐτοῦ</u> (v. 8b).

20. Similarly, Westcott, *Hebrews* 26; McCullough 369, 378 n. 103. In view of the parallel function of καί in 2:13; 10:30, 37–38 just mentioned, this explanation of the added καί is to be preferred over alternative proposals—that καί does not mark a fresh quotation (as in v. 10a) but simply introduces the parallel line (as in v. 10b) (Moffatt, *Hebrews* 13 n. 1); that καί is a simple connecting link, not a wedge splitting a single citation into two segments (Hort, "Hebrews" 3); that the insertion of καί merely confirms the symmetry that the author has created by transferring ἡ from the second to the first ῥάβδος; or that καί was necessary to make possible or to ease the transition from second person (ὁ θρόνος σου) to third person (ῥάβδος τῆς βασιλείας αὐτοῦ) (see §B.2 below).

21. The Palestinian Syriac version lacks any equivalent for either αὐτοῦ or σου. In spite of the tendency of scribes to add pronouns to remove ambiguity and the difference of this reading from the LXX text, a reading without either αὐτοῦ or σου may safely be regarded as a secondary variant, perhaps designed to avoid the awkward αὐτοῦ or what was taken to be a redundant σου after ὁ θρόνος σου in the previous line.

22. Zuntz (64) points to Heb. 1:8b (καὶ ἡ ῥάβδος τῆς εὐθύτητος ῥάβδος); 8:12; and 12:13 as other instances where 𝔓[46] agrees with "the bulk of 'Alexandrian' witnesses" and gives the correct reading against all or almost all the other textual evidence. Other defenders of the originality of αὐτοῦ include Hort, "Hebrews" 3–5; Nairne, *Hebrews* 33–34; Spicq, *Hébreux* 1:418, 2:18–19, Kistemaker 24–25; Bruce, *Hebrews* 10 n. 45 ("probably"); Schröger 60 and n. 4; Buchanan, *Hebrews* 11, 20.

3. A scribe, finding αὐτοῦ, would tend to make the text conform to the LXX quotation, which includes three other uses of σου, thereby removing an exegetical difficulty.
4. If αὐτοῦ is original, the insertion of καί may be readily explained as an attempt to ease the transition from second to third person.
5. It is possible that the author of Hebrews was influenced in his decision to alter the σου of the LXX by a passage (viz., 2 Sam. 7:12–16) that is closely related to Psalm 45 [LXX 44] (he has already cited 2 Sam. 7:14 in Heb. 1:5). That passage reads ἑτοιμάσω τὴν βασιλείαν αὐτοῦ . . . καὶ ἀνορθώσω τὸν θρόνον αὐτοῦ (MT: את־כסא ממלכתו) ἕως εἰς τὸν αἰῶνα . . . καὶ ἡ βασιλεία αὐτοῦ (MT: וממלכתך) ἕως αἰῶνος ἐνώπιον ἐμοῦ, καὶ ὁ θρόνος αὐτοῦ ἔσται ἀνωρθωμένος εἰς τὸν αἰῶνα.

b. Arguments in Favor of σου

1. The external evidence supporting σου is both ancient (cop^{sa,bo}) and, unlike that for αὐτοῦ, widely distributed geographically. (Alexandrian: A Ψ 33 81 104 326 1739 1881; Western: D it vg; Byzantine: K *Byz Lect*).
2. This variant agrees with the LXX text being cited and accords with the other four instances of the second-person singular pronoun (σε or σου) in the quotation.
3. There is no other instance of αὐτοῦ in the LXX of Psalm 44, whereas σου occurs twelve times at the end of a phrase or sentence in verses 3–12.
4. Scribes may have changed σου to αὐτοῦ because ὁ θεός in verse 8a was taken as a nominative (either subject or predicate) and therefore supplied a natural antecedent for αὐτοῦ.
5. Even if the addition of καί in effect created two separate quotations in verse 8, a change of person from ὁ θρόνος σου (v. 8a) to αὐτοῦ (v. 8b) to ἠγάπησας (v. 9a) is decidedly awkward.
6. If θρόνος signifies "reign" and βασιλεία "kingly reign," this parallelism between verse 8a and verse 8b would lead one to expect τῆς βασιλείας σου to match ὁ θρόνος σου.

These two sets of arguments are more evenly balanced than some writers have recognized, but with most textual critics and the majority of commentators[23] I opt for σου as the more primitive text. However, a decision about the more probable original reading in verse 8b does not determine how ὁ θεός is to be taken in verse 8a, for just as it is possible to read σου yet trans-

23. For exceptions, see n. 22 above. In the 25th edition of the NA text αὐτοῦ was preferred (p. 549), but in the 26th (= UBS^3) σου (p. 564).

late ὁ θεός as a nominative (e.g., Moffatt),[24] it is also possible to prefer αὐτοῦ yet take ὁ θεός as a vocative (e.g., JB).[25] With this said, it remains true that σου accords better with a vocative and αὐτοῦ with a nominative.

C. ὁ θεός in Hebrews 1:8

1. As a Nominative

If ὁ θεός is nominative, it may be either subject ("God is your throne") or predicate ("your throne is God").[26] Almost all proponents of the view that ὁ θεός is a nominative prefer the former translation,[27] which is reflected in the English translations of Moffatt,[28] Goodspeed, Cassirer, and TCNT and in the margins of the RSV, NEB, and NRSV. No modern English version, it seems, has the translation "your throne is God" in its text and very few commentators support it,[29] although word order is in its favor, as well as the parallel structure (viz., subject-predicate) of verse 8b. This view that ὁ θεός is a nominative is generally defended on three grounds.

a. Old Testament Parallels

B. F. Westcott (*Hebrews* 26) observes that "the phrase 'God is Thy throne' is not indeed found elsewhere, but it is in no way more strange than Ps. lxxi.3, '[Lord] be Thou to me a rock of habitation. . . . Thou art my rock and my fortress,'" and other comparable passages.[30]

A distinction must be drawn, however, between affirming that God is a person's rock, fortress, refuge, or dwelling place and that he is a person's throne. As a "rock of refuge . . . towering crag and stronghold" (Ps. 71:3 NEB) God provides secure protection, a "safe retreat" (Ps. 91:2, 9), for his people.

24. "He says of the Son, God is thy throne for ever and ever, and thy royal sceptre is the sceptre of equity" (*Hebrews* 11).

25. "But to his Son he says: 'God, your throne shall last for ever and ever'; and: 'his royal sceptre is the sceptre of virtue.'" So also NEB, NASB, REB; Kistemaker 25. Those who affirm that the reading αὐτοῦ *requires* that ὁ θεός be construed as a nominative (Westcott, *Hebrews* 26; Hort, "Hebrews" 5; K. J. Thomas 305; Metzger, *Commentary* 663) have overstated their case.

26. The range of possible renderings is narrower than is the case with אלהים in Psalm 45:7 (see chapter VIII above). Ὁ θρόνος σου ὁ θεός could not mean "your divine throne" (which would require ὁ θρόνος σου ὁ θεῖος) or "your throne is divine" (= ὁ θρόνος σου θεῖος or possibly ὁ θρόνος σου τοῦ θεοῦ), far less "your throne is God's throne" (possibly = ὁ θρόνος σου τοῦ θεοῦ, but note ἡ ῥάβδος . . . ῥάβδος τῆς βασιλείας σου in v. 8b) or "your throne is like God's throne."

27. For example, Westcott, *Hebrews* 24–26; Milligan 90–91 (but cf. 77 and n. 1); Moffatt, *Hebrews* 11 (but cf. 13–14); T. H. Robinson 10 (tentatively); K. J. Thomas 305.

28. Moffatt renders Ps. 45:6 as "your throne shall stand for evermore," probably following Wellhausen, Duhm, and others who take אלהים to be an Elohistic alteration of an original יִהְיֶה read as יהוה (cf. Moffatt, *Hebrews* 13). See further §B.1.a in chapter VIII above.

29. Of the commentators consulted, only Hort ("Hebrews" 3–5) and Nairne (*Hebrews* 31, 33–34; *Priesthood* 306) opt for "thy throne is God."

30. He also cites Deut. 33:27; Ps. 90:1; 91:1–2, 9; Isa. 26:4 (RV); cf. Isa. 22:23 and Zech. 12:8.

But whether "throne" signifies dynasty, kingdom, or rule, the concepts of "God" and "throne" are too dissimilar to permit a comparable metaphor. That is, unlike these other affirmations, "God is your throne" is elliptical[31] and must mean "God is the foundation of your throne."[32] In a similar way, "your throne is God" must mean "your throne is founded on (or, protected by) God," for, whatever θρόνος may signify by metonymy, it does not belong to the category of the divine.

b. Syntactical and Semantic Considerations

First, if ὁ θεός is a vocative, αὐτοῦ in verse 8b is left without an antecedent, "θρόνος and αἰών being out of the question" (Hort, "Hebrews" 4). Even if αὐτοῦ be *vera lectio*, ὁ θεός can be construed as vocatival (see §B.2 above), for the καί which the author adds to his LXX text effectively creates two distinct citations in verse 8 so that the movement from second person (σου) to third person (αὐτοῦ) within this verse occasions no particular difficulty. Therefore the antecedent of αὐτοῦ could be the Son (τὸν υἱόν, v. 8a) who has been addressed as θεός.

Second, since in verse 7a λέγει πρός can mean only "say about," not "say to," it is probable that the parallel [λέγει/εἴρηκεν][33] πρός in verse 8a should have an identical sense, which would indicate that ὁ θεός is nominative, not vocative: "But about the Son [he says], 'God is your throne.'"

This argument is robbed of its validity if the contrast between verse 7 and verse 8 that is marked by μὲν . . . δέ includes the repeated πρός as well as ἄγγελοι–υἱός. Λέγειν πρός in verse 13 (cf. τίνι . . . εἶπεν in v. 5) clearly means "say to," so that πρός in verse 8a may mark a transition from one meaning of λέγειν πρός (viz., "say about") to another (viz., "say to"), especially since one must understand "to the Son he says" before the unambiguous vocatives σὺ . . . κύριε in the intervening verse 10. (I shall return to this point below in §C.2.) In any case, it would not be improper to translate verse 8a as "but with respect to the Son [he says]: 'Your throne, O God, is for ever and ever'" (similarly RSV, Barclay, and NRSV; Lane 21).

c. Context

First, the contrast between verse 7 and verse 8 does not relate to being but to function. The author is not comparing the ever-changing being of created angels with the eternal nature of the divine Son, but rather their tran-

31. "God is your stronghold" means "God protects you," but "God is your throne" means neither "God rules you" nor "God occupies your throne."

32. Significantly, Westcott paraphrases "God is thy throne" (or, "thy throne is God") by "thy kingdom is founded upon God, the immovable Rock" (*Hebrews* 25–26), and Hort by "your kingdom rests on God" ("Hebrews" 3).

33. G. Kittel speaks of the "arbitrary interchange" of the tenses of λέγειν in vv. 5–13 (εἶπεν, v. 5; λέγει, vv. 6–7; εἴρηκεν, v. 13) (*TDNT* 4:109 n. 160).

sient service with his eternal kingship. As F. J. A. Hort expresses it: "To the Son, unlike the angels . . . is ascribed first the function of Divine kingship (8, 9), and then the function of Divine creation (10ff.)."[34]

There can be little doubt that one emphasis in these two verses is the contrast between the angels' service and Christ's dominion; they perform radically different functions. But function cannot be divorced from being. The mutability of angels' functions as servants of God—first wind, then fire—implies the dependent creatureliness of angelhood. So also the eternality of Christ's reign implies the immutability of his person (cf. Heb. 13:8). If there is, then, this dual contrast in verses 7–8,[35] the ascription of the title θεός to Jesus to denote his godhood cannot be deemed inappropriate.

Second, if ὁ θεός is a vocative ("O God") and the Father thus addresses the Son, this must be the climax of the argument, so that any further development would have the effect of weakening or obscuring, rather than strengthening, the case (thus Wickham 8).

In that verse 4 states the central theme that the writer develops in Hebrews 1–2, it may be said to represent the focal point of the two chapters, so that what follows verse 4 is an explication of the Son's superiority over angels. If verse 8 contains an address to the Son as "God," it may be described as pivotal, since in that case it applies to Jesus the divine title implied in verse 3a and it is the first of three terms of address (in vv. 8, 10, 13) in which the Father speaks to the Son. Certainly verses 10–12, introduced by the address σὺ . . . κύριε, cannot be deemed anticlimactic, for the title κύριος, as applied to Jesus, is no less elevated than the title θεός, and the verses from Psalm 102 cited there in reference to Jesus originally applied to Yahweh (as also in the case of v. 6). The role of Jesus as God's agent in creation (vv. 10–12) and as God's coregent (v. 13) is an implication of his sonship as significant as his essential divinity (v. 8a); the verses that follow verse 8 further illustrate the theme of the Son's consummate superiority and therefore strengthen the writer's argument.

2. As a Vocative

The strength of the case for taking ὁ θεός as a vocative (= ὢ θεέ, as in 10:7)[36] certainly does not rest solely in the weakness of the alternative. Several converging lines of evidence make that case particularly strong.

34. "Hebrews" 6; cf. Westcott, *Hebrews* 26.

35. See further the discussion below, §C.2.d.

36. The articular nominative of address is an established NT usage (BDF §147). See chapter IV §A.3.c. The pre-Christian papyri seem to lack instances of this *enallage* of case (N. Turner, *Syntax* 34). It should be observed that the elements of harshness, superiority, and impersonality that sometimes attach to the use of the idiom in Classical Greek are lacking in the almost 60 NT examples (cf. Moulton, *Prolegomena* 70; N. Turner, *Syntax* 34). On the vocative of θεός in the LXX, see above, chapter VIII n. 78.

a. Psalm 45:7 (LXX 44:7)

From the analysis of five proposed translations of Psalm 45:7a, we reached the conclusion that the traditional rendering, "Your throne, O God, is for ever and ever," is not simply readily defensible but remains the most satisfactory solution to the exegetical problems posed by the verse.[37] In the LXX version it is even more probable that ὁ θεός is a vocative, for the king is addressed as a "mighty warrior (δυνατέ)" not only in verse 4 but also in verse 6 where there is no corresponding גבור in the MT. This dual address heightens the antecedent probability, given the word order, that in the next verse ὁ θεός should be rendered "O God." One may therefore affirm with a high degree of confidence that in the LXX text from which the author of Hebrews was quoting[38] ὁ θεός represents a vocatival אלהים.[39]

b. Word Order

If ὁ θεός were a subject nominative ("God is your throne"), one might have expected the word order ὁ θεὸς ὁ θρόνος σου κτλ. to avoid any ambiguity of subject. Alternatively, if ὁ θεός were a predicate nominative ("your throne is God"), ὁ θρόνος σου θεὸς κτλ. or ὁ θρόνος σου εἰς τὸν αἰῶνα τοῦ αἰῶνος θεός might have been expected (cf. Heb. 3:4: ὁ δὲ πάντα κατασκευάσας θεός).[40] On the other hand, a vocative immediately after σου would be perfectly natural.[41]

c. Meaning of λέγειν πρός and the Structure of 1:8–13

We should note, first of all, that of the 35 NT uses of λέγειν πρός, only in 2 cases (Rom. 10:21; Heb. 1:7),[42] Hebrews 1:8a apart, does the expression mean "say/speak about." Elsewhere the sense is either "say to" (26 exam-

37. See above, chapter VIII §B.2, §C.5.

38. That the author was following the LXX closely is shown by (1) the identity between v. 9 and Ps. 44:8 (LXX); (2) the reproduction of the Septuagint's εἰς τὸν αἰῶνα τοῦ αἰῶνος in v. 8a, a *hapax legomenon* in the epistle (cf. εἰς τοὺς αἰῶνας τῶν αἰώνων, 13:21; εἰς τοὺς αἰῶνας, 13:8; εἰς τὸν αἰῶνα, 5:6; 6:20; 7:17, 21 [all citations of Ps. 110:4]; 7:28; and the distinctive εἰς τὸ διηνεκές, 10:12, 14); and (3) the fact that adequate reasons may be suggested for his departure from the LXX reading in v. 8b (see §B.1 above).

39. In the Psalter there are 63 instances of ὁ θεός as a vocative.

40. When the term θεός is predicative, NT writers show only a slight preference for the anarthrous nominative (16 uses) over the articular (13 uses in eight verses), whether εἶναι be expressed or unexpressed. But significantly, of these 13 articular uses, all but one (Heb. 11:10, where ὁ θεός is the predicate in a relative clause) have some qualification added to θεός, such as a noun in the genitive (e.g., Acts 7:32), an adjective (e.g., 1 John 5:20), or a substantival participle (e.g., 2 Cor. 4:6). See further, chapter I §B.2 above.

41. Cf. σὺ . . . κύριε (1:10); πεπείσμεθα δὲ περὶ ὑμῶν, ἀγαπητοί (6:9); [ἡ παράκλησις] ἥτις ὑμῖν ὡς υἱοῖς διαλέγεται, Υἱέ μου (12:5); παρακαλῶ δὲ ὑμᾶς, ἀδελφοί (13:22).

42. Possibly also Mark 12:12 = Luke 20:19, if the Matthean parallel (21:45), where περί replaces πρός, indicates that πρὸς αὐτοὺς εἶπεν means "speak with reference to" rather than "speak against" (see BDF §239.(6)).

ples) or "say/speak (something) for/against" (6 examples).[43] If the parallelism between verse 7a and verse 8a suggests that πρός should bear the same sense in verse 8a as in verse 7a (viz., "about, concerning, in reference to"),[44] predominant NT use of λέγειν πρός points equally strongly in the opposite direction, namely, that the preposition should be translated "to" in verse 8a (as in 7:21; see RSV). This latter presumption is strengthened by considerations of structure in verses 8–13.

1. Where λέγειν is used with τινί or τίνι (as in v. 5), πρός τινα (as in 5:5; 7:21), or πρὸς τίνα (as in v. 13) and is followed by a second-person address (σύ, v. 5; [σὺ] κάθου, v. 13; 5:5; 7:21), the meaning must be "say to," not "say about."
2. Accordingly, when in verse 10a a second-person address (σὺ . . . κύριε) is found after an implied πρὸς τὸν υἱὸν λέγει (supplied from vv. 7a and 8a), it is likely that the sense is "[to the Son he says,] 'You, O Lord. . . .'"
3. But verses 8–9 and verse 10 are joined by a simple καί, indicating that the quotation in verses 10–12 makes points comparable to those of verses 8–9,[45] so that [λέγειν] πρός in verse 8a probably has the same meaning as in verse 13 ("say to") and the ambiguous ὁ θεός that immediately follows will probably be a second-person address.

d. Context

In establishing the superiority of Jesus over angels, the author draws a series of contrasts between them in verses 4–14. The antithesis between verse 7 and verses 8–9 that is marked by the strongly adversative μὲν . . . δέ is twofold: the angels serve (τοὺς λειτουργούς), but the Son reigns (ὁ θρόνος σου . . . ἡ ῥάβδος); in their service of God the angels change their form (πνεύματα . . . πυρὸς φλόγα),[46] but in his rule of equity the divine Son

43. Mark 12:12; Luke 12:41; Acts 23:30; 1 Cor. 6:5; 7:35; 2 Cor. 7:3.

44. Thus, e.g., Delitzsch, *Hebrews* 1:72, 75; Westcott, *Hebrews* 24–25; Kistemaker 148–49; Vanhoye 71; Buchanan, *Hebrews* 11.

45. This point is not vitiated by the view that the inserted καί in v. 8b introduces what is virtually a separate quotation (see §B.1 above), for it remains true that vv. 8–9 technically form one quotation, being introduced by the single introductory formula πρὸς δὲ τὸν υἱόν.

46. In v. 7 ποιεῖν may mean "cause to be like" or, more probably, "cause to change into" (but not "cause to act through"). In one case the writer is saying that the functions angels perform as God's subordinate agents are as varied and transitory as the natural elements of wind and fire or that the angels are like wind for swiftness and fire for strength (as in the Targum of Ps. 104:4). In the other case, the point is that angels themselves are transformed first into winds and then into fiery flames. Davidson (48) comments: "This idea is not to be pressed so far as to imply that the angelic essence undergoes a transformation into material substance, but only that the Angels are clothed with this material form, and in their service assume this shape to men." K. J. Thomas observes that the addition of ὡς ἱμάτιον to the Septuagintal text of Ps. 101:27b [MT 102:27b] cited in Heb. 1:12 "emphasizes the frequency and casualness with which creation (which includes the angels) is changed: the

continues for ever (ὁ θεός εἰς τὸν αἰῶνα τοῦ αἰῶνος). One contrast relates to function, the other to nature.[47] Over against the variability of angelic function, the author sets the stability of the Son's throne and the constancy of his rectitude. Over against the evanescence and impermanence of angelic form, the author sets the eternality and divinity of the Son's person.[48] Whereas the angels are addressed *by* God, the Son may be addressed *as* God.[49] On this view verses 10–12 reinforce and extend the antitheses. While angels are creatures of divine fiat, the Son himself is the divine Creator. While they are mutable, he is immutable (σὺ δὲ διαμένεις . . . σὺ δὲ ὁ αὐτὸς εἶ). Never could it be said concerning the Son, ὁ ποιῶν τὸν υἱὸν αὐτοῦ πνεῦμα καὶ τὸν λειτουργὸν αὐτοῦ πυρὸς φλόγα. From this I conclude that to interpret ὁ θεός as a vocative does full justice to the flow of argument in the immediate context.

Some scholars are reluctant to express a preference as to whether ὁ θεός is nominative or vocative in verse 8, declaring that both interpretations are admissible and make good sense.[50] But the overwhelming majority of grammarians,[51] commentators,[52] authors of general studies,[53] and English trans-

creation will be changed even 'as a garment'. This is surely a special reference to the angels, of whom it has been said, 'They are new every morning' (Ḥagigah 14a)" (305–6). See further Bruce, *Hebrews* 18 and n. 81.

47. Similarly Lünemann 91–92.

48. If the objection be raised that v. 8a says merely that the Son's throne, not his person, is eternal, it should be observed that θρόνος here means "reign" (cf. ῥάβδος, v. 8b) rather than "dynasty," and that an eternal reign (v. 8a) implies an eternal ruler (cf. 5:6; 7:3, 28; 13:8).

49. The author avoids the use of even the collective titles θεοί (cf. אלהים in Ps. 8:6 [LXX, ἀγγέλους]; 97:7; 138:1) and υἱοὶ θεοῦ (cf. בני האלהים in Gen. 6:2, 4; and Job 1:6; 2:1 [LXX, οἱ ἄγγελοι τοῦ θεοῦ]) in reference to the angels.

50. For example, Robertson, *Grammar* 465; Robertson, *Pictures* 5:339; Dods 255.

51. Winer 182; Buttmann 140; B. Weiss, "Gebrauch" 335; BDF §147.(3); C. F. D. Moule, *Idiom Book* 32 (although ὁ θεός is "conceivably" a true nominative); N. Turner, *Syntax* 34 (ὁ θεός as a nominative is "only just conceivable"); N. Turner, *Insights* 15; Zerwick and Grosvenor 655. Also BAGD 358a.

52. Calvin, *Hebrews–Peter* 13–14; Alford 4:20; Lünemann 84, 92; Farrar, *Hebrews* 38; Delitzsch, *Hebrews* 1:76–77; Riggenbach 21–22; Windisch, *Hebräerbrief* 16–18; Spicq, *Hébreux* 1:288, 2:19; Kuss, *Hebräer* 37, 45–46, 146–47; Héring 10; Strathmann, *Hebräer* 79–80; O. Michel, *Hebräer* 118; Hewitt 56–57; Montefiore, *Hebrews* 47; Bruce, *Hebrews* 19–20, 23; Bruce, "Hebrews" 1009 §881b; Hughes 64; Guthrie, *Hebrews* 76; Hagner, *Hebrews* 13–14; R. M. Wilson 41; Attridge 49 (but see n. 5), 58–59; Lane 21, 29.

53. Warfield, *Lord* 278; van der Ploeg 206; E. Stauffer, *TDNT* 3:105; Stauffer 114; Wainwright, *Trinity* 58–60 (= "Confession" 286–87); V. Taylor, *Person* 95–96; V. Taylor, *Essays* 85; B. Reicke, *TDNT* 6:723; Synge 4–5; Snell 42, 58; Cullmann, *Christology* 310; Kistemaker 25–26, 98, 137; M. Barth 72; C. F. D. Moule, *Birth* 99; Barclay, *Jesus* 25–26; Vanhoye 71; A. T. Hanson, *Jesus* 162 ("in all likelihood"); Brown, *Reflections* 23–25 (= "Jesus" 562–63); de Jonge and van der Woude 316; Glasson, "Plurality" 271; Filson 39, 43; Sabourin, *Names* 303; Schröger 61–62, 262; E. Schweizer, *TDNT* 8:370 n. 255; R. N. Longenecker, *Christology* 137, 139; R. N. Longenecker, *Exegesis* 178–80; Swetnam, *Jesus* 143, 153; D'Aragon 200; Dey 137, 147–49, 153; Horton 168; J. W. Thompson, *Beginnings* 135 (= "Structure" 358); A. F. Segal 213, 215 n. 91; Dunn, *Unity* 260; Hanson and Hanson 81; Loader, *Sohn* 25 and n. 19, who cites Ahlborn, *Septuaginta-Vorlage* (see n. 14 above) 113–14; Dussaut 21; Allen 240; Williamson, "Incarnation" 6–7; Ulrichsen 66; Meier 513–17, 532 (who argues for "a general symmetry between the movement of thought in the seven Christological designations in Heb. 1,2b–4 and the movement of thought in the seven OT citations in 1,5–14," 523).

lations[54] construe ὁ θεός as a vocative ("O God"). Given the affirmation of verse 3 that the Son is the effulgence of God's glory and the visible expression of his being, it is difficult to avoid the conclusion that when the author affirms further that God the Father addresses[55] his Son as θεός[56] at his resurrection[57] he intends to signify that, equally with the Father, Jesus possesses the divine nature.[58]

D. ὁ θεός in Hebrews 1:9

With the precise parallelism between σου ὁ θεός (v. 8) and σε ὁ θεός (v. 9) and the high probability that ὁ θεός is vocatival in verse 8, it would seem eminently reasonable to suppose that verse 9b should be translated as "therefore, O God (= Jesus), your God (= the Father) has anointed you. . . ." Not surprisingly, a considerable number of exegetes have adopted this view and therefore maintain that Jesus is addressed as "God" in two successive verses.[59] The only modern English versions that reflect this interpretation

54. KJV, Weymouth, Berkeley, RSV, NEB, NASB, JB, GNB, NAB[1], NIV, NAB[2], NRSV, REB.

55. It seems probable that in each of the seven OT passages cited in vv. 5–13 God is the speaker (thus also Schröger 252; Williamson, *Philo* 512–14; R. N. Longenecker, *Exegesis* 164, 168). This must be the case in vv. 5a, 5b, 6, 10–12, 13. In v. 7 it would be permissible to translate "and concerning the angels it (Scripture) says" (similarly Buchanan, *Hebrews* 11) were it not for the fact that nowhere does the author use the expression ἡ γραφὴ λέγει (or even the noun γραφή). For him the words of Scripture are words spoken by God even where the OT does not describe them as such (as in 1:8) and even where the words cited are about God (as in 1:7) (cf. Metzger, "Formulas" 306 n. 16).

56. The presence of the article with θεός in Heb. 1:8 reflects normal Biblical Greek usage (see BDF §147.(3)) and has no special theological significance. See n. 36.

57. One need not suppose that the author believed either that vv. 8–9 were spoken by the Father only once or that the Son was appropriately addressed as θεός only after his resurrection, but it seems probable that he was thinking particularly of the exaltation of Jesus at his resurrection. The verbs ἠγάπησας and ἐμίσησας (v. 9) probably refer to the earthly life of Jesus (see §E.2 below and n. 93). If so, the consequent "anointing" would allude to the unsurpassed jubilance of Christ upon his reentry into heavenly glory (cf. 12:2; John 17:5) and his endowment with full messianic dignity and honors. But vv. 8–9 form a unit (even if the inserted καί of v. 8b in effect creates two quotations) since there is a single introductory formula, so that v. 8a belongs principally to a postresurrection setting.

58. That the expression ὁ θεός refers to the Son's possession of the divine nature is recognized, *inter alios*, by Stevens, *Theology* 504; Spicq, *Hébreux* 2:20; Montefiore, *Hebrews* 47; Swetnam, *Jesus* 149–50, 153–54; Hagner, *Hebrews* 14; Lane 29. But Hurst argues that the main interest of the author in Heb. 1–2 is not in a preexistent divine being who becomes man, but in a human figure who is raised to an exalted status, so that when the royal title "God" is applied to Jesus in Heb. 1:8, he is being presented as ideal king, elevated above his comrades as God's representative to the people (*Hebrews* 113–14; "Christology" 159–60, 163).

59. Lünemann 93–94; Delitzsch, *Hebrews* 1:80; B. Weiss, "Gebrauch" 335; Windisch, *Hebräerbrief* 16; H. Schlier, *TDNT* 2:472; van der Ploeg 206; Spicq, *Hébreux* 1:288, 2:19–20; Kuss, *Hebräer* 45–46, 146–47; Héring 10; Stauffer 114; E. Stauffer, *TDNT* 3:105; Strathmann, *Hebräer* 79; Cullmann, *Christology* 310; O. Michel, *Hebräer* 118; Vanhoye 71, 176–77; Montefiore, *Hebrews* 47; Bruce, *Hebrews* 19 (quite possible); Brown, *Reflections* 24 and n. 40 (= "Jesus" 562 and n. 40); de Jonge and van der Woude 314, 316; Filson 39, 43 and n. 17 ("probable"); Sabourin, *Names* 303; Schröger 63–64; R. N. Longenecker, *Christology* 139; Swetnam, *Jesus* 153; W. Grundmann, *TDNT* 9:564; Dunn, *Unity* 54, 260; Loader, *Sohn* 25 n. 24; Dussaut 21; Attridge 49, 59–60.

are the NEB and REB,[60] although they do not render אלהים in Psalm 45:8 [Engl. v. 7] as a vocative.[61]

But there are several compelling reasons why this view, although "eminently reasonable" and grammatically admissible, should be rejected in favor of the translation that takes ὁ θεός as a nominative and the following ὁ θεός σου as being in apposition: "Therefore God, your God, has anointed you. . . ."

First, in the LXX (as in the MT) there is a significant parallelism between Psalm 44:3c and 44:8b:

v. 3c διὰ τοῦτο εὐλόγησέν σε ὁ θεὸς εἰς τὸν αἰῶνα
v. 8b διὰ τοῦτο ἔχρισέν σε ὁ θεὸς ὁ θεός σου

In verse 3c ὁ θεός cannot be vocative, which suggests that in the parallel verse 8b it should be construed as nominative, not vocative. While one cannot be sure that the author of Hebrews had a copy of the Greek text of the whole psalm before him or that he had recently read the whole psalm, it would not be inappropriate to suggest, given the verbal identity between Hebrews 1:9 and Psalm 44:8 (LXX), that this parallelism within the psalm influenced his understanding of the phrase ὁ θεὸς ὁ θεός σου.

Second, since the author was not averse to adjusting the LXX text to avoid ambiguity,[62] one might have expected him, just as he altered the subject-predicate order in verse 8b to create parallelism, to alter the position of ὁ θεός in verse 9b to read διὰ τοῦτο, ὁ θεός, ἔχρισέν σε ὁ θεός σου in order to remove ambiguity, had he regarded the first ὁ θεός as a vocative.

Third, the phrases ὁ θεὸς ὁ θεός μου (Ps. 21:2 [MT 22:2]; 42:4 [MT 43:4]; 62:2 [MT 63:2]; cf. 50:16 [MT 51:16]), ὁ θεὸς ὁ θεὸς ἡμῶν (Ps. 66:7 [MT 67:7]),[63] and ὁ θεὸς ὁ θεός σου (Ps. 49:7 [MT 50:7]) are sometimes found in the LXX Psalter, and in each case the first ὁ θεός is nominative. The author of Hebrews generally derives his OT quotations from the Greek OT.[64]

Finally, the reason that the author cites verse 8 as well as verse 7 of Psalm 44 (LXX) may not simply be that ἔχρισεν corresponds to Χριστός or that παρά introduces a further comparison (cf. παρ' αὐτούς, 1:4) between

60. "Therefore, O God, thy God has set thee above thy fellows, by anointing with the oil of exultation" (NEB; similarly REB).

61. "So God, your God, has anointed you above your fellows with oil, the token of joy" (NEB; similarly REB). On the difficulty of rendering אלהים here by "O God," see above, chapter VIII §C.4 and §D.

62. McCullough (378) classifies the modifications of the text of OT quotations that may safely be traced to the author of Hebrews into three groups: adjustments (1) to make the quotation fit into the context more easily, (2) to emphasize important points in the quotation, and (3) to avoid ambiguity.

63. Ps. 66:7b is the closest parallel to Heb. 1:9b in the Psalter: εὐλογήσαι ἡμᾶς ὁ θεὸς ὁ θεὸς ἡμῶν.

64. K. J. Thomas 303, 325.

Christ and the angels,[65] but primarily to demonstrate that to address the exalted Son as "God" is to compromise neither the primacy of the Father nor the subordination of the Son. It is as appropriate for the Son to address the Father as "my God" as it is for the Father to address the Son as "God." What is more, the phrase "God, your God" may reflect the author's awareness that he has given ὁ θεός a distinctive application in verse 8 and his consequent desire to affirm that while the Son is *totus deus* he is not *totum dei*.

E. Significance of a Vocatival ὁ θεός in Hebrews 1:8

1. Within Hebrews 1–2

Just as the whole doctrinal portion of the epistle (1:1–10:39) focuses on the superiority of Jesus, so its first segment (1:1–2:18) seeks to establish the superiority of Jesus to angels. After the exordium (1:1–4) he is shown to be superior *because of his godhood* (1:5–14): he has obtained a vastly superior title and office (ὄνομα, 1:4) as the divinely begotten Son (1:5);[66] as preeminent heir ("firstborn") he enjoys unrivaled dignity and a unique relation to God (1:6a; cf. v. 2: "heir of all things"); he is the object of angelic worship (1:6b);[67] in his person he is divine (1:8a); in the exercise of his divine sovereignty he is scrupulously just (1:8b); he has a superior joy (1:9); he is the unchangeable Lord of creation, which includes the angels (1:10–12); and he is God's exalted coregent (1:13).[68] Then, after the first of the several exhor-

65. It is unclear whether μέτοχοι in 1:9 refers to angels (thus, e.g., Lünemann 94–95; Schröger 64 ["very probably"]; Héring 10; Meier 516), Christians (cf. 2:11; 3:14) (Bruce, *Hebrews* 21), or all who have fellowship with God, especially the angels (Hewitt 58) or people in general (Spicq, *Hébreux* 2:20; E. H. Riesenfeld, *TDNT* 5:735).

66. Εἶπεν in v. 5 alludes to (γάρ) the word γενόμενος in v. 4, suggesting that Jesus' receipt of the incomparable name of "Son" preceded or was coincident with his exaltation (v. 3b). It is not that his sonship was inaugurated at the resurrection, but the full exercise of the rights and privileges attaching to that name began with his enthronement (cf. Rom 1:4).

67. Angelic service (v. 7) involves the worship of the Son (v. 6; cf. Rev. 5:11–13) as well as ministry to and for Christians (v. 14). It is uncertain when this service of worship is rendered. If πάλιν is construed with εἰσαγάγῃ, the reference will be either to Christ's return from death or to his second advent ("when he again brings . . ."); but if πάλιν is taken with δέ, it introduces a new quotation ("and again, when . . ."; cf. 1:5; 2:13; 4:5) and the phrase may refer to God's bringing his Son into the world by the incarnation or God's "introducing" his Son to the world as rightful heir of the universe at the exaltation.

68. In his successive contrasts, some explicit, some implicit, between the Son and the angels in vv. 4–13, the author's intent has been to show his readers the incomparability of the Son, not to call into question the divinely ordained function of angels. He concludes, therefore, with a positive assessment of their role: they are "all ministering spirits sent out to serve, for the benefit of those who are to inherit salvation" (v. 14). Yet even here there are implicit contrasts. The Son, too, was sent, but whereas he came but once (1:6; 10:5) they are repeatedly sent (ἀποστελλόμενα). His mission also was to serve, but whereas they are ministering spirits, he was God's incarnate servant (10:5–7, 9). Whereas their role is to support those destined to receive salvation, his service was actually to achieve that salvation (2:10; 5:9).

tations (2:1–4) that are interspersed throughout the letter, the author demonstrates the superiority of Jesus over the angels *in spite of his manhood* (2:5–18):[69] God has subjected the world to come to the Son of Man (2:5–8), not to angels; although temporarily "lower" than the angels, he is now permanently "higher," being "crowned with glory and honor" (2:7, 9); because he assumed human nature and died, he emancipated humanity and became "a merciful and faithful high priest in God's service," roles that angels could never perform (2:14–17).[70]

One may therefore isolate the contribution of verse 8 to the argument of Hebrews 1–2 as being to show that the superiority of Jesus to angels does not reside simply in his having distinctive titles, an exalted status, or redemptive functions, but preeminently in his belonging to a different category—that of deity.[71] Just as he is set apart from sinners because he is "holy and without fault or stain" (7:26), so he is set apart from angels because he may be appropriately addressed as θεός:[72] to which of the angels did God ever say, "Your throne, O God, will endure for ever and ever"? No angel was ever dignified by the title θεός because no angel shared intrinsically in the divine nature.[73] This use of θεός in reference to Jesus is all the more significant because the author carefully avoids using the term unnecessarily in 1:1–14, preferring to use a circumlocution (1:3; cf. 8:1) and to leave the subject of successive verbs of saying unexpressed (1:5–7, 13).

69. Swetnam, however, contends that 2:5–18 treats of the Son's inferiority to the angels, his humanity, while 1:5–2:4 focuses on his superiority, his divinity ("Form" 372–75).

70. For the author of Hebrews there is no question of Jesus' having assumed angelic nature and therefore being merely equal to angels. He voluntarily assumed human nature and became for a short period "lower than the angels" because it was both appropriate (v. 10) and necessary (v. 17) for the Son to be completely identified with God's "sons to be" if he was to perform high-priestly service on their behalf. The rank he assumed was inferior to that of angels but the function he performed was certainly not. Heb. 2:16 seems to mean either that Jesus did not "take to himself" angelic nature but human nature or that it was not his concern to bring help to angelic beings but to humankind.

71. Similarly Spicq, *Hébreux* 2:20.

72. But Smith has argued that "the adjective κρείττων . . . is used not of natural but of official superiority. . . . The whole argument turns not on personal dignity, but on dignity of function in the administration of the economy of salvation" (26–27, 29).

73. Πάντες (1:14) excludes the possibility of an exceptional angelic figure such as Michael or Melchizedek eclipsing the supremacy of Christ: "Are they not *all* ministering spirits . . . ?" 11 Q Melchizedek, a document that may be dated ca. A.D. 50, illustrates the fact that in the use of at least one representative of one stream of first-century A.D. Jewish thought—a stream that may be designated "nonconformist Judaism"—the term אלוהים ("heavenly one") could be applied, it would appear, to Melchizedek and other angelic beings in the heavenly court (cf. Ps. 82:1): "(9) As it is written (10) concerning him (Melchizedek) in the hymns of David who said, 'Elohim [has ta]ken his stand in the congre[gation of El], in the midst of the Elohim he gives judgment'" (cf. אלוהיך in reference to Melchizedek in lines 24–25, alluding to Isa. 52:7, and אלי in line 14 referring to heavenly beings). Melchizedek is exalted high above (line 11) the angelic assembly of God (10) who are his helpers (14) in enacting the judgment of God (13) in the year of jubilee (9) from the hand of Belial and "all the spirits of his lot" (12–13, 26). See further de Jonge and van der Woude 301–23; Horton, esp. 64–82, 152–72; Demarest 120–28.

In addition, from one point of view 1:8a serves as a fulcrum within Hebrews 1. If ὁ θεός is a vocative, it is the first of three terms of address in this chapter, all referring to Jesus and all within OT quotations drawn from the Psalms: ὁ θεός (v. 8 = Ps. 44:7 LXX), κύριε (v. 10 = Ps. 101:26 LXX),[74] and [σὺ][75] κάθου (v. 13 = Ps. 109:1 LXX). Whether these OT passages had already been associated in a "testimony book" of christological texts or in the liturgical usage of the early church, it is impossible to say, but the christological confession of Thomas (ὁ κύριός μου καὶ ὁ θεός μου, John 20:28) shows how readily the titles θεός and κύριος could be juxtaposed in the worship of Jesus.

But verse 8a looks backward as well as forward. When the Son is said to be "the radiant light of God's glory (ὢν ἀπαύγασμα τῆς δόξης)" (v. 3 JB) and to bear "the imprint of God's nature (χαρακτὴρ τῆς ὑποστάσεως αὐτοῦ)" (v. 3), he is being described as the intrinsic possessor of the nature of God[76] without actually being given the generic title of "God." What verse 3 implies, verse 8 makes explicit: the Son is rightly addressed as θεός inasmuch as he is the exact representation of the very being of ὁ θεός. Verse 8 also alludes to the expression ἄγγελοι θεοῦ in verse 6,[77] where θεοῦ and αὐτῷ refer to different persons.[78] It is wholly appropriate, indeed imperative, that the angels *of God* worship Jesus, the firstborn, for he is by nature included within the generic category denoted by θεός and therefore is a legitimate and necessary object of adoration.[79]

If in fact verse 8a makes a distinctive and forceful contribution to the argument of Hebrews 1 in the manner suggested, it is scarcely adequate to claim, as V. Taylor does, that "the divine name is carried over with the rest of the quotation" and the writer "has no intention of suggesting that Jesus is God,"[80] so that "nothing can be built upon this reference."[81] Even if the author was not consciously applying a divine title to Christ, one cannot

74. On the differences between the MT and LXX in this citation, see Bruce, *Hebrews* 21–23; Schröger 66–71.

75. It could plausibly be argued that κύριε should be supplied here, since the psalm begins εἶπεν ὁ κύριος τῷ κυρίῳ μου.

76. So also Sabourin, *Names* 286. In patristic exegesis the former phrase was taken to imply that the Son was consubstantial with the Father (community of essence), and the latter that the Son should not be identified with the Father (distinction of persons). However, "to the degree that God's glory is His nature," δόξα and ὑπόστασις may be synonymous (U. Wilckens, *TDNT* 9:421), "both words . . . describing God's essence" (H. Köster, *TDNT* 8:585). According to G. Kittel, δόξα denotes "the divine mode of being," a sense that "is true of all the NT authors. Even writers like Lk. and the author of Hb., who have such a feeling for Greek, are no exception" (*TDNT* 2:247).

77. On the OT source of the quotation in v. 6, see Schröger 46–53.

78. On this latter point see Glasson, "Plurality," esp. 271.

79. Cf. Vanhoye 71: "Si les anges *de Dieu* (1,6) doivent se prosterner devant le premier-né, c'est qu'il partage la dignité de Dieu lui-même."

80. *Essays* 85 (= "Jesus" 117).

81. *Person* 96.

assume that he failed to recognize the theological import of such an incidental application. Further, I would suggest that even the more positive assessment of A. W. Wainwright (*Trinity* 60 = "Confession" 287) that "the Deity of Christ, which is relevant but not necessary to the argument, is only mentioned in passing" fails to do justice to the significance of this address in the flow of the argument. O. Cullmann, on the other hand, seems justified in his claim (*Christology* 310) that the psalm is quoted by the author precisely because of this address, "O God" (which he finds also in v. 9).

But to suggest that verse 8a is pivotal within the chapter is not to claim that the address ὁ θεός is the zenith or the principal affirmation of the chapter. Of the three main titles given to Jesus in Hebrews 1, υἱός is the title on which attention is focused (vv. 2, 5 *bis*, 8a), so that θεός (v. 8) and κύριος (v. 10) may be said to explicate two aspects of that sonship, viz., divinity and sovereignty. The principal point in the chapter is that the exalted Son is vastly superior to the angels (vv. 4–5, 13) as a divine King who is worshiped (vv. 6–9) and as a sovereign Creator who is changeless (vv. 10–12). In that verse 4 enunciates the theme of the superiority of the Son to angels that is to be developed, it forms the focal point of Hebrews 1–2.

The reference to the Son as "God" in 1:8 occurs within a citation from Psalm 45,[82] one of seven OT quotations in 1:5–14. Five or possibly six[83] of these are drawn from the Psalms, the author's favorite mine from which to quarry passages that illuminate the nature of the person and work of Christ. Of the seven quotations, only 2 Samuel 7:14, Psalm 110:1, and perhaps Psalm 2:7 seem to have had messianic overtones in any Jewish circles at the beginning of the Christian era.[84] Nevertheless the author of Hebrews, whose exegetical method was "unashamedly Messianic,"[85] proceeded on the assumption that his Christian addressees would recognize the validity of his handling of the OT, even if the messianic application of some of the texts had not yet become common Christian tradition. There is little to support the conjecture of F. C. Synge that in Hebrews 1 the author has made use of a "testimony book" collection of "Son" passages that already was deemed authoritative in the church.[86] More plausible, but still incapable of demonstration, is the proposal of R. G. Hamerton-Kelly (243–47) that before their use in Hebrews 1 to demonstrate Christ's superiority to angels,

82. In other OT citations in Hebrews, ὁ θεός does not refer to Christ: 2:13 (Isa. 8:18); 9:20 (Exod. 24:8); 10:7 (Ps. 40:8 [MT v. 9]) (Kistemaker 137 n. 3).

83. The uncertainty arises from the fact that the citation in v. 6 may be dependent on Deut. 32:43 (LXX) or, less directly, Ps. 97:7 [LXX 96:7]. See n. 77 above.

84. See the discussion of Kistemaker 17–29.

85. Williamson, *Philo* 535.

86. 1–7, 53–54. Synge notes that all the passages cited in Heb. 1 represent God as speaking to or of someone who shares heaven with him, someone whom Synge calls "the Heavenly Companion." On this "testimony book" hypothesis, see Kistemaker 91–92; R. N. Longenecker, *Exegesis* 179–80.

the seven quotations formed a "block" of traditional christological texts, selected primarily to interpret Jesus' resurrection and exaltation but then applied to prove his "protological" preexistence. I prefer the view that the author inherited as christological "proof texts" the two or three passages that probably were interpreted messianically in some contemporary Jewish exegesis (viz., 2 Sam. 7:14; Ps. 110:1; and perhaps Ps. 2:7) while the other scriptural illustrations of Christ's supremacy were the product of his own exegesis.[87] Yet the possibility should not be excluded that all five or six psalms cited in Hebrews 1 were already grouped together, not in a testimony book or as an orally transmitted set of christological texts, but as portrayals of the exalted status and roles of Jesus that were sung or recited in early Christian worship.[88]

As for the use made of Psalm 45:7–8 in Hebrews 1, there is both "shift of application and modification of text," as B. Lindars describes the phenomenon (*Apologetic* 17). A poet's address to the king at the royal wedding becomes the Father's address to his Son at the resurrection-exaltation. The eternity of the "throne" no longer denotes the perpetuity of the Davidic dynasty but the endless character of Christ's dominion (v. 8). The psalm pointed forward to the coming king-Messiah of David's house who would personally embody all aspects of the ideal theocratic rule. In Hebrews 1 the attributes of this ideal king—love of justice, hatred of iniquity—have become the past accomplishments of the Messiah-Son,[89] so that he is exalted by the Father to his right hand to receive incomparable heavenly accolades (v. 9).[90] (Modification to the text has already been discussed in §B.1 above.)

2. Within the Whole Epistle

What contribution does a vocative ("O God") in the context of 1:8–9 make to wider themes or emphases in the epistle? There are three principal areas of contribution: the paradox of Jesus' deity and humanity,[91] the subordination motif, and Christ's eternality.

In 1:8–9 there are juxtaposed an explicit assertion of Jesus' intrinsic deity ("O God") and the clear implication of his real humanity: "You have loved righteousness and hated iniquity" (v. 9a). The aorists ἠγάπησας and

87. Similarly Dey 153.

88. Just as Jesus had used the Psalms in his prayers (Luke 23:46; cf. Ps. 31:5 [MT v. 6]) and worship (Matt. 26:30), so the early church did in their prayers (Acts 4:24–30) and worship (Rev. 15:3–4).

89. The term ῥάβδος (v. 8b), denoting the royal scepter rather than the shepherd's staff, points not only to the divine sovereignty of the exalted Jesus but also to his messianic status (see SB 3:679).

90. For an attempt to trace in Heb. 1:5–2:4 the various stages of a royal enthronement ceremony of the (putative) OT pattern, see Swetnam, *Jesus* 142–45, 148; similarly M. Barth 72–73.

91. On the two basic ways in which pre-Chalcedon Greek commentators dealt with the deity-humanity christological paradox as presented by the data in Hebrews, see Young.

ἐμίσησας are not so much gnomic, implying that the Son is always devoted to the maintenance of the divine justice,[92] as constative, indicating that during his earthly mission the Son had been constantly committed to upholding justice and doing God's will.[93] In Psalm 45 the unsurpassed joy of the king on his wedding day is seen as a fitting consequence of his love of justice and repudiation of evil. Here in Hebrews 1 the Father's exaltation of his Son to heavenly glory and honor is viewed as the natural outcome and divine acknowledgment (διὰ τοῦτο) of his earthly life spent in "fulfilling all righteousness" (cf. Matt. 3:15).

Sometimes the elements of this divine-human paradox are expressed elsewhere in the epistle in close juxtaposition,[94] but generally the author is content to stress one or other aspect as his argument demands. That he believes in the full deity of Jesus is clear: Jesus is described as the perfect representation of God's glory and nature (1:3); he not only existed before he appeared on earth (10:5), before Melchizedek (7:3), before human history began (1:2), or before the universe was created (1:10), but he also existed and exists eternally (7:16; 9:14; 13:8); like his Father[95] he may be called "Lord";[96] he is creator (1:10), sustainer, (1:3), and heir (1:2) of the universe, that is, everything in time and space (τοὺς αἰῶνας, 1:2); he is "Son" (υἱός)[97] and "the Son of God" (ὁ υἱὸς τοῦ θεοῦ),[98] the timeless ὤν of 1:3 pointing to a natural, not adoptive, sonship;[99] he is worshiped by angels (1:6) and is the object of human faith (12:2); he is sovereign over the world to come (2:5); and passages referring to Yahweh in the OT are applied to him.[100]

No less evident is the writer's emphasis on the real and complete humanity of Jesus. He assumed human nature with all its weaknesses and limitations (2:11, 14, 17), apart from sin (4:15; 7:26); he belonged to the tribe of Judah (7:14) and "Jesus" was his human name;[101] he experienced human emotions (5:7), temptation (4:15), suffering (5:8; 13:12), and death (2:9; 12:2); he believed in and feared God (2:13; 5:7) and offered prayer to him (5:7); he exhibited human virtues such as fidelity (2:17; 3:2) and obedience

92. As, perhaps, in the LXX (see the MT).

93. These verbs are interpreted as referring to the earthly life and ministry of Jesus by, *inter alios* Lünemann 93; Westcott, *Hebrews* 26–27; Riggenbach 23 n. 53; Windisch, *Hebräerbrief* 18; Spicq, *Hébreux* 2:19; Strathmann, *Hebräer* 80; O. Michel, *Hebräer* 119; Hughes 65.

94. For example, 1:1–3; 2:17; 4:14; 5:8–10; 7:14; 10:29.

95. 7:21; 8:8, 11; 10:16, 30.

96. 1:10; 2:3; 7:14; 13:20.

97. 1:2, 5 *bis*; 3:6; 5:5, 8; 7:28; cf. ὁ υἱός in 1:8.

98. 4:14; 6:6; 7:3; 10:29.

99. Westcott, *Hebrews* 425.

100. 1:6; 1:10–12; 3:7–11, 15.

101. 2:9; 3:1; 6:20; 7:22; 10:19; 12:2, 24; 13:12, 20. For emphasis, Ἰησοῦς is always placed at the end of a clause (except in 13:12).

(10:7); he gave teaching while on earth (2:3); and he endured the hostility of sinners (12:3).

Perhaps the most remarkable feature of 1:8–9 is the sequence ὁ θεός . . . ὁ θεὸς ὁ θεός σου. The God who addresses his Son as "God" is also God to his Son, even his exalted Son. Whether ὁ θεός in verse 9 is nominative or vocative, ὁ θεός σου remains. In addition, the eternal sovereignty that Jesus now exercises was accorded him as a gracious gift of God (v. 8a), λέγειν πρός here referring not simply to the imparting of information but rather to the granting of a gift and the assignment to a special task (cf. v. 13).[102] Also, it was the Son's God who anointed him with the "oil of gladness" (v. 9). This element of the subordination of Jesus to his Father, a characteristic of NT Christology,[103] is much in evidence elsewhere in Hebrews. The Son was dependent on God for his appointment as heir of the universe (1:2) and to the office of high priest (3:2; 5:5, 10), for his "introduction" into the world (1:6), for the preparation of his body (10:5), for his resurrection (13:20), and for his exaltation to his Father's right hand (1:13).

Finally, Christ's eternality. "Your throne, O God, is for ever and ever" affirms that Christ's personal rule is eternal and implies that Christ, as ruler, is also eternal.[104] Εἰς τὸν αἰῶνα τοῦ αἰῶνος (v. 8a) anticipates the phrase εἰς τὸν αἰῶνα of Psalm 110:4 (109:4 LXX) cited three times by the author in reference to the eternity of the Melchizedekian order of priesthood (5:6; 6:20; 7:17).[105] Jesus is a priest "forever" after the order of Melchizedek, and the treatment in Hebrews of the relationship between these two figures constitutes "the culmination of the epistle's argument,"[106] "the kernel and focus of the entire Epistle."[107] Other statements that are reminiscent of this theme of Christ's eternal nature are "your years will never end" (1:12); "the power of an indestructible life" (7:16); "he continues for ever . . . he is able for all time (εἰς τὸ παντελές) to save those who draw near to God through him, since he always lives to make intercession for them" (7:24–25); "through his eternal spirit (διὰ πνεύματος

102. Similarly B. Reicke, *TDNT* 6:723, who compares πρὸς τὸν Ἰσραὴλ λέγει (Rom. 10:21).

103. For example, for Paul, see 1 Cor. 3:23; 11:3; 15:24, 28; for Peter, 1 Pet. 1:21; 2:23; cf. Acts 3:13, 26; for the fourth evangelist, John 5:30; 10:36; 14:28. Here, as elsewhere, this letter is (in the words of Williamson, *Philo* 579–80) "in the centre of the mainstream of primitive Christian theology."

104. The translation "God is your throne for ever and ever" asserts the permanence or eternality of God's support or protection of Christ's dominion. The implication of Christ's personal eternality is present but less obvious.

105. In addition, Allen notes (238–39) that τῆς βασιλείας σου. ἠγάπησας δικαιοσύνην (vv. 8b–9a) foreshadows the explanation in 7:2 of the meaning of Melchizedek's name, βασιλεὺς δικαιοσύνης: "For the author the royal, righteous and eternal Son of Hebrews 1:8–9 would hardly have failed to suggest the Melchizedek-type priesthood."

106. Spicq, *Hébreux* 2:203.

107. Demarest 2.

αἰωνίου)" (9:14);[108] "Jesus Christ is the same yesterday and today and forever (εἰς τοὺς αἰῶνας)" (13:8).[109]

F. Conclusion

Two general conclusions may now be stated. First, although some slight degree of uncertainty remains as to whether אלהים in Psalm 45:7 (MT) is a vocative, there can be little doubt that the LXX translator construed it so (see chapter VIII) and that the author of Hebrews, whose quotations of the OT generally follow the LXX, assumed that the Septuagintal ὁ θεός in Psalm 44:7 was a vocative and incorporated it in this sense into his argument in chapter 1, an argument that was designed to establish the superiority of the Son over the angels. The appellation ὁ θεός that was figurative and hyperbolic when applied to a mortal king was applied to the immortal Son in a literal and true sense.[110] Jesus is not merely superior to the angels. Equally with the Father he shares in the divine nature (ὁ θεός, v. 8) while remaining distinct from him (ὁ θεός σου, v. 9). The author places Jesus far above any angel with respect to nature and function, and on a par with God with regard to nature but subordinate to God with regard to function. There is an "essential" unity but a functional subordination.

Second, given the vocative ὁ θεός in 1:8, it cannot be deemed impossible for the comparable ὁ θεός in 1:9 to be translated "O God," but this interpretation seems improbable.

108. On the interpretation of this ambiguous phrase, see Hughes 358–60.
109. See further on this theme, J. W. Thompson, *Beginnings* 134–40 (= "Structure" 358–63).
110. Similarly Spicq, *Hébreux* 2:19.

X

Our God and Savior (2 Peter 1:1)

> Συμεὼν Πέτρος δοῦλος καὶ ἀπόστολος Ἰησοῦ Χριστοῦ τοῖς ἰσότιμον ἡμῖν λαχοῦσιν πίστιν ἐν δικαιοσύνῃ τοῦ θεοῦ ἡμῶν καὶ σωτῆρος Ἰησοῦ Χριστοῦ.

Stated simply, the principal exegetical issue at stake in 2 Peter 1:1 is this: Does the phrase ὁ θεὸς ἡμῶν καὶ σωτὴρ Ἰησοῦς Χριστός refer to two persons (God and Jesus Christ) or only to one person (Jesus Christ)? That is, should we render this phrase "our God, and the Savior Jesus Christ," or "our God and Savior, (who is) Jesus Christ"? After grappling with this issue and discussing the pros and cons of each translation, we shall be ready to examine the meaning of the whole verse.[1]

A. Arguments for a Reference to Two Persons

R. F. Weymouth translates 2 Peter 1:1 as referring to two persons: "Simon Peter, a bondservant and Apostle of Jesus Christ: To those to whom there has been allotted the same precious faith as that which is ours through the righteousness of our God and of our Saviour Jesus Christ."[2]

1. The Position of ἡμῶν

It is sometimes argued that the position of the pronoun ἡμῶν after θεοῦ distinguishes θεός from σωτήρ.[3] Two parallel passages illustrate the point.

Titus 2:13	τῆς δόξης	τοῦ μεγάλου	θεοῦ	καὶ σωτῆρος ἡμῶν	Ἰησοῦ Χριστοῦ
2 Thess. 1:12	τὴν χάριν	τοῦ	θεοῦ ἡμῶν	καὶ κυρίου	Ἰησοῦ Χριστοῦ
2 Peter 1:1	ἐν δικαιοσύνῃ	τοῦ	θεοῦ ἡμῶν	καὶ σωτῆρος	Ἰησοῦ Χριστοῦ

If ἡμῶν binds θεοῦ and σωτῆρος together in the first instance ("our God-and-Savior"), it separates θεοῦ from its coordinated substantive in the sec-

1. For a defense of the Petrine authorship of 2 Peter, see E. M. B. Green, *2 Peter–Jude* 13–39, and *Reconsidered*; in defense of the position that the letter belongs to the decade 80–90 and was penned by a prominent member of a "Petrine circle" in Rome, see Bauckham, *Jude–2 Peter* 138–62.

2. The ASV (1901) probably reflects this understanding in its translation "of our God and the Saviour Jesus Christ," especially since the earlier English RV (1881) on which the ASV was dependent reads "of our God and Saviour." But ASV's "of our God and the Saviour," along with the KJV rendering "of God and our Saviour Jesus Christ" (reading σωτῆρος ἡμῶν), *could* be construed as referring to one person, certainly if "and" is epexegetic. Only Weymouth's "and of our Saviour" puts the matter beyond doubt.

3. For example, Winer 130; E. Stauffer, *TDNT* 3:106 n. 268; Rahner 135 n. 4. There is no reason to follow BDF §276.(3) in preferring the reading κυρίου (א Ψ *pc* vg^{mss} syr^{ph} cop^{sa}) over θεοῦ in 2 Pet. 1:1.

ond and third cases: "our God and the Lord Jesus Christ" (2 Thess. 1:12), "our God and the Savior Jesus Christ" (2 Pet. 1:1).

But such grammatical reasoning is faulty, for when two substantives are under the *vinculum* of a single article, a personal pronoun applies to both, whether it precedes both (e.g., 2 Pet. 1:10: ὑμῶν τὴν κλῆσιν καὶ ἐκλογήν) or follows either of the substantives (e.g., Eph. 3:5: τοῖς ἁγίοις ἀποστόλοις αὐτοῦ καὶ προφήταις; 1 Thess. 3:7: ἐπὶ πάσῃ τῇ ἀνάγκῃ καὶ θλίψει ἡμῶν).[4] Thus one finds three times elsewhere in 2 Peter τοῦ κυρίου ἡμῶν καὶ σωτῆρος Ἰησοῦ Χριστοῦ (1:11; 2:20 [𝔓[72] ℵ A C P Ψ read ἡμῶν]; 3:18), where no commentator distinguishes κύριος from σωτήρ. In 1:1 ἡμῶν would be limited to θεοῦ only if an article (τοῦ) were added to σωτῆρος.

2. The Parallel Construction in 2 Peter 1:2

1:1	ἐν δικαιοσύνῃ	τοῦ θεοῦ ἡμῶν	καὶ σωτῆρος Ἰησοῦ Χριστοῦ
1:2	ἐν ἐπιγνώσει	τοῦ θεοῦ	καὶ Ἰησοῦ τοῦ κυρίου ἡμῶν[5]

Verse 2 "clearly distinguishes between God and Christ, and it is natural to let that interpret this [v. 1], as there seems no reason for identity here [v. 1] and distinction there [v. 2]" (Mayor 81–82; cf. Windisch, *Briefe* 84; Austin 274).

Although θεὸς . . . καὶ σωτήρ (v. 1) and θεὸς καὶ Ἰησοῦς (v. 2) have a formal similarity, there are two significant differences. The former phrase, but not the latter, was a stereotyped formula used by Jews in reference to Yahweh, the one true God, and by Gentiles when referring to an individual god or deified ruler.[6] Invariably the referent was a single deity or ruler, not two. Moreover, σωτήρ is a title, whereas Ἰησοῦς is a proper name; it is possible to speak of "our God and Savior, Jesus Christ," but hardly of "God and Jesus, our Lord." It is doubtless for these two reasons that most of the English ver-

4. On this point see Middleton 433–34; Robertson, *Grammar* 785; E. D. Burton 389. Although he distinguishes θεός from σωτήρ, Weymouth rightly construes ἡμῶν with both nouns.

5. P Ψ 1852 2464 *pc* vg[st] read ἐν ἐπιγνώσει τοῦ κυρίου ἡμῶν. This shorter reading is preferred by some commentators (e.g., Bigg 235, 251–52; Strachan, "2 Peter" 124; Chaine 38) and translations (Moffatt, JB, NJB) because (1) in 2 Peter Jesus alone is the object of ἐπίγνωσις (1:3, 8; 2:20) or γνῶσις (3:18, which may form an *inclusio* with 1:2); (2) this is *brevior lectio*, perhaps corrected to conform to a dual subject discerned in v. 1; (3) the singular αὐτοῦ in v. 3 points to a single antecedent in v. 2; and (4) a scribe influenced by Pauline salutations (where God and Jesus are associated in reference to "grace and peace" in 11 of 13 cases) may have added τοῦ θεοῦ καὶ Ἰησοῦ. But the majority of textual critics (e.g., WH, NA[26], UBS[3]) and commentators (e.g., Schelkle 186 n. 1; Kelly, *Peter–Jude* 299; Fuchs and Reymond 42–43) prefer the longer reading, on the grounds that (1) it is the better attested reading, witnessed by 𝔓[72] (which omits καί before Ἰησοῦ) ℵ A B C K L (ℵ A L *al* add Χριστοῦ after Ἰησοῦ); (2) it is *difficilior lectio*, given the singular αὐτοῦ in v. 3 and the author's use of ἐπίγνωσις; and (3) the shorter reading may be explained as a scribal correction to accord with singular referents in vv. 1b and 3a and the author's custom (1:3, 8; 2:20) of making Christ alone the object of ἐπίγνωσις or γνῶσις.

6. See the discussion above on Titus 2:13 (chapter VII §B.1).

sions which translate verse 1 as "by the righteousness of our God and Savior, Jesus Christ" or some similar rendering, translate verse 2 with some such rendering as "by the knowledge of God *and of* Jesus our Lord" (viz., RV, Goodspeed, TCNT, NASB, Berkeley, RSV, NEB, NAB¹, GNB, NIV, NAB², REB, NRSV).

3. Deviation from a Stereotyped Formula

According to E. Käsemann (*Essays* 183 n. 2; cf. Windisch, *Briefe* 84), the combination ὁ κύριος (ἡμῶν) καὶ σωτήρ, found in 1:11, 2:20, 3:2, and 3:18, is a stereotyped christological formula referring to a single person, Ἰησοῦς Χριστός. Since the use of ὁ θεὸς ἡμῶν in 1:1 instead of ὁ κύριος ἡμῶν deviates from this stereotype,[7] two persons must be referred to, not one.

But with equal validity one could argue, as O. Cullmann in fact does (*Christology* 314), that in 1:1 θεός is simply a variant of the more common κύριος (note also ἡμέρα κυρίου in 3:10 and ἡ τοῦ θεοῦ ἡμέρα in 3:12), so that here, as in the other four passages, there is a single referent. And C. H. Moehlmann (17) actually finds in 2 Peter 1:1 the climax of an "evolution" he claims to have found in the use of σωτήρ that is "traceable in the Pastoral Epistles and II Peter: God our *soter*, Jesus Christ our *soter*, Our Lord and *soter* Jesus Christ, our God and *soter* Jesus Christ."

B. Arguments for a Reference to One Person

When translated with reference to one person, 2 Peter 1:1 would read, "Simon Peter, a slave and apostle of Jesus Christ, To those who have received a faith as privileged as ours through the righteousness of our God and Savior, Jesus Christ" (similarly RV, Moffatt, Goodspeed, TCNT, NASB, Berkeley, RSV, NEB, JB, NAB¹, GNB, NIV, NJB, NAB², REB, NRSV).

1. The Single Article (or, the Anarthrous σωτήρ)

As in the case of Titus 2:13, the most convincing explanation of the anarthrous σωτῆρος in 2 Peter 1:1 is that two coordinate nouns referring to the same person are customarily linked by a single article (see the discussion above, chapter VII, §B.2).[8]

7. ℵ Ψ *pc* vg^{mss} syr^{ph} cop^{sa} actually read κυρίου in place of θεοῦ, under the influence of the four parallels in 2 Peter.

8. An appeal to the single article here as an indication of a christological use of θεός is made by Robertson (*Grammar* 127, 785–86; "Article" 184–85, 187), Zerwick (*Greek* §185); Zerwick and Grosvenor (717), C. F. D. Moule (*Idiom Book* 109–10), and N. Turner (*Syntax* 181 n. 3; *Insights* 16) among the grammarians; and Bigg (250–51), Chaine (36, who compares ὁ πατὴρ καὶ σωτήρ in Philo, *Praem. Poen.* 39 and τὸν μόνον δεσπότην καὶ κύριον ἡμῶν in Jude 4), Kelly (*Peter–Jude* 297), Schelkle (185), and Fornberg (142) among the commentators.

Now it is true that (1) the article is not required with the second noun if the distinction between the two nouns is regarded as obvious or is assumed; (2) σωτῆρος is shown to be definite by the Ἰησοῦ Χριστοῦ that follows, so that an article is not required; and (3) the single article may be accounted for by the writer's conceptual association of two separate items. But against these three arguments one may urge the following corresponding rejoinders.

Although the clear distinction between θεός and Ἰησοῦς in verse 2 might suggest that a similar distinction between θεός and σωτήρ is obvious or assumed in verse 1, the fact remains that elsewhere in 2 Peter whenever an anarthrous σωτήρ is attached by καί to another noun in the same case (viz., in 1:11; 2:20; 3:2, 18) there is a single referent, Jesus Christ. If the author had wished to distinguish the two persons unambiguously, he could have written either τοῦ θεοῦ ἡμῶν καὶ Ἰησοῦ Χριστοῦ τοῦ σωτῆρος ἡμῶν (cf. v. 2) or τοῦ θεοῦ ἡμῶν καὶ τοῦ σωτῆρος (ἡμῶν) Ἰησοῦ Χριστοῦ.

That σωτῆρος is definite is incontestable. It is definite not only because of the following proper name but also because it occurs in a monotheistic context in conjunction with θεός and in the singular number. But its definiteness does not in itself account for its anarthrous state, for a definite noun more often than not is articular, while proper names or quasi–proper names as well as titles (however σωτήρ be regarded) are sometimes articular and sometimes anarthrous.

How is the exegete to determine whether ὁ θεὸς ἡμῶν and σωτὴρ Ἰησοῦς Χριστός are distinct yet joint sources or possessors of δικαιοσύνη, or whether there is a single source or possessor of "righteousness," namely "our Savior God, Jesus Christ"? The latter alternative seems more probable for two reasons. First, as C. Bigg observes: "It is hardly open for anyone to translate in I Pet. i.3 ὁ Θεὸς καὶ πατήρ by 'the God and Father,'[9] and yet here [in 2 Pet. 1:1] to decline to translate ὁ Θεὸς καὶ σωτήρ by 'the God and Saviour'" (251). Second, in contemporary religious language the expression (ὁ) θεὸς (καὶ) σωτήρ always referred to one deity or ruler, not two. For example, when in 166 B.C. Prusias II of Bithynia addressed Roman senators as θεοὶ σωτῆρες,[10] he was not distinguishing certain senators who were θεοί from others who were σωτῆρες; all of them were "savior-gods." This point in fact becomes my second main argument that favors a reference to one person in 1:1.

2. The Stereotyped Formula θεὸς καὶ σωτήρ

In his brief monograph on the *Theos Soter* formula as the explanation of the primitive Christian use of σωτήρ in reference to Jesus, C. H. Moehlmann

9. On the θεὸς καὶ πατήρ combination, see E. D. Burton 386–92.
10. Polybius, *Hist.* 30:16 (cited by Bruce, "Pattern" 65 n. 5).

demonstrates how widespread was the God-Savior idea in the Mediterranean world of the first century A.D.: "On the coins that passed from hand to hand, on statue in marketplace or along the roadside, in local cults, in mystery religion convocations, on altar and on temple the inhabitant of the Graeco-Roman world beheld *soter*. No living person could escape contact with some *theos soter*" (32).[11] In all these settings the θεὸς σωτήρ formula never refers merely to a conceptual association of two separate deities, but invariably to a single god; the θεός is none other than the σωτήρ.[12] In its alternative form, ὁ θεὸς καὶ σωτήρ, the term σωτήρ is anarthrous because of the personal identity between the σωτήρ and the θεός: "God who is (epexegetic καί) the Savior."[13]

Peter may well be borrowing a conventional formula from pagan usage and applying it to the church's Lord to whom it properly belongs. But one should not overlook the possibility[14] that just as Paul interprets Isaiah 45:23 christologically in Philippians 2:10–11 so Peter may be relating to Christ the threefold description of Yahweh in Isaiah 45:21 (אל־צדיק ומושיע, "a righteous God and a Savior") when he writes ἐν δικαιοσύνῃ τοῦ θεοῦ ἡμῶν καὶ σωτῆρος Ἰησοῦ Χριστοῦ.

3. The Use of σωτήρ in 2 Peter

1:1	τοῦ	θεοῦ	ἡμῶν	καὶ σωτῆρος Ἰησοῦ Χριστοῦ
1:11	τοῦ	κυρίου	ἡμῶν	καὶ σωτῆρος Ἰησοῦ Χριστοῦ
2:20	τοῦ	κυρίου	ἡμῶν	καὶ σωτῆρος Ἰησοῦ Χριστοῦ
3:2	τοῦ	κυρίου		καὶ σωτῆρος
3:18	τοῦ	κυρίου	ἡμῶν	καὶ σωτῆρος Ἰησοῦ Χριστοῦ

11. To refer to Moehlmann's careful documentation of this point is not to concur with his thesis that "during the first decades of its life, Christianity promulgated a soter-less soteriology" (2) or his conclusion that "Jesus was not called *soter* until he was also called *theos* and this first occurred in the period after Paul" (65).

12. Similarly Moulton, *Prolegomena* 84; N. Turner, *Syntax* 181. Winer enunciates the principle that "a repetition of the Article is not admissible before connected nouns which, for instance, are merely predicates of one and the same person, as in . . . 2 Pet. i.11 τοῦ κυρίου ἡμῶν καὶ σωτῆρος Ἰ. Χρ." (126 n. 2). Yet he rejects the potentially parallel instance of this principle in 1:1. Robertson (*Grammar* 785–86) notes that this anomaly in Winer's reasoning was rectified in P. W. Schmiedel's (8th) edition of Winer's *Grammar*. Schmiedel cites the structural parallels to 1:1 in 2 Pet. 1:11; 2:20; 3:2, 18 and comments that grammar demands that one person be meant (158), although he includes Eph. 5:5 and 2 Thess. 1:12 as further instances!

13. If δικαιοσύνη is in fact predicated of two persons in 2 Pet. 1:1, it need not carry a different meaning with each person. Nor need one concur with Bigg (252) that "if the righteousness is one and the same, it becomes exceedingly difficult to keep God and Jesus Christ apart." For in the Pauline salutations, "one and the same" χάρις . . . καὶ εἰρήνη are regularly traced to a twofold source (e.g., Gal. 1:3).

14. This suggestion was made by one of my students, Roger W. Handyside.

Several observations may be made about the use of σωτήρ in 2 Peter: (1) it is always anarthrous and refers to Jesus Christ;[15] (2) it never stands alone but is always linked with a preceding articular noun, either κυρίου (four times) or θεοῦ (once); and (3) the ὁ κύριος (ἡμῶν) καὶ σωτήρ combination always refers to a single person. The use of σωτήρ elsewhere in 2 Peter strongly suggests that the onus of proof rests with any who would deny that in 1:1 also there is a reference to only one person, Jesus Christ.

4. The Doxology to Christ in 2 Peter 3:18

New Testament doxologies are regularly addressed to God,[16] sometimes "through Jesus Christ" (Rom. 16:27; Jude 25; cf. 1 Pet. 4:11), but on at least four occasions (2 Tim. 4:18; 2 Pet. 3:18; Rev. 1:5–6; 5:13) a doxology is addressed directly to Christ (cf. Rev. 5:12). In 2 Peter 3:18 there is no possible ambiguity as to the addressee (. . . Ἰησου Χριστοῦ. αὐτῷ κτλ.), such as there is in Romans 9:5, Romans 16:27, 1 Peter 4:11, or Hebrews 13:21. (See further Westcott, *Hebrews* 464–65). As an ascription of praise to a divine person, a doxology betrays a speaker's or writer's immeasurably high estimate of the addressee. An author who can address a doxology to Christ would have little difficulty in applying the term θεός to him. There is no reason to deny that in 2 Peter 1:1 Jesus Christ is called "our God and Savior."

C. The Meaning of the Verse

1. The Author

a. Συμεὼν Πέτρος

Συμεών ("Symeon" or "Simeon"), the Greek transliteration of the original Hebrew name שמעון, is a form found only here and in Acts 15:14. Elsewhere in the NT we find the apostle Peter referred to by his nickname Πέτρος ("Peter," "rock"), by the genuinely Greek name Σίμων ("Simon"; see BDF §53.(2)d),[17] or by Κηφᾶς, the Greek form of the Aramaic term כיפא ("stone"). Some regard the author's use of this unusual form Συμεών as an indication of the letter's authenticity (e.g., Green, *2 Peter–Jude* 59); Peter is using the name familiar to Jewish Christians (cf. Acts 15:14) and familiar in his youth. Others see it as an attempt by a pseudonymous writer to create verisimilitude for his stance as a protagonist of apostolic orthodoxy (e.g.,

15. Given the close link between τῶν ἀποστόλων and τοῦ κυρίου καὶ σωτῆρος and the historical sequence "prophets-Savior-apostles" in 3:2, there can be no doubt that the "Lord and Savior" in this verse is Jesus Christ.

16. Luke 2:14; Rom. 11:36; 2 Cor. 11:31; Gal. 1:5; Eph. 3:21; Phil. 4:20; 1 Tim. 1:17; 1 Pet. 5:11; Jude 24–25; Rev. 5:13; 7:12.

17. In 2 Pet. 1:1 Σίμων is read by 𝔓[72] B Ψ vg cop (see Metzger, *Commentary* 699).

Barnett 168) or as a reflection of current Palestinian Christian usage maintained by the Petrine circle in Rome to which the author belonged (Bauckham, *Jude–2 Peter* 167).

b. δοῦλος καὶ ἀπόστολος Ἰησοῦ Χριστοῦ

The term *slave* or *bond-servant* (cf. Jude 1) establishes identity of status between author and readers, whether Jew or Greek, since all equally were the willing slaves of Christ the Lord (cf. 2 Pet. 2:1; 1 Cor. 7:22; Eph. 6:6; Rev. 2:20). On the other hand, the term *apostle* (cf. 1 Pet. 1:1) points to a distinction of office, emphasizing apostolic commission and authority (cf. 1 Pet. 5:1 for a similar identity-distinction sequence).

2. The Addressees

a. τοῖς . . . λαχοῦσιν πίστιν

Originally signifying "obtain by lot," λαγχάνω came to mean "receive" by divine appointment or influence, quite apart from human merit or initiative. What the addressees had been "chosen to have" (Louw and Nida §57:127) was πίστις, that is, transmitted apostolic teaching about God's salvation in Christ (*fides quae creditur, Glaubenslehre*) as well as the personal trust to embrace this faith (*fides qua creditur*).[18]

b. ἰσότιμον ἡμῖν . . . (πίστιν)

The adjective ἰσότιμος should be distinguished from ἴσος; Peter did not write ἴσην πίστιν, "equal faith."[19] Again, if the meaning were simply "of the same kind" (NASB; BAGD 381b; Louw and Nida §58:34), the much more common word ὅμοιος might have been expected. F. Field has observed that whereas πολύτιμος is a derivative of τιμή in the sense of *pretium*, ὁμότιμος and ἰσότιμος invariably derive their meaning from τιμή in the sense of *honor*. Thus πολύτιμος, "of great value"; ὁμότιμος, "of the same honor"; and ἰσότιμος, "of equal honor." As applied to πίστις, this latter adjective means "equally privileged" (*Notes* 240)[20] or, one may paraphrase, "that brings parity of dignity, status, and rights within the kingdom of God." Field comments, "'Ἰσοτιμία is properly *aequalitas honoris*, but comes to be used for *equality* in general, *par conditio et ius*" (*Notes* 240).

18. Some scholars opt for the objective (*quae*) sense alone (e.g., BAGD 663c, noting that πίστις lacks an object here; R. Bultmann, *TDNT* 6:213; Chaine 35; Kelly, *Peter–Jude* 296; Schelkle 185; Reumann 171), others for the subjective (*qua*) sense alone (e.g., Winer 200; Cranfield, *Peter–Jude* 172; E. M. B. Green, *2 Peter–Jude* 68). Fuchs and Reymond (44–45) argue convincingly for a combination of objective and subjective senses.

19. See, however, Zerwick, *Analysis* 546 ("of equal value"; so also NAB^2); GNB, NIV, and NRSV, "as precious as ours."

20. So also MM 307 s.v.; TCNT; Chaine 35 ("également honorable"); Spicq, *Pierre* 208; Bauckham, *Jude–2 Peter* 165, 168; similarly Moffatt, Goodspeed, NEB, and REB; RSV has "of equal standing."

The comparison implied by ἰσότιμον ἡμῖν,[21] "(a faith) of equal privilege with ours" (Kelly, *Peter–Jude* 295), is not merely between the apostles and Christians of the postapostolic era (as Schelkle [184] proposes), but between apostles and nonapostles (Spicq, *Pierre* 208; cf. 2 Pet. 3:2), between eyewitnesses and noneyewitnesses (Chaine 36; cf. John 20:29; 1 Pet. 1:8), or between Jewish Christians and Gentile believers (Mayor 81; H. Hanse, *TDNT* 4:2; cf. Acts 11:15, 17; 15:8–9).

c. ἐν δικαιοσύνῃ τοῦ θεοῦ ἡμῶν καὶ σωτῆρος Ἰησοῦ Χριστοῦ

The prepositional phrase ἐν δικαιοσύνῃ should not be construed with πίστιν,[22] for nowhere in the NT is "righteousness" the object of faith, and faith is nowhere depicted as coming "through righteousness." Nor does the phrase belong solely with λαχοῦσιν (as Zerwick, *Analysis* 546)[23] but rather it modifies the whole expression τοῖς ἰσότιμον ἡμῖν λαχοῦσιν πίστιν: "To those who have received a faith as privileged as ours, by virtue of[24] the righteousness possessed and exercised by our God and Savior, Jesus Christ."[25] Δικαιοσύνη here does not bear its distinctively Pauline sense of a new and right relationship with God,[26] for there faith antedates righteousness, righteousness being granted on the basis of faith (ἐπί/διὰ πίστεως), whereas here parity in the faith is obtained through "righteousness." As elsewhere in 2 Peter (viz., 2:5, 21; 3:13; cf. 1 Pet. 2:24; 3:14), δικαιοσύνη is not a divine gift but a moral attribute, uprightness of character and conduct. In 1:1 one need not restrict its sense to "impartiality," although that meaning arises naturally from the context, for the term refers here to the divine benevolence in granting "faith" (1:1b) and "everything necessary for a life of godliness" (1:3), and the divine faithfulness in fulfilling promises,[27] espe-

21. Ἡμῖν is a case of the so-called abbreviated comparison (cf. Matt. 5:20), where ἡμῖν = τῇ ἡμῶν πίστει (Winer 623; cf. BDF §185.(1); N. Turner, *Syntax* 220) or τῇ ἐμετέρᾳ [*sic*] πίστει (Zerwick, *Analysis* 546).

22. ℵ has εἰς δικαιοσύνην, perhaps under the influence of passages such as Rom. 4:5, 9, 22.

23. On this view, one might have expected λαχοῦσιν to be placed after πίστιν.

24. "En [vertu de]" (Chaine 37; Zerwick, *Analysis* 546). Ἐν bears this same sense in 1:2, although Huther (*General Epistles* 292, citing de Wette; similarly Mayor 82) finds a locatival as well as an instrumental sense in the preposition: ἐν "states in what the increase of grace has its origin, and by what it is effected."

25. Θεοῦ and σωτῆρος are possessive/subjective genitives, with Ἰησοῦ Χριστοῦ in epexegetic apposition. This seems preferable to saying that τοῦ θεοῦ ἡμῶν καὶ σωτῆρος is predicative, being a double attribute of Ἰησοῦ Χριστοῦ. To construe these words to mean "our God and Savior of Jesus Christ" (with Ἰησοῦ Χριστοῦ as an objective genitive) is unjustifiable, for while the expression "the God of our Lord Jesus Christ" occurs once in the NT (Eph. 1:17; cf. Mark 15:34; John 20:17; Rev. 1:6; and E. D. Burton 389–90), one never finds "our God of Jesus," far less "(the) Savior of Jesus Christ," a notion which, in this unqualified form, would be abhorrent to NT writers.

26. Reumann, however, tentatively proposes that since the phrase is not [illegible] righteousness/justice *of God*," the author may have recast a Pauline term or phrase christocentrically: "(The) righteousness/justice of *Jesus Christ* our God and savior" (173).

27. Cf. Spicq (*Pierre* 208): "Cet attribut divin de bienveillance active et de fidélité aux promesses."

cially the promise that Gentiles would be incorporated into the people of God (cf. Acts 15:14–18, citing Amos 9:11–12), as well as to the divine freedom from προσωπολημψία (cf. Acts 10:34–35; 15:8–9).

3. Conclusion

The conclusion seems inescapable that in 2 Peter 1:1 the title ὁ θεὸς ἡμῶν καὶ σωτήρ is applied to Jesus Christ, a view endorsed by the great majority of twentieth-century commentators with varying degrees of assurance,[28] and by most grammarians[29] and authors of general works on Christology[30] or 2 Peter.[31]

What function does this title of Christ serve in the salutation? At both the beginning (1:2–3, 8) and end (3:18) of the letter, the author draws attention to his readers' need to advance in their knowledge of Jesus Christ; this is the principal protection he offers his readers against the specious arguments and ethical libertinism of the false teachers who were harassing them. An early reminder of the deity and saving power of that Lord would have been totally apt.

The overall sense of 2 Peter 1:1 is that, by virtue of the benevolence, faithfulness, and impartiality of "our God and Savior, Jesus Christ," the addressees have received personal faith and the corporate faith. And though they may not be apostles or Jews and may never have seen or heard Jesus in person, yet they enjoy parity of spiritual status and identity of spiritual privilege with the apostles, Jews, and the companions of Jesus. In the heavenly city there are no second-class citizens, for Christ guarantees ἰσοτιμία to all.

28. In the following list, an asterisk signifies that the commentator stresses the late date of 2 Peter when noting that θεός is used of Jesus: Bigg 235, 248, 250–52; Strachan, "2 Peter" 123; *James 10; *Moffatt, *Epistles* 177; Chaine 36–37; Cranfield, *Peter–Jude* 173; Barnett 169–70; *Schelkle 185; *J. Schneider, *Briefe* 102–3; Stöger 74; Reicke 150; Spicq, *Pierre* 208; Lenski, *Epistles* 252–53; E. M. B. Green, *2 Peter–Jude* 68–69; *Kelly, *Peter–Jude* 295, 297–98; *Schrage 125; *Grundmann 67 and *TDNT* 9:565 n. 464; *Fuchs and Reymond 42, 44–45; *Bauckham, *Jude–2 Peter* 168–69. The only major dissenting voices among the twentieth-century commentators seem to be Mayor (81–82), Windisch (*Briefe* 84), Schlatter (*Briefe* 97–98), and Preisker (84), although at an earlier time there was Alford (4:390), Huther (*General Epistles* 291–92), Plumptre (164), and von Soden (214).

29. Middleton 432–35; H. J. Rose in Middleton 432 n. 1; Robertson, *Grammar* 127, 785–86; Robertson, "Article" 184–85, 187; BDR §276 n. 3 (dropping the "cf." of BDF §276.(3) and the expressed preference for the textual variant τοῦ κυρίου); Zerwick, *Greek* §185; Zerwick and Grosvenor 717; N. Turner, *Syntax* 181 n. 3; N. Turner, *Insights* 16; C. F. D. Moule, *Idiom Book* 109–10.

30. Bousset 314; Warfield, *Studies* 269–70; Moehlmann 17, 58; Lebreton, *History* 371; Bultmann, *Theology* 1:129; cf. Bultmann, *Essays* 276; Metzger, "Jehovah's Witnesses" 79; Wainwright, *Trinity* 65 (= "Confession" 285); Cullmann, *Christology* 314; Barclay, *Jesus* 32; Bruce, "God" 51; W. Foerster, *TDNT* 7:1018 n. 70 ; Brown, *Reflections* 22–23 (= "Jesus" 560–61); Deichgräber 181; Sabourin, *Names* 302; Sabourin, *Christology* 126, 143–44; R. N. Longenecker, *Christology* 137–39; Schillebeeckx, *Jesus* 303; Reymond 288–91. Those who distinguish θεός from Ἰησοῦς Χριστός in the verse include E. Stauffer, *TDNT* 3:106 n. 268; and Rahner 135 n. 4.

31. Fornberg 142–43; Danker 78; Reumann 171, 173. Käsemann (*Essays* 183 n. 2) dissents.

XI

The True God (1 John 5:20)

Οἴδαμεν δὲ ὅτι ὁ υἱὸς τοῦ θεοῦ ἥκει καὶ δέδωκεν ἡμῖν διάνοιαν ἵνα γινώσκομεν τὸν ἀληθινόν, καὶ ἐσμὲν ἐν τῷ ἀληθινῷ, ἐν τῷ υἱῷ αὐτοῦ Ἰησοῦ Χριστῷ. οὗτός ἐστιν ὁ ἀληθινὸς θεὸς καὶ ζωὴ αἰώνιος.

It is a curious fact that in the case of 1 John 5:20, where the central issue is simple—what is the antecedent of οὗτος?—and the Greek straightforward, scholarly opinion is more evenly divided over the question of whether θεός is predicated of Jesus than is the case with any other verse discussed in this book. This ambiguity is reflected in virtually all English translations, for if they begin a new sentence at οὗτος, it begins with either "He is" or "This is," where the antecedent of the pronoun is just as uncertain as it is at first sight in Greek.[1]

Whether 1 John 5:14–21 be called a postscript (Dodd, *Epistles* 133–34), an appendix (Bultmann, *Epistles* 83, 85), or an epilogue (Vellanickal 276 n. 43), these verses fall into two clear sections:[2] verses 14–17 give directions about prayer; verses 18–21 state three reasons for Christian confidence, each introduced by οἴδαμεν ὅτι, and conclude with an exhortation (v. 21).[3] These three Christian certainties are (1) the divine protection of the believer from sin and from the evil one (v. 18), (2) the divine origin of the believer and the satanic grip on the world (v. 19), and (3) knowledge of and fellowship with the true God through his incarnate Son (v. 20).

For clarity of reference I shall refer to the six segments of 1 John 5:20 in the following manner:

20a	οἴδαμεν δὲ ὅτι ὁ υἱὸς τοῦ θεοῦ ἥκει
20b	καὶ δέδωκεν ἡμῖν διάνοιαν
20c	ἵνα γινώσκομεν τὸν ἀληθινόν
20d	καὶ ἐσμὲν ἐν τῷ ἀληθινῷ

1. The only way a reference to Christ could be made unambiguous would be to translate ". . . Jesus Christ who is . . ." or "The latter is. . . ."

2. Bultmann (*Epistles* 2, 83) believes that 5:14–21 is an appendix composed by an "ecclesiastical redactor" and added to a postscript (5:13) that states the purpose of the epistle. For a contrary view, viz., that 5:13–21 stems from the same author as penned the rest of the epistle, see Nauck 135–46. The issues involved in the hotly contested question of the authorship of 1 John and its relation to 2–3 John and the Gospel of John are carefully discussed by Brown, *Epistles* 14–35, who holds that while the same author (the "Presbyter") wrote the three epistles, he is in all probability not to be identified with the fourth evangelist. I shall be assuming the hypothesis that the Gospel and the three epistles were all the work of John the son of Zebedee.

3. The structure of 5:18–20 is analyzed by Nauck 134–35 and esp. Vellanickal 281–86, who finds in these three verses "three rhythmic developments marked by οἴδαμεν" and "a quasi-concentrical structure" (283), viz., A B C (v. 18) A′ C′ (v. 19) B′ A″ (v. 20).

20e ἐν τῷ υἱῷ αὐτοῦ Ἰησοῦ Χριστῷ
20f οὗτός ἐστιν ὁ ἀληθινὸς θεὸς καὶ ζωὴ αἰώνιος

A. The Textual Variants

There is one important textual question in the verse. The object of (ἵνα) γινώσκομεν[4] is found in five forms.

1. τὸν ἀληθινόν

The variant printed in UBS[3] and NA[26], τὸν ἀληθινόν, has support from the two families that have been clearly isolated within the Catholic Epistles (Alexandrian: B 81; Byzantine: K 056 0142 *Byz Lect*) and best accounts for the rise of the other readings. Its starkness as a substantival adjective used as a divine title (only in 1 John 5:20 *bis* and Rev. 3:7), "the true one", "him who is the truth," makes it the most difficult reading, for in the LXX and NT ἀληθινός is generally accompanied by a noun.

2. τὸ ἀληθινόν

Supported by ℵ* it^{r} cop$^{sa,bo^{mss}}$, τὸ ἀληθινόν relieves the starkness of the titular τὸν ἀληθινόν and seems to be a modification of that reading based on John 8:32: καὶ γνώσεσθε τὴν ἀλήθειαν, καὶ ἡ ἀλήθεια ἐλευθερώσει ὑμᾶς (cf. 1 John 2:21).

3. τὸν ἀληθινὸν θεόν

Although the third variant is read by the Alexandrian witnesses A Ψ 33 323 1739 1881 and other "mixed type" manuscripts (326 614 630 945 1505 2495), may conceivably have given rise to the first reading by haplography (ΑΛΗΘΙΝΟΝΘ̄Ν̄), and is true to the sense of the verse, it is probably secondary since (1) it is a longer reading than either of the variants above;

4. The variant γινώσκωμεν (NA[26]) has Alexandrian (Ψ 1739) and Byzantine (K *Byz*) support and is preferred by most scholars on the ground that the present indicative after ἵνα is due to "corruption of the text" (thus BDF §369.(6), "of course"; BAGD 377a, "prob[ably]"; Westcott, *Epistles* 196, followed by Law 411, speaks of a "corrupt pronunciation" of γινώσκωμεν; on the textual interchange between ο and ω, especially in the endings -ομεν and -ωμεν, see Robertson, *Grammar* 200–201). Ἵνα followed by the future indicative is not uncommon (see the references in Brooke 150–51) but the present indicative after ἵνα is rare—only here and in 1 Cor. 4:6 and Gal. 4:17, according to Robertson, *Grammar* 325, 984. Although, then, many dismiss γινώσκομεν as a secondary reading, probably a misspelling arising from the confusion of ο and ω (Abbott, *Grammar* §2114), there are two compelling reasons for preferring the indicative: it is found in proto-Alexandrian (ℵ B*), later Alexandrian (A 33 81), and Byzantine (L 049) witnesses; when ἵνα bears a consecutive sense ("so that we know"), the mood denoting reality (the indicative) accords with the reality expressed (Abel §65(a), remark III).

(2) ἀληθινός is adjectival, not substantival, in the Fourth Gospel[5] and in 1 John 2:8 and 5:20f; and (3) under the influence of ὁ ἀληθινὸς θεός in 5:20f and ὁ μόνος ἀληθινὸς θεός in John 17:3, it removes the ambiguity of τὸν ἀληθινόν (which, grammatically, could refer either to God or to the Son of God; cf. 5:20a), and therefore is a less difficult reading than the first.[6]

4. τὸν θεὸν τὸν ἀληθινόν

Only minuscule 629 reads τὸν θεὸν τὸν ἀληθινόν, which is a secondary variation of the third reading, reflecting the alternative attributive position of the adjective seen in Isaiah 65:16 *bis* (LXX), τὸν θεὸν τὸν ἀληθινόν.

5. *Patrem* (= τὸν πατέρα)

A variant found in Ambrose, *patrem*, probably represents a scribal effort to remove all ambiguity from either τὸν ἀληθινόν or τὸν ἀληθινόν θεόν by excluding any possible reference to the Son of God (5:20a).

We can therefore be confident that ἵνα γινώσκομεν τὸν ἀληθινόν was the original text.

B. The Identity of ὁ ἀληθινός (τὸν ἀληθινόν . . . ἐν τῷ ἀληθινῷ)

Ἀληθινός is a favorite Johannine word, occurring nine times in the Fourth Gospel, four times in 1 John, and ten times in the Apocalypse (there are only five other NT uses). Sometimes ἀληθινός does not differ in meaning from ἀληθής, another common Johannine term, but where a distinction obtains, ἀληθινός (Latin *veras*) "signifies truth of being, *verity*; while ἀληθής signifies truth of statement, *veracity*" (Latin *verax*) (Findlay 428 n. 1). R. C. Trench puts it succinctly (28): "The ἀληθής fulfils the promise of his lips, the ἀληθινός fulfils the wider promise of his name." Accordingly I prefer to render ὁ ἀληθινός as "the True One" (Law 412), "him who is true" (REB), or "Him who is real" (Moffatt), rather than "the truthful One" (Malatesta 319–20) or even "He who is the truth" (Smalley 292, 306–7).

Two considerations lead me to believe (with BDR §263 and n. 1) that τὸν ἀληθινόν and τῷ ἀληθινῷ refer to the same person, viz., God (τοῦ θεοῦ). First, both the sequence of thought and Johannine theology make it improbable that τὸν ἀληθινόν refers to the Son of God. Since καὶ δέδωκεν follows

5. John 1:9; 4:23, 37; 6:32; 7:28; 8:16 v.l.; 15:1; 17:3; 19:35.

6. Among English versions, τὸν ἀληθινὸν θεόν is (apparently) preferred by TCNT, Moffatt, GNB, JB (but not NJB), and REB. But it is possible that any one of these versions is translating τὸν ἀληθινόν and adds "God" to remove any ambiguity of referent.

immediately after ἥκει (whose subject is ὁ υἱὸς τοῦ θεοῦ), it is inappropriate to make an implied ὁ θεός the subject of δέδωκεν (*pace* Bengel 5:154), especially since both verbs are perfective in sense ("has come . . . and has given": the fact and consequences of the coming and the giving remain).[7] The result of the Son's gift of insight or apprehension (διάνοια)[8] is knowledge of ὁ ἀληθινός. If "the true one" here were the Son of God, one would have expected αὐτόν or τὸν υἱόν in the place of, or standing before, τὸν ἀληθινόν: "so that we know him/the Son of God, the true one," or simply "so that we know him/the Son of God." And it is more in keeping with Johannine theology to say that the Son imparts the understanding that brings a knowledge of the Father (cf. John 1:18; 14:7) than to affirm that the aim or result of the Son's gift of insight to believers is their knowledge of himself. The Son's mission is the revelation of the Father, not of himself. That τὸν ἀληθινόν in fact refers back to τοῦ θεοῦ in the phrase ὁ υἱὸς τοῦ θεοῦ is confirmed by three of the secondary textual variants discussed above, viz., τὸν ἀληθινὸν θεόν, τὸν θεὸν τὸν ἀληθινόν, and *patrem*.

Second, ἐν τῷ ἀληθινῷ more naturally refers to God than to the Son of God. If ἐν τῷ ἀληθινῷ did in fact refer to Christ, (1) John would probably have continued either with τῷ υἱῷ τοῦ θεοῦ, Ἰησοῦ Χριστῷ or with Ἰησοῦ Χριστῷ υἱῷ θεοῦ—that is, ἐν would be omitted before a phrase that was in epexegetic apposition,[9] and αὐτοῦ would be omitted, as lacking a natural antecedent in τῷ ἀληθινῷ; and (2) αὐτοῦ would have to refer back to τὸν ἀληθινόν (= the Father), but then Jesus would be both ὁ ἀληθινός and the Son of ὁ ἀληθινός. There can be no doubt that αὐτοῦ finds its most natural antecedent in τῷ ἀληθινῷ, which would then refer to the Father.

If, then, the first two uses of ἀληθινός in this verse refer to God, ἐν τῷ υἱῷ αὐτοῦ Ἰησοῦ Χριστῷ will not be in epexegetic apposition to ἐν τῷ ἀληθινῷ ("in the one who is true, namely, in his Son, Jesus Christ"), although such an understanding of the relation between the two phrases seems to be reflected in the translation "even in his Son Jesus Christ" (RV, ASV, Moffatt, NIV).[10] The second ἐν phrase is either modal or causal. If modal, the meaning

7. This emphasis on the ongoing results of the act of giving is lost in the reading ἔδωκεν (A Ψ 049 33 *al*). Nor should ἥκει be treated simply as equivalent to ἐφανερώθη (1:2; 3:5, 8) (as Bonnard 116 asserts). The gift has become a permanent possession (Abbott, *Grammar* §2454) and the incarnation is irreversible.

8. This assumes that ἵνα is ecbatic (see n. 4 above). But Bultmann (*Epistles* 89 and n. 33) and Bonnard (116) construe ἵνα as epexegetic (= ὅτι), introducing the content of the διάνοια, not the result or (as for many commentators) the purpose of the δέδωκεν.

9. "Before a noun in apposition the preposition is regularly not repeated" (Winer 421, citing Luke 23:51; Eph. 1:19; 1 Pet. 2:4). Winer concurs that in 1 John 5:20 τῷ υἱῷ is not in apposition to τῷ ἀληθινῷ.

10. But it is possible that "even" here means not "that is," but "and what is more." In the latter case, however, one would have expected ἐν τῷ ἀληθινῷ <u>καὶ</u> ἐν τῷ υἱῷ αὐτοῦ. Cf. 1 John 1:3, μετὰ . . . καὶ μετά . . . , and 2 John 3, παρὰ . . . καὶ παρά. . . .

of ἐν is "by our union with" (TCNT), "through" (Goodspeed), or "by being in" (Law 412; Zerwick, *Analysis* 560; Stott 195).[11] If causal, ἐν bears the sense "because we are in" (Malatesta 321; J. Schneider, *Briefe* 188; similarly NEB, NAB¹) or "by virtue of our being in" (Alford 4:514; similarly Haupt 343; Brooke 152; Bultmann, *Epistles* 89–90).[12] Ἐν τῷ υἱῷ αὐτοῦ expresses the means by which the εἶναι ἐν τῷ ἀληθινῷ is effected or states the reason why believers can be said to be "in the true one."

On this view John is affirming that, in addition to enjoying an ever-deepening knowledge (γινώσκομεν, present tense) of God, believers are, in very truth (καί), in living fellowship with God[13] through being incorporated in the person of his Son, Jesus Christ.

One difficulty needs to be faced. The precise notion of "being in" God is unparalleled in the Johannine corpus. The nearest parallels are "being in us" (Father and Son; John 17:21) and "abiding in God/the Father" (1 John 2:24; 4:15–16). But even in the absence of a precise parallel, one is justified in assuming that if John could use the expressions θεὸν ἔχειν (2 John 9a) and τὸν πατέρα ἔχειν (1 John 2:23 *bis*; 2 John 9b) in addition to the phrases ἐν ἡμῖν εἶναι and ἐν τῷ θεῷ μένειν mentioned above, he might equally be able to say εἶναι ἐν τῷ ἀληθινῷ, referring to God. Perhaps this unique turn of phrase was used as the antithesis of ἐν τῷ πονηρῷ κεῖσθαι (v. 19).

C. The Antecedent of οὗτος

Three preliminary points must be established. First, it seems incontestable that οὗτος points backward, not forward. If John were defining ὁ ἀληθινὸς θεός as ζωὴ αἰώνιος, "this is the true God, namely (καί) eternal life," the καί would have been omitted before ζωὴ αἰώνιος—at least if Johannine usage of the prospective οὗτος elsewhere be a guide (1 John 2:22; 5:4, 6; Rev. 20:14).[14]

Second, it is unnatural to find two separate subjects in 5:20f. Such an expedient takes two forms. Some see the Father as ὁ ἀληθινὸς θεός and the Son or the knowledge of the true God as ζωὴ αἰώνιος. Findlay (428), for

11. Stott comments (195): "In this way the first two sentences of verse 20 teach the necessity of the mediation of Jesus for both the knowledge of God and communion with God."

12. A. Harnack's suggestion (*Studien* 110 n. 1) that ΟΝΤΕΣ has been accidentally omitted after Χριστῷ, owing to the following ΟΥΤΟΣ, is an unnecessary conjecture, although a modal or causal ὄντες correctly represents the sense (see Schnackenburg, *Johannesbriefe* 291 n. 1).

13. As at 3:1 καὶ ἐσμέν introduces an independent statement, unrelated to either οἴδαμεν ὅτι or ἵνα.

14. Often in the Johannine Epistles a prospective οὗτος is followed by a defining ἵνα (1 John 3:11, 23; 5:3; 2 John 6 *bis*) or ὅτι clause (1 John 1:5; 5:9, 11, 14). But such a construction would be inappropriate in 1 John 5:20, for here it is not something impersonal such as a "message" or "testimony" or "commandment" that is being defined (on the hypothesis of a prospective οὗτος), but a divine person who could scarcely be defined by a mere proposition: "This is the true God, namely that. . . ."

example, renders 5:20f as "this is the true God, and (here, in this knowledge, is) eternal life" (similarly Dodd, *Epistles* 140). And Smalley (292, 307) proposes "he is the real God, and this is eternal life" (similarly NJB). But whether one reckons on an implied οὗτος after καί, referring to Jesus Christ, or on a case of prozeugma, so that αὕτη is implied after καί,[15] the predicate would need to be ἡ ζωὴ αἰώνιος to indicate the interchangeability of the concept (the Son/this knowledge/being in the true one *is* eternal life, and vice versa) and to preserve the parallelism of the sentence (cf. οὗτος . . . ὁ ἀληθινὸς θεός). Stated in another way, the anarthrous state of ζωή indicates a conceptual conjunction between ζωή and θεός so that both terms may be predicated of a single subject (οὗτος).

The other way two distinct subjects are found in 5:20f is by referring οὗτος to ὁ ἀληθινός and Ἰησοῦς Χριστός simultaneously. W. E. Vine believes that the singular οὗτος reflects "the inseparable unity of the Father and the Son in the one Godhead" (109): "*This* (the undivided, indivisible Father and Son) *is the true God*. . . . Christ is the embodiment, as well as the source, of the life which springs from God" (109–10). Such diction, however, where a singular pronoun refers to two persons of the Trinity, is unparalleled in the NT, although on occasion two separate subjects (Father and Son) are followed by a singular verb.[16] If it had been the author's intent to predicate ὁ ἀληθινὸς θεὸς καὶ ζωὴ αἰώνιος of two persons, he would have begun the sentence with οὗτοι or οἱ δύο or οὗτοι οἱ δύο εἰσίν (cf. 1 John 5:8b and the textual variants in 5:7–8).

The third preliminary point is this. Although in 5:20c–d there are two substantival uses of the adjective ἀληθινός, it is unnecessary for the sake of consistency to treat ὁ ἀληθινὸς θεός in 5:20f as a further instance, with θεὸς καὶ ζωὴ αἰώνιος in epexegetic apposition: "He [Christ] is the truthful One, God and Life eternal" (Malatesta 320). In the other two NT cases (viz., John 4:23; 17:3) where ἀληθινός stands between the article and a noun it is clearly attributive[17] and the onus of proof certainly rests on any exegete who would treat ἀληθινός as substantival in 5:20f, especially given the almost precise parallel in John 17:3: τὸν μόνον ἀληθινὸν θεόν.

These prolegomena have established that in 5:20f οὗτος is retrospective, not prospective; that ζωὴ αἰώνιος must be construed with ὁ ἀληθινὸς θεός, not directly with οὗτος or an implied αὕτη; that οὗτος has a single not a dual referent; and that ἀληθινός is adjectival, not substantival.

15. Winer (162) credits G. C. F. Lücke with holding this latter view, on which he comments "not impossible, but in my opinion unnecessary." Several English versions have "This is . . . , (and) this is . . ." (viz., Moffatt, NEB, GNB, JB).

16. 1 Thess. 3:11; 2 Thess. 2:16–17; cf. Rev. 22:3–4.

17. Ἀληθινός in fact generally stands in the alternative attributive position in the NT, e.g., τὸ φῶς τὸ ἀληθινόν, John 1:9 and 1 John 2:8; also John 6:32; 15:1; Heb. 8:2; Rev. 3:14; 6:10.

There are no fewer than seven possible antecedents of οὗτος. A representative advocate for each view may be mentioned.

1. the epistle's teaching about God (Dodd, *Epistles* 140)
2. v. 20 in general (Ewald, as cited by Huther, *General Epistles* 485)
3. Ἰησοῦ Χριστῷ (R. N. Longenecker, *Christology* 137)
4. υἱῷ (Ebrard 347)
5. τῷ ἀληθινῷ (Brooke 152)
6. αὐτοῦ (Robertson, *Grammar* 703, 707)
7. τοῦ θεοῦ (v. 19) (Buttmann 104)

These seven options may be reduced effectively to three: a general concept defined by what precedes (options 1 and 2 above), Jesus Christ (3 and 4), or God the Father (5–7).

1. A General Concept Defined by What Precedes

C. H. Dodd avers that οὗτος has "a wider and vaguer reference" than to the person of Jesus Christ. "The writer is gathering together in his mind all that he has been saying about God—how He is light, and love; how He is revealed as the Father through His Son Jesus Christ; how He is faithful and just to forgive our sins; how He remains in us—and *this*, he adds, *is the real God*" (*Epistles* 140). H. Ewald, on the other hand, focuses more narrowly on the first two sentences in verse 20 and especially οἴδαμεν and ἐσμέν: "This, both these things together, that we know and that we are all this, this is the true God and eternal life."[18]

It is not impossible that the masculine pronoun οὗτος should encapsulate some preceding idea or set of ideas[19] such as teaching about the knowledge of God through Christ, for the τοῦτο that one might have expected in such a case is nowhere used in the Johannine corpus without a grammatical (as opposed to a conceptual) antecedent (see 1 John 4:3).[20] The real difficulty with this proposal is twofold: it is arbitrary to prefer an impersonal antecedent, such as certain concepts or teaching, when there are two possible personal antecedents, viz., God and Jesus Christ; if οὗτος had an impersonal antecedent, the word order οὗτος ἐστιν (ἡ) ζωὴ αἰώνιος καὶ ὁ ἀληθινὸς θεός would be more natural, with "the true God" forming the per-

18. As cited by Huther, *General Epistles* 485. Westcott appears to endorse such a view when he writes that "the pronoun gathers up the revelation indicated in the words which precede" (*Epistles* 196; cf. 167, 218). But it is clear that he takes οὗτος in a personal sense when he continues, "This Being—this One who is true, who is revealed through and in His Son, with whom we are united by His Son—is the true God and life eternal" (*Epistles* 196).

19. On the function of οὗτος as summing up what precedes, see Abbott, *Grammar* §2386.

20. Ταῦτα would be inappropriate with the two singulars following.

sonal climax after two impersonal references: "This is eternal life—and the true God."

2. Jesus Christ (either Ἰησοῦ Χριστῷ or τῷ υἱῷ αὐτοῦ)

a. Ἰησοῦ Χριστῷ as the Nearest Antecedent

Locally, Ἰησοῦ Χριστῷ is the nearest antecedent of οὗτος and there is the necessary accord of number and gender. "Οὗτος does, as a rule, refer to what is near or last mentioned and ἐκεῖνος to what is remote" (Robertson, *Grammar* 702, who, however, refers οὗτος in this verse to God).

But one should not overlook the deictic use of οὗτος (see Buttmann 104; Winer 157; N. Turner, *Syntax* 13, 44; Zerwick, *Greek* §214).[21] Just as ἐκεῖνος may have a proximate antecedent which is of secondary import in the context (e.g., Matt. 17:27, where ἐκεῖνον refers to στατῆρα; Acts 3:13, where ἐκείνου refers to Πιλάτου), so οὗτος may have a remote or "nonimmediate" antecedent which is nevertheless dominant in the writer's mind (e.g., Matt. 3:3, 17; Acts 4:11; 7:19; 8:26). There are two notable instances in the Johannine Epistles.

1 John 2:22	Τίς ἐστιν ὁ ψεύστης εἰ μὴ ὁ ἀρνούμενος ὅτι Ἰησοῦς οὐκ ἔστιν ὁ Χριστός; οὗτός ἐστιν ὁ ἀντίχριστος.
2 John 7	Ὅτι πολλοὶ πλάνοι ἐξῆλθον εἰς τὸν κόσμον, οἱ μὴ ὁμολογοῦντες Ἰησοῦν Χριστὸν ἐρχόμενον ἐν σαρκί· οὗτός ἐστιν ὁ πλάνος καὶ ὁ ἀντίχριστος.

Pointers to what was dominant in John's mind in 1 John 5:20 may be found in τὸν ἀληθινόν . . . ἐν τῷ ἀληθινῷ . . . αὐτοῦ, all three expressions referring to God.[22] There is also the significant point that elsewhere in 1 John ἐκεῖνος is exclusively the demonstrative pronoun that refers to Christ (1 John 2:6; 3:3, 5, 7, 16; 4:17).[23]

b. Jesus as ζωή

In two passages in the Fourth Gospel (11:25; 14:6) Jesus is identified as "the Life" (ἐγώ εἰμι . . . ἡ ζωή). And just as "life" existed in the preexistent Logos (John 1:4: ἐν αὐτῷ ζωὴ ἦν), "eternal life" resides in and is experienced through the incarnate Son of God (1 John 5:11: ζωὴν αἰώνιον . . .

21. Buttmann, Winer, and N. Turner all cite 1 John 5:20 as an example of this deictic usage.

22. In the light of this grammatical phenomenon of a deictic οὗτος and the two instances in the Johannine Epistles, it is improper for Dodd to assert that "in strict grammar, the word 'this' should refer to the last person named" (*Epistles* 140).

23. "In the Epistle, it [ἐκεῖνος] is the pronoun used to denote Christ, as being the Person always before the writer's mind as his example" (Abbott, *Grammar* §2382).

αὕτη ἡ ζωὴ ἐν τῷ υἱῷ αὐτοῦ ἐστιν). In 1 John 1:2 ἡ ζωὴ ἡ αἰώνιος is both Jesus himself and the divine life revealed in him. In keeping with such usage it would be natural for John to affirm of Jesus οὗτός ἐστιν . . . ζωὴ αἰώνιος.

It is true that the emphasis throughout the Johannine corpus is on the Father as the source of the (eternal) life that is in his Son (e.g., John 5:26; 10:28), rather than on God as himself life or eternal life. But it is only a small step from the statement ὁ πατὴρ ἔχει ζωὴν ἐν ἑαυτῷ (John 5:26) or the characterization of God as ὁ ζῶν πατήρ (John 6:57) to the absolute identification οὗτός ἐστιν . . . ζωὴ αἰώνιος. In any case, whether 1 John 5:20c describes the Son or the Father, the statement is unique, for nowhere does John assert that either person "is life eternal," using both the present tense (ἐστιν) and the adjective (αἰώνιος).

c. ἀληθινός as Applied to Jesus

On five occasions in the Johannine literature the adjective ἀληθινός is applied to Jesus. He is the true light (John 1:9; 1 John 2:8), the true bread (John 6:32), the true vine (John 15:1), and the true witness (Rev. 3:14). Then, since he is called θεός in John 1:1, μονογενὴς θεός in John 1:18, ὁ θεός μου in John 20:28, and ὁ ἀληθινός in Revelation 3:7, it would seem unobjectionable for him to be called ὁ ἀληθινὸς θεός in 1 John 5:20. One could even argue that the change in this verse from two substantival uses of ἀληθινός to an adjectival use marks a change of referent, from God to Jesus.

As for John's use of θεός in the Fourth Gospel in reference to the preexistent Logos (John 1:1), the incarnate Son (John 1:18), and the risen Lord (John 20:28), we should not overlook the fact that in the first two cases θεός is anarthrous and in the third case it is articular simply because a vocatival nominative followed by a possessive pronoun is invariably articular.[24] Given this calculated nonuse of the article with θεός, it would be strange if such grammatical precision were compromised by equating Jesus Christ with ὁ θεός.[25] Support for applying ὁ ἀληθινὸς θεός to God may be found in the repeated τὸν θεὸν τὸν ἀληθινόν in Isaiah 65:16 (LXX), in the unambiguous τὸν μόνον ἀληθινὸν θεόν in John 17:3 (where a distinction is drawn between "the one true God" and "the one whom you sent, Jesus Christ"),[26] in the application of ἀληθινός to God in John 7:28 and Revela-

24. On these three verses, see above chapters II, III, IV.

25. Similarly Winer and Schmiedel 216. The difficulty of referring the absolute statement οὗτός ἐστιν ὁ ἀληθινὸς θεός to Christ is highlighted by two proponents of this view. Schnackenburg (*Johannesbriefe* 291) observes that this verse "admittedly has an extraordinary terseness, since without any restriction the full identity (*die volle Identität*) (note the article!) of Jesus Christ with 'the true one' (God) mentioned earlier is affirmed." The same sentiment is expressed by Schunack (106) who adds that the expression of this "full identity" in such an abbreviated form is unique, although Johannine theology paves the way (cf. John 1:1, 18; 20:28; 1 John 1:1–2).

26. On this verse, see below, chapter XII §B.

tion 6:10, and in the twofold use of ὁ ἀληθινός in reference to God in 1 John 5:20c–d.

d. Christological *Inclusio*

If οὗτος = Jesus Christ, then 1 John, like the Fourth Gospel (1:1; 20:28), begins and ends with a crucial christological affirmation that points to or expresses the deity of Christ (1:2; 5:20).

This is true in a general sense, but there is the difference that whereas in the Gospel θεός is applied to Jesus at the beginning and end, in the First Epistle it is the concept of Jesus as (ἡ) ζωὴ (ἡ) αἰώνιος, not an explicit statement of his deity, that is the common feature.

e. οὗτός ἐστιν in 1 John 5:6

Since οὗτός ἐστιν in 5:20f echoes 5:6 (Malatesta 322 n. 11), the referent in 5:20 will be the same as in 5:6, viz., Jesus Christ. A. Škrinjar (153) goes one step further: this "very solemn description" (ὁ ἀληθινὸς θεός) is introduced by οὗτός ἐστιν, to which there corresponds in the Gospel the christological formula ἐγώ εἰμι.[27]

The parallel with 5:6 is only verbal, for there οὗτός ἐστιν is prospective, not retrospective as it is in 5:20. Nor can any correspondence between οὗτός ἐστιν and ἐγώ εἰμι be pressed, for whereas the "I am" formula is frequent and is used exclusively of Jesus in the Gospel, οὗτός ἐστιν occurs only three times in the First Epistle, once clearly referring to Jesus (5:6) and once not (2:22). But this is not to doubt that οὗτός ἐστιν in 5:20, whatever its referent, forms an *inclusio* with αὕτη ἐστίν at the beginning of the epilogue (5:14) (Malatesta 320 n. 3).

Convinced by the arguments rehearsed above (viz., §C.2.a–e), a large number of scholars refer οὗτος to Jesus Christ[28] and therefore believe that the author is unequivocally asserting that "his (God's) Son, Jesus Christ" is ὁ ἀληθινός θεός. Those who discuss the matter further express this relation between Jesus and "the true God" in various ways. A. Corell, for instance, speaks only of the "absolute affinity" that always exists between Christ and

27. Bonnard (116) detects a polemical and exclusive tone in this οὗτος: "It is he and no other who is truly God and life for mankind."

28. Among the commentators are Ebrard 346–48; Lias 421–22; Chaine 223–24; J. Schneider, *Briefe* 188; Schnackenburg, *Johannesbriefe* 291–92; Bultmann, *Epistles* 90; Bruce, *Epistles* 128; Haas 129–30; Houlden, *Johannine Epistles* 14, 138; Balz 204; Marshall, *Epistles* 254–55; Wengst 224; Bonnard 116; Schunack 106; Brown, *Epistles* 625–26. Among general writers are Warfield, *Studies* 272–73; Bousset 238–39, 317–18; McGiffert 37–38; R. Bultmann, *TDNT* 2:865, 870 and n. 322; E. Stauffer, *TDNT* 3:106; Stauffer 114, 283 n. 354; Bonsirven, *Theology* 381; Corell 140; Cullmann, *Christology* 310; E. Schweizer, *TDNT* 6:439; Rahner 135; Škrinjar 152–53; Brown, *Reflections* 19, 23 (= "Jesus" 558, 561); Sabourin, *Names* 302; J. Schneider, *NIDNTT* 2:82; R. N. Longenecker, *Christology* 137, 139; Malatesta 320, 322 and n. 11; Reymond 310–12; Casey, *Prophet* 158. On the patristic data, see Plummer 128; Chaine 223; R. Bultmann, *TDNT* 2:865 n. 293; Brown, *Epistles* 625.

God (140). Both R. Schnackenburg (*Johannesbriefe* 291) and G. Schunack (106) use the expression "die volle Identität," emphasizing (respectively) that this total identity is here affirmed "ohne Einschränkung" or "uneingeschränkt." But, one may ask, identity of what? No one, of course, suggests identity of person, since John clearly distinguishes ὁ υἱὸς τοῦ θεοῦ from ὁ ἀληθινός (= ὁ πατήρ) in 5:20a–c. The only other option would seem to be identity of nature. Accordingly, H. Balz (204) explains his phrase "selbst wirklicher Gott" by "vom Wesen Gottes selbst" and J. Schneider affirms that this Johannine confessional formula asserts "the full unity of essence" ("die vollkommene Wesenseinheit") of Christ and God (*TBNT* 2:607; similarly *Briefe* 188). The Achilles' heel of such proposals is the presence of the article.[29] Although he propounds an odd solution to the problem, J. H. A. Ebrard is correct that "in declaring *what* any one is, the predicate must have no article; in declaring *who* any one is, the predicate must have the article" (347).[30]

3. God the Father (either τῷ ἀληθινῷ or αὐτοῦ or τοῦ θεοῦ)

In the course of evaluating the case for Jesus Christ as the antecedent of οὗτος, several arguments in favor of God as the antecedent were mentioned:

1. Οὗτος may be deictic, referring back not to the nearest antecedent but to the dominant thought in the writer's mind (cf. the use of οὗτος in 1 John 2:22; 2 John 7) as seen in the sequence τὸν ἀληθινόν . . . ἐν τῷ ἀληθινῷ . . . αὐτοῦ.
2. In 1 John the demonstrative pronoun used to refer to Jesus is invariably ἐκεῖνος, not οὗτος.
3. Ἀληθινός is applied to God in Isaiah 65:16 *bis* (LXX) (τὸν θεὸν τὸν ἀληθινόν), John 7:28, and Revelation 6:10.
4. It is very improbable that John would jettison two explicit and precise distinctions found in the Fourth Gospel by speaking of Jesus as ὁ θεός (cf. John 1:1, 18)[31] and as ὁ ἀληθινὸς θεός (cf. John 17:3).

To these arguments four additional points may be added.

29. Cf. Chaine (223–24): "Le Fils est vrai Dieu comme le Père." One thinks of the Nicene Creed's Θεὸν ἀληθινόν.

30. Ebrard can affirm that John teaches that the Son of God is "identical with the ἀληθινὸς Θεός Himself" (347) only because he (Ebrard) believes that "ὁ ἀληθινὸς Θεός is simply no other than a definition of the Divine collective personality in opposition to the creature (and here in opposition to false gods); and One is called ὁ ἀληθινὸς Θεός, in such case as His internal trinitarian relation is out of view" (348).

31. The use of the article with θεός μου in John 20:28 is grammatically conditioned (cf. above chapter IV §A.3) and without special theological significance.

a. Parallels to 1 John 5:20f

The closest verbal parallel to 5:20f is found in John 17:3 rather than in John 14:6. Now it is true that in the latter case ἀληθινός matches ἀλήθεια and ζωὴ αἰώνιος parallels ζωή, but in the former ὁ ἀληθινὸς θεός recalls ὁ μόνος ἀληθινὸς θεός and ζωὴ αἰώνιος corresponds to ἡ αἰώνιος ζωή. And it is there, in John 17:3, that the title ὁ ἀληθινός θεός is applied to the Father as *opposed* to the Son, who is depicted as the messenger of "the one true God" (ὃν ἀπέστειλας).[32] Also, wherever the articular nominative ὁ θεός is found in the Gospel (fourteen instances) or elsewhere in 1 John (twelve cases), it refers to the Father. This leads me to suggest that if John had intended to affirm that God's Son was ὁ ἀληθινὸς θεός, John 17:3 indicates that he would probably have written something like οὗτος καὶ κτλ., "He (God's Son, Jesus Christ) *also* is the true God and life eternal."

b. God as ζωή

We have seen that whether the predicate ἐστιν . . . ζωὴ αἰώνιος applies to God *or to Christ,* it is an unparalleled assertion in precisely this form (viz., with the present tense and this adjective). It is therefore unjustified for J. Schneider to reject the application of the predicate to God on the ground that John nowhere says of God that he is eternal life (*Briefe* 188). If the knowledge of the true God is eternal life (John 17:3), and if God "has life in himself" (John 5:26) so that he may be termed "the living Father" (John 6:57), there would be little difficulty in affirming that he "is life eternal." By this John means not merely that God is eternally the essence of all life and "eternally the Living One" (Law 413) but also that all eternal life granted to believers through his Son (John 10:28) stems from him and him alone. It is not exactly that he has eternal life and imparts it; rather he is eternal life and therefore is its only source. Ζωὴ αἰώνιος is anarthrous, I suggest, for two reasons: to indicate the intimate link between true deity and eternal life, viz., that the true God is eternally and essentially the living one and all those who have eternal life derive it from him; and to indicate a nonreciprocating proposition, viz., that, while God by nature and as revealed in Christ is eternal life, eternal life cannot be precisely equated with God. In any case John never writes ἡ ζωὴ αἰώνιος, only ζωὴ αἰώνιος (as here) or ἡ αἰώνιος ζωή.

32. The differences between John 17:3 and 1 John 5:20c are twofold. In the Gospel the object of the believer's knowledge is twofold—the only true God and the one whom he sent, Jesus Christ; in the Epistle the object is single ("he who is true") and the means of gaining this knowledge is also specified (". . . by being in his Son, Jesus Christ"). Also, in John 17:3 eternal life consists in knowing God and Jesus Christ, whereas in 1 John 5:20 God (or Christ) is actually identified with eternal life.

c. Contextual Support

The immediate and wider contexts support a reference to the Father. First, ὁ ἀληθινός twice refers to the Father in 5:20c–d, and while a change of referent is not impossible one would expect an identity of referent when ὁ ἀληθινὸς θεός occurs in the next sentence, even if ἀληθινός has become adjectival. In this case a clear progression is evident within 5:20: ὁ θεός—ὁ ἀληθινός (*bis*)—ὁ ἀληθινὸς θεός, all in reference to the Father.[33] Second, there are two indications that the phrase ἐν τῷ υἱῷ αὐτοῦ Ἰησοῦ Χριστῷ is of secondary import:[34] word order shows that the main assertion is ἐσμὲν ἐν τῷ ἀληθινῷ, "we are in union with this (anaphoric τῷ) true one"; the repeated ἐν reveals the sense to be not "namely in," but either "by being in" or "because we are in" (see §B above) so that the phrase introduced by ἐν is subsidiary or even parenthetical (as Harnack proposes, *Dogma* 110 n. 1) and not essential for the completion of sense. And the addition Ἰησοῦ Χριστῷ is even less central, for it is in epexegetic apposition to τῷ υἱῷ αὐτοῦ. If all this be so, the dominant line of thought in 5:20c–f will be τὸν ἀληθινόν . . . ἐν τῷ ἀληθινῷ . . . οὗτος. . . . Third, if οὗτος = God, this verse provides the final member of a trilogy of affirmations found in 1 John: God is φῶς (1:5), ἀγάπη (4:8, 16), and ζωὴ αἰώνιος (cf. πνεῦμα, John 4:24).

d. Apparent Tautology

Defenders of the equation οὗτος = Jesus Christ frequently draw attention to the apparent tautology that results if οὗτος refers to the Father. "To choose the more distant antecedent—that is, the Father—injects a tautology, if not an inanity, into the verse, for one does not need to be informed that the Father, who admittedly has just been twice identified already as the 'true One,' is 'the true God'" (Reymond 311).

To begin with, we should observe that there is no simple repetition: "This (true one) is the true God." On the one hand, just as the article with ἀληθινῷ is anaphoric, referring back to what has been said with respect to τὸν ἀληθινόν, so οὗτος gathers up all that has preceded in the verse. "This true one, whom believers now know because of his Son's coming and gift of insight and with whom they are now united in fellowship, this one (οὗτος)

33. In certain respects this happens to be closely parallel to the progression found within the Prologue of the Fourth Gospel: θεός (1:1)—μονογενής (1:14)—μονογενὴς θεός (1:18), all in reference to the Logos-Son.

34. With regard to Bousset's suggestion that this phrase is a gloss that introduces the assertion of Christ's full deity into the context (238–39; cf. 317–18), Brown aptly observes (*Epistles* 625–26, without explicitly referring to Bousset) that "the well-attested Johannine pattern of sequential phrases referring to Father and Son militates against this." For a critique of O'Neill's view (*Puzzle* 61) that all of v. 20 is a Christian addition to the last (5:13b–21) of twelve Jewish poetic admonitions that make up 1 John, see Smalley 294.

is the true God and life eternal."[35] Also, οὗτος stresses that it is only the Father of Jesus Christ who is the true God. On the other hand, in the predicate of verse 20f there is not simply repetition (ἀληθινός) but also expansion (θεός and ζωὴ αἰώνιος).

Then again, a twofold progression is represented by verse 20f. There is a development within the chapter from "God *gave* us eternal life" (5:11) to God "*is* eternal life" (5:20), and within verse 20 from ὁ θεός to ὁ ἀληθινός (*bis*) to ὁ ἀληθινὸς θεός.

Finally, the combination ὁ ἀληθινὸς θεός is designed to prepare the way for verse 21 with its warning against the worship of false gods: "He is the real God. . . . Little children, guard yourselves against false gods" (Smalley's rendering, 292). Whether εἴδωλα is understood literally as pagan idols, or by metonymy as paganism in general or as false images or heretical conceptions of God (e.g., 1 John 2:21–23, 26–27; 4:1–6), or as any substitute for the worship of the true God,[36] the "true God–false gods" antithesis, so common in both Testaments (e.g., Isa. 45:16–22; 1 Cor. 8:4–6; 1 Thess. 1:9–10), is clearly present in the transition from verse 20 to verse 21.[37]

4. Conclusion

Although it is certainly possible that οὗτος refers back to Jesus Christ, several converging lines of evidence point to "the true one," God the Father, as the probable antecedent. This position, οὗτος = God, is held by many commentators,[38] authors of general studies,[39] and, significantly, by those grammarians who express an opinion on the matter.[40]

35. Cf. the function of οὗτος in John 1:2: this λόγος who was θεός (cf. John 1:1c) "was in the beginning with God" (cf. John 1:1a–b).

36. See the very thorough canvassing of the options in Brown, *Epistles* 627–29.

37. This seems preferable to saying that ὁ ἀληθινὸς θεός is contrasted with ὁ πονηρός (v. 19) in whom there is no ἀλήθεια (John 8:44).

38. Huther, *General Epistles* 484–86; Alford 4:514; Haupt 343–45; Westcott, *Epistles* 196; Holtzmann 239; Law 412–13; Brooke 152–53; Dodd, *Epistles* 140; Preisker 135; Stott 195–96; Smalley 308–9; Grayston 147–48.

39. Findlay 428; Harnack, *Dogma* 110 n. 1; Dupont, *Christologie* 223–24; W. F. Howard, *John* 188 n. 1; Wainwright, *Trinity* 71; V. Taylor, *Person* 126 and n. 1; Segond, "Jean" 351.

40. Winer 157; Buttmann 104; Winer and Schmiedel 216; Robertson, *Grammar* 703; N. Turner, *Syntax* 13, 44; Zerwick and Grosvenor 733 ("almost certainly"; but in the earlier Zerwick, *Analysis* 560, a preference was expressed for οὗτος = Christ). See also BAGD 37a, 340c.

XII

Other Texts

In chapters II–XI we have considered the nine major NT texts in which the term θεός has been thought by many to apply to Jesus. But in three cases—Acts 20:28, Hebrews 1:9, and 1 John 5:20—the evidence was judged to be insufficiently strong to warrant any firm conclusion that θεός functioned there as a christological title. In the present chapter we shall briefly consider the other passages which on occasion have been adduced as evidence of this use.[1]

A. Matthew 1:23

> Ἰδοὺ ἡ παρθένος ἐν γαστρὶ ἕξει καὶ τέξεται υἱόν, καὶ καλέσουσιν τὸ ὄνομα αὐτοῦ Ἐμμανουήλ, ὅ ἐστιν μεθερμηνευόμενον μεθ' ἡμῶν ὁ θεός.

Matthew 1:23 is the first of Matthew's "formula citations" and reflects the LXX version of Isaiah 7:14,[2] to which the evangelist has added ὅ ἐστιν κτλ. The issue is whether μεθ' ἡμῶν ὁ θεός should be translated "God with us"[3] or "God is with us,"[4] that is, whether μεθ' ἡμῶν is attributive and functions as an adjective or is predicative and functions as an adverb. It should be observed immediately that both of the above translations are feasible, for in both Hebrew (GKC §141f) and Greek (N. Turner, *Syntax* 294–98, 309–10) the copula may be omitted.

That Matthew attaches special significance to the name Ἐμμανουήλ is incontestable: he has included in his citation of Isaiah 7:14 a line (καὶ καλέσουσιν . . . Ἐμμανουήλ) which was not directly germane to his purpose of showing that the virginal conception and the birth of Jesus were the fulfill-

1. Other verses sometimes alleged to contain a christological application of θεός include Luke 1:16–17; 8:39; 9:43; 1 Thess. 4:9 (assuming θεοδίδακτοι = διδακτοὶ θεοῦ [John 6:45] = taught by Jesus); 1 Tim. 1:1; 5:21; 2 Tim. 4:1; Titus 1:3; 3:4; Heb. 3:4 (see Bruce, *Hebrews* 93 n. 14 for this possibility); James 1:1; Jude 4. In a brief article in 1956 Oke proposed, largely on the basis of the anarthrous θεός, that the doxology in 1 Tim. 1:17 was addressed to Christ, not God, and should be translated as "now to the King of the ages, immortal, invisible, alone divine, be honour and glory for ever and ever" (368). Against this novel proposal I would observe that (1) an anarthrous θεός may refer to the Father (see chapter I §B.3.b) and is unlikely to be adjectival in import when it is qualified by an adjective (μόνῳ); (2) although Christ is the theme of the preceding paragraph (1 Tim. 1:12–16) and the addressee of some NT doxologies (2 Tim. 4:18; 2 Pet. 3:18; Rev. 1:5–6; 5:13), the remarkable similarities between the doxology of 1 Tim. 6:15–16, in which God the Father is incontestably the addressee, and that in 1:17 (βασιλεῦς, μόνος, immortality, invisibility) and the unparalleled use of the terms ὁ βασιλεὺς τῶν αἰώνων, ἄφθαρτος, and ἀόρατος in reference to Christ, make it certain that the doxology of 1 Tim. 1:17 is addressed to God.

2. See Gundry, *Use* 89–91.

3. RV, Weymouth, Goodspeed, Williams, Berkeley ("God-with-us"), RSV, NASB, NIV.

4. TCNT, NEB, GNB, JB ("God-is-with-us"), NAB[1], NAB[2], Cassirer, NRSV (but cf. RSV), REB.

ment of Scripture; in addition, he has added a translation of the Hebrew expression עמנו אל that the LXX had simply transliterated.

In arguing in favor of the translation "God with us," J. C. Fenton notes the *inclusio* in Matthew 1:23 and Matthew 28:20 (μεθ' ἡμῶν ὁ θεός—ἐγὼ μεθ' ὑμῶν εἰμι) and equates the ἐγώ of 28:20 with the ὁ θεός of 1:23: "Matthew is saying that Jesus is God" (81). But one may recognize the presence of *inclusio* without drawing Fenton's conclusion. The Messiah Jesus is now always with his obedient disciples (28:20) because God once deigned to visit his people in this Messiah (1:23). Is it likely that Matthew, whose favorite designation for Jesus is υἱὸς θεοῦ,[5] would *preface* his Gospel with ὁ θεός as a christological title?[6]

Fenton also emphasizes that in Matthew μετά + the genitive almost always means "in the company of" rather than "in favor of" and therefore is more readily applicable to the Son than the Father (81). In the nature of the case, most uses of μετά in the Gospels denote a literal "being with," but one should not overlook its figurative use "of aid or help *be with someone, stand by, help someone* of God's help" (BAGD 509a, citing [with a "cf."] Matt. 1:23). Perhaps the closest verbal parallel in the NT to μεθ' ἡμῶν ὁ θεός is found in 2 Corinthians 13:11: ὁ θεὸς . . . ἔσται μεθ' ὑμῶν. In both texts (εἶναι) μετά denotes divine aid and favor.

Whereas the MT of Isaiah 7:14 reads the third-person singular וְקָרָאת (referring to the child's mother) and the LXX the second-person singular καλέσεις (referring to Ahaz), Matthew has the impersonal third-person plural καλέσουσιν, "they (= people) will call him (Immanuel)." If these people are the followers of Jesus, "Immanuel" could here be portrayed as the post-Easter christological confession of the church, comparable to Thomas's confession, "My Lord and my God" (John 20:28).[7] It is unnecessary, however, to restrict this confession to a post-Easter setting when θεός became an occasional title of Jesus. For when, during the public ministry of Jesus, people glorified God that he had intervened in human history to bring physical or spiritual healing through Jesus, they were in effect giving Jesus the name "Immanuel"—in the person of Jesus "God is with us" to save. For

5. See Matt. 4:3, 6; 8:29; 14:33; 16:16; 26:63; 27:40, 43, 54; and cf. ὁ υἱός μου in 2:15; 3:17; 17:5. Kingsbury contends "that 1:23 is Matthew's 'thumbnail definition' of the predication Son of God, and that his entire Gospel may be seen as an attempt to elaborate on the implications of this passage and others that are similar to it (cf., e.g., 14:27; 18:20; 28:20)" (53; cf. 163).

6. It is the Fourth Gospel that moves from θεός (1:1) to a vocatival ὁ θεός μου (20:28).

7. Cf. Gundry, *Matthew* 25: "This revision turns the quotation into a prediction of the church's confession. . . . 'They' are the church, the people he [Jesus] saves. . . . He is with his people to save them from their sins, not merely in behalf of God, but as God." If the rendering "God is with us" finds support in the dual use of עמנו אל in Isa. 8:8, 10, the translation "God with us" looks to the messianic title אל גבור in Isa. 9:6 [MT v. 5] (cf. Isa. 10:21) for justification, for if Isa. 7:1–9:7 is considered a closely integrated unit containing the prophetic message to Judah (cf. the parallels with the message to Ephraim, Isa. 9:8–11:16) (as Motyer [122–23] argues), Isa. 7:14 could be interpreted in the light of Isa. 9:6.

instance, the crowd at Nain who had witnessed Jesus' raising of the widow's son "glorified God" with the words "God has visited his people" (Luke 7:16), which is equivalent to saying "Jesus is Immanuel" (cf. also Luke 1:68–69).

In favor of the translation "God is with us," it is true that the translation of עמנו אל that Matthew supplies, μεθ' ἡμῶν ὁ θεός, simply reproduces the word order of the Hebrew, but if ὁ θεός were in fact a title of Jesus,[8] one might have expected the translation to be either ὁ μεθ' ἡμῶν θεός or ὁ θεὸς μεθ' ἡμῶν (or the more correct Greek ὁ θεὸς ὁ μεθ' ἡμῶν). That is, word order suggests that μεθ' ἡμῶν is predicative rather than attributive, functioning as an adverb rather than as an adjective.

There are only three occurrences of עמנו אל in the OT, all in Isaiah. Twice the LXX translates the expression by μεθ' ἡμῶν (κύριος) ὁ θεός (Isa. 8:8, 10), and once it transliterates the phrase (Isa. 7:14). Matthew cites the transliteration found in Isaiah 7:14, but when he chooses to add a translation he uses the rendering found in Isaiah 8:8, 10 where, according to BDB 769a, עמנו אל is a "declaration of trust and confidence, *with us is God!*" That is, the meaning of μεθ' ἡμῶν ὁ θεός seems almost indistinguishable from ὁ θεὸς ὑπὲρ ἡμῶν (cf. Rom. 8:31).

There are therefore strong reasons for believing that in Matthew 1:23 μεθ' ἡμῶν ὁ θεός signifies that in Jesus God is present to bring salvation to his people rather than that Jesus, as ὁ θεός, is personally present with his people. Matthew is not saying, "Someone who is 'God' is now physically with us," but "God is acting on our behalf in the person of Jesus."

B. John 17:3

> Αὕτη δέ ἐστιν ἡ αἰώνιος ζωὴ ἵνα γινώσκωσιν σὲ τὸν μόνον ἀληθινὸν θεὸν καὶ ὃν ἀπέστειλας Ἰησοῦν Χριστόν.

Reviving the interpretation of Augustine, W. Bousset has proposed (317) that in John 17:3 τὸν μόνον ἀληθινὸν θεόν should be supplied after Ἰησοῦν Χριστόν:[9]

ἵνα	γινώσκωσιν	σὲ	τὸν μόνον ἀληθινὸν θεὸν
	καὶ	ὃν ἀπέστειλας Ἰησοῦν Χριστόν	[τὸν μόνον ἀληθινὸν θεόν]

8. It is clear that Ἰησοῦς, not Ἐμμανουήλ, was the actual, personal name by which the promised Son was known (Matt. 1:25; cf. 1:21). So at most Ἐμμανουήλ is titular.

9. Bousset is prompted to make this proposal by the use of ὁ ἀληθινὸς θεός in 1 John 5:20, which he takes to be a description of Christ. But see chapter XI.

Such an understanding should not be dismissed as impossible. Nevertheless it labors under the difficulty that, although with copulated expressions (here σέ and ὃν κτλ.) it is perfectly regular for a single word such as a possessive pronoun or an adjective to appear with the first expression and yet apply to both,[10] one would expect a longer phrase such as τὸν μόνον ἀληθινὸν θεόν to be repeated with both expressions or else to stand after the second expression, rather than standing only with the first (as here).

As the text reads, there is clear parallelism, with each object of γινώσκωσιν defined by a proper name in epexegetic apposition:

ἵνα	γινώσκωσιν	σὲ	τὸν μόνον ἀληθινὸν θεὸν
	καὶ	ὃν ἀπέστειλας	Ἰησοῦν Χριστόν[11]

The two appositive phrases are not set in opposition,[12] for ὃν ἀπέστειλας identifies Jesus Christ as the person whom the one true God sent as his revealer (cf. John 1:18). Yet the two phrases do distinguish Ἰησοῦς Χριστός from ὁ μόνος ἀληθινὸς θεός, the Son from the Father, as is consistently the case throughout the Fourth Gospel. In this regard John 17:3 expresses in Johannine idiom Paul's distinction between εἷς θεὸς ὁ πατήρ and εἷς κύριος Ἰησοῦς Χριστός (1 Cor. 8:6).

C. Galatians 2:20

> Ζῶ δὲ οὐκέτι ἐγώ, ζῇ δὲ ἐν ἐμοὶ Χριστός· ὃ δὲ νῦν ζῶ ἐν σαρκί, ἐν πίστει ζῶ τῇ τοῦ υἱοῦ τοῦ θεοῦ τοῦ ἀγαπήσαντός με καὶ παραδόντος ἑαυτὸν ὑπὲρ ἐμοῦ.

There are four textual variants to note in Galatians 2:20:

10. For example, ὑμῶν τὴν κλῆσιν καὶ ἐκλογήν (2 Pet. 1:10); ἐν πάσῃ σοφίᾳ καὶ συνέσει πνευματικῇ (Col. 1:9).

11. This analysis seems much more probable than the suggestion that σέ is parallel to Ἰησοῦν as object and τὸν μόνον ἀληθινὸν θεόν to Χριστόν as predicate ("as the one true God . . . as Messiah"):

ἵνα	γινώσκωσιν		σὲ	τὸν μόνον ἀληθινὸν θεὸν
	καὶ	ὃν ἀπέστειλας	Ἰησοῦν	Χριστόν

Against this I would urge that (1) a predicative Χριστός is almost always articular in the Fourth Gospel (1:20, 25; 3:28; 4:29; 7:26, 41; 10:24; 11:27; 20:31 [9:22 is the one exception]); (2) the combination Ἰησοῦς Χριστός occurs in John 1:17 and it would be unwarranted to separate the two terms when both are anarthrous (contrast Col. 2:6: τὸν Χριστὸν Ἰησοῦν τὸν κύριον, "the Messiah, Jesus the Lord"); and (3) when followed by a direct, personal object γινώσκω is usually used absolutely rather than in a construction such as "know someone to be/as something."

12. It is, by implication, the false gods of paganism—not Christ—who are contrasted with the one true God (cf. 1 Thess. 1:9–10; 1 John 5:20–21).

1. τοῦ θεοῦ	Byzantine: 330 (twelfth century A.D.)
2. τοῦ θεοῦ τοῦ υἱοῦ	Byzantine: 1985 (A.D. 1561)
3. τοῦ θεοῦ καὶ Χριστοῦ	proto-Alexandrian: $\mathfrak{P}^{46}$ B
	Western: D* G it^{d,e,g} Victorinus-Rome Pelagius
4. τοῦ υἱοῦ τοῦ θεοῦ	proto-Alexandrian: א
	later Alexandrian: A C Ψ 33 81 104 326 1739 1881 cop^{bo}
	Western: it vg Adamantius Ambrosiaster Jerome Augustine
	Byzantine: K *Byz Lect*

If any one of the first three variants represents the original text, there would be or could be a christological use of θεός, for the following phrase τοῦ ἀγαπήσαντος κτλ. alludes to the self-sacrificing death of Jesus.[13]

Although τοῦ θεοῦ is both the shortest and the most difficult reading (since it is either patripassian or involves an unqualified use of θεός in reference to Jesus) and could have prompted the second and third readings, it cannot be deemed original, given the slight and late external support.

With its notion of "God the Son," unparalleled in the Pauline corpus, τοῦ θεοῦ τοῦ υἱοῦ is undoubtedly difficult, which might have caused a scribe to substitute καὶ Χριστοῦ for τοῦ υἱοῦ (to give the next reading) or to transpose τοῦ θεοῦ and τοῦ υἱοῦ (to produce the last reading). But again external support is very meager. Moreover, it is difficult to account for the first reading, for an error of eye by which a scribe passed from the first to the second τοῦ would produce τοῦ υἱοῦ, not τοῦ θεοῦ.

There are, then, only two variants worthy of serious consideration.

In favor of the third reading, τοῦ θεοῦ καὶ Χριστοῦ, one may mention the early and strong external testimony (proto-Alexandrian and Western) and the parallel expression ὁ θεὸς καὶ Χριστός Ἰησοῦς in the Pastorals (1 Tim. 5:21; 2 Tim. 4:1). If one translates the phrase "(by faith in) God who is Christ" (epexegetic καί), there are numerous Pauline parallels for the concept of Christ as the object of faith (e.g., Gal. 2:16; 3:22; Rom. 3:22, 26; 10:11–13). Alternatively, if one prefers the more natural sense, "(by faith in) God and in Christ," one may appeal to Romans 4:5, 4:24, 1 Thessalonians 1:8, and Titus 3:8 as evidence that Paul sometimes also presented God as the object of the Christian's faith.

13. Although τοῦ ἀγαπήσαντός με could refer to the Father, the conjoined description (note the single article and μὲ . . . ἐμοῦ) παραδόντος ἑαυτὸν ὑπὲρ ἐμοῦ could refer only to the Son (cf. Gal. 2:20a, 21b; 1:4; Titus 2:14), so that both participles must therefore refer to Jesus.

The principal difficulty with this reading is the matter of the derivation of variants. Why would a scribe forfeit a reference to Χριστός as an object of faith when verse 16 has mentioned this three times[14] or change a dual object of faith, "God and Christ," into a single object of faith?

With regard to external evidence, the last reading, τοῦ υἱοῦ τοῦ θεοῦ, enjoys wide geographical distribution as well as strong support from all three families of witnesses. The expression ὁ υἱὸς τοῦ θεοῦ is a characteristically Pauline expression[15] and (ἡ) πιστὶς . . . τοῦ υἱοῦ τοῦ θεοῦ is paralleled by Ephesians 4:13. As for the origin of the other variants, B. M. Metzger plausibly suggests that "it is probable that in copying, the eye of the scribe passed immediately from the first to the second τοῦ, so that only τοῦ θεοῦ was written (as in ms. 330); since what followed was now incongruous, copyists added either τοῦ υἱοῦ or inserted καὶ Χριστοῦ" (*Commentary* 593).[16]

Consideration of both external and internal evidence leads to the conclusion that the original reading was τοῦ υἱοῦ τοῦ θεοῦ, the preference of NA[26] and of UBS[1,2,3] (with a "B" rating). Galatians 2:20 is therefore not a text in which Jesus is called θέος.

D. Ephesians 5:5

> Τοῦτο γὰρ ἴστε γινώσκοντες, ὅτι πᾶς πόρνος ἢ ἀκάθαρτος ἢ πλεονέκτης, ὅ ἐστιν εἰδωλολάτρης, οὐκ ἔχει κληρονομίαν ἐν τῇ βασιλείᾳ τοῦ Χριστοῦ καὶ θεοῦ.

Because there is no decisive grammatical reason why the final phrase of Ephesians 5:5 could not mean "in the kingdom of Christ who is God," with καί being epexegetic, one may concur with N. Turner (*Insights* 16; cf. Zerwick, *Greek* §185) that such a rendering should be seriously considered. On the other hand, there must be weighty reasons why none of the twenty major English versions reflects this sense,[17] although several notable scholars of last century espoused the view.[18] These "weighty reasons" may be summarized as follows.

14. Or once, if πίστις (Ἰησοῦ) Χριστοῦ means "the faith(fulness) of Christ" or "the faith which comes from Christ." Berkeley and NRSV mg render Gal. 2:20 "by the faith of the Son of God."

15. Rom. 1:4; 2 Cor. 1:19; Eph. 4:13; and ὁ υἱὸς αὐτοῦ in Rom. 1:3, 9; 5:10; 8:29; 1 Cor. 1:9; Gal. 1:16; 4:4, 6b; 1 Thess. 1:10.

16. Since the reading τοῦ θεοῦ καὶ Χριστοῦ is found in 𝔓[46] (about A.D. 200), this explanation of the derivation of variants assumes that the alteration from τοῦ υἱοῦ τοῦ θεοῦ to the simple τοῦ θεοῦ (as reflected in the twelfth-century minuscule 330) occurred at a very early date.

17. Indeed, several English versions exclude this sense by rendering "(in the kingdom) of Christ and of God" (Weymouth, RSV, NEB, GNB, NAB[1], NIV, NAB[2], Cassirer, NRSV, REB). Similarly Berkeley ("of the Christ and God") and Barclay ("which is Christ's and God's"). JB and NJB follow the reading of 𝔓[46] and Tertullian (τοῦ θεοῦ): "(The kingdom) of God."

18. For example, Middleton 362–67; Godet, *Romans* 141; Philippi 72 ("he who is Christ and God"); Liddon, *Romans* 153.

Epexegetic καί is never used to identify two proper names or a proper name and a title. If the meaning were "in the kingdom of Christ, who is God," one would expect either ἐν τῇ βασιλείᾳ τοῦ Χριστοῦ ὅς ἐστιν θεός (cf. Gal. 3:16; Eph. 1:14) or possibly ἐν τῇ βασιλείᾳ τοῦ Χριστοῦ τοῦ λεγομένου θεοῦ (cf. Col. 4:11). It is true that both ὁ Χριστός and θεός could be titles, but no one suggests that the sense is "the Messiah who is 'God.'" At least ὁ Χριστός here is a proper noun (and probably also θεός), so that my point remains valid.

In any case the true epexegetic καί ("that is to say, namely") is very rare in the NT.[19] Also, it is "always used to particularize" (BDF §442.(9)), so that if a single word is being defined by what follows καί, the definition is usually a phrase rather than a single word.[20]

The anarthrous state of θεοῦ is an inconclusive argument either way, for as a virtual proper noun θεός is sometimes anarthrous and sometimes articular (cf. Robertson, *Grammar* 786; N. Turner, *Syntax* 174) and a comprehensive pattern of usage is difficult to discern. If the absence of the article with θεοῦ is significant in the present instance, it shows not that Christ and θεός are in some sense identified but that they are intimately related as joint possessors and governors of a single kingdom.[21] As surely as the kingdom belongs to the one, it belongs to the other.[22]

It is highly improbable that Paul would introduce a profound, unqualified doctrinal affirmation (Christ is θεός) in an incidental manner, in a context where the assertion is not crucial to the flow of argument. In Romans 9:5, on the other hand, where also an anarthrous θεός follows ὁ Χριστός, Paul's declaration of the deity of Christ is integral to the argument and ὁ ὤν (= ὅς ἐστιν) links the two terms (see chapter VI).

It is true that elsewhere in Paul's letters ἡ βασιλεία is associated with either God[23] or Christ,[24] but not with both. But Revelation 11:15 at least shows that "our Lord and his Anointed" could be jointly associated with the

19. A careful distinction should be drawn between epexegetic καί (as in Matt. 8:33b; Mark 1:19c; John 1:16; Acts 5:21b), ascensive καί ("and indeed," "even"; John 5:25a; 1 Cor. 2:2), and adjunctive καί ("also"; Rom. 13:11), although some authorities treat them in conjunction.

20. For example, in John 1:16 χάριν ἀντὶ χάριτος explicates πληρώματος; in Matt. 8:33 τὰ τῶν δαιμονιζομένων explains πάντα.

21. Cf. the function of the single article in the series in Eph. 3:18 and with the pairs in Eph. 2:20 and 3:12.

22. Middleton (362) rightly observes that to make it unambiguous that separate persons were intended, τοῦ could have been added before θεοῦ, but the parallel he cites (Acts 26:30: ὁ βασιλεὺς καὶ ὁ ἡγεμών) does not involve proper names. When two *prima facie* personal nouns (such as Χριστός and θεός) are joined by καί, one should assume that καί is copulative, not epexegetic. It is precisely this point that counts against a christological use of θεός in 1 Tim. 1:1; 5:21; 2 Tim. 4:1; and James 1:1 (see n. 1).

23. Rom. 14:17; 1 Cor. 4:20; 6:9–10; 15:50; Gal. 5:21; Col. 4:11; 2 Thess. 1:5; cf. 1 Thess. 2:12.

24. Col. 1:13; 2 Tim. 4:1, 18; cf. 1 Cor. 15:24. Other NT references to the βασιλεία of Christ include Matt. 13:41; 16:28; Luke 1:33; 22:29–30; 23:42; John 18:36; and 2 Pet. 1:11.

kingdom in early Christian thought. What makes Ephesians 5:5 distinctive is its word order "Christ–God"[25] and its clarification that there is only a single kingdom—Christ's kingdom is God's kingdom—although there is joint ownership and governance. One and the same kingdom belonged to and was ruled by both Christ and God.[26] Such an emphasis serves to intensify Paul's warning that no immoral person will ever gain a place in that holy, consummated kingdom.

E. Colossians 2:2

> Ἵνα παρακληθῶσιν αἱ καρδίαι αὐτῶν συμβιβασθέντες ἐν ἀγάπῃ καὶ εἰς πᾶν πλοῦτος τῆς πληροφορίας τῆς συνέσεως, εἰς ἐπίγνωσιν τοῦ μυστηρίου τοῦ θεοῦ, Χριστοῦ.

There are more than fifteen textual variants in Colossians 2:2, eloquent testimony to the difficulties that Paul's accumulated genitives created for scribes. NA[26] and UBS[1,2,3] (with a "B" rating) are justified in preferring the reading τοῦ θεοῦ, Χριστοῦ,[27] for it is supported by two proto-Alexandrian texts (𝔓[46] and B) and two Western fathers (Hilary and Pelagius; also a manuscript of the Vulgate) and best explains the rise of the other variants. Scribes sought to clarify the meaning of τοῦ μυστηρίου τοῦ θεοῦ Χριστοῦ by resorting to omission, explanation, or amplification.

a. Original	
1. τοῦ θεοῦ Χριστοῦ	𝔓[46] Hilary Pelagius Ps-Jerome
b. Omission	
2. τοῦ θεοῦ	D[b] H P 69 424* 436* 462 1881 1912 cop[sa ms]
3. τοῦ Χριστοῦ	81 1241 1462 1739 (omits τοῦ) Euthalius
c. Explanation	
4. τοῦ θεοῦ ὅ ἐστιν Χριστός	D* it[ar,d,e,x] Pelagius Augustine Vigilius

25. This unusual word order is inverted by F G bo[ms] Ambrosiaster to give τοῦ θεοῦ καὶ Χριστοῦ, perhaps under the influence of ὁ θεὸς καὶ Χριστός in 1 Tim. 5:21 and 2 Tim. 4:1. Τοῦ Χριστοῦ τοῦ θεοῦ ("of God's Messiah"; cf. Ps. 2:2) is read by 1739* vg[ms].

26. When Paul declares that at the end Christ will surrender his kingdom to God the Father (1 Cor. 15:24) he may be indicating how he distinguished the kingdom of Christ from the kingdom of God: in the interadvent period the one and only kingdom of God may *also* be called the kingdom of Christ (but cf. 2 Tim. 4:18) since Christ himself embodies the kingdom of God, so that to belong to Christ's kingdom here is to inherit God's kingdom hereafter (cf. 1 Cor. 15:23, 50; Col. 1:13) and to serve Christ is to work for the kingdom of God (cf. Col. 4:11–12).

27. See also the discussions in WH 2: appendix 125–26; Metzger, *Commentary* 622 and *Text* 236–38.

	Reading	Witnesses
5.	τοῦ θεοῦ ὅ ἐστιν περὶ Χριστου	eth
6.	τοῦ θεοῦ τοῦ ἐν Χριστῷ	33 Clement (omits second τοῦ) Ambrosiaster
7.	τοῦ θεοῦ τοῦ ἐν Χριστῷ Ἰησου	arm
8.	τοῦ θεοῦ καὶ Χριστοῦ	l^{809*} Cyril-Alexandria
d.	Amplification	
9.	τοῦ θεοῦ πατρὸς Χριστοῦ	ℵ* 048 216 440
10.	τοῦ θεοῦ πατρὸς τοῦ Χριστοῦ	A C 4 cop^{bo,sa} Ps-Jerome
11.	τοῦ θεοῦ πατρὸς καὶ τοῦ Χριστοῦ	0208 441 1908 syr^{p} Chrysostom Theodore^{lat}
12.	τοῦ θεοῦ πατρὸς καὶ τοῦ Χριστοῦ Ἰησοῦ	vg^{cl} cop$^{bo^{ms}}$
13.	τοῦ θεοῦ πατρὸς καὶ τοῦ κυρίου ἡμῶν Χριστοῦ Ἰησοῦ	one Vulgate manuscript
14.	τοῦ θεοῦ καὶ πατρὸς τοῦ Χριστοῦ	ℵ^{b} Ψ 1962 1984 1985 2127 $l^{603,809mg}$ syr^{h}
15.	τοῦ θεοῦ καὶ πατρὸς καὶ τοῦ Χριστοῦ	D^{c} K 104 326 *Byz Lect* Theodoret John-Damascus

Even when the textual question has been resolved in favor of the reading τοῦ θεοῦ Χριστοῦ, grammatical ambiguities remain. There are three options.[28]

Χριστοῦ could be a possessive genitive: "the mystery of Christ's God," "that open secret of God, the Father of Christ" (Moffatt). Although the phrase ὁ θεὸς τοῦ κυρίου ἡμῶν Ἰησοῦ Χριστοῦ (Eph. 1:17) affords an approximate parallel to the expression ὁ θεὸς Χριστοῦ,[29] one would have expected ὁ θεὸς τοῦ Χριστοῦ[30] (on the canon of Apollonius and to avoid stark juxtaposition) if the sense were "the God of Christ"; in any case it would seem inappropriate for Paul to emphasize the subordination of Christ when the teaching he was opposing apparently undermined the sovereignty of Christ (cf. Col. 1:18; 2:8, 17, 19).

Χριστοῦ could be in epexegetic apposition to τοῦ θεοῦ: "the mystery of God, who is Christ." Such a bold, explicit, unqualified identification of ὁ θεός with Χριστός would not only negate Paul's general reservation of ὁ

28. Although D^{b} H P 436* 1881 cop$^{sa^{ms}}$ read simply τοῦ θεοῦ ("God's mystery, in which (ἐν ᾧ) . . ."), Χριστοῦ should not be dismissed as an early gloss that found its way into the text.

29. Cf. Rom. 15:6; Col. 1:3; see also Mark 15:34; John 20:17; Heb. 1:9; Rev. 1:6.

30. Note the articular Χριστοῦ in readings 10–12, 14–15.

θεός for the Father but also outstrip the milder Χριστὸς ὁ θεὸς ἡμῶν which is found in Ignatius (*Rom.* 6:3) but not in the NT.

Χριστοῦ could be in epexegetic apposition to τοῦ μυστηρίου: "God's mystery, which is Christ" (thus most grammarians, commentators, and English versions).[31] This sense is supported by Colossians 1:27 (cf. Col. 1:26; 4:3; Eph. 3:4–6) and is reflected in a textual variant that has strong Western support—τοῦ θεοῦ ὅ ἐστιν Χριστός (no. 4 above). Also, verse 3 may explain why Christ can be called God's mystery, viz., "for (causal ἐν) in him lie hidden all God's treasures of wisdom and knowledge."

In this verse, then, Χριστός is identified as τὸ μυστήριον τοῦ θεοῦ, not as ὁ θεός.

F. 2 Thessalonians 1:12

> . . . ὅπως ἐνδοξασθῇ τὸ ὄνομα τοῦ κυρίου ἡμῶν Ἰησοῦ ἐν ὑμῖν, καὶ ὑμεῖς ἐν αὐτῷ, κατὰ τὴν χάριν τοῦ θεοῦ ἡμῶν καὶ κυρίου Ἰησοῦ Χριστοῦ.

There are two possible translations of the last phrase of 2 Thessalonians 1:12:[32] (1) "according to the grace of our God and Lord, namely Jesus Christ" or (2) "according to the grace of our God and the Lord Jesus Christ."

The first rendering has a few supporters,[33] although no English version finds a single referent in the verse.[34] Two points may be stated in its favor. First, since in 2 Thessalonians 1:10–12 OT formulas that refer to Yahweh are applied to Christ,[35] it is conceivable that the divine title θεός is also given to Jesus here. Second, it is possible that ἡ χάρις τοῦ θεοῦ ἡμῶν καὶ κυρίου Ἰησοῦ Χριστοῦ is a variation of Paul's common formula ἡ χάρις τοῦ κυρίου (ἡμῶν) Ἰησοῦ Χριστοῦ.[36] A further argument is indecisive. In

31. For example, "the mystery of God—namely Christ" (NAB[1]); "God's mystery, that is, Christ himself" (NRSV). Berkeley has "a knowledge of Christ, the mystery of God." Whereas JB and NJB follow textual variant 2, Williams adopts variant 3.

32. It would be extremely arbitrary to render the phrase "according to the grace of our God and the God of the Lord Jesus Christ," where both ἡμῶν and κυρίου Ἰησοῦ Χριστοῦ are possessive genitives dependent on τοῦ θεοῦ (although John 20:17 parallels the concept). If this had been Paul's intent, he would have undoubtedly referred to Christ first, since the Christian's sonship is dependent on Christ's.

33. For instance, Cremer 281; Warfield, *Studies* 68–70; Bultmann, *Theology* 1:129; Petzke 193; N. Turner, *Insights* 16 (who oddly renders the crucial phrase as "our lord and God Jesus Christ"). It is significant that Middleton himself demurs (379–82) at Granville Sharp's defense of the rendering "of our God and Lord."

34. Most English versions have "of our God and the Lord Jesus Christ." At least four versions even more explicitly exclude the possibility of a single referent by inserting "of" before "the Lord Jesus Christ" (Weymouth, Berkeley, GNB, NAB[1]).

35. Cf. G. Kittel, *TDNT* 2:254, who cites Ps. 88:8 (LXX [MT 89:8]); Isa. 24:15; 59:19 (cf. also 66:5).

36. Thus R. N. Longenecker, *Christology* 138–39, who inclines toward seeing θεός as a christological title in this verse.

Pauline benedictions Christ is the sole source of χάρις (eight instances).[37] But this fact must be balanced against the observation that in Pauline salutations the Father and Christ are generally mentioned as the joint source of χάρις (nine instances)[38] and that 2 Thessalonians 1:12 is neither a salutation nor a benediction.

Support for the second understanding of the verse comes from six directions.[39]

1. The formula θεὸς καὶ κύριος in reference to one person is not found in the NT or LXX and is rare elsewhere,[40] whereas the threefold appellation κύριος Ἰησοῦς Χριστός is a fixed and common formula,[41] occurring some 48 times in the Pauline corpus.
2. We have already seen that an epexegetic καί between two personal names or between a title and a personal name is highly unlikely (see above §D and n. 22).
3. Elsewhere in Paul's letters, whenever θεός and κύριος Ἰησοῦς Χριστός are conjoined or occur in close proximity (viz., within the same sentence), two persons are always being referred to (31 instances).
4. Five times in the Thessalonian letters (ὁ) θεὸς (καὶ) πατὴρ ἡμῶν refers to God as distinct from Christ.[42] Also, there are three passages where no πατήρ is conjoined to ὁ θεὸς ἡμῶν but the reference is clearly to the Father.[43]
5. Earlier in the same sentence ὁ θεὸς ἡμῶν refers to the Father (v. 11) as distinct from ὁ κύριος ἡμῶν Ἰησοῦς (v. 12a).[44]
6. The fact that κυρίου is anarthrous is insignificant. As virtually a proper name, κύριος, like θεός, sometimes has the article and sometimes lacks it (N. Turner, *Syntax* 174). In the combination κύριος Ἰησοῦς Χριστός in Paul's writings, κύριος is articular 34 times (29 times with ἡμῶν attached) but anarthrous 14 times (10 examples being in the salutations).

37. Rom. 16:20; 1 Cor. 16:23; 2 Cor. 13:13; Gal. 6:18; Phil. 4:23; 1 Thess. 5:28; 2 Thess. 3:18; Philem. 25.

38. Rom. 1:7; 1 Cor. 1:3; 2 Cor. 1:2; Gal. 1:3; Eph. 1:2; Phil. 1:2; 2 Thess. 1:2; 1 Tim. 1:2; Philem. 3.

39. One cannot legitimately argue that the position of ἡμῶν serves to distinguish ὁ θεός from κύριος Ἰησοῦς Χριστός (*pace* E. Stauffer, *TDNT* 3:106 n. 268), for the reasons outlined above in chapter X §A.1.

40. See MM 287; Neufeld 80 n. 5.

41. These facts are also relevant to the combination θεοῦ καὶ κυρίου Ἰησοῦ Χριστοῦ δοῦλος in James 1:1 (cf. 2:1).

42. 1 Thess. 1:3; 3:11, 13; 2 Thess. 1:1, 2 (cf. 2 Thess. 2:16: ὁ θεὸς ὁ πατὴρ ἡμῶν).

43. 1 Thess. 2:2; 3:9; 2 Thess. 1:11.

44. In Titus 2:11–14 (one sentence in Greek), ὁ θεός refers first to the Father (v. 11), then to the Son (in the formula θεὸς καὶ σωτήρ, v. 13) (see chapter VII), but the difference between Titus 2:11–14 and 2 Thess. 1:11–12 is that in the latter passage a distinction is drawn between ὁ θεὸς ἡμῶν (v. 11) and ὁ κύριος ἡμῶν Ἰησοῦς (v. 12a) before the second reference to ὁ θεὸς ἡμῶν (v. 12b).

G. 1 Timothy 3:16

> Καὶ ὁμολογουμένως μέγα ἐστὶν τὸ τῆς εὐσεβείας μυστήριον· ὃς ἐφανερώθη ἐν σαρκί. . . .

The issue in 1 Timothy 3:16 is purely textual, for if the reading θεός be preferred in the place of ὅς, this would be an unambiguous use of θεός in reference to Jesus Christ, given the clause that follows ("was manifested in the flesh"). The textual data are as follows (from UBS^{3} 724).

1.	ὅς	ℵ* A* C* G^{gr} 33 365 442 2127 l^{599} syr^{hmg,pal} goth eth^{pp} Origen^{lat} Epiphanius Jerome Theodore Eutherius$^{acc. to Theodoret}$ Cyril Cyril$^{acc. to Ps-Oecumenius}$ Liberatus
2.	ὅ	D* it^{ar,c,d,dem,div,f,g,mon,x,z} vg Ambrosiaster Victorinus-Rome Hilary Pelagius Augustine
3.	ὅς or ὅ	syr^{p,h} cop^{sa,bo} arm eth^{ro} Ephraem?
4.	θεός	ℵ^{e} A^{2} C^{2} D^{c} K L P Ψ 81 104 181 326 330 436 451 614 629 630 1241 1739 1877 1881 1962 1984 1985 2492 2495 *Byz Lect* Gregory-Nyssa Didymus Chrysostom Theodoret Euthalius

The external evidence seems decisively to favor the reading ὅς. Although the reading θεός can claim the support of later Alexandrian (Ψ 81 104 326 1739 1881), Western (181), and Byzantine (L *Byz Lect*) witnesses, ὅς is attested by important witnesses that are proto-Alexandrian (ℵ*), later Alexandrian (A* C* 33), and Western (G^{gr}) in text type. In addition, one may assume that the variant ὅ arose as a correction of ὅς to align the relative with the preceding neuter noun μυστήριον. If this assumption is correct, the testimony that supports ὅ (Western: D* it vg), as well as the witnesses that presuppose either ὅς or ὅ (syr^{p,h} cop^{sa,bo} arm eth^{ro} Ephraem?), afford support for ὅς. In fact, all the ancient versions presuppose the relative pronoun, whether ὅς or ὅ, and the earliest uncial in the original hand that reads θεός (viz., Ψ) dates from the eighth or ninth century. Also, the earliest patristic citation of θεός dates from the last third of the fourth century (WH 2: appendix 133),[45] whereas Origen (d. 254) more than a century earlier testifies to ὅς.

The situation is not altered when we consider the internal evidence. Coming after the neuter noun μυστήριον, the masculine relative pronoun ὅς is the harder reading and was therefore more prone to scribal correction ("the removal of an apparent solecism," WH 2: appendix 133). A change from OC to Θ̄C involved only "two slight touches" (Farrar, "Readings" 383); on the other hand, a change in the opposite direction would have created

45. Either Gregory of Nyssa (d. 394), Didymus of Alexandria (d. 398), or Chrysostom (d. 407).

two grammatical difficulties—the lack of concord with μυστήριον and the absence of an explicit antecedent. Θεός arose probably because a scribe misread OC as the abbreviation Θ̄C or wished to replace a "weak" relative pronoun (ὅς) that lacked an antecedent with a "strong" substantive (θεός) as the subject of the series of six finite verbs that follow.[46]

With regard to the author's propensities, an anarthrous θεός as subject is rare (11 times in the NT, of which 9 are in Paul; never elsewhere in the Pastorals), whereas ὁ θεός as subject is found 262 times in the NT (107 in Paul) (see chapter I §B.1). Ὅς, however, not uncommonly begins a christological hymn or affirmation (Phil. 2:6; Col. 1:15; Heb. 1:3). If Christ was recognized as τὸ μυστήριον τοῦ θεοῦ (Col. 2:2), the transition from τὸ τῆς εὐσεβείας μυστήριον to ὅς becomes explicable, even if awkward: "It is he (God's mystery, Christ) who was manifested in the flesh." Alternatively, as WH suggests (2: appendix 134), if the verse is part of an early Christian hymn, the antecedent of ὅς would have occurred in the preceding context that has not been quoted.

The strength of the external evidence favoring ὅς, along with considerations of transcriptional and intrinsic probability, have prompted textual critics virtually unanimously to regard ὅς as the original text, a judgment reflected in NA^{26} and $UBS^{1,2,3}$ (with a "B" rating).[47] Accordingly, 1 Timothy 3:16 is not an instance of the christological use of θεός.

H. Conclusion

The conclusion we have reached about each of the "secondary" passages discussed in this chapter is identical—and negative. In every case textual or grammatical considerations rule out the possibility that Jesus is called θεός. This, then, leaves seven NT texts in which, with various degrees of probability, θεός is used as a christological title, viz., John 1:1, 18; 20:28; Romans 9:5; Titus 2:13; Hebrews 1:8; and 2 Peter 1:1. To these passages we now turn again in the final chapter.

46. The reading ὁ θεός found in minuscule 88 may have arisen as a conflation of θεός and the ambiguous letter *omicron* or because θεός is generally articular when it is the subject.

47. See further WH 2: appendix 132–34; Elliott 58–59; and esp. Ward, who summarizes in detail all the data (as it stood in 1865) and concluded from his study, which did not seek to defend any one reading, that "in point of antiquity, the great preponderance [of Greek manuscripts] is for ὅς" (10), that "the versions may confidently be adduced as unanimously supporting ὅς" (14), and that "there is no proof on either side ['orthodox' or 'heretic'] of any intentional corruption of the sacred text" (50). For a defense of θεός as the original reading, see Field, *Notes* 204–8.

XIII

Conclusions: *Theos* as a Christological Title

A. The Use of θεός in the Pre-Christian Era

Chapter I discussed the three common Hebrew terms that are rendered by θεός in the LXX: אל, אלהים, and יהוה. All three words are used of the God of Israel but only the first two can also refer to a particular pagan deity or, as generic appellatives, designate deity as such. יהוה, however, is exclusively a proper noun, denoting Israel's covenant God, never a common noun, and therefore, unlike אל and אלהים, it never refers to angels or human beings.

In extrabiblical literature, θεός has three primary referents. As applied to gods, it may refer to a particular god (or even goddess), to the supreme god, Zeus, or to deity in general, whether viewed in personal or impersonal terms. As applied to human beings, the title θεός was used to describe famous heroes, politicians, philosophers, patriarchs, renowned rulers, self-styled servants of God, or even people as intelligent beings. And Jewish writers roughly contemporary with the writing of the NT, such as Philo and Josephus, use θεός or ὁ θεός to refer to the God of Israel.

For any Jew or Gentile of the first century A.D. who was acquainted with the OT in Greek, the term θεός would have seemed rich in content since it signified the Deity, the Creator of heaven and earth, and also could render the ineffable sacred name, Yahweh, the covenantal God, and yet was capable of extremely diverse application, ranging from the images of pagan deities to the one true God of Israel, from heroic people to angelic beings. Whether one examines the Jewish or the Gentile use of the term θεός up to the end of the first century A.D., there is an occasional application of the term to human beings who perform divine functions or display divine characteristics.

B. The Use of θεός in the New Testament

Of the 1,315 uses of θεός in the NT, 78.4% are articular and 21.6% are anarthrous. No uniform distinction may be drawn between ὁ θεός and θεός, since (1) as a *nomen rectum* θεός is articular or anarthrous generally depending on the state of the preceding noun (the canon of Apollonius); (2) within single NT books the same preposition is found with both an articular and an anarthrous θεός, with apparently no difference of meaning; and (3) as a virtual proper name, θεός shares the imprecision with regard to articular use that characterizes proper names in general. Yet occasionally ὁ θεός and θεός are distinguishable, as when the anarthrous θεός emphasizes "godhood" (a theological distinction), or when the articular θεός is always found with certain words (e.g., ἐνώπιον) or phrases (e.g., κύριος ὁ θεός) or is generally found with personal pronouns (syntactical distinctions without theological import).

An analysis of the use of (ὁ) θεός as a subject or predicate with the verb εἶναι expressed or unexpressed shows that the NT writers prefer ὁ θεός (45 examples) over θεός (5) as the subject, but θεός (16) over ὁ θεός (8) as the predicate. Of these 24 predicative uses of (ὁ) θεός, the term is usually qualified if it is articular and often qualified if it is anarthrous. Generally, then, the NT avoids a statement such as "X is (ὁ) θεός" unless that θεός is further defined.

Each strand of the NT affords clear testimony that customarily θεός, whether articular or anarthrous, refers to the trinitarian Father. Four converging lines of evidence support this conclusion: (1) the frequent compound appellative θεὸς πατήρ where the second noun is in epexegetic apposition (e.g., Gal. 1:1); (2) the various trinitarian formulations where ὁ θεός must denote the Father (e.g., 2 Cor. 13:13); (3) the many places where ὁ θεός is distinguished from κύριος Ἰησοῦς Χριστός, as in epistolary salutations (e.g., James 1:1); and (4) uses of (ὁ) θεός in contexts where reference is made to fatherhood, sonship, regeneration, or brotherhood (e.g., John 6:32–33). Whenever (ὁ) θεός is found in the NT, we are to assume that ὁ πατήρ is the referent unless the context makes this sense impossible. Nowhere is it appropriate to render ὁ θεός by "the divine Essence" or "the Godhead."

C. The Application of θεός to Jesus Christ

From the detailed exegetical analysis in chapters II–XII, I conclude that it is certain that the term θεός is applied to Jesus Christ in John 1:1 and John 20:28, very probable in Romans 9:5, Titus 2:13, Hebrews 1:8, and 2 Peter 1:1, probable in John 1:18, and possible but not likely in Acts 20:28, Hebrews 1:9, and 1 John 5:20 (see table 5). Other passages to which appeal is sometimes made include Matthew 1:23, John 17:3, Galatians 2:20, Ephesians 5:5, Colossians 2:2, 2 Thessalonians 1:12, and 1 Timothy 3:16. In none of these latter verses is a christological use of θεός at all likely. In subsequent discussion in this chapter I shall therefore assume that θεός is applied to Jesus in seven NT passages: John 1:1, John 1:18; John 20:28, Romans 9:5, Titus 2:13, Hebrews 1:8, and 2 Peter 1:1.

No NT writer makes the explicit assertion ὁ Ἰησοῦς ἐστιν θεός (or ὁ θεός). Nevertheless John has the absolute statement θεὸς ἦν ὁ λόγος (1:1), the dramatic collocation μονογενὴς θεός (1:18), which in expanded form would read μονογενὴς υἱὸς ὅς ἐστιν θεός, and the exclamation by which Thomas addressed Jesus, ὁ κύριός μου καὶ ὁ θεός μου (20:28), from which one may legitimately extrapolate two christological formulas: ὁ Ἰησοῦς ἐστιν κύριος (cf. the formula κύριος Ἰησοῦς) and ὁ Ἰησοῦς ἐστιν θεός (see chapter IV §C.2.a). In Romans 9:5 ὁ Χριστὸς ὁ ὢν θεός could be

TABLE 5. *Jesus as θεός in the New Testament*

Probability Level	*Text*	*Date of Book or Event*	*Problem(s)*	*Type of Ascription*	*Associated Title and Concept*	*Setting*	*Translation*
Certain	John 1:1	90s	punctuation grammatical	designation: θεός	λόγος (revelation)	preincarnation	And the Word was God.
	John 20:28	30 (or 33)	grammatical historical	address: ὁ θεός μου	κύριος (sovereignty)	postresurrection	In response Thomas said to him, "My Lord and my God!"
Very Probable	Rom. 9:5	ca. 57	punctuation grammatical	doxology: θεός	Χριστός (messiahship)	timeless	To them belong the patriarchs, and from their ranks, as far as human descent is concerned, came Christ, who is supreme over all as God blessed forever. Amen.
	Titus 2:13	ca. 63	grammatical	designation: ὁ μέγας θεός	σωτήρ (salvation)	postresurrection	As we wait for our blessed hope, the appearing of the glory of our great God and Savior, Jesus Christ.
	Heb. 1:8	60s	textual grammatical contextual	address: ὁ θεός	υἱός (sonship)	postresurrection	But to the Son he says, "Your throne, O God, is for ever and ever."
	2 Peter 1:1	ca. 65	textual grammatical	designation: ὁ θεὸς ἡμῶν	σωτήρ (salvation)	postresurrection	To those who have received a faith as privileged as ours, by virtue of the righteousness of our God and Savior, Jesus Christ.
Probable	John 1:18	90s	textual grammatical	designation: θεός	μονογενής (unique sonship)	incarnation	The only Son, who is God and who resides in the Father's heart—he has revealed him.

extrapolated from ὁ Χριστὸς τὸ κατὰ σάρκα, ὁ ὢν ἐπὶ πάντων θεὸς κτλ. The writer to the Hebrews has God address his Son using the vocatival ὁ θεός (1:8), which implies ὁ υἱός ἐστιν θεός. And from Titus 2:13 and 2 Peter 1:1 one may deduce that Ἰησοῦς Χριστός ἐστιν ὁ θεὸς καὶ σωτὴρ ἡμῶν.

In spite of the neatness and attractiveness of the view, the evidence does not support the frequently repeated thesis that Jesus Christ is θεός but not ὁ θεός. Given the general NT oscillation between θεός and ὁ θεός when referring to the Father, it should occasion no surprise that if θεός is used of Jesus (as in John 1:1, 18; Rom. 9:5), ὁ θεός also should occasionally refer to him (as in 2 Pet. 1:1 and Titus 2:13, not to mention the two uses of the vocatival ὁ θεός in John 20:28 and Heb. 1:8). As far as the NT is concerned, the crucial distinction is not between the meaning of θεός with the article and its meaning without the article, but between predominant usage (where both θεός and ὁ θεός denote the Father) and exceptional usage (where either θεός or ὁ θεός may denote the Son).[1]

When it is applied to Jesus, the title θεός is generally qualified—by an epithet (μέγας, Titus 2:13) or descriptive clause or phrase (ὁ ὢν εἰς τὸν κόλπον τοῦ πατρός, John 1:18; εὐλογητὸς εἰς τοὺς αἰῶνας, Rom. 9:5), by an accompanying substantive (μονογενής, John 1:18; κύριος, John 20:28; σωτήρ, Titus 2:13 and 2 Pet. 1:1), or by a possessive pronoun (μου, John 20:28; ἡμῶν, Titus 2:13 and 2 Pet. 1:1). John 1:1 and Hebrews 1:8 are the only exceptions. Yet such syntactical qualification is not tantamount to theological qualification. Jesus is no less θεός because he is described as ὁ μέγας θεός, as εὐλογητὸς εἰς τοὺς αἰῶνας, as ὁ θεὸς καὶ σωτὴρ ἡμῶν, or is addressed as ὁ θεός μου. The word or words added to θεός are not an apology for an exceptional usage, or a theological modification of a daring linguistic innovation, but rather form a description of the status or function of Jesus as θεός.

There is no evidence that the use of θεός as christological appellation was restricted to a particular geographical location or theological milieu. It occurs in literature that was written in Asia Minor (the Fourth Gospel, Titus?), Achaia (Romans), and possibly Judea (Hebrews) and Rome (2 Peter), and that was addressed to persons living in Asia Minor (Fourth Gospel, 2 Peter?), Rome (Romans, Hebrews?), and Crete (Titus). Second, it is evidenced in a Jewish Christian setting (John 1:1, 18; 20:28; Heb. 1:8; 2 Pet. 1:1) as well as in a Gentile Christian milieu (Rom. 9:5; Titus 2:13).

1. Nor does (ὁ) θεός ever refer to both the Father and the Son together, although such a referent has occasionally been suggested in Rom. 9:5 (Heil 134 n. 3) or detected in 1 Thess. 3:11 (Hogg and Vine 103) and 1 John 5:20 (Vine 109). Richardson alleges that in the epistles of Ignatius this is the most characteristic use of θεός (e.g., *Tr.* 11:1–2), expressing an almost inseparable nexus of will (40, 44).

D. Limitations to the Use of θεός in Reference to Jesus Christ

The application to Christ of the title θεός is exceedingly rare—only seven certain, very probable, or probable instances out of a total of 1,315 NT uses of θεός. From an analysis of representative scholarly views concerning the nine texts discussed in chapters II–VII and IX–XI, it may be seen that the majority of scholars hold that θεός is applied to Jesus no fewer than five times and no more than nine times in the NT.[2] The same range characterizes the principal modern English translations of the NT (1 John 5:20 apart).[3] Reasons for the relative infrequency of θεός as a christological title are discussed below in §G.

The very rarity of the designation of Jesus as "God" is evidence that θεός never becomes a proper name when used of Jesus but remains a descriptive title. In accord with this, one never finds θεός applied to Jesus without an accompanying identification of the person so titled. In John 1:1 it is the λόγος who is θεός; in John 1:18, μονογενὴς (υἱός); in John 20:28, αὐτός = ὁ Ἰησοῦς; in Romans 9:5, ὁ Χριστός; in Titus 2:13 and 2 Peter 1:1, Ἰησοῦς Χριστός; and in Hebrews 1:8, υἱός. Unless the context refers explicitly to Jesus as the person of whom the title θεός is being predicated, this term will refer to the

2. The following authors are listed in descending order according to the number of passages where they hold that θεός refers to Jesus (note that D'Aragon reckons Heb. 1:8 and 1:9 as one passage):

10	M. J. Erickson	7	H. W. Attridge	5	H. Alford
	R. N. Longenecker		W. Barclay		J. Bonsirven
9	O. Cullmann		H. M. Faccio		R. Bultmann
	E. Stauffer		E. J. Fortman	4	J. Schneider
	B. B. Warfield		K. Rahner	3	G. Lindeskog
8	R. E. Brown		A. T. Robertson	2	G. H. Boobyer
	J. L. D'Aragon		L. Sabourin		G. B. Winer
	A. C. McGiffert		A. W. Wainwright		
	R. L. Reymond	6	C. Hodge		
	N. Turner		J. Lebreton		

3. The following figures necessarily *exclude* 1 John 5:20, which remains ambiguous in this regard, for "he" or "this" (οὗτος) could refer to either God or Jesus Christ:

8	Montgomery		TCNT		REB
	NASB	6	Cassirer		Weymouth
	NIV		GNB	5	Barclay
	Williams		Goodspeed		RSV
7	Berkeley		NAB^{1}	4	ASV
	JB		NAB^{2}		Moffatt
	NRSV		NEB		
	RV		NJB		

In these twenty-two English versions, the eight verses most commonly translated as having a christological use of θεός are as follows (in descending order of frequency and again excluding 1 John 5:20; for a narrower analysis of English versions see Perry, "God")

22	John 1:1	18	Titus 2:13		Rom. 9:5
	John 20:28	17	Heb. 1:8	10	John 1:18
20	2 Pet. 1:1	13	Acts 20:28		

Father and be a virtual proper name. Although ὁ υἱὸς τοῦ θεοῦ occurs (where ὁ θεός = the Father), never does one find ὁ πατὴρ τοῦ θεοῦ (where ὁ θεός = Jesus). No NT writer says anything comparable to τὸ πάθος τοῦ θεοῦ μου (Ignatius, *Rom.* 6:3) or ὁ θεὸς ὁ ἀγαπήσας με καὶ παραδοὺς ἑαυτὸν ὑπὲρ ἐμοῦ (the reading of minuscule 330 in Gal. 2:20, in the genitive case).

In the seven instances in which θεός refers to Jesus, the usage is usually (Rom. 9:5 being the only exception) accompanied by a statement in the immediate context that makes an explicit personal distinction between the Son and God the Father. That is, there is a remarkable juxtaposition of statements that imply the substantial oneness of Son and Father and statements that express a personal distinction between them. Thus one finds ὁ λόγος ἦν πρὸς τὸν θεόν immediately before θεὸς ἦν ὁ λόγος (John 1:1). In John 20 the same Jesus who is addressed as ὁ θεός μου (v. 28) himself refers to his Father as ὁ θεός μου[4] (v. 17). The verse that follows 2 Peter 1:1, where Ἰησοῦς Χριστός is called ὁ θεὸς ἡμῶν καὶ σωτήρ, distinguishes ὁ θεός from Ἰησοῦς ὁ κύριος ἡμῶν (2 Pet. 1:2). Similarly, in successive verses in Hebrews 1, Jesus is addressed by the words ὁ θεός (v. 8) and the one who anointed him is referred to as ὁ θεὸς ὁ θεός σου (v. 9). Immediately after John has described the λόγος as μονογενὴς θεός (John 1:18) he adds ὁ ὢν εἰς τὸν κόλπον τοῦ πατρός. Finally, the same sentence that portrays Ἰησοῦς Χριστός as ὁ μέγας θεὸς καὶ σωτὴρ ἡμῶν (Titus 2:13) speaks of ἡ χάρις τοῦ θεοῦ σωτήριος πᾶσιν ἀνθρώποις (Titus 2:11). And even in Romans 9:5 where there is no explicit distinction between Son and Father, (τῶν συγγενῶν μου . . . ἐξ ὧν) ὁ Χριστός is qualified by τὸ κατὰ σάρκα, a phrase that could not be predicated of the Father.

Linked with the preservation of this inviolate distinction between the Son and the Father is the fact that although he is θεός Jesus is never called either πατήρ or κύριος ὁ θεός (= יהוה אלהים)[5] or ὁ μόνος ἀληθινὸς θεός.[6] Never is he termed θεός in a place where a reference to (ὁ) πατήρ is found; the Father is never called ὁ πατὴρ τοῦ θεοῦ. And in binitarian and trinitarian passages or formulations, only the Father, never the Son (or Spirit), is called ὁ θεός (e.g., binitarian: 1 Cor. 1:3; 8:6; trinitarian: 12:4–6; 2 Cor. 1:21–22; 13:14). Moreover, while the expressions ὁ θεὸς ὁ πατήρ, ὁ θεὸς πατήρ, ὁ θεὸς καὶ πατήρ, θεὸς πατήρ, and θεὸς καὶ πατήρ are found, one never finds ὁ θεὸς ὁ υἱός,[7] ὁ θεὸς υἱός, ὁ θεὸς καὶ υἱός, θεὸς υἱός, or θεὸς καὶ υἱός.

4. In this verse τόν qualifies θεόν μου as well as πατέρα μου and πατέρα ὑμῶν.

5. On the contrary, Jesus refers to his Father as κύριος ὁ θεός by implication in Matt. 4:7, 10.

6. On ὁ ἀληθινὸς θεός in 1 John 5:20, see chapter XI.

7. Minuscule 1985 has this reading in Gal. 2:20 (see chapter XII §C). Note also the rendering of μονογενὴς θεός by "God the only Son" in some English versions (viz., TCNT, NAB[1], NIV [1973, 1978]). Cf. also θεὸς Χριστός, the reading of 𝔓[72] in Jude 5.

E. Date of the Emergence of θεός as a Christological Title

There is a widespread tendency in modern scholarship to regard the application of the title θεός to Jesus as a late development in Christology, dating at the earliest from the late 50s (when Rom. 9:5 was written) and not becoming at all frequent until the end of the century. A typical spokesman of this prevailing view is J. L. D'Aragon. He finds two clear instances of θεός applied to Jesus (John 20:28; 2 Pet. 1:1), three very probable (John 1:1; 1 John 5:20; Heb. 1:8–9), and three probable (John 1:18; Rom. 9:5; Titus 2:13). Observing that the oldest traditions (viz., the Synoptic Gospels, Acts, and the early Pauline Epistles) lack examples of the usage, D'Aragon claims that apart from Romans 9:5, which itself is "relatively old (about 56–58)," the references to Jesus as θεός do not occur until after 80 (Titus 2:13; Heb. 1:8–9) or 90 (John 1:1, 18; 20:28; 2 Pet. 1:1; 1 John 5:20). He concludes that the practice of calling Jesus "God" was a late development, occurring sporadically in first-century Christianity (201).

Such a reconstruction of the first-century history of the use of θεός as a christological title rests on four assumptions, each of which is at least open to question.

First, it is assumed that the date of the first use of θεός as a title of Jesus may be determined by its first literary occurrence: because θεός is first applied to Jesus in Romans 9:5, the christological use of the title is thought to have begun in the mid-50s. It is axiomatic in all literary study, however, that a clear distinction must be drawn between the date of the composition of a book and the date of the material contained in it.[8] The point does not seem to have been given the attention it warrants, for it implies that no definitive *terminus a quo* may be placed on the christological use of θεός solely on the basis of literary occurrence. Certainly, it is no more difficult to explain an apparent "gap" in usage between the 30s (if John 20:28 be a confession actually uttered by Thomas) and the 50s (Rom. 9:5) than between the 50s (Rom. 9:5) and the 80s (on D'Aragon's dating).

A second assumption commonly made is that Thomas's confession is a Johannine creation and therefore not the earliest use of θεός in reference to Jesus. Considerable attention was given to this matter above (see chapter IV §§B–C), where I argued that the probability can be reasonably estab-

8. While Brown acknowledges the truth of this ("New Testament occurrence does not create a usage but testifies to a usage already extant," *Reflections* 31 n. 54 = "Jesus" 567 n. 54), it does not seem to affect his verdict, for he asserts that "quite clearly the use of 'God' for Jesus belongs to the second half of the period" (viz., 30–100) that may be called "New Testament times" (*Reflections* 31 = "Jesus" 567).

lished that Thomas testified to the deity of Jesus during his encounter with the risen Lord.[9]

A third support for the allegedly late occurrence of θεός as a title for Jesus is often found in the observation that "time must pass" before the emerging consciousness of the deity of Christ on the part of the disciples could have come to sufficient maturity to permit any formulation of that truth.[10] In reply, I observe, first of all, that it is not the passage of time in itself but dramatic events that effect any deepening or broadening of human thought. The fact needs no demonstration that reaction to a brief crisis may be more determinative for the maturation of thought than endless exposure to undemanding circumstances. The resurrection of Christ is just such an unexpected dramatic crisis that catalyzed creative theological thought. Second, there is no need to restrict the development of Thomas's christological thought to the week between Christ's resurrection and his appearance to Thomas and the other disciples (John 20:19, 26). This week of concentrated theological reflection simply formed the climax of a prolonged period spent in observing the deeds of Jesus and in meditating on his words.[11] Third, there is a certain inconsistency on the part of some who claim that the christological use of θεός must be a late development (presumably because θεός is an elevated title not unrelated to ontology) and yet insist that the title is purely functional in import. If, as a christological title, θεός merely denotes "God acting for us," it is not clear why, from a theological standpoint, the use must be a late development; if it is deemed a necessarily late development, this must be *ex hypothesi* because it represents an advance from functional to ontic Christology.

Last, Titus is often assumed to be non-Pauline and 2 Peter non-Petrine and they are dated, along with Hebrews, late in the first century or even early in the second century.[12] But without a late dating for these three epistles the developmental theory regarding the use of θεός would need serious

9. Wainwright ("Confession" 290) is one of the few scholars who recognize that "the possibility cannot be excluded that Thomas accorded full divine honours to Jesus" (his later *Trinity* [63] has "entirely excluded").

10. For example, Fitzmyer, *Aramean* 131. See the preliminary discussion of this issue in chapter IV §B.2.c.

11. C. F. D. Moule traces the various NT estimates of Jesus to "changes only in perception" (*Origin* 3) and observes that "in evolution, the more complex species generally belong to a later stage than the more simple; but in development, there is nothing to prevent a profoundly perceptive estimate occurring at an early stage, and a more superficial one at a later stage: degrees of perception will depend upon individual persons and upon circumstances which it may be impossible to identify in any intelligibly chronological sequence" (Moule is not here commenting on John 20:28, however).

12. Assigning a late date to the Pastorals and 2 Peter (seen as documents contemporary with the Ignatian letters), Wainwright proposes that their uninhibited use of ὁ θεός (Titus 2:13; 2 Pet. 1:1) in reference to Jesus represents a failure to exercise the "subtle restraint" shown by their predecessors, who use either an anarthrous θεός (John 1:1, 18; Rom 9:5) or an articular θεός as a vocative (John 20:28; Heb. 1:8) ("Confession" 297–98).

modification, for if the hands of the apostles Paul and Peter are detected in Titus and 2 Peter, and if Hebrews is dated before the fall of Jerusalem, this provides three instances in the 60s of the christological use of θεός.

The following chronological order may be proposed for the seven instances where θεός refers to Jesus.

John 20:28	30 (or 33)
Romans 9:5	ca. 57
Titus 2:13	ca. 63
2 Peter 1:1	ca. 65
Hebrews 1:8	60s
John 1:1	90s
John 1:18	90s

On this view, the Christian use of θεός as a title for Jesus began immediately after the resurrection (30 or 33; John 20:28), continued during the 50s (Rom. 9:5) and 60s (Titus 2:13; Heb. 1:8; 2 Pet. 1:1) and extended into the 90s (John 1:1, 18).

F. Origin of the Usage

Proposals regarding the historical stimulus that gave rise to the application of the title θεός to Jesus are closely connected with the date advocated for the first use of the title. For example, if Titus 2:13 is taken to be the earliest instance of this usage and if the Pastorals are regarded as the work of a Paulinist at the end of the first century, it may be plausibly suggested that Jesus was first called θεός in opposition to the blasphemous arrogation of the title by Domitian in the flourishing imperial cult. On the other hand, if John 20:28 has a claim to historical reliability, it is natural to associate the origin of the christological use of θεός with the resurrection appearances of Christ. Any proposal regarding origin, then, is predetermined by two factors: (1) the isolation of the earliest NT instance of the application of θεός to Jesus; and (2) the dating given to the document in which the example occurs or to the incident that involves the description of Jesus as θεός.

Among the proposals that have been made are the following:

1. Polemic against the emperor cult: Under the stimulus of the pagan deification of the emperor and the ascription to him of divine honors and titles, the early Christians applied to Christ similar titles (such as θεός) they had derived from the LXX.[13]

13. Chaine writes: "A l'encontre des apothéoses humaines, Jésus-Christ est proclamé Dieu et Sauveur" (37, commenting on 2 Pet. 1:1). Deissmann (342–44) speaks of a "polemical parallelism" between the imperial cult and the cult of Christ.

2. The ascription of the title κύριος to Jesus: Once the title κύριος was applied to Jesus in the postresurrection confession κύριος Ἰησοῦς, it was inevitable that ultimately the appellative θεός should also be used of him, given the partial interchangeability of יהוה (= κύριος) and אלהים (= θεός) in Jewish usage and the Septuagintal combination κύριος ὁ θεός.[14]
3. The worship and liturgy of the early church: That instances of the christological use of θεός occur in contexts that are doxological (Rom. 9:5; Titus 2:13; 2 Pet. 1:1), hymnic (John 1:1, 18), liturgical (Heb. 1:8), or confessional (John 20:28) points to the liturgical origin of the usage.[15] In support of this theory, the famous statement of Pliny the Younger is sometimes cited. Writing about A.D. 112 as governor of Pontus-Bithynia, Pliny reports the testimony of certain Christians that "they were in the habit of meeting on a fixed day before daybreak and reciting an antiphonal hymn to Christ as god (God?) (*carmenque Christo quasi deo dicere*)" (*Letters* 10:96).
4. The resurrection appearances of Jesus: Personal confrontation with the risen Jesus (John 20:24–29) convinced Thomas that Jesus must share God's nature (ὁ θεός μου) and sovereignty (ὁ κύριός μου), for his resurrection in a glorified form demonstrated his final conquest of death, and his effusion of the Holy Spirit (John 20:22) showed his equality with the Father (cf. John 14:16, 26; 15:26; 16:7).

If John 20:24–29 is an historical episode,[16] it marks Thomas's "Damascus." As later with Paul, a personal appearance of the risen Christ caused a drastic change of attitude that led to the recognition of the divinity of Jesus. In John 2:22 the evangelist notes that the resurrection transformed the disciples' spiritual perception. For Paul, Jesus "was designated Son of God in power . . . through his resurrection from the dead" (Rom. 1:4); for Thomas and John, he was shown to be "God" by his resurrection from the dead. But to trace the initial stimulus for the christological use of θεός to the influence of the resurrection[17] is not to deny that the way was pre-

14. For statements or variations of this view, see Bousset ("the deification of Jesus develops gradually and with an inner necessity out of the veneration of the Kyrios in the earliest Christianity. The Kyrios becomes the θεὸς Ἰησοῦς Χριστός"; 317; cf. 322 n. 309, 330); Cullmann (*Christology* 237, 306–7, 311, 314 [the christological designation θεός is a variant of κύριος]); R. N. Longenecker (*Christology* 136, 140); Barrett (*John* 476); Lindars (*John* 615).

15. Brown, *Reflections* 34–37 (= "Jesus" 570–71); *Gospel* 1:24, 2:1047; similarly Stauffer 114. Cf. the observation of Coggan (80): "Christolatry preceded Christology."

16. See chapter IV §B.

17. It is significant that in none of the four Gospels is a person said to have used θεός of Jesus during the period of his preresurrection ministry. However, writing (the Prologue of the Fourth Gospel) in the 90s, John can refer to the incarnate Son as θεός (John 1:18).

pared for the ascription by the Septuagintal conjunction of κύριος and θεός in various combinations[18] or that subsequently the confession of Jesus as "God" found a natural home in the liturgical usage of the early church and formed a convenient means of rebutting imperial claims to divinity.

Moreover, several factors in intertestamental Judaism[19] may have been conducive to the use of θεός as a christological appellation, without necessarily providing the conceptual resources or framework[20] for this remarkable departure from customary Jewish practice:

1. Speculation regarding the status and function of the Logos and of Wisdom as personifications of God's immanence[21]
2. The creation of a hierarchy of angels who act as intermediaries between God and humankind or between God and creation, with an individual figure such as Michael or Gabriel as the principal archangel
3. The elevation of past heroes of the Jewish people, such as Enoch and Elijah, to become God's agents at the final judgment

18. See above, chapter IV §C.1.

19. For a detailed treatment of the following data, see Hurtado, *One God* 17–92; Hurtado, "Shape" 380–89; and, more briefly, Dunn, "Christianity" 307–33; Casey, *Prophet* 78–94. Casey seeks to account for what he regards as the rapid development of Pauline Christology to the point where in the 50s Paul "very probably" calls Jesus θεός (Rom. 9:5) by appealing to the blossoming in intertestamental Judaism of intermediary figures who assumed some of the functions of God and enjoyed an elevated status—figures such as the Davidic king, Abel, Elijah, Michael, Melchizedek, Moses, Enoch, and Wisdom. But the case of Jesus was unique in that his combined functions surpassed those of any single Jewish intermediary and he alone rather than God or the law was the focus of the early Christian community's identity ("Chronology").

20. *Pace* Hurtado, *One God* 21, 50, 93, 115, 123–24. For an evaluation of Hurtado's book, see Rainbow.

21. According to Dunn, in pre-Christian Judaism "the Sophia-Logos imagery is simply a way of speaking of God's own activity in creation, revelation and salvation" ("Christianity" 322; cf. 318–21, 329–30). Just as Sophia and Logos were not thought of as heavenly beings distinct from God but rather as ways of expressing the one God's presence in the world, so in Christianity Christ as Sophia-Logos incarnate was understood not as being distinct from God but as the clearest expression of the presence of God himself (334). "Christ is divine in no other sense than as God immanent, God himself acting to redeem as he did to create" (330). One questions the aptness of MacKinnon's description of Dunn's Christology as "this admittedly sophisticated adoptionism" ("Review" 363), for Dunn holds that the impersonal Sophia-Logos actually became incarnate in the person of Jesus of Nazareth ("Christianity" 330–31, 335; *Christology* 212, 244), and even this type of "incarnation" would exclude "adoptionism." Rather it would now (in his article "Christianity") more nearly seem to be a diluted form of apotheosis, for, on Dunn's view, the exalted person who is Jesus of Nazareth enjoys a continuing "postexistence" without being "any more divine than the earthly Jesus," but whose destined return as Savior will be "the appearing of the glory of our great God" (Titus 2:13) ("Christianity" 334–35).

4. The use of אלהים in reference to Melchizedek and other angelic beings in the heavenly court (as in 11 Q Mel, ca. A.D. 50; see chapter IX n. 73)[22]

The suggestion is not that these factors in any sense generated or even shaped belief in the deity of Christ but that they contributed to the creation of a sympathetic religious environment in which the early Christians occasionally applied the title θεός to Jesus, who was a contemporary figure or a figure of the recent past, as opposed to an abstract figure such as Wisdom or a figure of the distant past such as Enoch, Moses, or Elijah.

G. Reasons for the Infrequency of the Usage

Few scholars find more than nine NT uses of θεός as a title of Jesus (see n. 2 above). On no reading of the data could the claim be allowed that the early Christians regularly called Jesus θεός or ὁ θεός. It would be specious reasoning to argue that since what is assumed by an author comes to expression infrequently and spasmodically, the usage was in fact far more common in the early church than the documents would indicate. On the other hand, given the fewness of the instances of the usage and the fact that Paul has at most two examples, Peter one, and the author of Hebrews one, there is a danger that appeal should be so constantly made to the regular NT usage of θεός for the Father that it should be thought impossible for any writer ever to use θεός of Jesus. Just as a writer must be permitted to use certain words only once, so on principle a writer must be allowed certain theological *hapax* (or *dis* or *tris*) *legomena*.

Certain inadequate explanations of the infrequency of the usage may now be briefly stated and dismissed. First, the sparse use was not because at this point faith was outstripping reason and the early Christians felt unable to accommodate the new christological data within the consistent theological framework of hereditary Jewish monotheism. The presence of *any* examples of the usage in the early church's documents discounts this explanation. If the early church was embarrassed by the ascription of θεός to Jesus[23] or if the ascription was regarded as heterodox by some elements

22. On the relation of 11 Q Mel to Jewish monotheism, see Ashton 149–50. It is Fuller's view that "shortly before the NT period not surprisingly, Hellenistic Jewish thinkers were beginning to move beyond the functional thinking of the OT and traditional Judaism in the direction of ontology, and as a result were advancing to a distinction within the deity, between God as he is in himself and God going out of himself in revelatory and salvific activity" ("Jesus" 109, citing Hanson and Hanson [104] approvingly, 111). In the christological hymns of the NT and in the later stratum of the Fourth Gospel is found an incipient ontological Christology, "a christology which identifies the ego of Jesus with an aspect of the Being of God" ("Jesus" 115; cf. Fuller and Perkins 131).

23. Bousset speaks of "the half-instinctive, half-traditional reluctance to speak without embarrassment of the deity of Christ" that is evident in the NT but abandoned in the Ignatian epistles (321).

in the church, it is strange that four NT writers (John, Paul, the author of Hebrews, and Peter) should have examples which represent both a Jewish Christian setting (John 1:1, 18; 20:28; Heb. 1:8; 2 Pet. 1:1) and a Gentile Christian milieu (Rom. 9:5; Titus 2:13). Second, it cannot be said that the infrequency is due to a conviction that θεός was too sacred a title to apply to Jesus or else was capable of being applied hyperbolically to humans and therefore was a demeaning title for Jesus. Both of these criteria, however, if valid, would have also excluded the christological use of κύριος, a title which occurs frequently throughout the epistles in reference to Jesus. Third, the paucity of examples of the employment of the title θεός for Jesus cannot be attributed to the belief that κύριος was itself such an adequate title to express the deity of Christ that the use of θεός was virtually superfluous. This suggestion erroneously assumes that κύριος and θεός are virtually indistinguishable in content. Rather, as a christological title κύριος is primarily functional in significance, denoting sovereignty, whereas θεός is principally ontological, denoting deity.[24]

What positive reasons may be advanced to account for this phenomenon?[25]

First, in all strands of the NT, θεός generally signifies the Father (see chapter I §B.4). When we find the expression θεὸς πατήρ we may legitimately deduce that ὁ θεός ἐστιν ὁ πατήρ. And since πατήρ refers to a particular person (not an attribute), the identity between ὁ θεός and ὁ πατήρ *as proper names* referring to persons must be numerical: "God" is to be equated with "the Father." If Jesus were everywhere called θεός, so that in reference to him the term ceased to be a title and became a proper noun[26] like Ἰησοῦς, linguistic ambiguity would be everywhere present.

Another reason why θεός regularly denotes the Father and rarely the Son is that such usage is suited to protect the personal distinction between Son and Father (see above §D)[27] which is preserved everywhere in the NT, but

24. See above, chapter IV §C.2, and below in the present chapter, §J.1.

25. The rarity with which the NT calls Jesus θεός corresponds to the rarity with which prayer was addressed to the risen Lord in the early church (see Acts 1:24; 7:59–60; 9:10–17; 22:16, 19; 1 Cor. 1:2; 16:22; 2 Cor. 12:8; Rev. 22:20). To judge by the NT data, neither practice was common in the apostolic period. Generally Jesus was called κύριος (e.g., 1 Cor. 8:6) and prayer was addressed to God the Father (e.g., Eph. 2:18; 3:14).

26. If θεός *were* a proper name when used of Jesus, no adequate reason could be given for the infrequency of the use and one should expect to find statements such as "I have been crucified with God; it is no longer I who live, but God who lives in me, and the life I now live in the flesh I live by faith in God who loved me and gave himself for me" (cf. Gal. 2:20).

27. Similarly Cotter 284; H. N. Ridderbos, *Jesus* 73. In describing the unity that exists between God and Christ it is probably wiser to speak of "the complete unity of being" ("die vollkommene Wesenseinheit"; J. Schneider, *TBNT* 2:607) than of "identification" (e.g., Mackintosh 120; Küng 685), for this latter term may easily be misinterpreted to mean either "personal equation" or mere "copartnership." "Short of thoroughgoing identification of persons, the unity expressed by their conjunction seems to be complete" (Warfield, *Studies* 64).

nowhere more dramatically than where the Father is called "the God of our Lord Jesus Christ" (Eph. 1:17)[28] or "his God and Father" (Rev. 1:6) and where Jesus speaks of "my God" (Matt. 27:46 = Mark 15:34; John 20:17; cf. Rev. 3:2, 12), or, in an address to Jesus reference is made to "your God" (Heb. 1:9). God was the one to whom Jesus prayed, the one he called his Father (e.g., Matt. 11:25). It was ὁ λόγος, not ὁ θεός, of whom John said σὰρξ ἐγένετο (John 1:14).[29]

Closely related to this second reason is a third. The element of "subordinationism" that finds expression not only in the four authors who use θεός as a christological appellation[30] but also elsewhere in the NT may have checked any impulse to use θεός regularly of Jesus. By customarily reserving the term θεός for the Father, NT writers were highlighting the fact, whether consciously or unconsciously, that while the Son is "subordinate" to the Father, the Father is not "subordinate" to the Son. One finds the expression "the Son of God" where God is the Father, but never "the Father of God" where God is the Son.[31]

A fourth reason that may be suggested for the comparatively rare use of θεός as a christological ascription was the danger recognized by the early church that if θεός were applied to Jesus as regularly as to the Father, Jews would have tended to regard Christianity as incurably deuterotheological and Gentiles would probably have viewed it as polytheistic. If θεός were the personal name of the Father *and* the Son, Christians would have been hard pressed to defend the faith against charges of ditheism, if not polytheism, however adamant their insistence on their retention of monotheism.[32]

Fifth, behind the impulse generally to reserve the term θεός for the Father lay the need to safeguard the real humanity of Jesus against docetic or monophysitic sentiment in its embryonic form. In the early years of the church there was a greater danger that the integrity of the human "nature" of Jesus should be denied than that his divinity should be called into question, witness the fact that docetism not Arianism was the first christological deviation.

Finally, the relative infrequency of the use of θεός for Jesus corresponds to the relatively infrequent use of ontological categories in NT Christology which is functional in emphasis (see §J.1 below).

28. That the Father is the "God of Jesus" is also a legitimate inference from the expression ὁ θεὸς καὶ πατὴρ τοῦ κυρίου ἡμῶν Ἰησοῦ Χριστοῦ found in 2 Cor. 1:3; Eph. 1:3; 1 Pet. 1:3; cf. 2 Cor. 11:31.

29. Cf. D'Aragon 201–2.

30. For example, (for John) John 5:19, 30; 10:36; 14:28; 17:3; (Paul) 1 Cor. 3:23; 11:3; 15:28; (*Auctor*) Heb. 1:2–3; 5:5, 10; (Peter) 2 Pet. 1:17; and see V. Taylor, *Person* 57–60 (for Paul), 96 (Hebrews), 104–7 (John); and Barrett, *Essays on John* 19–36.

31. Since subordination does not imply inferiority (see Crawford, "Christ"), it does not argue against the description of Jesus as θεός (*contra* Schmeichel 505).

32. Fortman proposes that Paul preferred κύριος over θεός as a title for Jesus because with its greater flexibility in meaning κύριος would not so easily offend monotheists (19). Cf. Mackintosh 419–20.

H. The Cruciality of the Johannine Testimony

As one considers the significance of John's three uses of θεός in reference to Jesus, it becomes apparent that the witness of the Fourth Gospel is of paramount importance.[33] Several reasons may be given for this.

First, in John 1:1 and John 20:28 we have the two incontestable NT instances of θεός as a christological title, instances that reflect the earliest historical application of the title (John 20:28) and the latest literary application in the NT documents (John 1:1).

Second, all three Johannine instances of a christological use of θεός are strategically placed and essential to the flow of thought. The Fourth Gospel begins (1:1) as it ends (20:28), the Prologue begins (1:1) as it ends (1:18), with an unequivocal assertion of the deity of Christ which is crucial to the argument being developed. Unless the Logos was "God by nature" (θεός, 1:1), unless the only Son fully shared the divine nature (θεός, 1:18), there could not be assurance that the revelation of the Father achieved through the Son as Logos was accurate. In the θεότης of the λόγος and the μονογενής, John saw a guarantee of the reliability of God's self-disclosure. And in John 20, by placing the climactic confession of Thomas immediately before the last dominical beatitude ("blessed are those who have not seen and yet believe," 20:29) and his overall statement of purpose (20:30–31), the evangelist indicates that belief in the messiahship and divine sonship of Jesus (20:31a) involves recognition of his lordship and deity (20:28) and brings divine blessing (20:29b) and eternal life (20:31b).

Third, in the deceptively simple assertion θεὸς ἦν ὁ λόγος (John 1:1c) John gives the one undeniably ontological use of θεός when the term refers to Jesus.[34] Some seem to read this statement as if it were comparable to Exodus 7:1. Just as Moses, God's representative to Pharaoh, could be depicted as "God" to Pharaoh (אלהים לפרעה), so Jesus, God's representative to humans, can be described as "God" to believers. What is overlooked is that in Exodus 7:1, as also in the similar passage Exodus 4:16 (where Moses is said to be as "God" to Aaron, תהיה־לו לאלהים), it is a case of one person's being θεός *to another*. It is precisely the absence of this ingredient—ἡμῖν, καθ' ἡμᾶς, or εἰς ἡμᾶς—that shows John 1:1c to be ontological, not functional, in import. With ἦν linking subject and predicate and standing without some such qualification as "for us" or "in relation to us," the most straightforward interpretation must relate θεός to nature, not function. Before time began and before the Father was revealed, the Logos

33. Indeed, some scholars (e.g., Lindeskog 234–36) believe that the appellation θεός is applied to Jesus only in the Fourth Gospel.

34. That a Johannine title may retain a qualitative sense is illustrated in the use of υἱὸς ἀνθρώπου in John 5:27 (see Moloney, *Son of Man* 81–82).

enjoyed an independent existence in active relation to the Father. But to say that θεός here has an ontological sense is not, of course, to deny the functional overtones of the Logos Christology in John 1.[35] And even in John 20:28, where significantly one finds μου not ἐμοί, the presence of μου does not convert into a functional assertion what otherwise would be an ontological affirmation. Thomas is not saying, "To me, you are Lord and God," but "Lord and God, I worship you!" The situation is less clear in John 1:18 where there are not only textual but also translational difficulties. But if the reading μονογενὴς θεός is preferred and the translation "the only Son, who is God" be preferred (see chapter III §C.2), once again θεός has ontic significance.[36] Described as θεός in John 1:1 and 1:18 and addressed as ὁ θεός μου in John 20:28, Jesus the Word is seen to be not only human (cf. σάρξ in John 1:14) but also divine, not only subordinate to the Father (e.g., John 14:28) but also essentially one with him.[37] John's perpetual distinction between the fully human Son who obeys and the divine Father who directs is not incompatible with their unity of being or nature which comes to clearest expression in John 1:1c.[38]

Fourth, the three Johannine verses under consideration refer to the three successive stages of the "career" of Jesus. Before (John 1:1), during (John 1:18), and after (John 20:28) his incarnate life on earth, Jesus was θεός. What is more, the evangelist shows that the deity of Christ is no phenomenon of the past. In John 1:1 John says that in the beginning the Word *was* θεός; in 1:18 the appositive θεός implies that the only Son *is* θεός; and in 20:28 John affirms through Thomas that Jesus *is* κύριος and θεός. If John 1:18 is to be understood this way, this will be the only NT text in which the incarnate Son is called θεός. He who is fully divine and intimately

35. Cf. Pannenberg 122.

36. Cf. the verdict of Casey: "In the author of the Fourth Gospel we meet a Gentile who has allowed the deity of Jesus to assume consistently expounded ontological status" ("Chronology" 130; similarly in his *Prophet* 23–24, 167). See also n. 79 below.

37. Mastin ("Christology" 48–51) also vigorously argues that in John 1:1, 18; 20:28 θεός refers to the nature of the Logos or Jesus. But a more "official" sense of θεός seems to be implied by Ashton's provocative observation that "in the Fourth Gospel the whole heavenly count is encapsulated in the person of Jesus; apart from the Father he alone is given the title [θεός] (cf. 1:1; 1:18, reading μονογενὴς θεός; 20:28)" (149).

38. This dual concept of "distinction of person–community of essence" also comes to expression in John 10:30, ἐγὼ καὶ ὁ πατὴρ ἕν ἐσμεν, which refers neither to personal identity (which would require εἷς ἐσμεν) nor simply to agreement of will and purpose (since John 10:28b, 29b implies at least an equality of power). The unity is less moral or dynamic than essential or substantial. Son and Father are one in the sense that the image conforms to its prototype (cf. Col. 1:15), the reflection to its source (cf. Heb. 1:3) (see further Pollard, "Exegesis"). One may agree with Loader's conclusion concerning Johannine Christology that "the precise character of the Son's being *theos* is not defined" (*Christology* 229) if he simply means that a formal definition is lacking. But a precise, informal definition is supplied by the immediate contexts of 1:1, 18; 20:28 and by Johannine passages such as 5:17–18; 10:22–39. Loader himself leans toward a functional interpretation of θεός, although he allows for (unspecified) ontological implications (*Christology* 159, 161, 166, 168, 173).

acquainted with the Father revealed God the Father during his earthly life (including his death and resurrection). The implication is that throughout this lifelong act of disclosure,[39] the only Son was what he had always been and what he was at the time of writing—θεός.[40]

Whatever be judged the source of this threefold use of θεός in the Fourth Gospel,[41] it represents the high point of NT usage of θεός as a christological appellative and, with regard to frequency, the midpoint between the sparse references elsewhere in the NT and the relatively profuse usage in Ignatius.[42]

I. θεῖος, θεότης, θειότης, and θεός

Let us assume that some New Testament author wished to state explicitly that Jesus fully possessed the divine nature. What linguistic options were open to him? There would seem to be four.

First, he could use (τοῦ) θεοῦ as an adjectival genitive, meaning "divine," and say something like Χριστός θεοῦ ἐστιν. But not only is there no instance of this meaning among the 689 NT uses of (τοῦ) θεοῦ, such a sentence would more naturally mean "Christ is God's" or "Christ belongs to

39. That ἐξηγήσατο is a constative aorist embracing the whole of Christ's earthly life seems evident from the subsequent Johannine insistence that the words and deeds of Jesus constitute a revelation of the Father (e.g., John 5:19, 30, 36–38; 7:16; 8:26, 38; 10:30, 38; 12:49; 14:6–10; 17:4, 6, 8).

40. To embrace this interpretation of John 1:18 is not to endorse the verdict of Käsemann who describes John's "christology of glory" as "naive docetism" (*Testament* 26), with its picture of "the incarnation as a projection of the glory of Jesus' pre-existence and the passion as a return to that glory which was his before the world began" (20; cf. 9–10), of the Son of Man as "God, descending into the human realm and there manifesting his glory" (13), of "Jesus as God walking on the face of the earth" (75). More moderate is his observation that "not merely from the prologue and from the mouth of Thomas, but from the whole Gospel he [the insightful reader] perceives the confession, 'My Lord and my God'" (9; cf. 13). On Käsemann's view see M. M. Thompson, *Humanity*; Morris, *Jesus* 43–67.

41. Mastin suggests that the source of the evangelist's usage may be controversy between Jews and Christians about the person of Jesus (e.g., John 5:17–18; 8:58–59; 10:30–39) ("Christology" 48, 50–51), although he (guardedly) maintains his earlier view ("Cult") that John 20:28 may possibly have arisen as a counterblast to the state theology of the imperial cult ("Christology" 46). On the other hand, Reim (*Studien* 259–60) traces Johannine usage of θεός as a christological title to Wisdom theology in which Wisdom is depicted as sharing the life and knowledge of God (e.g., Wisd. 8:3–4; 9:9). But writing ten years later (in 1984), Reim concurs with Mastin in seeing controversy with the Jews as the stimulus for the evangelist's christological use of θεός (so also Matsunaga 136–41) and argues that a messianic understanding of Ps. 45 in Johannine circles prompted the controversy ("Jesus"). For his part, Radcliffe places John's Gospel and therefore 1:1 and 20:28 after the expulsion of the Christians from the synagogues and the emergence of Christianity as a new religion, when an exclusive form of monotheism had been rejected by the Johannine churches (52–58). Finally, Neyrey believes that Thomas's confession was born in controversy but came to maturity as the creed or "formal boundary line" (163) that distinguished authentic Johannine Christians from both the synagogue and certain apostolic churches. It reflects the value they placed on the heavenly and spiritual spheres (as opposed to the earthly and fleshly) and expresses an "ideology of revolt" ("Divinity" 163, 170–71).

42. There are at least thirteen uses in the Ignatian letters (*Eph. prooem.*; 1:1 *bis*; 7:2; 15:3; 18:2; 19:3; *Rom. prooem. bis*; 3:3; 6:3; *Smyr.* 1:1; *Poly.* 8:3), which together are approximately one-twentieth the length of the NT.

God" (θεοῦ being a possessive genitive), as in fact Χριστὸς . . . θεοῦ does in 1 Corinthians 3:23.

Second, he could call Jesus θεῖος. Now while this adjective could be used of deity and all that belonged to deity, more often in Classical and Hellenistic Greek it was employed in a diluted sense—"sent by the gods," "sacred to a god," "superhuman," "extraordinary" (see LSJ 788). Accordingly one could speak of divine wine, divine physique, or a divine monster. In reference to persons, such as heroes or wise men or prophets, the word described someone who stood in a close relation to the Godhead ("divine," "inspired," "extraordinary")[43] rather than someone fully sharing divine attributes. The substantival form of the adjective (τὸ θεῖον) denoted "the divine" or "the divine being," without reference to a particular god.[44] Although it was often used by Philo and Josephus to refer to the one true God (perhaps in their effort to accommodate non-Jewish sensibilities),[45] it would doubtless have struck NT writers as too abstract and philosophical an expression to apply to Jesus, just as the Jews who translated the OT into Greek refrained from ever using τὸ θεῖον of God.[46] The adjective θεῖος occurs only three times in the NT: attributively, of δύναμις (2 Pet. 1:3) and φύσις (2 Pet. 1:4), and substantivally, of "the divine being" (τὸ θεῖον, Acts 17:29).[47]

Third, a NT writer could refer to Jesus as θεότης or θειότης. Both these terms are found once in the New Testament (viz., Col. 2:9 and Rom. 1:20 respectively), but again, any bald statement equating Jesus with "deity" or "divinity" would have sounded as abstruse and impersonal in Greek as it does in English.[48] What Paul does affirm, however, is that "in him (Christ) there dwells in bodily form the total plenitude of deity (πᾶν τὸ πλήρωμα

43. Cf. Holladay 57–58, 189–90, 237. On θεῖος in Josephus, see pp. 47–67; in Philo, pp. 177–98. MM 285 indicates that in the papyri and inscriptions θεῖος commonly bears an "imperial" connotation. For example, in a calendar inscription from Priene (ca. 9 B.C.) the birthday of Augustus is said to be τὴν τοῦ θηοτάτου Καίσαρο[ς γ]ενέθλιον, "the birthday of the most divine Caesar."

44. For example, Herodotus 1:32; Thucydides 5:70; Xenophon, *Mem.* 1:4:18. Also see above, chapter I n. 113.

45. See E. Stauffer, *TDNT* 3:122–23.

46. Apart from 29 uses of θεῖος in the "free Greek" of 2–4 Maccabees (25 instances in 4 Maccabees), there are only 6 occurrences of this adjective in the LXX: πνεῦμα θεῖον (Exod. 31:3; 35:31; Job 27:3; 33:4), διαθήκη θεία (Prov. 2:17), πᾶσα διήγησις θεία (Sirach 6:35).

47. Note also the textual variant τὸ θεῖον in Acts 17:27 (read by D Iren Clem) and in Titus 1:9 (read by 460, a thirteenth-century minuscule). Seven times in the NT one finds (τὸ) θεῖον [θυμίαμα], "the divine incense" = burning sulfur, brimstone.

48. It is commonly asserted that θεότης is to θεός what θειότης is to θεῖος: θεότης refers to personality or nature, "Deity" or "deity" (*deitas*; Gottheit, das was Gott ist), θειότης to attributes or qualities, "godhood," (*divinitas*; Göttlichkeit, das was Gottes ist). Nash has subjected this traditional distinction to penetrating analysis and concluded "that the two terms covered a common field, that they fought for existence, and that θεότης triumphed" (26): "Ὁ θεός, used as Christians used it, its powers insured against the dissipation of polytheism, was every way superior to τὸ θεῖον; θεότης shared its kinsman's fortunes. . . . On the ear of the impassioned Christian feeling for the Personality of God τὸ θεῖον struck cold and hard; and θειότης shared its emotional limitations" (27–28).

τῆς θεότητος)" (Col. 2:9), meaning that Jesus possesses all the divine essence and attributes.[49]

Fourth, he could speak of Jesus as θεός. True, as seen in chapter I, the term θεός was capable of extremely diverse application in first-century usage, being applied to a particular god (or even goddess), to the supreme God, or to deity in general, not to mention famous persons who might be so described with hyperbole or flattery. But in the LXX θεός translates the three principal Hebrew terms for God in the OT: אל, אלהים, and יהוה. Here, then, was the most natural Greek term for any Christian writer to use in affirming the godhood of Jesus of Nazareth, in affirming that he participates in the divine nature intrinsically and fully and personally.

Of course, these observations do not in themselves prove that the term θεός bears this sense when it is applied to Jesus, but at least they establish an *a priori* case in favor of such a meaning.

J. The Significance of the Christological Use of θεός

There are, I would suggest, two main ways in which θεός Christology makes a unique contribution to NT Christology as a whole.

1. θεός Is a Christological Title That Is Primarily Ontological in Character

If there is one christological issue on which a scholarly consensus has been reached, it is that NT Christology is functional in emphasis. This was one of the principal findings of O. Cullmann in his thorough and influential work, *The Christology of the New Testament*, which appeared in German in 1957. In his introduction he states, "When it is asked in the New Testament 'Who is Christ?', the question never means exclusively, or even primarily, 'what is his nature?', but first of all, 'what is his function?'" (3–4). However, in his conclusion, alongside his acknowledgment that "we can neither simply speak of the person apart from the work or [*sic*] of the work apart from the person" (326), one finds the less guarded assertion that "functional Christology is the only kind which exists" (326). By this he seems to mean that the person of Christ ("i.e., his unique relation to God") can be known only in his work (325–26, 330). "All Christology is *Heilsgeschichte* and all *Heilsgeschichte* is Christology" (326). Accordingly he believes that "Jesus Christ was God in so far as God reveals himself to the world" (267); "Jesus Christ is God in his self-revelation" (325). The NT des-

49. Col. 2:9 and John 1:1 both assert the deity of Christ, but in complementary ways. The former affirms that all that God essentially is, is in Christ; the latter, that all that God essentially was, the Logos was.

ignation of Jesus as θεός bears no relation to later Greek speculation about substance and natures (306, 326).[50]

All this comes perilously close to denying that any ontological affirmation about Jesus is made in the NT or that θεός is ever ontological in sense when used of Jesus. Such denial becomes explicit when G. H. Boobyer asserts that when NT writers referred to Jesus as θεός "they were not assigning Jesus equality of status with God, and certainly did not intend to say that ontologically he *was* truly God. They meant that he was God functionally" (260).

That NT Christology is primarily functional cannot be denied. But several points should not be overlooked.

The presupposition of functional Christology is ontological Christology. Christ *performs* divine functions because he is divine. His ability to act "divinely" rests on his being divine.[51] Behind Christ *pro nobis* is Christ *in se*. Temporally, being precedes doing. Logically, doing presupposes being.[52]

Behind the conviction that the NT is free of ontological Christology there often lies a preference for the dynamic "Hebraic" categories of action, purpose, and event over the static "Greek" categories of being and substance.[53] What must not be forgotten, however, is that ontological categories were not foreign to biblical thought, a point argued persuasively and at length by L. Malevez,[54] who rightly observes that once we concede that the Logos exists independently of salvation history and independently of the Father, Christology cannot be exclusively functional (285–90).

One of the most significant recent developments in the study of New Testament theology has been the demonstration by religious philosophers that

50. But Cullmann later somewhat modified his position to allow that the dogma formulated at the Council of Chalcedon "corresponds to what the Christology of the New Testament presupposes" ("Reply" 43).

51. So also Boismard, *Prologue* 123 ("the function which Christ fulfils is based on his nature, his being"); cf. the review of Cullmann's *Christology* by Pittenger ("Review").

52. On this functional-ontological dilemma, see Runia, esp. 95–97. Schillebeeckx (*Report* 21–27) regards function and nature as indistinguishable: "In 1 John 4.8 and 16b God's nature is 'love of mankind'" (23), so that "the dichotomy between functional christology and substance christology [is] a false one" (21). As Temple rightly observes, only someone who is truly divine can have the value of God (*Christus* 133n.). Any value judgment about Jesus implies some underlying ontological reality (Pittenger, *Incarnate* 120, 122).

53. A corollary of this impatience with ontology often seems to be the repudiation of Christology which is done "from above." But Gunton rightly affirms (17–18) that "in Christology, matters of method and content are closely related: the way a Christology is approached cannot be separated from the kind of Christology that emerges, and a Christology from below is hard put to avoid being a Christology of a divinized man." See further the final chapter entitled "The Neo-Antiochene Solution" in Lawton 302–24. To these two classical approaches to Christology ("from above," "from below"), Berkhof (267) adds "from behind" (i.e., from the perspective of OT redemptive history) and "from before" (i.e., from the perspective of Christian experience and human history).

54. But see *per contra* Dix 79–81.

the use of concepts such as "substance," "essence," or "nature" is not only legitimate and advantageous but also inevitable in describing the person of Christ. One thinks, for instance, of D. M. MacKinnon's 1972 essay on "'Substance' in Christology: A Cross-Bench View"[55] and his 1982 review of J. D. G. Dunn's 1980 monograph, *Christology in the Making*; E. L. Mascall's critique (122–25) of J. Hick's 1966 essay, "Christology at the Cross Roads"; T. F. Torrance's 1980 treatment of *The Ground and Grammar of Theology* (esp. 146–75); H. P. Owen's 1984 volume, *Christian Theism* (27–51); and above all G. C. Stead's monumental work, published in 1977, entitled *Divine Substance.*

To find in the term θεός a reference to the divine nature is not anachronistic and does not involve reading the NT in the light of Nicene or Chalcedonian Christology.

If one acknowledges that NT Christology is primarily functional, this does not imply that it is exclusively functional. In safeguarding the primary emphasis of NT Christology—which is undoubtedly soteriological not ontological—one must beware of denying the presence of secondary or tertiary interests. John 1:1 has been shown to be undeniably ontological in import (see §H above) and it has been argued that this also is the most natural interpretation of John 1:18 and 20:28. What is true of John may not unreasonably be thought to apply to the other four NT christological uses of θεός. The anarthrous θεός in Romans 9:5, following the ontic articular participle ὁ ὤν, emphasizes Christ's being fully divine. Again, the ontological interest of the author of Hebrews is apparent in the immediate context: the Son is said to bear "the very stamp of his (God's) nature" (Heb. 1:3). Then it can scarcely be denied that a writer who calls Jesus Christ "our God and Savior" (2 Pet. 1:1) and then speaks of believers' future participation in the θεία φύσις (2 Pet. 1:4) could think in ontological terms when using θεός of someone other than the Father. This leaves Titus 2:13, which could as readily conform to the meaning of ὁ θεὸς καὶ σωτήρ in 2 Peter 1:1 as be the one exceptional NT usage: behind Jesus' role as σωτήρ lies his nature as θεός.

The close interrelationship of ontic and functional Christology is well illustrated by the fact that when the title θεός is ascribed to Jesus, the immediate context refers to his role as Creator or Revealer (John 1:1, 18; Heb. 1:8), Savior (Titus 2:13; 2 Pet. 1:1), or Lord over all (John 20:28; Rom. 9:5).[56]

55. "If we think or speak of Christ as subordinate to the Father, or ask if he is subordinate, and co-equal, or argue whether as a person—understood in Boethius' terms as *individua substantia rationabilis naturae*—he is distinguished from his Father, we are immediately involved willy-nilly in the use of and reconstruction of ontological notions" (MacKinnon 288).

56. This interrelationship is also illustrated by the fact that some of the words or phrases that qualify θεός in a christological application have functional overtones: κύριος (John 20:28), σωτήρ (Titus 2:13; 2 Pet. 1:1), μέγας (Titus 2:13).

The use of θεός as a christological title shows not that Jesus is God-in-action or God-in-revelation but rather that he is God-by-nature.[57] Not only are the deeds and words of Jesus the deeds and words of God. The nature of Jesus is the nature of God; what God is, Jesus is. By nature, as well as by action, Jesus is God.

2. θεός Is a Christological Title That Explicitly Affirms the Deity of Christ

The traditional interpretation that understands the deity or divinity of Jesus as his possession of the divine nature has been frequently called into question in recent christological discussions.[58] "Divinity" has been equated by some writers with divine significance, with ultimacy, with developed spiritual sensitivity to God, with total permeation by God (ἔνθεος, "filled with God"),[59] or with heightened spiritual communion with God. P. Tillich, for example, prefers christological concepts that reflect "dynamic relation" rather than "static essence." Because God is "beyond essence and existence," his essential or divine nature being his eternal creativity, there is no meaningful way in which Jesus of Nazareth may be said to have a "divine nature." He could not have been simultaneously beyond essence and existence and personally involved in the human existential predicament of finitude, temptation, and mortality. Talk of a static unity of two natures must give way to the assertion that the eternal and essential unity of God and humans became a historical and dynamic reality in Jesus as the Christ.[60] In Jesus' being, unity between God and humans is reestablished, the New Being becomes real (147–50).

57. In my previous exegetical discussion of each of the seven verses just mentioned, I cited numerous scholars who held that as a christological appellation θεός bears this sense of "God by nature," "Gott von Art."

58. For a summary and critique of contemporary approaches to Christology, see Fitzmyer, *Scripture* 3–32, 58–96; and Erickson 89–379.

59. "It is credibly and conceptually possible to regard Jesus as a wholly God-informed person, who retrieved the theistic inputs coded in the chemistry and electricity of brain-process for the scan of every situation, and for every utterance, verbal and non-verbal" (Bowker 187). Bowker carefully distinguishes this use of information theory in the service of Christology from Sanday's proposal (159) that the "subliminal consciousness" was the proper *locus* of the Deity of the incarnate Christ: "To talk in informational terms is *not* to talk, as Sanday did, of the insertion of God-items into aspects, or perhaps even into delimited locations, of brain behaviour. Exactly the reverse, it is to talk about the consistency with which the codes of theistic possibility are retrieved in the scan and construction of *all* thought and action; and this is not in any way to confine the nature of God in Christ to intellect or concept alone" (Bowker 188). Thus, one may speak simultaneously of "a wholly real presence of God" and "a wholly human figure, without loss or compromise" (188).

60. Cf. Bultmann: "The formula 'Christ is God' is false in every sense in which God is understood as an entity which can be objectivized, whether it is understood in an Arian or Nicene, an Orthodox or a Liberal sense. It is correct, if 'God' is understood here as the event of God's acting" (*Essays* 287; cf. 280–81; followed by Austin 273, 275).

But "dynamic" and "static" categories of thought are not mutually exclusive but essentially complementary,[61] for logically doing presupposes being. The Dutch philosopher C. van Peursen may well be right in his analysis of the three fundamental ways in which humans have represented reality: the mythological, the ontological, and the functional.[62] However, even if it may be said that the *history* of Christology has in general been marked by a sequential movement from one category of thought to another—from substantives to substances to verbs (J. A. T. Robinson, *Face* 183)—it seems abundantly clear that the christological data of the NT evidence all three ways of thinking. Within the first chapter of the Fourth Gospel, for example, Jesus Christ is λόγος (1:1, 14), θεός (1:1c, 18), and ὁ βαπτίζων ἐν πνεύματι ἁγίῳ (1:33), representing the categories of mythology, ontology, and function as delineated by van Peursen. One's choice, then, is not between affirming that Jesus "represents to us the reality of what God is"[63] and saying that "what God is, Jesus is."[64] It is only because of his divine nature that Jesus can perform exclusively divine functions. He does not become divine simply because he represents Deity. The title θεός enshrines the truth that in relation to other persons Jesus is unique in kind and not merely degree. He, and he only among persons who have walked the earth, shares in the godhood of the Father. This divinity qualifies him to be the Father's agent *par excellence*.[65]

For all its current popularity, "agency Christology," as defended, for example, by G. W. Buchanan ("Christology") or A. E. Harvey (*Jesus* 161–65; "Agent"), does less than full justice to the NT data.[66] In the first chapter of Hebrews, prophets, angels, and the Son are all divine agents, carrying out the will of their Principal. Agency is the highest common denominator. But the author is concerned to show a distinction of agency. "In times past" God had mediated his revelation through various prophets, but "in these last

61. Tillich himself seems to recognize this. He prefers his "New Being" Christology over Schleiermacher's *Urbild* Christology precisely because of its ontological nature. Whereas "essential God-manhood" has an ontological character, the notion of the superior God-consciousness of Jesus is anthropological. Again, the New Being participates in and conquers human existence, while the *Urbild* expresses the transcendence of true humanity over human existence (150).

62. Cited by J. A. T. Robinson, *Face* 33; cf. 182–85; *Exploration* 40.

63. J. A. T. Robinson, *Face* 100; cf. 113–14 (Jesus "is a man who in all that he says and does as man is the personal representative of God: he stands in God's place, he *is* God to us and for us"), 180–211.

64. Butterworth is right in recognizing (in his article review of J. A. T. Robinson's *Human Face of God*) that "traditional christological statements which use the concept of divinity may well have an abiding value irreplaceable by other non-ontological ways of speaking" (81).

65. On the notion of agency, see §J.2 above.

66. A colorful depiction of "agency Christology" may be found in Cupitt's description (30) of Paul's view of the relation between God the Father and Jesus Christ as "something like that between King and ambassador, employer and omnicompetent secretary, or Sultan and Grand Vizier. Christ is God's right hand man: all God does, he does through Christ, and all approach to God is through Christ. All traffic, both ways, between God and the world is routed through Christ."

days," he embodied his revelation in his Son: "prophethood" is contrasted with sonship (ἐν υἱῷ, 1:2). Angels continue to be God's instruments as they assume a variety of forms (1:7), but the Son's nature is divine and his sovereignty is eternal (1:8). The focus of attention is not the parity of status between prophets, angels, and the Son as God's agents, but the incomparable superiority of the Son. Jesus is the Father's agent *par excellence* precisely because he is his Son *per essentiam*. An agent may intermittently act on God's behalf and therefore be "God to us" without actually sharing God's nature. But an agent who everywhere and always and unerringly is God functionally must also be God essentially. If it is always true that *ubi Christus ibi Deus*, then Christ must be *totus deus*. Christ is God's fully accredited agent—and more.

To recognize that the godhood of the Son is indistinguishable from the godhood of the Father is not, of course, to jeopardize the personal distinction between Son and Father. Jesus is *totus deus* but not *totum dei*. He is all that God is without being all there is of God. There is a numerical unity of essence but not a numerical identity of person. Although Jesus shares the divine essence fully and personally, he does not exhaust the category of Deity of the being of God. To use the distinction made in the Johannine Prologue, ὁ λόγος was θεός (1:1c) but ὁ θεός was not ὁ λόγος (cf. 1:1b).

While other christological titles such as κύριος and υἱὸς θεοῦ imply the divinity of Jesus,[67] the appellation θεός makes that implication explicit.[68] For example, in the first recorded use of θεός in reference to Jesus (viz., John 20:28), θεός is associated with and follows κύριος. Once κύριος was applied to Jesus in his postresurrection state, it was natural to use θεός also, not merely as a variant of κύριος, but as making explicit the implication of κύριος. To designate Jesus as θεός or ὁ θεός is to affirm his deity *expressis verbis*. Certainly the NT doctrine of the deity of Christ does not stand or fall depending on the number of times Jesus is called θεός. Even if the title were never used of Jesus, his deity is apparent, for example, in his being the object of human and angelic worship and of saving faith; the exerciser of exclusively divine functions such as agency in creation, the forgiveness of sins, and the final judgment; the addressee in petitionary prayer; the possessor of all divine attributes; the bearer of numerous titles used of Yahweh in the OT; and the coauthor of divine blessing (see appen-

67. On κύριος, see Cullmann, *Christology* 234–37, 306–7; and V. Taylor, *Names* 51 ("implicit in the recognition of the lordship of Jesus is the acknowledgment of his essential divinity"); on υἱὸς θεοῦ see E. Schweizer, *TDNT* 8:387 (who has doubt that for John υἱὸς θεοῦ presupposes a "unity of essence"); Marshall, "Development."

68. Applying his "developmental" approach to NT Christology to the NT use of θεός in reference to Jesus, C. F. D. Moule comments that "it is far from clear that this designation is alien to the *implications* of what is demonstrably 'there' at an early date or that it is incompatible with authentic evidence about what Jesus was" (*Origin* 137; cf. 4).

dix II).[69] Faith in the deity of Jesus does not rest on the existence or validity of a series of "proof texts" in which Jesus may receive the title θεός but on the general and unambiguous testimony of the NT corroborated at the bar of personal experience.[70] With this said, the significance of θεός as a christological ascription must not be minimized. The use of θεός in reference to Jesus makes explicit what other christological titles imply and confirms what may be established on other grounds, viz., the deity of Jesus Christ.

If, then, θεός is a christological title that is primarily ontological in nature, unequivocally affirming the deity of Christ, and if its use in early Christian worship and theology, however infrequent, may be dated from the resurrection of Jesus, then we cannot maintain that an ontological concern in Christology is restricted to the later strata of the NT.[71] There is no linear development from an early functional Christology to a later ontic Christology.[72] Consequently, although the development of Christology after NT times may be legitimately viewed as having (inevitably) reversed NT christological emphases by highlighting the ontological over the functional, it should not be regarded as having imported into the discussion an element foreign to NT christological thought.

Did the four NT writers who applied the title θεός to Jesus regard this dramatic departure from Jewish custom a compromise or an abandonment of their hereditary monotheism?[73] Apart from Paul's εἷς θεὸς καὶ πατὴρ πάντων in Ephesians 4:6, written subsequently to Romans 9:5, there is no explicit use of the εἷς θεός formula by these writers after they had used θεός as a christological ascription. But perhaps 1 Corinthians 8:4–6 indicates how Paul and other NT authors reformulated their monotheism to accommodate their belief in the deity of Christ.

The LXX version of the beginning of the *Shemaᶜ* (Deut. 6:4) reads κύριος ὁ θεὸς ἡμῶν κύριος εἷς ἐστιν. Paul concurs with the Corinthians in this basic affirmation (οἴδαμεν . . . ὅτι οὐδεὶς θεὸς εἰ μὴ εἷς, 1 Cor. 8:4) but pro-

69. See also Argyle, *God* 91–97; "Evidence."

70. Cf. Temple, *Christus* 112, 113 and n. 2.

71. See *per contra* Styler, esp. 399–400, 403.

72. But France argues ("Uniqueness" 211–12) for a *progression* from functional to ontological thinking and language: "Worship preceded Christological formulation, Christians found themselves led to think and speak of Jesus in divine terms, or at least in terms which implied divinity, and to pray to him and worship him, and *therefore*, as a result of this 'functional' approach, were obliged to think out and express in ever more 'ontological' terms what was his relationship with the Father" (211). Ontological formulation "is the proper, indeed the inevitable, outcome of the more functional thinking of the earlier period" (212).

73. On monotheism in the OT, see Vriezen 23–25, 175–80; Labuschagne, esp. 142–49 and the literature cited on 142 n. 3; and Sawyer with the response by Clements. On monotheism in modern Judaism, see M. H. Vogel in *EJ* 12:260–63 (where the three ingredients of monotheism are depicted as, first, the "personal-ness" (*theos*), then the arithmetical oneness and ontological uniqueness (*mono-*) of ultimate being); Lapide in Lapide and Moltmann 25–44.

ceeds to restate the undifferentiated generic εἷς θεός of the *Shema*>in a binitarian formulation, εἷς θεὸς ὁ πατὴρ . . . καὶ εἷς κύριος Ἰησοῦς Χριστός (8:6), which indicates that in Paul's view ὁ πατήρ + Ἰησοῦς Χριστός = εἷς θεός.[74] That is, Paul did not regard εἷς κύριος as an addition to the *Shema*> but as a constituent part of a christianized *Shema*.>[75] Εἷς θεός in 8:6 is not contrasted with εἷς κύριος, as if they were generically distinct, but with θεοὶ πολλοὶ (ἐν οὐρανῷ) in 8:5, just as εἷς κύριος is opposed to κύριοι πολλοὶ (ἐπὶ γῆς). Apparently, then, the solution Paul proposed to the theological problem created by the Christ event was to use the expression εἷς θεός only of the Father (cf. Eph. 4:6), never of Jesus, although θεός could occasionally be used of Jesus, while the expression εἷς κύριος was applied exclusively to Jesus (cf. Eph. 4:5), never to the Father, although κύριος was often applied to the Father.[76] It would seem that Paul never relinquished his inherited Jewish monotheism[77] but reformulated it so as to include Christ within the Godhead.[78] In light of other monotheistic statements scattered throughout the NT, it is safe to assume that no NT writer regarded the surrender of monotheism as the corollary of belief in the essential deity of Christ.[79]

74. Ὁ πατήρ is in epexegetic apposition to εἷς θεός, and Ἰησοῦς Χριστός to εἷς κύριος.

75. Reference may be made to three articles that usefully discuss 1 Cor. 8:4–6: J. M. Robinson; Giblin 529–37; and de Lacey.

76. According to R. D. Wilson ("Names" 393), there are 120 examples in the NT of κύριος = God and 368 instances of κύριος = Christ. It is generally true that in Paul ὁ κύριος refers to Jesus Christ, and κύριος to Yahweh (cf. Zerwick, *Greek* §169), but grammatical principles sometimes affect the articular state of the noun (see appendix I).

77. Rom. 9–11 affords a striking illustration of this. I have argued (in chapter VI) that Rom. 9:5b contains a doxology to Christ as θεός; yet the climactic doxology at the end of these three chapters is ascribed to God the Father (Rom. 11:36). That is, a theological and monotheistic framework is retained (note ἐξ αὐτοῦ . . . δι' αὐτοῦ . . . εἰς αὐτόν . . . αὐτῷ) in spite of a dramatic christological affirmation. The Jewish scholar Lapide points to the subordinationist passages in Paul (he cites 1 Cor. 3:22–23; 8:6; 11:3; 12:6; Eph. 4:6) as evidence that Paul retained his monotheism (in Lapide and Moltmann 39). A. F. Segal has argued that controversy over "two powers in heaven"—the usual rabbinic terminology for any heresy that threatened strict monotheism—was one of the central issues that led to the separation of Christianity from Judaism. "The basic heresy involved interpreting scripture to say that a *principal angelic or hypostatic manifestation in heaven was equivalent to God*" (x). The earliest "two powers" heretics (in the view of the rabbis) were those first-century Christians who claimed there were two *complementary* powers in heaven (viz., God and Christ), while Gnostics were the later heretics of this variety with their postulation of two *opposing* powers in heaven (see esp. ix–xii, 147–55, 205–19, 260–67). The basic concept that developed into heresy was the idea of a complementary figure in heaven, "God's principal assistant" who bore the divine name (xi, 218–19, 262).

78. Cf. Hagner, "Christology" 34–36. Hurtado prefers to speak of a "mutation" (*One God* 93–128; "Shape" 379, 390) or "*functional* re-definition" ("Shape" 379) of monotheism. However, with his stress on the influence of primitive Christian experience in the development of Christology, he also can speak of the Jewish Christians' "redefinition" of their devotion to God so as to include the veneration of Jesus (*One God* 11).

79. For monotheistic statements involving εἷς, see Mark 12:29, 32; Rom. 3:30; Gal. 3:20b; Eph. 4:6; 1 Tim. 2:5a; James 2:19. Statements with μόνος: John 17:3; Rom. 16:27; 1 Tim. 1:17; cf. 1 Tim. 6:15–16. See further Mauser. But according to Casey, the elevation of Jesus to the ontological status of

K. "Jesus Is God" as a Theological Formulation in English

Nowhere in the NT do we read that ὁ Ἰησοῦς ἐστιν θεός (or ὁ θεός).[80] The nearest comparable affirmation is found in John 1:1 (θεὸς ἦν ὁ λόγος). But before "*Jesus is* God" may be inferred from "*the Word was* 'God,'" one must assume or establish that in the Prologue of the Fourth Gospel the Word is Jesus (see chapter II §D.2) and that an ontological statement about a divine person is a timeless affirmation. That is, the theological proposition "Jesus is God" introduces an element of systematization which, although true to NT thought, goes beyond actual NT diction. Certainly, if we use this proposition frequently and without qualification, we are negating the general NT reservation of the term θεός as a virtual proper name referring to the Father.

When the appellation θεός is applied to Jesus in the NT, there is always the wider linguistic and theological context in which ὁ Ἰησοῦς is distinguished from ὁ θεός (see §D and §G above) or is depicted as subordinate to ὁ θεός (see §G above and n. 21). If the formulation "Jesus is God" is used without qualification, it fails to do justice to the whole truth about Jesus[81]—that he was the incarnate Son, a man among human beings, and that in his "postexistence" he retains his humanity, albeit in glorified form[82]—and therefore tends toward docetism (with its denial of the real humanity of Jesus), monophysitism (with its denial of the two natures of Jesus), or Sabellianism (with its claim that Jesus as Son was a temporary mode of the Divine Monad, exhausting the category of Deity). There are two ways in which this danger of misrepresentation may be avoided. The first is to prefer an assertion that incorporates both aspects of the truth—Christ's divinity and his humanity. Jesus is the God-man (θεάνθρωπος, a term coined by Origen),[83] God and man,[84] God Incarnate,[85] God in his self-

"God" occurred after 70 when Jews in the Johannine community were expelled from the synagogue and were therefore forced to make their "identity decision." They took on Gentile self-identification, removed the restraint of Jewish monotheism, and declared the deity and incarnation of Jesus. In this way, a "Jewish prophet" became a "Gentile God" (*Prophet* 23–38, 97–98, 156–59, 169, 176).

80. But see above §C.

81. This, presumably, is what Pittenger means when he cites (with approval) the remark of J. F. Bethune-Baker (no reference given) that responsible theology has never called Jesus God *absolutely* ("Words" 210).

82. See M. J. Harris 413–15.

83. *Princ.* 2:6:6.

84. Cf. the title of Pannenberg's book *Jesus—God and Man*; Sturch 337 (who proposes "God in kenosis").

85. Ferré 67 ("Jesus Christ is God Incarnate, not God in Himself"); Morris, *Cross* 372; Owen 27.

revelation,[86] God Manifest.[87] The second way is to qualify the affirmation "Jesus is God" by observing that this is a nonreciprocating proposition.[88] While Jesus is God, it is not true that God is Jesus. There are others of whom the predicate "God" may be rightfully used. The person we call Jesus does not exhaust the category of Deity.

Another possible difficulty about the unqualified assertion "Jesus is God" is linguistic. Probably under the influence of biblical usage, the word *God* in English is used principally as a proper noun identifying a person, not as a common noun designating a class.[89] Evidence of this may be seen in the fact that we cannot speak of "a God" or of "Gods," only of "a god" and of "gods."[90] The "person" identified is generally the God of the Judeo-Christian monotheistic tradition, or God the Father of Jesus and of the Christian, or the Godhead (as traditionally understood in Christian theology to refer to three persons subsisting in one essence).[91] Since, then, the word *God* may be used only to identify, not to describe, it cannot be used predicatively without suggesting equivalence or numerical identity.[92] But Jesus is neither

86. Cullmann, *Christology* 325–26; cf. 265–67.

87. Knight 42; Balz 204 (Christ is "der offenbare Gott," and "Wer Gott unter Umgehung Christi haben will, hat nicht den wirklichen Gott"). The expression "God as man" tends to be docetic, "God in man" adoptionist, and "God with man" immanentalist or synergistic.

88. See the discussion of this matter in chapter II §D.3.a.(4).

89. Similarly Denney, in a letter cited in Darlow 363; Pieper 62; Sturch 327–31. Cf. *COED* 1:1168 s.v. "God" §I.1.a: "The use of *God* as a proper name has throughout the literary period of English been the predominant one."

90. Cf. Baillie 80, 119. As a proper name in Greek, θεός may be articular or anarthrous. As a proper name in English, "God" is anarthrous, except when it is qualified (e.g., "the God and Father of our Lord Jesus Christ"), although even this is not invariable (e.g., "God the Father").

91. Mueller (257) has the curious comment that "the term *God*, when used in its proper sense, is never a generic term, but always a proper noun, since it always designates the divine Essence which exists but as one (*una numero essentia divina*)."

92. Hick 156–57 (cf. Caird, *Language* 9–10, 100–101) distinguishes four principal uses of the copula "is": the "is" (1) of predication (e.g., "Jesus Christ is divine"), (2) of class membership ("Jesus Christ is human"), (3) of definition ("a quadrilateral is a four-sided plane figure"), and (4) of identification ("Jesus Christ is God"), which may refer to qualitative identity or numerical identity. This latter category may be subdivided ("Christology" 161) into self-identity (X is identical with itself), identity through time (X at time t^1 is identical with X at time t^2), and identity by continuity or inclusion (the pseudopodium of an amoeba is one, or continuous, with the amoeba as a whole). A variation of this third type of numerical identity is a continuity of event, rather than a continuity of entity or substance. It is in this sense of "continuous identity of action" that one may speak of the numerical identity of the *agapēing* of Jesus with the divine *Agapēing* (161–62). The "one continuous event in virtue of which we can say that Jesus was God's attitude to mankind incarnate" involves "a qualitative identity between Jesus' *agapē* and the divine *Agapē*" ("an identity . . . of moral pattern," 163) and "a direct causal connection between Jesus' attitudes to his fellow human beings and God's attitudes to them" (164). In the place of the *homoousia* one should proclaim the *homoagapē*, since to the modern mind the continuity-of-*agapēing* formulation may be more intelligible than the oneness-of-substance formulation (165–66). In a similar vein Montefiore affirms that "in Jesus the divine activity was fully present so far as is possible in human personality. Because the early fathers held that substance was the regulative concept of Christology, they could not but credalize as they did. But if activity replaces substance, there is *metabasis eis allo genos*. By saying that the divine activity was

the Father nor the Trinity. Unlike Greek (which has the articular and anarthrous states of the noun), English has no way of modifying a noun so that inherent qualities are emphasized; this is the difficulty with translating θεὸς ἦν ὁ λόγος in John 1:1 by "the Word was God." On the other hand, there is no consistency in disallowing in theological English a usage that is comparable with what is actually found in the religious Greek of the NT, viz., an exceptional use of θεός in which it is a generic title applied to Jesus. Indeed, living on the other side of the trinitarian controversies and centuries of theological usage, the modern speaker of English probably has less difficulty with an exceptional use of the term *God* than the first-century Jew had with a special use of θεός.

Whenever the generic title θεός is applied to Jesus it may be appropriately rendered by "God." The formulation "Jesus is God" may be said to systematize NT teaching, but without the context afforded by the text of the NT it is wise to qualify the assertion by incorporating a reference to the humanity, sonship, or incarnation of Christ or by noting that the proposition is nonreciprocating. And it is necessary to recognize that the meaning attached to "God" in this case, viz., "one who is by nature divine," is exceptional.

L. General Conclusion

The general conclusion of this investigation may be stated in the following way. While the NT customarily reserves the term θεός for the Father, occasionally it is applied to Jesus in his preincarnate, incarnate, or postresurrection state. As used of the Father, θεός is virtually a proper name. As used of Jesus, θεός is a generic title, being an appellation descriptive of his *genus* as one who inherently belongs to the category of Deity.[93] In this usage θεός points not to Christ's function or office but to his nature.[94] When this title is anarthrous (John 1:1, 18; Rom. 9:5), the generic element is emphasized. When it is articular (John 20:28; Titus 2:13; Heb. 1:8; 2 Pet. 1:1), the titular aspect is prominent.

---

fully present in Jesus of Nazareth, we are exactly translating the essence of Chalcedon into a different thought-form" ("Christology" 171). But on the appropriateness of "substance" terminology, see Stead, esp. 267–75, and §J.1 above.

93. The word *generic* needs careful definition. As used here, it does not refer to a class that incorporates many divine beings, but to a category involving a single entity ("God"), a category which nevertheless is distinguishable from other categories. It is the same use of *genus* as when one describes God as *sui generis*.

94. In the sentence "Winston Churchill was a Britisher and a prime minister," "Winston Churchill" is a proper noun, "Britisher" a generic title, and "prime minister" an official title. A parallel sentence would be "Jesus is God and King."

In the christological use of θεός we find both the basis and the zenith of NT Christology: the basis, since θεός is a christological title that is primarily ontological in character and because the presupposition of the predominantly functional Christology of the NT is ontological Christology; the zenith, because θεός is a christological title that explicitly and unequivocally asserts the deity of Christ.

Appendix **I**

The Definite Article in the Greek New Testament: Some General and Specific Principles

In several of the verses that are discussed in this book, the presence or absence of the article with θεός is a matter of considerable importance. Rather than have the discussion of various aspects of the syntax of the Greek article scattered throughout the book, it was thought preferable to provide a systematic though brief treatment of this issue in one place to which reference could be made at the appropriate junctures.

A. General Principles

1. Originally Greek had no article, ὁ ἡ τό being a demonstrative pronoun.[1] Strictly speaking, therefore, the Greek article is a pronoun, while the noun to which it is attached is in apposition.[2] How this pronoun became an article is clearly seen in Homeric usage, such as ὁ δ' ἔβραχε χάλκεος Ἄρης (*Iliad* 5:859), "but he, brazen Ares, shouted," which easily becomes "but brazen Ares (ὁ Ἄρης) shouted."[3]

Unlike English, which restricts the use of the article to substantives, Greek employs the article freely, with participles, infinitives, adjectives, adverbs, phrases, clauses, and sentences, as well as with nouns—even articular nouns.[4] Not without reason has the article been described as a distinctive Greek contribution to Indo-European languages (cf. Robertson, *Grammar* 754, 756).

2. Since originally the article was a demonstrative pronoun,[5] it is not surprising that the basic function of the article is *deictic*, to add precision to thought by emphasizing individuality or identity. The article is the index finger of the Greek language, drawing special attention to a particular per-

1. Jannaris, *Grammar* §§236, 558–59, 1195–98. Middleton, however, prefers to speak of the article as originally a relative pronoun that referred to some object *already* present to the mind of the speaker (6 n. 1).

2. Middleton (4, 13–14) refers to the article as the subject, and the adjunct annexed to the article as the predicate, of an assumptive proposition in which the "participle of existence" is expressed or (as is usual) understood. Thus in the phrase Ῥώσκιος ὁ υἱὸς καὶ κληρονόμος τοῦ τεθνηκότος, ὁ is the subject, υἱὸς καὶ κληρονόμος forms the predicate, with ὤν being "understood": "He (Roscius) being both son and heir of the deceased" (60).

3. This example is cited by R. W. Moore 61–62. Citing Stummer's research, Milden notes (8) that "in the Iliad ὁ, ἡ, τό is used as a pronoun 3,000 times, as an article 218 times, i.e., in the ratio of 14:1; in the Odyssey it is found as a pronoun 2,178 times, as an article 171 times, i.e., in the ratio of 13:1."

4. For example, οἱ τοῦ Χριστοῦ, 1 Cor. 15:23; τὰ τοῦ θεοῦ, Matt. 22:21; Ἰάκωβος ὁ τοῦ Ζεβεδαίου, Matt. 10:2.

5. There are several traces of this Homeric usage (which is not uncommon in the papyri—MM 436 §1) in the NT: ὁ μὲν . . . ὁ δέ, "the one . . . the other" (e.g., Acts 17:32); ὁ δέ ("but he"), ἡ δέ, οἱ δέ (e.g., John 4:32); Acts 16:12 (on which see C. F. D. Moule, *Idiom Book* 111); and the quotation from Aratus (*Phaen.* 5) in Acts 17:28 (τοῦ [= τούτου] γὰρ καὶ γένος ἐσμέν). See further BDF §§249–51. Whereas in Homer (and, to a lesser degree, in the papyri) the pronominal use of ὁ ἡ τό predominates over the articular, the reverse is true in both Classical and Hellenistic Greek (cf. Moulton, *Prolegomena* 81).

son, object, fact, or idea.[6] Even without the article a noun *may* be definite,[7] but the presence of the article as "the existing symbol of definiteness" (Winer 139) guarantees this specificity (thus ἡ βίβλος, "the book in question") and often introduces an additional element of particularity ("this book"—and not that, where ἡ = αὕτη ἡ) or exclusiveness ("this book"—and no other).

3. Correspondingly, the absence of the article before a noun often indicates that the speaker or writer is thinking less of a *particular* person or thing as distinctive from others than of the *quality* or *nature* of that person or thing.[8] Attention is being drawn to the distinctive content of a term. For example, when, in Hebrews 1:1–2, the author declares that God has in the last days spoken ἐν υἱῷ ("in a Son"), he is highlighting the contrast between two modes of divine speech (λαλήσας . . . ἐλάλησεν)—the prophetic (ἐν τοῖς προφήταις, where the article is generic) and the filial.

The principal distinctives of articular and anarthrous nouns may be summarized as follows.

4. An articular noun may be:

a. Anaphoric, alluding to someone or something previously mentioned (= "the aforesaid")[9] or familiar to the author (and his audience).[10]

b. Generic, specifying (in the singular) a class or species as represented by an individual[11] or (in the plural) a class as such and not as an aggregate of individuals.[12]

6. Significantly, when the article is used in Homer as a pronoun, it often marks a contrast; e.g., τὴν δ' ἐγὼ οὐ λύσω (*Iliad* 1:29), "but *her* I will not let go" (cited by R. W. Moore 61).

7. Although Modern Greek has an indefinite article (ἕνας, μιά, ἕνα), this was not the case in Classical or Hellenistic Greek where the absence of the definite article often denoted indefiniteness. Sometimes, however, the function of the indefinite article was performed in Attic Greek by the indefinite pronoun τις and in Hellenistic Greek by τις (e.g., ἄνθρωπός τις, Luke 10:30) and the cardinal numeral εἷς (e.g., εἷς γραμματεύς, Matt. 8:19). Cf. Jannaris, *Grammar* §237.

8. Cf. Moulton, *Prolegomena* 82–83; Zerwick, *Grammar* §§171, 176. No commentator has shown himself more aware of this principle than E. D. Burton in his massive commentary on Galatians (see, e.g., 21, 89, 225, 228, 282), although on occasion he does not seem to make sufficient allowance for the operation of Apollonius's canon or for the influence of stylistic variation in explaining why a particular noun is anarthrous.

9. For example, John 4:43 (cf. 4:40); 2 Cor. 3:17 (cf. 3:16); 5:4 (cf. 5:1); Gal. 3:23 (cf. 3:22); James 2:14b (cf. 2:14a).

10. Cf. MM 437 §9, citing P Oxy 1:117 line 17 (2d–3d cent. A.D.): τὴν ἀδελφὴν ἀσπάζου καὶ τὴν Κύριλλαν, "greet your sister and Cyrilla." Milden summarizes (9) Apollonius's classification of the principal uses of the article thus: "(1) κατ' ἐξοχήν, *par excellence*, e.g., ὁ ποιητής = Homer; (2) κατὰ μοναδικὴν κτῆσιν, e.g., ὁ βασιλεὺς σὺν τῷ στρατεύματι—our possessive use; (3) κατ' αὐτὸ μόνον ἁπλῆν ἀναφοράν. The last is the commonest of all, and in it, as Apollonius saw, is to be found the essential characteristic of the Greek article, viz., ἀναφορά."

11. For example, ὁ μισθωτός = hirelings (John 10:12); ὁ κλέπτης = thieves (John 10:10). But this usage may also be represented in English by "a hireling" or "the hireling."

12. For example, οἱ νεκροὶ ἐν Χριστῷ (1 Thess. 4:16).

c. An abstract noun concretely applied.[13] In general, articular abstract nouns and anarthrous concrete nouns call for special exegetical attention.[14]

d. Possessive in meaning, where the article functions as a possessive pronoun or adjective.[15]

e. An indication of a reciprocating proposition, if the subject also is articular.[16]

5. An anarthrous noun may be:

a. Indefinite, lacking any special stress upon individual identity.[17]

b. Definite, since (1) some words (such as proper names) are by nature always definite;[18] (2) definiteness is not expressed only by the article but may also be indicated by an accompanying genitive or possessive pronoun; (3) two nouns in regimen[19] may be both anarthrous and yet definite;[20] (4) Biblical Greek sometimes reflects the Semitic idiom in which the noun in the construct state, even if definite, is anarthrous (see MH 430); and (5) there is a tendency for nouns to be anarthrous that are used in familiar or stereotyped expressions that may date from the prearticular age of Greek—expressions such as idiomatic prepositional phrases.[21] Similarly, nouns that appear in headings, lists, or proverbs tend to lack the article.[22]

13. Zerwick, *Greek* §176. For example, while χάριτι in Eph. 2:5 denotes grace as a divine *quality* that effects human salvation, τῇ χάριτι in Eph. 2:8 probably refers to that particular *act* of divine grace by which salvation was procured (although the article may be simply anaphoric) (so also N. Turner, *Syntax* 176). But Gildersleeve and Miller (2:259 §567) find in the easy passage from the articular to the anarthrous form in Classical Greek evidence that there was there "no vital difference" between articular and anarthrous abstract nouns (citing Plato, *Meno* 99A [ἡ ἀρετή] and 99E [ἀρετή]; also 100B [ἡ ἀρετὴ . . . ἀρετή]).

14. Zerwick, *Greek* §179 (citing υἱός and πατήρ in Heb. 12:7 as examples of anarthrous concrete nouns used qualitatively).

15. For example, Ἀνανίας . . . ἐπιθεὶς ἐπ᾽ αὐτὸν τὰς χεῖρας κτλ. (Acts 9:17).

16. The reciprocity involved may point to an actual identity or to a conceptual identity.

17. For example, John 1:6: ἐγένετο ἄνθρωπος, ἀπεσταλμένος παρὰ θεοῦ.

18. See the analyses of Nevius, *Mark* and *Gospels*; Funk 136–39; Fee, "Article." On classical usage, see Gildersleeve.

19. That is, where one noun is "governing" (*nomen regens*) and the other noun is "governed" (*nomen rectum*). For example, in the phrase ὁ λόγος τοῦ θεοῦ the word ὁ λόγος is *nomen regens* and the word τοῦ θεοῦ is *nomen rectum*.

20. See the discussion of the canon of Apollonius below, §B.1.

21. There is a certain similarity between Greek and English at this point: note the classical εἰς ἄστυ ("to town"), the κατὰ πόλιν ("in town") of the papyri, and the phrase ἐν οἰκίᾳ ("at home") in Luke 8:27. See MM 436 §5.

22. For example, 1 Pet. 1:1 (heading and list); 4:1b, 8b (proverbs).

c. Qualitative, emphasizing the intrinsic qualities of the particular person or thing signified.[23] Whereas articular nouns identify, anarthrous nouns may describe.
d. An indication of the predicate in the sentence (where the subject is articular),[24] since a predicate further defines an individual person or thing already specified.
e. An indication of a nonreciprocating proposition if the subject is articular.[25]

Against this background we may better understand the operation of three special principles regarding the use of the article that are of particular relevance to some of the verses discussed in the body of this book.

B. Three Specific Principles

1. The Canon of Apollonius

Apollonius Dyscolus, a native of Alexandria who lived in the second century A.D., is the principal source for the history of Greek grammar from the second century B.C. down to his own day. He was acclaimed by Priscian, the famous Latin grammarian of the sixth century A.D., as "a most distinguished model of the art of grammar (*maximus auctor artis grammaticae*)."[26] To him we owe the formulation of the grammatical principle that nouns in *regimen* generally either both have the article or both lack it.[27] Thus, one must say either λέοντος σκυμνίον or τὸ τοῦ λέοντος σκυμνίον. Both mean "the cub of the lion." Commenting on the impossibility of τὸ σκυμνίον λέοντος, T. F. Middleton observes that "the accuracy of a philosophical language denies, that of λέοντος, which is indefinite, there can be any definite σκυμνίον. Exactly as the insertion of the Article before the governed Noun . . . is made necessary by its insertion before the Noun which governs, so the indefiniteness of the governed will cause the governing Noun to assume the indefinite form" (48).

23. See Moulton, *Prolegomena* 83: "For exegesis, there are few of the finer points of Greek which need more constant attention than this omission of the article when the writer would lay stress on the quality or character of the object."

24. For example, John 8:42 (εἰ ὁ θεὸς πατὴρ ὑμῶν ἦν . . .); Rom. 1:9a; Phil. 1:21 *bis*. On occasion, however, the subject may be anarthrous and the predicate articular—as when the subject is a proper name (e.g., 1 John 4:15).

25. For example, 1 John 4:8: ὁ θεὸς ἀγάπη ἐστίν.

26. Cited by P. B. R. Forbes, "Apollonius (15)," in *OCD* 72.

27. Ἢ . . . ἀμφότερα χωρὶς ἄρθρου, λέοντος σκυμνίον ἔδραμεν· ἢ ἀμφότερα συνενεχθήσεται, τὸ τοῦ λέοντος σκυμνίον ἔδραμεν (*De Syntaxi seu Constructione Orationis*, ed. F. Portus and F. Sylburgius [Frankfurt: Wechelus, 1590], p. 90 §1:42).

New Testament usage accords with this canon. So one finds, for example, ἐν τῷ πνεύματι τοῦ θεοῦ in 1 Corinthians 6:11 but ἐν πνεύματι θεοῦ in 1 Corinthians 12:3. A notable instance, again involving (τοῦ) θεοῦ as *nomen rectum*,[28] occurs in 1 Corinthians 15:10: <u>χάριτι</u> δὲ <u>θεοῦ</u> εἰμι ὅ εἰμι, καὶ ἡ χάρις αὐτοῦ ἡ εἰς ἐμὲ οὐ κενὴ ἐγενήθη, ἀλλὰ περισσότερον αὐτῶν πάντων ἐκοπίασα, οὐκ ἐγὼ δὲ ἀλλὰ <u>ἡ χάρις τοῦ θεοῦ</u> ἡ σὺν ἐμοί.

Apparent exceptions to the canon[29] may often be accounted for by reference to other grammatical principles, viz.:

a. That predicative nouns are not infrequently anarthrous,[30] especially when they precede the verb,[31] for example, Acts 16:17: οὗτοι οἱ ἄνθρωποι δοῦλοι τοῦ θεοῦ τοῦ ὑψίστου εἰσίν.[32]
b. That Biblical Greek sometimes reflects the Hebrew idiom[33] in which a noun in the construct state or a noun to which a pronominal suffix is attached is anarthrous. For example, when לימיני of Psalm 110:1 appears in NT citations or allusions, one finds ἐν δεξιᾷ τοῦ θεοῦ (Rom. 8:34; Col. 3:1; Heb. 10:12; 1 Pet. 3:22 v.l.) or ἐκ δεξιῶν τοῦ θεοῦ (Acts 7:55–56).[34]
c. That a noun is generally articular when a personal pronoun or an attributive adjective accompanies it. Thus 2 Peter 1:1: ἐν δικαιοσύνῃ τοῦ θεοῦ ἡμῶν καὶ σωτῆρος Ἰησοῦ Χριστοῦ.[35]
d. That the absence of the article before the second of two nouns joined by καί indicates that the writer views the nouns as a conceptual unit.[36] For instance, Paul describes Timothy as τὸν ἀδελφὸν ἡμῶν καὶ συνεργὸν τοῦ θεοῦ (1 Thess. 3:2).[37]
e. That the vocative is never articular, for example, Mark 5:7 (= Matt. 8:29; Luke 8:28): υἱὲ τοῦ θεοῦ.

28. All the following examples cited in the text under §B.1 involve (ὁ) θεός as either *nomen regens* or *nomen rectum*.
29. Apollonius himself recognized (*De Syntaxi* 90) that proper names do not always conform to his general canon.
30. This is because the article is a marker of what is already known, while a predicate generally introduces some *new* fact about the subject (Gildersleeve and Miller 2:324).
31. See the discussion of "Colwell's rules" below, §B.3.
32. Thus also (involving (ὁ) θεός) Matt. 4:3, 6; 5:34; 27:40; Luke 4:3, 9; Acts 17:29; Rom. 9:8; 1 Cor. 15:15a; 2 Cor. 4:4b; Eph. 2:19; 5:1; Col. 1:15; 3:12 (?); 1 Thess. 4:3; James 4:4 *bis*; 1 Pet. 5:12; Rev. 20:6.
33. But see GKC §§127–28 for apparent exceptions.
34. Also Acts 10:3; 27:23 (?); Rom. 1:1 (*si vera lectio*); 2:5; 15:7; 2 Cor. 1:12b; Eph. 2:22; Rev. 15:2.
35. Also Rom. 16:26; 2 Pet. 1:2; and possibly Titus 1:3.
36. See the more detailed discussion below, §B.2.
37. Also Acts 2:23; Eph. 5:5.

f. That indeclinable proper names are generally anarthrous in the genitive case. Thus Matthew 22:32 (= Mark 12:26): ἐγώ εἰμι ὁ θεὸς Ἀβραὰμ καὶ ὁ θεὸς Ἰσαὰκ καὶ ὁ θεὸς Ἰακώβ.
g. That πᾶς is anarthrous when it means "every" (see N. Turner, *Syntax* 144–200)—thus Colossians 4:12: ἐν παντὶ θελήματι τοῦ θεοῦ, "in every part of God's will."[38]

When (τοῦ) θεοῦ is *nomen rectum*, the word order is generally AABB (e.g., ὁ ναὸς τοῦ θεοῦ); this is always the case in the Gospels. However, an ABBA order (e.g., ὁ τοῦ θεοῦ ναός) is sometimes found outside the Gospels.[39] Only relatively rarely does θεοῦ precede the anarthrous noun on which it depends.[40]

2. The Article with Copulated Nouns

In his controversial book *Remarks on the Uses of the Definitive Article in the Greek Text of the New Testament; Containing Many New Proofs of the Divinity of Christ, from Passages, Which Are Wrongly Translated in the Common English Version*, first published in 1798 (second edition, 1802; third edition, 1803), Granville Sharp formulated and applied to the NT a rule regarding the repetition or nonrepetition of the article with copulated substantives:

> When the copulative καί connects two nouns of the same case [viz., nouns (either substantive, or adjective, or participles) of personal description respecting office, dignity, affinity, or connection, and attributes, properties or qualities good or ill] if the article ὁ, or any of it's [*sic*] cases preceeds [*sic*] the first of the said nouns or participles, and is not repeated before the second noun or participle, the latter always relates to the same person that is expressed or described by the first noun or participle; i.e. it denotes a further description of the first named person (4–5, rule I).

Following M. Zerwick's lead (Greek §184; cf. N. Turner, *Syntax* 181), one may simplify and extend the rule as follows: With two (or more) coordinated nouns, the repetition of the article distinguishes, while a single article

38. There are only two exceptions (involving the word θεός) to the canon of Apollonius that are not accounted for by the seven categories of exception listed above—Matt. 22:32 (οὐκ ἔστιν ὁ θεὸς νεκρῶν ἀλλὰ ζώντων, B L Γ Δ f^1 33 *pc*), where there is textual uncertainty and where the Marcan parallel (12:27) reads θεὸς νεκρῶν; and Eph. 2:8 (καὶ τοῦτο οὐκ ἐξ ὑμῶν, θεοῦ τὸ δῶρον), where either the desire to highlight the juxtaposition of the contrasted ἐξ ὑμῶν and θεοῦ or the inverted word order (cf. the more usual τὸ δῶρον (τοῦ) θεοῦ) accounts for the anarthrous θεοῦ.

39. Viz., Acts 13:36; Rom. 10:3a (cf. 10:3b); 2 Cor. 1:19; 11:7; 2 Tim. 3:17; 1 Pet. 3:20; 4:14 v.l., 17b; 2 Pet. 3:5, 12; Jude 4.

40. Viz., Matt. 14:33; Acts 12:22; Rom. 3:5a; 13:4 *bis*; 1 Cor. 1:24 *bis*; 2:7a; 3:9 *ter*; 2 Cor 6:4; Titus 1:7; Heb. 6:5; 1 Pet. 2:16. On θεοῦ τὸ δῶρον in Eph. 2:8, see above n. 38.

associates the notions in a conceptual unity[41] (or sometimes an identity). This restatement goes beyond Sharp's formulation in two regards—it applies the rule to more than persons and singulars and it explains the significance of the repeated article (not simply the significance of the nonrepetition).[42] Several NT examples[43] illustrate the principle.

a. The Repetition of the Article

(1) Acts 26:30: Ἀνέστη τε ὁ βασιλεὺς καὶ ὁ ἡγεμὼν ἥ τε Βερνίκη. The three articles make it clear that three different persons rose up. Had Luke written ὁ βασιλεὺς καὶ ἡγεμών he would have implied that King Herod Agrippa II was also governor of Judea (which was not the case).

(2) Alluding to himself and Apollos, Paul comments (1 Cor. 3:8) ὁ φυτεύων . . . καὶ ὁ ποτίζων ἕν εἰσιν. By repeating the article Paul implies that the roles of planter and waterer should not be confused or identified; distinct tasks and separate individuals are indicated.

b. The Nonrepetition of the Article

(1) In Ephesians 4:11 (καὶ αὐτὸς ἔδωκεν) τοὺς μὲν ἀποστόλους, τοὺς δὲ προφήτας, τοὺς δὲ εὐαγγελιστάς is followed by the phrase τοὺς δὲ ποιμένας καὶ διδασκάλους. The absence of the article before διδασκάλους, particularly after the thrice-repeated τοὺς δέ,[44] could imply that Paul is thinking of only four (not five) types of persons, the last being the pastor-teacher ("pastors who are, by virtue of their function, also teachers"), that there are no pastors who are not teachers. But an equally possible explanation of the anarthrous διδασκάλους is that, while Paul distinguished the role of the pastor from that of the teacher, here he associates them (presumably

41. Another way that Greek can express close conceptual association is through disagreement in number between subjects and their verb. In John 1:17, for example, ἡ χάρις καὶ ἡ ἀλήθεια . . . ἐγένετο (not ἐγένοντο) shows that John so naturally thought of truth when he thought of grace, and grace when he thought of truth, that the two formed a single theological unit of thought. Note also the remarkable instances in 1 Thess. 3:11 and 2 Thess. 2:16–17.

42. Wallace has shown that Sharp recognized that his first rule did not apply to proper names, plurals, or impersonal constructions (63–66). Wallace himself examines the 71 NT examples of the article–noun–καί–noun plural construction and classifies 60 of these instances into one of five semantic categories: (1) two entirely distinct groups, though united, (2) two overlapping groups, (3) the first group as a subset of the second group, (4) the second group as a subset of the first group, and (5) two identical groups (67–79).

43. Regarding classical usage, Gildersleeve and Miller observe (2:277 §603) that although (1) theoretically the repetition of the article demands separate consideration of the nouns involved and the absence of the article suggests unity, (2) in practice the distinction is not always observed. The examples cited are, for the first group, οἱ στρατηγοὶ καὶ οἱ λοχαγοί (Xenophon, *An.* 3:5:14), "the generals and the captains" (as distinct classes of officers), but οἱ στρατηγοὶ καὶ λοχαγοί (*An.* 1:7:2), "the generals and captains" (officers as distinct from privates); for the second group, τὸ ὅμοιον καὶ τὸ ἀνόμοιον καὶ τὸ ταὐτὸν καὶ ἕτερον (Plato, *Theat.* 186A), "the like and the unlike and the identical and different."

44. If it were simply a case of stylistic variation, καὶ τοὺς διδασκάλους might have been expected.

because of their similar functions as ruling and teaching elders) in a single category (viz., pastors-and-teachers) over against the other three groups (viz., apostles, prophets, evangelists). In one case, there are four types of persons and four conceptual categories; in the other, five types and four categories. From the viewpoint of grammar alone, a verdict of *non liquet* must be passed.[45]

(2) The formula ὁ θεὸς καὶ πατὴρ (ἡμῶν), so common in Pauline greetings,[46] affords an example of this rule in which theological considerations show that it is not a matter of unity in concept (θεός and πατήρ actually referring to two persons) but of actual identification (θεός is no other than πατήρ). In this regard it is instructive to compare (ἀπὸ) θεοῦ πατρὸς (ἡμῶν) in 2 Corinthians 1:2, Ephesians 1:2, and 1 Peter 1:2[47] with ὁ θεὸς καὶ πατὴρ (τοῦ κυρίου ἡμῶν Ἰησοῦ Χριστοῦ) in the following verse in each case. Moreover in 2 Corinthians 1:3 one finds both ὁ θεὸς καὶ πατήρ and ὁ πατὴρ (τῶν οἰκτιρμῶν) καὶ θεὸς (πάσης παρακλήσεως).

c. The Repetition and Nonrepetition of the Article

(1) Particularly interesting is the comparison of ἐν τῇ Μακεδονίᾳ καὶ ἐν τῇ Ἀχαΐᾳ in 1 Thessalonians 1:7 with ἐν τῇ Μακεδονίᾳ καὶ Ἀχαΐᾳ in 1 Thessalonians 1:8.[48] In the former case, the two provinces are themselves distinguished; in the latter, they are considered a unit and distinguished from ἐν παντὶ τόπῳ ("in every place, everywhere").[49]

(2) Acts 15:23: οἱ ἀπόστολοι καὶ οἱ πρεσβύτεροι ἀδελφοὶ τοῖς κατὰ τὴν Ἀντιόχειαν καὶ Συρίαν καὶ Κιλικίαν ἀδελφοῖς τοῖς ἐξ ἐθνῶν χαίρειν. In the first phrase ("the brethren, both the apostles and the elders," RSV) the repeated article before πρεσβύτεροι (as in Acts 15:4, 6, 22) indicates that within the Jerusalem church the elders were distinguishable from the apostles as holders of a separate office. Yet the two groups could also be regarded (from an Antiochene perspective?) as a single administrative unit representing the whole Jerusalem church, as is clear from Acts 15:2 (Paul, Barnabas, and some others from Antioch were appointed to go up πρὸς τοὺς ἀποστόλους καὶ πρεσβυτέρους εἰς Ἰερουσαλήμ) and 16:4 (Paul and Silas promulgate the decisions reached ὑπὸ τῶν ἀποστόλων καὶ πρεσβυτέρων τῶν ἐν Ἱεροσολύμοις).

45. On the basis of his analysis of article–noun–καί–noun plural constructions (see n. 42 above), Wallace argues that the "pastors" formed a subset of the "teachers": "All pastors are to be teachers, though not all teachers are to be pastors" (83).

46. See above, chapter I §B.4.d.

47. Appositives that follow an anarthrous θεός may themselves be anarthrous in stereotyped expressions such as epistolary introductions (BDF §268.(2)).

48. However ℵ C D F G Ψ read καὶ ἐν τῇ Ἀχαΐᾳ in 1:8.

49. Cf. ἡ Ἰουδαία καὶ Σαμαρεία in Acts 1:8; 8:1.

In Acts 15:23 the absence of an article before Συρίαν[50] and Κιλικίαν suggests that the apostolic letter was intended primarily for the Gentiles of the Antioch-Syria-Cilicia region. The placement of the whole phrase κατὰ . . . Κιλικίαν between τοῖς and ἀδελφοῖς tends to confirm this point. M. Zerwick, however, goes one step further, declaring that "the letter of the council of Jerusalem, by joining under the same article the three regions to which it was addressed (Acts 15,23) may perhaps be said rather to discourage a wider promulgation of its contents" (*Greek* §184).

d. Summary

Thus it may be seen that a repeated article shows unambiguously that nouns are separate items. Its nonrepetition indicates that the nouns involved are to be considered not separately but corporately or as having a single referent.

3. Colwell's "Rules"

a. The Origin and Statement of the Rules

As a result of his investigation of C. C. Torrey's theory of the Aramaic origin of the Gospel of John (esp. 323–24) and in particular Torrey's claim that some nouns stand without the article in Greek because of the underlying Semitic anarthrous construct state, in 1933 E. C. Colwell was led to study three passages in John (viz., 1:49; 5:27; 9:5) that had been cited by Torrey as examples. It was the interesting variation in word order in these verses, especially John 1:49 (σὺ εἶ ὁ υἱὸς τοῦ θεοῦ, σὺ βασιλεὺς εἶ τοῦ Ἰσραήλ), that first suggested to Colwell that the variable quantum was not definiteness but word order.[51]

Colwell tabulated his results after analyzing all the definite predicate nouns in the NT with regard to their articular status and their position in relation to the verb ("Rule" 17):

1. Definite predicate nouns with the article	244
a. After the verb	229 (94%)
b. Before the verb	15 (6%)
2. Definite predicate nouns without the article	123
a. After the verb	26 (21%)
b. Before the verb	97 (79%)

50. 𝔓[45] reads τὴν Συρίαν.
51. Colwell, "Rule."

Colwell observes that the close relation between word order and the use of the article in these cases can be shown by a different grouping of the same figures:

1. Definite predicate nouns after the verb	255
a. With the article	229 (90%)
b. Without the article	26 (10%)
2. Definite predicate nouns before the verb	112
a. With the article	15 (13%)
b. Without the article	97 (87%)

On the basis of these and other findings, Colwell claims that certain rules may be "tentatively formulated to describe the use of the article with definite predicate nouns in sentences in which the verb occurs. (1) Definite predicate nouns here regularly take the article. (2) The exceptions are for the most part due to a change in word-order: (a) Definite predicate nouns which follow the verb (this is the usual order) usually take the article; (b) Definite predicate nouns which precede the verb usually lack the article; (c) Proper names regularly lack the article in the predicate; (d) Predicate nominatives in relative clauses regularly follow the verb whether or not they have the article" ("Rule" 20).

b. Evaluation of the Rules

(1) There can be no doubt that the formulation of these rules that cover NT usage represented a significant advance on the three general observations concerning the use of the article with predicate nouns that are found in the older NT grammars (e.g., Robertson, *Grammar* 767–68), viz., (a) that predicate nouns tend to be anarthrous; (b) that predicate nouns that are generic are anarthrous;[52] and (c) that predicate nouns in convertible propositions are articular.[53]

With this said, one should not overlook the definite limitations of the rules.

(2) Colwell himself notes ("Rule" 16–17, 17 n. 12) that the rules do not apply to constructions where there is an ellipsis of the copula or to qualitative nouns. And it is clear from the last two rules that proper names (2c) and predicate nominatives in relative clauses (2d) are themselves exceptions to the principal exceptions (viz., 2a and 2b). Examples that fitted any of these four categories were not included in Colwell's statistical analysis.

(3) It must remain uncertain whether the inference Colwell drew from his study may stand, viz., that a predicate noun which precedes the copula

52. For example, Luke 17:16: καὶ αὐτὸς ἦν Σαμαρίτης.
53. For example, Matt. 13:38: ὁ δὲ ἀγρός ἐστιν ὁ κόσμος.

"is *indefinite* in this position only when the context demands it" ("Rule" 21). In fact the reverse would seem to be the case, as Colwell himself first stated it: "A predicate nominative which precedes the verb cannot be translated as an indefinite or a 'qualitative' noun solely because of the absence of the article; if the context suggests that the predicate is *definite*, it should be translated as a definite noun in spite of the absence of the article" ("Rule" 20). The difficulty is simply this. How can one determine the definiteness of a noun which is anarthrous? For example, is προφήτης definite or indefinite in Mark 11:32 and John 4:19? The only indisputable datum about an anarthrous noun is that it lacks the article. Particularly in the application of rule 2b—often referred to as "Colwell's rule"—a considerable element of subjectivity comes into play[54] and there is the constant danger of arguing in a circle by assuming from the context that a particular anarthrous predicate noun is definite and then finding in its placement before the copula the confirmation of its definiteness. Whether in the subject or predicate, an articular noun is definite with regard to what is signified. An anarthrous noun in the subject or predicate, on the other hand, may be either indefinite or definite, but the presumption ought to be that it is either (1) *indefinite*[55] (since Greek has, in the article, a means of making definiteness unambiguous), until it has been shown to be definite from the context (both immediate and general),[56] or (2) *qualitative*,[57] whatever be its state of definiteness.[58] This leads me to affirm that one may not infer (as is often done) from rule 2b that anarthrous predicate nouns which precede the verb are usually definite. Indeed, such nouns will usually be qualitative in emphasis.

On this latter point, the primary finding of P. B. Harner in his analysis of predicate nouns in Mark and the Fourth Gospel was that "anarthrous predicate nouns preceding the verb may be primarily qualitative in force yet may

54. For instance, Nelson (72) finds in four verses in Mark (viz., 2:28; 3:35; 12:35; 15:39) definite predicate nouns that are anarthrous since they precede the verb (= Colwell's rule 2b), whereas Harner (77–81) adduces the same examples (along with four others in Mark: 6:49; 11:17, 32; 14:70) as instances where the definiteness or indefiniteness of the predicate noun is less prominent than its qualitative force.

55. For example, as subject (John 1:4), as predicate (Mark 6:49).

56. Thus, it seems, the ambiguous ἀληθῶς οὗτος ὁ ἄνθρωπος υἱὸς θεοῦ ἦν of Mark 15:39 should be rendered as "truly this man was the Son of God" in accordance with Mark's intention in the passion narrative and in his whole Gospel. See Bratcher.

57. For example, Mark 14:70.

58. From this viewpoint, two more recent statements of the principle behind rule 2b are preferable. Nelson writes: "An anarthrous predicate nominative before the verb can be, and indeed should be where the context indicates, translated as definite and certainly not qualitative" (64; compare, however, his statements on 44, 60–61). Then there is Greenlee ("Article" 164): "With the verbs 'to be' and 'to become,' a predicate noun regularly does *not* have the article if it is written preceding the verb, regardless of whether it is definite or not, and the context must be the deciding factor in its interpretation" (similarly his *Grammar* 23).

also have some connotation of definiteness. The categories of qualitativeness and definiteness, that is, are not mutually exclusive, and frequently it is a delicate exegetical issue for the interpreter to decide which emphasis a Greek writer had in mind" (87). In Mark the anarthrous predicate nouns in all 8 instances in which they precede the verb (viz., 2:28; 3:35; 6:49; 11:17, 32; 12:35; 14:70; 15:39) were found to be qualitative in force (76–81). Of the 53 examples in the Fourth Gospel of an anarthrous predicate expression preceding the verb, Harner judged (82–83) that (1) in 41 cases[59] the qualitative force of the predicate substantive is more prominent than its definiteness or indefiniteness; (2) in 26 cases[60] the predicate could not be definite; and (3) in 11 instances[61] the predicate may be definite, but clear indications of definiteness are lacking.

(4) It seems *a priori* unlikely that the largely mechanical and external factor of word order should itself account for the presence or absence of the article.[62] This becomes evident when one alters the word order of a particular statement and then adds or omits the article in accordance with the rules, for the result may be theologically inadmissible. For instance, if one found in John 1:1c ὁ λόγος ἦν ὁ θεός instead of θεὸς ἦν ὁ λόγος, a serious ambiguity if not contradiction would be present, for the previous clause (ὁ λόγος ἦν πρὸς τὸν θεόν) distinguishes the person of the Logos from the person of the Father (ὁ θεός). Therefore the absence of the article before θεός in John 1:1c must be accounted for on grounds other than mere word order.[63]

The other factors (in addition to word order) that may account for the presence or absence of the article in any given case have been dealt with in the foregoing discussion.

59. Viz., John 1:12, 14; 2:9; 3:4, 6 *bis*, 29; 4:9; 6:63, 70; 7:12; 8:31, 33, 34, 37, 39, 42, 44 *bis*, 48; 9:17, 24, 25, 27, 28, 31; 10:1, 2, 8, 13, 33, 34, 36; 12:6, 36, 50; 13:35; 15:14; 17:17; 18:35 (cited by Harner on p. 83 n. 20), to which may be added John 1:1 (84–87), giving the total of 41 cases.

60. Viz., John 1:14; 2:9; 3:4, 6 *bis*; 4:9; 6:63; 7:12; 8:31, 44 *bis*, 48; 9:8, 24, 25, 27, 28, 31; 10:1, 8, 33, 34; 12:6, 36; 18:26, 35 (Harner 83 n. 21).

61. Viz., John 1:12; 6:70; 8:33, 34, 37, 39; 9:17; 12:50; 13:35; 15:14; 17:17 (Harner 83 n. 21).

62. Similarly Zerwick, *Greek* §175. But see *per contra* Colwell, "Rule" 15–16, and Nelson 30–32, 58–59 (both of whom cite examples where a textual variant that adds or omits the article also changes word order).

63. See above, chapter II §D.3.a.(3).

Appendix II

An Outline of the New Testament Testimony to the Deity of Christ

This outline does not purport to be in any sense an exhaustive analysis of the NT witness to Christ's deity. Rather it is a sketch of one approach—a rather traditional approach—to this theme. Other complementary or supplementary approaches abound, such as the creative treatment of Jesus' implicit claim to deity in his parables by P. B. Payne or R. T. France's documentation from the Synoptic Gospels of Jesus' assumption of the role of Yahweh (*Jesus* 150–59). For a brief discussion of the NT verses that seem, at first sight, to call Jesus' divinity into question, see R. E. Brown, *Reflections* 6–10 (= "Jesus" 548–51).

A. Implicit Christology
  1. Divine functions performed by Jesus
    a. In relation to the universe
      (1) Creator (John 1:3; Col. 1:16; Heb. 1:2)
      (2) Sustainer (1 Cor. 8:6; Col. 1:17; Heb. 1:3)
      (3) Author of life (John 1:4; Acts 3:15)
      (4) Ruler (Matt. 28:18; Rom. 14:9; Rev. 1:5)
    b. In relation to human beings
      (1) Healing the sick (Mark 1:32–34; Acts 3:6; 10:38)
      (2) Teaching authoritatively (Mark 1:21–22; 13:31)
      (3) Forgiving sins (Mark 2:1–12; Luke 24:47; Acts 5:31; Col. 3:13)

(4) Granting salvation or imparting eternal life (Acts 4:12; Rom. 10:12–14)
(5) Dispensing the Spirit (Matt. 3:11; Acts 2:17, 33)
(6) Raising the dead (Luke 7:11–17; John 5:21; 6:40)
(7) Exercising judgment (Matt. 25:31–46; John 5:19–29; Acts 10:42; 1 Cor. 4:4–5)

2. Divine status claimed by or accorded to Jesus
   a. In relation to his Father
      (1) Possessor of divine attributes (John 1:4; 10:30; 21:17; Eph. 4:10; Col. 1:19; 2:9)
      (2) Eternally existent (John 1:1; 8:58; 12:41; 17:5; 1 Cor. 10:4; Phil. 2:6; Heb. 11:26; 13:8; Jude 5)
      (3) Equal in dignity (Matt. 28:19; John 5:23; 2 Cor. 13:14; Rev. 22:13; cf. 21:6)
      (4) Perfect revealer (John 1:18; 14:9; Col. 1:15; Heb. 1:1–3)
      (5) Embodiment of truth (John 1:9, 14; 6:32; 14:6; Rev. 3:7, 14)
      (6) Joint possessor of the kingdom (Eph. 5:5; Rev. 11:15), churches (Rom. 16:16), Spirit (Rom. 8:9; Phil. 1:19), temple (Rev. 21:22), divine name (Matt 28:19; cf. Rev. 14:1), and throne (Rev. 22:1, 3)
   b. In relation to human beings
      (1) Recipient of praise (Matt. 21:15–16; Eph. 5:19; 1 Tim. 1:12; Rev. 5:8–14)
      (2) Recipient of prayer (Acts 1:24; 7:59–60; 9:10–17, 21; 22:16, 19; 1 Cor. 1:2; 16:22; 2 Cor. 12:8)
      (3) Object of saving faith (John 14:1; Acts 10:43; 16:31; Rom. 10:8–13)
      (4) Object of worship (Matt. 14:33; 28:9, 17; John 5:23; 20:28; Phil. 2:10–11; Heb. 1:6; Rev. 5:8–12)
      (5) Joint source of blessing (1 Cor. 1:3; 2 Cor. 1:2; Gal. 1:3; 1 Thess. 3:11; 2 Thess. 2:16)
      (6) Object of doxologies (2 Tim. 4:18; 2 Pet. 3:18; Rev. 1:5b–6; 5:13)

B. Explicit Christology
1. Old Testament passages referring to Yahweh applied to Jesus
   a. Character of Yahweh (Exod. 3:14 and Isa. 43:11 alluded to in John 8:58; Ps. 101:27–28 LXX [MT 102:28–29] quoted in Heb. 1:11–12; Isa. 44:6 alluded to in Rev. 1:17)
   b. Holiness of Yahweh (Isa. 8:12–13 [cf. 29:23] quoted in 1 Pet. 3:14–15)

   c. Descriptions of Yahweh (Ezek. 43:2 and Dan. 10:5–6 alluded to in Rev. 1:13–16)
   d. Worship of Yahweh (Isa. 45:23 alluded to in Phil. 2:10–11; Deut. 32:43 LXX and Ps. 96:7 LXX [MT 97:7] quoted in Heb. 1:6)
   e. Work of Yahweh in creation (Ps. 101:26 LXX [MT 102:27] quoted in Heb. 1:10)
   f. Salvation of Yahweh (Joel 2:32 [MT 3:5] quoted in Rom. 10:13; cf. Acts 2:21; Isa. 40:3 quoted in Matt. 3:3)
   g. Trustworthiness of Yahweh (Isa. 28:16 quoted in Rom. 9:33; 10:11; 1 Pet. 2:6)
   h. Judgment of Yahweh (Isa. 6:10 alluded to in John 12:41; Isa. 8:14 quoted in Rom. 9:33 and 1 Pet. 2:8)
   i. Triumph of Yahweh (Ps. 68:18 [MT v. 19] quoted in Eph. 4:8)
2. Divine titles claimed by or applied to Jesus
   a. Son of Man (Matt. 16:28; 24:30; Mark 8:38; 14:62–64; Acts 7:56)
   b. Son of God (Matt. 11:27; Mark 15:39; John 1:18; Rom. 1:4; Gal. 4:4; Heb. 1:2)
   c. Messiah (Matt. 16:16; Mark 14:61; John 20:31)
   d. Lord (Mark 12:35–37; John 20:28; Rom. 10:9; 1 Cor. 8:5–6; 12:3; 16:22; Phil. 2:11; 1 Pet. 2:3; 3:15)
   e. Alpha and Omega (Rev. 22:13; cf. 1:8; 21:6, of the Lord God)
   f. God (John 1:1, 18; 20:28; Rom. 9:5; Titus 2:13; Heb. 1:8; 2 Pet. 1:1)

Bibliography

Abbot, *Authorship* — E. Abbot. *The Authorship of the Fourth Gospel and Other Critical Essays.* 2 vols. Boston: Ellis, 1888.

Abbot, "Reading" — E. Abbot. "On the Reading 'Church of God,' Acts xx.28." *Bibliotheca Sacra* 33 (1876): 313–52. Reprinted in Abbot, *Authorship* 294–31.

Abbot, "Titus" — E. Abbot. "On the Construction of Titus ii.13." *Journal of Biblical Literature* 1 (1881): 3–19. Reprinted in Abbot, *Authorship* 439–57.

Abbot, "Construction" — E. Abbot. "On the Construction of Romans ix.5." *Journal of Biblical Literature* 1 (1881): 87–154.

Abbot, "Discussions" — E. Abbot. "Recent Discussions on Romans ix.5." *Journal of Biblical Literature* 3 (1883): 90–112.

Abbott, *Vocabulary* — E. A. Abbott. *Johannine Vocabulary.* London: Black, 1905.

Abbott, *Grammar* — E. A. Abbott. *Johannine Grammar.* London: Black, 1906.

Abbott, *Contributions* — E. A. Abbott. *"The Son of Man"; or, Contributions to the Study of the Thoughts of Jesus.* Cambridge: Cambridge University Press, 1910.

Abel — F. M. Abel. *Grammaire du grec biblique, suivie d'un choix de papyrus.* Paris: Gabalda, 1927.

Aejmelaeus — L. Aejmelaeus. *Die Rezeption der Paulusbriefe in der Miletrede* (Apg 20:18–35). Helsinki: Suomalainen Tiedeakatemia, 1987.

Aland — K. Aland. "Neue neutestamentliche Papyri II." *New Testament Studies* 9 (1962–63): 303–13.

Alexander — J. A. Alexander. *The Acts of the Apostles.* London: Nisbet, 1884.

Alford — H. Alford. *The Greek Testament.* 4 vols. in 2. Reprinted Chicago: Moody, 1958 (= 1849–61 original).

Allen — L. C. Allen. "Psalm 45:7–8 (6–7) in Old and New Testament Settings." Pp. 220–42 in *Christ the Lord: Studies in Christology Presented to Donald Guthrie.* Edited by H. H. Rowdon. Leicester: Inter-Varsity, 1982.

Allis — O. T. Allis. "'Thy throne, O God, is for ever and ever': A Study in Higher Critical Method." *Princeton Theological Review* 21 (1923): 236–66.

Althaus — P. Althaus. *Der Brief an die Römer.* Göttingen: Vandenhoeck & Ruprecht, 1966.

Amiot — F. Amiot. "Deum nemo vidit unquam: Jo., 1,18." Pp. 470–77 in *Mélanges bibliques rédigés en l'honneur de André Robert.* Paris: Bloud & Gay, 1957.

Andersen — F. I. Andersen. *The Hebrew Verbless Clause in the Pentateuch.* Nashville: Abingdon, 1970.

Anderson — A. A. Anderson. *The Book of Psalms,* vol. 1. London: Oliphants, 1972.

Andrews — E. Andrews. *The Meaning of Christ for Paul.* New York: Abingdon, 1949.

Argyle, *God* — A. W. Argyle. *God in the New Testament.* London: Hodder, 1965.

Argyle, "Evidence" — A. W. Argyle. "The Evidence for the Belief That Our Lord Himself Claimed to Be Divine." *Expository Times* 61 (1949–50): 228–32.

Ashton — J. Ashton. *Understanding the Fourth Gospel.* Oxford: Clarendon, 1991.

Attridge — H. W. Attridge. *The Epistle to the Hebrews.* Philadelphia: Fortress, 1989.

Austin M. R. Austin. "Salvation and the Divinity of Jesus." *Expository Times* 96 (1984–85): 271–75.

Bahr G. J. Bahr. "Paul and Letter Writing in the Fifth [*sic*] Century." *Catholic Biblical Quarterly* 28 (1966): 465–77.

Baillie D. M. Baillie. *God Was in Christ.* London: Faber, 1956.

Balz H. R. Balz. "Die Johannesbriefe." In *Die "katholischen" Briefe: Die Briefe des Jakobus, Petrus, Johannes und Judas.* By H. R. Balz and W. Schrage. 11th edition. Göttingen: Vandenhoeck & Ruprecht, 1973.

Barbel J. Barbel. *Christos Angelos.* Bonn: Hanstein, 1944.

Barclay, *Jesus* W. Barclay. *Jesus as They Saw Him.* London: SCM, 1962.

Barclay, "Themes" W. Barclay. "Great Themes of the New Testament, II: John i.1–14." *Expository Times* 70 (1958–59): 78–82, 114–17.

Barnett A. E. Barnett. "The Second Epistle of Peter." *IB* 12:166–206.

Barrett, *Romans* C. K. Barrett. *A Commentary on the Epistle to the Romans.* London: Black, 1962.

Barrett, *Pastoral Epistles* C. K. Barrett. *The Pastoral Epistles.* Oxford: Clarendon, 1963.

Barrett, *NT Essays* C. K. Barrett. *New Testament Essays.* London: SPCK, 1972.

Barrett, *John* C. K. Barrett. *The Gospel according to St. John.* 2d edition. London: SPCK, 1978.

Barrett, *Essays on John* C. K. Barrett. *Essays on John.* Philadelphia: Westminster, 1982.

Barrett, "Elders" C. K. Barrett. "Paul's Address to the Ephesian Elders." Pp. 107–21 in *Studies in Honour of Nils Alstrep Dahl: God's Christ and His People.* Edited by J. Jervell and W. A. Meeks. Oslo: Universitetsforlaget, 1977.

K. Barth, *Romans* K. Barth. *The Epistle to the Romans.* ETr. London: Oxford University Press, 1933.

K. Barth, *Dogmatics* K. Barth. *Church Dogmatics*, vol. 2.2: *The Doctrine of God.* ETr. Edinburgh: Clark, 1957.

M. Barth M. Barth. "The Old Testament in Hebrews." Pp. 53–78 in *Current Issues in New Testament Interpretation: Essays in Honor of Otto A. Piper.* Edited by W. Klassen and G. F. Snyder. New York: Harper & Row, 1962.

Bartlet J. V. Bartlet. *The Acts.* Edinburgh: Jack, 1901.

Bartsch H. W. Bartsch. "Röm. 9,5 und 1. Clem. 32,4: Eine notwendige Konjektur im Römerbrief." *Theologische Zeitschrift* 21 (1965): 401–9.

Bauckham, *Jude–2 Peter* R. J. Bauckham. *Jude, 2 Peter.* Waco, Tex.: Word, 1983.

Bauckham, "Worship" R. J. Bauckham. "The Worship of Jesus in Apocalyptic Christianity." *New Testament Studies* 27 (1980–81): 322–41.

Bauer W. Bauer. *Das Johannesevangelium.* 2d edition. Tübingen: Mohr, 1925.

Bauernfeind O. Bauernfeind. *Kommentar und Stüdien zur Apostelgeschichte.* Reprinted Tübingen: Mohr, 1980 (= 1939 original).

Beasley-Murray G. R. Beasley-Murray. *John.* Waco, Tex.: Word, 1987.

Becker J. Becker. *Das Evangelium nach Johannes.* 2 vols. Gütersloh: Mohn, 1979–81.

Bengel J. A. Bengel. *Gnomon of the New Testament.* ETr. Revised and edited by A. R. Fausset. 5 vols. Edinburgh: Clark, 1863.

Benoit P. Benoit. *The Passion and Resurrection of Jesus Christ.* ETr. New York: Darton, Longman & Todd, 1969.

Bentzen A. Bentzen. *King and Messiah.* London: Lutterworth, 1955.

Berkhof H. Berkhof. *Christian Faith.* ETr. Grand Rapids: Eerdmans, 1979.

Bernard, *Pastoral Epistles* J. H. Bernard. *The Pastoral Epistles.* Cambridge: Cambridge University Press, 1899.

Bernard, *John* J. H. Bernard. *A Critical and Exegetical Commentary on the Gospel according to St. John.* 2 vols. Edinburgh: Clark, 1928.

Bernhardt — K. H. Bernhardt. *Das Problem der altorientalischen Königsideologie im Alten Testament.* Leiden: Brill, 1961.

Best — E. Best. *The Letter of Paul to the Romans.* Cambridge: Cambridge University Press, 1967.

Bethge — F. H. K. Bethge. *Die paulinischen Reden der Apostelgeschichte.* Göttingen: Vandenhoeck & Ruprecht, 1887.

Beyer — K. Beyer. *Semitische Syntax im Neuen Testament,* vol. 1.1. 2d edition. Göttingen: Vandenhoeck & Ruprecht, 1968.

Bigg — C. Bigg. *A Critical and Exegetical Commentary on the Epistles of St. Peter and St. Jude.* 2d edition. Edinburgh: Clark, 1902.

Black — M. Black. *An Aramaic Approach to the Gospels and Acts.* 3d edition. Oxford: Clarendon, 1967.

Blank — J. Blank. *Das Evangelium nach Johannes.* 2 vols. Düsseldorf: Patmos, 1977–81.

Blass — F. Blass. *Euangelium secundum Iohannem cum variae lectionis delectu.* Leipzig: Teubner, 1902.

Boismard, *Prologue* — M. E. Boismard. *St. John's Prologue.* ETr. Westminster, Md.: Newman, 1957.

Boismard, "Sein" — M. E. Boismard. "'Dans le sein du Père' (Jo., 1,18)." *Revue Biblique* 59 (1952): 23–39.

Bonnard — P. Bonnard. *Les Épîtres Johanniques.* Genève: Labor & Fides, 1983.

Bonsirven, *Témoin* — J. Bonsirven. *Le témoin du verbe: Le Disciple Bien-aimé.* Toulouse: Apostolat de la Prière, 1956.

Bonsirven, *Theology* — J. Bonsirven. *Theology of the New Testament.* ETr. Westminster, Md.: Newman, 1963.

Boobyer — G. H. Boobyer. "Jesus as 'Theos' in the New Testament." *Bulletin of the John Rylands Library* 50 (1967–68): 247–61.

Bousset — W. Bousset. *Kyrios Christos.* ETr. New York: Abingdon, 1970.

Bowker — J. W. Bowker. *The Religious Imagination and the Sense of God.* New York: Oxford University Press, 1978.

Boyle — M. O. Boyle. "Sermo: Reopening the Conversation on Translating Jn 1,1." *Vigiliae Christianae* 31 (1977): 161–68.

Bratcher — R. G. Bratcher. "A Note on υἱὸς θεοῦ (Mark xv.39)." *Expository Times* 68 (1956–57): 27–28.

Braun — F. M. Braun. *Jean le théologien,* vol. 3.1: *Le mystère de Jésus-Christ;* vol. 3.2: *Le Christ, notre Seigneur.* Paris: Gabalda, 1966–72.

Briggs, *Prophecy* — C. A. Briggs. *Messianic Prophecy.* New York: Scribner, 1886.

Briggs, *Psalms* — C. A. Briggs and E. G. Briggs. *A Critical and Exegetical Commentary on the Book of Psalms,* vol. 1. Edinburgh: Clark, 1906.

Brooke — A. E. Brooke. *A Critical and Exegetical Commentary on the Johannine Epistles.* Edinburgh: Clark, 1912.

Brown, *Gospel* — R. E. Brown. *The Gospel according to John.* 2 vols. Garden City, N.Y.: Doubleday, 1966.

Brown, *Reflections* — R. E. Brown. *Jesus, God and Man: Modern Biblical Reflections.* Milwaukee: Bruce, 1967.

Brown, *Epistles* — R. E. Brown. *The Epistles of John.* Garden City, N.Y.: Doubleday, 1982.

Brown, "Historicity" — R. E. Brown. "The Problem of Historicity in John." Pp. 143–67 in his *New Testament Essays.* Milwaukee: Bruce, 1965.

Brown, "Jesus" — R. E. Brown. "Does the New Testament Call Jesus God?" *Theological Studies* 26 (1965): 545–73. Reprinted in R. E. Brown, *Reflections* 1–38.

Broyles — S. E. Broyles. "What Do We Mean by 'Godhead'?" *Evangelical Quarterly* 50 (1978): 223–29.

Bruce, *Romans* — F. F. Bruce. *The Epistle of Paul to the Romans.* Grand Rapids: Eerdmans, 1963.

Bruce, *Paraphrase* — F. F. Bruce. *An Expanded Paraphrase of the Epistles of Paul.* Exeter: Paternoster, 1965.

Bruce, *Epistles* — F. F. Bruce. *The Epistles of John.* London: Pickering & Inglis, 1970.

Bruce, *John* — F. F. Bruce. *The Gospel of John.* Grand Rapids: Eerdmans, 1983.

Bruce, *Acts (NIC)* — F. F. Bruce. *Commentary on the Book of the Acts.* 2d edition. Grand Rapids: Eerdmans, 1989.

Bruce, *Hebrews* — F. F. Bruce. *Commentary on the Epistle to the Hebrews.* 2d edition. Grand Rapids: Eerdmans, 1990.

Bruce, *Acts* — F. F. Bruce. *The Acts of the Apostles.* 3d edition. Grand Rapids: Eerdmans, 1991.

Bruce, "God" — F. F. Bruce. "'Our God and Saviour': A Recurring Biblical Pattern." Pp. 51–66 in *The Saviour God: Comparative Studies in the Concept of Salvation Presented to Edwin Oliver James.* Edited by S. G. F. Brandon. New York: Barnes & Noble, 1963.

Bruce, "Hebrews" — F. F. Bruce. "Hebrews." Pp. 1008–19 in *Peake's Commentary on the Bible.* Edited by M. Black and H. H. Rowley. London: Nelson, 1962.

Bruce, "Speeches" — F. F. Bruce. "The Speeches in Acts: Thirty Years After." Pp. 53–68 in *Reconciliation and Hope: New Testament Essays on Atonement and Eschatology Presented to L. L. Morris.* Edited by R. Banks. Grand Rapids: Eerdmans, 1974.

Bruston — C. Bruston. *Du texte primitif des Psaumes.* Paris: Sandoz & Fischbacher, 1873.

Buchanan, *Hebrews* — G. W. Buchanan. *To the Hebrews.* Garden City, N.Y.: Doubleday, 1972.

Buchanan, "Christology" — G. W. Buchanan. "Apostolic Christology." Pp. 172–82 in *Society of Biblical Literature Seminar Papers*, vol. 25. Edited by K. H. Richards. Atlanta: Scholars Press, 1986.

Bultmann, *Theology* — R. Bultmann. *Theology of the New Testament.* 2 vols. ETr. London: SCM, 1952–55.

Bultmann, *Essays* — R. Bultmann. *Essays Philosophical and Theological.* ETr. London: SCM, 1955.

Bultmann, *John* — R. Bultmann. *Gospel of John: A Commentary.* ETr. Philadelphia: Westminster, 1971.

Bultmann, *Epistles* — R. Bultmann. *The Johannine Epistles.* ETr. Philadelphia: Fortress, 1973.

Bultmann, "Untersuchungen" — R. Bultmann. "Untersuchungen zum Johannesevangelium, B: θεὸν οὐδεις ἑώρακεν πώποτε." *Zeitschrift für die Neutestamentliche Wissenschaft* 29 (1930): 169–92. Reprinted in his *Exegetica*, pp. 174–97. Edited by E. Dinkler. Tübingen: Mohr, 1967.

Burkitt, *Beginnings* — F. C. Burkitt. *Christian Beginnings.* London: University of London Press, 1924.

Burkitt, *Church* — F. C. Burkitt. *Church and Gnosis.* Cambridge: Cambridge University Press, 1932.

Burkitt, "Romans" — F. C. Burkitt. "On Romans ix 5 and Mark xiv 61." *Journal of Theological Studies* 5 (1904): 451–55.

Burkitt, "Punctuation" — F. C. Burkitt. "The Punctuation of New Testament Manuscripts." *Journal of Theological Studies* 29 (1928): 397–98.

Burney — C. F. Burney. *The Aramaic Origin of the Fourth Gospel.* Oxford: Clarendon, 1922.

E. D. Burton — E. D. Burton. *A Critical and Exegetical Commentary on Paul's Epistle to the Galatians.* Edinburgh: Clark, 1912.

H. F. Burton — H. F. Burton. "The Worship of the Roman Emperors." *Biblical World* 40 (1912): 80–91.

Buttenwieser — M. Buttenwieser. *The Psalms.* Reprinted New York: Ktav, 1969 (= 1938 original).

Butterworth — R. Butterworth. "Bishop Robinson and Christology": Review of *The Human Face of God* by J. A. T. Robinson. *Religious Studies* 11 (1975): 73–85.

Buttmann — A. Buttmann. *A Grammar of the New Testament Greek.* Andover, Mass.: Draper, 1873.

Cadbury, "Titles" — H. J. Cadbury. "The Titles of Jesus in Acts." *BC* 5:354–75.

Cadbury, "Speeches" — H. J. Cadbury. "The Speeches in Acts." *BC* 5:402–27.

Cadman	W. H. Cadman. *The Open Heaven: The Revelation of God in the Johannine Sayings of Jesus.* Edited by G. B. Caird. Oxford: Blackwell, 1969.
Caird, *Language*	G. B. Caird. *The Language and Imagery of the Bible.* Philadelphia: Westminster, 1980.
Caird, "Hebrews"	G. B. Caird. "The Exegetical Method of the Epistle to the Hebrews." *Canadian Journal of Theology* 5 (1959): 44–51.
Calès	J. Calès. *Le Livre des Psaumes*, vol. 1. Paris: Beauchesne, 1936.
Caloz	M. Caloz. *Étude sur la LXX Origenienne du Psautier.* Göttingen: Vandenhoeck & Ruprecht, 1978.
Calvin, *Hebrews–Peter*	J. Calvin. *The Epistle of Paul the Apostle to the Hebrews and the First and Second Epistles of St Peter.* ETr. Edinburgh: Oliver & Boyd, 1963.
Calvin, *Acts*	J. Calvin. *The Acts of the Apostles*, vol. 2. 2d edition. ETr. Edited by D. W. Torrance and T. F. Torrance. Grand Rapids: Eerdmans, 1973.
Caragounis	C. C. Caragounis. *The Ephesian Mysterion: Meaning and Content.* Lund: Gleerup, 1977.
Carson, *Responsibility*	D. A. Carson. *Divine Sovereignty and Human Responsibility.* London: Marshall, 1981.
Carson, *John*	D. A. Carson. *The Gospel according to John.* Grand Rapids: Eerdmans, 1991.
Casey, *Prophet*	M. Casey. *From Jewish Prophet to Gentile God.* Louisville: Westminster/John Knox, 1991.
Casey, "Chronology"	M. Casey. "Chronology and the Development of Pauline Christology." Pp. 124–34 in *Paul and Paulinism: Essays in Honour of C. K. Barrett.* Edited by M. D. Hooker and S. G. Wilson. London: SPCK, 1982.
Cassuto	U. Cassuto. *The Documentary Hypothesis and the Composition of the Pentateuch.* ETr. Jerusalem: Magnes, 1961.
Cerfaux, *Christ*	L. Cerfaux. *Christ in the Theology of St. Paul.* ETr. Edited by G. Webb and A. Walker. New York: Herder, 1959.
Cerfaux, *Church*	L. Cerfaux. *The Church in the Theology of St. Paul.* ETr. New York: Herder, 1959.
Cerfaux and Dupont	L. Cerfaux and J. Dupont. *Les Actes des Apôtres.* 2d edition. Paris: Cerf, 1958.
Cerfaux and Tondriau	L. Cerfaux and J. Tondriau. *Le culte des souverains dans la civilisation gréco-romaine.* Tournai: Desclée, 1957.
Chaine	J. Chaine. *Les Épîtres Catholiques.* 2d edition. Paris: Gabalda, 1939.
Champion	L. G. Champion. *Benedictions and Doxologies in the Epistles of Paul.* Oxford: Kemp Hall, 1935.
Chantraine	P. Chantraine. *Dictionnaire étymologique de la langue grecque: Histoire de mots*, vol. 2. Paris: Klincksieck, 1970.
Chase	F. H. Chase. *The Credibility of the Book of the Acts of the Apostles.* London: Macmillan, 1902.
Cheyne, *Psalter*	T. K. Cheyne. *The Origin and Religious Contents of the Psalter.* London: Paul, Trench, Trübner, 1891.
Cheyne, *Psalms*	T. K. Cheyne. *The Book of Psalms*, vol. 1. London: Paul, 1904.
Clark	A. C. Clark. *The Acts of the Apostles.* Oxford: Clarendon, 1933.
Clements	R. E. Clements. "Monotheism and the Canonical Process." *Theology* 87 (1984): 336–44.
Clines	D. J. A. Clines. "The Psalms and the King." *Theological Students' Fellowship Bulletin* 71 (1975): 1–6.
Coggan	D. Coggan. *The Prayers of the New Testament.* London: Hodder, 1967.
Colwell, *Greek*	E. C. Colwell. *The Greek of the Fourth Gospel.* Chicago: University of Chicago Press, 1931.
Colwell, "Rule"	E. C. Colwell. "A Definite Rule for the Use of the Article in the Greek New Testament." *Journal of Biblical Literature* 52 (1933): 12–21.
Colwell, "Papyri"	E. C. Colwell. "Scribal Habits in Early Papyri: A Study in the Corruption of the Text." Pp. 370–89 in *The Bible in Modern Scholarship.* Edited by J. P. Hyatt. Nashville: Abingdon/London: Carey Kingsgate, 1965.

Combrink — H. J. B. Combrink. "Some Thoughts on the Old Testament Citations in the Epistle to the Hebrews." *Neotestamentica 5* (1971): 22–36.

Conzelmann — H. Conzelmann. *Acts of the Apostles.* ETr. Philadelphia: Fortress, 1987.

Corell — A. Corell. *Consummatum est.* London: SPCK, 1958.

Cotter — A. C. Cotter. "The Divinity of Jesus Christ in Saint Paul." *Catholic Biblical Quarterly* 7 (1945): 259–89.

Countess — R. H. Countess. "The Translation of θεός in the New World Translation." *Bulletin of the Evangelical Theological Society* 10 (1967): 153–60.

Couroyer, "Review" — B. Couroyer. Review of *L'expression de la louange divine et de la prière dans la Bible et en Égypt* by A. Barucq. *Revue Biblique* 72 (1965): 281–86.

Couroyer, "Psaume xlv" — B. Couroyer. "Dieu ou roi? Le vocatif dans le Psaume xlv (vv. 1–9)." *Revue Biblique* 78 (1971): 233–41.

Craigie — P. C. Craigie. *Psalms 1–50.* Waco, Tex.: Word, 1983.

Cranfield, *Peter–Jude* — C. E. B. Cranfield. *I and II Peter and Jude.* London: SCM, 1960.

Cranfield, *Romans* — C. E. B. Cranfield. *A Critical and Exegetical Commentary on the Epistle to the Romans*, vol. 2. Edinburgh: Clark, 1979.

Cranfield, *Shorter Commentary* — C. E. B. Cranfield. *Romans: A Shorter Commentary.* Edinburgh: Clark, 1985.

Cranfield, "Comments" — C. E. B. Cranfield. "Some Comments on Professor J. D. G. Dunn's Christology in the Making with Special Reference to the Evidence of the Epistle to the Romans." Pp. 267–80 in *The Glory of Christ in the New Testament: Studies in Christology in Memory of George Bradford Caird.* Edited by L. D. Hurst and N. T. Wright. New York: Oxford University Press, 1987.

Crawford, "Christ" — R. G. Crawford. "Is Christ Inferior to God?" *Evangelical Quarterly* 43 (1971): 203–9.

Crawford, "Pittenger" — R. G. Crawford. "Pittenger on the Divinity of Christ." *Modern Churchman* 15 (1971–72): 121–22.

Cremer — H. Cremer. *Biblico-Theological Lexicon of New Testament Greek.* 3d edition. ETr. Edinburgh: Clark, 1883.

Cullmann, *Christology* — O. Cullmann. *The Christology of the New Testament.* ETr. London: SCM, 1959.

Cullmann, "Reply" — O. Cullmann. "The Reply of Professor Cullmann to Roman Catholic Critics." *Scottish Journal of Theology* 15 (1962): 36–43.

Culpepper — R. A. Culpepper. "The Pivot of John's Prologue." *New Testament Studies* 27 (1980–81): 1–31.

Cupitt — D. Cupitt. *The Debate about Christ.* London: SCM, 1979.

Dahl — N. A. Dahl. "The Neglected Factor in New Testament Theology." *Reflection* 73 (1975): 5–8.

Dahl and Segal — N. A. Dahl and A. F. Segal. "Philo and the Rabbis on the Name of God." *Journal for the Study of Judaism in the Persian, Hellenistic and Roman Periods* 9 (1978): 1–28.

Dahood — M. Dahood. *Psalms*, vol. 1. Garden City, N.Y.: Doubleday, 1966.

Dana and Mantey — H. E. Dana and J. R. Mantey. *A Manual Grammar of the Greek New Testament.* New York: Macmillan, 1957.

Daniélou, *Anges* — J. Daniélou. *Les anges et leur mission d'après les pères de l'église.* 2d edition. Brussels: Chevetogne, 1953.

Daniélou, *Theology* — J. Daniélou. *The Theology of Jewish Christianity.* ETr. London: Darton, Longman & Todd, 1964.

Danker — F. W. Danker. "2 Peter 1: A Solemn Decree." *Catholic Biblical Quarterly* 40 (1978): 64–82.

D'Aragon — J. L. D'Aragon. "Jésus de Nazareth était-il Dieu?" Pp. 193–217 in *Jésus: De l'histoire à la foi.* Edited by J. L. D'Aragon et al. Montreal: Fides, 1974.

Darlow — T. H. Darlow (ed.). *William Robertson Nicoll: Life and Letters.* London: Hodder & Stoughton, 1925.

Davidson — A. B. Davidson. *The Epistle to the Hebrews.* Edinburgh: Clark, n.d.

de Ausejo — S. de Ausejo. "Es un himno a Cristo el prólogo de San Juan?" *Estudios Bíblicos* 15 (1956): 381–427.

de Boor, *Apostelgeschichte* — W. de Boor. *Die Apostelgeschichte.* Wuppertal: Brockhaus, 1965.

de Boor, *Römer* — W. de Boor. *Der Brief des Paulus an die Römer.* 2d edition. Wuppertal: Brockhaus, 1967.

de Fraine — J. de Fraine. *L'aspect religieux de la royauté israélite.* Rome: Pontifical Biblical Institute, 1954.

Deichgräber — R. Deichgräber. *Gotteshymnus und Christushymnus in der frühen Christenheit: Untersuchungen zu Form, Sprach und Stil der frühchristlichen Hymnen.* Göttingen: Vandenhoeck & Ruprecht, 1967.

Deissmann — A. Deissmann. *Light from the Ancient East.* ETr. Reprinted Grand Rapids: Baker, 1965 (= 1927 original).

de Jonge and van der Woude — M. de Jonge and A. S. van der Woude. "11Q Melchizedek and the New Testament." *New Testament Studies* 12 (1965–66): 301–26.

de Kruijf — T. C. de Kruijf. "The Glory of the Only Son (John i 14)." Pp. 111–23 in *Studies in John Presented to Professor Dr. J. N. Sevenster.* Edited by T. C. de Kruijf. Leiden: Brill, 1970.

de Lacey — D. R. de Lacey. "'One Lord' in Pauline Christology." Pp. 191–203 in *Christ the Lord: Studies in Christology Presented to Donald Guthrie.* Edited by H. H. Rowdon. Leicester: Inter-Varsity, 1982.

de la Potterie, *Vérité* — I. de la Potterie. *La vérité dans Saint Jean.* 2 vols. Rome: Pontifical Biblical Institute, 1977.

de la Potterie, "L'emploi" — I. de la Potterie. "L'emploi dynamique de εἰς dans Saint Jean et ses incidences théologiques." *Biblica* 43 (1962): 366–87.

Delitzsch, *Hebrews* — F. Delitzsch. *Commentary on the Epistle to the Hebrews.* 2 vols. ETr. Edinburgh: Clark, 1886.

Delitzsch, *Psalms* — F. Delitzsch. *Biblical Commentary on the Psalms,* vol. 2. ETr. 2d edition. London: Hodder, 1902.

Delling — G. Delling. *Wort und Werk Jesu im Johannes-Evangelium.* Berlin: Evangelische Verlagsanstalt, 1966.

Demarest — B. Demarest. *A History of Interpretation of Hebrews 7, 1–10 from the Reformation to the Present.* Tübingen: Mohr, 1976.

Denney — J. Denney. "St. Paul's Epistle to the Romans." *EGT* 2:555–725.

DeVine — C. F. DeVine. "The 'Blood of God' in Acts 20:28." *Catholic Biblical Quarterly* 9 (1947): 381–408.

Dewailly — L. M. Dewailly. "'La parole parlait à Dieu'?" *Revue de Théologie et de Philosophie* 100 (1967): 123–28.

Dey — L. K. K. Dey. *The Intermediary World and Patterns of Perfection in Philo and Hebrews.* Missoula, Mont.: Scholars Press, 1975.

Dibelius — M. Dibelius. *Die Pastoralbriefe.* 2d edition. Tübingen: Mohr, 1931.

Dibelius and Conzelmann — M. Dibelius and H. Conzelmann, *The Pastoral Epistles.* ETr. Philadelphia: Fortress, 1972.

Dittenberger — W. Dittenberger. *Sylloge Inscriptionum Graecarum,* vol. 2. 4th edition. Hildesheim: Olms, 1960.

Dix — G. Dix. *Jew and Greek.* Westminster: Dacre, 1953.

Dodd, *Romans* — C. H. Dodd. *The Epistle to the Romans.* London: Hodder & Stoughton, 1932.

Dodd, *Epistles* — C. H. Dodd. *The Johannine Epistles.* London: Hodder & Stoughton, 1946.

Dodd, *Interpretation* — C. H. Dodd. *The Interpretation of the Fourth Gospel.* Cambridge: Cambridge University Press, 1953.

Dodd, *Tradition* — C. H. Dodd. *Historical Tradition in the Fourth Gospel.* Cambridge: Cambridge University Press, 1963.

Dodd, *Studies* — C. H. Dodd. *More New Testament Studies.* Grand Rapids: Eerdmans, 1968.

Dodd, "Appearances"	C. H. Dodd. "The Appearances of the Risen Christ: An Essay in Form-Criticism of the Gospels." Pp. 9–35 in *Studies in the Gospels: Essays in Memory of R. H. Lightfoot.* Edited by D. E. Nineham. Oxford: Blackwell, 1955. Reprinted in Dodd, *Studies* 102–33.
Dodd, "Problems"	C. H. Dodd. "New Testament Translation Problems II." *Bible Translator* 28 (1977): 101–16.
Dods	M. Dods. "The Epistle to the Hebrews." *EGT* 4:219–381.
Dreyfus	F. Dreyfus. *Did Jesus Know He Was God?* ETr. Chicago: Franciscan Herald, 1989.
G. R. Driver, *Documents*	G. R. Driver. *Aramaic Documents of the Fifth Century* B.C. Oxford: Oxford University Press, 1957.
G. R. Driver, "Study"	G. R. Driver. "The Modern Study of the Hebrew Language." Pp. 73–120 in *The People and the Book.* Edited by A. S. Peake. Oxford: Clarendon, 1925.
G. R. Driver, "Psalms"	G. R. Driver. "The Psalms in Light of Babylonian Research." Pp. 109–75 in *The Psalmists.* Edited by D. C. Simpson. Oxford: Oxford University Press, 1926.
G. R. Driver, "Yahweh"	G. R. Driver. "The Original Form of the Name 'Yahweh': Evidence and Conclusions." *Zeitschrift für die Alttestamentliche Wissenschaft* 46 (1928): 7–25.
S. R. Driver	S. R. Driver. *A Treatise on the Use of the Tenses in Hebrew.* Oxford: Clarendon, 1892.
du Bose	W. P. du Bose. *The Ecumenical Councils.* 4th edition. New York: Scribner, 1910.
Duhm	B. Duhm. *Die Psalmen.* Leipzig: Mohr, 1899.
Dunn, *Baptism*	J. D. G. Dunn. *Baptism in the Holy Spirit.* London: SCM, 1970.
Dunn, *Unity*	J. D. G. Dunn. *Unity and Diversity in the New Testament.* London: SCM, 1977.
Dunn, *Christology*	J. D. G. Dunn. *Christology in the Making.* London: SCM, 1980.
Dunn, *Romans*	J. D. G. Dunn. *Romans 9–16.* Dallas: Word, 1988.
Dunn, *Partings*	J. D. G. Dunn. *The Partings of the Ways.* Philadelphia: Trinity, 1991.
Dunn, "Christianity"	J. D. G. Dunn. "Was Christianity a Monotheistic Faith from the Beginning?" *Scottish Journal of Theology* 35 (1982): 303–36.
du Plessis	I. J. du Plessis. "Christ as the 'Only Begotten.'" *Neotestamentica* 2 (1968): 22–31.
Dupont, *Discours*	J. Dupont. *Le discours de Milet: Testament pastoral de Saint Paul (Actes 20,18–36).* Paris: Cerf, 1962.
Dupont, *Christologie*	J. Dupont. *Essais sur la christologie de Saint Jean: Le Christ, parole, lumière et vie; la gloire du Christ.* Bruges: L'Abbaye de Saint-André, 1951.
Durand	A. Durand. "La divinité de Jésus-Christ dans S. Paul, Rom. ix,5." *Revue Biblique* 12 (1903): 550–70.
Dussaut	L. Dussaut. *Synopse structurelle de l'Épître aux Hebreux: Approche d'analyse structurelle.* Paris: Cerf, 1981.
Dwight, "Notes"	T. Dwight. Supplementary Notes in H. A. W. Meyer, *Critical and Exegetical Hand-book to the Epistle to the Romans.* New York: Funk & Wagnalls, 1889.
Dwight, "Romans"	T. Dwight. "On Romans ix.5." *Journal of Biblical Literature* 1 (1881): 22–55.
Easton	B. S. Easton. *The Pastoral Epistles.* New York: Scribner, 1948.
Eaton, *Psalms*	J. H. Eaton. *Psalms.* London: SCM, 1967.
Eaton, *Kingship*	J. H. Eaton. *Kingship and the Psalms.* London: SCM, 1976.
Ebrard	J. H. A. Ebrard. *Biblical Commentary on the Epistles of St. John.* ETr. Edinburgh: Clark, 1860.
Eichrodt	W. Eichrodt. *Theology of the Old Testament,* vol. 1. ETr. Philadelphia: Westminster, 1961.

Eissfeldt — O. Eissfeldt. "'My God' in the Old Testament." *Evangelical Quarterly* 19 (1947): 7–20.

Ellicott — C. J. Ellicott. *The Pastoral Epistles of St. Paul.* 5th edition. London: Longmans, 1883.

Elliott — J. K. Elliott. *The Greek Text of the Epistles to Timothy and Titus.* Salt Lake City: University of Utah Press, 1968.

Ellis — E. E. Ellis. "Background and Christology of John's Gospel: Selected Motifs." *Southwestern Journal of Theology* 31 (1988–89): 24–31.

Elwell — W. Elwell. "The Deity of Christ in the Writings of Paul." Pp. 297–308 in *Current Issues in Biblical and Patristic Interpretation: Studies in Honor of Merrill C. Tenney.* Edited by G. F. Hawthorne. Grand Rapids: Eerdmans, 1975.

Emerton — J. A. Emerton. "The Syntactical Problem of Psalm xlv.7." *Journal of Semitic Studies* 13 (1968): 58–63.

Engnell — I. Engnell. *Studies in Divine Kingship in the Ancient Near East.* 2d edition. Oxford: Blackwell, 1967.

Enz — J. J. Enz. "The Book of Exodus as a Literary Type for the Gospel of John." *Journal of Biblical Literature* 76 (1957): 208–15.

Erickson — M. J. Erickson. *The Word Became Flesh: A Contemporary Incarnational Christology.* Grand Rapids: Baker, 1991.

Ewald, *Psalms* — H. A. von Ewald. *Commentary on the Psalms,* vol. 1. ETr. London: Williams & Norgate, 1880.

Ewald, *Syntax* — H. A. von Ewald. *Syntax of the Hebrew Language of the Old Testament.* ETr. Edinburgh: Clark, 1881.

Faccio — H. M. Faccio. *De divinitate Christi juxta S. Paulum, Rom. 9,5.* Jerusalem: Franciscan Printing Press, 1945.

Fahy — T. Fahy. "A Note on Romans 9:1–18." *Irish Theological Quarterly* 32 (1965): 261–62.

Farrar, *Hebrews* — F. W. Farrar. *The Epistle of Paul the Apostle to the Hebrews.* Cambridge: Cambridge University Press, 1894.

Farrar, "Readings" — F. W. Farrar. "A Few Various Readings in the New Testament." *Expositor,* 1st ser., 9 (1882): 375–93.

Fee, *Timothy–Titus* — G. D. Fee. *1 and 2 Timothy; Titus.* 2d edition. Peabody, Mass.: Hendrickson, 1988.

Fee, "Sinaiticus" — G. D. Fee. "Codex Sinaiticus in the Gospel of John: A Contribution to Methodology in Establishing Textual Relationships." *New Testament Studies* 15 (1968–69): 23–44.

Fee, "Article" — G. D. Fee. "The Use of the Definite Article with Personal Names in the Gospel of John." *New Testament Studies* 17 (1970–71): 168–83.

Fee, "Critique" — G. D. Fee. "The Text of John in *The Jerusalem Bible:* A Critique of the Use of Patristic Citations in New Testament Textual Criticism." *Journal of Biblical Literature* 90 (1971): 163–73.

Fee, "Contribution" — G. D. Fee. "The Text of John in Origen and Cyril of Alexandria: A Contribution to Methodology in the Recovery and Analysis of Patristic Citations." *Biblica* 52 (1971): 357–94.

Fennema — D. A. Fennema. "John 1.18: 'God the Only Son.'" *New Testament Studies* 31 (1985–86): 124–35.

Fenton — J. C. Fenton. "Matthew and the Divinity of Jesus: Three Questions concerning Matthew 1:20–23." Pp. 79–82 in *Studia Biblica 1978,* vol. 2: *Papers on the Gospels.* Edited by E. A. Livingstone. Sheffield: JSOT Press, 1980.

Ferré — N. F. S. Ferré. "Is the Basis of the World Council Heretical?" *Expository Times* 74 (1962–63): 66–68.

Feuillet, *Prologue* — A. Feuillet. *Le prologue du Quatrième Évangile.* Paris: Desclée de Brouwer, 1968.

Feuillet, *Mystère* — A. Feuillet. *Le mystère de l'amour divin dans la théologie johannique.* Paris: Gabalda, 1972.

Feuillet, *Christologie*	A. Feuillet. *Christologie paulinienne et tradition biblique.* Paris: Desclée de Brouwer, 1973.
Field, *Origenis*	F. Field. *Origenis Hexaplorum quae supersunt.* 2 vols. Oxford: Clarendon, 1875.
Field, *Notes*	F. Field. *Notes on the Translation of the New Testament.* Cambridge: Cambridge University Press, 1899.
Filson	F. V. Filson. *"Yesterday": A Study of Hebrews in the Light of Chapter 13.* London: SCM, 1967.
Findlay	G. G. Findlay. *Fellowship in the Life Eternal.* London: Hodder & Stoughton, 1919.
Finegan	J. Finegan. *Encountering New Testament Manuscripts.* Grand Rapids: Eerdmans, 1974.
Fitzmyer, *Aramean*	J. A. Fitzmyer. *A Wandering Aramean: Collected Aramaic Essays.* Missoula, Mont.: Scholars Press, 1979.
Fitzmyer, *Scripture*	J. A. Fitzmyer. *Scripture and Christology.* New York: Paulist, 1986.
Fornberg	T. Fornberg. *An Early Church in a Pluralistic Society: A Study of 2 Peter.* Lund: Gleerup, 1977.
Fortman	E. J. Fortman. *The Triune God: A Historical Study of the Doctrine of the Trinity.* Westminster: Philadelphia, 1972.
Fortna	R. T. Fortna. *The Gospel of Signs.* Cambridge: Cambridge University Press, 1970.
Fowler	W. W. Fowler. *Roman Ideas of Deity.* Reprinted Freeport, N.Y.: Books for Libraries, 1969 (= 1914 original).
France, *Jesus*	R. T. France. *Jesus and the Old Testament.* Downers Grove, Ill.: Inter-Varsity, 1971.
France, "Uniqueness"	R. T. France. "The Uniqueness of Christ." *Churchman* 95 (1981): 200–217.
Franklin	E. Franklin. *Christ the Lord: A Study in the Purpose and Theology of Luke–Acts.* Philadelphia: Westminster, 1975.
Fuchs and Reymond	E. Fuchs and P. Reymond. *La Deuxième Épître de Saint Pierre; l'Épître de Saint Jude.* Neuchâtel: Delachaux & Niestlé, 1980.
Fuller, *Foundations*	R. H. Fuller. *The Foundations of New Testament Christology.* New York: Scribner, 1965.
Fuller, "Christology"	R. H. Fuller. "Pre-existence Christology: Can We Dispense with It?" *Word and World* 2 (1982): 29–33.
Fuller, "Jesus"	R. H. Fuller. "The Theology of Jesus or Christology: An Evaluation of the Recent Discussion." *Semeia* 30 (1984): 105–16.
Fuller and Perkins	R. H. Fuller and P. Perkins. *Who Is This Christ? Gospel Christology and Contemporary Faith.* Philadelphia: Fortress, 1983.
Funk	R. W. Funk. *The Syntax of the Greek Article: Its Importance for Critical Pauline Problems.* Ph.D. dissertation, Vanderbilt University, 1953.
Gaster	T. H. Gaster. "Psalm 45." *Journal of Biblical Literature* 74 (1955): 239–51.
Gealy	F. D. Gealy. "The First and Second Epistles to Timothy and the Epistle to Titus." *IB* 11:343–551.
Gesenius	H. Gesenius. *Gesenius' Hebrew and Chaldee Lexicon to the Old Testament Scriptures.* ETr. London: Bagster, 1846.
Gianotti	C. R. Gianotti. "The Meaning of the Divine Name YHWH." *Bibliotheca Sacra* 142 (1985): 38–51.
Giblin	C. H. Giblin. "Three Monotheistic Texts in Paul." *Catholic Biblical Quarterly* 37 (1975): 527–47.
Gifford	E. H. Gifford. *The Epistle of St. Paul to the Romans.* London: Murray, 1886.
Gildersleeve	B. L. Gildersleeve. "On the Article with Proper Names." *American Journal of Philology* 11 (1890): 483–87.
Gildersleeve and Miller	B. L. Gildersleeve and C. W. E. Miller. *Syntax of Classical Greek from Homer to Demosthenes.* 2 vols. New York: American Book Company, 1900–1911.

Giles	K. N. Giles. "Luke's Version of the Term 'ἐκκλησία' with Special Reference to Acts 20.28 and 9.31." *New Testament Studies* 31 (1985): 135–42.
Glasson, *Moses*	T. F. Glasson. *Moses in the Fourth Gospel.* London: SCM, 1963.
Glasson, "Plurality"	T. F. Glasson. "'Plurality of Divine Persons' and the Quotations in Hebrews 1.6ff." *New Testament Studies* 12 (1965–66): 270–72.
Godet, *Romans*	F. Godet. *Commentary on St. Paul's Epistle to the Romans,* vol. 2. ETr. Edinburgh: Clark, 1892.
Godet, *John*	F. Godet. *Commentary on the Gospel of St. John.* 3 vols. ETr. Reprinted Grand Rapids: Zondervan, 1969 (= 1877 original).
Goodenough	E. R. Goodenough. *By Light, Light.* Amsterdam: Philo, 1969.
Goppelt	L. Goppelt. *Theology of the New Testament.* 2 vols. Edited by J. Roloff. Grand Rapids: Eerdmans, 1981–82.
Gordon, "אלהים"	C. H. Gordon. "אלהים in Its Reputed Meaning of *Rulers, Judges.*" *Journal of Biblical Literature* 54 (1935): 139–44.
Gordon, "Psalm 82"	C. H. Gordon. "History of Religion in Psalm 82." Pp. 129–31 in *Biblical and Near Eastern Studies: Essays in Honor of William Sanford LaSor.* Edited by G. A. Tuttle. Grand Rapids: Eerdmans, 1978.
Goulder	M. D. Goulder. *The Psalms of the Sons of Korah.* Sheffield: University of Sheffield, Department of Biblical Studies, 1982.
Granbery	J. C. Granbery. *Outline of New Testament Christology.* Chicago: University of Chicago Press, 1909.
Grant	F. C. Grant. "'Only-Begotten': A Footnote to the RSV." *Bible Translator* 17 (1966): 11–14.
Grayston	K. Grayston. *The Johannine Epistles.* London: Marshall, 1984.
E. M. B. Green, *Reconsidered*	E. M. B. Green. *2 Peter Reconsidered.* London: Tyndale, 1961.
E. M. B. Green, *2 Peter–Jude*	E. M. B. Green. *The Second Epistle General of Peter and the General Epistle of Jude.* 2d edition. Grand Rapids: Eerdmans, 1987.
H. C. Green	H. C. Green. "The Composition of St. John's Prologue." *Expository Times* 66 (1954–55): 291–94.
Greenlee, *Introduction*	J. H. Greenlee. *Introduction to New Testament Textual Criticism.* Grand Rapids: Eerdmans, 1964.
Greenlee, *Grammar*	J. H. Greenlee. *A Concise Exegetical Grammar of New Testament Greek.* 5th edition. Grand Rapids: Eerdmans, 1986.
Greenlee, "Article"	J. H. Greenlee. "The Greek Definite Article." *Bible Translator* 1 (1950): 162–65.
Greenlee, "Preposition"	J. H. Greenlee. "The Preposition εἰς in the New Testament." *Bible Translator* 3 (1952): 12–14.
Griffiths	J. G. Griffiths. "A Note on the Anarthrous Predicate in Hellenistic Greek." *Expository Times* 62 (1950–51): 314–15.
Grundmann	W. Grundmann. *Der Brief des Judas und der zweite Brief des Petrus.* Berlin: Evangelische Verlagsanstalt, 1974.
Gundry, *Use*	R. H. Gundry. *The Use of the Old Testament in St. Matthew's Gospel.* Leiden: Brill, 1967.
Gundry, *Matthew*	R. H. Gundry. *Matthew.* Grand Rapids: Eerdmans, 1982.
Gunkel	H. Gunkel. *Die Psalmen.* 4th edition. Göttingen: Vandenhoeck & Ruprecht, 1926.
Gunton	C. E. Gunton. *Yesterday and Today: A Study of Continuities in Christology.* Grand Rapids: Eerdmans, 1983.
Guthrie, *Mind*	D. Guthrie. *The Pastoral Epistles and the Mind of Paul.* London: Tyndale, 1956.
Guthrie, *Hebrews*	D. Guthrie. *The Letter to the Hebrews.* Leicester: Inter-Varsity, 1983.
Guthrie, *Pastoral Epistles*	D. Guthrie. *The Pastoral Epistles.* 2d edition. Grand Rapids: Eerdmans, 1990.

Haas — C. Haas. *A Translator's Handbook on the Letters of John*, by C. Haas, M. de Jonge, and J. L. Swellengrebel. London: United Bible Societies, 1972.

Haenchen, *Acts* — E. Haenchen. *The Acts of the Apostles.* ETr. Philadelphia: Westminster, 1971.

Haenchen, *John* — E. Haenchen. *John*, vol. 1: *A Commentary on the Gospel of John, Chapters 1–6.* ETr. Philadelphia: Fortress, 1984.

Haenchen, "Probleme" — E. Haenchen. "Probleme des johanneischen 'Prologs.'" *Zeitschrift für Theologie und Kirche* 60 (1963): 305–34.

Haering — T. Haering. *Der Römerbrief des Apostels Paulus.* Stuttgart: Calwer, 1926.

Hagner, *Use* — D. A. Hagner. *The Use of the Old and New Testaments in Clement of Rome.* Leiden: Brill, 1973.

Hagner, *Hebrews* — D. A. Hagner. *Hebrews.* London: Harper, 1983.

Hagner, "Christology" — D. A. Hagner. "Paul's Christology and Jewish Monotheism." Pp. 19–38 in *Perspectives on Christology: Essays in Honor of Paul K. Jewett.* Edited by M. Shuster and R. Muller. Grand Rapids: Zondervan, 1991.

Hahn — F. Hahn. *The Titles of Jesus in Christology.* London: Lutterworth, 1969.

Hamerton-Kelly — R. G. Hamerton-Kelly. *Pre-existence, Wisdom, and the Son of Man.* Cambridge: Cambridge University Press, 1973.

A. T. Hanson, *Jesus* — A. T. Hanson. *Jesus Christ in the Old Testament.* London: SPCK, 1965.

A. T. Hanson, *Pastoral Letters* — A. T. Hanson. *The Pastoral Letters.* Cambridge: Cambridge University Press, 1966.

Hanson and Hanson — A. T. Hanson and R. P. C. Hanson. *Reasonable Belief.* New York: Oxford University Press, 1980.

R. P. C. Hanson — R. P. C. Hanson. *The Acts.* Oxford: Clarendon, 1967.

Harman — A. M. Harman. "The Syntax and Interpretation of Psalm 45:7." Pp. 337–47 in *The Law and the Prophets: Old Testament Studies Prepared in Honour of Oswald Thompson Allis.* Edited by J. H. Skilton. Nutley, N.J.: Presbyterian & Reformed, 1974.

Harnack, *Dogma* — A. von Harnack. *History of Dogma*, vol. 1. ETr. Reprinted New York: Dover, 1961 (= 1894 original).

Harnack, *Date* — A. von Harnack. *The Date of the Acts and of the Synoptic Gospels.* ETr. New York: Putnam, 1911.

Harnack, *Studien* — A. von Harnack. *Studien zur Geschichte des Neuen Testaments und der alten Kirche*, vol. 1: *Zur neutestamentlichen Textkritik.* Berlin: de Gruyter, 1931.

Harner — P. B. Harner. "Qualitative Anarthrous Predicate Nouns: Mark 15:39 and John 1:1." *Journal of Biblical Literature* 92 (1973): 75–87.

J. R. Harris, *Prologue* — J. R. Harris. *The Origin of the Prologue to St. John's Gospel.* Cambridge: Cambridge University Press, 1917.

J. R. Harris, "Athena" — J. R. Harris. "Athena, Sophia and the Logos." *Bulletin of the John Rylands Library* 7 (1922–23): 56–72.

M. J. Harris — M. J. Harris. *From Grave to Glory: Resurrection in the New Testament.* Grand Rapids: Zondervan, 1990.

Harrison — E. F. Harrison. "Romans." *EBC* 10:1–171.

Harvey, *Jesus* — A. E. Harvey. *Jesus and the Constraints of History.* London: Duckworth, 1982.

Harvey, "Agent" — A. E. Harvey. "Christ as Agent." Pp. 239–50 in *The Glory of Christ in the New Testament: Studies in Christology in Memory of George Bradford Caird.* Edited by L. D. Hurst and N. T. Wright. New York: Oxford University Press, 1987.

Hasel — G. F. Hasel. "Recent Translations of Genesis 1:1: A Critical Look." *Bible Translator* 22 (1971): 154–67.

Hasler, *Briefe* — V. Hasler. *Die Briefe an Timotheus und Titus (Pastoralbriefe).* Zurich: Theologischer Verlag, 1978.

Hasler, "Epiphanie" — V. Hasler, "Epiphanie und Christologie in den Pastoralbriefen." *Theologische Zeitschrift* 33 (1977): 193–209.

Hatzidakis — G. N. Hatzidakis. *Einleitung in die neugriechische Grammatik.* Leipzig: Breitkopf & Härtel, 1892.

Haupt — E. Haupt. *The First Epistle of St. John.* ETr. Edinburgh: Clark, 1879.

Heil — J. P. Heil. *Paul's Letter to the Romans.* New York: Paulist, 1987.

Helbing — R. Helbing. *Grammatik der Septuaginta: Laut- und Wortlehre.* Göttingen: Vandenhoeck & Ruprecht, 1907.

Held — M. Held. "Studies in Biblical Homonyms in the Light of Akkadian." *Journal of the Ancient Near Eastern Society of Columbia University* 3 (1970): 46–55.

Hemer, *Acts* — C. J. Hemer. *The Book of Acts in the Setting of Hellenistic History.* Edited by C. H. Gempf. Reprinted Winona Lake, Ind.: Eisenbrauns, 1990 (= 1989 original).

Hemer, "Speeches" — C. J. Hemer. "The Speeches of Acts, I: The Ephesian Elders at Miletus." *Tyndale Bulletin* 40 (1989): 77–85.

Hendriksen, *Timothy–Titus* — W. Hendriksen. *Commentary on I and II Timothy and Titus.* Grand Rapids: Baker/London: Banner of Truth, 1959.

Hendriksen, *Romans* — W. Hendriksen. *Exposition of Paul's Epistle to the Romans*, vol. 2: *Chapters 9–16.* Grand Rapids: Baker, 1981.

Hengstenberg — E. W. Hengstenberg. *Commentary on the Psalms.* ETr. Edinburgh: Clark, 1846.

Héring — J. Héring. *The Epistle to the Hebrews.* ETr. London: Epworth, 1970.

Herkenne — H. Herkenne. *Das Buch der Psalmen.* Bonn: Hanstein, 1936.

Hewitt — T. Hewitt. *The Epistle to the Hebrews.* London: Tyndale, 1960.

Hick — J. Hick. "Christology at the Cross Roads." Pp. 139–90 in *Prospect for Theology: Essays in Honour of H. H. Farmer.* Edited by F. G. Healey. London: Nisbet, 1966.

E. Hirsch — E. Hirsch. *Studien zum vierten Evangelium.* Tübingen: Mohr, 1936.

S. R. Hirsch — S. R. Hirsch. *The Psalms*, vol. 1. New York: Feldheim, 1960.

Hodge, *Theology* — C. Hodge. *Systematic Theology*, vol. 1: *Introduction*, part 1: *Theology.* Reprinted Grand Rapids: Eerdmans, 1965 (= 1871 original).

Hodge, *Romans* — C. Hodge. *Commentary on the Epistle to the Romans.* Reprinted Grand Rapids: Eerdmans, 1953 (= 1886 original).

Hofius — O. Hofius. "Struktur und Gedankengang des Logos-Hymnus in Joh 1 1–18." *Zeitschrift für die Neutestamentliche Wissenschaft* 78 (1978): 1–25.

Hoftijzer — J. Hoftijzer. "The Nominal Clause Reconsidered." *Vetus Testamentum* 23 (1973): 446–510.

Hogg and Vine — C. F. Hogg and W. E. Vine. *The Epistles of Paul the Apostle to the Thessalonians.* London: Holness, 1914.

Holladay — C. R. Holladay. *Theios Aner in Hellenistic-Judaism.* Missoula, Mont.: Scholars Press, 1977.

Holtzmann — H. J. Holtzmann. *Evangelium, Briefe und Offenbarung des Johannes.* 2d edition. Freiburg: Mohr, 1893.

Holtzmann and Bauer — H. J. Holtzmann and W. Bauer. *Evangelium, Briefe und Offenbarung des Johannes.* 3d edition. Edited by W. Bauer. Tübingen: Mohr, 1908.

Hort, *Dissertations* — F. J. A. Hort. *Two Dissertations.* London: Macmillan, 1876.

Hort, *James* — F. J. A. Hort. *The Epistle of St. James.* London: Macmillan, 1909.

Hort, "Hebrews" — F. J. A. Hort. "Hebrews 1.8." Unpublished manuscript in the 1894 R. L. Bensly Collection in the Cambridge University Library, n.d.

Horton — F. L. Horton Jr. *The Melchizedek Tradition.* Cambridge: Cambridge University Press, 1976.

Hoskyns — E. C. Hoskyns. *The Fourth Gospel.* 2d edition. London: Faber, 1947.

Houlden, *Johannine Epistles* — J. L. Houlden. *A Commentary on the Johannine Epistles.* London: Black, 1973.

Houlden, *Pastoral Epistles* — J. L. Houlden. *The Pastoral Epistles.* Philadelphia: Trinity, 1989.

G. E. Howard, "Hebrews" — G. E. Howard. "Hebrews and the Old Testament Quotations." *Novum Testamentum* 10 (1968): 208–16.

G. E. Howard, "Tetragram" — G. E. Howard. "The Tetragram and the New Testament." *Journal of Biblical Literature* 96 (1977): 63–83.

W. F. Howard, *John* — W. F. Howard. *Christianity according to St. John.* London: Duckworth, 1943.

W. F. Howard, "Gospel" — W. F. Howard. "The Gospel according to St. John: Introduction and Exegesis." *IB* 8:435–811.

Hughes — P. E. Hughes. *A Commentary on the Epistle to the Hebrews.* Grand Rapids: Eerdmans, 1977.

Humbert — J. Humbert. *La disparition du datif en grec (du Ier au Xe siècle).* Paris: Champion, 1930.

Hunger — H. Hunger. "Zur Datierung des Papyrus Bodmer II (𝔓66)." Anzeiger der Österreichischen Akademie der Wissenschaften, phil.-hist. Klasse, 1960/4: 12–33.

Hupfeld and Nowack — H. Hupfeld and W. Nowack. *Die Psalmen*, vol 1. Gotha: Perthes, 1888.

Hurst, *Hebrews* — L. D. Hurst. *The Epistle to the Hebrews: Its Background of Thought.* Cambridge: Cambridge University Press, 1990.

Hurst, "Christology" — L. D. Hurst. "The Christology of Hebrews 1 and 2." Pp. 151–64 in *The Glory of Christ in the New Testament: Studies in Christology in Memory of George Bradford Caird.* Edited by L. D. Hurst and N. T. Wright. New York: Oxford University Press, 1987.

Hurtado, *One God* — L. W. Hurtado. *One God, One Lord: Early Christian Devotion and Ancient Jewish Monotheism.* Philadelphia: Fortress, 1988.

Hurtado, "Shape" — L. W. Hurtado. "The Binitarian Shape of Early Christian Devotion and Ancient Jewish Monotheism." Pp. 377–91 in *Society of Biblical Literature Seminar Papers*, vol. 24. Edited by K. H. Richards. Atlanta: Scholars Press, 1985.

Huther, *General Epistles* — J. E. Huther. *Critical and Exegetical Handbook to the General Epistles of James, Peter, John and Jude.* ETr. New York: Funk & Wagnalls, 1887.

Huther, *Timothy–Titus* — J. E. Huther. *Critical and Exegetical Hand-book to the Epistles to Timothy and Titus.* ETr. New York: Funk & Wagnalls, 1890.

Isaac — J. Isaac. *La révélation progressive des personnes divines.* Paris: Cerf, 1960.

Jacob — E. Jacob. *Theology of the Old Testament.* ETr. New York: Hodder, 1958.

Jacquet — L. Jacquet. *Les Psaumes et le coeur de l'homme*, vol. 2. Gembloux: Duculot, 1977.

Jacquier — E. Jacquier. *Les Actes des Apôtres.* Paris: Gabalda, 1926.

James — M. R. James. *The Second Epistle General of Peter and the General Epistle of Jude.* Cambridge: Cambridge University Press, 1912.

Jannaris, *Grammar* — A. N. Jannaris. *An Historical Greek Grammar.* New York: Macmillan, 1897.

Jannaris, "Logos" — A. N. Jannaris. "St. John's Gospel and the Logos." *Zeitschrift für die Neutestamentliche Wissenschaft* 2 (1901): 13–25.

Jendorff — B. Jendorff. *Der Logosbegriff: Seine philosophische Grundlegung bei Heraklit von Ephesos und seine theologische Indienstnahme durch Johannes den Evangelisten.* Bern: Lang, 1976.

Jeremias — J. Jeremias. *Die Briefe an Timotheus und Titus.* 9th edition. Göttingen: Vandenhoeck & Ruprecht, 1968.

A. R. Johnson, *Kingship* — A. R. Johnson. *Sacral Kingship in Ancient Israel.* Cardiff: University of Wales Press, 1955.

A. R. Johnson, "Divine Kingship" — A. R. Johnson. "Living Issues in Biblical Scholarship: Divine Kingship and the Old Testament." *Expository Times* 62 (1950–51): 36–42.

E. E. Johnson — E. E. Johnson. *The Function of Apocalyptic and Wisdom Traditions in Romans 9–11.* Atlanta: Scholars Press, 1989.

Jones — W. H. S. Jones. "A Note on the Vague Use of θεός." *Classical Review* 27 (1913): 252–55.

Joüon — P. Joüon. *Grammaire de l'hébreu biblique.* Rome: Pontifical Biblical Institute, 1947.

Karris	R. J. Karris. *The Pastoral Epistles.* Wilmington, Del.: Glazier, 1979.
Käsemann, *Essays*	E. Käsemann. *Essays on New Testament Themes.* ETr. London: SCM, 1964.
Käsemann, *Testament*	E. Käsemann. *The Testament of Jesus.* ETr. Philadelphia: Fortress, 1968.
Käsemann, *Questions*	E. Käsemann. *New Testament Questions of Today.* ETr. London: SCM, 1969.
Käsemann, *Romans*	E. Käsemann. *Commentary on Romans.* ETr. London: SCM, 1980.
Käsemann, *People*	E. Käsemann. *The Wandering People of God.* ETr. Minneapolis: Augsburg, 1984.
Keck, "Jesus"	L. E. Keck. "Jesus in New Testament Christology." *Australian Biblical Review* 28 (1980): 1–20.
Keck, "Renewal"	L. E. Keck. "Toward the Renewal of New Testament Christology." *New Testament Studies* 32 (1985–86): 362–77.
Kelly, *Pastoral Epistles*	J. N. D. Kelly. *The Pastoral Epistles.* New York: Harper, 1963.
Kelly, *Peter–Jude*	J. N. D. Kelly. *The Epistles of Peter and Jude.* New York: Harper, 1969.
Kidner	D. Kidner. *Psalms 1–72.* London: Inter-Varsity, 1973.
J. S. King	J. S. King. "The Prologue to the Fourth Gospel: Some Unresolved Problems." *Expository Times* 86 (1974–75): 372–75.
P. J. King	P. J. King. *A Study of Psalm 45 (44).* Rome: Pontificia Universitas Lateranensis, 1959.
Kingsbury	J. D. Kingsbury. *Matthew: Structure, Christology, Kingdom.* Reprinted Minneapolis: Fortress, 1989 (= 1975 original).
Kirk	K. E. Kirk. *The Epistle to the Romans.* Oxford: Clarendon, 1937.
Kirkpatrick	A. F. Kirkpatrick. *The Book of Psalms.* Cambridge: Cambridge University Press, 1902.
Kissane	E. J. Kissane. *The Book of Psalms*, vol. 1. Dublin: Browne & Nolan, 1953.
Kistemaker	S. Kistemaker. *The Psalm Citations in the Epistle to the Hebrews.* Amsterdam: van Soest, 1961.
Kittel	R. Kittel. *Die Psalmen.* 2d edition. Leipzig: Deichart, 1914.
Klijn and Reinink	A. F. J. Klijn and G. J. Reinink. *Patristic Evidence for Jewish-Christian Sects.* Leiden: Brill, 1973.
Knight	R. Knight. "Creator and Created." *Hibbert Journal* 45 (1946): 38–43.
Knox	R. A. Knox. *A New Testament Commentary*, vol. 2. London: Burns, Oates & Washbourne, 1954.
König	E. König. *Die Psalmen.* Gütersloh: Bertelsmann, 1927.
Kramer	W. Kramer. *Christ, Lord, Son of God.* ETr. London: SCM, 1966.
Kränke	E. Kränke. *Jesus der Knecht Gottes.* Regensburg: Pustet, 1972.
Kraus, *Psalmen*	H. J. Kraus. *Psalmen*, vol. 1. 5th edition. Neukirchen: Neukirchener Verlag, 1978.
Kraus, *Theologie*	H. J. Kraus. *Theologie der Psalmen.* Neukirchen: Neukirchener Verlag, 1979.
Kümmel	W. G. Kümmel. *The Theology of the New Testament.* ETr. Nashville: Abingdon, 1973.
Küng	H. Küng. *Does God Exist?* ETr. Garden City, N.Y.: Doubleday, 1978.
Kuss, *Hebräer*	O. Kuss. *Der Brief an die Hebräer.* 2d edition. Regensburg: Pustet, 1966.
Kuss, *Römerbrief*	O. Kuss. *Der Römerbrief übersetzt und erklärt*, vol. 3. Regensburg: Pustet, 1978.
Kuss, "Römer"	O. Kuss. "Zur Römer 9,5." Pp. 291–303 in *Rechtfertigung: Festschrift für Ernst Käsemann zum 70. Geburtstag.* Edited by J. Friedrich, W. Pöhlmann, and P. Stuhlmacher. Tübingen: Mohr, 1976.
Kysar	R. Kysar. "Christology and Controversy: The Contributions of the Prologue of the Gospel of John to New Testament Christology and Their Historical Setting." *Currents in Theology and Mission* 5 (1978): 348–64.

Labuschagne — C. J. Labuschagne. *The Incomparability of Yahweh in the Old Testament.* Leiden: Brill, 1966.

de Lagarde — P. de Lagarde. *Prophetae Chaldaice.* Leipzig: Teubner, 1872.

Lagrange, *Jean* — M. J. Lagrange. *Évangile selon Saint Jean.* Paris: Gabalda, 1947.

Lagrange, *Romains* — M. J. Lagrange. *Saint Paul: Épître aux Romains.* Paris: Gabalda, 1950.

Lambrecht — J. Lambrecht. "Paul's Farewell-Address at Miletus (Acts 20,17–38)." Pp. 307–37 in *Les Actes des Apôtres: Traditions, rédaction, théologie.* Edited by J. Kremer. Gembloux: Duculot, 1979.

Lampe — G. W. H. Lampe. *God as Spirit.* Oxford: Clarendon, 1977.

Lane — W. L. Lane. *Hebrews 1–8.* Dallas: Word, 1991.

Langbrandtner — W. Langbrandtner. *Weltferner Gott oder Gott der Liebe.* Frankfurt am Main: Lang, 1977.

Lapide and Moltmann — P. Lapide and J. Moltmann. *Jewish Monotheism and Christian Trinitarian Doctrine.* ETr. Philadelphia: Fortress, 1981.

Lattey, "Codex Vaticanus" — C. Lattey. "The Codex Vaticanus on Romans ix.5." *Expository Times* 34 (1922–23): 331.

Lattey, "Codex Ephraemi" — C. Lattey. "The Codex Ephraemi Rescriptus on Romans ix.5." *Expository Times* 35 (1923–24): 42–43.

Law — R. Law. *The Tests of Life: A Study of the First Epistle of St. John.* Edinburgh: Clark, 1909.

Lawton — J. S. Lawton. *Conflict in Christology.* London: SPCK, 1947.

Leaney — A. R. C. Leaney. *The Epistles to Timothy, Titus and Philemon.* London: SCM, 1960.

Lebreton, *History* — J. Lebreton. *History of the Dogma of the Trinity from Its Origins to the Council of Nicaea*, vol. 1: *The Origins.* ETr. London: Burns, Oates & Washbourne, 1939.

Lebreton, "Théologie" — J. Lebreton. "La théologie de la Trinité d'après Saint Ignace d'Antioche." *Recherches de Science Religieuse* 15 (1925): 97–126, 393–419.

Leenhardt — F. J. Leenhardt. *The Epistle to the Romans.* ETr. London: Lutterworth, 1961.

Lenski, *Romans* — R. C. H. Lenski. *The Interpretation of St. Paul's Epistle to the Romans.* Columbus: Lutheran Book Concern, 1936.

Lenski, *John* — R. C. H. Lenski. *The Interpretation of St. John's Gospel.* Reprinted Minneapolis: Augsburg, 1961 (= 1942 original).

Lenski, *Epistles* — R. C. H. Lenski. *The Interpretation of the Epistles of St. Peter, St. John and St. Jude.* Minneapolis: Augsburg, 1966.

Levey — S. H. Levey. *The Messiah: An Aramaic Interpretation.* Cincinnati: Hebrew Union College, 1974.

Lias — J. J. Lias. *The First Epistle of St. John.* Chicago: McClurg, 1887.

Liddon, *Divinity* — H. P. Liddon. *The Divinity of Our Lord and Saviour Jesus Christ.* London: Rivingtons, 1889.

Liddon, *Romans* — H. P. Liddon. *Explanatory Analysis of St. Paul's Epistle to the Romans.* Reprinted Minneapolis: James & Klock, 1977 (= 1899 original).

Lietzmann — H. Lietzmann. *A History of the Early Church.* 2 vols. ETr. Cleveland: World, 1961.

J. B. Lightfoot — J. B. Lightfoot. *The Apostolic Fathers. Clement, Ignatius, and Polycarp.* 2 parts in 5 vols. 2d edition. Reprinted Peabody, Mass.: Hendrickson, 1989 (= 1889–90 original).

R. H. Lightfoot — R. H. Lightfoot. *St. John's Gospel.* Edited by C. F. Evans. Oxford: Clarendon, 1956.

Lindars, *Apologetic* — B. Lindars. *New Testament Apologetic.* London: SCM, 1961.

Lindars, *John* — B. Lindars. *The Gospel of John.* London: Oliphants, 1972.

Lindeskog — G. Lindeskog. "Theoskristologien i Nya Testamentet." *Svensk Exegetisk Årsbok* 37–38 (1972–73): 222–37.

Loader, *Sohn* — W. R. G. Loader. *Sohn und Hoherpriester.* Neukirchen: Neukirchener Verlag, 1981.

Loader, *Christology* W. R. G. Loader. *The Christology of the Fourth Gospel: Structure and Issues.* New York: Lang, 1989.

Loader, "Structure" W. R. G. Loader. "The Central Structure of Johannine Christology." *New Tstament Studies* 30 (1984): 188–216.

Lock W. Lock. *A Critical and Exegetical Commentary on the Pastoral Epistles.* Edinburgh: Clark, 1924.

Lohfink G. Lohfink. *Die Sammlung Israels: Eine Untersuchung zur lukanischen Ekklesiologie.* Munich: Kösel, 1975.

Loisy A. Loisy. *Quatrième Evangile.* 2d edition. Paris: Nourry, 1921.

B. W. Longenecker B. W. Longenecker. *Eschatology and Covenant.* Sheffield: JSOT Press, 1991.

R. N. Longenecker, *Christology* R. N. Longenecker. *The Christology of Early Jewish Christianity.* London: SCM, 1970.

R. N. Longenecker, *Exegesis* R. N. Longenecker. *Biblical Exegesis in the Apostolic Period.* Grand Rapids: Eerdmans, 1975.

R. N. Longenecker, "Acts" R. N. Longenecker. "Acts." *EBC* 9:205–573.

Lorimer W. L. Lorimer. "Romans ix.3–5." *New Testament Studies* 13 (1966–67): 385–86.

Louw J. P. Louw. "Narrator of the Father: ἐξηγεῖσθαι and Related Terms in Johannine Christology." *Neotestamentica* 2 (1968): 32–40.

Louw and Nida J. P. Louw and E. A. Nida. *Greek-English Lexicon of the New Testament Based on Semantic Domains,* vol. 1. 2d edition. New York: United Bible Societies, 1989.

Lumby J. R. Lumby. *The Acts of the Apostles.* Cambridge: Cambridge University Press, 1912.

Lünemann G. Lünemann. *Critical and Exegetical Handbook to the Epistle to the Hebrews.* ETr. Edinburgh: Clark, 1882.

Lyonnet S. Lyonnet. *Quaestiones in Epistulam ad Romanos.* Rome: Pontifical Biblical Institute, 1962.

Lyonnet and Sabourin S. Lyonnet and L. Sabourin. *Sin, Redemption, and Sacrifice: A Biblical and Patristic Study.* Rome: Pontifical Biblical Institute, 1970.

McCullough J. C. McCullough. "The Old Testament Quotations in Hebrews." *New Testament Studies* 26 (1979–80): 363–79.

McGaughy L. C. McGaughy. *Toward a Descriptive Analysis of εἶναι as a Linking Verb in New Testament Greek.* Missoula, Mont.: University of Montana Press, 1972.

McGiffert A. C. McGiffert. *The God of the Early Christians.* New York: Scribner, 1925.

Macgregor G. H. C. Macgregor. *The Gospel of John.* London: Hodder & Stoughton, 1928.

Macintosh A. A. Macintosh. "The Meaning of אלהים in Psalm 45:6." *Trivium* 1 (1966): 182–83.

McKenzie J. L. McKenzie. "The Appellative Use of El and Elohim." *Catholic Biblical Quarterly* 10 (1948): 170–81.

MacKinnon, "Substance" D. M. MacKinnon. "'Substance' in Christology: A Cross-Bench View." Pp. 279–300 in *Christ, Faith and History: Cambridge Studies in Christology.* Edited by S. W. Sykes and J. P. Clayton. Cambridge: Cambridge University Press, 1972.

MacKinnon, "Review" D. M. MacKinnon. Review of *Christology in the Making* by J. D. G. Dunn. *Scottish Journal of Theology* 35 (1982): 362–64.

Mackintosh H. R. Mackintosh. *The Doctrine of the Person of Jesus Christ.* 2d edition. Edinburgh: Clark, 1913.

Macquarrie J. Macquarrie. *Jesus Christ in Modern Thought.* Philadelphia: Trinity, 1990.

McReynolds — P. R. McReynolds. "John 1:18 in Textual Variation and Translation." Pp. 105–18 in *New Testament Textual Criticism: Essays in Honour of Bruce M. Metzger.* Edited by E. J. Epp and G. D. Fee. Oxford: Clarendon, 1981.

Mahoney — R. Mahoney. *Two Disciples at the Tomb: The Background and Message of John 20.1–10.* Bern: Lang, 1974.

Malatesta — E. Malatesta. *Interiority and Covenant: A Study of εἶναι ἐν and μένειν ἐν in the First Letter of Saint John.* Rome: Pontifical Biblical Institute, 1978.

Malevez — L. Malevez. "Nouveau Testament et théologie fonctionnelle." *Recherches de Science Religieuse* 48 (1960): 258–90.

Manson — W. Manson. *The Epistle to the Hebrews.* London: Hodder & Stoughton, 1951.

Marmorstein — A. Marmorstein. *The Old Rabbinic Doctrine of God,* vol. 1: *The Names and Attributes of God.* London: Oxford University Press, 1927.

Marshall, *Luke* — I. H. Marshall. *Luke: Historian and Theologian.* Grand Rapids: Zondervan, 1971.

Marshall, *Origins* — I. H. Marshall. *The Origins of New Testament Christology.* Downers Grove: Ill.: InterVarsity, 1976.

Marshall, *Epistles* — I. H. Marshall. *The Epistles of John.* Grand Rapids: Eerdmans, 1978.

Marshall, *Acts* — I. H. Marshall. *The Acts of the Apostles.* Grand Rapids: Eerdmans, 1980.

Marshall, "Development" — I. H. Marshall. "The Development of Christology in the Early Church." *Tyndale Bulletin* 18 (1967): 77–93.

Marshall, "Redemption" — I. H. Marshall. "The Development of the Concept of Redemption in the New Testament." Pp. 153–69 in *Reconciliation and Hope: New Testament Essays on Atonement and Eschatology Presented to L. L. Morris.* Edited by R. Banks. Grand Rapids: Eerdmans, 1974.

Martin — R. P. Martin. *Carmen Christi.* Cambridge: Cambridge University Press, 1967.

Mascall — E. L. Mascall. *Theology and the Gospel of Christ.* London: SPCK, 1977.

Masson — C. Masson. "Pour une traduction nouvelle de Jean 1:1b et 2." *Revue de Théologie et de Philosophie* 98 (1965): 376–81.

Mastin, "Cult" — B. A. Mastin. "The Imperial Cult and the Ascription of the Title θεός to Jesus (John xx.28)." Pp. 352–65 in *Studia Evangelica,* vol. 6. Edited by E. A. Livingstone. Berlin: Akademie-Verlag, 1973.

Mastin, "Christology" — B. A. Mastin. "A Neglected Feature of the Christology of the Fourth Gospel." *New Testament Studies* 22 (1975–76): 32–51.

Matsunaga — K. Matsunaga. "The 'Theos' Christology as the Ultimate Confession of the Fourth Gospel." *Annual of the Japanese Biblical Institute* 7 (1981): 124–45.

Mauser — U. Mauser. "Εἷς θεός und μόνος θεός in biblischer Theologie." Pp. 71–87 in *Einheit und Vielfalt biblischer Theologie.* Jahrbuch für Biblische Theologie 1. Neukirchen-Vluyn: Neukirchener Verlag, 1986.

Mayor — J. B. Mayor. *The Epistle of St. Jude and the Second Epistle of St. Peter.* London: Macmillan, 1907.

Mayser — E. Mayser. *Grammatik der griechischen Papyri aus der Ptolemäerzeit,* vol. 2.2: *Satzlehre.* Berlin: de Gruyter, 1934.

Meecham — H. G. Meecham. "The Anarthrous θεός in Jn. i.1 and I Corinthians iii.16." *Expository Times* 63 (1951–52): 126.

Meier — J. P. Meier. "Symmetry and Theology in the Old Testament Citations of Heb. 1,5–14." *Biblica* 66 (1985): 504–33.

Mettinger — T. N. D. Mettinger. *King and Messiah.* Lund: Gleerup, 1976.

Metzger, *Text* — B. M. Metzger. *The Text of the New Testament: Its Transmission, Corruption and Restoration.* 2d edition. New York: Oxford University Press, 1968.

Metzger, *Studies* — B. M. Metzger. *Historical and Literary Studies.* Leiden: Brill, 1968.

Metzger, *Commentary*	B. M. Metzger. *A Textual Commentary on the Greek New Testament.* New York: United Bible Societies, 1971.
Metzger, "Formulas"	B. M. Metzger. "The Formulas Introducing Quotations of Scripture in the NT and the Mishnah." *Journal of Biblical Literature* 70 (1951): 297–307.
Metzger, "Translation"	B. M. Metzger. "On the Translation of John i.1." *Expository Times* 63 (1951–52): 125–26.
Metzger, "Jehovah's Witnesses"	B. M. Metzger. "The Jehovah's Witnesses and Jesus Christ." *Theology Today* 10 (1953): 65–85.
Metzger, "Reconsideration"	B. M. Metzger. "A Reconsideration of Certain Arguments against the Pauline Authorship of the Pastoral Epistles." *Expository Times* 70 (1958–59): 91–94.
Metzger, "Punctuation"	B. M. Metzger. "The Punctuation of Romans 9:5." Pp. 95–112 in *Christ and Spirit in the New Testament: Festschrift in Honour of C. F. D. Moule.* Edited by B. Lindars and S. S. Smalley. Cambridge: Cambridge University Press, 1973.
E. Meyer	E. Meyer. *Ursprung und Anfänge des Christentums.* 3 vols. Stuttgart: Cotta, 1921–23.
H. A. W. Meyer, *John*	H. A. W. Meyer. *Critical and Exegetical Hand-book to the Gospel of John.* ETr. Revised and edited by F. Crombie; supplementary notes by A. C. Kendrick. New York: Funk & Wagnalls, 1884.
H. A. W. Meyer, *Romans*	H. A. W. Meyer. *Critical and Exegetical Hand-book to the Epistle to the Romans.* ETr. Supplementary notes by T. Dwight. New York: Funk & Wagnalls, 1889.
Michaelis	W. Michaelis. *Zur Engelchristologie im Urchristentum.* Basel: Majer, 1942.
H. J. Michel	H. J. Michel. *Die Abschiedsrede des Paulus an die Kirche Apg 20,17–38: Motivgeschichte und theologische Bedeutung.* Munich: Kösel, 1973.
O. Michel, *Römer*	O. Michel. *Der Brief an die Römer.* 4th edition. Göttingen: Vandenhoeck & Ruprecht, 1966.
O. Michel, *Hebräer*	O. Michel. *Der Brief an die Hebräer.* 12th edition. Göttingen: Vandenhoeck & Ruprecht, 1966.
Middleton	T. F. Middleton. *The Doctrine of the Greek Article.* Preface and notes by H. J. Rose. 2d edition. London: Rivingtons, 1841.
Milden	A. W. Milden. *The Limitations of the Predicate Position in Greek.* Baltimore: Murphy, 1900.
Miller, *Prologue*	E. L. Miller. *Salvation-History in the Prologue of John: The Significance of John 1:3–4.* Leiden: Brill, 1989.
Miller, "God"	E. L. Miller. "'The *Logos* was God.'" *Evangelical Quarterly* 53 (1981): 65–77.
Milligan	G. Milligan. *The Theology of the Epistle to the Hebrews.* Edinburgh: Clark, 1899.
Milligan and Moulton	W. Milligan and W. F. Moulton. *Commentary on the Gospel of St. John.* Edinburgh: Clark, 1898.
Minn	H. R. Minn. *The Golden Prologue.* Melbourne: Bacon, n.d.
Moehlmann	C. H. Moehlmann. *The Combination Theos Soter as Explanation of the Primitive Christian Use of Soter as Title and Name of Jesus.* Rochester: Du Bois, 1920.
Moffatt, *Hebrews*	J. Moffatt. *A Critical and Exegetical Commentary on the Epistle to the Hebrews.* Edinburgh: Clark, 1924.
Moffatt, *Epistles*	J. Moffatt. *The General Epistles.* London: Hodder & Stoughton, 1928.
Moloney, *Son of Man*	F. J. Moloney. *The Johannine Son of Man.* Rome: Las, 1976.
Moloney, "John"	F. J. Moloney. "John 1:18: 'In the Bosom of' or 'Turned towards' the Father?" *Australian Biblical Review* 31 (1983): 63–71.
Montefiore, *Hebrews*	H. W. Montefiore. *A Commentary on the Epistle to the Hebrews.* London: Black, 1964.

Montefiore, "Christology"	H. W. Montefiore. "Towards a Christology for Today." Pp. 147–72 in *Soundings: Essays concerning Christian Understanding.* Edited by A. R. Vidler. Cambridge: Cambridge University Press, 1966.
Moody	D. Moody. "God's Only Son: The Translation of John 3:16 in the Revised Standard Version." *Journal of Biblical Literature* 72 (1953): 213–19.
G. F. Moore	G. F. Moore. *Judaism in the First Centuries of the Christian Era.* 3 vols. Reprinted New York: Schocken, 1971 (= 1927 original).
R. W. Moore	R. W. Moore. *Comparative Greek and Latin Syntax.* London: Bell, 1957.
Morris, *Preaching*	L. Morris. *The Apostolic Preaching of the Cross.* London: Tyndale, 1955.
Morris, *Cross*	L. Morris. *The Cross in the New Testament.* Grand Rapids: Eerdmans, 1965.
Morris, *Studies*	L. Morris. *Studies in the Fourth Gospel.* Grand Rapids: Eerdmans, 1969.
Morris, *John*	L. Morris. *The Gospel according to John.* Grand Rapids: Eerdmans, 1971.
Morris, *Theology*	L. Morris. *New Testament Theology.* Grand Rapids: Zondervan, 1986.
Morris, *Romans*	L. Morris. *The Epistle to the Romans.* Grand Rapids: Eerdmans, 1987.
Morris, *Jesus*	L. Morris. *Jesus Is the Christ: Studies in the Theology of John.* Grand Rapids: Eerdmans, 1989.
Motyer	J. A. Motyer. "Context and Content in the Interpretation of Isaiah 7:14." *Tyndale Bulletin* 21 (1970): 118–25.
C. F. D. Moule, *Idiom Book*	C. F. D. Moule. *An Idiom Book of New Testament Greek.* 2d edition. Cambridge: Cambridge University Press, 1960.
C. F. D. Moule, *Origin*	C. F. D. Moule. *The Origin of Christology.* Cambridge: Cambridge University Press, 1977.
C. F. D. Moule, *Birth*	C. F. D. Moule. *The Birth of the New Testament.* 3d edition. London: Black, 1982.
H. C. G. Moule, *Epistle*	H. C. G. Moule. *The Epistle to the Romans.* London: Pickering & Inglis, n.d.
H. C. G. Moule, *Romans*	H. C. G. Moule. *The Epistle of Paul the Apostle to the Romans.* Cambridge: Cambridge University Press, 1899.
Moulton, *Prolegomena*	J. H. Moulton. *A Grammar of New Testament Greek*, vol. 1: *Prolegomena.* 3d edition. Edinburgh: Clark, 1908.
Moulton, "Notes"	J. H. Moulton. "Notes from the Papyri." *Expositor,* 6th ser., 3 (1901): 276–77.
Mowinckel, *Psalms*	S. Mowinckel. *The Psalms in Israel's Worship.* ETr. Oxford: Blackwell, 1962.
Mowinckel, *Psalmenstudien*	S. Mowinckel. *Psalmenstudien*, vols. 1–4. Amsterdam: Schippers, 1966.
Mowinckel, "Elements"	S. Mowinckel. "General Oriental and Specific Israelite Elements in the Israelite Conception of the Sacral Kingdom." Pp. 283–93 in *The Sacral Kingship.* Numen Supplement 4. Leiden: Brill, 1959.
Mueller	J. T. Mueller. *Christian Dogmatics.* St. Louis: Concordia, 1955.
Mulder	J. S. M. Mulder. *Studies on Psalm 45.* Oslo: Witsiers, 1972.
Mullins	T. Y. Mullins. "Ascription as a Literary Form." *New Testament Studies* 19 (1973): 194–205.
Munck, *Acts*	J. Munck. *The Acts of the Apostles.* Garden City, N.Y.: Doubleday, 1967.
Munck, *Christ*	J. Munck. *Christ and Israel: An Interpretation of Romans 9–11.* ETr. Philadelphia: Fortress, 1967.
Munck, "Discours"	J. Munck. "Discours d'adieu dans le Nouveau Testament et dans la littérature biblique." Pp. 155–70 in *Aux sources de la tradition chrétienne: Mélanges offerts à M. Maurice Goguel.* Neuchâtel: Delachaux & Niestlé, 1950.
G. Murray	G. Murray. *Five Stages of Greek Religion.* 2d edition. London: Watts, 1935.
J. Murray	J. Murray. *The Epistle to the Romans*, vol. 2. Grand Rapids: Eerdmans, 1965.
Murtonen	A. Murtonen. *A Philological and Literary Treatise on the Old Testament Divine Names* אל, אלוה, אלהים, *and* יהוה. Helsinki: Societas Orientalis Fennica, 1952.

Nairne, *Priesthood* A. Nairne. *The Epistle of Priesthood.* 2d edition. Edinburgh: Clark, 1915.

Nairne, *Hebrews* A. Nairne. *The Epistle to the Hebrews.* Cambridge: Cambridge University Press, 1917.

Nash H. S. Nash. "Θειότης–Θεότης, Rom. i.20; Col. ii.9." *Journal of Biblical Literature* 18 (1899): 1–34.

Nauck W. Nauck. *Die Tradition und der Charakter des ersten Johannesbriefes.* Tübingen: Mohr, 1957.

Neil W. Neil. *The Acts of the Apostles.* London: Marshall, 1973.

Nelson D. M. Nelson Jr. *The Articular and Anarthrous Predicate Nominative in the Greek New Testament.* Ph.D. dissertation, Southern Baptist Theological Seminary, Louisville, 1944.

Neufeld V. H. Neufeld. *The Earliest Christian Confessions.* Leiden: Brill, 1963.

Nevius, *Mark* R. C. Nevius. *The Divine Names in Mark.* Salt Lake City: University of Utah Press, 1964.

Nevius, *Gospels* R. C. Nevius. *The Divine Names in the Gospels.* Salt Lake City: University of Utah Press, 1967.

Neyrey, "Divinity" J. H. Neyrey. "'My Lord and My God': The Divinity of Jesus in John's Gospel." Pp. 152–71 in *Society of Biblical Literature Seminar Papers Series*, vol. 25. Edited by K. H. Richards. Atlanta: Scholars Press, 1986.

Neyrey, "Gods" J. H. Neyrey. "'I Said: You Are Gods': Psalm 82:6 and John 10." *Journal of Biblical Literature* 108 (1989): 647–63.

Nicol W. Nicol. *The Sēmeia in the Fourth Gospel: Tradition and Redaction.* Leiden: Brill, 1972.

Nilsson M. P. Nilsson. *Geschichte der griechischen Religion.* 2 vols. 2d edition. Munich: Beck, 1955–61.

North C. R. North. "The Religious Aspects of Hebrew Kingship." *Zeitschrift für die Alttestamentliche Wissenschaft* 9 (1932): 8–38.

Noth M. Noth. "Gott, König, Volk im Alten Testament." *Zeitschrift für Theologie und Kirche* 47 (1950): 157–91. ETr. in his *Laws in the Pentateuch and Other Studies*, pp. 145–78. Philadelphia: Fortress, 1966.

Nygren A. Nygren. *Commentary on Romans.* London: SCM, 1952.

Obermann J. Obermann. "The Divine Name YHWH in the Light of Recent Discoveries." *Journal of Biblical Literature* 68 (1949): 301–25.

O'Brien P. T. O'Brien. *Introductory Thanksgivings in Letters of Paul.* Leiden: Brill, 1977.

Oepke A. Oepke. "Δικαιοσύνη θεοῦ bei Paulus in neuer Beleuchtung." *Theologische Literaturzeitung* 78 (1953): 257–64.

Oesterley W. O. E. Oesterley. *The Psalms*, vol. 1. London: SPCK, 1939.

Oke C. C. Oke. "A Doxology Not to God But Christ." *Expository Times* 67 (1955–56): 367–68.

Olshausen H. Olshausen. *The Epistle of St. Paul to the Romans: A Biblical Commentary on the New Testament.* Edinburgh: Clark, 1856.

O'Neill, *Puzzle* J. C. O'Neill. *The Puzzle of 1 John: A New Examination of Origins.* London: SPCK, 1966.

O'Neill, *Romans* J. C. O'Neill. *Paul's Letter to the Romans.* Harmondsworth: Penguin, 1975.

O'Rourke J. J. O'Rourke. "Εἰς and ἐν in John." *Bible Translator* 25 (1974): 139–42.

von der Osten-Sacken P. von der Osten-Sacken. *Christian-Jewish Dialogue: Theological Foundations.* ETr. Philadelphia: Fortress, 1986.

O'Toole R. F. O'Toole. *The Christological Climax of Paul's Defense.* Rome: Pontifical Biblical Institute, 1978.

Owen H. P. Owen. *Christian Theism.* Edinburgh: Clark, 1984.

Paap A. H. R. E. Paap. *Nomina Sacra in the Greek Papyri of the First Five Centuries A.D.* Leiden: Brill, 1959.

Pancaro S. Pancaro. *The Law in the Fourth Gospel.* Leiden: Brill, 1975.

Pannenberg W. Pannenberg. *Jesus: God and Man.* ETr. Westminster: Philadelphia, 1968.

Parke-Taylor — G. H. Parke-Taylor. *Yahweh: The Divine Name in the Bible.* Waterloo, Ontario: Wilfrid Laurier University Press, 1975.

Parry — R. St. J. Parry. *The Pastoral Epistles.* Cambridge: Cambridge University Press, 1920.

Patterson — R. D. Patterson. "A Multiplex Approach to Psalm 45." *Grace Theological Journal* 6 (1985): 29–48.

Paulsen — H. Paulsen. *Die Briefe des Ignatius von Antiochia und der Brief des Polykarp von Smyrna.* 2d edition. Tübingen: Mohr, 1985.

J. B. Payne — J. B. Payne. *The Theology of the Older Testament.* Grand Rapids: Zondervan, 1962.

P. B. Payne — P. B. Payne. "Jesus' Implicit Claim to Deity in His Parables." *Trinity Journal* 2 (1981): 3–23.

Perowne — J. J. S. Perowne. *The Book of Psalms.* 3d edition. London: Bell, 1873.

A. M. Perry — A. M. Perry. "Translating the Greek Article." *Journal of Biblical Literature* 68 (1949): 329–34.

V. Perry, "Jehovah's Witnesses" — V. Perry. "Jehovah's Witnesses and the Deity of Christ." *Evangelical Quarterly* 35 (1963): 15–22.

V. Perry, "God" — V. Perry. "Does the New Testament Call Jesus God?" *Expository Times* 87 (1975–76): 214–15.

Petzke — G. Petzke. *Die Traditionen über Apollonius von Tyana und das Neue Testament.* Leiden: Brill, 1970.

Philippi — F. A. Philippi. *Commentary on St. Paul's Epistle to the Romans*, vol. 2. ETr. Edinburgh: Clark, 1879.

Pieper — F. Pieper. *Christian Dogmatics*, vol. 2. ETr. St. Louis: Concordia, 1951.

Pietersma — A. Pietersma. "Kyrios or Tetragram: A Renewed Quest for the Original LXX." Pp. 85–101 in *De Septuaginta: Studies in Honour of John William Wevers.* Edited by A. Pietersma and C. Cox. Ontario: Benben, 1984.

Piper — J. Piper. *The Justification of God: An Exegetical and Theological Study of Romans 9:1–23.* Grand Rapids: Baker, 1983.

Pittenger, "Review" — W. N. Pittenger. Review of *The Christology of the New Testament* by O. Cullmann. *Theology Today* 17 (1960): 255–58.

Pittenger, "Words" — W. N. Pittenger. "A Matter of Words." *Modern Churchman* 14 (1970–71): 209–11.

Plummer — A. Plummer. *The Epistles of S. John.* Cambridge: Cambridge University Press, 1886.

Plumptre — E. H. Plumptre. *The General Epistles of St. Peter and St. Jude.* Cambridge: Cambridge University Press, 1889.

Podechard — M. E. Podechard. "Notes sur les Psaumes." *Revue Biblique* 32 (1923): 28–38.

Pollard, *Christology* — T. E. Pollard. *Johannine Christology and the Early Church.* Cambridge: Cambridge University Press, 1970.

Pollard, "Exegesis" — T. E. Pollard. "The Exegesis of John x.30 in the Early Trinitarian Controversies." *New Testament Studies* 3 (1956–57): 334–49.

Pollard, "Cosmology" — T. E. Pollard. "Cosmology and the Prologue of the Fourth Gospel." *Vigiliae Christianae* 12 (1958): 147–55.

Pope — M. H. Pope. *El in the Ugaritic Texts.* Leiden: Brill, 1955.

Porter — J. R. Porter. "Psalm xlv.7." *Journal of Theological Studies* 12 (1961): 51–53.

Prast — F. Prast. *Presbyter und Evangelium in nachapostolischer Zeit: Die Abschiedsrede des Paulus in Milet (Apg 20,17–38) in Rahmen der lukanischen Konzeption der Evangeliumsverkündigung.* Stuttgart: Katholisches Bibelwerk, 1979.

Prat — F. Prat. *The Theology of Saint Paul.* 2 vols. ETr. Westminster, Md.: Newman, 1926.

Preisker — H. Preisker. *Die katholischen Briefe.* 3d edition. Tübingen: Mohr, 1951.

Prestige, *God* — G. L. Prestige. *God in Patristic Thought.* London: SPCK, 1952.

Prestige, "Eusebius"	G. L. Prestige. "Ἀγέν[ν]ητος and γεν[ν]ητός, and Kindred Words in Eusebius and the Early Arians." *Journal of Theological Studies* 24 (1923): 486–96.
Prestige, "Athanasius"	G. L. Prestige. "Ἀγέν[ν]ητος and Cognate Words in Athanasius." *Journal of Theological Studies* 34 (1933): 258–65.
Prümm	K. Prümm. *Die Botschaft des Römerbriefes*. Freiburg: Herder, 1960.
Pusey	E. B. Pusey. *Daniel the Prophet*. 3d edition. Oxford: Parker, 1869.
Rackham	R. B. Rackham. *The Acts of the Apostles*. 4th edition. London: Methuen, 1909.
Radcliffe	T. Radcliffe. "'My Lord and My God': The Locus of Confession." *New Blackfriars* 65 (1984): 52–62.
Rahlfs	A. Rahlfs. *Psalmi cum Odis*. 2d edition. Göttingen LXX 10. Göttingen: Vandenhoeck & Ruprecht, 1967.
Rahner	K. Rahner. "Theos in the New Testament." Pp. 79–148 in his *Theological Investigations*, vol. 1. ETr. Baltimore: Helicon, 1961.
Rainbow	P. A. Rainbow. "Jewish Monotheism as the Matrix for New Testament Christology: A Review Article." *Novum Testamentum* 33 (1991): 78–91.
Rawlinson	A. E. J. Rawlinson. *The New Testament Doctrine of the Church*. London: Longmans, 1929.
Regard	P. F. Regard. *Contribution à l'étude des prépositions dans la langue du Nouveau Testament*. Paris: Leroux, 1918.
Reicke	B. Reicke. *The Epistles of James, Peter and Jude*. Garden City, N.Y.: Doubleday, 1964.
Reim, *Studien*	G. Reim. *Studien zum alttestamentlichen Hintergrund des Johannesevangeliums*. Cambridge: Cambridge University Press, 1974.
Reim, "Jesus"	G. Reim. "Jesus as God in the Fourth Gospel: The Old Testament Background." *New Testament Studies* 30 (1984–85): 158–60.
Renié	J. Renié. *Actes des Apôtres*, vol. 11.1 of *La Sainte Bible*. Edited by L. Pirot and A. Clamer. Paris: Letouzey & Ané, 1951.
Rese	M. Rese. "Die Vorzüge Israels in Röm. 9,4f. und Eph. 2,12: Exegetische Anmerkungen zum Thema Kirche und Israel." *Theologische Zeitschrift* 31 (1975): 211–22.
Reumann	J. Reumann. *Righteousness in the New Testament*. Philadelphia: Fortress, 1982.
Reymond	R. L. Reymond. *Jesus, Divine Messiah: The New Testament Witness*. Phillipsburg, N.J.: Presbyterian & Reformed, 1990.
Richardson	C. C. Richardson. *The Christianity of Ignatius of Antioch*. New York: Columbia University Press, 1935.
Richter	G. Richter. *Studien zum Johannesevangelium*. Edited by J. Hainz. Regensburg: Pustet, 1977.
H. N. Ridderbos, *Jesus*	H. N. Ridderbos. *Paul and Jesus*. ETr. Philadelphia: Presbyterian & Reformed, 1958.
H. N. Ridderbos, *Theology*	H. N. Ridderbos. *Paul: An Outline of His Theology*. ETr. Grand Rapids: Eerdmans, 1975.
H. N. Ridderbos, *Romeinen*	H. N. Ridderbos. *Aen de Romeinen*. Kampen: Kok, 1977.
N. H. Ridderbos	N. H. Ridderbos. "The Psalms: Style-Figures and Structure (Certain Considerations, with Special Reference to Pss. xxii, xxv, and xlv)." *Oudtestamentische Studiën* 13 (1963): 43–76.
Riggenbach	E. Riggenbach. *Der Brief an die Hebräer*. Leipzig: Deichert, 1913.
Ringgren	H. Ringgren. *Israelite Religion*. ETr. London: SCM, 1966.
Robert and Tournay	A. Robert and R. Tournay. *Le Cantique des Cantiques*. Paris: Gabalda, 1963.
Roberts	R. L. Roberts. "The Rendering 'Only Begotten' in John 3:16." *Restoration Quarterly* 16 (1973): 2–22.

Robertson, *Divinity* — A. T. Robertson. *The Divinity of Christ in the Gospel of John.* New York: Revell, 1916.

Robertson, *Pictures* — A. T. Robertson. *Word Pictures in the New Testament.* 5 vols. New York: Long & Smith, 1932.

Robertson, *Grammar* — A. T. Robertson. *A Grammar of the Greek New Testament in Light of Historical Research.* 4th edition. Nashville: Broadman, 1934.

Robertson, "Article" — A. T. Robertson. "The Greek Article and the Deity of Christ." *Expositor,* 8th ser., 21 (1921): 182–88.

J. A. T. Robinson, *Honest* — J. A. T. Robinson. *Honest to God.* London: SCM, 1963.

J. A. T. Robinson, *Exploration* — J. A. T. Robinson. *Exploration into God.* London: SCM, 1967.

J. A. T. Robinson, *Face* — J. A. T. Robinson. *The Human Face of God.* London: SCM, 1973.

J. A. T. Robinson, *Redating* — J. A. T. Robinson. *Redating the New Testament.* London: SCM, 1976.

J. A. T. Robinson, *Truth* — J. A. T. Robinson. *Truth Is Two-Eyed.* London: SCM, 1979.

J. A. T. Robinson, *Priority* — J. A. T. Robinson. *The Priority of the Fourth Gospel.* London: SCM, 1985.

J. A. T. Robinson, "Use" — J. A. T. Robinson. "The Use of the Fourth Gospel for Christology Today." Pp. 61–78 in *Christ and Spirit in the New Testament: Festschrift in Honour of C. F. D. Moule.* Edited by B. Lindars and S. S. Smalley. Cambridge: Cambridge University Press, 1973.

J. A. T. Robinson, "John" — J. A. T. Robinson. "Dunn on John." *Theology* 85 (1982): 332–38.

J. M. Robinson — J. M. Robinson. "The Witness of Paul." Pp. 133–45 in *Who Say Ye That I Am? Six Theses on the Deity of Christ.* Edited by W. C. Robinson. Grand Rapids: Eerdmans, 1949.

T. H. Robinson — T. H. Robinson. *The Epistle to the Hebrews.* London: Hodder & Stoughton, 1933.

Roloff — J. Roloff. *Die Apostelgeschichte.* 17th edition. Göttingen: Vandenhoeck & Ruprecht, 1981.

Romaniuk — K. Romaniuk. *L'amour du Père et du Fils dans la sotériologie de Saint Paul.* 2d edition. Rome: Pontifical Biblical Institute, 1974.

Ropes — J. H. Ropes. *The Text of Acts. BC* 3. London: Macmillan, 1926.

Rosenthal — F. Rosenthal. *A Grammar of Biblical Aramaic.* Wiesbaden: Harrassowitz, 1961.

Rostron — S. N. Rostron. *The Christology of Paul.* London: Scott, 1912.

Rowland — C. Rowland. *The Open Heaven.* London: SPCK, 1982.

Runia — K. Runia. *The Present-Day Christological Debate.* Leicester: Inter-Varsity, 1984.

Sabourin, *Names* — L. Sabourin. *The Names and Titles of Jesus.* ETr. New York: Macmillan, 1967.

Sabourin, *Psalms* — L. Sabourin. *The Psalms. Their Origin and Meaning.* ETr. 2d edition. New York: Alba, 1970.

Sabourin, *Christology* — L. Sabourin. *Christology: Basic Texts in Focus.* ETr. New York: Alba, 1984.

Sahlin — H. Sahlin. *Zur Typologie des Johannesevangeliums.* Uppsala: Lundequistska, 1950.

Sanday — W. Sanday. *Christologies Ancient and Modern.* Oxford: Oxford University Press, 1910.

Sanday and Headlam — W. Sanday and A. C. Headlam. *A Critical and Exegetical Commentary on the Epistle to the Romans.* Edinburgh: Clark, 1902.

J. N. Sanders — J. N. Sanders. *A Commentary on the Gospel according to St. John.* Edited and completed by B. A. Mastin. New York: Harper, 1968.

J. T. Sanders	J. T. Sanders. *The New Testament Christological Hymns: Their Historical Religious Background.* Cambridge: Cambridge University Press, 1971.
Sawyer	J. F. A. Sawyer. "Biblical Alternatives to Monotheism." *Theology* 87 (1984): 172–80.
Schedl	C. Schedl. "Neue Vorschläge zu Text und Deutung des Psalmes xlv." *Vetus Testamentum* 14 (1964): 310–18.
Schelkle	K. H. Schelkle. *Die Petrusbriefe; Der Judasbrief.* Freiburg: Herder, 1961.
Schildenberger	J. Schildenberger. "Zur Textkritik von Ps 45 (44)." *Biblische Zeitschrift* 3 (1959): 31–43.
Schillebeeckx, *Jesus*	E. Schillebeeckx. *Jesus: An Experiment in Christology.* ETr. London: Collins, 1979.
Schillebeeckx, *Christ*	E. Schillebeeckx. *Christ: The Christian Experience in the Modern World.* ETr. London: SCM, 1980.
Schillebeeckx, *Report*	E. Schillebeeckx. *Interim Report on the Books "Jesus" and "Christ."* ETr. London: SCM, 1980.
Schlatter, *Johannes*	A. Schlatter. *Der Evangelist Johannes.* Stuttgart: Calwer, 1930.
Schlatter, *Briefe*	A. Schlatter. *Die Briefe des Petrus, Judas, Jakobus, der Brief an die Hebräer.* Stuttgart: Calwer, 1950.
Schlatter, *Gerechtigkeit*	A. Schlatter. *Gottes Gerechtigkeit: Ein Kommentar zum Römerbrief.* Stuttgart: Calwer, 1965.
Schlier	H. Schlier. *Der Römerbrief.* Freiburg: Herder, 1977.
Schmeichel	W. Schmeichel. "Does Luke Make a Soteriological Statement in Acts 20:28?" Pp. 501–14 in *Society of Biblical Literature Seminar Papers,* vol. 21. Edited by K. H. Richards. Chico, Calif.: Scholars Press, 1982.
Schmithals	W. Schmithals. *Der Römerbrief.* Gütersloh: Mohn, 1988.
Schnackenburg, *Johannesbriefe*	R. Schnackenburg. *Die Johannesbriefe.* 5th edition. Freiburg: Herder, 1975.
Schnackenburg, *John*	R. Schnackenburg. *The Gospel according to St. John.* 3 vols. ETr. New York: Crossroad, 1980–82.
G. Schneider	G. Schneider. *Die Apostelgeschichte,* vol. 2. Freiburg: Herder, 1982.
J. Schneider, *Briefe*	J. Schneider. *Die Briefe des Jakobus, Petrus, Judas und Johannes.* 9th edition. Göttingen: Vandenhoeck & Ruprecht, 1961.
J. Schneider, *Johannes*	J. Schneider. *Das Evangelium nach Johannes.* 2d edition. Berlin: Evangelische Verlagsanstalt, 1978.
Schoedel	W. R. Schoedel. *Ignatius of Antioch.* Philadelphia: Fortress, 1985.
Schonfield, *Authentic NT*	J. Schonfield. *The Authentic New Testament.* New York: New American Library, 1958.
Schonfield, *Original NT*	J. Schonfield. *The Original New Testament.* San Francisco: Harper, 1985.
Schoonenberg	P. Schoonenberg. *The Christ.* ETr. New York: Seabury, 1971.
Schrage	W. Schrage. "2. Petrusbriefe." In *Die "katholischen" Briefe: Die Briefe des Jakobus, Petrus, Johannes und Judas.* By H. Balz and W. Schrage. 11th edition. Göttingen: Vandenhoeck & Ruprecht, 1973.
Schröger	F. Schröger. *Der Verfasser des Hebräerbriefes als Schriftausleger.* Regensburg: Pustet, 1968.
Schulz	S. Schulz. *Das Evangelium nach Johannes.* Göttingen: Vandenhoeck & Ruprecht, 1972.
Schunack	G. Schunack. *Die Briefe des Johannes.* Zurich: Theologischer Verlag, 1982.
C. A. A. Scott, *Dominus*	C. A. A. Scott. *Dominus Noster: A Study in the Progressive Recognition of Jesus Christ Our Lord.* Cambridge: Heffer, 1918.
C. A. A. Scott, *Christianity*	C. A. A. Scott. *Christianity according to St. Paul.* Cambridge: Cambridge University Press, 1927.
E. F. Scott, *Fourth Gospel*	E. F. Scott. *The Fourth Gospel: Its Purpose and Theology.* 2d edition. Edinburgh: Clark, 1908.

E. F. Scott, *Pastoral Epistles* — E. F. Scott. *The Pastoral Epistles.* London: Hodder, 1936.

Scrivener — F. H. A. Scrivener. *A Plain Introduction to Criticism of the New Testament*, vol. 2. 4th edition. Edited by E. Miller. London: Bell, 1894.

A. F. Segal — A. F. Segal. *Two Powers in Heaven: Early Rabbinic Reports about Christianity and Gnosticism.* Leiden: Brill, 1977.

M. H. Segal — M. H. Segal. "El, Elohim, and YHWH in the Bible." *Jewish Quarterly Review* 46 (1955): 89–115.

Segond, "Jean" — A. Segond. "1re Épître de Jean chap. 5:18–20." *Revue d'Histoire et de Philosophie Religieuses* 45 (1965): 349–51.

Sharp — G. Sharp. *Remarks on the Uses of the Definitive Article in the Greek Text of the New Testament.* 3d edition. London: Vernor & Hood, 1803.

Shedd — W. G. T. Shedd. *A Critical and Doctrinal Commentary on the Epistle of St. Paul to the Romans.* Reprinted Minneapolis: Klock & Klock, 1978 (= 1879 original).

Sickenberger — J. Sickenberger. *Der Briefe des Heiligen Paulus an die Korinther und Römer.* Bonn: Hanstein, 1932.

Siegert — F. Siegert. *Argumentation bei Paulus gezeigt an Röm 9–11.* Tübingen: Mohr, 1985.

Simpson, *Words* — E. K. Simpson. *Words Worth Weighing in the Greek New Testament.* London: Tyndale, 1949.

Simpson, *Pastoral Epistles* — E. K. Simpson. *The Pastoral Epistles.* Grand Rapids: Eerdmans, 1954.

Skilton — J. H. Skilton. "Romans 9:5 in Modern English Versions: A Study in Syntax and Doctrine." Pp. 104–30 in *The New Testament Student*, vol. 2: *The New Testament Student at Work.* Edited by J. H. Skilton. Philadelphia: Presbyterian & Reformed, 1975.

Škrinjar — A. Škrinjar. "Theologia primae epistolae Joannis." *Verbum Domini* 42 (1964): 3–16, 49–60; 43 (1965): 150–80.

Smalley — S. S. Smalley. *1, 2, 3 John.* Waco, Tex.: Word, 1984.

Smith — W. R. Smith. "Christ and the Angels: Hebrews I." *Expositor*, 2d ser., 1 (1881): 25–33.

Snell — A. Snell. *New and Living Way.* London: Faith, 1959.

von Soden — H. von Soden. *Hebräerbrief, Briefe des Petrus, Jakobus, Judas.* 3d edition. Freiburg im Breisgau: Mohr, 1899.

Spicq, *Hébreux* — C. Spicq. *L'Épître aux Hébreux.* 2 vols. Paris: Gabalda, 1953.

Spicq, *Pierre* — C. Spicq. *Les Épîtres de Saint Pierre.* Paris: Gabalda, 1966.

Spicq, *Épîtres Pastorales* — C. Spicq. *Saint Paul: Les Épîtres Pastorales.* 2 vols. 4th edition. Paris: Gabalda, 1969.

Stählin — G. Stählin. *Die Apostelgeschichte.* 3d edition. Göttingen: Vandenhoeck & Ruprecht, 1966.

Stauffer — E. Stauffer. *New Testament Theology.* ETr. New York: Macmillan, 1955.

Stead — C. Stead, *Divine Substance.* Oxford: Clarendon, 1977.

Stevens, *Johannine Theology* — G. B. Stevens. *The Johannine Theology.* New York: Scribner, 1894.

Stevens, *Pauline Theology* — G. B. Stevens. *The Pauline Theology.* New York: Scribner, 1903.

Stevens, *Theology* — G. B. Stevens. *The Theology of the New Testament.* 2d edition. Edinburgh: Clark, 1911.

Stöger — A. Stöger. *Der Brief des Apostels Judas; der zweite Brief des Apostels Petrus.* Düsseldorf: Patmos, 1962.

Stott — J. R. W. Stott. *The Epistles of John.* Grand Rapids: Eerdmans, 1964.

Strachan, *Fourth Gospel* — R. H. Strachan. *The Fourth Gospel: Its Significance and Environment.* 3d edition. London: SCM, 1941.

Strachan, "2 Peter" — R. H. Strachan. "The Second Epistle General of Peter." *EGT* 4:81–148.

Strathmann, *Johannes* — H. Strathmann. *Das Evangelium nach Johannes.* 8th edition. Göttingen: Vandenhoeck & Ruprecht, 1955.

Strathmann, *Hebräer* — H. Strathmann. *Der Brief an die Hebräer.* 8th edition. Göttingen: Vandenhoeck & Ruprecht, 1963.

Stuhlmacher — P. Stuhlmacher. *Der Brief an die Römer.* Göttingen: Vandenhoeck & Ruprecht, 1990.

Sturch — R. L. Sturch. "Can One Say 'Jesus Is God'?" Pp. 326–40 in *Christ the Lord: Studies in Christology Presented to Donald Guthrie.* Edited by H. H. Rowdon. Leicester: Inter-Varsity, 1982.

Styler — G. M. Styler. "Stages in Christology in the Synoptic Gospels." *New Testament Studies* 10 (1963–64): 398–409.

Suriano — T. Suriano. "Doubting Thomas: An Invitation to Belief." *Bible Today* 53 (1971): 309–15.

Šurjanský — A. J. Šurjanský. *De mysterio verbi incarnati ad mentem b. Iohannis apostoli libri tres.* Rome: Athenaei, 1941.

Swetnam, *Jesus* — J. Swetnam. *Jesus and Isaac.* Rome: Pontifical Biblical Institute, 1981.

Swetnam, "Form" — J. Swetnam. "Form and Content in Hebrews 1–6." *Biblica* 53 (1972): 368–85.

Synge — F. C. Synge. *Hebrews and the Scriptures.* London: SCM, 1959.

Tarelli — C. C. Tarelli. "Johannine Synonyms." *Journal of Theological Studies* 47 (1946): 175–77.

Tasker — R. V. G. Tasker. *The Greek New Testament, Being the Text Translated in the New English Bible.* Oxford: Oxford University Press, 1961.

J. R. Taylor — J. R. Taylor. "A Note on St. John i.18." *Expository Times* 18 (1906–7): 47.

L. R. Taylor — L. R. Taylor. *The Divinity of the Roman Emperor.* Reprinted Chico, Calif.: Scholars Press, 1981 (= 1931 original).

V. Taylor, *Names* — V. Taylor. *The Names of Jesus.* London: Macmillan, 1953.

V. Taylor, *Romans* — V. Taylor. *The Epistle to the Romans.* London: Epworth, 1955.

V. Taylor, *Person* — V. Taylor. *The Person of Christ in New Testament Teaching.* London: Macmillan, 1958.

V. Taylor, *Essays* — V. Taylor. *New Testament Essays.* London: Epworth, 1970.

V. Taylor, "Jesus" — V. Taylor. "Does the New Testament Call Jesus 'God'?" *Expository Times* 73 (1961–62): 116–18. Reprinted in V. Taylor, *Essays* 83–89.

Temple, *Christus* — W. Temple. *Christus Veritas.* London: Macmillan, 1925.

Temple, *John* — W. Temple. *Readings in St. John's Gospel.* London: Macmillan, 1945.

Tenney — M. C. Tenney. *John: The Gospel of Belief.* Grand Rapids: Eerdmans, 1948.

Thayer — J. H. Thayer. *Greek-English Lexicon of the New Testament.* Reprinted Grand Rapids: Zondervan, 1962 (= 1886 original).

Theobald — M. Theobald. *Im Anfang war das Wort: Textlinguistische Studie zum Johannesprolog.* Stuttgart: Katholisches Bibelwerk, 1983.

D. W. Thomas — D. W. Thomas. *The Text of the Revised Psalter.* London: SPCK, 1963.

K. J. Thomas — K. J. Thomas. "The Old Testament Citations in Hebrews." *New Testament Studies* 11 (1964–65): 303–25.

J. W. Thompson, *Beginnings* — J. W. Thompson. *The Beginnings of Christian Philosophy: The Epistle to the Hebrews.* Washington: Catholic Biblical Association of America, 1982.

J. W. Thompson, "Structure" — J. W. Thompson. "The Structure and Purpose of the Catena in Heb 1:5–13." *Catholic Biblical Quarterly* 38 (1976): 352–63. Reprinted with revisions in J. W. Thompson, *Beginnings* 128–40.

M. M. Thompson — M. M. Thompson. *The Humanity of Jesus in the Fourth Gospel.* Philadelphia: Fortress, 1988.

Thumb — A. Thumb. *Handbook of the Modern Greek Vernacular.* ETr. Edinburgh: Clark, 1912.

Thüsing — W. Thüsing. *Gott und Christus in der paulinischen Soteriologie,* vol. 1: *Per Christum in Deum: Das Verhältnis von Christozentrik zur Theozentrik.* 3d edition. Münster: Aschendorff, 1986.

Tillich — P. Tillich. *Systematic Theology,* vol. 2. Chicago: University of Chicago Press, 1957.

Torrance — T. F. Torrance. *The Ground and Grammar of Theology.* Charlottesville, Va.: University of Virginia Press, 1980.

Torrey — C. C. Torrey. "The Aramaic Origin of the Gospel of John." *Harvard Theological Review* 16 (1923): 305–44.

Tournay, "Psaume cx" — R. Tournay. "Le Psaume cx." *Revue Biblique* 67 (1960): 5–41.

Tournay, "Ps. xlv" — R. Tournay. "Les affinités du Ps. xlv avec le Cantique des Cantiques et leur interprétation messianique." Pp. 168–212 in *Congress Volume: Bonn 1962.* Vetus Testamentum Supplement 9. Leiden: Brill, 1963.

Trench — R. C. Trench. *Synonyms of the New Testament.* 2d edition. London: Macmillan.

C. H. Turner — C. H. Turner. "Ὁ υἱός μου ὁ ἀγαπητός." *Journal of Theological Studies* 27 (1926): 113–29.

H. E. W. Turner — H. E. W. Turner. *Jesus the Christ.* London: Mowbrays, 1976.

N. Turner, *Syntax* — N. Turner. *A Grammar of New Testament Greek*, vol. 3: *Syntax.* Edinburgh: Clark, 1963.

N. Turner, *Insights* — N. Turner. *Grammatical Insights into the New Testament.* Edinburgh: Clark, 1965.

N. Turner, *Style* — N. Turner. *A Grammar of New Testament Greek*, vol. 4: *Style.* Edinburgh: Clark, 1976.

N. Turner, *Words* — N. Turner. *Christian Words.* Edinburgh: Clark, 1980.

N. Turner, "Eternal Word" — N. Turner. "St. John's Eternal Word." *Evangelical Quarterly* 22 (1950): 243–48.

Ulrichsen — J. H. Ulrichsen. "Διαφορώτερον ὄνομα in Hebr. 1,4: Christus als Träger des Gottesnamens." *Studia Theologica* 38 (1984): 65–75.

Vaganay — L. Vaganay. "La finale du Quatrième Évangile." *Revue Biblique* 45 (1936): 512–28.

van der Ploeg — J. van der Ploeg. "L'exégèse de l'Ancien Testament dans l'Épître aux Hébreux." *Revue Biblique* 54 (1947): 187–228.

Van Groningen — G. Van Groningen. *Messianic Revelation in the Old Testament.* Grand Rapids: Baker, 1990.

Vanhoye — A. Vanhoye. *La structure litteraire l'Épître aux Hébreux.* Paris: Desclée de Brouwer, 1963.

van Peursen — C. van Peursen. "Man and Reality: The History of Human Thought." *Student World* 56 (1963): 13–21. Reprinted in *A Reader in Contemporary Theology*, pp. 115–26. Edited by J. Bowden and J. Richmond. 2d edition. London: SCM, 1971.

Vaughan — C. J. Vaughan. *St. Paul's Epistle to the Romans.* London: Macmillan, 1874.

de Vaux — R. de Vaux. *Ancient Israel*, vol. 1. ETr. London: Darton, Longman & Todd, 1961.

Vellanickal — M. Vellanickal. *The Divine Sonship of Christians in the Johannine Writings.* Rome: Pontifical Biblical Institute, 1977.

Vine — W. E. Vine. *The Epistles of John.* Reprinted Grand Rapids: Zondervan, 1970.

Vogels — H. J. Vogels. *Novum Testamentum Graece et Latine*, vol. 1. 3d edition. Freiburg: Herder, 1949.

Vriezen — T. C. Vriezen. *An Outline of Old Testament Theology.* ETr. Oxford: Blackwell, 1960.

Wainwright, *Trinity* — A. W. Wainwright. *The Trinity in the New Testament.* London: SPCK, 1962.

Wainwright, "Confession" — A. W. Wainwright. "The Confession 'Jesus Is God' in the New Testament." *Scottish Journal of Theology* 10 (1957): 274–99. Reprinted (with a few changes) in A. W. Wainwright, *Trinity* 53–74.

Wallace — D. B. Wallace. "The Semantic Range of the Article–Noun–καί–Noun Plural Construction in the New Testament." *Grace Theological Journal* 4 (1983): 59–84.

Ward — W. H. Ward. "An Examination of the Various Readings of 1 Timothy iii:16." *Bibliotheca Sacra* 22 (1865): 1–50.

Warfield, *Lord* — B. B. Warfield. *The Lord of Glory*. London: Hodder & Stoughton, 1907.

Warfield, *Christology* — B. B. Warfield. *Christology and Criticism*. New York: Oxford University Press, 1929.

Warfield, *Studies* — B. B. Warfield. *Biblical and Theological Studies*. Edited by S. G. Craig. Philadelphia: Presbyterian & Reformed, 1952.

Warner — H. J. Warner. "Romans ix.5." *Journal of Theological Studies* 48 (1947): 203–4.

Watson — D. F. Watson. "Paul's Speech to the Ephesian Elders (Acts 20.17–38): Epideictic Rhetoric of Farewell." Pp. 184–208 in *Persuasive Artistry: Studies in New Testament Rhetoric in Honor of George A. Kennedy*. Edited by D. F. Watson. Sheffield: JSOT Press, 1991.

Webster — W. Webster. *The Syntax and Synonyms of the Greek Testament*. London: Rivingtons, 1864.

Weiser — A. Weiser. *The Psalms*. ETr. London: SCM, 1962.

B. Weiss, *Römer* — B. Weiss. *Handbuch über den Brief des Paulus an die Römer*. 6th edition. Göttingen: Vandenhoeck & Ruprecht, 1881.

B. Weiss, *Theology* — B. Weiss. *Biblical Theology of the New Testament*. 2 vols. ETr. Edinburgh: Clark, 1882–83.

B. Weiss, *Johannes* — B. Weiss. *Das Johannes-Evangelium*. 9th edition. Göttingen: Vandenhoeck & Ruprecht, 1902.

B. Weiss, *Commentary* — B. Weiss. *A Commentary on the New Testament*, vol. 2. ETr. New York: Funk & Wagnalls, 1906.

B. Weiss, "Gebrauch" — B. Weiss. "Der Gebrauch des Artikels bei den Gottesnamen." *Theologische Studien und Kritiken* 84 (1911): 319–92, 503–38.

Wellhausen — J. Wellhausen. *The Book of Psalms*. ETr. London: Clarke, 1898.

Wendland — P. Wendland. "Σωτήρ: Eine religionsgeschichtliche Untersuchung." *Zeitschrift für die Neutestamentliche Wissenschaft* 5 (1904): 335–53.

Wengst — K. Wengst. *Der erste, zweite und dritte Brief des Johannes*. Gütersloh: Mohn, 1978.

Westcott, *Hebrews* — B. F. Westcott. *The Epistle to the Hebrews*. 3d edition. London: Macmillan, 1920.

Westcott, *Gospel* — B. F. Westcott. *The Gospel according to St. John*. Reprinted London: Clarke, 1958 (= 1880 original).

Westcott, *Epistles* — B. F. Westcott. *The Epistles of St. John*. 3d edition. Reprinted Grand Rapids: Eerdmans, 1966 (= 1892 original).

Wettstein — J. J. Wettstein. *Novum Testamentum Graecum*. 2 vols. Reprinted Graz: Akademische Verlag, 1962 (= 1752 original).

Wevers — J. W. Wevers. *Genesis*. Göttingen LXX 1. Göttingen: Vandenhoeck & Ruprecht, 1974.

White — N. J. D. White. "The Epistle to Titus." *EGT* 4:185–202.

Whiteley — D. E. H. Whiteley. *The Theology of St. Paul*. Oxford: Blackwell, 1964.

Wickham — E. C. Wickham. *The Epistle to the Hebrews*. London: Methuen, 1910.

Wiesinger — A. Wiesinger. *Biblical Commentary on St Paul's Epistles*. ETr. Edinburgh: Clark, 1851.

Wikenhauser — A. Wikenhauser. *Das Evangelium nach Johannes*. Regensburg: Pustet, 1957.

Wilckens — U. Wilckens. *Der Brief an die Römer*. Neukirchen-Vluyn: Neukirchener Verlag, 1980.

Wiles, *Gospel* — M. F. Wiles. *The Spiritual Gospel*. Cambridge: Cambridge University Press, 1960.

Wiles, "Generation" — M. F. Wiles. "Eternal Generation." *Journal of Theological Studies* 12 (1961): 284–91.

C. S. C. Williams — C. S. C. Williams. *A Commentary on the Acts of the Apostles*. London: Black, 1957.

D. J. Williams — D. J. Williams. *Acts*. Peabody, Mass.: Hendrickson, 1985.

R. R. Williams, *Acts*	R. R. Williams. *The Acts of the Apostles.* London: SCM, 1953.
R. R. Williams, "Binitarianisms"	R. R. Williams. "Overlapping Binitarianisms in the New Testament." Pp. 30–36 in *Studia Evangelica,* vol. 5.2: *The New Testament Message.* Edited by F. L. Cross. Berlin: Akademie-Verlag, 1968.
Williamson, *Philo*	R. Williamson. *Philo and the Epistle to the Hebrews.* Leiden: Brill, 1970.
Williamson, "Incarnation"	R. Williamson. "The Incarnation of the Logos in Hebrews." *Expository Times* 95 (1983–84): 4–8.
R. D. Wilson, "Old Testament"	R. D. Wilson. "The Names of God in the Old Testament." *Princeton Theological Review* 18 (1920): 460–92.
R. D. Wilson, "Names"	R. D. Wilson. "The Names for God in the New Testament." *Princeton Theological Review* 19 (1921): 392–433.
R. D. Wilson, "Psalms"	R. D. Wilson. "The Names of God in the Psalms." *Princeton Theological Review* 25 (1927): 1–39.
R. M. Wilson	R. M. Wilson. *Hebrews.* Grand Rapids: Eerdmans, 1987.
Windisch, *Hebräerbrief*	H. Windisch. *Der Hebräerbrief.* Tübingen: Mohr, 1913.
Windisch, *Briefe*	H. Windisch. *Die katholischen Briefe.* Tübingen: Mohr, 1930.
Winer	G. B. Winer. *A Grammar of the Idiom of the New Testament.* ETr. Andover, Mass.: Draper, 1872.
Winer and Schmiedel	G. B. Winer. *Grammatik des neutestamentlichen Sprachidioms.* Edited by P. W. Schmiedel. 8th edition. Göttingen: Vandenhoeck & Ruprecht, 1894.
Young	F. M. Young. "Christological Ideas in the Greek Commentaries on the Epistle to the Hebrews." *Journal of Theological Studies* 20 (1969): 150–63.
Zahn, *Johannes*	T. Zahn. *Das Evangelium des Johannes.* 2d edition. Leipzig: Deichert, 1908.
Zahn, *Römer*	T. Zahn. *Der Brief des Paulus an die Römer.* Leipzig: Deichert, 1910.
Zahn, *Introduction*	T. Zahn. *Introduction to the New Testament.* 3 vols. ETr. Reprinted Grand Rapids: Kregel, 1953 (= 1909 original).
Zehnle	R. Zehnle. "The Salvific Character of Jesus' Death in Lucan Soteriology." *Theological Studies* 30 (1969): 420–44.
Zeller	D. Zeller. *Der Brief an die Römer.* Regensburg: Pustet, 1985.
Zerwick, *Greek*	M. Zerwick. *Biblical Greek Illustrated by Examples.* ETr. Rome: Pontifical Biblical Institute, 1963.
Zerwick, *Analysis*	M. Zerwick. *Analysis philologica Novi Testamenti graeci.* 3d edition. Rome: Pontifical Biblical Institute, 1966.
Zerwick and Grosvenor	M. Zerwick and M. Grosvenor. *A Grammatical Analysis of the Greek New Testament.* 3d edition. Rome: Pontifical Biblical Institute, 1988.
Ziesler	J. Ziesler. *Paul's Letter to the Romans.* Philadelphia: Trinity, 1989.
Zuntz	G. Zuntz. *The Text of the Epistles.* Schweich Lectures 1946. London: Oxford University Press for the British Academy, 1953.

Author Index

Subject Index

Index of Principal Greek Terms and Phrases

Reference Index

Detailed or important discussions are indicated by an asterisk.
References to the Septuagint are indicated by LXX.

Old Testament

Proverbs

Song of Solomon

Isaiah

Old Testament Apocrypha

Old Testament Pseudepigrapha

4 Ezra

New Testament

Matthew

Mark

Luke

John

Acts

Romans

1 Corinthians

Philippians

Colossians

1 Thessalonians

2 Thessalonians

1 Timothy

2 Peter

1 John

2 John

3 John

Jude

Revelation

Other Ancient Authors and Writings

Murray J. Harris, former professor of New Testament exegesis and theology at Trinity Evangelical Divinity School and warden of Tyndale House, Cambridge, received his Ph.D. from Manchester, where he studied under F. F. Bruce. Harris wrote the commentary on 2 Corinthians for the Expositor's Bible Commentary, and has begun a twenty-volume series, Exegetical Guide to the Greek New Testament, with the publication of *Colossians and Philemon.*